Praise for *Eye of the Storm*

"*Eye of the Storm* is a magnificent addition to the art and literature of the Civil War. Just when it seemed that nothing could be unearthed about America's Armageddon, along comes the unexpected: a sensational discovery of a long-hidden treasure trove of sketches and a diary of riveting descriptive prose."

–Stephen B. Oates, author of *The Whirlwind of War: Voices of the Storm, 1861–1865*

"[*Storm*] has made [a] big splash among historians and others who value new and authentic insights into the Civil War years. Sneden's important record now casts fresh light on momentous events."

–Ann Lloyd Merriman, *Richmond Times-Dispatch*

"Considered one of the richest and most detailed descriptions of Civil War soldier life ever written."

–Catherine Fox, *The Atlanta Journal-Constitution*

"[Sneden's] book is unique in the crowded field of Civil War histories. There is nothing like it for realistic detail of the day-to-day life of a common soldier, and to add to it, the pictures are drawn with painstaking care. . . . It is, in all, a vast reality we moderns have never seen before in a Civil War narrative."

–Duncan Spencer, *The Washington Times*

"This richly illustrated account of one man's Civil War belongs in the library of anyone interested in knowing what it was really like to fight for the American Union."

–Geoffrey C. Ward, coauthor of *The Civil War: An Illustrated History*

"Sneden's record in words and pictures is remarkable and unique. You have never read–or seen–a Civil War memoir like this one."

–John Jakes, author of the *North and South* Trilogy

"Perhaps one of the most complete descriptions of the Civil War battlefield experiences (Army of the Potomac) and prison life (Andersonville) ever written. Skillfully executed, *Eye of the Storm* may one day be considered a classic."

–*Library Journal*

"Editors Bryan and Lankford, of the Virginia Historical Society . . . have excerpted the more important sections of this compellingly straightforward account and provided more than 70 color illustrations of battlefields, city layouts and other scenes that caught Sneden's precise, cartographic eye. The end result is a pleasing palate of vivid . . . descriptions and terrific watercolors from a patriotic man."

–*Publishers Weekly*

"'Spectacular,' 'gripping,' 'unprecedented,' and 'unique in every sense' are overused phrases in describing a new book. Yet each applies here. Robert Sneden's diary-memoir of service in the 40th New York is extraordinary in itself. His scores of watercolors of scenes in the field have no equal in Civil War art."

–James I. Robertson, Jr., author of *Stonewall Jackson: The Man, the Soldier, the Legend*

"Robert Knox Sneden bequeathed a rich store in pictorial and narrative material to students of the Civil War. His drawings and paintings depict many places for which we have no other pictorial representations. This highly unusual account, which is enhanced by the editors' excellent work, quickly should take its place among the invaluable published primary sources on the conflict."

–Gary W. Gallagher, author of *Lee and His Army in Confederate History*

"A prize find. Unusually full and dramatic, Sneden's *Eye of the Storm* is one of the most fulsome and significant prison memoirs to come out of the war. The wonderful drawings and maps only further gild an already golden human and historical document."

–William C. Davis, author of *Lincoln's Men: How President Lincoln Became Father to an Army and a Nation*

"Robert Knox Sneden saw too much of the Civil War, from the slaughter of battlefields to the horrors of Andersonville. But Sneden was an astute observer, who left behind a wonderful legacy in words, drawings, and maps. *Eye of the Storm* is a splendid book."

–Jeffry D. Wert, author of *A Brotherhood of Valor*

"Robert Sneden's detailed eyewitness sketches of Confederate prisons–and Andersonville in particular–offer unique glimpses of scenes that were, for the most part, never recorded by any camera or any better artist."

–William Marvel, author of *Andersonville: The Last Depot*

1863

Eye of the Storm

A Civil War Odyssey

Written and Illustrated by

Private Robert Knox Sneden

Edited by Charles F. Bryan, Jr.,
and Nelson D. Lankford

A Touchstone Book
Published by Simon & Schuster
New York London Toronto Sydney Singapore

To Floyd and Libby Gottwald

Touchstone
Rockefeller Center
1230 Avenue of the Americas
New York, NY 10020

FIRST TOUCHSTONE EDITION 2002
TOUCHSTONE and colophon are registered trademarks of Simon &Schuster, Inc.
Designed by Kim Llewellyn
Manufactured in the United States of America
1 3 5 7 9 10 8 6 4 2

The Library of Congress has catalogued the Free Press edition as follows:

Sneden, Robert Knox, b. 1832.
Eye of the storm : a Civil War odyssey / written and illustrated by Robert Knox Sneden; edited by Charles F. Bryan, Jr., and Nelson D. Lankford.
p. cm.
1. Sneden, Robert Knox, b. 1832. 2. United States—History—Civil War, 1861–1865—Personal narratives. 3. United States—History—Civil War, 1861–1865—Campaigns. 4. Soldiers—United States—Biography. 5. Andersonville Prison—Biography. 6. Prisoners of war—Georgia—Andersonville—Biography.
I. Bryan, Charles F. II. Lankford, Nelson D. III. Title.
E601.S667 2000
973.7'3—dc21 00-26453

ISBN 0-684-86365-0
0-684-86366-9

Contents

Preface

In 1994, four tattered scrapbook albums, containing some five hundred vivid Civil War watercolor drawings and maps by Union soldier Robert Knox Sneden, were consigned to an art dealer who specializes in Southern works. When the dealer initially approached the Virginia Historical Society by phone, the institution's curators were naturally curious, but skeptical. When they finally examined firsthand what the dealer had described, however, they realized they were looking at a remarkable collection of artwork that had dropped from sight for many decades, languishing in a Connecticut bank vault since the Great Depression. A generous gift from Mr. and Mrs. Floyd D. Gottwald, Jr., of Richmond enabled the Historical Society to acquire the collection.

The Historical Society realized that it had made a significant acquisition. Over the years, previously unknown drawings, paintings, and sketches have turned up here and there. But not major collections. Most were known and accounted for. Never before had so many original watercolors appeared from nowhere like these. The Historical Society staff launched an all-out effort to learn more about the Union soldier who had captured so much of Virginia's lost landscape, but who left faint tracks in the documentary record himself.

Their investigation led to Sneden's service records at the National Archives and the inevitable genealogists, who helped fill in details about the man and his background. Further research led them to a ninety-five-year-old local and family historian, who in turn reported that the great-grandson of Robert Sneden's brother lived in upstate New York. He was the present owner, she alleged, of the Union soldier's illustrated wartime diary/memoir.

Little of this diary/memoir had been known to historians before. *The Century Collection of Civil War Art*, a book published in 1974, however, gave a tantalizing hint. A brief passage noted that nearly three dozen engravings on the Peninsula Campaign were by a Robert K. Sneden, who kept an extensive wartime diary with illustrations. "Little is known of Sneden's life beyond his wartime experiences," it further noted, and "the fate of his diary is a mystery. . . . It seems to have disappeared."

A call by the Historical Society to the artist's great-great-nephew confirmed that he did indeed own the diary/memoir. Actually, he said that it was in five volumes, but he had shut them away years ago in a mini–rental bin in Arizona. Through a complicated arrangement, the owner retrieved the documents and brought them to the Historical Society for examination, with the right to purchase. The five volumes turned out to contain nearly five thousand handwritten pages and hundreds more watercolors. Unfortunately, Volume 2, covering most of May and June 1862, had been missing for more than a century, according to the owner. Nevertheless, Mr. and Mrs. Gottwald were generous once again, and by the end of 1997, the Historical Society added the other significant body of Sneden's work to its collections.

Although originally described as a "diary," the five volumes are a memoir based on a diary. In the introduction to his first volume, Sneden states: "In these volumes an authentic and generally correct account is given of the movements and Battles fought by 'The Army of the Potomac' . . . which has been compiled from a diary kept during the time by the author." Indeed, in his narrative Sneden notes that he mailed diary entries and pictures home during the war. He stated that he kept a shorthand diary in secret while incarcerated as a prisoner of war. Apparently using his original diaries and several published sources as the basis of his account, Sneden put pen to paper and wrote his wartime narrative probably over a period of many years beginning in the late 1870s. At the same time, presumably he compiled the separate scrapbook albums of drawings, many of which may have been his original wartime images. Like many Civil War artists, both professional and amateur, he probably made hasty sketches in the field in pencil or pen and ink. He then refined and colored them later, possibly after the war. We know that a few of his drawings were done later, copied from other pictures that he could not have seen until after the war. The vast majority of the eight hundred or so drawings, however, were based on his original sketches made in the field.

Perhaps Sneden tried to publish his memoir. In the 1870s and 1880s, a steady stream of Civil War publications rolled off the presses, many of which were bestsellers. Sneden may have hoped that his magnum opus would bring him much needed income to support a struggling career as an architect. Portions of his account discuss the war beyond his own experiences. He analyzes strategy, relates the movement of armies, including the enemy's, reports the strengths of opposing forces, and critiques army leadership. He occasionally interjects information that could have been known to him only well after the event. He may have been trying to publish a history of the Civil War combining his personal story with a more general account. There is no evidence, however, that any such effort by Sneden bore fruit.

Because his original wartime diaries have never been found, it is impossible to know how detailed or accurate they were. Like most diarists, when time did not allow, he probably reconstructed events several days or longer after they occurred. From checking other reliable sources, it is clear that at times he misdated events or confused them with other happenings. In a few instances he freely lifted dialogue and other information from sources that were published after the war. This edited version of his account notes the few places in which his information is inaccurate, questionable, or borrowed. Nevertheless, the amount of detail he provides on things he saw, heard, did, or had done to him strongly suggests that he is the sole source of information for all but a small portion of the account. His descriptions of events and his portrayal of key personalities with whom he associated can be corroborated in numerous other sources. For Sneden, as for many veterans, the Civil War was the most important event of his life, and details of those years were burned in his memory.

Together, his narrative and art constitute one of the most important Civil War documents ever produced. Memoirs of the war are commonplace, but the overwhelming volume of Sneden's account and his incredible detail—from the terror of being roused from sleep at pistol-point by his captors one cold November night to despondently swatting flies in his Andersonville shanty—make his story perhaps the most complete description of Civil War battlefield experience and prison life ever written. Hundreds of watercolor sketches and maps provide a visual chronicle of almost every place Sneden went. It is as though he had a video recorder and kept it running throughout the war.

Unlike many Civil War narratives, Sneden's avoids giving the reader postmortem discussions of political or philosophical issues. He shuns diatribes on the evils of the South or the righteousness of the Union cause, though both opinions can be inferred from his matter-of-fact recounting of the ordinary soldier's life. Sneden suffered terribly during his imprisonment, and the perspective of writing after the war ended did not lessen his hatred for his enemies. The desire for retribution, though never far from his mind, is tempered by the analytical detachment of a surveyor and mapmaker. He describes houses, fortifications, and the physics of artillery shells in flight. In the same clinical detail, he delineates the appearance of a mangled corpse lying on the ground and the horrific death in battle of an artilleryman.

It is in Sneden's analytical detachment, devoid of the flowery language and sentimentality typical of nineteenth-century memoirs, that the value of his account lies. His experience rings true to modern ears. As the years carry us farther and farther from the Civil War, we find it harder to understand what it was like for those who lived through it. We can visit the battlefields, but they seem parklike. We can watch the work of filmmakers, but their images are too languid or contrived. We can read the books of thousands of authors and still not catch the spirit and the suffering of the Civil War. The surest way for us to reach back to the events of 1861–1865 is through the record set down by a man who was there. By means of Robert Sneden's words and his art, we learn about the defining experience of his existence: a terrible war in which he was a participant, victim, and chronicler. His remarkable Civil War story, hidden away for decades, can now be told.

ARMY DIARY
OF THE
WAR OF THE
REBELLION.
1861-5.
1863
BY R. K. SNEDEN. OF THE
40th N.Y. VOLS. (Mozart Regt.)
AND TOPOGRAPHICAL ENGINEER OF THE
3RD ARMY CORPS.
ARMY OF THE POTOMAC.

Prologue

Little is known of Robert Sneden's life before the Civil War. Small scraps of scattered evidence reveal that he was born in the Canadian maritime province of Nova Scotia in 1832, the great-grandson of a Loyalist who had fled New York at the end of the American Revolution. When he was eighteen years old, he moved with his parents and two siblings to the teeming metropolis of New York City. Once there, he apparently decided to become an architect and engineer, two professions that flourished in a city that kept up a never-ending demand for factories, public buildings, commercial structures, and housing. The nature and extent of his education for these fields are a mystery. His early schooling was most likely shaped in his native Nova Scotia. In America, Sneden probably followed the route of self-education and apprenticeship, learning his craft from practitioners. He also began to dabble in art. His *Sneden's Landing, opposite Dobb's Ferry, Hudson River, N.Y.*, painted in 1858, and another Hudson River landscape are his earliest known works. The paintings reflect more the hand of an architectural draftsman than a formally schooled artist. Rather than planning a career in art, Sneden probably took up landscape painting in conjunction with a developing career as an architect and engineer who needed to make the "architectural and perspective drawings" that he mentioned on his business card after the war.

Although Robert Sneden's life in the 1850s is shrouded in mystery, it is reasonable to assume that he became swept up in the turmoil of 1860–61 as the nation plunged into civil war. Listing 50 Wall Street in the heart of the city's financial and commercial district as his mailing address in 1861, he would have been aware of the growing concern surrounding him

SNEDEN'S LANDING

Opposite Dobbs Ferry, Hudson River, N.Y., 1858. © Collection of the New-York Historical Society.

in business circles. Nowhere was the prospect of conflict more deeply dreaded than in the nation's largest city, which depended heavily on the South. Wall Street served as the banker and broker of the Southern states. A majority of manufactured goods going to the South passed through the port of New York. The prospect of losing Southern markets and hundreds of millions of dollars in credit greatly concerned the city's business community. Most New Yorkers had little sympathy for the abolitionist crusade, fearing that emancipation would free millions of slaves who might come north to flood the community. The city was overwhelmingly Democratic in its politics, and in the presidential election of 1860, 62 percent of voters cast their ballots for candidates other than Abraham Lincoln. Given Sneden's less than sympathetic comments on African Americans during the war, we can guess that his political leanings followed those of most of his fellow New Yorkers.

Yet the Confederate attack on Fort Sumter on April 12, 1861, resulted in a powerful change in public attitude. Most New Yorkers were shocked and outraged by the assault on the national flag. An angry mob descended on the offices of the Southern-leaning *New York Herald* and demanded that the publisher fly the Stars and Stripes. When President Lincoln called for 75,000 volunteers to put down the rebellion, New Yorkers responded with overwhelming displays of support. A few days after Fort Sumter, a massive crowd of more than 100,000 people jammed Union Square for a rousing war rally. Tens of thousands of men flooded recruiting stations, anxious to do their part to save the Union. By April 23, six regiments from New York City had been dispatched to protect the national capital in Washington. In the meantime, more regiments were being formed. Indeed, by year's end the city placed sixty-six regiments in the field.

One of the regiments formed shortly after Fort Sumter was the 40th New York Volunteers or Mozart Regiment, the name given the unit by Mayor Fernando Wood to recognize the Mozart Hall political faction of the city's Democratic party. Although he did not sign up as a soldier at first, Robert Sneden decided to do his part for the Union and got himself appointed as the regiment's assistant quartermaster, no doubt through social or business contacts. For whatever reason, he served as an unpaid civilian and did not officially join the army for several months. He recorded few details of his early war experience, but general comments he made later and other sources indicate that it was a time of both exhilaration and frustration.

Although the 40th eventually turned into an effective fighting unit, the regiment led a chaotic existence in the early weeks of the war. Bright-eyed men from New York City and Brooklyn who had signed up expecting to wear handsome uniforms, shoulder muskets, and head to the front within days were disappointed. The city's Union Defense Committee struggled mightily to arm and equip scores of regiments being formed, but the process was slow going. Enlisted men and officers grumbled. Some early recruits left the 40th to join other units that were already uniformed, especially the gaudily clad Zouaves. The quarters of the regiment at the city's old ironworks in Manhattan were grim and provided little room for drill. Armed guards confined the enlisted men to camp after nine at night, although officers were allowed to leave and imbibe freely at nearby saloons. With no officers around to supervise, whiskey managed to find its way into the enlisted men's quarters, and many an evening ended with discontented Mozarters slugging it out among themselves.

After nearly a month confined to the ironworks, the men of the 40th were moved from one set of unsatisfactory quarters to another. The regiment boarded barges pulled by tugboats and steamed ten miles north of the city to Yonkers on the Hudson River. There the men were crowded into a large, brick flour mill that doubled as a barracks and drill hall. Two weeks of constant drilling on the upper floors of the mill, however, stirred up such clouds of dust that it was difficult to hear the barking of orders over a cacophony of coughing and sneezing. Finally, the regiment was moved to a large field in the northern suburbs of Yonkers, and at last the men had decent surroundings. Tents were spread over a plateau that overlooked the placid Hudson, across which wafted cooling breezes. At long last, every soldier was issued a uniform, smoothbore musket, and accoutrements, the distribution of which must have kept the quartermaster staff running ragged. Sneden was put in charge of forwarding quartermaster and commissary supplies by steamer from the regimental recruiting office in Manhattan to the camp at Yonkers.

Now the business of real soldiering began. Long hours of drill, dress parades, rigid inspections, and the tedium of guard duty became a way of life. Despite the drastic change from the civilian world to the military, the men of the 40th New York would later look back on the time at Yonkers with nostalgia. Being a soldier seemed like play. Local farmers supplied the men with fresh vegetables and succulent strawberries. Dress parades were fre-

VIEW OF BARRACKS OF THE MOZART REGIMENT
At Yonkers, N.Y., June 1861.

quently attended by visiting dignitaries and attractive young women who usually brought cakes and other delicacies to the boys in their bright new blue uniforms. Nevertheless, the men were anxious to go to "the seat of war" in Virginia before the fighting ended with certain Union victory.

Finally word raced through the camp that it was time to head to the front. Excitement was intense. Mayor Fernando Wood and a large delegation of city officials traveled to Yonkers on July 3 to present the Mozarters with a beautiful silk flag surmounted by a gold eagle and emblazoned with the motto "E Pluribus Unum." Looking straight at the men, the mayor exclaimed: "If that flag falls, every man will fall with it; if it conquers, every man in the regiment will conquer with it. . . . It must never be humbled in the dust. We look to you for its defense, knowing that you will defend it to the last." The soldiers cheered lustily and were then formed up by their officers to show off their martial skills in a formal dress parade. The men then returned to camp and began preparing for the trip south.

The following morning, Independence Day, was one that veterans of the regiment would never forget. At first light a tattoo of drumbeats summoned everyone to the camp

ENCAMPMENT OF THE MOZART REGIMENT AT YONKERS, N.Y.
Known as Camp Wood. July 3, 1861.

flagstaff, where, standing bareheaded, the men lifted their voices in chorus to sing "The Star-Spangled Banner" and "America." Then amid nervous laughter, the neophyte soldiers ate breakfast, rolled their blankets, packed knapsacks, filled canteens, struck their tents, formed up, marched out of camp, and paraded through the streets of Yonkers. Throngs of men, women, and children waved handkerchiefs and shouted words of encouragement as the 40th New York, 1,030 men strong, tromped up the gangplank of the steamer *Red Jacket*, which would take the regiment to a railhead in New Jersey. The sounds of laughing soldiers and the shrill toot of the boat's whistle melted away as the *Red Jacket* pulled out and disappeared in the distance downriver.

Three days later, when the Mozarters arrived in Washington by train, anxious to meet the enemy, Robert Sneden was not with them. Still a civilian, he stayed behind, charged with a sizable cleanup job at Yonkers. The regiment had left the camp a mess. Boxes, barrels, tin plates and cups, and clumps of straw littered the grounds. Sneden invited local residents to take whatever they wanted, and then he had the campground cleaned up to turn back over to its owner. He sold all of the surplus stores of foodstuffs left behind and carefully prepared the paperwork to send to regimental headquarters, now in Virginia. Then, for reasons that are not clear, Sneden traveled to Boston, possibly to sign up more recruits for the 40th New York, four companies of which already were composed of Massachusetts men. While there, he would have received the shocking news of the disastrous Union defeat at Bull Run in Virginia on July 21.

Before the battle, many people on both sides had expected the war to be a short one. But in the aftermath of the first big action, it became evident that a quick conclusion of the conflict was no longer possible. Amateur armies had to be turned into efficient fighting forces. In the North, a lust to avenge Bull Run caused a whole new wave of recruits to don the uniform of blue. No longer content to remain a civilian in the backwaters of the war, Sneden decided to follow suit and join his comrades of the 40th New York, who had been kept out of the Bull Run battle but were drilling earnestly for the next fight.

Chapter One

To the Front!

For most men going to the front in the late summer of 1861, war was a great adventure. The Union army had been bloodied at Bull Run in July, but for tens of thousands of green soldiers pouring into Washington in the following weeks, the horrors of combat, the misery of disease, the exhaustion of long marches, and the drudgery of camp life were unknown. Robert Sneden was no exception. Traveling initially from Boston to New York and then on to Washington in late August, at first Sneden squeezed himself onto a train filled with new soldiers, mostly Irish immigrants, who drank and caroused their way south. Then boarding another crowded train in New York, he sat with an old acquaintance, Henry Gotleb, a captain in the 40th New York heading to the front. Sleep was all but impossible, not so much from the lurching and rattling of the train as it chugged through the night, but because of its human cargo. Like adolescent boys on their way to summer camp, the soldiers sang and brawled long into the night. So many fights broke out that finally several men were locked in the baggage car under guard. Early the next morning, a bleary-eyed Sneden arrived in Washington and checked into a hotel. He wasted little time in his room.

Sneden's curious eye for his environment would serve him well in the army. Little escaped his observation. Although no more than an overgrown town, the Washington he entered teemed with activity. He saw long wagon trains, rumbling artillery caissons, blue-clad regiments of infantry, and herds of cattle clogging the narrow dirt streets all the way to the camps across the Potomac River. He bought an "outfit for active service in the field." He played

Chapel on hill for hospital, 40th Regiment · House on the telegraph road · Guardhouse of 40th and General John Sedgwick's headquarters · Flank battery and rifle pit built by 40th and 3rd and 4th Maine Regiments

ENCAMPMENT OF THE 40TH NEW YORK VOLUNTEERS (MOZART REGIMENT), LEESBURG TURNPIKE, VA.

tourist and visited several public buildings, closing his day by eavesdropping on conversations at the bar crowded with officers at Willard's Hotel.

The next day, Sneden took a ferry across the Potomac to Alexandria, then rode out to rejoin his comrades in the 40th New York camped on the Leesburg Turnpike. The 40th was only one small element of a growing host being formed under the command of the hero of the hour, General George B. McClellan. Newly christened the Army of the Potomac, it comprised nearly 100,000 men, who were stationed in encampments springing up on the outskirts of Washington and on the Virginia side of the Potomac. In these camps the troops were issued equipment and introduced to the discipline of army life. For weeks on end, the men learned marching movements, how to fire their weapons, and bayonet practice.

This energetic drilling of the Army of the Potomac continued for the next several months, but from the beginning Robert Sneden's war was different. Even though he officially enlisted as a private in E Company of the 40th New York, apparently he was spared many of the travails of basic training. Probably through previous arrangement, Sneden immediately picked up his quartermaster duties when he was detailed as an assistant to the brigade commissary. Working at General John Sedgwick's brigade headquarters and tenting with an officer, he recorded that he "soon learned to figure out how much a brigade could eat daily, which was enormous!"

Almost at once Sneden developed a pattern that would mark his time in the army. Although an enlisted man, he mingled freely with officers. In these early months of the war, he seemed to have plenty of free time to move about, frequently visiting the camps of other regiments and the picket lines. He took a keen interest in the ring of fortifications and earthworks going up around the city. And from the beginning, he made maps and drew sketches of what he observed. Only two days after Sneden's arrival in the field, General Sedgwick had him prepare a map of area encampments. Apparently someone had informed the general of Sneden's prewar talents.

In addition to maps and drawings, Sneden kept his journal. In it he provided detailed insights into army life when the war was still a novelty and few men had died. At first, enemy soldiers were little more than distant figures observed on the picket lines on the far horizon. He reported occasional clashes with Rebel patrols, but for the most part his early journal reveals an army struggling more with boredom, alcohol abuse, incompetent officers, internal squabbling, army politics, and disease. From his initial entries, he manifested a deep prejudice toward officers who did not look after the interest of enlisted men or who were arrogant. West Pointers were particular targets of his written barbs. Weather was a constant factor, often determining the success or failure of a day. After one particularly stormy night, for example, he noted that bareheaded soldiers rushed about wildly in two feet of mud and water "yelling and swearing loud enough to paralyze any of the chaplains." It was the equivalent of the Phony War during the relatively bloodless winter of 1939–40 on the Western Front of Europe. Like those early soldiers of World War II, Sneden and his army comrades would have to wait several months to experience hard war.

September 29, 1861

The 40th Regiment had a sham fight today which resulted in filling up the hospital with as many wounded and maimed men as if there had been a big skirmish with the enemy. Colonel [Edward J.] Riley took one half of the regiment while Major [Richard T.] Halstead* took the other half. Both set out in different directions to meet a mile away on unknown ground. Yet neither officers or men knew where skirmish lines were thrown forward, while the men clambered over fences, through mud and over walls. In about an hour both parts came together again, and a heavy rolling fire opened with blank cartridge.

The howitzer gun was fired rapidly, but it [was] upset several times by the recoil, and the rammer was fired away during the excitement. The major handled his part of the regiment with more skill than the colonel, who with a company were made prisoners in fun, and locked up in a barn. They broke out though the boarding and being now excited charged the major's men, firing their muskets within ten feet of each other so that many were burnt and singed by the wads. Riley endeavored to stop the fight, which was getting

*Riley served as commander of the 40th New York until his resignation from the army in June 1862. As major, Halstead was third in command of the regiment.

serious, when some company fired their ramrods (iron ones) at him. These struck the ground all around him, and bounded, tingling in the air, doing him no harm. The major stopped the fight after a while, and bough litters had to be made to bring those who were hurt into camp. The colonel has many enemies in the regiment, caused by favoritism, and being too much of a martinet. There is no chance of the 40th indulging in this little pastime of hurting each other to no purpose for some time to come.

The 40th Regiment have built a log guard house for delinquents at the entrance of the camp or Post No. 1. The only light is admitted to the inside by a narrow slit in the flat roof. It is kept pretty much full most of the time. Lieutenant Beaumont of [the] 4th U.S. Cavalry, an aide to General Sedgwick, inspects the brigade every morning and his direst threat to any soldier who does not come up to the requirements of drill or cleanliness is that "he will put him in the Mozart guard house." So all have a holy horror of being put there. Sometimes the drunken soldiers who are put there have to be put in irons. They yell and make the air blue with curses all night. Some "hard cases" are "bucked and gagged" at the foot of the flag pole. This treatment makes many enemies of the colonel among the men. Many openly swear that they will shoot him the first time they have a battle with the enemy. The men will do anything to please most of the other officers of the regiment. . . .

October 7, 1861

There was the first exchange of prisoners of war today at Richmond. The fifty-seven officers were sent under flag of truce to Fortress Monroe, Virginia and three officers had all been captured at Bull Run, 21st July last. Fifty-seven Rebel officers were exchanged for them, some of high rank. The returned prisoners tell the most horrible stories of their treatment while in Libby Prison, Richmond,* some of which are hard to credit. Major Potter said that he was marched five miles in a burning hot sun with nothing on but his shirt, the Rebels having appropriated all the rest of his clothes for their own use! The Rebel guards hurried him up too with the point of the bayonet. They were half starved, plundered of everything, and closely confined like hogs in a pen. The Rebel jailor—one Richard Turner—was a hard and cruel reprobate. Years ago, while a cadet at West Point, he forged something, was tried and dismissed [from] the service in disgrace. He now vented his spite on all Union officers who fell into his power. There were several other Rebel prisons in Richmond where our private soldiers were confined. . . .

October 21, 1861

I went today to the camp of General [Edwin V.] Sumner's division at the [Episcopal] Seminary. . . . From there I rode out to Bailey's Cross Roads and up to Munson's Hill

* Sneden must have added this name later. Libby Prison did not open until March 1862. Perhaps Sneden is referring to the prison set up in Ligon's Warehouse and Tobacco Factory, which was housing prisoners of war.

now evacuated by the enemy. The 5th Michigan and 35th New York regiments were encamped in the vicinity. At the cross roads I noticed that the large building on the corner had been entirely stripped of its clapboards, roofs and all other woodwork which would serve to make camp fires. Nothing but the skeleton frame remained. The other houses and barns were badly shattered by the enemy's shot and shell just before they evacuated the works on the hill top. I made a careful sketch and went to the Rebel works. The work itself was a miserable attempt at military engineering. The picket line was composed of little huts built of logs, with low breastworks of earth and palisades built in all sorts of shapes and angles. The position however commanded our whole lines while Washington and Arlington could be plainly seen as well as many of the new forts which we recently had built. . . .

November 16, 1861

Captain [John M.] Cooney of the 38th New York Regiment made plans and started the work on a Log Theatre for the amusement of men and officers in the camps of the brigade. Many officers subscribed a certain amount of work for this purpose. Axe men were detailed to chop down every tree on Fowle's Plantation and the neighboring one to get suitable logs for a building to hold 1,500 to 2,000 men. The warehouses of Alexandria long since empty were to furnish the flooring. Sails from the vessels now rotting at the wharves were to be used inside over the logs for walls, while all the house painters and artists were at work designing scenery to be painted on ship sails for canvas. There were more volunteers for these works than wanted, and nearly every soldier now would sooner work hard all day digging on the new redoubt than go on picket.

The whiskey ration was the great desiration. Three gallons of whiskey was drawn from the brigade commissary for 100 men. One gallon of this was mixed with three buckets of water and a gill given to each hard working soldier morning and evening. The remaining two gallons was kept in the officers' tents for their own use and card playing and drinking went on until midnight sometimes. The officers did not work at all, as they knew little or nothing of how it should be done. They looked on and gave a few directions. Still being an officer settled their right to the lion's share of the whiskey, or "commissary" as it was called so they thought. Many of them had swelled heads in the morning and probably had to go out on picket duty at that.

The men get on sprees while in Alexandria on few hours' leave, and fill the guard house on their return to camp. An officer can go to Washington, see the sights and have a good time at Willard's Hotel or elsewhere. The privates must stick to the Virginia mud. Many fights take place between the men belonging to different regiments while returning to camp in a semi drunken condition. Sometime a whole company in camp have to be turned out armed to march and quell and arrest the rioters. The 40th New York guard house is generally full of prisoners.

November 20, 1861

A grand review of the Army of the Potomac who were encamped on the Virginia side of the river was had today. All the brigades marched out of their camps at 5 a.m. with bands playing and flags flying. Every gun, button and brass work was polished up and as many had new uniforms lately issued, the army looked splendid. The ground selected was a large plateau in the vicinity of Bailey's Cross Roads. . . . It was a fine, though cold and windy day. Patches of snow were on the ground when we arrived there about 10 a.m., which made it muddy in places. Many regiments had overcoats on the men. Ours had not as the colonel wanted to show off the fine uniforms. The brigades were drawn up in columns while General McClellan and staff with President Lincoln rode up and down the lines while the bands played and a battery fired salutes.

There were thousands of citizens and officials from Washington and elsewhere among the spectators, and hundreds of ladies in carriages or on horseback. The French Princes de Joinville, Duc de Chartres, [Comte] de Orléans, who were on McClellan's staff, rode with him. The heavy and light artillery with cannon polished up like gold, and the ugly looking black Parrott guns [rifled cannon] were drawn up in a long line, while the cavalry were massed in squadrons. Then about 2 p.m. all marched past in review. . . . About half of the men had to stand in the cold wind for hours. Nearly everyone was thoroughly chilled. Many soon filled up the camp hospitals. . . .

The President with his body guard . . . was cheered from end to end of the long lines of troops. As the 40th Regiment marched past the reviewing point they were applauded by the spectators for their fine martial appearance and correct marching. The review lasted until 5 p.m. and all were not off the ground until darkness had set in. As the men had brought no rations and had been up and marching since five in the morning, all were hungry, thirsty, and cold. They got to camp much quicker than on going out to the review. They were all much elated and no one ever can forget the splendid military sight [it] afforded. All the cooks in camp were at work for half of the night when we returned at 7 p.m. in a drizzling rain.

December 1, 1861

Several [officers of the 40th New York] have resigned and left—Captain H. E. Gotleb . . . Captain Foster . . . and Major Halstead. Political huckstering for higher grades in promotion makes eternal discord among the officers in most regiments. The officers, from the colonel down to the lowest in rank know very little of the principles of military art. And the soldier says that their officers know no more than they do about drill or discipline, and overstep their authority. Hence there is no superiority of knowledge on the part of the officers over the soldiers, and no superior social position admitted by him. The popularity of the officer would be lost if he were rough on the soldiers, or showed himself too exacting in the service. To the volunteer soldier the officer is simply a comrade who wears a different uniform.

He is obeyed in everyday routine of duty but only voluntarily. The soldiers don't trouble themselves about him when circumstances become serious. From the point of view of American equality there is no good reason to obey him. The habits which are created by universal suffrage also are often reproduced on the field of battle. By a tactical agreement the regiment marches against the enemy, advances under fire, and begins to deliver its volleys. The men are brave enough and get killed and wounded, and then when they think they have done enough for military honor, they all march off together! The colonel perhaps gives an impulse and entreats them by begging or cursing to stay, but his efforts are generally useless, more especially if he is not popular in the regiment. As to the other officers, they never think of it. Why should they attempt to stay the retreat when the majority of the regiment has made up its mind to retrograde? A company or two perhaps hold out longer than some of the others, but being left alone without any support they must fall back also, or be cut to pieces. Time and discipline will alone counterbalance this state of things now so prevalent among the troops. Colonel Riley is a good disciplinarian, and enforces his orders, even if he has to fill the guard house with prisoners all the time. Consequently he has many enemies among the rougher classes of men in his command.

The pickets of the 40th Regiment were fired into last night by skulkers in the woods between Mrs. Scott's and Stout's houses. None of our men were hit. One had his gun struck by a bullet which tore the lock off, just as he was about to fire. Sergeant Wells of the 40th Regiment was shot dead last night by mistake while placing his picket line through a woods in the dark. After placing the line with orders to fire on anyone seen approaching without challenging them in some manner he was the first one to do so and while climbing a fence was shot dead. His body was brought into camp, placed in a metallic coffin and sent to New York. He was a native of Halifax, Nova Scotia. The coffin and expenses were paid for by the four Nova Scotians who belonged to the 40th. Wells was a fine fellow. . . .

By recent orders all the regimental wagons have been reduced in number and officers' baggage limited in quantity. Brigade drills are held every fine afternoon and a marked efficiency is shown in the military evolutions and precision of drill. Colonel Riley has had 40 in large white figures painted on the back of every man's knapsack which number can be seen at an incredible distance. He also introduced the high stiff leather stocks [collars], which the regular army wear. The men stood the infernal invention for about ten days, when they threw them all over the camp ground. A few kept wearing them . . . yet there were not a dozen worn in the regiment. Riley introduced the black feather worn in the hats of regular army, but the men destroyed them.

December 2, 1861

I went out on picket today with part of a company of the 40th Regiment. At the first post at Olivet Church, several dead horses lay in the road as there had been some skirmishing here last night. I have not seen any dead cavalrymen so far. . . .

From Olivet Church I went to our picket reserve station at Stout's farm. Here was a spacious two story frame house with log barns and hayricks, and a fine spring of water. The chimney stacks were built on the outside gable ends, as is common in Virginia. From here Fort Ward was in view, and the cupola of the seminary showed above the tree tops in the distance. Old man Stout [a Southern sympathizer] had a fine farm with lots of fodder about three months ago, but our men found a lot of old fashioned muskets and sabres secreted in a dry well on the premises. When they were seized of course and sent to Fort Lyon, old man Stout was sent with them. The wife and daughter still lived at the house. They were rabid "Secesh." Our men picketed outside the house and used fence rails or anything else handy to keep up their camp fires. They made raids too on all the other houses within sight, bought milk, eggs, and chickens when they had money to pay for them, and "sequestered" them if they had no money—or exchanged sugar, coffee or tobacco for them. I got lots of persimmons from three trees and filling a haversack with them returned to camp.

December 3, 1861

The brigade's theatre was completed and opened for inspection today. . . . Some old scenery for the stage had been bought at Washington. The orchestra is to be made up from some of the 3rd Maine Regiment band, while a good Negro minstrel troupe from G and H companies of the 40th will perform on the off nights. There are several amateur actors in the 38th New York, prominent of whom is Captain Cooney. Regular comedians will be hired at Washington to come out here . . . to act when all is ready. The prices are $5 for the upholstered boxes, 50¢ for gallery seats, and 25¢ for seats on the ground floor.

There were six boxes near the proscenium stalled off from a gallery which ran around the room like that of any church. Some seats had straw cushions made of canvas sails, rough pine seats were on the ground floor, while a piano from some Rebel house was in the orchestra. Suitable dressing rooms were behind the stage which had only sliding scenes. A restaurant built as an annex was fitted with long pine tables and seats.

December 4, 1861

Some skirmishing was had last evening near Annandale, on the Little River Turnpike between thirty men of 3rd New Jersey under Colonel [George W.] Taylor and forty Rebel cavalry. Taylor placed telegraph wires across the road when the charging Rebel horsemen were thrown. Seven or eight killed and three captured, including a Rebel lieutenant. We lost one man killed. An old camp peddler was seized by our men and hung to a tree. He visited our camps selling hardware, etc., and made plans and estimates of the forces very accurately, which were found on him. He was run up two or three times for a minute or so and then let down before he confessed that he was a Rebel spy. The last time he went up he stayed there.

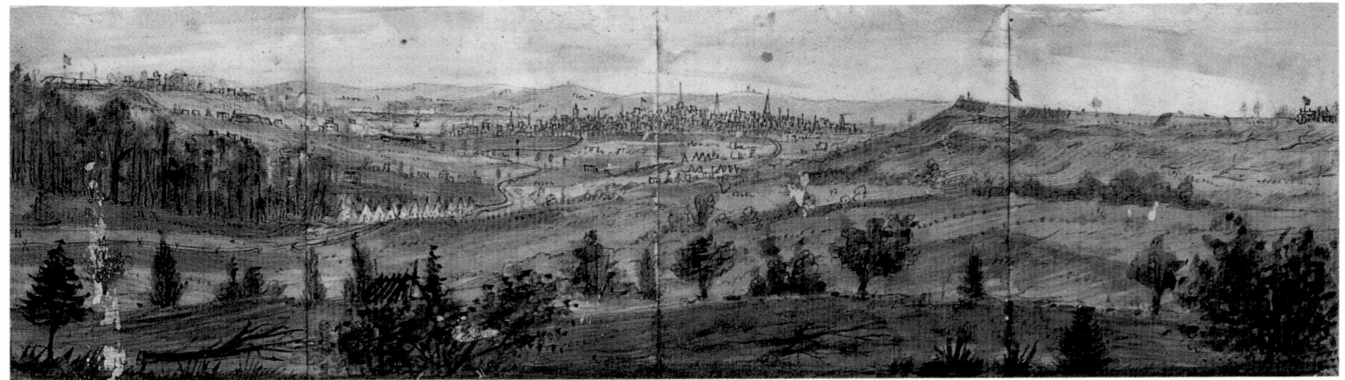

VIEW OF FORT LYON, ALEXANDRIA AND FORT ELLSWORTH, VA.
From rear of the camp of the 40th New York Regiment, October 1861.

December 25, 1861

Have had snow for past eight hours. It laid six to eight inches deep on everything. Many tents had to be taken down and repitched. Could not have dress parade or drill today. All were eating and drinking all they could get. Rations of whiskey were served to the brigade and the 40th guard house was full of drunken soldiers before sundown. Many officers got leave yesterday to go to Washington for forty-eight hours. General Sedgwick never leaves camp and insists on brigade drill every fine afternoon. . . .

January 1, 1862

Snow all day. I went to camps of 40th New York, 6th Michigan, and 63rd Pennsylvania regiments. After paying New Year's calls went by ambulance over Aqueduct Bridge to Georgetown and Washington, returning by steamer to Alexandria where I stayed overnight with friends. Willard's Hotel corridors were full of colonels, majors and generals as usual. Very few privates were to be seen anywhere. Had good supper at Gantier's and went to the Variety Theatre in evening. The provost guard took several officers from the audience during the performance as they could not show their passes, having overstayed their limit. The knowing ones borrow a suit of civilian's clothes from a friend when they overstay their time, and unless the lynx eyed officer of the guard don't recognize them they are not questioned of course. All men and officers in uniform are compelled to show their passes to the officer of the provost guard or go to the central guard house in arrest until he can get the marshall to let him off. The theatres are visited every night about 9 p.m. by this guard. Citizens are not bothered at all.

By early 1862, the combination of Sneden's mapmaking skills and a desperate demand for men with those abilities resulted in a turning point in his army career. At the beginning of the war, military authorities in the North, as well as the South, had a critical need for maps. Few maps were available, and many of them were obsolete or so inaccurate that military commanders found them nearly worthless. One officer in Virginia complained that they "knew no more about the topography of the country than they did about Central Africa."

As a result of this deficiency, both Union and Confederate armies devoted substantial manpower to producing maps suitable for military use. Soldiers with any background in surveying and the making of maps were actively sought. Once recruited and put to work at headquarters, army topographers were given special treatment and allowed a fair degree of freedom to move about and do their jobs. Private Sneden began making maps for his brigade commander within days of arrival in camp. Soon after the beginning of the new year, however, his services were demanded at an even higher level, divisional headquarters. For the next two years, Sneden had an eye on the war that few of his contemporaries ever did.

January 5, 1862

The redoubt and rifle trenches on the camp ground and across the turnpike were inspected by Captain William Heine, topographical engineer on General [Samuel P.] Heintzelman's* staff of division [headquarters] at Fort Lyon today. He is a Prussian officer sent by his government to observe the conduct of the war. Same as the French princes, who are attached to General McClellan's staff. I went over the ground with him, and he made up his mind to have me detached from my regiment and do topographical duty with him at Fort Lyon. . . .

The snow is yet on the ground, about six inches deep, but the wagon wheels on the roads cut this up and churns it into filthy red paste. All the cavalry who return from picket [duty] are splashed with this filthy, vile smelling compound from head to foot. They have a hard time of it to keep themselves and accouterments clean.

January 8, 1862

I went out on picket today with three companies of the 40th Regiment. Roads were horrible slush and mud a foot deep. We waded and plunged through it until we got to Olivet Church when we went through the wood roads to the respective picket posts. At the Rebel commodore French Forrest's house, I stayed most of the time. The house was being wantonly destroyed inside by our men. Ceilings had been punched through and nearly all

*Samuel Peter Heintzelman (1805–1880), a West Point graduate and career army officer, commanded one of the Army of the Potomac's twelve divisions.

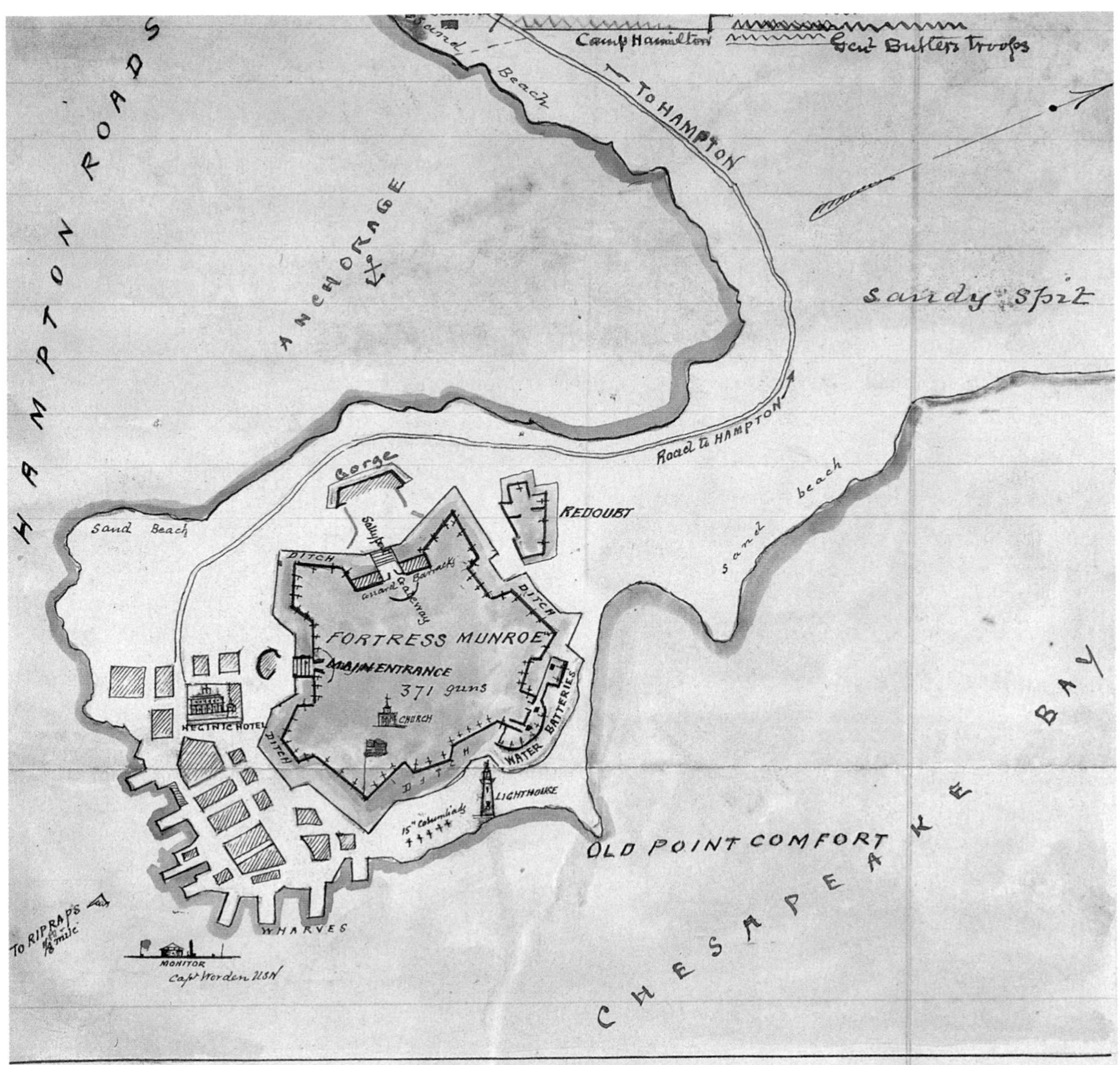

PLAN OF FORTRESS MUNROE Va 1862.

Area of outside walls 65 acres. Granite walls 35 ft. high Embrasures intended for 42 pdrs
Ditch 75 to 150 ft wide. Tide ebbs and flows in Ditch 8 to 15 ft daily. 42 embrasures
War garrison. 2450 men Cost $2.400.000 No of Guns 1862 371

Many Embrasures were enlarged and heavier guns mounted (some 200 pdr Parrots) in 1862

The fort was planned by Genl Simon Bernard Corps of Engineers formerly and Officer of French Army under Napoleon
The foundations of the Fort were laid in March 1819. under Maj Charles Gratiot. The post was first
occupied by Battery C. 3rd U S Artillery June 1823. Capt M. P. Lomax Commanding USA.
The site was occupied by a small Fort as early as 1608.

the furniture used for firewood including handsome wardrobes, staircases, etc. The piano had been gutted and stood on the outside of the house, being used for a horse bin to feed cavalrymen's horses. I went then over to Stout's and up the railroad track where some of the 1st New Jersey were passing on picket duty near Edsall's Hill. Several dead horses lay in the road near Mount Olivet Church, showing that the enemy had driven our cavalry outpost last night, two or three were wounded only. A dead cavalryman has not been found yet so far on our picket lines, and the saying is "Who ever saw a dead cavalryman?"

I visited an outpost at 9:30 p.m. with the relief guard and while returning one of the sentinels let [his] musket drop which went off. This alarmed the reserve post at Stout's farm house who scrambled out and made noise enough to be heard half a mile away. The false alarm brought about sixty men and muskets to intercept our return. And it was as much as good luck would have it that they had not fired into us on meeting. If there had been a fog, they would have done so without challenging. The men and officers are very slack while on picket. They look upon this duty as a sort of excursion in the woods, plunder is the main object. And as most of the officers are tame and good natured the men have pretty much their own way. Some officers return to camp with their detachments before others have come to relieve the posts! All because the new guard is an hour or so beyond the regular time. They thus leave the gaps open long enough for the Rebel farmers to pass out free.

January 10, 1862

Cold windy weather. Mud is all frozen on the roads which makes the rumbling of the long line of army wagons heard for a long distance. I went down to the head of Aqueduct Bridge to see Fort Corcoran and other works now all completed and armed with field artillery [and] rode up the Little River Turnpike to Pimmit Run to see the new military road just finished by our engineers. [I] returned by way of Arlington. In [the] afternoon I received an order to report to Captain William Heine . . . [at General Heintzelman's headquarters] at Fort Lyon for duty. [I] packed up my traps and got there about sundown, [where I] had a cordial welcome from Heine and Captain Israel Moses who was adjutant general. [I] slept in a Sibley tent* which was with others in front of the house, and nearly froze before the morning as the wind blew a cold gale and there was no stove in the tent. I found Edward Niven of the 40th here, detailed as a clerk to Captain Moses and Lieutenant [Leavitt] Hunt, assistant adjutant general. . . .

January 12, 1862

I met General Heintzelman for the first time today and was accorded a genial reception. He went over several large maps with me and gave instructions for my work. As Captain

*A large conical tent able to accommodate up to twenty soldiers.

Heine was a poor draughtsman on map work I had it all my own way. General [Irvin] McDowell [another division commander] whose headquarters are at the Arlington House has for a long time caused his engineer officers to make surveys and maps from actual reconnaissances of all the country between the Potomac and the enemy's lines, and a lot of draughtsmen have compiled a very elaborate map six or eight feet long and broad. These in small sheets have been lithographed by the Bureau of Maps and Engineering at Washington of which Colonel [Israel C.] Woodruff is chief. These sheets are in turn distributed to the several commanding officers for practical use in placing their picket lines, reserves, etc. Parts of these maps have to be enlarged, and are supplied to commanding officers who have orders to make a reconnaissance or attack on the enemy when the time arrives for them to move. Skeleton maps are then made, with a blue line for infantry march and a red one for artillery marked on each particular road. I began on a large cloth tracing of all the county below Fort Lyon to below Pohick Church and the Occoquan. . . .

I moved my sleeping quarters from the tent out in front of this house to a front room on the second floor of it. I work at my maps on the first floor where the telegraph instruments are, and the continual ticking and hammering bothers me considerably. I bought a strong and very powerful spy glass for $8 and with this from the flat roof of the house swept the panoramic scenery from Washington to miles down river. The accumulation of red earth forts, and long lines of rifle trenches was wonderful, while the long lines of canvas topped army wagons were in full view climbing hills or losing themselves in the valleys.

Captain Heine . . . has all this section of country under his supervision, and by constant scouting with map in hand extends information as to roads, bridges, Rebel earthworks and forces, while every house is marked on the map where rabid secessionists live or congregate. A [Southern civilian] scout regularly employed by the secret service goes with him on nearly every adventure. He lived at Accotink but the Rebels ostracized him long ago for being a Union man, and have set many traps to kill him which thus far has failed. Of course he knows every road and inhabitant in the vicinity from Alexandria to the Occoquan having lived here for years. Sometimes Heine has a boat expedition [of] five or six soldiers who formerly were sailors [who] are detailed from some regiment to go with him. They seize a boat at night in Belmont Bay or elsewhere and row along shore, landing here and there to capture Rebels in their own homes, seize mails brought across the Potomac from Port Tobacco or other places and confiscate and bring in powder, guns, homemade bullets or anything contraband of war. At times they have narrow escapes of being themselves captured.

The city of Alexandria can be seen below the hill, [along with] the white tents of thousands of men encamped for miles up and down river. On a fine moonlight night the scene is charming. Now and then the sullen boom of artillery is heard down river for an hour at a time, showing that the enemy are alive and [firing] their land batteries on the lower Potomac. We sit on the piazza smoking our pipes on fine nights and listen to this music for hours.

Telegraphic lines run from here to Arlington House, headquarters of General McDowell, and to the "Marshall House" at Alexandria, from thence over Long Bridge to the War Department at Washington. Two [telegraph] operators are stationed here, Nichols and Theodore Moreland, both from Pittsburgh, Pennsylvania. One relieves [the] other when they have to be at their instruments all night. One must be always "very wide awake." . . . The operators are dressed in a neat uniform, not enlisted men, and get from $60 to 80 per month, out of which they must clothe and feed themselves. Inviolable secrecy is enforced as to what messages they transmit and they must be perfect "know nothings" as to any inquiries as to what is going on. All are sworn to this.

January 21, 1862

. . . On account of the muddy camp grounds no brigade drills have been had for some time, dress parade, and inspections go on every day as usual. There are many deaths every day in camp or hospital, and funerals are numerous. Some of the men are sent home, where they came from, others are buried in little patches of woods near their camps. The cavalry are drilling constantly despite the mud. Colonel Sir Percy Wyndham and Colonel [William W.] Averell drill the cavalry squadrons around these headquarters, as there is level ground.

January 24, 1862

We have had several storms since [the] 15th. About sixteen inches now covers the ground, making it very uncomfortable for camping out. I had to leave my Sibley tent in front of the house where I had slept at nights and am now quartered with the general's staff in the second floor of Ballenger's house. Can now keep up a good fire day and night in the large chimney place. Captain Heine . . . makes frequent reconnaissances down the lower Potomac towards Accotink and Colchester, and has been fired on repeatedly by Rebel pickets. He seized a Rebel mail from a sailboat which came from the Maryland side, below Piscataway, which gave important information concerning the forces at Colchester and below. "Bushwhackers" infest all the country below Pohick Creek. Our pickets are along this stream but seldom see an enemy.

On one of his scouts Heine picked up a large Negro who deserted to our lines from a company of wood choppers at work on a Rebel earthwork at Colchester. He has him now as servant and guide, and black Harry now is dressed in cavalry uniform with sabre and pistol and a good horse. As he knows every road and path in the vicinity of Colchester and Accotink his services are valuable to Heine and would fight to the death before allowing himself to be captured. Harry is the first black cavalryman of the war.

I went over to the camp of the 63rd Pennsylvania Regiment today to see my friends Lieutenants [William H.] Jeffries and [Hugh B.] Fulton and had dinner and a good time generally. This regiment is in a fine state of discipline and drill and is commanded by Colonel

VILLAGE OF ACCOTINK, VA.

Alexander Hays. Most of the regiment came from Pittsburgh, Pennsylvania and are a splendid body of men. The roads and camps were six to eight inches deep in red mud and slush. Long lines of army wagons were stalled in it, doubling up the mule teams was necessary, while the cracking of whips and volleys of blood curdling oaths from the drivers and wagon masters was something fearful. As a defense to the enemy this Virginia mud is as good as several regiments to their numbers as it prevents us from raiding or attacking them for neither army can march two miles in the filthy red pasty mud. I made several sketches and returned to quarters at 10:30 p.m., tired out with struggling through the stumpy fields and muddy approaches to Fort Lyon. . . .

January 25, 1862

. . . Professor Lowe* was here, making ascensions in his balloon, which was held by fifteen enlisted men by three long ropes and a portable windlass. He had just finished his observations when the snow shut out his view and compelled him to pack up his balloon in two wagons and return to Alexandria. The balloon was up 1,000 feet. Lowe was observing the country towards Colchester, and saw earthworks being constructed by the enemy from there to Aquia Creek on the lower Potomac, which he of course marked on his map.

A reserve picket was here at the church, which stood in an open glade where four roads met. The forest had been cut for a long ways from it. Pohick Church was a substantial two story brick structure with white marble quoins and trimmings, and old colonial gambrel roof. It had neither tower or cupola however. It had been designed by Washington and was

*Thaddeus S. C. Lowe (1832–1913) was the driving force behind the establishment of the Union army's balloon corps. Used extensively by McClellan in the upcoming campaign, the program inexplicably was abandoned by the Union high command in 1863.

built of bricks imported from England in 1765.* Here Washington attended service, with all the old first families of the time. . . . Washington drove from Mount Vernon to church in his coach with four horses, tandem fashion as did the others. Now the church was in a ruinous condition. Windows were all broken out, doors gone, pews nearly gone, being used for fire wood by our pickets. The ceilings broken by the rain coming through the roof, walls discolored black by smoke, etc. The mahogany pulpit was half cut away and carried off for relics, while the cornerstone had been unearthed and the contents carried off. Washington had lain this stone in 1765 and the soldiers who got it out must have found valuable relics. There was not much left for the relic hunters now even the sconces and door knobs and hinges were gone. The owner was in the Rebel army and the house had no furniture. From here our picket line was strung along the banks of Pohick Creek. . . .

Three weeks after being assigned to division headquarters, Sneden's mapmaking duties were interrupted by his participation in a raid. The intrepid Captain Heine brought Sneden close to his first taste of action in dramatic form.

January 30, 1862

A reconnaissance and expedition started this morning for Colchester and Occoquan on the lower Potomac. The object was to ascertain the nature and force of the enemy at those places and what works have been erected as seen from the balloon. Also to secure all the Rebel mail carriers, who crossed over at night from the Maryland shore, particularly one known as Old Potter who lived with his son-in-law Haslip near Colchester.

Lieutenant Colonel Burke with fifty men of the 37th New York Volunteers and a squadron of Averell's 3rd Pennsylvania Cavalry composed the force. Captain Heine . . . [and] his Negro cavalryman went also. I got leave to go on my first raid. I got a good horse at Alexandria and all left there about 6 a.m. We went by the gravel road to Wright's. Thence to Pohick Church where we took the road to Hanover's house on the other side of Pohick Creek. Professor Lowe was up in the balloon at Pohick Church. We rested and had supper about 5 p.m. before crossing. The cavalry had the lead with skirmish line thrown out after we had passed the road which led to Colchester on the Occoquan River. The men had forded the head of Pohick Creek, and the delay caused by taking off their shoes, and wringing the water out of their stockings, made it dark before the route was resumed, but a full moon coming up soon after made everything visible and we jogged on without seeing anyone. The country was level with large clearings bordered by thick underbrush and pine trees. We found some Negroes further on who were chopping wood, and from whom we got informa-

*Built in 1769–1774, the church was probably designed by James Wren, not Washington, who served on the vestry.

tion of the enemy's whereabouts. Many of these broke away for the woods when we first came in sight in terror. It was decided to make a flank movement to the right as the Negroes gave us information that old man Potter was then at Haslip's house.

We got to within 1,000 yards of the river above Colchester and saw in the clear moonlight the line of Rebel earthworks on the other side, but could not tell if guns were mounted in them or not. Strict silence was ordered. Still the men managed to make quite a loud noise for their canteens were clanging and the sabres of the cavalrymen jangled incessantly. Lights were seen in Colchester and in other houses in the clearings, but no alarm was then given. At last we got near Haslip's house when a halt was called to prepare for action.

The cavalry being dismounted, crept on the ground towards Haslip's house which was a two story frame structure on a knoll, and surrounded it completely. Lights were in all the windows on the first floor and a dance was in progress inside. Heavy feet were keeping time to a fiddle at a great rate. One solitary sentinel was dozing on the front porch steps with his musket a few feet away from him. The moon was now hidden in a thick cloud for a time. One of our cavalrymen now crawled on all fours behind the sentinel and laid him out with one blow from the stock of his carbine, without making any noise. The whole force of twenty now advanced to within fifteen feet of the house on all sides, and Heine yelled "Surrender you d____d Rebels instantly!" The lights were immediately extinguished amid much swearing inside. Then all was quiet for a minute. No answer coming back, about twenty carbines were leveled at the clapboards of the first floor and discharged simultaneously. Then there were heard women screaming, men cursing and yelling, all striving to get upstairs.

Captain Heine now burst open the front door holding a pistol cocked in one hand and a dark lantern in another. As he did so two shots were fired at him from the top of the stairs. Both missed hitting him however, one shot knocked the lantern out of his hand. Those in the house now opened a fusillade from the windows of the second story on our men on the outside, who ranged themselves close up to the clapboarding and as the enemy leaned out overhead to fire they were shot at by others of our men fifty or sixty feet away in the open ground. Twenty of our men took cover behind fence corners and opened fire on the windows on all sides of the house. Three Rebels fell out of the windows to the ground dead or wounded. The firing ceased in about five minutes, and the Rebels surrendered amid cries of rage and much swearing.

Our men had to get into the house by the windows as the doors were barricaded with furniture after Heine had been first driven out. Inside were found a Rebel major and six soldiers of Texan Rangers all of whom were either dead or mortally wounded. Two more were dead on the outside where they had fallen out of the upper story windows, beside the unlucky sentinel. The fiddler, who was not a soldier, was unharmed as were old man Potter and his two daughters-in-law.

Potter had vanished all at once before the candles were relighted. Heine followed all over the house looking for him. He climbed up a ladder into the attic and found the old fellow in bed covered up between two of the women who belonged to the house! He was soon dragged downstairs, amid yells and cursings of these women despite his vigorous resistance. He was seventy years old but yet very strong and an ugly customer to handle. He bit, yelled, and kicked like a wild animal and four men had all they could do to get him bound and out of the house. He had been using his double barreled shotgun vigorously on our men all the while. He was securely bound with a rope and lashed behind one of our cavalrymen and brought off. The fiddler was served the same way.

In the melee one of our men was killed and four badly wounded. The dead man was brought off by us. One of the women (Mrs. Disney) showed fight all the time, and yelled to give the alarm at Colchester, not very far away. She was then seized, bound, and lashed behind another cavalryman and brought off. Old man Potter was only half dressed and would have frozen had not one of our men wrapped him up in blankets used for the horses. The enemy at Colchester hearing the firing were thoroughly alarmed, and began shelling the woods at random from their earthwork battery across the Occoquan River, so this hurried up the raiding party somewhat, and all soon left, taking a bye road piloted by black Harry the servant of Captain Heine who knew the country thoroughly. The Texans were left where they fell, and such was the hurry that their arms were not brought off, which was the only thing that General Heintzelman blamed the raiding party for.

After riding hard a mile or so we halted, and could hear the jingle of cavalry sabres of Rebels in pursuit. Shells were bursting at intervals in the woods but not within 500 yards of us. They soon stopped firing. We turned into another bye road and making a wide detour to the right, went to another house occupied by another Haslip, surrounded it and took two young men prisoners without any resistance. Also a Mrs. Bates, a noted Rebel contrabandist.* These were all tied behind the saddles of three cavalrymen and we went slow although the cold was intense, and reached Fort Lyon about 3 o'clock in the morning.

The prisoners were brought into the telegraph room before a good fire, where they dozed until morning. They had lost their defiant attitudes except old Potter and were nearly frozen before arriving. All were anxious, asked many questions, but it was against orders to talk to them. The night telegraph operator, myself, and one cavalryman as guard were the only ones who sat up with them all night. I went to bed at 5 a.m., for some rest after the hard riding of the night before. The general saw the prisoners in the morning, and sent them all under guard to [the] provost marshal at Alexandria, from whence they were transferred to the Old Capitol Prison in Washington.

February 1, 1862

Professor Lowe is staying here for a few days. [He] has several small balloons with him to use in an experimental way, from this high hill he can see many miles in all directions. Some

* Contrabands were escaped slaves, but in this context Sneden probably was using the term to refer to a smuggler.

of our more sanguine generals want him to cut his balloon loose . . . sail over the enemy's camps and drop live shells on the fellows below. Lowe won't do it however as it would be murder, not war. If the enemy ever took prisoner [of] one who would do this, he would meet a varied kind of death at once. Balloons are now used frequently at Pohick Church and on our front lines at Chain Bridge, whence Munson's Hill and all the country up river can be observed. A gas wagon is attached to the balloon [partly] with which the balloon is only one half or one third inflated, then it rises 1,000 feet or more, and is held on the ground by two or three long ropes by a lot of soldiers who are detailed for the purpose. [They] are paid 25c per day in addition to their regular pay, work or no work as may be. . . .

February 10, 1862

Fine and cold. I went over to the 40th Regiment camp today and while returning on foot through a clump of trees came near being shot by a company of the 40th who were practicing at a target and whom I did not see. I had walked past the target just as a volley was fired. The bushes and trees were hit all around me and I had a "close call." I did not stop for further investigation but continued on to Fort Lyon. . . .

February 12, 1862

A small riot was in progress this forenoon at Alexandria caused by the provost guard seizing liquors from some of the Secesh bar rounds. Two or three companies of the 38th New York Regiment went down to quell it. Several were arrested and sent to the slave pen. The people of Alexandria contrive to sell whiskey to soldiers who go there from the camps on a few hours' furlough. The soldiers are generally robbed of their money and [end] up in the guard house. All liquors are confiscated and seized by the provost marshal Captain Andrew Porter, but it can be had at all times nevertheless by those who know where to find it. The soldiers get drunk, fight among themselves, and are arrested. The slave pen is used as a jail and many dozens are there every day and night to sober up before they can return to their camps.

I went to the brigade theatre this evening. . . . Miss Julia Hudson, from one of the Washington theatres played to a large audience of officers and soldiers. The play was "His Last Legs." Several ladies were in the audience, [including] officers' wives, etc. The hackmen made $8 and $5 fares for each coach. Theatre closed at 11:30 p.m. . . .

February 15, 1862

Snowing all day. Three inches fell. The artillerymen at Fort Lyon were practicing at the guns all the forenoon. The concussion of the 100 pounder Parrotts shook these headquarters to the foundation. The clerks could not write as usual while I could not make a straight line, owing to the firing. In the evening [at] 9 p.m. we had a fine serenade at these headquarters by the 26th New York Regiment band, which are now stationed at Fort Lyon. Artillery firing was heard down river from 10 to 12 p.m., supposed to be [General Joseph] Hooker's batteries shelling Cockpit Point. Fine moonlight night with no wind made the cannonading very distinct, and it sounded grand. The view from headquarters of the river smooth as glass was enchanting. We smoked our pipes on the piazza until after midnight.

February 22, 1862

Washington's birthday. Salutes were fired from the guns in the Navy Yard Washington, as also from Forts Lyon, Ellsworth and Fort Corcoran at sunrise and at noon. The heavy guns at Fort Lyon shook these headquarters and made the window sashes rattle greatly. I could not do any drawing while the firing lasted. The Rebel flags which were recently captured at Fort Donelson [Tennessee] were presented to the War Department today in the presence of a large crowd of spectators and military men. Speeches were made by Secretary [of War Edwin M.] Stanton and others from the balcony of that building.

I went to Washington today with Nichols our telegraph operator here. Willard's and other hotels there were crowded with our officers as usual, and the way they "practiced at the bar" was enough to craze a poor lawyer! Long lines of army wagons lined Pennsylvania Avenue and hundreds of beef cattle were being driven over Long Bridge. I made purchases needed, dined at Gantier's, and returned by Aqueduct Bridge. [I] went to the camp of the 40th, saw [a] dress parade, and went to the Log Theatre in the evening. Miss Susan Denin and Benjamin Rogers from Washington played in "Eddystone Lighthouse." The theatre was crowded, many ladies from Washington being there. At 11:30 p.m., when the show was over Nichols and I indulged in an oyster supper in the restaurant attached to the theatre. A ball was in progress in the theatre, which lasted until far into the morning. Washington city was illuminated at night.

February 25, 1862

The 2nd Michigan, 63rd Pennsylvania, and 38th New York regiments with two batteries of artillery had a heavy skirmish with the enemy this morning at Nelson's house, Pohick. Our lines were drawn in to Wright's house, on the gravel road. Captain Chapman and Lieutenant Jeffries of 63rd Pennsylvania called on me for maps in [the] vicinity of Pohick Church which were furnished them. In the skirmish we lost one killed, two wounded. Three women were brought in as prisoners. They were Mrs. Disney, Mrs. Plunkett, and Mrs. Wright. They were proved to have sent their Negroes to the Rebel lines at night, giving information of our forces at Wright's, where our rescue picket post is. They were all sent to the Old Capitol Prison Washington. Colonel James Kerrigan of 25th New York Volunteers was dismissed [from] the army by a court martial. "Too much rye" was the main cause of his disgrace. There are lots of other officers who would benefit the service if they too were cashiered. . . .

By late winter 1862, George McClellan had assembled the largest fighting force ever seen in the Western Hemisphere—nearly 150,000 men. The army was the product of diligent training, but "Little Mac" conspicuously kept it out of action. While Yankee forces threatened key points on the Mississippi River and scored victories in North Carolina, Tennessee, and Arkansas, the mighty Army of the Potomac lay dormant. President Lincoln and Secretary of War Stanton indulged McClellan's reluctance for months, but their tolerance had dissolved. To them it was essential that McClellan break the hold of the Rebel army at Manassas, and, above all, capture Richmond, the Confederate capital.

At last, the general devised a plan that would outflank the Confederates, an amphibious landing on the Rappahannock River northeast of Richmond. When the enemy army withdrew from Manassas to the line of the Rappahannock, however, an agitated Lincoln permitted McClellan to execute an alternative plan of advancing on Richmond by water. McClellan would sail his army down the Potomac River into the Chesapeake Bay and land at the tip of the Virginia Peninsula, that piece of history-rich land framed by the York and James rivers. There the aged Fort Monroe, still in Federal hands, would serve as a solid base for an advance seventy miles up the Peninsula to Richmond.

Throughout March, McClellan worked tirelessly to launch the operation. He gathered a massive flotilla of some four hundred ships and boats on the wharves of the Potomac near Washington. In the next weeks, this armada transported nearly ninety thousand troops and vast numbers of animals, equipment, and artillery to Fort Monroe. McClellan had embarked the largest amphibious operation the world had ever seen. Private Sneden observed these events with keen interest while continuing his regular excursions.

March 1, 1862

Fine—cold high winds—new arms—clothing and ammunition have been furnished the troops in camp on this side [of] the Potomac, and orders were read on parade that a forward movement on the enemy will soon be made, which was received with prolonged cheering by the men. Of course where to was not mentioned. The army now being fully equipped and well drilled are ready to go anywhere as the monotony and muddy camps make all very impatient to "On to Richmond" or anywhere else. At these headquarters it is known among a few that we will embark for the Virginia Peninsula. I have been for several days working on maps showing country from Fort Monroe to Yorktown, Virginia, making enlarged tracings on cloth from the smaller maps furnished by the Topographical Bureau at Washington. Yorktown is the objective point, where the Rebel General [John B.] Magruder is entrenched with more than 10,000 men.

I went to the log theatre. This evening Susan Denin played in two French comedies. The house was crowded. The band of [the] 63rd Pennsylvania Regiment . . . serenaded at these headquarters 9 to 10 p.m. It was fine moonlight and from this high elevation the music could be heard a long distance. Lieutenants Jeffries and Fulton of [the] 63rd sat with us smoking until after midnight. . . .

March 3, 1862

The enemy are reported to have evacuated Fairfax Court House and vicinity. A brigade started out there this morning to see for themselves. The number of regimental wagons have been lessened. The surplus are sent to Alexandria for shipment when orders come to move. There are many deaths in camp. Every day a soldier's funeral takes place. The 40th Regiment have lost several officers, among them Lieutenant [John M.] Turnbull and Captain [James W.] George. Exposure and whiskey causes frequent deaths among officers mostly. . . . The ceaseless click of the telegraph instruments here is kept up nearly all night while I work on maps until long past midnight. . . .

March 8, 1862

Fine weather. With Captain Heine I went down on a reconnaissance toward Occoquan. Got to [George] Mason's plantation about 11 a.m., thence to Pohick Church, where . . . two balloons [were] making observations from a height of 2,000 feet. Professor Lowe and a lot of scientific men were here also from Washington. The enemy had withdrawn all their picket lines along our whole front from Munson's Hill to Colchester. From the balloon large volumes of smoke was seen over the woods in several places down river, which shows that the enemy are falling back toward Manassas and Centreville and are burning their log house camps. Scores of Negroes from below the Occoquan are daily coming into our lines, who declare that the whole Rebel army has moved south. We found many of the inhabitants in the region of Accotink and Pohick who had left their houses with their Negroes and gone with the Rebels. So the chances now are that the bushwhackers won't trouble us for a while. Old Capitol Prison at Washington is nearly full of Rebel sympathizers and bushwhacking farmers.

A squadron of Averell's cavalry was pushed to Occoquan and beyond who met none of the enemy's forces. All the earthworks and batteries on the other side of the Occoquan and on its steep banks had been deserted. In Colchester very few people were seen, and these only old men. The women on the doorsteps wanted to know "where we . . . were going." The road ran along high bluffs on the banks of the Occoquan and the view down river was fine, not a solitary sail was to be seen either on Pohick Bay or the Potomac. Many houses on the road were entirely deserted. Fences were few. No live cattle of any kind were seen. Doors were hanging by one hinge and the whole country looked deserted everywhere outside the villages of Colchester and Accotink. This last village has a pre-

VIEW OF THE MANSION AT MOUNT VERNON, VA.
Sketched December 23, 1861.

ponderance of Union Quaker folks. The people seemed poor, as no business of any kind was doing. Fishing and raising corn is all that the inhabitants can do. Not more than 200 people were in the town who turned out in the streets to see us pass through.

I left the escort and revisited Mount Vernon on our homeward march. Two of us rode over a greater portion of the estate. We did not go through the house, but entered our names on the register book in the grand hall. We then visited both tombs and also gathered leaves to press for mementoes. Got some large acorns.

I noticed now that the carved marble eagle which was on the lid of the sarcophagus had been broken off and carried away by some vandal looking for relics! These wretches spare nothing sacred or profane so long as they can get a relic of some sort. The only way that I saw for the wretch to obtain the eagle was to thrust the butt end of his musket through the open barred grating of the arched entrance and break off the emblem from the face of the slab. No one could climb into the chamber as the iron spike heads of the gate went up to within a foot of the center of the arched door. The claws of the eagle remained on the slab but the remainder had vanished. I was here last [December] when everything in and about the tomb were intact. The custodian of the estate at the mansion did not know of this vandalism until I informed him of it. He does not go over the grounds very often, as he stands a chance at night especially, of being shot by either our or Rebel pickets who sometimes are on the grounds prowling around after something of use while in camp.

March 17, 1862

. . . I went to Alexandria this afternoon and made a good sketch of Christ Church, which was the first Episcopal Church built there in 1773. Washington and the first families used to attend there. It was locked and I could not get inside. It seemed in good repair. While the inscriptions on the tombstones were very quaint—many stones were chiseled with armorial bearings, but the weather had obliterated all the finest executed designs—many had sunk to only a few inches out of the ground.

In returning I had to make a cross cut over deserted fields full of stumps so as to avoid the steady streams of wagons which were all going from their camps towards Alexandria. Many regiments had to encamp as best they could on the wet flat ground below Fort Lyon, as they could not be embarked on account of night coming on, while the wagons stood in the streets of Alexandria all night for the same cause. I reached headquarters about 10 p.m. where I found everyone getting ready for a move. Stocks of dried meat and ham had to be packed in old soap boxes [and] demijohns of whiskey filled. These had patent tops with locks. Baggage had to be cut down to the smallest possible quantity and five days' rations were being cooked in the kitchens of the house and by small fires on the outside. For some days I had prepared myself for the campaign by buying things needed at Washington and now packed my map box, instruments, etc., and cleaned up my new acquisition—the double barrel shot gun—making a cover for it from a rubber blanket.

March 19, 1862

Fine and windy. [Israel B.] Richardson's brigade of Sumner's corps embarked on steamers today from Alexandria. These are mostly Michigan regiments and are a fine body of well drilled men. The 40th New York broke camp at noon. I went over to see them off. They marched off their camp ground at 2:30 p.m. and went down the Leesburg Pike to Alexandria. The Brigade Theatre was sold to Mr. Fowle, the owner of the plantation on which it was built, who intends to turn it into a tobacco curing house where the leaves of tobacco are dried by smoke by small fires built on the floor. I did not hear the price paid, but Fowle got a large building built of logs, such as he could not build with all his Negro help in ten years. . . .

March 21, 1862

The headquarters flag was struck at noon today in fog and a drizzly rain, and our headquarters at Ballenger's house, Fort Lyon, ceased to exist, as all had been prepared for moving. This was done after dinner. Our stuff was then hauled to the wharf at Alexandria where the fast river steamer *Kent* had been selected for General Heintzelman and his staff and about 100 other officers. At 2 p.m. the fleet began to slowly sail and steam

HEADQUARTERS OF MAJOR GENERAL SAMUEL P. HEINTZELMAN
At Ballenger's house. Fort Lyon, Va., March 1862.

down the Potomac amid the cheers of the soldiers, booming of guns in salute and the playing of several bands. The sun had now come out and shone on the white steamers crowded with blue uniforms or the red ones of the Zouaves—glistening muskets and bayonets and the white sails of the sailing vessels, while the smoke of the saluting guns from Fort Lyon gave an impressive and fine effect. The Army of the Potomac had now started on its career of glory and fame never to be forgotten by those who participated in it or shared its fortunes and victories. The fleet of 400 odd vessels slowly sailed down the Potomac until lost in the haze beyond Fort Washington and Mount Vernon. . . .

At 6:30 p.m. . . . General Heintzelman, commanding [the] III Army Corps* embarked on board the small fast sailing steamer *Kent* from the wharf foot of King Street, Alexandria with his staff, etc. Among those who accompanied us were Mr. Ed Hall, special war artist of *Frank Leslie's Illustrated Newspaper* . . . and Mr. [Thomas B.] Gunn, correspondent of [the *New York*] *Times*, and [Samuel] Wilkeson of the *Tribune*. . . .

We made our supper, everyone for himself in the cabin (had no cooks or stewards aboard). By 8 p.m. the tide had now fallen so low that the boat was aground, and we had to lie at the wharf until morning, much to our disgust. All turned in for sleep at midnight, leaving a solitary guard on deck to prevent stragglers from boarding us. Mules were being hoist-

* Before launching the Peninsula Campaign, McClellan grouped his twelve divisions into four corps and designated senior generals for each, including Heintzelman, who commanded the III Corps. As such, Sneden now worked in a headquarters just below army level.

ed into barges, horses were neighing and soldiers were yet embarking most of the night. The whole fleet was anchored some miles down river, and the hundreds of lights on board lit up the whole lower bay making a fine sight. We passed over our evening in admiring these, eating and drinking and smoking our pipes.

March 22, 1862

Fine clear day and warm. All were up at 7 a.m. and on deck. General Heintzelman had not stayed on board during the night with us. . . . We had to wait for him until he did come, which was at 10 a.m. when the steamer cast off the lines, and soon we were going down under full steam to overtake the fleet below. About 11 a.m. [we] came up to the fleet now under weigh but going slow and very much together, the steamers leading. Some vessels were not more than sixty to eighty feet apart. The bands played and the crowded decks filled with soldiers [who] were cheering and calling to one another. Our boat seemed very fast and outran the fleet, when we slowed up to let them catch up. We steamed quite close to Fort Washington going slow. Mr. Hall, the artist for *Frank Leslie's*, made a sketch of the fleet for his paper.

The fleet sailed in double columns and the shouting and jokes passed by the soldiers to each other on other vessels afforded much merriment. Whiskey seemed to be plentiful on board some of them. The bands stopped playing after we had passed Fort Washington. The whole garrison were looking at us from the parapets and wharf at the foot of the high bluff on which it was built. No one was seen anywhere at Mount Vernon, though all the inhabitants along [the] shore were out to see the great [armada] pass. Lots of little and big Negroes rolled their eyes in amazement no doubt. As we arrived off Cockpit Point the Rebel earthworks loomed up on the steep clay banks. They, as well as those below, had long been evacuated by the enemy. General Hooker's forces had been withdrawn from them to his old camps on the Maryland side of the river . . . and was soon to follow to Fort Monroe. General Heintzelman wanted to send him maps and dispatches.* I was selected to carry them. The *Kent* slowed up and the dory boat was lowered into which I soon jumped and was pulled ashore by two of the crew. The whole fleet was two or more miles in advance. It was about 4 p.m. and low tide, so the boat was beached in the mud flats and I had to get out and jump from rock to rock until I reached the foot of the bluff which was wooded and steep to climb. Not a soldier was in sight when I got at the top of the bluff. I pulled out a white handkerchief and waved it vigorously for a minute, when one of our cavalrymen came out of a clump of trees and rode toward me with carbine at rest. I yelled to him not to shoot, which he was intelligent enough to understand. I gave him the maps and dispatches for General Hooker and scrambled down the bluff to the boat. The cavalryman could not see the steamer from his post as she was below the bluff in the river, and took me for a Secesh offi-

*Hooker's division was now part of Heintzelman's corps.

Stump Neck and Chickamaxen Creek — Mrs. Budd's house and Rebel battery on hill — Potomac River

BUDD'S FERRY, LOWER POTOMAC RIVER, MD.
Rebels ran mail across to Maryland side nearly every night in boats.

cer who wanted to surrender. I regained the boat with both feet wet and returned on board the *Kent*, when we made all speed to catch up with the fleet, now nearly out of sight in a bend of the Potomac below Budd's Ferry.

I made sketches of all the deserted Rebel batteries at Evansport [and] Quantico Creek, while Mr. Hall did the same for his newspaper. We overhauled the fleet at about 8 p.m. The vessels were now brilliant with hundreds of lights which reflected on the smooth waters making the scene very beautiful. Mr. Hall had another chance to make a sketch.

The *Kent* now passed the fleet and kept in the lead until off the Rappahannock River. After a good supper I kept the deck until past midnight. The moon came out, making the shores and headlands plainly visible. The white sandy beach and dark black pine trees throwing deep shadows on the water made a charming picture, while the churning of wheels and screws from 330 steamers made a strange noise as the echoes reverberated from the heavily wooded shore. Many lights moving about were seen at Aquia Creek where there is a long wharf and deserted earthen forts left by the enemy when they fell back from the whole Potomac River front. With a good map I noted every headland and shore with interest. I walked the deck with Colonel Alexander Hays of the 63rd Pennsylvania until nearly morning, then turned in.

March 23, 1862

I was on deck by 6 a.m., the wind had freshened during the night and the fleet now were bowling before a stiff breeze. The ships were much scattered, while all the fastest steamers were going slow so that the vessels could keep up together. By 11 a.m. this was effected and

THE REBEL BATTERY AT EVANSPORT, LOWER POTOMAC, VA.

two lines were kept again as the order of sailing, we were now off the entrance of the York River. Several large and small islands densely wooded were off the [starboard] beam, which had a refreshing look and as the wind was off shore we could smell the pine trees. A tall thin column of black smoke rose above the forest beyond the islands, which no doubt was a signal to the enemy at Gloucester and Yorktown that the "Yankees" had come at last to investigate matters for themselves. The shores along here to Old Point Comfort were low and sandy, with forest quite close down to the water's edge. No signs of life or any houses were visible. Two or three fishing boats were hauled up high and dry along the entrances of Poquoson River and Back River which empty into Chesapeake Bay at this point.

About 12:30 noon we rounded the point and came into Hampton Roads, and passing the lighthouse and the frowning walls of Fortress Monroe landed at a wharf up near the hotel. The whole fleet rounded the point and came to an anchor between the Rip Rap battery in the Roads and the fort, and about 300 yards from it several of the larger steamers with [General Charles Smith] Hamilton's division of III Corps tied up at the wharves while hundreds of soldiers disembarked and stacked arms all along the beach for a mile, while their officers made a rush for the hotel to get something to eat and drink. All was bustle and hurry until midnight to land the troops first. As fast as one steamer was emptied of troops she would haul out and anchor while another filled the place. There were but two large wharves available for a large vessel, one was the U.S. government wharf, this was soon crowded. General McClellan did not come with the fleet but stayed at Washington to see all the forces and vessels off. . . .

[I] went ashore about 3 p.m. and to the Hygeia Hotel of course. Here I found oysters such as I never saw before for size and quality at 50¢ a dozen and got a canteen filled with good ale. All the cooks were hard at work, the rooms and bar was crowded with our officers, all talking, eating, drinking, and smoking. I went all over the place and out on the sand spit and rear of the fort. Saw several [unmounted] monster guns near the lighthouse at the point.

I was called on to furnish maps to General Heintzelman and after a while got at the box containing them in the steamer's cabin. The general and several other officers were in the fort consulting General [John E.] Wool* as to the situation and approaches to Yorktown twenty-four miles up the Peninsula where the enemy under Magruder . . . were to dispute our going farther. Fortunately I had several duplicate tracings on cloth made at Fort Lyon weeks ago, which were furnished to generals in III, II, and IV Corps. General Wool had coast survey maps only. Mine had been enlarged from more recent surveys and reconnaissances made by the engineer officers of General [Benjamin F.] Butler when he was here last April and were more valuable now than any others. My map box was of hardwood, six feet long and two feet wide by two feet deep. It had strong iron hinges with hasps and padlock with handles so as to carry in the wagons. These maps and my instruments were ever my constant care. . . .

By 3:30 p.m. Hamilton's division . . . had all landed and at 4 o'clock all were on the march to Hampton. About three miles from Fort Monroe a light drizzling rain now fell which in no wise dampened the ardor of the troops who all went forward gayly but without music except the tap of the drum. Our headquarter wagons and horses had now been landed and packed and I with the rest went forward at 4 p.m. General [Erasmus D.] Keyes' IV Corps were to follow us of the III as soon as practicable. Coming to Hampton Creek the troops crossed on one pontoon bridge to the ruined town while the wagons crossed on another. The generals of III and IV Corps were far in the advance to select their headquarters and to direct the troops to their several campgrounds.

After they had crossed I walked from Fort Monroe with some officers of [the] 40th Regiment and our two telegraph operators. . . . We found the town in utter ruin, nothing but tumbled down walls and blackened chimneys, which stuck up in all directions amid charred timbers and debris of all kinds. Magruder burnt the whole place down 7th August last to prevent General Butler's troops from holding it after [the] battle of Big Bethel.

The general's tent, with those of the staff was pitched at the corner of Main Street and that [street] which led to the church now in ruins. The courthouse, roofless and thoroughly gutted, adjoined the ground selected. The ruins of a large church or bank was opposite. A circular building near was said to be the ruins of Secretary Floyd's† house. The chimney of the ruined court house served our cooks well in getting supper. The telegraph tent was soon up and the operator at work on the newly strung wires to Fort Monroe. The clerks

*Union commander at Fort Monroe.

† Sneden may have thought this was the home of former Secretary of War John B. Floyd, but there is no evidence that Floyd ever lived in Hampton.

ADVANCE OF THE ARMY UP THE PENINSULA
Major General George B. McClellan commanding.

had to sleep in the empty wagons tonight. I tented with Moreland and Nichols, but the incessant click of the instruments near my head kept me awake nearly all night. It came on to rain at 9 p.m. continuing all night. The infantry regiments marched past up the main street and into the large open fields a short way above our headquarters where they camped for the rest of the night. They filed past until 2 a.m. . . . All was quiet. The glare on the sky of the numerous camp fires could be seen miles away. The rain splashed down and the troops marched past in silence most of the night.

March 24, 1862

. . . At 3 p.m. I went over the ruins of the town and down to the creek. A durable trestle bridge had been built by our engineers on the stumps or spiles of the former one which had been burnt. Army wagons were going over it in a steady stream and were winding away up the main street to the green fields, now white with tents in all directions. Crossing over the pontoon bridge I came upon the remains of our old earthworks built by General Butler's troops in April 1861 and from there made a sketch of Hampton and its ruined buildings. Keeping through the town I came upon the ruins of St. John's Episcopal Church. The fire had gutted it completely. The tower had fallen down all in a heap, roofs clean gone, and nothing but bare walls left standing. Not a piece of woodwork of any kind could be seen but a few ends of timbers sticking up out of piles of burnt bricks, some of the fine trees

around the graveyard were scorched black and dead, others were in full leaf. Notable [was] a very large willow tree whose trunk must have been eight or nine feet at the base. Many of the marble monuments had been thrown down and smashed. Most of these were fine monuments of white marble erected to officers of the old army and navy of the United States for years back. Other tombs of brick with sandstone or slate slabs were everywhere, some surrounded with wooden fences, others with handsome iron fences. Most of the wooden fences had been used as firewood by Butler's troops when here. A low brick wall ran around the whole graveyard, broken at the top to give room for field artillery. A deep and wide ditch had been dug by Butler's troops on two sides of the graveyard the size of which was about one acre. The church was built [of bricks] brought from England. I made two sketches of the church and copies of several tombstones. . . .

March 25, 1862

Fine and warm. Fitz-John Porter's* division [of the III Corps] arrived at Fortress Monroe on [the] 24th [and] marched up today and went into camp. I revisited the ruined town and St. John's Church today, and made several sketches. The army marched through the town until

*Porter (1822–1901) was one of McClellan's favorite generals. He rose to command the V Corps, a post he held until cashiered from the army in 1863, after an exhaustive investigation for disobedience of orders at Second Bull Run.

FRONT VIEW OF ST. JOHN'S CHURCH, HAMPTON, VA.

late at night, large bonfires were made to light their way. The fire shone on the tall burnt chimneys, making quite a theatrical effect. General McClellan has not yet arrived from Washington. General Sumner who is second in command is at the wharves most of the day, directing movements and disembarkation.

March 26, 1862

Rain and slight snow. Our picket lines were advanced at daylight this morning to the South West Branch and reconnoitering was had towards Little and Big Bethel by the cavalry and some regiments of infantry. The enemy were met in small force. We had five killed and a few wounded. Enemy's loss unknown, as they kept in dense woods. Hundreds of soldiers are roaming over the ruined town and churchyard. There is nothing of any use to them to be found, but they have broken and upset tombs in the churchyard of St. John's and unearthed coffins and skeletons looking for jewelry and coffin plates for relics! Skulls, and parts of skeletons are lying among the tombs. This will be stopped.

March 27, 1862

[General Daniel E.] Sickles' and Keyes' troops march through the town today and went into camp. A gunboat expedition was sent to the mouth of [the] York River and going up towards Yorktown and found the enemy entrenched in strong batteries at Gloucester Point opposite Yorktown, who fired a few shots from their heavy guns at them. None hit however. The gunboats withdrew without any firing. The [Confederate ironclad] *Merrimac* is still behind Craney Island. We don't want her to come out from there either, as she would destroy our vessels at anchor off Fort Monroe. There are over 500 vessels and steamers there now landing troops and stores, horses and ammunition. Fifteen batteries have now landed and gone into camp. A brigade have formed a camp on the sandy ground between Fort Monroe and Hampton. It is called Camp Hamilton. A large building near the water which had been used for a seminary or college of some kind has been fitted up by our surgeons for an hospital. I work hard on maps until sundown, and have but little room as I still am in the telegraph tent with the operators. I detailed Mr. [William] Goldsby of [the] 40th Regiment for my cook. . . .

March 30, 1862

The enemy fired several shots from their heavy guns at Sewell's Point at our fleet of transports anchored off Fort Monroe today. All of them missed though several came near hitting. Professor Lowe with two large war balloons arrived at camp today. He has a gas making apparatus on wheels. Twenty-five soldiers were detailed to assist in working and lowering the balloon, which will be held by two or three ropes 1,000 feet long on [a] windlass. Troops and stores of all kinds are still being landed at the wharves at Fortress Monroe. White tents cover the large fields in all directions. Dress parades and music [are] had every fine afternoon. Artillery firing was heard in the direction of Newport News about 5 p.m. We thought surely that the *Merrimac* had come out to try her luck. All the men in camp listened a long while but only a few shots were fired then stopped.

April 1, 1862

Fine day. I walked to Fort Monroe and had oysters at the Hygeia Hotel. Met several of my old acquaintances whom I had not seen since leaving Alexandria. I walked the beach to the rear of the fort and watched with my glass the fleet at anchor and the Rebel batteries at Sewell's Point. . . . I [then] went on some of the wharves where many vessels and steamers were discharging gun carriages, bales of hay, and stores of all kinds. One wharf was piled with gunpowder in kegs and grape and cannister. I saw a soldier rolling some of the kegs and smoking his pipe at the same time. I got off that wharf as soon as I could. . . .

Last evening a Rebel gunboat steamed out from behind Pig Point, which is opposite Newport News and shelled the camps of our troops there. Our men ran back out of range. A few tents were knocked down and destroyed but no one was hurt. This was the firing we heard yesterday. I walked along shore to Hampton and crossed the pontoon bridge, long lines of wagons were going toward Hampton and the camps beyond. I visited the camps of the 40th New York and 63rd Pennsylvania regiments, saw my friends and a dress parade of [the] 63rd and got to headquarters at 8 p.m. Some of the camps are on swampy ground and a heavy rain would drown out half the men. Up the road from our headquarters I came upon a graveyard triangular in shape with a brick wall all around it. No church or any other building was near it. It was getting dark [and] I could not then make out the inscriptions on the many tombs and head stones. These graves had not been broken into as the ones in St. John's churchyard there. I picked up half a skull of some infant which I use for a soap dish.

Chapter Two

Under Fire

With thousands of troops streaming onto the tip of the Virginia Peninsula, expectations ran high that the army would be in motion soon. Scouting reports indicated that a small force of Confederates under John Magruder held a line of entrenchments at Yorktown, a mere fifteen miles up the road. A confident George McClellan fully expected to brush aside these Rebels and easily take the old Revolutionary War battlefield in two or three days. Excited Union soldiers anticipated a triumphal march to Richmond.

The Federal advance began well enough on April 4. The Confederates put up little resistance, and by nightfall Union troops had marched twelve miles. The following day, however, rain, poor roads, inaccurate maps, overly cautious generals, and an unexpected surprise at Yorktown conspired to bring McClellan to an abrupt halt. Reports from his scouts revealed that the Confederate fortifications were not limited to the immediate Yorktown vicinity; instead they ran completely across the Peninsula. Even more alarming were reports that Magruder was resisting with a much stronger force than anticipated. In reality, the Confederates had only eleven thousand men; but Magruder put on a dramatic show of force by firing his cannon, double-timing his troops to and fro, and ordering his men to cheer as if reinforcements had arrived.

The Confederate determination to stand and fight was something McClellan had not anticipated. As much as the rain, it dampened his urge for rapid movement. After a two-day reconnaissance, he decided on a formal siege of a position that he could have carried immedi-

ately by assault. Settling into a month-long siege, McClellan's delay enabled the Confederates eventually to move most of their main army under Joseph E. Johnston to the lines at Yorktown. Still the Federals held an advantage of almost two to one.

Removed from his comfortable quarters in northern Virginia, Private Sneden now experienced real campaigning for the first time. Cold rain, gluelike mud, wagon-clogged roads, and the sometimes maddening actions of officers became part of his daily routine. Those annoyances, however, could not interfere with the important job he had to do. "The maps of the Peninsula are perfectly unreliable," George McClellan complained. Most were decades old and often failed to show the numerous streams that slowed troop movements. As a result, Union army topographers stayed busy at Yorktown.

Sneden spent long hours bending over drafting tables, often relying on the most modern of available scientific methods, including reports from Professor Lowe's balloons, to prepare maps. He also was not afraid to go up on the lines to do his job. He, like some other mapmakers, regularly exposed himself to enemy fire to get accurate surveys of the landscape. On one occasion he found himself the object of target practice from a Confederate artillery crew. For a soldier, however, Sneden led a charmed existence, and he knew it. He freely admitted that his comrades in the trenches were not so fortunate.

April 2, 1862

. . . General McClellan arrived today at Fortress Monroe by steamer. A call was made for all the generals to meet at the fort to consult [on] the situation and decide on future movements. At 5 p.m. orders were read at dress parade for a forward movement at once. Three days' rations to be cooked immediately. Forty rounds of ammunition per man. So at night the sky was aglow with camp fires in every direction.

A very violent thunderstorm with torrents of rain began at 10 p.m., which soon drowned the fires out. The wind blew a gale, making the camp lakes of water and keeping the men up until daylight to prevent their tents and belongings from being swept away. The thunder crashed among the chimneys around our headquarters in the ruins, while blinding sheets of lightning in quick succession made us all nervous and miserable. Some of us stood against the low brick walls or in the open, as some of the chimneys might tumble on us. We had fortunately ditched our tents days ago, so we were not flooded out, yet everything was dripping wet at midnight when the storm was at its height. The mules brayed and horses neighed in mortal terror of the terrific crashes of thunder. It beat all any of us had ever heard in the North. The storm moderated . . . but did not wholly abate [and] sleep was impossible until 4 a.m. I laid down in the telegraph tent, on rubber blankets and straw on the ground where it was dry. . . .

April 3, 1862

. . . Orders were given for the whole army to march tomorrow morning, which was hailed by cheers from the regiments at dress parade. The cooking of rations has been continuous all day as the storm of last night put a stop to anything pertaining to camp duty. Batteries of artillery, ammunition wagons, and all the available troops at Fort Monroe marched through the town and past these headquarters all day and until near midnight. Large bonfires lit their way through at night. I had exhausted my stock of maps and worked steadily on skeleton maps to be used by officers on the march. The maps which General Wool had were faulty, being old. As yet the most reliable ones have to be proved by our going over the ground. All are in ignorance of the obstacles to be met with from the general down to private soldier. The coast survey maps are accurate only for the rivers, but only show a few hundred yards on either shore. So we will have to march and fight on unknown ground. The enemy know, or ought to know every road and bye path by which they can concentrate or elude our forces. They have made a stand at Yorktown however. All other works between here and there can be easily outflanked when we go forward. I made a duplicate map of Yorktown taken from one used by General Butler's engineers and scouts when here in April last, and from it the fortifications look very formidable. I went with others over the ruined town this afternoon and to St. John's Church. Some of our fellows had dug out the corner stone and carried away the contents, valuable no doubt. . . .

April 4, 1862

. . . The whole army here and in this vicinity broke camp at 5 a.m. and moved by column of divisions towards Big Bethel and Howard's Bridge. The day was fine and quite warm. Roads [were] very muddy from last night's rain storm, [but] the green grass and trees and bright sky gave energy to the scene. Bright uniforms, polished arms, flags flying, and bands playing as the men marched out of their respective camps made a fine picture while the white wagon tops moving slowly in endless lines through the dark pines added to its beauty.

Everything [was] packed and loaded in the wagons at these headquarters at 6:30 a.m. The headquarter flag was struck with the tents at 7 a.m. and we began our first march toward the enemy. The cavalry escort with general and staff set out . . . while the wagon guard marched along with the wagons. Clerks, cooks and all [were] afoot but not armed. We went up [the] road through parts of the III Corps, all of whom were in motion. I saw and hailed friends in [the] 40th New York beyond the triangular graveyard. Over a vast treeless plain the army now moved as if on parade, everything burnished up bright. Gay uniforms, bands, and flags disappeared in long lines into the deep woods beyond leading to Big Bethel. Two regiments of cavalry led the advance with several batteries of horse artillery. I saw General McClellan with his staff inspecting the troops as they marched by with cheers. The staff officers were gorgeously dressed. . . .

Rifle pits and earthworks on hill | General McClellan's headquarters at house on hill | Morrel's mill | Rebel earthworks and log barracks

HOWARD'S BRIDGE AND RUINS OF MORREL'S MILL, POQUOSON RIVER, VA.
Advance of Union army into the Peninsula, April 4, 1862.

The army is advancing in two columns. General Keyes commanding the IV Corps . . . forms the left and General Heintzelman of the III Corps . . . [is] on the right. All went forward in fine order, the wagon trains keeping on the road with the artillery and ammunition trains, while the troops marched in column on both sides of them and across the fields or clearings at the route step. The bands soon ceased to play and everyone had to settle down in a steady tramp through the swampy grounds and muddy roads. "On to Richmond" was yelled from one regiment to another.

The pools of water from the recent rain storm had settled in the narrow road and overspread it on both sides for hundreds of feet. As our officers did not want to march their men through these, regiments were echeloned and partly jammed together in making the necessary detours to avoid them. There were no houses seen for some three or four miles. Fences were all gone, here and there a deserted log house. [I saw] no animals of any kind or inhabitants until after we had gone several miles. A halt of ten minutes was had every half hour so as to give a breathing spell to men and animals. I had to keep with our headquarter wagons, so as to forward any maps which might be called for by General Heintzelman now far ahead. . . . The roads grew worse and worse for the center of the advancing column as they were cut up by the hundreds of wagons and artillery ahead of us. The mules balked and tried to lay down in the muddy road. Teamsters lashed and swore at them until "the air was blue." Our train came up to Little Bethel about noon time. It was little enough as there were but three houses to be seen, with a few old rickety slab barns surrounded with broken fences. . . .

During the time of halting artillery fire was heard in front. This soon ceased and all moved on. About 2:30 p.m. we came to Big Bethel. The approaches to it were marshy and the stream had been dammed up, causing the banks to overflow. . . . The Rebel position was strong in front, but could be flanked easy by wading the stream, here not over four feet deep. Large semicircular rifle trenches enfiladed the only crossing at the bridge. Felled trees were laying in all directions. . . . Columns of black smoke now showed themselves above the tree tops in the advance caused by the enemy burning houses in their retreat to Howard's Bridge and beyond. The column moved on at a quicker pace while the artillery and wagons struggled through the sloughs of red mud and water found everywhere.

I went through the church and barracks. Nothing of value was left in them, [only] piles of dirty straw and broken boxes and barrels. Heaps of dirty rags and cast off clothing littered the barracks, and bunks were in the church made from the pews. A sickening odor pervaded the whole place. There were no platforms in the redoubt for guns but field artillery had been used. Dead trees and stumps stuck up in the stream and over most of the hillside. In one of the log houses was found a quantity of rusty bacon, which had a vile smell. Dirty rags, straw and old clothes were scattered everywhere.

From 5 to 6 p.m. the troops stacked arms on the road side, cooked coffee, and had their suppers, then resumed the forward march. Large fires were built along the road and left burning to light the way of those coming behind us. . . . We plunged along in the mud and water until near midnight lit by the fires on the roadside, [until] a halt was called and everyone bivouacked where he could. . . . I slept in the wagon as did the clerks, while the guard laid anywhere in the mud as it was bright starlight. . . . The mules brayed all the rest of the night. A bright light on the sky told where the enemy were burning houses or barns in the advance. Some musketry firing had been heard at sundown, but no one near us knew anything of what caused it. A squadron of cavalry came up past where we were sleeping which awoke us all up. The general and staff did not ride back to our wagons, nor had we seen them for many hours. I was lulled to sleep by the braying of mules and snoring of teamsters. Once in a while a solitary owl would hoot away off.

April 5, 1862

It rained hard from 5 a.m. to 10 a.m., when it cleared off quite hot. At 5:30 a.m., all had resumed the march on Howard's Bridge. General McClellan [and staff] passed from the rear up towards the head of the marching columns amidst great cheering from the troops. Their gorgeous uniforms were splashed all over with the beautiful red mud of Virginia. . . . The roads were in a horrible state, but we had to plunge through it as best we could. . . . Everyone enjoyed this march despite the oceans of mud which we had waded through as [if it] would have been a huge picnic. The troops were not hurried and no enemy of any account had been met with so far. . . . [At last] we camped off the road while the troops kept marching past until near midnight. . . . Thousands of camp fires lit up the tall trunks of the pine trees, while the frogs croaked in the marsh all night.

April 6, 1862

. . . We broke bivouac at 5:30 a.m., hitched teams and crossed over to the high ground and slowly went on towards Yorktown. . . . All the infantry marched in the fields and woods which bordered it, the wagons and artillery using the road. No straggling was allowed to the houses which were seen in the distance. . . . The roads were very much cut up by the wagons and artillery away ahead of us and frequent and long halts were made caused by wagons breaking down and the balking of the mule teams. At such times the teamsters would soon build small fires and boil coffee. We came to a cross roads and turned our headquarter teams off to the left where we got mired up to the axles several times, while fence rails were freely used under the wheels. I rode on the tongue of one of our wagons, and we plunged through the pools of liquid red mud like a ship in a chop sea. We were all spattered with the vile stuff.

Some artillery firing was heard away ahead of us at 2:30 p.m. The wagons were all halted or had stuck in the mud, while the infantry pressed on eagerly, their clothes spattered up to the knees. The mules wallowed in the mud and cleared themselves completely from their harness in one or two rolls. There was vehement swearing and lashing of whips by the teamsters when we would go 500 feet more ahead and stick again. This traveling was very tedious and did not help to keep any in good humor. . . .

As the heads of two wagon trains approached through an open space a narrow fenced road was ahead some hundreds of feet away. Both wagon masters started their trains at the same time to get preference of the lead and both trains of wagons approached the road at a full gallop. Both entered the gorge at the same time but as there was not room for two wagons abreast, the wagons ran side by side until the wheels were locked and everything brought up with a jerk. [This] threw many teamsters and the mules headlong into the mud. I held on like grim death during the rush, but had to tumble into my wagon now as the wheels were striking the corners of the zig zag or worm rail fence, throwing the rails completely over on the mules, who were now unmanageable. After much swearing and ordering we managed to extricate the mules from the teamsters and resumed our way. We passed a long row of low log sheds which had been cavalry stables for the enemy's horse. Some bacon was found in them. Our men would eat nothing which they found left by the enemy for fear of being poisoned.

I left the wagon and making a cut across the fields came to Grafton Church near Dr.

Power's house. It was a neat brick building, but being locked I did not get in. I had sent maps to General Heintzelman who was at the head of the corps, now arriving in front of Yorktown a few miles ahead by an orderly sent back for them. The orders were to park the headquarters train at Dr. Power's house, as it was sundown. This was soon done when we all went at work to cut brush for fires and cook supper. . . . General Heintzelman and staff with escort now arrived from the front and we unloaded two or three wagons and pitched two tents and a fly and made the headquarters in the lawn in front of the house. A light mizzling rain began to fall after 7 p.m., which lasted until midnight. The troops now had hundreds of camp fires burning for miles around and the rail fences and old barns had to suffer. . . . All was quiet at midnight. Fires were kept up all night, and for miles the glow shone on the murky clouds overhead. I and others found good dry quarters in Dr. Power's carriage house and having plenty to eat and drink, left the guards to take care of us while we slept. . . . A cavalry brigade went past near morning and the jangle of sabres woke us all up at once as we thought the enemy were on us. All slept in quiet thereafter. . . .

The following day, Sneden and his comrades reached an abandoned sawmill, the place selected by Heintzelman for his new headquarters. Located near the center of the Union line, the site provided good views of Yorktown and the extensive network of enemy earthworks and trenches. For the next month, the grounds of the sawmill served as Sneden's home in the field.

April 7, 1862

. . . The enemy have not fired a gun today. They can be seen mounting guns on their parapets. Engineers are very busy making reconnaissances and new maps. The rain held up at noon but a thick fog prevailed along the swampy front of the enemy's position. I went out to reconnoiter for myself and went out on the right in front of the wooded ravine which runs up from the crooked Wormsley Creek. I met two regiments of infantry with a battery stationed in the open ground with pickets thrown out to a peach orchard below Yorktown. Below the ravine Pennsylvania troops were in bivouac while farther in the woods were the shelter tents of [Fitz-John] Porter's troops. All were cooking and eating, the fog was so thick that nothing could be seen further than 200 yards.

I met Captain Heine, who with three soldiers, were tearing down long strips of sawn boards five to six inches wide, which were nailed here and there to trees along our front line. These were range marks put up by the enemy to aim their artillery with. They were nailed in an upright position against the trunks of the trees and being of new scantling could be seen at one and a half miles distant very plainly. These were all removed by Captain

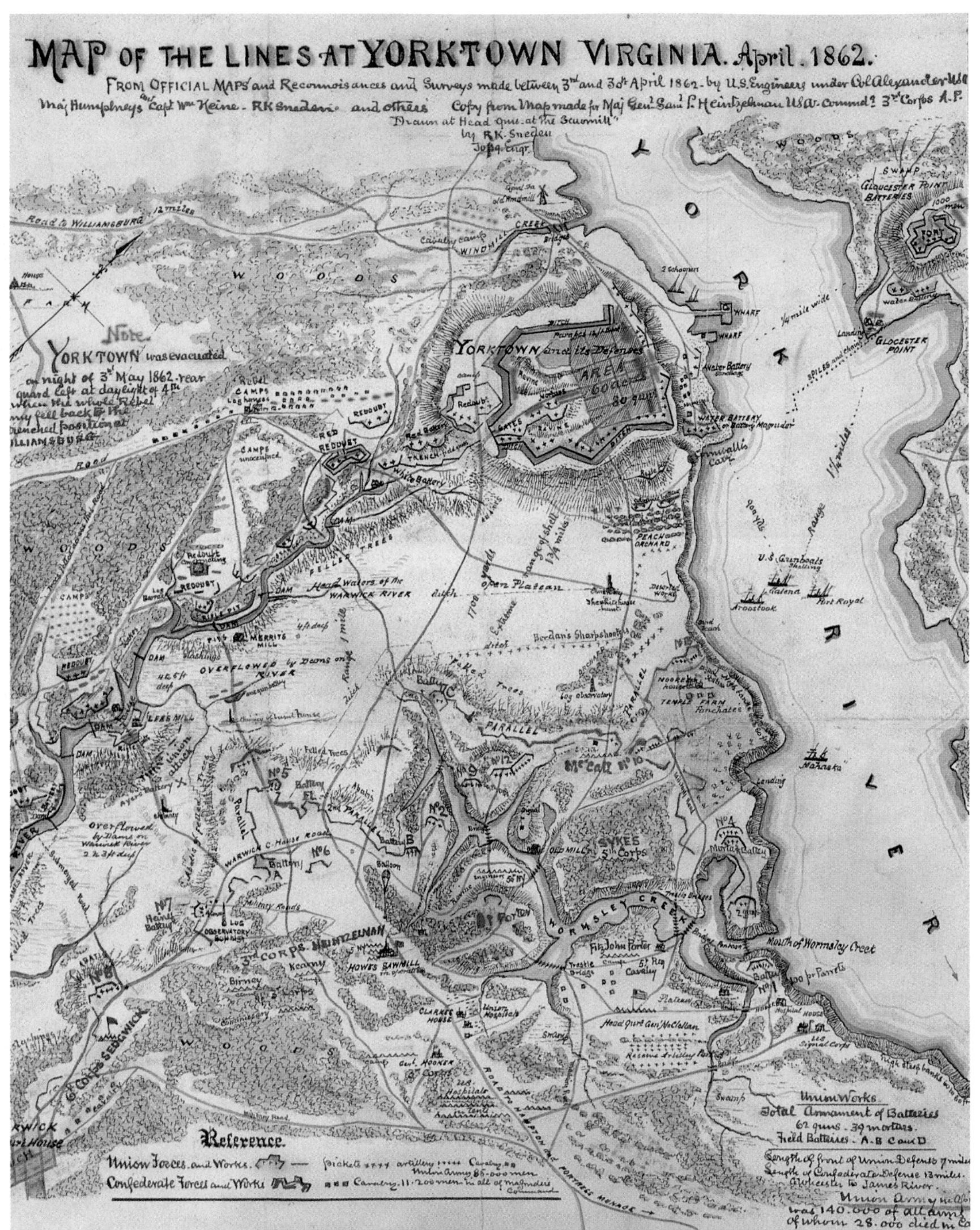

MAP OF THE LINES AT YORKTOWN, VA.

From official maps and reconnaissance made between April 3 and 30, 1862 by U.S. Engineers under Colonel Alexander, U.S.A., Major Humphreys and Captain William Heine. R. K. Sneden and others. Copy from map made for Major General Samuel P. Heintzelman, U.S.A. command, III Corps A. P. Drawn at headquarters at the sawmill.

Heine, who had now left General Heintzelman's staff, being transferred to staff of General Birney.* Lieutenant [Orlando] L. Wagner of the regular army engineers [was] appointed in his stead. He reported today for duty and a tent was put up on the staff line for him. I turned over all the maps to him later.

Our front line extends four miles from Warwick Court House to the York River. We have now 53,000 men here, of whom 42,000 are with the colors and ready for battle. The enemy are known to have 13,000 and every engineer officer as well as others wonder why McClellan doesn't order an immediate assault on the left of our position on Lee's Mill, where the enemy have only a few men to defend their unfinished earthworks. General Heintzelman says that he could with his command storm the whole line of works there and shut the enemy up in Yorktown by seizing the road in the rear of that place which leads to Williamsburg. But by McClellan's orders, no general is permitted to bring on a battle until all our forces are up. One corps alone could take the place in an hour. Disgust at the inactivity is very manifest among most officers of all grades. . . .

April 9, 1862

. . . [Professor Lowe's] balloon went up for the first time this forenoon. Thousands of soldiers swarmed out from their camps in the woods to see it. It ascended from the strip of woods just across the road from these headquarters and was held by two ropes attached to the basket car. It was only partially inflated and rose like a bird to an elevation of 900 feet. It was made of yellow colored cloth varnished on the outside and glistened in the bright sunshine. On it was painted in colors an immense head portrait of General McClellan. The ramparts of Yorktown soon swarmed with the enemy to see it, but all at once they disappeared as if by orders. The balloon remained up three hours. Lowe and two officers were in it, who kept their glasses on the enemy's line of earthworks constantly. They could see, of course, the inside of the enemy's works, sketch the outlines of parapets, and count the guns already mounted, and note their bearings. From this, the draughtsman can make the maps and plans which they are waiting for. . . . The balloon came down at 5 p.m.

The enemy were observed getting three large guns mounted on their main parapets. Our artillery fire prevented them from doing any work on them for the time being. Our sharpshooters under Colonel Berdan† were pushed up closer from the peach orchard [and] reported that the enemy had lots of Negroes helping them to mount the guns. Several were shot. . . .

Several of our regiments are camped out in the open plain about the center of our line in

* David B. Birney commanded a brigade in Heintzelman's corps.

† Hiram Berdan commanded a regiment of sharpshooters armed with special rifles, including finely crafted target pieces with telescopic sights.

Earthworks in woods | Yorktown. Peach orchard below hill | Howe's Sawmill | Headquarters III Corps | Balloon | Hamilton Road | Rebel works at Gloucester Point, York River | Encampment of Fitz-John Porter's I Corps

VIEW OF YORKTOWN, VA., FROM REAR OF HOWE'S SAWMILL,
Headquarters III Corps A. P., April 1862.

plain sight to the enemy and within artillery range. But they have dress parade while the bands play as usual, as the enemy have not as yet mounted guns in the works to any extent. These regiments will have to take cover very quickly when the enemy are ready to open on them. Many wonder why they are so exposed. . . . It rained hard after dark and a dense fog set in at 11 p.m. I worked on maps until then. . . .

April 10, 1862

Engineers crawl out on hands and knees at night in front of the works at Lee's Mill and remain until daylight to discover what the enemy are doing. Captain Heine is the most adventurous of them all. He makes a very rough sketch of what is being done, while I make a perfect map for the general's use in my tent.

Our bough house mess tents are constructed of pine poles with flat roofs of thick pine branches, and afford much coolness and comfort when at meals. When it rains the sides are enclosed by canvas. A log fire is continually kept up in front of General Heintzelman's double wall tent. He and other officers sit there before the fire until nearly midnight discussing the situation while the adjutant general, Captain [Chauncey] McKeever keeps the orderlies or couriers galloping about with orders most of the night. All lights are put out at 9 p.m. The camps are well screened from the enemy's sight by the trees along the front line, but from the ramparts of Yorktown vast camps can be seen in the open fields in rear of the woods, while the sky is illuminated for miles on a dark night by thousands of camp fires. The regimental bands seldom play, while continuous drumming is heard at Yorktown every night, mostly by bass drums. . . .

April 12, 1862

. . . This morning at 7 a.m. cries of "the balloon is loose" and "look at her". . . startled most of us at headquarters while crowds of soldiers came running from all directions out of the woods to the front of the open plain to see it sail gracefully away high in [the] air with two long ropes dangling from the car or basket. It was going swiftly straight for Yorktown. All had our conjectures as to what it was going that way for. It rose two miles or more when about three quarters way across the immense open ground in our front struck an upper current of air and came slowly back to our lines in a slanting direction and suddenly dropped down in the woods where Birney's brigade were in camp. General Fitz-John Porter after a while made his appearance from that quarter, accompanied by three or four officers of Birney's staff to report to General Heintzelman.

The balloon had been moved since it had been fired on yesterday to his headquarters half a mile or so back of the sawmill. The ropes being securely fastened to a tree, Porter had ascended there yesterday to observe the enemy. This morning he unloosed one rope which held the balloon leaving one to hold it and tried to ascend again by himself. When the balloon arose the rope broke and set him free. He had been up with Lowe the balloonist many times before, but the idea of being loose and sailing at such a swift rate through the air had confused him, and he did not know how to manage a balloon either. It was dead calm on the earth's surface, but the balloon moved very rapidly nevertheless. As he passed over our heads . . . we shouted "pull the valve," but he did not heed or hear us. Lowe soon came up on horseback and went after his balloon. . . . The Rebels would have been delighted to have got the balloon with Fitz-John in it. We at headquarters did not care as long as they did not get the balloon.

. . . The balloon rose to about 1,600 feet [and] sailed across the plateau in our front and to [the] right over Yorktown. The general crouched down in the car as volleys of rifle balls were fired at the balloon by the enemy as the car descended lower down and directly over their works. Porter now threw over all the sand bag ballast attached to the balloon, when it rose quickly to a great height and striking an upper adverse current came sailing slowly back to us again to the camps of Birney's [brigade] below the sawmill. Porter, fearing that he would be carried beyond to the James River unless he could descend, became desperate, climbed out of the car and gave the valve line a hard jerk, which opened the valve wide. It also made him lose his grip on the ropes and he fell into the basket, one half of his body hanging over the side with the balloon 2,000 feet above the earth! Porter now was aware that he had pulled the valve too wide as the balloon now began to fall very rapidly and with a fearful rush, he could not close the valve again for the rope was far out of his reach away above his head in the netting. Even if he had the strength to reach it, he could not climb up and get it.

The balloon now began to be as limp as a rag and was tossing from side to side, but was descending straight into the camp. Seeing a large tree beneath him he took his chances for life by jumping into it, and in a second was hanging in the branches by one arm and leg, completely enfolded by the shattered balloon with the escaping gas filling his lungs at every breath. Help was at hand, however, and he was rescued by the soldiers of Birney's troops. The balloon was torn away, and he was lowered to the ground in an exhausted condition. . . .

On investigating, it was found that both ropes which held the balloon had become corroded by contact with the acid wagon tops, by which the gas is manufactured, and broke at the jerk when the balloon had got to the end of its tether. New ropes were of course attached to it. General Porter investigated the cause of the balloon ropes so suddenly snapping off when he made the ascent, and found out that the sergeant who had been detailed from the 50th New York engineer regiment had had some hard words with his captain who had charge of the balloon the evening previous. The sergeant, therefore, smeared the ropes with acid from the gas making wagon, which ate the ropes so that they broke like loose tow. As the captain generally made the ascent at an early hour, . . . the sergeant thought it would be a good thing for him to get loose once and go anywhere or nowhere. But the captain was not on the ground until later, when General Porter decided to go up alone. So he was carried off instead of the captain.*

April 13, 1862

. . . About 9 o'clock this morning all were surprised to see a large balloon slowly rise from the woods behind the enemy's works at Wynne's Mills. All our field glasses were brought into use at once. It went up about 700 feet and stayed up just seven minutes, when it was hauled down. Professor Lowe rode up to the sawmill, and on seeing it, recognized it as one which he had used in Charleston, South Carolina, some years ago. He said that it was a hot air balloon and was liable to take fire when in mid air, and therefore risky to manipulate. He knew of no aeronaut in the enemy's service. It was pulled down briskly, showing that something worked wrongly. In seven minutes they could not note much on our side. During this time the soldiers thronged from their camps to see it.

We get the New York papers in all the camps now every day. They are only two days old but are much sought for at 10¢ apiece. They are brought from Fort Monroe by young men who ride up from there on sorry looking horses. Mr. Wilkeson of the *Tribune* is at our headquarters. Mr. [Alfred] R. Waud takes the place of Mr. Hall as artist for *Frank Leslie's* paper. Several correspondents of the *New York Herald* and other papers bother the adjutant general for passes to go to the front line. They are refused in all cases here, but General Porter grants many which should stop, as the papers tell too much of what concerns the

* This paragraph appears earlier in Sneden's original manuscript, but it has been moved here for clarity.

army, while the Rebels get the northern papers nearly as regularly as we do. The press "should be muzzled" regarding all army matters, as the Rebel press is. . . .

I went on a tour of observation today along the Wormsley Creek shores and up river along the high bluffs. While here . . . [I] saw a lively contest between two of our side wheel gunboats and the Rebel batteries at Yorktown and those at Gloucester Point. It was a charming sight to see the gunboats move in circles and fire from their heavy bow guns. Slow, and with precision, their shell struck the parapets of the water battery, or "Battery Magruder," knocking the sandbags up in the air and dismounting a gun. There was much scampering about among the enemy's artillery men when this took place. Shells from the gunboats burst in and on the enemy's batteries at Gloucester Point. The enemy opened [fire] at once, two from the ramparts of Yorktown, four or five from the water battery there, and three from the water battery below Gloucester Point. The duel lasted for two hours. The enemy's shot struck the water very close to the vessels while shells burst in mid air. None struck the steamers, however, which kept moving all the while. Being on a bluff seventy feet above the York River, I had a fine view of the action.

With my powerful glasses I could look down into "Battery Magruder" and on the decks of our gunboats. I made a good sketch, then went down to the Moore house. . . . General McClellan with the French princes and staff had been on the roof of this ancient building looking at the fight and were just leaving when I got there.

April 15, 1862

Rain, probably brought on by the artillery firing yesterday. Lively picket firing on right and left of our lines began at daylight. This, with the saws in the mill in full operation, kept us all awake. Hundreds of new picks and shovels were dumped down this morning at these headquarters, and the III Corps will now have to do more digging than fighting by the way things look. Standing in the trenches ankle deep in mud and water shoveling mud is no easy thing in a hot sun under fire from the enemy day and night. Batteries of artillery are placed along the first parallel line to shell the enemy and keep his musketry fire down until the trench is deep enough to shelter the workmen. So artillery fire at intervals has been going on all day. We ought to have some of those fat "contrabands" up here from Fort Monroe to dig trenches and do the heavy work. The enemy so we hear have 3,000 [slaves] at work on the batteries now being constructed from Yorktown to Lee's Mills. What with picket duty and digging trenches, [our] men . . . are grumbling very much, which is not to be wondered [from] new troops on their first campaign.

The Rebels crowd up on their parapets daily, watching our operations. They look right down on us too from their elevated position, and by the lines of red earth thrown up can tell exactly where our trenches are located. Several of our batteries [are] armed but don't fire, as McClellan won't allow it until he can erect all of the batteries contemplated and then *all* will open fire at the same time. . . . Same as at [the siege of Sebastopol in the Crimean War], but we only waste our time and exhaust our men. The chances of a general assault now are not so good by half as they were two weeks ago. . . .

Constant drumming in [the] evening is heard at Yorktown. This is construed by the knowing ones to mean that the enemy are receiving reinforcements from [Benjamin] Huger at Norfolk, who has 8,000 men. These with Magruder's 13,000 would bring the enemy's forces up to 21,000 men. We can any day throw 65,000 men on the enemy's lines. If one half of these should attack at the same time at Lee's Mills and at the red battery outside the main ramparts of Yorktown, the Rebels would have to get out quick enough, thus saving all the military humbug of carrying on a protracted siege. . . .

The engineer corps are camped down the Hampton Roads near the headquarters of General McClellan and are controlled by him alone. There are twelve to fourteen draughtsmen there constantly making very pretty plans on paper of the different parallels, trenches, [and] batteries, which are now being constructed to the detriment of the private soldier by the exhaustive work which he has to perform. The private soldier will have to do the fighting part of the business after all, despite useless earthworks. The enemy have not a single gun thus far heavy enough to throw shot or shell into our lines as they are now placed, but the regular engineer officers think this a great opportunity to carry out their West Point ideas of how a siege should be carried out. [To them] the map and plan business is highly essential to its development, of course. But we should attack, and should have attacked without fail when we first came here April 5, giving the enemy no time or chance to construct new works on the road between here and Richmond and concentrate his now scattered forces behind them to oppose. . . .

April 16, 1862

In the afternoon, I went down to Heine's sunk[en] battery. . . . Two 20 pound Parrott guns had replaced two of smaller caliber. And the artillery men soon opened fire on the enemy's foremost battery across the Lee's Mills road. The Rebel flag was shot away twice. The enemy replied by three guns and the firing was good on both sides. Shells burst in mid air, leaving white curls of smoke, while solid shot crashed through the trees, bringing down huge limbs or splitting the trunks. The firing was slow at first but increased in vigor.

I was glad to lie down in a corner of the battery while the enemy's 42 pounder shot struck the ground twenty feet from the front of the battery and rebounded overhead into a strip of woods left there purposely to break shell fire. Heine stood up on the parapet, glass in hand, to note [the] effect of his battery on enemy. The enemy fired only round shot. This continued two and a half hours, when both batteries stopped firing. This was my first experience under fire in a battery and [I] was contented to "lie low" most of the time. . . .

UNION GUNBOATS SHELLING YORKTOWN, VA., AND GLOUCESTER POINT
From Panchates House, April 14, 1862.
April 22: eleven shells were thrown into Yorktown. April 17: sixteen shells thrown into Gloucester Point.

Very few people, not military men, have the true theory of an exploding shell. Pictorial papers represent them as exploding while in full flight in the air and the fragments flying in all directions, like the spokes from a wheel, which is the common idea. The laws of physics teach that if a shell is moving through the air with a velocity greater than that which its explosion is capable of giving to the fragments, none of them can possibly fall back of the place of explosion. If these velocities were exactly equal, the pieces of [the] shell on the side next to the mortar or gun would be just stopped by the explosion and so would fall perpendicularly to the ground, while those on the side opposite to the mortar or gun being propelled by two forces (that of the mortar and that of the explosion) would be thrown a greater distance forward. The pieces at right angles to the direction of [the] motion would be thrown at right angles to this direction if the velocities were equal. If not equal, they would be more obliquely backwards or forward, all according to the velocities.

If a shell explodes while moving rapidly over a body of water, the pieces all strike several rods in the advance of the place of explosion, some more, some less. The puff of smoke still remaining near the spot. Some move obliquely forward, some strike nearer, and some farther from the place of explosion. If a shell is stationary, or moving very slowly, the pieces of course fly in all directions. If it bursts when on the ground the pieces mostly fly upward. This last result saves many a soldier while lying flat on the ground to support a battery in action. As many shells burst in full sight not 300 feet away from our headquarters this theory was proved many times. While I had seen the enemy's shells burst near our gunboats on the river I watched the effect with much interest always.

April 17, 1862

. . . The enemy unmasked several new guns in their works along the Warwick River and shelled No. 7 battery vigorously. The return fire was slow and sure while the shells went screaming over the tree tops in several directions. Our signal corps men were posted on the highest tree tops and by signals directed the fire of our guns. Some of the trees were hit, but the signal men only climbed another. They suspend themselves when up in a tree by a strong leather strap for the feet, a sort of stirrup, while the officer with the book of code of signals calls off the number required to be signaled from the ground below the tree. A trestle work has been built on top of the sawmill at these headquarters on which three signal men are placed. They signal to Fitz-John Porter's headquarters and Hooker's, while the telegraph lines run there and to all the brigade, division, and corps headquarters, connecting with General McClellan's. At night the signal men use the torch instead of the flag. A flag in motion in a tree top or on a high elevation, house, [or] chimney, can be seen a very long way off on a clear day. The waving of it attracts the eye at once.

The balloon went up from a new position in the strip of woods near these headquarters. A telegraph operator went up in it with an instrument and a wire leading to another instrument on the ground below. The enemy began to shell the balloon when it had to be hauled down. As shells burst uncomfortably near, it was then carried back 200 feet or so and went up again. All the enemy's shot now fell short.

The firing at Heine's No. 7 battery today was continuous while the enemy had four guns going at the same time. While laying out a new [earthwork] to this battery this afternoon Lieutenant Wagner, the topographical engineer to General Heintzelman, was struck in the shoulder by a fragment of one of the enemy's shells and badly wounded. He was brought to these headquarters on a stretcher and after being given a glass of brandy, was carried to Clarke's house hospital down the road where he suffered amputation of the arm.

He with three engineer soldiers were measuring with a steel tape line in front of the battery. It being very warm he carried an umbrella to shade the plane table on which he was drawing his lines. Being dressed in full uniform covered with much gold lace, he drew the enemy's attention at once in the open ground in front of the battery. The first shell thrown went over his head and bounded into the trees behind the battery where it exploded. The next was a round shot which struck the plane table fairly though almost spent and upset Wagner and all his apparatus. The shot struck a glancing blow on his shoulder breaking his collar bone and otherwise wounding him. This was a good shot, the best the enemy have made so far from such a long distance. The next was a shell which burst so near that it wounded two of the other engineers, when all ran into the battery for safety. Lieutenant

Wagner was a regular officer who put on a great many West Point airs and had very little sympathy with any of the staff or those about headquarters.

By the constant beating of drums in Yorktown at different hours of [the] day and evening we surmise that the enemy are receiving reinforcements. General Joe Johnston is known to have superceded Magruder in command.* . . .

April 18, 1862

. . . As the sawmill has been hither to working day and night, orders are given to shut down at dark, as the lights used there help to give the enemy true range. More trees were cut and planted around our tents to act as a blind at night. All lights were ordered out at 8:30 p.m. I had to put up army blankets inside my tent so the light cannot shine through the canvas, as I have to work often until 11 p.m., on maps and plans of the batteries and trenches. . . .

I went over to General McClellan's headquarters today. . . . The camp was on a fine green level sward about twenty tents in quadrangular form. I had much difficulty to find a Lieutenant Perkins, a topographical engineer to whom I had lent some instruments. There were fifteen or more draughtsmen at work on maps and plans of the entrenchments, all old soldiers of the regular army in a large hospital wall tent. None of them knew Perkins, although I knew that he worked there as a draughtsman. At last an officer asked me if [Perkins] was in the volunteers. I said yes. [Then] his tent was pointed out to me at once. Regular army officers in this camp did not know any other officer unless of the regular army. I had a joke on Perkins and got what I went after, first opening a bottle of prime brandy, and returned to headquarters, first going to headquarters of General Porter.

The general there had a tall lookout made near his tent, which consisted of a tall pine tree with branches all cut off and rings or steps nailed on. [It] rested against another tall pine tree at an incline, strongly lashed at the top with rope. I climbed this and had a fine view of all our camps and looked inside our batteries constructing on Wormsley Creek. The ramparts of Yorktown and Gloucester Point and all the York River spread out like a panorama. General Porter said that he was "up a tree" half his time.

I left and went down by Wormsley Creek to the river and walked along shore under the high bluffs for a long distance. I sat on a boulder and made a good sketch of Gloucester Point and the water battery at Yorktown. I kept on up the shore as it was low tide and did not know that I was walking directly into the enemy's lines. The seventy foot bluff shut off all view on my right while the enemy's water battery in front attracted me by seeing several of the enemy standing on its sandbag parapets looking at me approach. I saw over the bluff a soldier's head, then he jumped out of a crevice of some kind, aimed his musket and yelled

*Sneden's observations were correct. By mid-April, Johnston had marched most of his army to the Yorktown line, bringing Confederate strength to sixty thousand men.

"Halt, or I'll fire." Not being armed, I soon explained matters, when he said that I was within range of the Rebel sharpshooters along the shore behind the rocks. I lost no time in walking very fast to a gully made in the bluff by the rains, crawling up the steep sides to the top, and coming out on a level ground near the burnt chimney. I then knew where I was and struck the ravine [and] made a long detour to the sawmill.

I met a train of heavy guns being drawn by twenty mules each which were going to Battery Number 9. The Negro drivers were lashing the mules for all they knew and yelling in an uncouth language only understood by the mule and the drivers. I met Captain Heine at headquarters, who wanted a map made at which I worked until midnight. The enemy continuing his fire on headquarters at that time. Round shot were used by them altogether. Many spent shot rolled past the encampment in the darkness. . . . The staff, clerks, and guard escorts, etc. were up all night, as there was a chance of being killed in one's sleep. Many "bunked" down in the sawdust in the mill, which recently has not been run at night.

April 19, 1862

. . . I went over to Captain Heine's tent . . . and worked on his battery plan. . . . About 11 a.m., the enemy began to shell the balloon near the sawmill, which was up 1,800 feet in the air. About 2 p.m., they opened seven or eight guns and shelled our whole line from right of it to centre. A 62 pounder shot struck within twenty feet of General Birney's tent and plunged into the earth five feet. It was dug out at once. Another came within fifty feet of where I was at work on the map, struck into a soft bank of earth four feet, it was dug out and found to be a copper shell different from any which was known. Fortunately it did not explode. It weighed sixty-five pounds. After this I could do no more work in a tent as I wanted to take my chances outside. The bombardment continued from 2 p.m. to 6:30 p.m. All their shot seemed to fall within 100 feet of our front lines, along the edge of the woods all going over the hundreds of men working in the trenches out in the open field in front. There was enough old iron piled up and laying around in the open to gladden the heart of any junk peddler. No one was hurt.

The hospitals in the III Corps are quite full of sick soldiers caused by overwork in the trenches in mud and water half the time. The officers all go to Clarke's house, which is used for hospital for them only. There are fine hospitals erected and covered with boughs and trees to keep them cool. I left General Birney's camp after seeing my friends in the 40th Regiment and supped on oysters, which are found in the York River and sold by Negroes in the camps at 50¢ per quart. [I] then walked through the woods to the sawmill.

April 20, 1862

Rain and fog. This is Easter Sunday, but no eggs are to be had. Lots of broken shells fired by the enemy are lying all over the ground along our front lines, which are gentle reminders of what we may expect in the future. Balloon did not go up today, and no work was done in the trenches. Bands played away down the road among the camps there, but none along the front line of camps.

Large piles of sawn lumber are stacked around the sawmill and tons of sawdust, which is used every day to make fresh clean paths to the camp. Seven or eight men of the 4th Maine Regiment, all old lumbermen, cut trees and haul them to the mill with teams of oxen, just as they would do when at home. The rasping of the saws makes a continuous noise while at work. Our food supplies are regular and excellent, and we actually grow fat. Those who work in the trenches grow thin and officers and men complain of being overworked. The field hospitals show it. Whiskey is scarce and can only be had at the sutler's* at $2 per bottle. Those who work in the trenches get their three gills a day, but the officers, by using water freely in the ration, manage to save enough of the pure stuff to keep themselves pretty full. . . .

Several hundred beef cattle are kept corralled in the woods adjoining [the] commissaries of the brigade camps. They and the mules make a continual racket, especially when artillery firing begins. Each animal is shot first, then butchered for rations. Sometimes they break loose and stampede through the woods, carrying with them all the mule teams which are at the time not hitched. Teamsters and butchers have a lively time of it to recover them. . . .

April 21, 1862

Clear and colder until 3 p.m., when it rained hard and a thick fog set in all night. Lieutenant Wagner . . . who was struck by a fragment of shell while laying out a flank entrenchment to Number 7 battery last Thursday, died this evening at Clarke's house hospital. After amputation of his arm, gangrene set in. His body was sent north. The deaths in hospitals average twelve to fifteen per day. Soldiers are seen picking up stray pieces of board around the sawmill to make coffins for their comrades who die in camp. . . .

April 22, 1862

. . . The French Prince de Joinville with Robert duc de Chartres visited General Heintzelman during the firing. . . . They all were sent from the French government to observe the conduct of the war. They sketched and kept regular notes and diaries of all they saw, but of course did not give anything to the newspapers. The reporters of the newspapers besiege headquarters of all the generals for military information and are a nuisance. They are forbidden to print many things, but they do it. The *New York Herald* prints war maps and diagrams with much accuracy. The enemy of course take the *Herald* and see it too.

*A sutler was a civilian businessman who provided goods to army personnel.

April 23, 1862

. . . I went out to see the batteries and trenches with a large map to correct errors or make additions. I first went to the picket line at the peach orchard. I was not allowed to go beyond the burnt chimneys as it was dangerous. I met California Joe* in a dry ditch near the chimneys and admired his six foot rifle with telescopic sights on it. It was very heavy in weight, had an octagon shaped barrel and silver mounted ornaments. Two weeks ago, before we had advanced our line of pickets to the chimney, a Rebel sharpshooter had climbed the inside flue of it at night, and by a stick set crosswise had fixed himself near the top from whence he shot several of our fellows from his covered perch. Joe came along and at the fourth shot brought the enemy down at 500 yards' distance. The other bullets had struck the bricks which were seen to chip off. The sharpshooter tumbled down the chimney flue in a doubled up position and stuck thus in the fireplace of the second story of the house before it had been burnt. Some days afterwards when our picket line was pushed forward the body was taken down and proved to be an Indian. He had been shot between the eyes and the back of his skull was all blown out! He was buried near the ruins. Joe was a dead shot and had often kept the enemy from firing a gun for half an hour at a time by shooting five, six, and seven one after another . . . through the embrasures.

April 28, 1862

. . . Moreland, telegraph operator for General Porter, called on me today and I took him down to Number 7 battery to see the artillery practice. The enemy were firing about one shot a minute, but soon fired three shots per minute from two guns over near Lee's Mills. While we were returning, the enemy opened from another gun, making it a crossfire. We hurried through patches of woods and small clearings and found ourselves in this crossfire. The shells were screaming overhead, splitting the trees and tumbling the branches down everywhere. At last the shells burst within thirty to forty feet of us while we stopped to try to discover a shelter. I picked out a small clump of trees . . . where some fallen logs were lying on top of each other. Just as we made up our minds to run for them, a shell came over the opening and burst at the foot of the very tree which we had selected. It lifted the tree by the roots and sent it skyward twenty feet or more, showers of stones and mud fell from the roots at the same time. We gained the pile of logs and laid down to watch further firing, considered it safe on the principle of saying that "a shot never strikes in the same place," and they didn't. We watched a signal man waving his flag from the top of a tall pine tree, the shell burst around him so that he had to come down. We could not even see the smoke from the enemy's guns for the clumps of trees and underbrush in which we were.

Returning we passed Captain Heine's log observatory. The enemy was trying his aim on it with round shot, which struck it several times, knocking out a few timber supports. Heine

*One of Hiram Berdan's sharpshooters, whose real name was Truman Head.

was up on it near the top with glass in hand. He did not come down until the shot came very near hitting him. We regained headquarters by noon. . . .

At 8 p.m., I went over to General Birney's camp and to Captain Heine's tent, where he and I worked on a map of the batteries until 11 p.m. In returning through the woods, it being foggy and very dark, I lost my way and got below General Hooker's headquarters, where I managed to fall into a wet ditch five or six feet deep and was covered with nasty red mud. This ditch had been dug since I was that way before and formed a part of an entrenched camp. Then a camp guard halted me and as I did not have the countersign, had to go to post 1 and see the officer in charge and being covered with mud was not known. After explaining matters and being detained an hour I got back to my tent disgusted.

By the end of April, McClellan had nearly one hundred heavy guns in position, ready to blast away at the enemy. The Union commander, still wanting every detail in place, set May 6 as the date for a mighty bombardment, followed by a massive assault that would crush the enemy army. Confederate commander Joseph Johnston, however, understood the consequences of remaining at Yorktown. In the dark of the night, he slipped his army out of the lines and dropped back to better defensive positions near Richmond, foiling McClellan's elaborate preparations for an attack. During all of this, the men in the ranks labored away while dodging enemy bullets and cannon shell. Like Robert Sneden, they sensed that something was afoot. The anticlimactic end of the siege, however, disappointed everyone in the Union ranks. It intensified a growing sense of doubt about McClellan.

May 2, 1862

. . . The enemy shelled all the batteries along the first and second parallels from 8 to 11 a.m. All those working in the unfinished works had to lie down flat until the storm of round shot and shell ceased. At one o'clock I happened to be returning to the sawmill from reconnoitering the water battery on the river and crossed in front of our battery line over the open plateau between the enemy and our line of works. When the enemy trained a gun on me, a round shot struck the ground not more than thirty feet in front of me, ploughing up the turf many yards. I stopped and surveyed the ramparts with my glass and distinctly saw the men in the embrasure sight and fire the gun again. This time a shell whizzed screaming over my head and burst beyond me over a hundred feet. The fragments tore up the ground viciously. I saw them getting another gun ready to fire when I made up my mind that they were practicing on me alone. So I ran about a hundred feet to the right, then about a hundred feet to the left and waited. Another shell came and burst behind me in the air, the fragments struck the sods and the dirt covered my back. I saw a dry ditch . . . and ran for it with all my might just as another shell burst in the air over my head but a good way up. I got to the ditch and laid down in it a minute to look through my glass, then crawled for a hundred feet or more and laid flat for some time. A shell burst in the ditch a hundred feet away, but the fragments flew in another direction.

I was satisfied that I was selected for a target and I made for a point of low woods and bushes which concealed our masked Battery C, and got safely into the work. I was covered all over with mud and dust thrown by the fragments of shell and counted myself lucky to escape, being considerably flustered running in the hot sun. When I got to headquarters, the general was very angry at me for exposing myself, saying that "I would come in with my head blown off some time." I had been seen by our whole right line of batteries and from headquarters.

While running into our lines I noticed a gun firing from the direction of the so-called "White Battery," but was so excited as not to see what the enemy were firing at. On getting to headquarters I found that they were shelling the sawmill and that a large missile had struck eight feet from the pole of my tent on the line and had exploded. [It tore] up a hole four or five feet deep and made an excavation for ten square feet in the gravelly soil. Fragments had struck and passed through the canvas and had knocked the telegraph tent next to it half over. [D.] Lathrop the operator was at work at the time but escaped being hit. If I had been in my tent working as usual on my map board, I would have stood a poor chance and not so good a one to escape being hit as I recently experienced in the open field.

While a crowd of guards and officers, etc. were examining the hole in the ground at my tent, the enemy opened fire again and we were all surprised to see a shell burst just beyond the sawmill, while in another minute a solid shot skipped across the road and crashed into the woods where the balloon was. This was followed by five or six more shot and shell, when the firing suddenly stopped. One gun on the enemy's works had got exact range and had thrown their missiles farther than at any time before. There was quite an excitement among the staff, orderlies, clerks, and guards in the camp during the firing. The sawmill shut down while the signal men on the roof scrambled to the ground.

The balloon was quickly hauled down and removed farther back while the sawdust flew near the mill covering all the workmen near it. One shell, the last one fired, went seven or eight hundred feet over the sawmill and burst in the woods near General Hooker's headquarters. General Heintzelman sat in front of his tent whittling a piece of wood and was the most composed of us all, although one solid shot went but a few feet over his head and just grazed the iron smoke stack of the sawmill. The balloon went up again and reported a large crowd gathered in one of the embrasures of the enemy's parapet while the gun which had done the firing was dismounted. . . .

We have . . . fit for duty 103,378 soldiers, while the enemy have not more than 50,000 if he has that! The Fabian policy* of McClellan has lost him much popularity and "Little

* "Fabian tactics" were named for ancient Roman consul Quintus Fabius Maximus Verrucosus Cunctator, who advocated a cautious, defensive strategy against Carthage.

Napoleon" stock is at a very low ebb among those dashing leaders as [Philip] Kearny,* Hooker, Sumner or [William F.] Smith. These generals, including Sedgwick and Heintzelman, never go to McClellan's headquarters to consult about the military situation. And many generals don't "pull together" at all, but pull in opposite directions. [This is] mostly caused by McClellan's "masterly" inactivity with siege operations on the brain, when we all know that we could have walked right over the Rebels when we came here first on April 4. Since then hundreds are sick in hospital while lots have been killed at Lee's Mill and on the picket line, good officers too, who cannot be replaced.

May 3, 1862

. . . Towards midnight much drumming was heard from Yorktown, all bass drums. They were making a hideous din. Numerous shells bursting high in [the] air lit up the whole plateau and made a fine sight, while the flashes of the guns along the parapets added to the fine theatrical display. None of their missiles reached our front line of woods nearest. They all went clean over all our works in the front, with few exceptions. All the guards were doubled in the front works, and long lines of men laid on the ground while the enemy's shot went over them. The firing was wild and to no purpose, as it was so much ammunition wasted. Three divisions were all under arms at midnight and strong forces put into batteries A, D, C, numbers 2, 5, 15, and 9 to prevent the capture of any of the guns there in position.

About 1:30 a.m., large fires were seen in the town and dull explosions followed once in a very little while. These fires seemed to be in the ravines among the parapets, as the glare reflected on the sides of the parapets. Then there would be louder explosions as of powder while at the wharf large piles of lumber and sheds were blazing furiously, lighting up the river. The flashes of explosives and two or three houses lit up the woods and York River for miles. Dull explosions were heard over at Gloucester Point, but no fires were seen. The cannonading grew weaker . . . and finally stopped. The other batteries along the Warwick River fired only a few rounds and ceased.

May 4, 1862

We were all astir at 4:30 this morning while the bugles sounded through all the various encampments and shortly after to "pack up." Three days' cooked rations were ordered and all the troops were under arms by noon. General Heintzelman went up in the balloon at dawn to reconnoiter from the old position near the sawmill. Clouds of gray and black smoke obstructed the enemy's parapets and the houses in Yorktown, which were now burning, while smothered explosions were noticed every little while. A magazine blew up . . . at sunrise, while the large piles of lumber near the wharf were in a bright blaze. There was no doubt now but that the enemy were getting away as fast as they could. They had in fact

* Kearny (1814–1862), who rose to command a division in the III Corps, was one of the Union army's most aggressive generals.

been "getting out all night." The occupants in the balloon reported large masses of the enemy's troops moving away from Lee's Mills, with large numbers of cavalry moving out of Yorktown on the Williamsburg road at Windmill Creek. Word had been sent to the officers in command of the picket lines at the peach orchard and in front of Lee's Mills to advance the lines up and into the enemy's works at early dawn. Two brigades were on the ground at 2 a.m. to support the movement, while yet the enemy were burning their camps. They did so and sent word that "the place was evacuated." The news spread rapidly through all the camps as the orderlies rode through them with dispatches from headquarters to the different commanders to get under arms at once.

Thousands of soldiers were in the open space in front of the sawmill to see for themselves and all was excitement and hurry when the bugles at 10 o'clock sounded "the assembly." General [Charles D. Jameson] of Kearny's division . . . were the first troops to enter the enemy's works about daylight. The 35th, 40th and 70th New York regiments . . . went across the plateau and entered the main works . . . planting their colors on the ramparts and trying to put out the fires in the town. . . . A black smoke from [the] Gloucester Point batteries showed that the enemy had fired the camps there and the garrison had crossed over in boats to Yorktown before daybreak.

We made a hurried breakfast at headquarters while all the cooks were hard at work cooking rations for the expected forward march. Our telegraph operator Lathrop started for the Rebel headquarters in Yorktown to secure any dispatches or memo left behind by the Rebel operator there at 7 a.m. He wanted me to go with him very much, but I would not as I then had not gotten my breakfast, although I had all my instruments and map box fully packed, so he went without me.

The whole army were much chagrined that the enemy had so cleverly "skipped out" after giving us all the hard work to construct fourteen batteries, corduroy numerous miles of road, etc. [It was] a whole month's work for nothing, and without the opportunity to see the grand "feu de enfer"* which McClellan had set his heart upon. All the fine guns stood up in the different batteries with ammunition piled in them for a forty-eight hours' continuous bombardment as monuments of McClellan's imbecility and "fortification on the brain." All were useless now, and must be sent back to Fort Monroe. The enemy. . . had given us the slip and would not wait, of course, to be killed when the batteries would open on the morning of the [6th] as intended. The "Little Napoleon stock" fell very low among officers who knew anything. . . .

At 11 a.m., the [troops] of Kearny and Birney moved across the plateau to Yorktown from which clouds of smoke were still rising. The bands were now once more in full blast, while the colors flying and bright uniforms with the polished arms glistening in the morning sun looked grand and imposing. . . . All our tents at headquarters at the sawmill had been struck and packed in the wagons. [Once] the general and staff mounted, we all moved over

*As roughly translated, "Fires of Hell."

The wharf McClellan's headquarters Union troops marching in

UNION ARMY MARCHING INTO YORKTOWN, VA.
View on Main Street, May 4, 1862.

the plain to Yorktown. The fleet of gunboats had got through the obstructions and had sailed up river shelling the woods as they went.

Word reached us before leaving that Lathrop, our telegraph operator, had been blown up by a torpedo [land mine] in one of the houses in Yorktown at 8 o'clock. He had been carried to the old grist mill with both legs blown off and had died in great agony. He had found the office of the Rebel operator, and while removing a ground wire had stepped on a hidden torpedo shell placed there by the enemy. [It] exploded, tearing out the whole side of the building. I was lucky in not going with him, as I fully intended doing so, but was too old a campaigner to lose my breakfast by not waiting for it.

The enemy had planted live shells with fuse attached in the main road leading into the works, and in houses, and buried them in the parapets and other places. Several large mines had been constructed in the ditches and ravines outside the parapets, in case our troops should assault. Some of the ditches forty feet wide were dry, others had five to eight feet of water in them. Many of these torpedo shells with friction primers attached had been tramped on and had exploded wounding and killing several of our men who were first into the works and town. . . . Some of the cavalry were also killed with their horses. One man picked up a jack knife [with] a string attached to it, which exploded a torpedo and blew him to fragments. Barrels half full of corn meal or potatoes in the houses had strings and levers attached which exploded a torpedo if moved.

Our sapper engineers after two hours' work had safely unearthed many of these cowardly missiles. Many were in groups, others planted at haphazard. Pieces of telegraph wire with a small piece of white cotton rag attached showed where some were taken out and where others were yet planted.

Yorktown contained only about forty houses. Many were of brick, unpainted and weather worn. The former custom house was [very] much dilapidated. A red flag was hung out of one of the windows showing that it had been used for a hospital. The old house, formerly headquarters of General Lafayette during or after the siege of 1781, was in a tumble down condition. . . . Our headquarters train came to a halt at a barrack looking place and I went over the town and ramparts making notes and sketching as rapidly as possible. The troops were moving across the plateau all day into the town, and they looked fine from the ramparts. General McClellan . . . made his headquarters in one of the best houses at the head of the main street while a tall flag staff put up by the Rebels floated a large national flag.

The Nelson house was the finest and best in the town. It had been built by Governor Nelson in colonial times. The bricks and white marble trimmings had been imported from England, and was the headquarters of Lord Cornwallis during the siege of 1781. . . . A red flag was still attached to the chimney on the roof, which we had all along plainly seen from the sawmill or on any part of our front line. This house had been the general headquarters of the Rebel generals Johnston and Magruder during the siege. It was not fired upon on account of the red hospital flag on the roof. When Number 1 battery opened fire on April 30, it could have been smashed with all in it. Jeff Davis himself held a council of war here only two days ago with Generals Robert E. Lee, Johnston, Magruder, [Daniel H.] Hill, and others relative to the evacuation. . . . If we had only known of it, our 200 pounder Parrott guns would have "hurried them up."*

Another headquarters of Rebel generals were at the grist mill below on the flats. Those of General Magruder, which were in a large brick house in the town, had been set on fire, and was now a smoking ruin. I went into a long frame building where a dinner or mess table was set for a dozen or more persons, tin plates, iron spoons, broken crockery, and a lot of wheat bread in loaves were strewed on the table and on the floor. The bread was not touched by our men for fear of poison. Neither was any of the water used from wells or cisterns for the same reason. Rough hemlock boards nailed to floor and supports served for seats in the absence of chairs, while on the floors of both stories were strewed tin cartridge boxes, rough dirty leather accouterments, dirty straw beds, torn and cast off clothing, meal bags, bloody, dirty rags and broken bottles. The stench was vile. The place had not been swept out in a month.

*Sneden's information must have been based on rumor. No such meeting of Confederate leaders occurred at any time during the Yorktown siege.

Every house in the town had been used for some military purpose. In some were medical stores, others which had probably been used as hospitals, were littered with bloody rags, broken boxes and barrels, dirty straw beds, tin cups, and wooden canteens made like small flat kegs with a strap or horse hide string. The old wooden church had been used for quartermaster stores. Rough leather cartridge boxes, mixed in with broken barrels and boxes, were all around and a pile of rusty bacon corn meal flour were lying on the floors and at the doors.

All the inhabitants had fled. A few old Negroes came out of their hiding places when we occupied the town in the morning. They gave all information that they were capable of when they were put at work at once to unearth the torpedoes, although they claimed to know nothing about them. Several wounded and dying Rebels were found on the second story of the Nelson house which had been used for hospital purposes for officers. They had been wounded by the bursting of a large gun on the ramparts two days ago while firing at the balloon and sawmill. . . . It blew off half way from the trunnion to [the] cascabel, upsetting the heavy timber carriage. It was overcharged at the time. This was fortunate for us at the sawmill, as the shot and shell were making it hot for us when the gun burst.

Governor Nelson's tomb was near the mansion. It was a white marble shaft, not very high, but very elaborately carved. A brick wall surrounded the Nelson house enclosing what was once a fine garden and valuable shrubs. These were now all trampled down. The houses were deserted, all the fences gone, and not a live chicken or pig could be found in the place. . . . The interior was finished in oak and walnut with mahogany doors. It now was defaced with dirt and all manner of hospital filth, though some of the heaviest furniture remained. The marble monument erected by Congress to commemorate the surrender of Cornwallis stood on the plateau a little off the main road leading from Hampton to Yorktown. It had been broken all up and carried off for relics by either our fellows or the Rebels. Only the foundation remained, and if this had not been too heavy to carry, would have been taken also by the "relic hunting fiend." . . .

The Night of May 4, 1862

General McClellan's headquarters were in a white house at the head of the main street and nearly opposite the Nelson house. A large national flag floated from a tall pole put up this forenoon. As the troops marched through I made a sketch. All moved off in fine spirits without music, and the columns of men and bayonets glistening in the setting sun moved down into the ravines by Windmill Creek, and into the unknown depths of the dark woods for hours. Generals Heintzelman, Kearny, and Birney rode at the head of the column with Hooker, whose troops had the lead. Light batteries of artillery moved with the column. All went forward at the "route step" and all moved as if in review. On the river our gunboats were shelling the woods over towards Gloucester Point (now deserted by the enemy). Others, with numerous small boats, were removing the sunken spiles across the channel, while

View of Fort Magruder. Battlefield of Williamsburg, Va.
Showing obstructions, rifle pits, and other redoubts.

the sun set in splendor over the scene, and everyone was joyous to be once more foot loose in pursuit of the enemy.

Soon our headquarter train of six wagons came along with the wagon guard of twenty men under Lieutenant Gray of [the] 3rd Maine. I had packed my map box and instruments before leaving headquarters in the morning and went with the wagon train so as to get any maps out which might be wanted by the general in advance. The wagons were packed with tents, mess chests, officers' baggage, and several demijohns of "red eye" with patent lock stoppers on each, which were carefully nursed from mishap by the teamsters. Three days' rations were ordered to be cooked before breaking camp. Still many had not time to do so. Such was the hurry in getting off. Forty rounds of cartridges were carried by each soldier, however, while many were overloaded. Others had thrown away their overcoats or had left them behind so as to lighten the march. The artillery moved with the wagons on the road while the troops had to march in columns of fours on each side of them on account of the narrowness of them.

We passed down a steep hill to Windmill Creek, which was bridged in several places,

then struck into the Yorktown and Williamsburg Turnpike or main road about 6:30 p.m. The dense woods overhung the road, while pools of black water could be seen under them. The roads were sandy but full of sloughs of mud and water, with here and there broken corduroy stuff sticking out of the red mud, and these mud holes were numerous. The wagon trains crawled along slowly, until an opening in the woods allowed one train to pass the other. After going two miles the wagons stuck in the mud every few minutes, while the mules were belabored unmercifully by the teamsters, while the air was blue with their swearing. Every wagon master tried to get his train ahead of the one before him and raced the teams when an opening appeared in the woods. Then wheels would be interlocked and the mules roll completely out of harness, so the same old scenes were repeated as when we traveled from Hampton to Yorktown a month ago. . . . The yells, cracking of whips, curses, and braying of the mules resounded through the woods for a great distance in many places. The road went down in a gully with high banks of gravel on either side with water a foot deep at the bottom. The men had then to take hold of the wheel spokes and turn them by main strength to get them through.

Soon we came to a narrow part of the road going downhill with a wet sandy bottom. Here our headquarter train stuck for half an hour and the mules had to be taken out of the rear wagons and hitched on in front. This gave us time to build a fire and have supper. When lighting our pipes, we kept along the edges of the woods and clearings. Very few houses were seen, and they were all deserted with windows broken and overrun with tall weeds and brambles in front and rear. About 9 p.m., we had a long halt of all the wagons and going ahead half a mile or more found the delay caused by a large uncultivated field which stretched on both sides of the road, along which and in the field were small heaps of fresh earth at intervals. These heaps were also in the middle of the road. The heaps of earth were thought to be planted torpedoes. So the artillery men were turning these over but found none. These were only shams placed by the enemy to cause delay. We did lose more than an hour's time trying to find out what the heaps meant. . . .

As we neared the Halfway House we came upon numerous Rebel army wagons which had been stalled in the mud. They were lying on their sides with all the wheels cut to pieces with axes. Nothing was found in the wagons but a few old salt bags. There were lots of dead mules strung out on the road for a mile or more lying on their backs, half smothered in mud, with their feet sticking up out of it. These had to be all removed by ropes before the line mules in our train would pass them, another delay of an hour.

An order came at 2 a.m. to halt the whole wagon trains, which was gladly complied with, while the battery horses now pulled the guns through to the front when they were parked near the Halfway House, an old wayside tavern near. The teamsters slept in their

THE WILLIAM AND MARY COLLEGE, WILLIAMSBURG, VA.
May 6, 1862.

Deserted hotel on Main Street | Factory | Record office | Court house Slate roof, wood shutters | Jail (burnt by the Rebels 18th May when they evacuated) | Headquarters of Colonel William Averell, 3rd Pennsylvania Cavalry

NEW KENT COURT HOUSE, VA.

May 19, 1862. Evacuated by the Rebels May 18.

The III Army Corps, Major General Samuel P. Heintzelman commanding, camped here May 18, 19, and 20, 1862. The enemy hastily evacuated as the 3rd Pennsylvania Cavalry, Colonel William Averell approached. The Rebels burnt the jail and all the houses were deserted by the inhabitants. The Union soldiers looted the court house and records office. Deeds and legal parchments were carried off by them. Two Rebel soldiers were left behind the Rebel army at two houses, desperately wounded. Three old women were the only persons in the town. General Heintzelman's headquarters were at the deserted house of Telemachus Taylor until the army resumed their forward march again May 20.

wagons while the patient army mule stood in harness during the rest of the night chewing on the tailboards of the wagon in front of him. Our headquarter wagon guard built a fire and we all had a good meal at 2:30 in the morning of May 5. I and others slept in our wagons. All of our sugar, salt, and hard bread had got wet with the rain which poured down steadily until long after daylight. The small streams in the bottom of the ravines in the woods where we had halted were turned into small mill races roaring all the while. The mules brayed unceasingly, which scared an owl or two away up in the pine trees, and everyone soon sought sleep as best he might.

Because the second volume of Sneden's diary/memoir is missing, unfortunately we lose the details of his life for nearly two months. From evidence drawn from notes in his scrapbook and a diary of General Heintzelman, it must have been a period of intense activity for Sneden, including firsthand observations of two battles. On May 5, Heintzelman's corps advanced on Williamsburg, where it fought a sharp battle just east of the old colonial capital. Sneden prepared a map for Heintzelman's official report of the battle. He also made detailed drawings of

View of Fair Oaks Station, Va., as Fortified by the III Corps
Known as the "Twin Houses." Headquarters of Major General Joe Hooker after the battle of Fair Oaks, Va., June 15, 1862.

the battlefield and an army hospital set up at the College of William and Mary. With sketch-book in hand, he then drew villages and crossroads as the Union army advanced slowly up the Peninsula to the Chickahominy River, only a few miles northeast of Richmond. And almost without fail, he made drawings of the houses that Heintzelman selected for his headquarters.

By the end of May, McClellan split his army, putting two corps, including Heintzelman's, on the south side of the Chickahominy River in preparation for an attack on the Confederate capital. Rather than wait for McClellan to act, however, the Rebels launched a heavy but unwieldy assault on the two exposed Union corps at Seven Pines and Fair Oaks. Heintzelman took command of the battlefield on the first day and was in the heat of action, having a horse shot from under him. We do not know of Sneden's whereabouts during the battle, but his scrapbook contains images of Fair Oaks sites, including buildings used as hospitals.

The two-day battle ended in a draw, but the butcher's bill for both sides was high, more than eleven thousand men. One casualty, however, stood out. At the end of the first day of battle, Confederate commander Joseph E. Johnston was severely wounded. The following day, President Jefferson Davis announced his replacement—Robert E. Lee. Within a matter of weeks, this bold new leader would change the course of the war. For Robert Sneden, the conflict would become a far deadlier business.

Chapter Three

Confusion and Darkness: The Seven Days

For nearly a month after the battle of Fair Oaks, the Army of the Potomac lay idle astride the Chickahominy River. Even though McClellan maintained a numerical advantage over his opponent, he acted as though he were in grave danger. His spies told him that the Confederates had 200,000 troops in Richmond, when in reality the Southern army had less than half that number. In mid-June, Confederate cavalry under General Jeb Stuart rode completely around the Federal army, disrupting communications and leaving the impression that the Rebels were everywhere. Despite constant entreaties from Washington, McClellan hesitated to act. With tentative plans to begin another siege, he said he needed more time to build bridges across the Chickahominy and to bring up his big guns. In the meantime, he kept up demands for reinforcements that he had been making since March. For a while it seemed as if Lincoln would comply; but the threat posed in the Shenandoah Valley by Stonewall Jackson's army permitted only one division to be sent to McClellan. In the meantime, he readjusted his army's disposition, moving all but one of his corps south of the Chickahominy.

In the Union camps, the men began to recover from the Fair Oaks battle and waited anxiously for the next move. They also went to work with pick and shovel to prepare for siege work. Drawings in Sneden's scrapbook indicate that he visited several key sites along the Union lines, including the army's great supply base at White House Landing and some of the bridges crossing the Chickahominy. With headquarters at Savage's Station, General Heintzelman spent long hours writing his after-action reports, no doubt enlisting the aid of

Sneden to prepare maps. Heintzelman grumbled constantly about fellow generals, about insults given and received, and about who deserved credit for this action or that. Rumors of impending plans and Confederate actions filled his pages. He rarely slept through the night, for although the army sat idle, its days and nights were frequently interrupted by sharp clashes on the picket line and the boom of cannonading. Sudden and violent thunderstorms brought only temporary relief from the rising heat and humidity of the oncoming summer.

While McClellan kept his soldiers relatively inert, his opponent, Robert E. Lee, made good use of this valuable time. He whipped the Confederate army into fighting shape, and he developed a bold plan to drive the Union host from Richmond. While part of his army held the Federals in check east of the city, Lee would launch a full-scale attack on the one isolated Union corps north of the Chickahominy, thereby threatening McClellan's supply line. The assault would also drive McClellan out of his entrenchments and force him to fight in the open. To ensure success, Lee brought Jackson's army from the Shenandoah Valley to join in the offensive.

The first round of what would be known as the Seven Days battles began on June 25. Rebel troops east of Richmond launched a short but violent assault on Heintzelman's corps at Oak Grove to make McClellan think that a strong army was in front of him. Then on June 26, the weight of Lee's attack fell on McClellan's right at Mechanicsville. The next day Jackson joined the assault at Gaines Mill. By late June 27, McClellan had seen enough; he decided to retreat to Harrison's Landing on the James River where his gunboats could protect him. Still the Confederates came on, hammering the Union army at every turn and threatening to cut off and capture large numbers of retreating soldiers.

Robert Sneden and his comrades in Heintzelman's corps found themselves caught in the middle of a maelstrom created by the Confederate offensive. Late on the afternoon of June 29, Rebel troops under General John Magruder attacked Union forces as they retreated from Savage's Station. Darkness saved the Union rear guard from a serious defeat. But as they withdrew during the night, the Federals abandoned huge quantities of supplies and more than two thousand sick and wounded men in a field hospital. Sneden's account begins on the eve of the battle of Savage's Station.

June 29, 1862

. . . After leaving our headquarters train stuck in the mud last night, I found my way [to Savage's Station] through the darkness and rain storm about 11:30 p.m. . . . I found the telegraph operators still here at work with a small instrument. I slept in the attic room of Savage's house on a pile of carpets which had been taken from the best rooms downstairs some time ago. Every room in the house was occupied by our surgeons and their assistants, who were probing wounds and putting on splints. The walls and floors were spattered with blood, and dozens of officers were lying on the floors and in hallways awaiting their turn. Some were moaning in pain, while others were fast asleep. A general feeling of despondency prevailed which was enhanced by the rain storm and the knowledge that the morning would bring another battle and that we would probably retreat through White Oak Swamp whether we repulsed the enemy or not. Several dead officers were boxed up in coffins in the main hall of the house, and the noise occasioned by moving them into wagons during the night kept many awake. I got but two and a half hours sleep. I went to the telegraph room where I found Generals Heintzelman, Sumner, [Winfield S.] Hancock, [William B.] Franklin, and others in close conversation "on the situation" and sending orders by the field telegraph to their commands in front. Orderlies came dashing up every moment for instructions or with dispatches. Long lines of army wagons were filing from the woods in our front across the wide fields opposite Savage's. Artillery and ammunition wagons blocked the main road to White Oak Swamp. A large train of baggage and platform cars with an engine attached was on the railroad track below the house, while details of men were loading them up with the reserve ammunition which had been stored in Savage's coach house and other buildings. These were soon destined to be set on fire and [they set off] for Long Bridge, and destruction. Huge piles of boxes of clothing, commissary stores, and bales of hay were also piled up across the railroad ready for the torch. Wounded men and officers were streaming in from the front. Some walking, others in ambulances, while hundreds of stragglers, some but very slightly wounded, were interspersed in the steady moving throng.

As our headquarters wagons were all on their way to Brackett's Ford on White Oak Swamp Creek, I had no way of getting anything to eat, but fortunately managed to get a breakfast from a surgeon assistant of our headquarters who was still on the ground. At 8 a.m. I went on foot off towards our right. . . . At Dr. Trent's, which has been used a second time by General McClellan as headquarters, everything betokened hasty exit. Wagons were loading up with baggage and tents. The cavalry escort were all mounted. As the general was moving to Savage's house, I found our troops strongly posted along the high ground which borders the Chickahominy. . . . All our wagons, guns, and men, had crossed the river during the night, leaving most of our wounded [from] Friday's battle in the enemy's hands. As most of the commissary stores had been burned by us in the retreat, these poor fellows will probably starve to death! Our troops were crossing all night, the last getting over about daybreak. The bridges were then blown up by our engineers. Large fires were kept burning all night on the picket line to deceive the enemy, as most of the force had been moved back from the river and were now behind the third line of defenses near Fair Oaks.

. . . All through the woods I met lines of wounded men hobbling towards Savage's by the railroad track. Many had been so badly wounded that they sat on the ground to die, but few ambulances were to be seen. And they were all full of dying and desperately wounded men. Thin streams of blood ran out of the sides and bottoms of these vehicles, while the drivers were lashing the horses, and going over stumps in a reckless manner, jolting the remaining life out of the occupants. No signs of the enemy were to be seen in the woods on the opposite side of the Chickahominy, but their camp fires during the night denoted a very large force. I heard much drumming off to the left, which I supposed were fresh troops coming from Richmond to reinforce.

... The atmosphere was very close and sultry, not a breath of air in the pine woods while the muddy roads and dead leaves gave out [a] sickening miasmatic odor. I returned to Savage's by the railroad track, first going through the now deserted camps . . . on hopes of meeting some quartermasters of my acquaintance, or of the 40th Regiment. But all had gone below Savage's and nothing but ragged blankets and broken tent poles were to be seen.

I came back with the stream of wounded and stragglers, who all thought our army had been defeated, but now said a "flank movement" was to be made in which "we would either go to Richmond or to hell!" I found that General McClellan had arrived from Dr. Trent's and a council of war was being held.

Savage's house had been cleared of all the wounded, and numerous officers seemed to fill the rooms. About 100 hospital tents were on the grounds now and they all seemed filled to repletion with wounded soldiers. Hundreds more wounded were in the barns, others were lying on rails, and on the ground back of the house, while amputations were being carried on by the exhausted surgeons and their assistants in front of the tents in the ruined garden. There are 2,500 sick and wounded here now. . . . Many [were] able to travel off last night with the retreating army, but General Heintzelman says "all who cannot get off by walking must be left behind to the enemy." Although there are as many as 500 ambulances, these, by General McClellan's orders must go empty! Probably he reserves these ambulances for officers only. The sick and wounded are as yet kept in ignorance of the ultimate evacuation of Savage's, and few officers even think we will not fall back further than White Oak Swamp and Bottom's Bridge, five and a half miles away. . . .

There had been sharp picket firing last night at 12 o'clock. Also more firing on the Nine Mile Road this morning from 6 to 7 a.m. Word came to Savage's at 9 o'clock that the enemy was crossing the Chickahominy at New Bridge, having now constructed a pontoon there, and another at Duane's Bridge. Artillery and infantry were crossing in large force, while another large body was endeavoring to repair and construct [a] bridge on the ruins of Alexander's and Grapevine bridges. About 9 a.m., heavy musketry firing, and rapid discharge of artillery [signaled] that the enemy had attacked General Smith's division of Sumner's command, who were in an entrenched position in Garnett's field near . . . Allen's farms. Couriers were instantly dispatched with orders for the troops to take position and deploy into the old rifle pits and earthworks which crossed the Williamsburg Stage Road. All was excitement and anxiety at these headquarters pending the result. I went up to the attic story of Savage's house, and saw the white clouds of battle smoke above the tree tops and the white puffs of bursting shells, while the musketry was very sharp and continuous. This lasted for a hour, when it died out. All was again quiet. . . .

The immense open space in front of Savage's was densely thronged with wagon trains,

HEADQUARTERS OF GENERAL GEORGE B. MCCLELLAN AT HOUSE OF DR. TRENT
Near Savage's Station, Va., June 1862.

artillery, caissons, ammunition trains, and moving troops. No drums beat or bands played, while the regimental colors were furled to the staffs. Officers tried to pacify [the men] and fight off the true meaning of the retrograde movement. Countless streams of wounded and stragglers, dirt begrimed, hungry, haggard looking from want of sleep, mixed themselves in with the trains and moving troops. Caissons were being hastily replenished with spare ammunition from Savage's coach house. Orderlies were galloping everywhere with dispatches, while Sumner and Franklin's troops were taking up a defensive position around Savage's house and adjacent open field. About 12 noon, General Heintzelman had word that the Rebels had constructed a bridge over the Chickahominy . . . near Dr. Trent's house, a mile and a quarter from here, and were crossing in force. Cavalry were at once sent off to ascertain the enemy's movements, and soon the information was verified. No . . . obstructions here had prevented the enemy from crossing. We had to hurry up movements of troops and make ready to destroy the immense quantities of stores by fire, as intended previously. . . .

I had dinner with the telegraph operators Moreland and Nichols. From an assistant surgeon, [I] got two cans of condensed milk and some hard bread to last me until I caught up with our wagon train in the [White Oak] Swamp, and although whiskey was in plenty, I preferred to fill a canteen with cold strong coffee for future use. "We ate, drank, and were merry, for tomorrow we die." After getting a "good square meal," I went to the hospital tents, as our chief medical director was now to inform those who were able to walk "to get away as fast as possible." The scene was melancholy, and distressing enough to move the heart of a Rebel. Some were dying every moment. [These] were wrapped in their blankets, placed on stretchers, and carried off back of the peach orchard, placed in shallow graves, and trenches, with their overcoats covered over them. [Then] the earth was shoveled in without further ceremony.

When the orders to leave were given, many grasped their muskets and hobbled off. Some of the younger and helplessly wounded soldiers cried like children, deploring their fate, after having fought so hard. Others indulged in cursing McClellan and the doctors for not taking them away in ambulances. They all could have been taken off days ago if we had disputed the enemy's crossing on the Chickahominy by even a show of earthworks at the bridgeheads. Although the trains to and from White House had been kept running to the last moment, bringing stores and provisions, and returning with crowded cars filled with wounded, the hospitals were always kept full by the influx of the wounded coming from the field hospitals in front. The trains had stopped running since 11 a.m. yesterday, and now lay on the track below the hospitals filled with shot, shell, and powder.

Those who could hobble or walk started from the hospitals and mixed in with the moving wagon trains. Some were taken up by the teamsters, others, carrying their guns, supported a comrade. Some limped on sticks or improvised crutches. Others staggered forward, resting every few steps to adjust their bloody bandages. But stimulated by the fear of the enemy, [they] again pressed on. The attending surgeons were completely exhausted, and used up for want of sleep. All had stopped performing "capital operations." The number of surgeons were totally inadequate for the wants of the wounded. The strain upon their nervous system by continually performing amputations in the midst of such scenes of misery was so great that in a short time the surgeon sinks under prostration which paralyzes every vital power. The most humane man, with the strongest nerves, breathing for days the poisoned atmosphere of festering wounds, gazing on the most ghastly sights, and hearing the piercing shrieks of the patients while undergoing the operations, is absolutely compelled to shut his eyes to the surroundings, and turn a deaf ear [to] the most imploring cries for aid. Many of those surgeons and assistants who have lately come here from Washington don't know their business any more than a drug clerk. The consequence is that they perform the most bungling of operations, while many of the sufferers have soon died, after passing through their unskillful hands. They were mere butchers! Others again performed quick and successful operations. And the wounded would patiently endure pain hours longer so that they would not fall into the hands of the unskilled operators. Not more than 300 wounded managed to get away, leaving 2,300 to fall into the enemy's hands. It is estimated that we have fully 5,000 wounded on this side of the Chickahominy. Not many were carried off by the ambulances, and those [few] are principally officers. . . .

Large quantities of medical stores and provisions for the use of the hospitals are packed away in the upper rooms of Savage's house. But in my opinion the Rebels will confiscate them to their own use, and our wounded and sick won't get much, if anything of them. As all our headquarter tents were left standing on the ground when our trains left yesterday, they have been since used for the sick with the exception of the large bell shaped tent, known as the

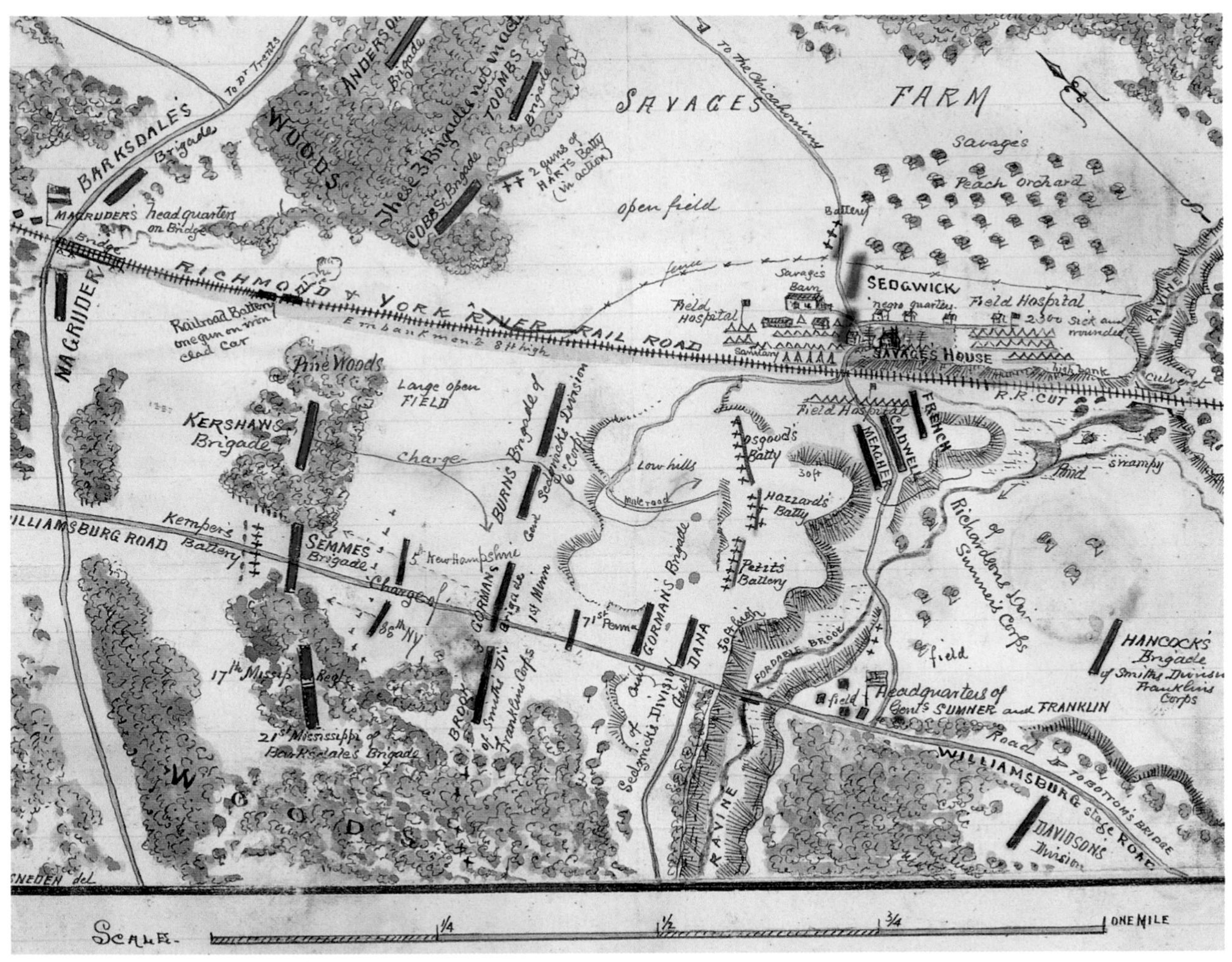

PLAN OF THE BATTLE OF SAVAGE'S STATION, VA.
Fought Sunday, June 29, 1862.

general's mess tent, and the one occupied by General Heintzelman. These will also be left behind when we go. I found my tent full of wounded officers. The grass was so saturated with blood, where the wounded had laid for days and nights together, that in the now hot sun, the stench was like that of a slaughter house! Swarms of large flies were everywhere.

The heat was intolerable. The large trees near Savage's house afforded the only shade. Under these were collected generals and other officers, orderlies with their horses, surgeons, quartermasters, commissary officers, and artillery officers, all giving and receiving orders for future movements. The surgeons and assistants occupied the several Negro quarters attached to Savage's house. Everyone was cooking and eating a hasty meal. Long trains of wagons were still coming from the woods in front and columns of troops in motion filled the fields in front of Savage's. Amid cracking of whips and braying of mules, all were hurrying to "the swamp road." Now and then [the] wheels would get locked, causing a short halt and much yelling by the teamsters. But again they would move on, only to get stuck lower down the road, and go on as before. Generals Heintzelman, Sumner, Sedgwick, Franklin, and their staff officers were consulting and giving orders. All were taking the situation coolly. No excitement showed itself in their faces, though all were more or less anxious. . . . I had furnished General Heintzelman with a good supply of maps before packing away those not to be used. These the general was now looking over in his tent, in company with Sumner and Franklin. . . .

About 3:30 p.m., some cavalry officer brought word that the enemy had crossed the Chickahominy at three points, and would be here in an hour's time. Orders were at once given by General Heintzelman "to fire the spare ammunition" . . . which could not be put on the train. A guard drove back all the soldiers around the log barn and coach house where the ammunition was stored. [They] got the wounded men away, and the officers crowded into Savage's house for shelter. Soon the fuse was fired, and the headquarters resembled a volcano! Shells went screaming and bursting in the air. Volumes of white smoke, mixed with flying timbers, enveloped the house and grounds for ten minutes. The carriage house was a sheet of flame and burned to the ground. The sides and roof of the ice house also took fire and was burnt all above ground. Twenty tons of ice had recently been put in it, and the contractor was lucky to get his pay for it three days ago. Several horses and mules were badly hurt by the flying shell but I did not hear of any men being hit. The hospitals were at a safe distance in the garden, and Savage's house was between the wounded and the ammunition.

At about 4:30, the train of seventeen cars, filled with hundreds of tons of shot and shell, and hundreds of barrels of gun powder and cartridges was fired. The locomotive engine under a high pressure of steam [had] been previously attached. The engineer ran slow for a few hundred feet, when he jumped off first pulling the throttle valve wide open. Immediately the train assumed the appearance of some living monster, and bounded off at a terrific speed, the driving wheels revolving faster every second. Each car was fired separately; and soon the whole train was enwrapped in billows of flame, out of which exploding shells were hurled in every direction and high in [the] air. Through the roofs and sides of the cars sprang hundreds of live shells, which burst in the woods on either side of the track, screaming like fiends in agony, while the thousands of moving troops looked on in amazement. The blazing and deadly train rushed towards Long Bridge, which had been previously destroyed by us, to plunge in the Chickahominy River a shattered wreck. . . . The speed attained by the train in running there (about six miles) must have been terrific.

As the army was not moving near the track, no fears were had as to its doing us any damage. While it was getting headway, the mules brayed in fright, and started on the full gallop, despite all the teamsters' efforts to hold them. Wheels were locked, and many a wagon was broken or upset by running into trees off the road. The excitement was now increased by the burning of the accumulated stores.

As the flame surmounted the different piles, crackled and hissed in the black smoke, our whole line of pickets now rushed in from the strip of woods in front to announce the enemy advancing in great numbers directly upon us. Orders were given to "fall in" immediately, which was quickly responded to by the troops. Trains were hurried off at full gallop, artillery wheeled into their positions and unlimbered. Orderlies galloped in every direction with orders, and for a few minutes everyone was excited by the approaching conflict. The heat was terrible. . . . Not a breath of air was felt. The sun threw its red glare on the red soil and railroad track, making it difficult to see clearly up towards Fair Oaks Station. About 5 p.m., thick clouds of dust were visible above the woods in this direction, and soon we heard the Rebels yelling like Comanche Indians.

They had found our deserted camps and probably were digging up the barrels of whiskey, or filling themselves with those left open. Yells in response were heard on our right towards Dr. Trent's and Dudley's houses, and soon long lines of the enemy debouched from the woods in plain view, while artillery could be seen struggling through the woods. The drivers frantically lash[ed] the horses to enable the guns to get into action. . . .

Sharpshooters took positions behind stone walls and in Savage's log barn to the right. The railroad embankments afforded cover for more. The men were all stern looking, determined, cool, and quiet. The sun had began to lose itself over the tree tops of the woods in front, and the heat was stifling. The Rebels, in large numbers, burst from the cover with loud yells [and] opened on us at once with artillery.

The enemy sent showers of shells into our lines. Two burst very close to where [the generals] were standing, covering them with dust and earth. Our batteries now vigorously replied, . . . plying the enemy with shell and spherical case shot. And for an hour the crash and concussion of air was so great that I could hardly keep my feet. The artillery duel slackened about 6:30, while the guns were covered with wet blankets to cool them off, and caissons were galloped with fresh ammunition to the front. The enemy's fire was badly directed, most of their fuse being cut too short, and thus far we had few casualties. A series of prolonged yells from the Rebels was now heard, and two strong lines were deployed in the field on our center and right, who soon came rushing to the charge. The setting sun glistening on their bayonets, as they came on in beautiful order of battle, with piercing yells and confidence. Our lines stood firm as a rock, 5,000 muskets were simultaneously pointed and discharged with a terrific crash! To [this] the enemy replied by double the number, when all in front was hid in smoke.

For a moment there was a pause, until the Rebel line came within close and certain range, when there was a terrific crash of musketry, while the artillery fire was redoubled. And the storm of lead was continuous and deadly on the approaching lines of the Rebels. They bravely rushed up, however, to within twenty feet of our artillery, when bushels of grape and canister from the cannon laid them low in rows. Large gaps were made in their alignments and whole companies tumbled to the ground at once. The ranks in their rear still came on stumbling over those already fallen, yelling and firing as they came. At the same moment a wild cheer from our troops in defiance could be heard above the roar of artillery and crash of musketry. Beaten back by the storm of lead and iron, the enemy hesitated, wavered, and fell back a short ways to the railroad, while fresh regiments of Rebels came up behind. [These] pressed the remains of the broken column once more to a renewed attack. Again our lines poured in a terrible crushing fire from 10,000 muskets, and again the enemy fell back in disorder and dismay. This time they fairly ran to the woods for cover, hotly plied by the far reaching artillery. Rush's Lancers* now charged them as they retreated, leaving all the ground in front covered with their dead and dying. And many a poor Rebel was speared in the back before reaching the woods. There the lancers encountered a terrible fire from the Rebel masses, and soon returned in some disorder, with their red pennons half stripped from their lances, and many spear heads broken off and lost. . . .

All this time the stores of boxes and barrels were fiercely burning, sending up black smoke high in air. The Rebels, no doubt now maddened at the chances of not recovering the plunder before being all destroyed, soon formed again in solid lines which looked irresistible, and came again to the attack with deafening yells as before. But they again met a terrific storm of lead and iron and stood off about 200 feet from our line firing at close range. For a moment the fire would somewhat slacken, when it would burst out anew by the instantaneous discharge of thousands of muskets, and the contest again redoubled.

After the Rebels had sustained their first repulse, and during a temporary lull in the firing, a shrill locomotive whistle was heard up the railroad at Fair Oaks Station. And soon appeared coming down the track towards us a nondescript car, which was roofed over at sides with railroad iron set at an angle, and from which in front projected a heavy gun. . . . A sort of railroad "Merrimac." A powerful locomotive pushed it along from behind. While all eyes were directed towards it, [its] big gun opened fire suddenly, and everyone looked for some place of shelter. It advanced slowly nearer, and threw another shot straight for Savage's house. There was some dodging among officers and cavalrymen. I dodged myself into a dry ditch, while the shot plunged into the soft earth behind me, throwing up showers of small stones and earth. One shot struck the remains of the ice house thirty feet from Savage's house. Another went overhead through the trees and beyond the hospital tents. Another had gone into the earth in front of the house. [Then] the railroad gun was suddenly withdrawn and steamed up fully half a mile on the track, where it continued the firing until dark.

I ascertained afterwards that the cause of its sudden retrograde movement was, that after it had got to the nearest point from Savage's house, General [William W.] Burns had thrown a regiment forward to tear up the track behind it, which being perceived, the train was backed up quickly for fear of capture. [Our] men having only a few artillery handspikes, did not get up a single rail before the engineer backed up in time. Two of our rifled gun batter-

*The 6th Pennsylvania Cavalry, organized by Englishman Richard H. Rush, was equipped with lances. Later in the war, the regiment abandoned these unwieldy weapons.

BATTLE OF SAVAGE'S STATION, VA.
June 29, 1862. Rebel ironclad car with cotton bales in action.

ies were then trained on the locomotive and gun, which would have ensured its destruction if the track had been promptly torn up behind. The gun was a heavy 32 pounder and was placed on two platform cars, with a hood built of railroad iron in front to protect the gunners. . . . Cotton bales were piled on both sides of the car, which concealed a hundred or more sharpshooters. Those engaged in trying to tear up the track had barely noticed that the engine was backing before taking cover. And when the moving gun passed, the occupants of the platform received a close sharp volley of musketry, which must have killed many of the men on it. The Rebels did not return the fire in passing our force, but hid behind the cotton bales. The back part of the iron shield or hood was, however, open, and two [of our] companies delivered their fire from ground higher than the floor of the car. I made a sketch of the ["Merrimac"] however, when it was nearest Savage's. The affair was novel, and caused general astonishment among officers and men. A detail of men were set at work tearing up the railroad track in front of Savage's which was within the lines held by our battle lines.*

As darkness began to settle on the field of battle, the enemy renewed their efforts to force our lines, but always met the same bloody repulse. They attacked on our extreme right, but were repulsed by the concentrated fire of our artillery on the road leading to Dudley's house when our lines were drawn closer in towards the rear of Savage's house.

During the battle, a Rebel battery had got the range of the hospital tents in the garden. Several were knocked down and many of the helplessly wounded were hurt anew or killed. There had been no hospital flag flying on the tents. Now one was hoisted, and a white flag of truce [was] sent to the battery of the enemy to inform them that they were firing on our sick and wounded. They received the flag and sent word for us "to take that 'ar battery out

*Nicknamed the "Land Merrimac" by its producer, the Confederate navy, this contraption was history's first armored railroad battery. Although momentarily terrifying, the weapon proved too cumbersome and was never used again by the Southern army.

Rebels charging the guns　　Gorman's and Burns's brigades　　Ravine

View of the Battle of Savage's Station, Va.
Sunday, June 29, 1862. Fought by Sumner's and Franklin's corps.

Union artillery Savage's house and railroad Field hospital

of thar." A section of [one of our batteries] had occupied the high knoll near the railroad, and within fifty feet of Savage's house and as many more from the hospitals. This was the reason the Rebels had shelled the grounds. The battery was then withdrawn, and the Rebels did not throw any more shot in the vicinity.

The ground in front of Savage's was crowded with troops in reserve, and were too numerous for their allotted space. The enemy's artillery had caused many casualties among the crowded ranks. It was now 8 p.m., and still the battle raged with terrific fury on both sides. Fresh regiments of Rebels constantly came into the field from out of the woods, amid terrific yells from their companions, hundreds of the Rebels were now crazy drunk from the effects of the whiskey found in our old camps. They fired their guns in the air, yelled and staggered forward to renewed charges, coming right up to the muzzles of the artillery, only to be blown away to atoms! Officers were seen vainly trying to get them into compact lines. They were crazy drunk, and attacked us in regiments and squads. The fighting was now desperate and deadly on both sides. . . . As it grew dark in the confusion and darkness made by the battle smoke, two regiments approached each other, and each reserved its fire, uncertain whether the other were friend or foe. . . . Both regiments discharged their muskets simultaneously into each other's faces not ten feet distant apart! The loss of the Rebels is unknown, but 200 [Union soldiers] fell dead or helplessly wounded!

Our artillery was now so overheated by rapid and long firing, that many of the pieces had to be withdrawn. The wagons had now all gone on towards White Oak Swamp and the road [was] clear for retreat of the troops. Orders were given for the men who had been fighting to withdraw in retreat, while the reserves were to hold the ground and still keep the Rebels at bay, and act as rear guard when all retreated. There was a lull in the firing as it now was quite dark. The Rebel artillery continued firing at short intervals, while their frenzied infantry made sudden charges on isolated groups of our men, cutting, slashing and yelling like fiends. Our men still fought firmly and followed up any success by charging with the bayonet. Still, numbers were falling every minute. And as all the ambulances had gone on in retreat to the swamp, all our dead and wounded were left on the field of battle where they had fallen. Our columns were drawn closer to Savage's house, while others were crowded in among the ammunition wagons now in retrograde movements on the road to White Oak Swamp. . . .

Night was coming on with every appearance of a rain storm. Wounded officers again filled Savage's house and grounds, while hundreds lay weltering in their blood all along the railroad, on the lawn, and on the grassy slopes, imploring not to be left in Rebel hands. Stragglers were crowding down the road in retreat, some carrying a wounded officer or comrade. All knew that they must march all night through an unknown swamp, and if needs be fight all the way on empty stomachs, for there was no time to cook anything now. . . . As General Heintzelman and his staff had moved off at sundown, I hastened to overtake them. I got a good supply of cold meat and hard bread from an assistant surgeon and mounted my horse and left Savage's.

It was now 9:30 p.m., and it was with great difficulty in the darkness and confusion of the retreating masses of troops and wagons, that I could pick my way. The firing had stopped since 9 o'clock when the Rebels had occupied Savage's. Their shrill and prolonged yells echoing through the woods attested their satisfaction in getting the provisions and wounded left there by stupid negligence of our officers. Nearly all could have been sent away if we had opposed the enemy while crossing the Chickahominy.

The enemy followed our rear guard a mile below Savage's. [They made] a desperate and last assault [striving] to break our formation, but our artillery fired without unlimbering the pieces, and [then] the double doses of grape laid many of them in the road. [Then] they gave it up as a bad job and retired, to our great relief.

The whole road before and behind me was densely crowded with men, wagons, pontoons on wheels, horses, and mule teams, hundred of stragglers and wounded men limped along in the surging throng. Teamsters were lashing and swearing at the mules, while the darkness increased as we entered patches of woods.

The clouds hung low and black which portended a heavy rain storm. The heat was yet very great and all the way from Savage's the men had thrown their overcoats, blankets, and knapsacks along the roadside, making the sides of the roads literally blue with clothes, which they were too exhausted to carry. The knapsacks had all been cut and gashed. And most of the clothes were similarly treated. All kept their guns, ammunition, and canteens. Very few had rations of any kind. Some had not eaten anything since early dawn, for the enemy had attacked us early in the morning, and all the forces had turned out in lines of battle. There were frequent halts in the moving mass of troops and wagons, when the current became clogged or stuck caused by the determined efforts of one teamster trying to pass the one ahead of him in the narrow road. There would then be a locking of wheels, cracking of whips, yells, and much swearing of teamsters. Although strict orders had been previously given "to make no noise on the march," this was little heeded by the vast crowds of troops and teamsters. Making fires also was prohibited. And although many small fires were started to make coffee, they were kicked out by the officers. Negro guides had been employed to show the roads to the advance, and they performed their mission faithfully.

Large numbers of our wounded fell out of [the] line of march, unable to go further from exhaustion and pain. And as we entered the dense pine woods many lay down to get a short sleep under the trees, who would probably be made to move on when the rear guard came up. I passed the Gartwrights' house or "Linden Farm" at 11 p.m. General Heintzelman had made his headquarters here when we advanced [on] May 25. The place had seen hard usage since then, fences had been all burnt, trees cut down, outhouses had disappeared. The house had been used for a hospital. Even now, sick and wounded were being hastily removed to ambulances in front of the entrances. . . .

I carried a good map of my own make with me, and in company with several officers went to a deserted house off the road to unfold it, and see the "situation" for ourselves. We found several of our men here. Some were asleep on the floor. Others were busily cooking coffee by a fire made in the chimney. All the windows had been covered with blankets and boards to prevent the light being seen from the road. It was now midnight and the rain began to come down steadily, which caused many to regret having thrown their overcoats away. The first thing done was to turn all the sleepers out of the house. We consulted the map, and afterwards made a midnight supper of the provisions which I fortunately had with me. The men were loath to leave the shanty, and it was only by telling them that "the rear guard was passing" and that the "Johnnies" would get them if they did not go on immediately, that they started for the road again. We put the fire out and left soon after. The long pent up rain now came down in torrents, while the thunder crashed and roared, and the lightning blinded us and scared the horses. Many of the men wrapped their rubber blankets around their muskets to keep them dry, preferring to get wet through in the storm. We had now fairly entered "The Swamp," and the woods were very dark and wet. The road was very fortunately of an alluvial light colored sand, which the rain hardened and made the travel comparatively easy.

If we had to go over the red mud roads we would have hopelessly stuck in the mud all night and the enemy would have overtaken us. Numerous owls screeched in the trees overhead, while all that we could see was the white road under our feet. The tall trees shut out the sky almost completely, while the sudden flashes of lightning lit up the long struggling lines of wagons and men in advance, and flashed on their muskets like a scene in a theatre. Several wagons broke down and were left by the wayside. One siege gun was abandoned and spiked, the horses had given out, pulling through the wet sand. There were ten horses harnessed to each gun. . . . This was the only gun which we left in the swamp. All the others, some 600 pieces, were brought through safely. Some delay was caused by the wagons breaking down, but everyone pushed forward while the storm raged and the rain poured down on us until 3 o'clock in the morning. The confusion which attended the march during the storm was very considerable and demoralizing. There were 3,000 wagons cooped up on a narrow road between Savage's and White Oak Creek. Infantry, cavalry, artillery, mules, horses, and stragglers, were promiscuously mixed without much order. . . . Many horses and mules fell from exhaustion. After being taken out of harness [they] were left to die by the wayside. Pine torches were used by artillerymen, for it was very dark, and the horses could not see the road ahead. These threw a flickering light on the vast column in motion, while the loud thunder and vivid lightning gave a fine scenic effect to the whole.

Although the distance from Savage's to the White Oak Creek was but about six miles, it was gray dawn before we came to the crossings or 4 o'clock in the morning of June 30. I with others turned off the road to the right, dismounted, and laid down under the large trees to get some sleep. We put our rubber blankets under us, and, with saddles for pillows, slept soundly for two hours. A fire could not be made, as all the underbrush was dripping wet. Water fit to drink was very hard to get. I was glad to drink rain water which had settled in the wheel ruts made by the passing artillery of yesterday. Near where we bivouacked was a rifle pit, which had been constructed by us some time ago to oppose the enemy. Crossing the swamp, it was now "in reverse," and of no use to us.

To reach safety on the James River, McClellan now moved his weary troops through the desolate mire of White Oak Swamp. Still the Confederates came on, and the nervous Federal commander informed Washington that his army was threatened with annihilation. On June 30, Union forces, including Heintzelman's III Corps, fought a fierce rearguard battle at Glendale (Frazier's and Nelson's farms). Lack of Confederate coordination and a determined stand by the Federals prevented Lee from cutting McClellan's army in two. By night, the Union commander retreated again, drawing his lines in tightly on Malvern Hill. With sketchbook in hand, Sneden witnessed these events unfold.

June 30, 1862

Foggy until 9 a.m., when it cleared off and the rest of the day [was] terribly hot. . . . I was roused from sleep at 5 a.m. with the admonition "to hurry," as the rear guard was crossing the bridges. This I found to be so, and Rush's Lancers were driving in the stragglers, who now were making the only good time during the retreat. [These] hurried in confused masses down the steep banks which bordered the creek to the bridges. The stream itself ran through a morass . . . but the marsh on either side was treacherous, and would have been impassable were it not for the three corduroy bridges which crossed both marsh and stream, and which had been constructed on Sunday morning by the engineers. A few tree stumps were scattered through the marsh, and but few trees impeded the artillery range from our guns now "in battery" on the other side.

All the wagons and troops had crossed . . . when the engineers proceeded to prepare the bridges for blowing up. The sappers were felling trees across the roads on both sides of the swamp to delay the enemy's advance. There was a wood road which ran from Savage's which we had not used, and knew nothing about until now. The enemy could have followed us on this road and cut off half our trains and rear guard, but now we all had crossed and were getting ready to dispute the crossings, while all the wagons were kept moving on to Malvern Hill, where Generals Porter and Keyes had already arrived and taken position. . . . General Heintzelman with the III Corps had crossed the creek at Braskett's Ford, a little above where the main line of retreat was made.

I therefore made my way there, and found our headquarters team in the woods in charge of Captain Weeks. The general and staff [were] just mounting their horses to place the command in a defensive position to repel the enemy. Two fly tents had been pitched, but the wagons were still loaded with mules hitched ready to move at a moment's warning. I found that we had no cooked rations left in the wagons. And Goldsby, the cook, had not been seen since Saturday morning. I had therefore to make my breakfast on two crackers and rain water taken from wheel ruts by means of a rubber drinking tube which I used as a syphon. I then went off to see how the troops would be posted, meeting General McClellan and staff reconnoitering our position from left to right. The fog now lifted, and the sun came out hot, which soon dried up the sandy soil. . . .

I saw the troops which had been recalled from the Chickahominy on our right, and learned that the bridges at Bottom's Bridge had been destroyed by them before retiring, and that Jackson's Rebel corps was now coming in on our right from White House on the Pamunkey [River]. It was thought the enemy would be delayed in this quarter some hours before he could reconstruct the broken bridges. Cavalry scouts . . . were thrown forward a mile in our front on the Charles City road, and the one by which we had retreated. The third or middle road was then discovered. This road was marked on my map, and partly shown on the photographic map issued to corp commanders a long time ago. But it had not been reconnoitered, and General McClellan did not know of its existence until this morning.

From our forces who had fallen back from Bottom's Bridge, I heard of the final destruction of the train which we fired and sent off from Savage's yesterday. They saw the train coming at terrific speed, a mass of flame and bursting shells. And such was the momentum, that when it reached the chasm on the Chickahominy River it sprang out full forty feet. And the engine and first car leaped over the first pier in the stream, and hung there suspended a perfect wreck, while the flames destroyed the remainder which stood on the track.

By 9:30 a.m., General McClellan had posted the troops to his satisfaction and about 10 o'clock he left with his staff and escort for Malvern Hill. Why he left was an enigma. He generally places the troops on the eve of a battle, then goes off to the rear some miles away, leaving his generals to fight it out as best they can without his further assistance. In the event of a victory he alone gets the credit. He would place the troops in position in the morning, then leave the field to seek a position for next day. . . .

At 10 o'clock our scouts and pickets came in [and] reported the enemy advancing in great numbers on all three roads in front of our position. Our immediate rear was secure, but we were liable to be flanked by Jackson coming in on our right, and by [General James] Longstreet who was following on the Charles City and New Market roads. The enemy could extend to the central road, still more to the left, and cut our trains now on the Quaker road in full retreat to Malvern Hill and Turkey Bend. All haste was now made to get the trains in motion. And many were going at full gallop.

Our headquarters wagons had not yet started, however, and by some stupidity or carelessness was the last to move off, and the last to reach Malvern. During the [ensuing] battle, Captain Weeks kept it running from one point to another all day. Being an artillery officer, [he] handled the train like so many artillery caissons, keeping it under fire most of the day, while the ammunition wagons crowding in, prevented its moving on. I was fortunate to espy

Rodger's red sutler wagon just moving off and succeeded in getting a bottle of brandy for $3, two pounds of cheese, some sardines and hard bread, buying all at war prices but glad enough to get them at any cost. I at once went in for a "good square meal," and while so engaged the enemy opened the battle from the other side of the swamp [with] thirty-one pieces of artillery. . . .

I took cover in some scrub oak brush for some time, but was compelled to leave for safer quarters in a deep gully. The enemy's shell burst in the tree tops, and ricocheted at all angles among the foliage, killing and wounding those who were not in a direct line of fire, and cutting the branches in every direction which fell on all sides. Now and then a 32 pounder shot would come in with a "swish," crashing into a tree trunk, [and] would split it for twenty feet upward, while the grape would hiss and crash through the undergrowth, compelling the sharpshooters to get back for shelter in the gullies. . . .

As our headquarters train was now about moving off to the Quaker road, I retired from the immediate front, being ordered to keep with the train, as maps might be called for. . . . The sun shone with great heat. There was no wind, and the woods were filled with sulphurous battle smoke, which greatly incites thirst. Water was very scarce, however, and cavalrymen with dozens of canteens slung on their horses, were exploring all the woods and gullies for it. A small stream ran across the Quaker road, a branch of which ran through woods on our right, but the steady stream of men and wagons going through them had made the water so muddy as not to be fit to drink. All the horses and mules had been watered there also. And to search in the woods farther to the right or left was dangerous, as the enemy were in occupation. All who could get water were making coffee, with arms stacked near them. . . .

Our train took the Long Bridge road, and arrived at the juncture of the Quaker road, and the first named road. A two story frame house was near here, with an old fashioned pole well in the yard. General Heintzelman made his headquarters here soon after. . . . The verandah was crowded with officers belonging to staffs. Four or five rather good looking young women were here too. They were refugees from some of the farm houses in the vicinity. They were all in mortal fear and trembling, and did not know where to go farther. The woman of the house was more in a defiant humor and complained that the soldiers had burnt her fences, stolen her poultry, and had ruined her cherry trees. [She] was very anxious to know if there was any probability of "a fight with wagon guns" near the house. (She meant artillery!) Maps were now called for, and I had to almost entirely unload one of the wagons before the map box was got at. The wagon had been repacked since leaving Savage's, and the wagon master had stowed it underneath everything else. I replaced it handy to get at in future.

Dozens of soldiers were getting water from the well, who soon had the water so muddy that they were driven off by Lieutenant Gray. A guard [was] placed on it to ensure more careful handling of the well pole. Soldiers were lying on the ground by the wayside all sound asleep, despite the roar of artillery. Others were cooking and eating a hurried meal. Long lines of stacked muskets shone in the hot sun, while hundreds of little fires were to be seen everywhere on [the] road, and in the large open fields across the Long Bridge road. There was not an inhabitant of the vicinity to be seen, excepting the women in the house. . . . Not a solitary Negro could be found to show us the roads. Our maps showed most of the main roads, yet there were many more unknown to us. And what we most feared was that Jackson could cross the Chickahominy on our right rear, and take our position at White Oak Creek in reverse.

No map could be found showing the roads in this direction, [so] scouts were sent to reconnoiter. At 2:30 p.m. a long and continuous crash of musketry was heard on the Charles City road not a mile away. [This] was soon accompanied by the rapid and spiteful firing of artillery [which] lasted until 3:30 when it suddenly ceased. The artillery firing at the crossings of the swamp had been unceasingly heard all the while. . . . The fighting was desperate, but the reserves now coming up poured in a terrible enfilading fire, which drove back the enemy in disorder with great loss. . . .

The enemy, finding the task impossible to cross the swamp, now had moved off to his right, and was approaching by the Charles City and New Market roads full on our position in front of the Quaker road. All our artillery at the swamp crossings were now withdrawn, and were galloping down the road furiously to take position in the road and fields in front of Heintzelman's headquarters. Soon [three of our] brigades came pouring out of the woods and down the Long Bridge road. Fences were torn down, artillery unlimbered, and all were awaiting the results in front. From over the tree tops could be seen the shells flying, which now covered the enemy's advance. General Heintzelman and staff mounted, and with the escort, went off into the woods.

Our headquarters train was hastily hitched up and went down the Quaker road towards Willis's Church at a smart trot. I mounted [but] stayed behind until the shells from the enemy ploughed the road and crashed through the house . . . which had been our headquarters. The women shrieked and ran from it as fast as they could go to the barn and woods some hundreds of yards southward. They were in mortal terror, but the soldiers yelled, and laughed at such an unexpected sight. The "wagon guns" had come after all. . . . [I] then followed the train, which I found halted near Willis's Church in an open field which adjoined the Quaker road.*

The battle now was raging on Nelson's Farm or Glendale, and the fighting was desperate and deadly in the extreme. The Rebel yells could be heard above the crashing musketry and the sharp reports of the rifle cannon. A line of battle smoke a mile long showed over the tree tops, with the puffs of bursting shells still higher in the air. The intervening strips of woods hid the fierce battle from view, until later in the day, when it came in full force on the Quaker road and around Willis's Church extending over Frazier's farm, and the hills and fields towards Malvern. All the wagon trains were now well on their way to Turkey Bridge on the James River. Our solitary headquarters train of five wagons [was] the only one left behind. Captain Weeks had ridden off to find General Heintzelman, leaving the wagons standing under fire!

The advance of the enemy was clearly marked by the battle smoke. And soon round shot

*The order of sentences in this paragraph has been altered slightly for clarity.

Nelson's house
Headquarters train in field below

Quaker Road
looking toward Malvern Hill

Willis's Methodist Church
Union hospital

Hooker's troops in battle
Enemy on hill

HEADQUARTERS OF MAJOR GENERAL SAMUEL P. HEINTZELMAN'S COMMAND, III ARMY CORPS
At Nelson's house, Quaker Road, during battle of Glendale, Va., Monday, June 30, 1862.

and shell flew over our heads in the open ground. The teamsters and wagon guard laid flat on the ground, while the iron storm went past. The enemy were outflanking us on the New Market road, and our position was hazardous. Our wagon train was cut off, and the teamsters were nervous. Under directions of Lieutenant Gray, the officer of the train guard, it was moved more to the rear and in line with Willis's Church which in some manner sheltered it from the shot and shell. This church was a plain frame building with a pediment in front overhanging the entrance, which was supported by columns. It stood twenty feet or more from the road, with a fine grove of trees in the rear. It had no spire or belfry, but looked quite pretty and neat. It had been used by us for a hospital since yesterday and several tents were pitched near, which were occupied by surgeons. I made a sketch of it.

There were about sixty wounded in the church who lay on the pew cushions on the floor. Many of the pews had been torn down and all the books carried off. . . . I left the train and rode up to the Quaker road to the former headquarters. I met numbers of ambulances filled with wounded, and stretcher bearers with their bleeding loads toiling slowly rearward. Most of our wounded had been brought from the battleground at the swamp crossings, but the dead were all left behind, as there was no time to bury them. . . . No one knew how many. Trees had been felled across the road leading back to the [White Oak] Swamp Creek. All the troops were filing down the Quaker road and taking positions along it, and in the large open space which bordered it. Long trains of ammunition wagons were moving to the rear, many having been emptied, were now full of wounded unable to walk.

WILLIS'S CHURCH ON THE QUAKER ROAD, VA.
Used as Union hospital during battle of Glendale, June 30, 1862.

The white wagon tops could be seen on the Charles City road away up in front, while the battle smoke hung over the woods along this and the New Market road. After [this] my attention was called to a large number of lame and wounded horses and mules who were being driven by a dozen or so of Rush's Lancers into the swampy woods off the Long Bridge road. These unfortunates were to be killed to prevent them falling into the enemy's hands. I followed and soon saw the poor animals slaughtered by lance and pistol. There were about 230 horses and mules. At the same time, about thirty empty wagons and several pontoons, still lashed to their carriages were set on fire and burnt entirely up. The smoke from these burning wagons rose high in the still air. The battle increased in intensity, and soon the shells and solid shot of the enemy crashed through the trees in the immediate vicinity, compelling all to get out as soon as possible. As I passed our late headquarters, the clapboard and shingles were flying in all directions. The few wounded who were in the house were running out in great haste, while a battery of artillery came along at full gallop to reply to the enemy, who now were reported as driving our troops before them down the Charles City road in front. I did not wait here much longer, but regained our headquarters train at Willis's Church. Here I found the teamsters laying flat on the ground in much alarm, while the round shot from a Rebel battery masked in the woods behind the church were flying over their heads. Captain

Weeks now rode up, and ordered the train to move down the Quaker road. Teamsters now lashed the mules into a sharp gallop, and away the train went up a hill amid clouds of dust.

The saddle had galled the back of my horse badly during the forenoon. And when the wagons moved off I had loosened the girths to apply a salve. [Then] a shell burst quite near me at the foot of a tree, which it lifted in the air, and a shower of mud and stones fell all around. My horse jerked himself away, and followed the train at full speed with the saddle under his belly, as I had not time to adjust the band. I was half blinded with sand, and fell into a ploughed field, as the horse jerked me over in his effort to get away. I scrambled up and ran for the train, just in time to catch the irons on the tail board of the last wagon, and was fairly dragged up the hill by it. The train went at full gallop all the way, and the exertion used me up completely. The wagon guard, having thrown their muskets into the wagons were running along side them, while the bullets hummed across the road lively, hitting the wagons and spluttering under our feet. If one of the mules had been hit, or had fallen, the train would have been wrecked as we were going full gallop, but we ran the gauntlet without any mishap. [We] kept right up the hill and turned into a ploughed field on high ground and which gave a view of all the battlefield along the Quaker road below us. Here we waited an hour or more. One of the wagon guard during the stampede had shot himself through the hand, losing his thumb and one finger, while carelessly putting his musket into the wagon with the barrel towards him.

Three or four started for water in a hollow nearby, while I climbed a large pine tree to get a better view of the battleground near Willis's Church below us. The enemy were still outflanking our left on the Central and New Market road. I could see their gun barrels shining through the woods for half a mile to our left and rear, and between us and Malvern Hill. . . . The roar of artillery and crash of musketry was terrific and continuous, while the Rebel yells could be heard above the din. Shells were bursting in the woods on both sides of the road, while high above the smoke of battle shells by dozens were bursting in the air. The immense shells from our gunboats, which had moved up the James River, came hurtling through the lines of both friend and foe, knocking down trees like tenpins and bursting with deafening concussions.

From the elevated position [I] occupied a fine view of our line on the Quaker road. The battle smoke hid the Rebel lines along the edge of the woods, while the flash of the artillery, and long lines of white smoke showed the positions of our infantry. . . . Behind us was a house, sunk in the bottom of a ravine, and a sergeant with two men loaded with canteens started to get water, leaving their arms in the wagons. In a short time they returned bringing full canteens and two Rebel prisoners. The sergeant had found a fine spring and while engaged in filling canteens they were joined by these thirsty Rebels looking for water also. Having left their muskets with the train, [our men] felt anxious enough, but kept at work filling. The Rebels were fully armed, and did not suspect but that they all were of the Rebel army. They had no cups to drink out of, however, which our men supplied, and while in the act of drinking, with their guns on the ground, they were pounced upon and made prisoners at the muzzles of their own rifles. They were dirty and savage looking in appearance, and showed resistance when searched, howling with rage and cursing vehemently at their easy capture. A blow on the head with a gun barrel quieted them. [Then] they were tied to the tailboard of wagons, with one arm lashed behind them by a small rope tied to the wrist and passed round the body. A large Bowie knife was taken from one and an old fashioned dirk knife from the other. [These] were concealed in their boots, which they were very loath to give up. They belonged to A. P. Hill's division, and said that "Longstreet and Hill had 70,000 men in the woods, that General Lee commanded in person, and that Jeff Davis was with him to see the Yanks licked." This accounted for the desperate fighting of the enemy. I rode back to the church to communicate this intelligence to Captain McKeever of our staff.

As the regiments to which the prisoners belonged were going down the New Market road, and might come in on our rear and capture the wagons, it was decided that [the wagons] must be removed at once. So they were moved out of the field, and down the hill to Willis's Church again. Here the two prisoners were turned over to the provost marshal, who had a hundred or more other prisoners in charge. The battle still continued all along the Quaker road and in the fields on either side. The heaviest firing being that of artillery. Shells from the enemy's batteries were bursting in the strip of wood back of the church and in the road. Our batteries were replying in the open space, while ammunition wagons were all along the road, the mules belonging to them dropping dead or wounded every minute. A squadron of Rush's Lancers were in and across the road to stop all straggling below the church. As there was nothing to do but wait the course of events the train was halted at the old spot close to Willis's Church.

I had to shift my position many times to avoid the enemy's shells, which came from behind the woods back of the church, and killed several mules attached to ammunition wagons to the left of the road. Their ranges were too high to sweep the road, and their fuses were cut too short to hurt many of us, for which we were thankful. Soon Captain McKeever rode up, and expressed much surprise and indignation as well he might, at the wagon train standing under fire when all others had gone on to Malvern. [He] ordered it to proceed there immediately. We soon moved off up the hill again, on the full gallop for the New Market road which led there. After my horse ran away from me as described previously, he came quietly back to the wagon train when we had halted on the hill and was soon caught. I decided to let the saddle gall him as much as it would sooner than loose the girths again. I had broken my single spur short off when I was thrown down in the ploughed field. . . . I soon had another, by going down the road to where our batteries were in action and finding a dead artilleryman on the road whose spurs I took without compunction, as he never would use them again.

I soon overtook our wagon train now en route for Turkey Creek Bridge and Malvern Hill. I noticed that [our] troops were falling back for new positions on the Quaker road. The surgeons were getting the wounded out of Willis's Church in a great hurry, while the few tents were being struck and put into two wagons, and the wounded into ambulances. Long rows of empty ammunition wagons were being filled with wounded likewise, and all haste was made to start them on the road to Malvern, which was soon accomplished. . . .

After we had gone a mile from Willis's Church we got out of the enemy's fire, but we knew that the Rebels were making for the point where the Quaker road ran into the New Market road, and would not show themselves from out of the woods until they had secured a position to head us off. So all the teams were kept on a full gallop until this point was passed. Captain McKeever and [Captain Samuel] McKelvey, chief of commissary, accompanied the train, and gave directions as to where we would make headquarters on our arrival at Turkey Creek.

Other officers rode constantly back and forth to hurry up all the wagons behind us. The sun was just setting when we came in view of the blue waters of the James River on our right, and the long spur of hills on our left, with a large plain or plateau fringed with heavy dark woods on two sides, and open undulating ground towards the river. The hill rose abrupt from the plateau, tall grass and corn covered its sides. A clump of woods was at the base of the salient point to our left, while a grove of trees and orchards were on its summit. A solitary house on top could only be seen from the plain below. The left wing of the army, now here at Malvern Hill under Generals Fitz-John Porter and Keyes, [was] lying in the path of the enemy. A dozen or so guns could be seen in battery half way up, and on the summit of the hill, but the infantry force was hardly visible. Not a musket showed itself and it was only by seeing the regimental colors here and there that a force would be guessed at on this slumbering volcano. Even the colors were wrapped tight to the staffs. Our train turned toward the James and we soon came to ground intersected by ravines and low marsh, through which ran Turkey Creek, an insignificant stream, which wound around the base of Malvern, and ran into the James through the marsh.

The stream was crossed by a good wooden bridge, and once over, the train was halted to select a position for headquarters. Two hundred or more wagons of the train passed [around] us, and down into the ravine and woods to the river. So our wagon train was the very last to come into our lines after all, excepting the ambulances and wagons still at the battleground on the Quaker road. We halted on the low ground about 300 yards from the river, and getting up two tent flies made headquarters under two or three solitary trees close beside a pile of old lumber and boards, formed [from] the debris of a shanty of some kind which had recently been torn down. Before reaching here, however we had passed through five or six lines of our infantry, most of whom were lying flat on the ground in the tall grass. [Their] presence could not be ascertained from the plain in front by an approaching enemy until close upon them so well were they concealed. Batteries of artillery stood up along the lines like war dogs. The artillerymen were all lying down beside their guns, watching the expected approach of the enemy, reported by signal flags as coming down the Kingsland and New Market roads near the James from direction of Fort Darling and Drury's Bluff. The U.S. gunboat *Mahaska* was at anchor a few hundred feet from shore, throwing the immense projectiles from 11 inch guns into the woods along the river road, and woods by which the Rebels were approaching. Another gunboat was farther up the river shelling the woods also. . . .

Along the river bank near our bivouac was a fringe of trees, and a long unpainted two story frame house, from the chimney top of which our signal men were vigorously waving their signal flags. But all eyes were turned on the placid blue river with pleasure, as it was the first river seen by any of us since leaving Yorktown. The Pamunkey was a narrow crooked affair compared with the James, here seen for miles north and south, winding among green fields and strips of forest. Our wagons were not unloaded, but everyone, including the clerks and guard, set about making shelter of the old boards fortunately found on the spot. Fires were made and all were making coffee while the provision boxes were overhauled only to find very little if anything in them. There was no meat of any kind to be had for love or money. Hard tack and coffee we were glad to get. . . .

I . . . constructed a shelter of broken boards and a rubber blanket, got supper, and around the camp fire revised my maps of the day's march, and overhauled others to define our present position. The night was fine and warm, bright starlight, while troops were on the move, shifting positions and bivouacking all around our quarters. Mules were braying, artillery moving, and the frogs croaking in the marsh along the river. The gunboats yet kept up a slow and steady fire two miles or more up river, shelling the woods, and driving the enemy back on New Market. They did not cease firing until 10 p.m. Camp fires twinkled in the woods all along the river and away up over Malvern Hill, looking like a park in the city after dark. Artillery and wagons were rumbling all night. And the troops having withdrawn from Glendale and White Oak Swamp, were marching in all night until daylight, but the noise thus made did not disturb our heavy slumber caused by the night marches and great fatigues of the past forty-eight hours. After dark, the old deserted house by the river was occupied by us for an hospital and ambulances were crossing Turkey Bridge with our wounded nearly all night.

The great Seven Days battles reached their climax at Malvern Hill north of the James River on July 1. Here McClellan's army took its stand at a strong defensive position formed by tightly massed Union artillery and determined riflemen. Lee, once again hoping to destroy the Federals, decided to attack. After numerous delays, the Confederates launched several disjointed assaults in the afternoon. Wave after wave of gray infantry were turned back with terrible carnage. By nightfall the Confederates were badly spent, but the battered Union army continued its withdrawal down the James to Harrison's Landing.

Sneden saw the battle firsthand. Despite witnessing a Union victory, however, he again vented his anger at the Union army commander. Little Mac had promised more than once that he would take the Confederate capital. Sneden and his comrades instead found themselves conducting a humiliating retreat. His account opens the morning of Malvern Hill.

July 1, 1862

. . . The sun rose in haze this morning and we had a very hot and sultry day. All were up at daylight cooking breakfast. . . . [We] awaited the enemy's movements all the forenoon. Berdan's sharpshooters, all along our immediate front . . . could only be heard firing slowly at the opposing line of skirmishers . . . while artillery shots were now and then exchanged. I made a sketch of the Haxall house by the river from our headquarters. I then went over the ground near the river, and crossing Turkey Bridge went some way along the base of Malvern Hill, and thence by the road which runs over its crest to the extreme point where it juts out into the plateau in front. . . . I busied myself in making several sketches until the enemy attacked [at 4 p.m.]. . . . The whole side of Malvern Hill seemed a vast sheet of fire. The smoke obscured everything from view. . . . The bursting shells could be seen dealing destruction on all sides to the yelling assailants.*

I went back to General [Porter's] headquarters at the Malvern house and made a sketch from the stone wall opposite. The staff tents were pitched in the front yard while the signal men were frantically waving their signal flags from the roof near the chimneys. When our forces first came here Sunday last the house was occupied by a Mr. Due. He had decamped with all the stock and slaves before we reached here. The house was now being filled with our wounded, while our surgeons were hard at work amputating limbs, which were in a ghastly heap near the house, [having been] thrown out of the windows by the assistants. Groans and piercing cries from those undergoing the surgeon's knife were heard on all sides, while the air was sultry and hot as an oven. Battle smoke in huge drifts was in the meadow below, and settled along the tree tops of the pine forest beyond. There was a lull in the firing for half an hour, broken by a gun now and then from the gunboats in the river which were moored close in shore. The artillerymen nearby were all stripped to the waist, while fresh ammunition wagons with six mules each were struggling up the incline road from the meadow below. Theodore Moreland, our telegraph operator, and myself sat on a rail fence which was built along the top of the stone wall . . . when a solid shot from the enemy's artillery struck the fence, throwing us over backward into the field below. We were not much hurt. But on the next section of rails several soldiers [who] had been likewise sitting a moment before were tumbled off also as another shot struck the wall and fence twenty feet away, killing two instantly. Another had his leg broken by a piece of the rail. Moreland and I got out of this as soon as possible, and went to near the crest of the cliff where our batteries could be seen resting in a long line. . . .

The enemy kept up a desultory artillery fire all along the edge of the woods in our front, while our guns . . . were slowly replying. To the right of where we stood I noticed quite a

*Several lines in this and the next few pages appear earlier in Sneden's original manuscript, but have been moved for clarity.

THE REBEL ATTACK ON WEEDEN'S BATTERY AND 14TH BROOKLYN REGIMENT
On west side of Crew's Hill. Battle of Malvern Hill, Va., July 1, 1862.

large depression in the corn field. . . . The spent shot or shell rolled into it, which would now and then explode. A large white dog of mongrel breed was amusing himself by chasing these shot . . . into the hollow, when a shell there burst and he was blown skyward in shreds. I heard afterwards that the dog was owned by one of our soldiers and had been in every battle including Fair Oaks, while his owner fought in the ranks.

We went down the hill to our temporary headquarters at its foot and got something to eat, but very little but hard tack, raw pork and weak coffee. Only one fly tent had been put up, and headquarters wagons were not unloaded as we did not know when or where we should be ordered to move any minute. . . .

Another lull in artillery firing on both sides lasted until 5:45 p.m., when terrific yells of the enemy and continuous roar of artillery showed that the Rebels were ready, and were now making their last charge on our lines. I scrambled and ran up the steep hill and got a partial view of the oncoming desperate assault from near the top of the cliff, the last desperate charge of the enemy.

About 6 p.m. by pushing out about twenty pieces of artillery from their front, followed by four lines of solid infantry colors flying, as if on parade, [they] advanced at a run with ter-

VIEW OF THE MALVERN HOUSE OR "WYATT HOUSE" ON MALVERN HILL, VA.
Headquarters of General Fitz-John Porter.

rifying yells, heard all above the crash of musketry and roar of artillery. We now opened on them with terrible effects. . . . Several times our infantry withheld their fire until the Rebel column, which rushed through the storm of canister and grape, [came] close up to the artillery. Our men then poured a single crashing volley of musketry and charged the enemy with the bayonet with cheers. [We] thus captured many prisoners and colors and drove the remainder in confusion from the field. These would rally under cover of the woods and charge again, but only to be met with the same murderous volleys of shot, shell, and bullets, leaving piles of dead and dying on the plateau along our front. Hundreds of poor maimed wretches were continually crawling on hands and knees across the open, many of whom were killed before they regained shelter in the woods. The Rebel cavalry were seen driving the remnants of regiments out of the woods into the open ground, and were shooting all those who did not keep in line and "face the music." As the charging columns came up to within 150 yards of our artillery, whole ranks went down at once, battle flags rose and disappeared. Officers on horseback threw their sword arm in the air and [tumbled] to the ground. Riderless horses were running in every direction, while officers on foot were far in advance of their commands, shouting and yelling like madmen.

The battle was at its height at 7:30 p.m. At this time the artillery ammunition began to run short. All the spare shot and shell brought from Savage's had been expended, and now the roads on the summit of Malvern were filled with fresh caissons of the reserve artillery going forward at a full gallop to replenish the guns in battery. Ambulances were upset, men and dead horses and mules were run over in the rush, while clouds of red dust and smoke prevented

U.S. gunboat *Galena* shelling the Rebels in the woods

Haxall's house
U.S. hospital and Signal Corps

U.S. gunboat *Mahaska* shelling the woods

HEADQUARTERS OF MAJOR GENERAL SAMUEL P. HEINTZELMAN
During the battle of Malvern Hill, Va., July 1, 1862, near Turkey Bridge.

wagon drivers from getting out of the way. The heat had been intense all day. Knapsacks were piled in large heaps. And the men fought with the least quantity of clothes possible. The enemy charged without knapsacks, and being thus not encumbered fought like fiends, and got into our lines twice in spite of all resistance but the steady roll of musketry, and grape and canister at close range made it impossible for any troops to hold the line and live. . . .

The battlefield at the foot of the slopes presented a shocking sight of dead, dying, and mangled corpses, while the numerous dead and wounded horses were crawling and kicking in death agony among them. They were generally shot to put them out of misery as soon as possible [while] fresh horses are brought up from the rear. When no spare horses are to be had, the guns have to be drawn out by hand. And if the enemy charges and surround the guns, they are spiked. The wheel spokes [are] cut with axes, or the gun is upset to prevent the enemy [from] using them on us. . . . As darkness set in the Rebels withdrew into the woods for shelter. The siege guns on the crest of Malvern and the gunboats continued to ply the enemy with shot and shell until 9:30 p.m., when all was quiet for the rest of the night, save the groans of the wounded and the rumbling of wagons and artillery.

General McClellan was not on the ground (as usual) until the battle was over. He was off with Commodore [John] Rodgers, who commanded the gunboats ten miles down [the] James River, selecting a *new* and safer position for the army for the morrow! When the enemy attacked us yesterday he was safe on board the *Galena*! Today he is safe enough where there is no enemy, thus depriving all his corps and division commanders of his abilities and counsel. . . . McClellan had first placed the troops in position this morning before leaving. . . . And as there was no headquarters staff, every general did as he pleased in changing battle lines during the day. But the Army of the Potomac has fought so many battles without General McClellan's supervision or assistance, that he is not missed when the fighting commences! His cautionary measures are so well known that the corps commanders win battles, and move troops to ensure the enemy's defeat, and are not hampered with McClellan's orders or presence, though McClellan gets all the credit. The fighting generals, such as Heintzelman, Sumner, Kearny, Hooker, Sedgwick, Richardson, and others, have a profound contempt for General McClellan's fighting qualities, and several officers high in command denounce him without stint. . . . The army was saved in spite of General McClellan's ignorance of the situation in the front of battle.

All the army wagons were moving both yesterday and today on the roads leading to Westover and Harrison's Bar or Landing some eight or ten miles down the James River. . . . I regained our headquarters camp about dark, first going over some of the ground where the hardest fighting had occurred which seemed to be where the Rebels had charged our massed guns. The ground was covered with dead and wounded men and horses. Many of the latter had been disemboweled completely by shell exploding under them. Soldiers of both sides lay in all the orchards, sheds and barns, torn and mangled, dead and dying. They made but little complaint, and suppressed their groans of pain for we had beaten the enemy at all points, and were victorious, as ever on open ground. Surgeons were very busy at work under trees, in barns, and in sheltered ravines. The flashes from the gunboat's ports lighted up the dark hollows, and the black woods across the plateau, while the shell screamed overhead, and crashed in the tree tops, making it a very "unhealthy place" for Rebels.

I met one of Berdan's sharpshooters, desperately wounded in the groin, and having yet another bullet in his leg. I could not persuade him to go to the hospital for treatment. He had made many a Rebel bite the dust during the day, and only was anxious to kill one more before he died. His rifle was loaded, and I helped him to a position at an old stone wall, where he said he would be ready for the enemy in the morning. He probably died before then.

Long lines of ambulances were passing our headquarters carrying ghastly wounded soldiers to the deserted house at Haxall's. . . . The sky drew dark and cloudy with appearance of rain, while the stunning reports of the heavy guns on the *Galena* and *Mahaska* reverberated for miles up and down the shores of the river. The red flashes and the shrieking shell lit up the woods and marsh, and the frogs croaked loud and hoarsely along the river bank. Signal lanterns were vigorously waving from the roof of "Crew's House," away up on the crest of Malvern, which were answered by others at the mastheads of the gunboats and from the roof of the old house on the bank of the river. Numerous lanterns and torches were sparkling and moving along the slopes of the hill, and into the plateau beyond, showing that the wounded were being cared for and removed. The glare of the enemy's camp fires reflected on the black clouds over the dark woods all along our front, and away to the right, which showed them to be in great force. The shells from the gunboats crashed through the trees at the rate of two per minute, while the ambulances, with their blood dripping burdens, wound down the center roads and across the marshy ground to the hospital at the old house by the river. . . .

All the paymasters, with their funds, had embarked on the gunboats during the forenoon. And the immense wagon trains had been moving down towards Harrison's Landing and Westover all day to the new position selected by McClellan and Captain Rodgers U.S.N. In consequence of the moving of these trains, provisions and forage were very scarce. Most of the haversacks of the men had been empty since last night and a limited supply of hard bread was all that could be had. Officers and men fared alike. And generals were glad to get hard tack and raw pork. Hard tack sold readily for 25¢ and 50¢ each.

All the sutlers had started early this morning, so we had to go hungry all day and night in hope of a better time on the morrow. The wounded fared badly, as there [were] no hospital supplies after noon today, and the large number of wounded used up all that had not gone forward in the wagons. There were over 2,000 wounded in the battles . . . at Malvern Hill. A great proportion, however, were not badly wounded, and could travel. The artillerymen suffered the most. As the enemy charged the guns, they had to fight with rammers and hand spikes, cold shot, or anything that came to hand. Many crawled under their guns and were bayoneted there by the Rebels. Some died while grasping the lanyards of the guns, others while biting cartridges, while others were disfigured beyond recognition and were bundles of bloody clothing.

About 9:30 p.m., an orderly came from General Heintzelman for maps of the country below Malvern Hill, which I sent. [I] learned that the general had been wounded by a spent bullet in the wrist yesterday at Glendale. All the general officers had headquarters at Wyatt's house in fly tents, pitched on the lawn among the trees. All the maps of General McClellan had been captured by the enemy during the retreat. And all we had to depend on were the coast survey maps, which only showed roads a mile or so back from the banks of the James River. I had projected roads from other maps on the copy I sent to the general, and was gratified to know that the night march was conducted by it afterwards. Orders came . . . to pack up and be ready to move at a moment's warning. Headquarters trains got the order first, and the troops an hour later. This order produced great dissatisfaction and excitement in the ranks . . . but more so from the general officers, who now knowing the real cause for the movement, were loud in their protestations against the order. [They] denounced McClellan for a coward or traitor! General Kearny protested against the movement vehemently. . . . Of course, but few knew of this feeling among officers.

And although every soldier was aware that the enemy had been bloodily repulsed, they cooked what they had to eat and fell in line without a murmur. The cries of the wounded were loud in despair, for not one quarter of them could be carried off, and they must fall into the enemy's hands. All who could walk now poured out of the hospitals with wounds yet uncared for, and the same scenes were enacted as at Savage's Station on Sunday last. Details of engineers were felling trees across the road to retard the enemy in pursuit, while Turkey

Creek Bridge was completely destroyed. Camp fires [were] built all along the crest and slopes of Malvern to deceive the enemy during the night. . . .

Sneden then saw a large group of Confederate prisoners of war from Magruder's division. He ambled over to them and struck up a conversation with some officers. He recorded his observations.

[The Rebel prisoners said that] their generals were completely at fault as to our movements from White Oak Bridge to . . . Malvern Hill. [They said that] "Magruder was crazy drunk and charged us repeatedly without orders," thus sacrificing them to no purpose. Half of Magruder's men were in the same condition, and nearly all the captured prisoners carried one canteen of whiskey and another of gunpowder. Their fixed ammunition had given out, and the rank and file had to make their own cartridges at night and during the lulls in the fighting. The prisoners were all hungry, but we had nothing much to eat ourselves, and they got nothing from us. They had plenty of Confederate money, however, and gave $20 of this stuff for a single cracker. I got the first $5 bill of the kind for a plug of tobacco. The prisoners were dressed in homespun clothes, some with jackets, others in long coats, like farmers. Their trousers were of dark jean, and were stuffed into heavy boots, much worn, and very muddy. The boots never were cleaned, and the leather could not be determined for the coatings of red mud.

Some had brass or white metal buttons, others were of stamped leather. A strip of blue braid on cuff and collar denoted infantry, while red braid was for artillerymen. A dirty slouch hat, and yet dirtier blanket of a mud color, and coarse texture made the dress of the Rebel soldier. All their knapsacks had been thrown down before they charged our lines, and the prisoners were now deploring their loss. Others had knapsacks and pouches made of ox hide, with the hair outside. Officers were dressed nearly the same as the men, with the exception of a sword belt and feather in hat.

At midnight, orders came for the troops to move, and soon regiments, brigades, and divisions filed down Malvern Hill in silence. Through the woods and low grounds the tramp of marching columns, rumbling of the artillery ammunition wagons, and ambulances were heard, all going nobody knew whither. Rain had now begun to fall, and the darkness was so intense that objects twenty feet distant could not be seen. This caused much confusion, and in half an hour the roads were crammed with moving wagons, artillery, infantry, and cavalry. Old scenes were renewed, and wheels locked, mules brayed, teamsters cracked their whips, and swore, while stragglers, and wounded men thronged in between wagons, on the road side, in fields and woods on both sides of the road, now slippery as glass from the peculiar consistency of Virginia mud. Mules went down, artillery stuck, teams had to be doubled and trebled, yet we moved on somewhat, but very slowly. Heads of columns got mixed with other brigades or divisions in the darkness, and men and officers lost their commands from the same cause, and thus swelled the number of stragglers every minute.

Most of our wounded were left in the enemy's hands! Very few of our dead were buried on the field. Several wagons were hacked to pieces and left behind. The horses had been all killed during the day. Large quantities of shot and shell and fixed ammunition had to be abandoned, but the siege guns were brought off, as well as all of our other artillery. I rode in company with Major Joe Dickinson of General Hooker's staff. Our headquarters train was 100 feet ahead, but the darkness was so intense that I could not see ten feet ahead of my horse's head. At 1:30 a.m. the rain came down heavily, the thunder roared and the lightning vividly flashed scaring the mules and horses, and wetting us through.

It was White Oak Swamp over again. We had but one road to retreat by, and the artillery and wagons moved on the road, while the infantry marched in the open ground both sides of them. Negro guides led the way. The 3rd Pennsylvania Cavalry . . . were left behind as rear guard to keep the camp fires burning all night and deceive the enemy. . . . The wagons and artillery, if stretched out, would cover forty miles of road. So they were kept closed up as much as possible, and a breakdown stopped the whole train. But as the troops moved over ground parallel with the road, and not on it, they experienced no impediment except from the thunderstorm and intense darkness. . . .

Our headquarters train had not gone over the first mile of road when the general's wagon at the head of the column was hopelessly wrecked by being run into by an artillery train. We met going down a steep grade, with a turn in the road. Here a battery was on one side of the turn waiting to fall in the line of wagons ahead. Our quartermaster (Captain Weeks) in his usual hurry, ordered our train to advance to close the gap, when the artillery train came down the bank suddenly into its position in line. The wheels of a brass gun struck the general's wagon, breaking both axles and knocking down the horses. I was just in time to save my box of instruments and double barreled gun, which were in the wagon. The general's clothing, demijohns, and sword were hastily distributed among our remaining train wagons, and amid terrific swearing of drivers and teamsters we resumed our march. All the whiskey in the demijohn was drunk by the drivers of the train before we reached Harrison's Landing, where there was more swearing by the staff officers to whom it belonged. The fine covered wagon was left a wreck on the roadside, while the driver mounted the horses and resumed the route. We plunged on in mud and darkness until at gray dawn, or 4 a.m. when the James River came in view.

Thus ended McClellan's grand campaign to take the capital of the Confederacy. With it went the hopes many people had for ending a war that had turned into something far more costly than anyone had imagined.

Chapter Four

Enough of Terrible Fighting

After its retreat to Harrison's Landing, the Army of the Potomac sat in wilting heat for the next six weeks licking its wounds and awaiting new orders. The army was safe enough. McClellan kept his men busy building fortifications, and Union gunboats in the James River discouraged major threats from the Confederates. He issued new uniforms and equipment to his battered troops. But despite the reprieve, the men in blue soon became an unhappy lot. Many still wondered why they had turned tail from Richmond after such a promising beginning to the campaign. The chief source of their discontent, however, was their environment on the river bottomland. Days and nights alike were steamy and endlessly hot. Shade provided little comfort. Men, horses, wagons, equipment, and arms were jammed together in the camps. Poor drinking water, imperfect sanitation, and swarms of insects only made the situation worse. As a result, disease and death spread quickly through the army. The monotony of life was interrupted by the infrequent visit of dignitaries, including President Lincoln, or by the Rebels, who occasionally lobbed artillery shells into camp. Many men, including Sneden, tried to cope with the miserable situation with whiskey.

Although the army was not actively campaigning, General Heintzelman kept his topographer busy surveying and mapping. Accordingly Sneden traveled freely throughout Harrison's Landing, and as always, he noted conditions in detail.

HARRISON'S LANDING: THE OLD HARRISON MANSION, BERKELEY LANDING, JAMES RIVER, VA.
Headquarters of General McClellan, July 1862.
Afterwards used for signal station and hospital, July 13, 1862.

July 4, 1862

Fine day and very hot 92 degrees in [the] shade. Our quartermaster, Captain Weeks, having obtained a new lot of tents from the supply vessels, had them on the ground by 9 a.m. today. Then our quarters were permanently pitched, and a detail of the wagon guard set about digging a well. Soon good water was struck. . . . This well was afterwards covered with an open bough shelter to keep off the rays of the hot sun. It was dug out in the plain a short ways from our line of tents, and the guard on post prevented stragglers from using it. General Kearny made his headquarters in the woods near us. And within a hundred feet, flag staffs were cut and the corps colors set at noon, at which time a national salute was fired by all the artillery in the army in honor of the day, and to let the enemy know that we had not been conquered quite yet.

A general inspection of troops and arms was had today at 10 a.m., which lasted until 4 p.m. Most of the stragglers had rejoined the regiments and the long lines of infantry with shining muskets and bayonets made a fine appearance. At 12 o'clock the artillery from left to right fired the salute. Those guns along our front line nearest the enemy were shotted and sent a storm of iron across the swamp and ravines into the woods. If any lurking Rebels were there, they must have been astonished. The regimental bands now played while General McClellan and dozens of other generals with their staff officers rode along the line. The men cheered and put their caps on the bayonet points, all was enthusiasm in the serried ranks, and the morale of the army was ascertained to be much better than supposed. The gunboats fired a salute at the same time, and the roar of 300 guns made the earth tremble, and echoed far up and down the James. After this, whiskey rations were issued to the whole army. . . .

During the evening the regimental bands played at all the headquarters of generals, lasting until midnight. This is the first music we have been treated to since leaving Williamsburg, and was fully appreciated by all. All the time we lay in front of Richmond, music by the bands was prohibited by General McClellan, so that the enemy would not know our position in the woods and swamps of the Chickahominy. There was no "reveille" or "tattoo" by the drum corps even. No bugles were heard, except during the hours of battle, which then transmitted orders. Consequently the army was continually in low spirits, and fought with less enthusiasm than if the music had been allowed. The only thing that held Hooker's decimated lines . . . at the battle of Williamsburg was the music from a band playing "the Flag of the Free," by General Heintzelman's personal orders. Hooker's men thought reinforcements were close at hand in the woods behind them, when in fact Kearny was struggling through muddy and overcrowded roads two miles in the rear to get to the front. Hooker held on though until Kearny did come up, and dashed at the enemy with victorious results. The regimental bands have suffered very much by swamp fevers, and casualties while under fire, and number not half of what a full band should. The drummers were also decimated, as many were mere boys, who cannot stand the exposure consequent on a campaign such as this has proved. . . .

Hospital tents were erected today in great numbers, which were soon filled with sick and wounded which count up [to] 12,000. Surgeons and their assistants are hard at work amputating and probing for bullets, many are dying hourly, and several steamers have arrived here expressly fitted up to carry the unfortunates home. Goldsby, our mess cook, had a good supper in consequence, and we did not feel very inquisitive as to where the chickens came from. The band played, whiskey punch was made and circulated freely until midnight, when all turned in, except the watchful sentinel. . . .

July 6, 1862

. . . I was ordered by General Heintzelman to ride over all the ground occupied by the III Corps, and locate the camps and commands on the map, which I am now making to a much larger scale than the one furnished by the topographical engineers at General McClellan's headquarters. Large details of men had been employed in constructing breastworks, felling trees, bridging, and repairing roads. And I found them all at work under engineer officers so doing, and as they got "the whiskey ration" for extra work all were happy and worked with a will. I got away from headquarters at 11 a.m., having a good map, field glass, and prismatic compass. As General Heintzelman wanted to know if General Hooker wanted more men to fell trees in his front, I went there first. I found the general in a worn out tent at the farthermost post on our left, and delivered the message. The general was in his shirt sleeves, for the sun was hot at this point, the forest prevented the cooling air from the river from reaching his quarters. A rough bed of boughs, and a table constructed of a barrel head nailed on three stakes, and a mess chest comprised the sole furniture of his tent. Two or three bottles of whiskey and a broken tumbler were on the table. And after trying the quality of the whiskey, I went over the log defenses and redoubt, which was being constructed quite near, with Captain Joseph Dickinson, assistant adjutant general to Hooker. . . .

July 8, 1862

. . . President Lincoln with several congressmen and military officers arrived here today. He and his suite landed at 4 p.m., and all the gunboats in the river fired salutes. The troops not on duty in the front were reviewed and the President, accompanied by General McClellan and staff rode along the lines amid salutes from several batteries and the music from the bands. The cheering by the troops was very weak however. The President looked ungainly on horseback. He wore a high silk hat and his black clothes were covered with dust. The brilliant staffs surrounding him made this all the more prominent. The troops were dismissed at sundown and returned to their several camps. We had a fine moonlight night, and the bands played at several headquarters of different generals, until 11 p.m. . . .

July 13, 1862

. . . At 2 p.m. I went over to the camps of [the] 3rd Maine and 40th New York regiments. The iron ovens were in full blast baking wheat bread for the division. We have good bread now, or "soft tack" (the army biscuit is called "hard tack" or "monitors"). . . . I [then] rode down to the landings, and visited General McClellan's headquarters at the old house at Westover. I made a sketch [of it]. . . and everything else of interest about the premises. . . . A signal station had been erected on the roof, and all the fences had been used for firewood. Trees had been cut down for bough houses along the river bank. Quartermaster's tents were pitched between the house and another house about 100 feet from it, which had been used for the former overseer of the plantation. The landing was crowded with wagons and teams, while sutlers were erecting shanties and tents along the river bank. Steamers and vessels were discharging stores, and dozens more laid at anchor in the placid James. I got some new maps from the topographical engineers attached to the headquarters, and found several draughtsmen (all soldiers detailed for this purpose) at work in one of the lower rooms. This gave me an opportunity to examine the interior, and from an old white headed slave I got much interesting history of the place.

The mansion was of brick, with white marble quoins and trimmings. Shutters were on the two stories, which wanted a coat of paint badly. Everything outside denoted neglect; and several old slaves yet occupied the quarters adjoining. The mansion has much interest as hav-

THE WESTOVER MANSION, HARRISON'S LANDING, JAMES RIVER, VA.
August 1862. Headquarters of General Fitz-John Porter. Former residence of Colonel Byrd.

ing been the residence of a family, who, for three generations were representatives of royalty in the colonial times. It still bears evidence of wealth and high standing of its former occupants. It stands about 300 feet back from the James River, and has old and antique gateways facing the road, and another more curious at the back. The house was built by Captain, afterwards Colonel [William] Byrd. The main hallway runs through the center, and is about ten feet wide, with a grand old staircase of mahogany having handsomely carved newels and rails. All the rooms on the first floor were twelve feet high. The rooms were all paneled and wainscoted throughout, with elaborately carved cornices. But a few articles of furniture remained, no carpets, or books in the library. The signal corps had quarters in the upper rooms. And rolls of blankets, numbers of signal flags, and lanterns and other traps littered the floor. There was a very handsome chimney piece in the parlor, the background of which was composed of rich black veined marble; while the border around the modern grate and the pediment above the mirror was of white marble. This was imported from Italy by Colonel Byrd. The mirror was smashed, and the pieces were being taken away by relic hunters piece by piece. Soon it will all be gone. At the back doors was a wide platform having marble steps, on the left of which stood the laundry and kitchen. On the right were other domestic wooden buildings, which a lot of cavalrymen were tearing down to make stables for their horses, which are kept ready saddled at headquarters at all times. Opposite the back door was a large gateway, with ornate wrought iron gates. The brick pillars were square, but most of the stucco on them had fallen off. They were about ten feet high, and were each surmounted by an eagle standing on a ball (the crest of the Byrd family). A cavalryman was trying to wrench one of these off, but I told the officer of the guard, and it was replaced with much unwillingness. After dark, probably this fellow would secure the relic unopposed.

. . . Beyond the gateway was a field, with stables on the right. All the fences had gone for firewood. The house had been occupied by a Mr. John Selden, who now was "non est." In the garden was the monument to Colonel Byrd. The family graveyard was some distance off, which I will visit at another time. The monument in the garden was much dilapidated, and some vandal had chipped off the escutcheon, which bore the arms of Colonel Byrd. The edges were also broken and carried off for relics! If the Selden family had remained at the mansion, this would not have occurred, as guards are always placed on occupied houses to prevent this very thing. During the Revolution, the Westover estate was visited by the English army, then under Cornwallis and Arnold, on January 8, 1781. . . .

July 20, 1862

Fine and hot, 90 degrees. A general review and inspection of the whole army here was had today. The different commands were all inspected on the ground which they occupied in the defenses. The III Corps were reviewed and inspected on the plain opposite these headquarters by Generals Heintzelman, Hooker, and Kearny. And the sight was very fine. The arms and accouterments glistened with the bayonets in the sun. Bands played, and the ragged battle flags flew to the winds. The brass Napoleon guns looked like burnished gold, while new uniforms and white leggings gave color to the display. Artillery salutes were fired as each army corps finished inspection. General McClellan, with a numerous and brilliant staff, personally inspected all the commands. . . . Regimental bands were serenading at each general's headquarters after dark. That which serenaded General Kearny must have been the worst one in the army. It was a regular "sheet iron band." I did not learn of which regiment. General Kearny gave this band a gallon of whiskey "to *go away*!" It was [a] "regular circus.". . .

July 23, 1862

. . . There is much discontent and grumbling among our general officers at our helpless position here. We can repulse an attack, but what is Lee doing in the meantime? Our newspapers and letters come regularly, but no one seems to know what the enemy is about. Our cavalry have made few reconnaissances and the balloon has left the landing. . . . General Hooker visited General Heintzelman this afternoon. The maps were spread on the mess table and our position freely discussed. General Kearny, who also was present, was very cutting on McClellan's operations, and advises a forward movement on Richmond without waiting for reenforcements. Music [was played] by the 1st New York regimental band at 7 p.m. at these headquarters. This is a fine band and ably led. They got their whiskey as usual.

THE COLE HOUSE ON RUFFIN'S PLANTATION OPPOSITE HARRISON'S LANDING, JAMES RIVER, VA.

July 30, 1862

. . . I made a sketch of the Cole house on the opposite side of the river, and while doing so, was surprised to see persons in the cupola of the tower surveying our position and surroundings. I climbed on one of the siege guns and from there got a better view. With my glass I could plainly ascertain the cupola to be occupied by Rebel officers, and about 200 cavalry were seen close to the house in rear, sheltered by a hedge. They must have been seen by the signal corps, and from their position could look down on the landing and decks of the gunboats as if from a balloon. . . .

July 31, 1862

Raining most of the day, with thunder and lightning storm in afternoon. We had the same kind of weather yesterday after 7 p.m., and are now used to discomfort and getting wet. Fresh beef and fresh wheat bread is now daily issued to the army, while the sutlers furnish pickles, cheese, sardines, and cheap brandy for a high price. I reported seeing Rebels at Cole's house yesterday, and was laughed at "as none could possibly be there without General McClellan knowing it." I have seen too many Rebels to have been mistaken. And the gray uniforms and slouch hats were seen without a glass, as the open windows of the cupola brought them in relief against the sky behind. . . .

At about 12:30 midnight, all were started from their sleep by rapid and heavy artillery firing on the James River at Westover Landing. All was excitement at headquarters immediately. Horses were called for and General Heintzelman, with most of the staff mounted, dashed off into the plain. The long roll beat in the camps near us. Divisions and brigades turned out in line and awaited orders. The firing grew more unsteady and finally stopped about 1:30 a.m. A thousand rounds were fired. The sonorous roar of the gunboats, now rapidly firing, was heard above the others. I climbed a tall pine tree, and as we were not more than two and a half miles from the river, saw the trail of the fiery shells bursting in the woods on the horizon, as the night was very dark and lowering the flashes of the guns lit up the plain for miles in our front. The general and staff returned soon, and orders sent to dismiss the troops under arms. The enemy had opened on us with artillery from forty-three pieces simultaneously!

One battery was at Coggin's Point. Two others at the Cole house, and two more above and opposite Berkeley Landing. (This was just as I had anticipated and now had my laugh.) The enemy's guns were of 32 pounder and 12 pounder caliber, the missiles from which crashed and smashed into the steamers and vessels at anchor, and into the camp of the 3rd Pennsylvania Cavalry near [Westover]. The contraband camp caught it also, and Negro women, children, and darkies ran in all directions for the woods, stampeding the horses and mules with their yells of affright. When the enemy first opened fire, the gunboat *Wachusetts* was some ways up river, and the *Cimerone* was the nearest one down below Coggin's Point. Both were on the night patrol, and soon steamed to the landing and immediately opened fire. In twenty minutes they had driven off the enemy and silenced his guns.*

August 1, 1862

Rain. I went down to the landing to ascertain the effect of the rumpus last night. I could plainly see and count twenty-seven Rebels at the Cole house across the river. They were no doubt looking for sunken vessels or steamers in the James, but none were found for their shot and shell had been thrown away for nothing. All the vessels and steamers had moved down river early this morning, but were anchored in a safer position below Herring Creek. The gunboats alone were in the river opposite the landings and I wondered why they did not shell the Cole house now as the Rebels were plainly seen in the cupola of the tower without the aid of glasses. But they did not man the guns, and I was disappointed accordingly. During the attack last night ten men and thirteen horses were killed, besides fifteen more wounded, some mortally. Several contrabands were also killed and wounded. The loss was mainly in Averell's cavalry. They were now moving their quarters farther back from the river. Many of our vessels and steamers were struck, but not much damage done, as the Rebels aimed quite high, and did not have time to play their "little game" long, before the screeching shells from our gunboats scattered them in the woods. . . .

At 5:30 p.m., 1,800 of our troops were assembled at Westover Wharf, who soon embarked on three or four steamers. A large detail of axe men went with them and under

*The Confederate troops and artillery in this action had been sent by General D. H. Hill from Petersburg to harass McClellan's army.

U.S. gunboat *Cimerone* Steamers landing troops from Harrison's Landing

U.S. TROOPS BURNING THE COLE HOUSE AND PLANTATION
Opposite Harrison's Landing, James River, on the night of August 1, 1862.

cover of the gunboats, the crews of which were "all at quarters." The force steamed across, landed at the ruined wharf, deployed, and went over the hill to the Cole house. This was set on fire, and soon the flames streamed out of every window and wrapt the fine dwelling in sheets of fire. The sun had just set, and the scene was grand.

I made a sketch on the spot. The axe men now felled the trees, destroyed the outbuildings, and the fire caught in the dry timber and brush, and at 6:30 p.m. the whole opposite bluff was a sheet of fire and smoke, which burnt clean over twenty acres of ground before morning. The troops were withdrawn at 10 p.m. while the fire raged unobstructed all night. I did not leave the landing until 9:30 p.m. The fire at this time had demolished the house and outbuildings and the woods were burning fiercely. The river was lit up for miles, and the rigging of the vessels shone like gold. Many officers and men came from their camps to see the fine sight. We had a fine serenade at headquarters . . . and whiskey punch flowed freely. General Kearny's favorite air is "The Mocking Bird," and the band leaders know that if this tune is well played they will be furnished whiskey "ad libitum." So we have this fine piece played over repeatedly, or as long as the musicians can see his instrument. Sometimes the whiskey prevents his so doing, when the band is dismissed without thanks.

The camps have now a neat and compact appearance and they are all sheltered from the sun as much as possible in woods. The work on the defenses still continues, and the troops are drilled every day when the weather permits. . . .

August 5, 1862

Fine but very hot in [the] afternoon, 93 degrees. . . . We cannot move anywhere at present as the 2,000 sick hamper us. They cannot be transported in wagons or ambulances when we leave here. Our headquarters, as well as the camps, are infested with thousands of flies, which are nearly as large as bees and sting nearly as bad. While eating our meals, the flies are so thick that we have to blow them off our food before putting [it] in our mouths.

They settle in hundreds among the brush, which composes the roof of our mess house. We explode loose powder under them, which brings down a shower of dead and wounded. Still there are just as many more in a few minutes afterwards. I had two trees cut in front of my tent, on the stumps of which I made a sort of trough with stiff paper, [which] was filled with powder. The flies lit on the stump in the thousands to get at the running sap, [and] piled up on each other three deep, completely covering the top. With a piece of touch paper fastened to the end of a long switch or twig, I would blow these fellows up several times a day. But still there were just as many more there ten minutes afterwards! We are not much troubled with mosquitoes, as we are on the edge of the woods, and no grass is on the plain in our front for them to hide in. The camps of [the] 38th and 40th [New York] are infested with mosquitoes, as they are near Rawlins Mill pond and the marshy ground which is around its borders. We had a fine moonlit night, and the 1st New York regimental band serenaded our headquarters until 11:30 p.m. All was gay and festive, and a new box of lemons were used for making the "military punch.". . .

While McClellan's men remained on the banks of the James River, a newly constituted Union army under the command of General John Pope prepared to move on Richmond from northern Virginia. Union strategists were certain that Robert E. Lee could not fend off an offensive from two directions. The basic concept was sound, but Lee had accurately sized up the situation and his opponents. He saw clearly that if Pope and McClellan joined forces, their strength could easily overwhelm him, and he knew that he had to act swiftly to prevent such a merger. Certain that McClellan would remain inactive for a while, he detached a large force under Stonewall Jackson and sent him north to deal with Pope in late July. Two weeks later, Lee followed with most of his remaining troops to take on Pope, still confident that McClellan would not threaten Richmond.

Although Little Mac talked of plans to advance on the important railhead of Petersburg and even of making another move toward Richmond, President Lincoln had little confidence in the general's offensive inclinations. The president also had become concerned over the fate of

Pope's army and the national capital. Despite objections from McClellan, on August 3, Lincoln ordered the Army of the Potomac to withdraw and join forces with Pope as soon as possible. McClellan, jealous of Pope and on less than good terms with the president, took his time removing his troops from the Virginia Peninsula. Not until August 16 did the last units of the army leave Harrison's Landing for the march down to Fort Monroe and embarkation for Alexandria. From there they were to march to join Pope. For Sneden and his comrades, the misery of life on the James River soon would be replaced by another form of hardship. They now retraced their steps through places they had advanced on with such high hopes earlier in the spring.

August 10, 1862

. . . All the heavy guns, and most of the ammunition are being shipped, and the sick leave at the rate of 800 per day. All the knapsacks of soldiers, officers' baggage, spare tents, and other material of war will be sent by vessels to Aquia Creek and Alexandria. Teams were at work nearly all of last night hauling, as [they] will be today, when the broiling sun goes down. All infantry are ordered to have five days' rations cooked in advance, and to move in light marching order. No tents will be carried, shelter tents for men, and six tent flies per regiment or staff headquarters each. The general impression in this army is that we will move on Richmond by way of Petersburg. Very few of the generals even know the route which eventually will be taken, all the rank and file know is that a "flank movement" will soon be made of some sort, very soon. The topographical engineers, who are hard at work duplicating maps of roads over which the army *will* march are about the only knowing ones in camp, but they are secret and "don't know," if questioned. As the enemy captured the map wagon of General McClellan during the recent retreat, they know as much as we do, and perhaps more of the country between here and Yorktown. . . .

The soldiers, as usual leave everything to their officers, who, in turn leave everything to the generals. And it don't make much matter to the soldiers which way he marches, as long as he moves in some direction. So that when the orders come to "pack up," they do so promptly without asking questions of any kind. As a strong force of our troops yet hold Coggin's Point, and all along up to Jordan's Point above, the enemy have made no further demonstrations since the midnight cannonade. . . .

August 14, 1862

Fine day. Marching orders were sent all the corps commanders this morning to be in readiness to move tomorrow on Yorktown via Williamsburg. There was much surprise manifested among officers who thought we would move on Malvern Hill and Richmond, or cross the James above Petersburg, and move on Manchester which is opposite Richmond, and where there are no fortifications at present. There was much discussion in camp, and although the officers knew little or nothing of the route of the march and "the objective point" all were glad to know that the army would move out of these burning arid plains and go *somewhere*, no matter where!

The corps of Fitz-John Porter (V) marched this morning, via Barrett's Ford on the Chickahominy, with orders to halt at Williamsburg until the rest of the army arrive there. These are the first troops to march. All the reserve artillery and ammunition wagons went with Porter. Nearly all the sick have been embarked. A few hundred remain at the temporary hospitals, who will be shipped tomorrow. . . . Most of the baggage, soldiers' knapsacks, [and] tents are now on board vessels and small steamers and nothing much will be left behind except empty barrels, deserted earthworks, and a few of the iron baking ovens, which are too bulky and heavy to get to the wharf. The whole of the III Corps were reviewed at 4 p.m. by General Heintzelman. [Hiram] Berry's and Birney's brigades looked especially fine. These all wore new clothes, white canvas leggings, and the *red diamond* corps badge looked especially neat. All the other corps wear their cloth badges or marks, and it is next to impossible for a soldier now to lose his command when on the march.* I was employed most of the day duplicating maps for the march route, and as all the headquarters tents were struck and packed ready for shipment, I worked in the general's tent. General Hooker came in after the review of the troops to see General Heintzelman and before going, made me an offer to go on his staff as captain and engineer. I declined respectfully, as I could not leave General Heintzelman at this important time and on the eve of a march. Besides, corps headquarters are always more preferable than those of division or brigade. . . .

Several corps moved camp during this afternoon, taking their position in order of march on the high ground of Evelynton Hills, and along Herring Creek. I was engaged working on maps until 11 p.m. when I packed up my instruments and map box, and slept in my new rubber tent for the first time, finding it to answer my expectations, though being cramped for room. General Kearny had a serenade at his quarters near us, and the last brewing of punch was held at midnight. All the vessels and steamers weighed anchor and got under weigh about 8 p.m. . . . Two . . . gunboats led the fleet. All the sick had been got aboard safely. Then came vessels and steamers of all kinds and sizes carrying horses, forage, stores, ammunition, tents, and all the baggage of the army. Several hundred contrabands, with women and children, were also on the vessels, and by 10 p.m. the landing was deserted. The fleet moved down river slowly. The moon was half full and reflected its rays on the smooth waters of the James, while the colored signal lanterns were in constant motion on the gunboats which brought up the rear. All the camps were ablaze until a late hour, the men were burning up empty barrels, tent poles . . . camp tables, and other debris, so that nothing of any possible use or value whatever should be left for the Rebels. . . .

* The III Corps was the first in the Army of the Potomac to wear distinctive badges for identification purposes. The practice did not become widespread or official until Joseph Hooker took command of the army in 1863.

August 15, 1862

Fine day and very hot, 92 degrees. The bugles sounded to "pack up" in all the camps at 6 o'clock this morning and soon all the tents were struck, packed in wagons, and sent to the wharf where two or three vessels yet remained taking on their last loads. . . . The wagon trains will move all night and they now are moving off in a steady stream across Herring Creek bridges. Our engineers have built three bridges across this creek, and the approaches to them are over long corduroy roads laid in the swampy ground which borders it. All the bridges across Kimmager's Creek were destroyed, and trees were felled across all the roads leading to Malvern Hill and Richmond. The whole army was in motion by noon, with its artillery and wagons. General McClellan went over the ground personally, superintending the movements, and was loudly cheered. Tents were struck at Heintzelman's and Kearny's headquarters at 7 a.m. Three wagons only to each headquarters were allowed and the guards rejoined their regiment as there was no use for them. A squadron of cavalry accompanied General Heintzelman as escort and guard. At 10 a.m. the whole plain in our front was covered with troops moving in column towards the bridges which crossed Herring Creek. Ammunition wagons having full loads, and ambulances empty, all were in light marching order. The men carried haversacks with ten days' rations, sixty rounds of ammunition, and their shelter tents. As the several generals rode along the moving columns they were loudly cheered, Hooker and Kearny especially.

[During the march] I was met on all sides with sullen and defiant remarks by the women who complained of the loss of their slaves or servants as they call them, which now forced them to do their own work. "Why don't the Yankees let us alone!" they would question, and then "You will never subjugate us." Some would ask for coffee and sugar, others for snuff or fine tobacco, the besotting habit of the lower and middle classes is swabbing their mouths and teeth with snuff. The women indulge in this dirty habit continually, both old and young. They carry little sticks with a swab on the end made of cotton, and rub the snuff on their gums, which serves to excite them in the same way that strong tea does old women. They address you with "I say, have you some fine 'bacca to give a lady? I haven't had a swab in a week." "Curse this war, but you 'uns will never conquer us." "Why don't you 'uns let us alone?" They were much alarmed at first as column after column of our army passed through the place without halting, but when they found that no battle was to be fought here, they became more quiet and conversant. . . .

August 18, 1862

Fine and very hot. Tents were struck at 5:30 a.m. and an hour later, the III Corps were all on the march again for Williamsburg. We made but ten miles yesterday, but our marches don't average six miles per day, though we could make fifteen if required. But McClellan is taking things easy though Pope is badly in want of reenforcements. And it is in a critical posi-

HEADQUARTERS, III ARMY CORPS, GENERAL SAMUEL P. HEINTZELMAN COMMANDING
Williamsburg, Va., August 18, 1862.

tion with the enemy confronting him in superior numbers. . . . Our route today was by the Williamsburg Stage road, the same over which we had advanced in May last. The telegraph poles stood like sentinels along it. The wires had been removed or destroyed. We passed the ruins of "Burnt Ordinary," which I sketched for the second time. And at 2:30 p.m., we entered Williamsburg and made our headquarters on a bye road, near William and Mary College. All our flies and tents were here put up. And the wagons were unloaded for the first time since leaving Harrison's Landing. I made a sketch of headquarters at sundown. The national flag floated from the college park and a red hospital flag from the steeple of the largest church in Williamsburg. . . . I went through Williamsburg before dark and to the college and monument which is in the park erected to Governor [Norborne Berkeley, Baron de] Botetourt in 1771. Several pieces of rough made artillery were here on grim black painted carriages. They were captured from the enemy by us when here . . . during the battle of May 5 last. The inhabitants kept close to their houses, and peered cautiously at us behind shutters and doors. All the stores had been sacked and no business was being done. There were guards on some of the churches and public buildings. No safe guards were on any of the houses, yet our men did not disturb the inhabitants in any manner. The troops were bivouacked in the open fields on the outskirts of the town and not in it. The Negro population were cooking "corn pones" for the soldiers, who repaid them in sugar, coffee, and money. . . . Bands were playing this evening at [the] headquarters of several generals, while the camp fires were seen all around the environs of the town, through which no soldier was permitted to go.

August 19, 1862

Fine but very hot, 96 degrees. Tents were struck at 7:30 a.m. and all were on the march again by 8:30. The roads were very dusty and the long black columns wound down the dreary road . . . towards Yorktown, where we will embark for Alexandria. About 10:30 a.m. our train came to near Fort Magruder and I left the column to go over once more the old battlefield. Generals Heintzelman, Kearny, Hooker, Sickles, and others rode over the ground.* No others left the marching column, as the men were prevented from leaving the line of march by previous orders from the generals commanding. The Rebel fort was just as we had left it 6th May last. The ditches were full of water but the parapets were much washed away by the rains. A heavy undergrowth of weeds and vines covered all the ground outside the main fort, among which, graves with stakes at their heads were numerous. On a trench, which was filled with dead, I found tomatoes growing plentifully. They were dead ripe, and I filled my pockets and everything else with them. I must have eaten several quarts before moving on. I stumbled over battered and rusty canteens, broken muskets, cartridge boxes and half burnt trees for a long while. And the briars, which were thickly growing all through the abatis, impeded my way. Skeletons of horses or mules half burned, were in heaps in the undergrowth. The half burnt trees were piled on some of these, showing where they had been felled on purpose to burn the dead animals when the army left here after the battle. Most of the log houses which the Rebels had used for barracks had disappeared. Several more had been burned. Many of the graves had stakes or slabs to mark them, but names of those buried had been obliterated by rain and sun so as to be illegible, as they had been written with a pencil. Some had initials cut in [them] with a knife, but wild vines and weeds covered the whole ground three feet high. By great exertion in the hot sun was I enabled to stumble my way through. As the wagon tops of our headquarters train were now out of sight ahead, I made haste to rejoin. . . .

About 3 p.m., we passed Whitaker's Mill. Old man Whitaker was grinding corn as if there was no war in the vicinity. The road here had been overflowed by water from the mill pond. And three inches of good sticky Virginia mud was over the corduroy built road underneath. Many of the mules fell in coming down the steep hill back of the mill. And some delay was had before the wagon trains proceeded. We kept on, and passed the Halfway House, once an old tavern. It had been burnt since we were here and nothing but chimney stacks showed where it once had stood. We crossed the ravines and Warwick road at 5:30 p.m., went through Yorktown and made headquarters . . . outside the fortifications, near the steep banks of the York River. All the tents were not up until 9 p.m. General Heintzelman remained at Yorktown all night. The clerks had to sleep in the wagons. I put up my rubber tent and laid smoking, looking at the river below me until near midnight. Bands were playing in the town,

* Fort Magruder was the main Confederate defensive position during the May 5 battle of Williamsburg. Hooker's and Kearny's divisions led the Union offensive.

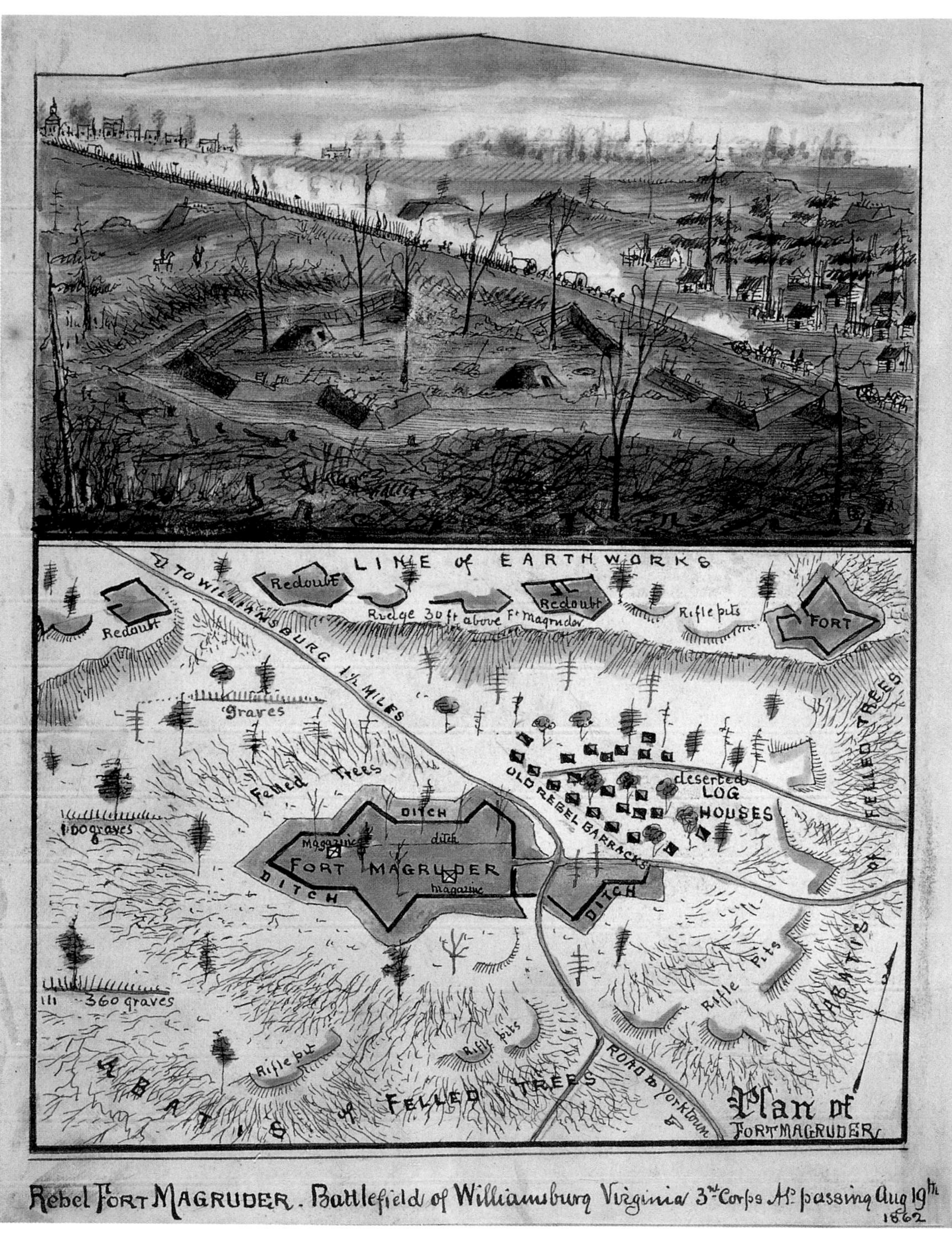

REBEL FORT MAGRUDER

Battlefield of Williamsburg, Va. III Corps passing August 19, 1862.
Army in retreat on Yorktown, Va.

and thousands of camp fires showed themselves all over the open ground, while the twinkling of lights from numerous steamers and vessels at anchor in the river made it impressive.

August 20, 1862

Fine day with good cool breeze from river. . . . General [Heintzelman] came into camp this forenoon, and soon after we removed our headquarters to a fine dry spot near the river bank from whence a fine view was had up and down the York. Whole regiments of soldiers were in swimming, as well as numberless horses and mules. We had marched over dusty roads for many miles and everyone went for the luxury of a swim who could get off duty. No Rebels were here now to interfere, and the air resounded with laughter, yells of delight, instead of Rebel yells. I went over [to] the deserted water battery, and the caves in the river bank. All were the same as I had seen them when here last, but the guns had been removed from the battery. These rough looking pieces of artillery were placed at intervals all along the bluffs of the town. Some were on the ramparts, others covered the wharf landing from the bluff on Main Street. . . .

Our old lines of entrenchments were plainly visible, but now all going to ruin. I saw with regret what an immense amount of labor and muscle had been thrown away in their useless construction by McClellan, when any one army corps could have broken the Rebel lines . . . and bagged the whole Rebel army in Yorktown. The sawmill had been burnt to the ground . . . and naked burnt chimneys showed only where houses had once been. Numerous vessels and steamers were anchored in the river, and others were crowded around the only wharf of the town. These were taking on board artillery and stores of every description, saved from the wreck of the campaign on the Peninsula. . . . I returned to our headquarters outside the town, when I made map tracings for General Heintzelman of around Warrenton and Culpeper . . . from lithographic maps furnished by [the] map bureau at Washington. . . .

August 21, 1862

Fine day. I went swimming in the York River at 6:30 a.m. Several hundred soldiers, with some officers were in the water at the same time. The bugles sounded "pack up" at 7:30 and our headquarter tents were struck by 9 o'clock. Long lines of troops moved from the town to the dreary looking wharf and began embarking on steamboats appropriated for transportation to Alexandria. Men had been embarked during the night, and several steamers were anchored off the landing, which were crowded with troops. Regiments stacked their arms all along the beach, and were awaiting their turn to embark, and as each steamer filled up, it steamed out in the river to make room for another. All the movements were made with precision and order. Staff officers were everywhere directing the embarkation. . . . Sentinels were posted all along the ramparts of the town, as the intention is to hold it after we have left. Brigade bands were playing in the town and on the beach.

Our headquarters train moved in and through Yorktown . . . and by 11 o'clock, the general, with staff, were all embarked on the steamer *Long Island*. General Heintzelman . . . occupied the best cabin, which was soon filled with the personal baggage, saddles, [and] demijohns. All the horses were left behind for another boat to bring on. We took on board 200 men and officers of [the] 105th Pennsylvania Regiment, and hauled off from the wharf at 12 noon. A dozen or more steamers, all laden with troops were now steaming down river, and our boat soon overhauled the fleet as she was a fast river steamer. Bands were playing and men cheering, flags flying, and the show was grand. But our spirits were not so buoyant as when another much larger fleet, filled with expectant troops left Alexandria in March last, "On to Richmond" then being the universal song.

Our steamer proved a fast sailer, and we led the fleet, by 3 p.m. We passed down the York River and with a northeast course crossed Mobjack Bay into the Chesapeake. The shores looked low and sandy, while pine forests came down to the beach, but the sea air was very refreshing, and despite a drizzling rain which set in at dark, very few went below until morning. Nearly all the soldiers slept on deck. At 10 p.m. we slowed our engines and kept in company with four or five larger steamers all laden with troops. Sounds of [conviviality] reached us across the water, while the signal lanterns communicated messages or orders from one steamer to another. The heavy swell in Chesapeake Bay sent many a soldier to his bunk with seasickness. Much whiskey was drank to keep this off. I kept the deck until after midnight, but as I could not sleep in the close cabin, I made my bunk on deck near the wheelhouse.

At 1:30 a.m. [August 22] we had arrived off the Piankatank River, and had to lay at anchor two hours off the bar on account of low tide. We were under weigh again and at 4:30 a.m. made Windmill Point, at the mouth of [the] Rappahannock River. At 7 we had passed Point Lookout and passed Mount Vernon and Fort Washington at noon, arriving at Alexandria at 2 p.m. . . .

The arrival of McClellan's troops came none too soon. John Pope, who had boasted earlier in the summer of certain success, found himself in serious trouble. Rarely has a general been more confused over the whereabouts of his opponent and what his own next move would be. He had suffered the indignity of losing official papers, maps, cash, and uniforms when Confederate cavalry raided his headquarters. Worse, Pope thought he was in the immediate presence of Lee's army with only the shallow Rappahannock River between them. In reality, Lee had boldly divided his army, sending half of it under Stonewall Jackson on a long march to the northwest, while holding the remainder to keep Pope occupied. Jackson sped his troops off behind the Bull Run Mountains, came swiftly east, and on August 26 swooped down on the Union army's base of supplies at Manassas Junction, twenty miles in Pope's rear.

MANASSAS JUNCTION, VA., ORANGE AND ALEXANDRIA RAILROAD
August 28, 1862. Destruction of railroad cars by the Rebels.

When Pope turned around to take care of this threat, Lee then followed Jackson's route, to join him east of the Bull Run Mountains.

Although Pope crowed that he had his opponent just where he wanted him, in reality he was falling into a trap himself. He set his troops marching back and forth to surround Jackson, but he could not find him. After setting a massive bonfire of the Federal supplies that he could not carry off, Jackson left Manassas Junction and took a concealed position in the woods and hills near the old Bull Run battlefield. There he waited to pounce. In the meantime, Pope wore his soldiers out looking for Jackson. He constantly begged that McClellan's troops be rushed forward to help him bag the Confederates. But again McClellan did little to aid his fellow commander. Of five army corps available, he slowly advanced only two to the battlefront, one of which was Heintzelman's.

For Sneden, the frenetic pace of activity and the uncertainty of hard campaigning returned. After arriving from the Peninsula on August 22, he was kept busy making maps, although he took a brief trip to Washington to purchase supplies and new equipment for the field. Everywhere he looked, fortifications were being strengthened in anticipation of an advance by Lee. Then late in the afternoon of August 25, Heintzelman and his staff, including Sneden, boarded a train in Alexandria and headed south for Pope's headquarters in

HEADQUARTERS OF GENERALS POPE AND HEINTZELMAN AT WARRENTON JUNCTION, VA.
Afternoon of August 28, 1862.

Warrenton, Virginia, passing through Manassas Junction. Once at their destination, the mapmaker sensed that matters were far from under control. There was obvious distrust between the Army of the Potomac men and their new commander. The generals were confused by reports of enemy moves. Driving rainstorms deepened the gloom of night. Then on the night of August 26, Sneden could distinctly see a huge fire glowing on the horizon toward Manassas. When word of Jackson's raid on the rail junction reached headquarters the next morning, Sneden and his colleagues packed up everything hastily and joined the army in pursuit of Jackson. By the next day, they had reached Bull Run Creek.

In the meantime, late on the afternoon of August 28, Jackson came out from hiding and attacked an unsuspecting Union column marching to join Pope's main body. Pope, now certain that he had Jackson in the bag, moved up the remainder of his army the following day and launched a series of uncoordinated attacks, which included the two divisions of Heintzelman's corps. Little did he know that Lee had brought up the rest of his army and had taken a position squarely on the Union left flank. Sneden would soon find himself in the midst of the largest battle of his wartime experience. His account picks up a day before the Second Battle of Bull Run or Manassas.

August 28, 1862

. . . Before leaving Warrenton Junction [yesterday] our headquarters and General Pope's were together in a clump of heavy pines. The wagons of each general were drawn up in two half circles, mules unhitched to the rear. One or two flies were spread among the trees for use of generals and staffs. General Pope sat in a large wicker arm chair smoking. His staff were in groups discussing the affair at Catlett's Station, and bewailing the loss of their personal baggage now being put in practical use by Jackson and Stuart. Pope's staff officers were gorgeously arrayed in different styles of uniform with all the gold lace and buttons which could be possibly be put on them. Pope himself had on a fine new major general's uniform the lapels being quilted inside with white satin!

The telegraph had been out for some hours, and where the different generals with their commands at this time were nobody seemed to know. General Heintzelman, with two of his staff sat on a felled tree perhaps fifty feet away from Pope, all looking fatigued and bespattered with mud. An orderly or courier galloped up, dismounted, and approached General Pope. [He] delivered him several dispatches and stood waiting until he had read the first one. He had forgotten to take off his hat. (This is not necessary in military etiquette.) Pope instantly opened on the poor orderly with a string of blood curdling oaths, which scared the orderly nearly out of his boots. General Pope's chief of staff said something not heard by us which made Pope more furious. He ordered his wagon guard to lash the unfortunate orderly to one of the wagon wheels which was near. This they slowly and reluctantly did. All at once artillery firing was heard off towards Sulphur or Warrenton Springs. Pope ordered up his horse mounted, and rode off with his staff scowling and swearing. The guard released the orderly, who mounted as quick as he could and galloped off in a different direction in mortal fear which provoked a laugh all around. Pope's action was plainly denounced by all present, as was plainly shown by their expression. Much comment was made by our staff and general who called it "an outrage to the service." That orderly will not be apt to take any more dispatches to Pope in a hurry.

Before leaving Bristoe Station, I went over most of the battlefield.* I made two or three sketches, and went into an old stone house near the railroad which had been occupied by the enemy during the battle. There was no furniture in it but two or three broken chairs and stools with a very rickety pine table. The rooms were fitted up in bunks all around the rooms. On the first floor in one of these laid a Rebel soldier with a musket between his knees. He was dead enough—had been struck in the forehead with a bullet which had come out at the back of the skull leaving a hole as large as a grape shot. He had been shot while in the act of loading. The bunk was full of dirty straw and covered with blood. The stench of blood and dirt made it unhealthy to stay long. Another dead Rebel was on the floor

*Sneden is referring to an engagement fought on August 27 near Bristoe Station between Confederate troops led by General Richard Ewell and Hooker's division. Ewell was driven back after sustaining several hundred casualties.

upstairs. The house had evidently been used for hospital purposes, the floor and yard was strewn with dirty and bloody gray clothing, torn blankets, hard looking shoes, old battered felt hats, [and] canteens, while the floor and walls was smeared all over with blood. The stench was terrible. I went up the track where another house stood on a high bank. This had no occupants. . . . A picket fence surrounded the lot and on it were hundreds of Rebel blankets torn and burnt. While on the ground were two or three hundred Rebel knapsacks, which were made of ox hide with the hair outside. Our men were rummaging them, getting letters, and tobacco, but nothing of any value. The Rebels had thrown off knapsacks and blankets to make a charge and never had the chance to get back to them again.

After much delay in waiting for ammunition trains and batteries we came up to Manassas during a shower of rain and waited three hours there [for] further orders from General Heintzelman, who with Hooker and Pope, were far ahead of most of the wagon trains. At about 5 p.m., we were ordered on to Bull Run [Creek] by the way of the lower fords. . . . We were soon off when the rain came down hard making our progress very slow. We were stalled several times but the guard, throwing their muskets into the wagons, laid hold of the wagons and spokes of the wheels, and by much exertion pushed them up the hills, the roads over which were of quicksand. We had no time to halt, for wagons were behind us, and before us, while at times the trains were on a full run, all trying as usual to get ahead of one another. Then wagons would lock wheels and the mules come to dead halt, which took a large amount of patience, and much swearing from teamsters to get once more started. . . . [We finally] turned towards Bull Run and arrived about 7 p.m. The sound of battle was heard by us during the whole time and up to 9 p.m. We put up one fly tent and then camped down for the night. . . . The width of Bull Run here was about 150 feet. Two or three small islands were here. . . . We felled a tree to get on the nearest one, [then] we built a large fire and cooked our suppers. I pitched my rubber tent on it and had water rushing on all sides during our stay. A trestle bridge had been thrown over the run near us by our engineers and the artillery trains rumbled over it constantly all night. We heard nothing of General Heintzelman or staff during the day. We made ourselves as comfortable as we could.

August 29, 1862*

The battle reopened this morning at daylight with artillery . . . on our extreme right. We had several large camp fires going by 5 a.m., and after a good breakfast, most of us went bathing in the run. Columns of troops were passing . . . over the trestle bridge, followed by the artillery. These passed up and over the opposite hill out of sight. At 7 [a.m.], lines of battle were formed on the crest of hills on [the] other side of Bull Run, while the roar of artillery and steady rolling of musketry showed that the battle was being continued with fury on

* Sneden marked this entry August 30, but from events he describes it probably should be dated August 29. Some sentences have been moved for clarity.

both sides. Our camp was between high banks on either side of the run and off the road so we were not interrupted by wagon trains or any stragglers.

So we smoked our pipes and watched the sky full of bursting shells over the hill top, while infantry were deploying along the ridges. Most of these were soon ordered to move forward while artillery alone were stationed in their places. The gurgling waters of Bull Run had a very pleasant effect on our tired nerves. And while everything was hot and dusty on the hills, we were in a shady, cool spot and enjoyed our situation until we had orders to move to Ball's house, which we were very loath to do. The wagon guard improved the time to clean all the muskets and accouterments which they needed badly while the cook overhauled the scanty amount of food left us. . . . I had sent off several maps to General Heintzelman by the orderly, which I knew would be most wanted, so I was now free to go anywhere, having left the map box in charge of Lieutenant Gray of our wagon guard.

About 3 p.m., I was crossing a rough stubble field which bordered on the Sudley Springs road on the right of our battle line when [our] troops . . . overtook me and passed rapidly on the double quick into a thin strip of woods about the center of the enemy's line. These were of [General Rufus] King's division. . . . Hooker's command was just beyond Dogan's house, while several of our batteries were taking position along a rocky ridge facing the enemy. Soon they unlimbered and opened a rapid fire, throwing their shells over the woods so as to reach the Rebels behind the embankment on the other side and into Jackson's headquarters, which were on another ridge beyond this.

The enemy replied with their artillery, and the air was soon filled with screeching shells and the thud of solid shot striking the ground and rebounding in all directions. I did not stay here longer than ten minutes as the missiles were too uncomfortably near. "It was not healthy" to stay over two minutes in any one place. I followed a ditch and lay down on the safe side of it, while I saw the desperate fighting at the edge of the woods and open ground on the left and up to the railroad embankment.

The Rebels had two or more pieces of Whitworth guns.* The peculiar screech of their missiles were heard above the whizzing of other projectiles. The Rebel artillery was fired at a high elevation and their shells burst mostly in rear of our lines for a long while. But they rectified this when our men were ordered to lie down. Still many were killed in this position while our artillery horses were cut up badly. For an hour the Rebels, being out of ammunition, fired pieces of railroad iron at us. Two pieces bound with telegraph wire, these would stick in the tree tops and slide down on our men's heads. This confused and mystified the troops who scattered and broke ranks continually. [They] thought it a new explosive until after it had been solved. . . .

I saw the head of one of our artillerymen taken off, shot within fifty feet of my position. His blood spattered his gun. He was pulled up by his arms a few paces away, the blood gush-

*An English rifled cannon that was used in small but well-publicized numbers by the Confederates.

ing in streams from his neck. . . . The other artillerymen kept on loading and firing without giving him further notice. All the guns of the battery were worked with great rapidity. The men were loading and firing like madmen. The wounded were crawling around on their hands and knees. Others were tearing up their shirts to make bandages for their bloody wounds . . . while from a low strip of bushes the Rebels were firing on our wounded in front who were crawling to our lines. The wounded and dying Rebels along our front in the open ground held up their hands in token of surrender, while piercing shrieks, yells, cheers, and oaths filled the air, heard above the deafening reports of the artillery and crash of musketry. . . . Having seen enough of the terrible fighting, I returned to our headquarters. . . .

At the end of the first day of battle, Pope was convinced that he was winning and that the enemy would retreat soon. He ignored reports of a large Confederate force under James Longstreet on his left flank. The Federal commander feebly probed enemy lines the next morning, but not until the afternoon did he launch his "pursuit" when he ordered a massive assault on Jackson's corps along a wide front. Two hours later, however, Longstreet unleashed five divisions of Confederates, who rolled forward to smash the Union left. The Rebels quickly overran a thin line of resistance. As Pope tried in vain to stem the tide on his left, Jackson hit him on the right. By nightfall, the Union army was crushed and driven north of Bull Run in disorder. The next day, Lee kept up the pressure, attacking at Chantilly, where General Phil Kearny, one of Sneden's heroes in the III Corps, was killed. Sneden again found himself in the heat of battle and then the chaos of retreat.

August 30, 1862

Fine day, very hot, roads dry and very dusty. . . . At 5 a.m. an orderly came from General Heintzelman to Lieutenant Gray of the guard ordering us to move [the] headquarters train across Bull Run to Ball's house . . . on [the] other side of that stream. So we packed up and moved over the trestle bridge and got there about 8:30 a.m. Our engineers were constructing bridges over Cub Run, and had bridged the gap at Stone Bridge which had previously been blown up by our engineers. The men were working up to their waists in water, but the stream was low and water warm. Men were felling trees and repairing roads at the different crossings of Cub Run and towards Stone Bridge on the Warrenton Turnpike. Long lines of army wagons were on all roads and in open fields while batteries were going down the turnpike at full gallop.

After waiting until 9:30 a.m. at Ball's house, I concluded to go over to the battlefield to see General Heintzelman, taking some maps with me for use. The battle had opened on our right by this time and the musketry fire continuous. I soon . . . got information of [how] our forces were posted and how to find General Heintzelman. . . . Generals Porter and [George]

Headquarter Teams of Major General Heintzelman, III Corps at Island Ford
During second battle of Bull Run, Va., August 30, 1862.

Sykes and some others whom I did not know [were] all in earnest conversation with Pope, getting their orders for the day as I supposed. I then went to Matthew's house on the Sudley road, where were several batteries all harnessed up waiting for orders. The house was full of our wounded. Keeping to the right I came among the troops of General Birney . . . and soon found General Heintzelman, who looked very much used up from constantly being in the saddle. I was returning to the Balls' house about 4 p.m., when the crashing fire of musketry amid the quick and spiteful fire of artillery on our left center and right told of the reopening of the battle. King's division of McDowell's corps were now in the front fighting the enemy, who were still behind the railroad embankment with much superior forces to ours. I watched the lines of infantry moving up the Sudley road and the batteries rushing over the stone bridge for a long while. [I] made sketches of the Robinson and Henry houses, and returned to our train at Ball's house. The firing was continuous and rolling. The smoke rose above the woods, while the air was alive with bursting shells from both sides of the turnpike and away north to the railroad embankment. . . .

I got back to Ball's house about 4:30 p.m. while our guard and teams were soon ready to move as ordered to Centreville only a mile or so away. This was [a] pretty good two story farm house with verandah. It stood on a hill among barns and other outhouses. One old woman and three young women were here, not a man or Negro on the premises. The old

PLAN OF SECOND BATTLE OF BULL RUN, VA.
Showing movement of troops from May 27 to September 1, 1862.

EASTERN VIEW OF CENTREVILLE, VA., FROM CUB RUN
Union army falling back evening of August 30, 1862.

woman was "tongue-lashing" our guard for taking the remnant of what was left of her chickens. One of our officers had shot most of them from the door step some hours before I got there. He had found a loaded musket in the house and coolly shot all that could be seen about the house [and] then had as coolly carried off the musket. Our wagon guard had appropriated what was left, besides two young pigs, on the ground that they were "secech." She cursed them for Yankee thieves, while the men cooked the grub, laughing at her and eating before her eyes. The girls were calling them all the vile names they could think up, but condescended to take some tobacco from one of our clerks. Then they would begin to denounce them as thieves, liars, cowards again. One of our quartermasters had found the barn quite full of hay. He soon was loading it up on two large carts to carry off while the mule teams were filling themselves at the same time.

I went into the house [and] found it pretty well furnished. [I] made myself at home for half an hour, and had "to take a vituperous tongue wagging" from the old dame myself. Behind some crockery in an open cupboard I saw a pistol. This I confiscated and found four barrels loaded. This was contraband of war, so I had a right to "sequester it." The women were furious, but I only laughed at them. At 5 p.m., while watching the battlefield just as the sun was going down behind the tree tops, came the outburst of the Rebel attack and advance on our left at Bald Hill and Henry House Hill. The shells were bursting in the air above the woods while the discharges of musketry and artillery was incessant and terrible in volume.

At 6 p.m., long lines of wagons and ambulances began to file past towards Centreville, while wounded stragglers came from all points across fields en route for the same place. I watched the smoke of battle which came nearer every minute [and] talked with some of our soldiers who were falling back leisurely and with some wounded officers whom I knew. One of our colonels rode past slowly, he had been shot through the head which now had swollen to three times its natural size! Another had been shot through both eyes. Some were limping, others were being carried in blankets, a terrible sight. The stragglers were prowling around chicken coops and barns, but got nothing as everything eatable had long since been confiscated. Our teams were now harnessed up and moved towards Centreville just as our busy quartermaster had carted off the last load of hay and fodder found in the barn. Then the women came out on the verandah of the house to give us a parting curse setting off bunches of fire crackers. As they did so, [they] cheered for Jeff Davis and sang "the Bonnie Blue Flag" and clapped their hands. We moved off in no good humor, and going to a road to the right which had very few wagon trains on it, kept on until halted by a breakdown of a train ahead of us.

As we were ascending all the while, the battlefield came in sight in the now deepening shades of evening. Artillery firing was heard at intervals. The flashes were all along the hills in rear of Stone Bridge, while the faint sputtering of musketry were heard still away to our right where [the troops of Generals] Birney, [Isaac] Stevens, [John] Robinson and [James] Ricketts were holding the enemy at bay while our army was falling back over Stone Bridge and the upper fords to form a line along Cub Run. The Warrenton Pike was now crowded with men and wagons. Our trains struck more to the right and came on a good road but as it was all uphill we had to go slow. We soon stumbled over dead mules and broken down wagons which had lain here since 1861. Dead mules laid on both sides of the road while broken down wrecks of army wagons were in the road and in the woods. These had to be removed before we could pass, which took up much of our time. The rain began to fall heavily at 8 p.m. which had the effect of stopping the musketry fire across Bull Run, but the artillery fire was continued at intervals until 10 p.m. Captain McKelvey, our commissary, now came to us and directed the course of the wagon train. We turned into an old field near a deserted house and bivouacked in a small clump of scrub oaks and pines. Soon all were busy building fires and cooking what we had in the wagons. Many were eating and cooking until daylight. One wagon with General Heintzelman's mess chest went to Centreville so that he could get supplies. He and [the] staff were away all night. Lanterns were seen moving all night on the old Rebel forts at Centreville, while the sound of hundreds of axes were heard on all sides. Our engineers were putting Centreville in a state of defense, pulling down houses and mounting guns. At 11:30 p.m. all was quiet. Occasionally a musket shot was heard down in the valley where our forces were holding the line of Cub Run. . . .

September 1, 1862

At about midnight orders came to move Pope's wagon trains. Some officer who wore a straw hat was in charge of it all! All the teamsters were Negroes and they all rode on the "off mule." Our wagon train of four wagons moved in company with Pope's wagons, and we were soon on the road to Sangster's Station. There was fortunately a quartermaster at Centreville of Kearny's division and from him I succeeded in getting a horse. The night was very dark with light showers of rain. The roads were heavy and a throng of stragglers crowded it, [along with] teamsters who had lost their horses, sutlers, coffee boilers, and numbers of wounded soldiers. All were tramping towards Alexandria. We went in a southeast direction. For two or three miles the road was good, but we soon afterwards came to sunken roads which lay between high banks of sand and pools of water at the bottom. Our wagon wheels stuck and the mules were unable to pull them through. The mules from the rear wagons were taken out and hitched to the foremost team while the guard threw their arms into the wagons and put shoulders to the wheels. They thus got every wagon pulled through by these double teams, although it took over an hour to go half a mile. We came to Pope's Run, which is a stream about 200 feet wide with high banks on either side. . . . Pope's wagons were in advance of ours. The Negro teamsters got bewildered when in the middle of the stream and the wagons were near capsizing. But the officer in the straw hat put his pistol to the teamsters' heads, which he swore he would blow off if one of them were upset. The darkies rolled their eyes wonderfully at this, but managed to get the train over without mishap. We got to Sangster's Station about 1:30 a.m. Fires were burning all around it while soldiers were sleeping and cooking around them.

As Pope's wagons were going to Fairfax Court House, Lieutenant Gray of the guard and myself concluded not to go there as the roads were blocked with wagon trains. I got out my maps and we decided to make for the Old Ox Road, which leads to Occoquan and thus get to Alexandria by a route not impeded by trains. So we left Pope's train, and struck out at a smart pace. While crossing a small bridge made of poles, one of our teamsters drove to near the edge in the darkness when the whole floor of the bridge tilted and threw the wagon completely upside down into the dry bed of a creek! The pole broke short off at the whiffletrees, and thus released the mules. We had to roll the wagon over, unload it, get [it] up again and reload it, which took more than an hour. The wagon top frame was smashed and the cover daubed with mud. So these were left behind. On the other side of the bridge was a sutler's wagon which had been wrecked. Both axles were broken while the contents lay on the ground in confusion. The sutler had ridden the horses off for help probably, and as no one had been left to care for the stock it fell a prize in to our hands. Sardines, whiskey, cheese, boots, and other clothing were in the wreck. We helped ourselves very liberally, put some of the stuff into our wagons, and then moved on. While at Sangster's Station I noticed that our quartermasters there were loading up a large number of wagons in a frenzy of haste as the Rebels were sure to come in on them from Union Mills. As we were now going on an unknown road precautions were taken to make no unnecessary noise, while a portion of the guard were to proceed 200 yards or more in advance of the train.

We found the Ox Road, and were going at a smart pace, when musketry firing was heard behind us at Sangster's Station as we thought. Our teams were put on the gallop for several miles. When coming to another sandy road in a valley, the mules could not pull through, and we had to double teams again. The firing did not last long. One horse fell dead in his harness, and we halted to rest the other animals for half an hour or more when I again consulted my map. We had passed but few houses. They were all deserted by their occupants. We found a house empty by the roadside, and letting the mules stand in the road, [we] went into it and cooked a grand supper from the provender found in the sutler's wagon. Huge wood fires blazed in the chimneys, and the flame came out of the top of them like blast furnaces. We made a "good square meal" and proposed to stay here for the rest of the night. So the teamsters and guard, [and] clerks bunked down on the floors before good fires. A guard was placed on the train and the mules fed on corn husks found in the barn. . . .

About 3 a.m. a clatter of horses' hoofs up the road alarmed the guard, who awoke us, and grasped his arms. Rebel cavalry might be coming and the guard was "very shaky" until an officer rode up wearing a straw hat, who I recognized as the one who had formerly led our train from Centreville to Sangster's. He was now pretty full of whiskey and dictated orders to us in a premptory manner. [He] ordered us to put the fires out immediately, and move the train as the Rebels were coming down the road after us. Our mules were completely used and would not budge an inch. So we concluded to stay where we were until daylight anyhow. The officer swore roundly and wanted Lieutenant Gray to take fifteen men of the guard and join his cavalrymen, eighteen in number, who had now ridden up and to go back to find out, or skirmish with the enemy. We could not see this military maneuver in the same light as the officer, although a sergeant and ten men were willing to do so. Our presence was to be with the wagon train, which could not be left on the road to be plundered by the rest of the cavalrymen who did not propose to skirmish. So we told him we would not go with him or anyone else. He was in a great rage and left us, saying "that he was going to Alexandria and that the enemy would get us." His force followed him. They were much demoralized by whiskey. We posted guards 100 feet from the house and slept quietly until daylight. At sunrise I consulted my map and knew just where we were. As I knew that the Rebel bushwhackers were thick around Occoquan and Colchester, I changed our route so as to reach Accotink. We took the road past Carmel Church so as to get on the Pohick road. And after a good breakfast, [we] started the wagon train down road towards Accotink. The roads were now good and we went as fast as the guard could keep up with the wagons. Their rifles were all loaded as we might come across bushwhackers in the clumps of pine trees which lined the way for a mile or more.

While the train was going downhill last night in the rain storm the mules broke into a wild gallop and one of the Negro teamsters who was riding the off mule, fell off, and was run over by two wagons, breaking both of his legs. The wagons could not be stopped at once, but when we did stop [we] had to go back to find him laying helpless in the road, half smothered in the mud. Most fortunately a small shanty was near in the windows of which a dim light was burning. So three of the other teamsters carried him there. Much hollering and pounding at the door brought out an old white wooled Negro, half scared to death, who after much persuasion allowed the teamsters to enter. So we left him to his care and kept on our way. This teamster was no doubt asleep on his mule when he fell off. No surgeon being with us we had to leave him behind and we had to hurry on our way.

We passed several large houses which looked to be deserted, as we saw no one for miles, not an animal of any kind was visible. The fences were mostly gone or lay broken down. We halted the trains several times while we gathered a bushel or two of apples from two or three orchards which bordered the road. The sun came out bright at noon, dispelling the cold damp fog of the morning. About 1 o'clock we came to Pohick Church, an old familiar landmark where once our picket reserves had been stationed. Heaps of ashes and old bough houses were all around it, while all the pews [and] flooring had been torn up and used for fuel and rickety shelters along the road and on the borders of the woods.

We now went on more leisurely. And about 3 p.m., [we] arrived safely at Accotink village, and halted the wagons in the main street while we built fires and cooked dinner and fed the mules. A crowd of small boys and ragged old men gathered around us and assured us that no bushwhackers or guerillas had been in the vicinity for a month. They were in great fear however that a Rebel force would follow us as below Occoquan they were all secesh, while in the village most of the inhabitants were Union. One man who had once been postmaster at Alexandria was a thorough Union man. And he pressed myself and Lieutenant Gray of the train guard to dine with him, which we gladly accepted as he lived close by. So we went and had a good square meal and a good time. We had not taken a meal inside of a house for a year. So the furniture [and] carpets, which were good, made it feel strange to us and we felt the want of air in the close room. We had been used to eating our meals in the woods or under bough houses or tent flies, off of logs or cracker boxes, on tin plates and iron forks. And the sight of china, plated forks and spoons, with a white table cloth, nearly took our breath away. We had ham and eggs, with plenty of milk and wheat bread and ate as much as we could without being hoggish.

All being ready, the mules were hitched up and we started for Alexandria at 4 p.m., taking the gravel road by way of rear of Mount Vernon. [We] arrived at the head of King Street, Alexandria about 8 p.m. From telegraph headquarters at the Marshall house on King Street, we got information of where General Heintzelman could be found, which camps we were soon at, situated in a field on the old Fairfax Turnpike near the slave pen. The general and staff welcomed us gladly as we and the train had been given up for captured. Soon the wagons were unloaded, our tents put up, fires built, and we settled down early for a good sleep which we were in much need of. I showed General Heintzelman the route on the map which we had taken and was given much credit for getting in safe. . . .

Generals Heintzelman, Birney, and everyone of the old III Corps were in low spirits for the stunning facts were known of the death of General Phil Kearny at Chantilly. His dead body had been sent in by General Lee by flag of truce, robbed of money, watch, diamonds, and everything valuable. And bitter were the curses of both officers and men at the vile treatment he had received from Jackson, at whose headquarters he had laid dead all night of September 1.* The body now was in the hands of Dr. Brown [in] Alexandria [for] embalming for shipment to New York. All flags on the forts and headquarters were at half mast while the whole Army of the Potomac mourned inconsolably the tragic death of the Ney of the Union army.† No officer in the army was so much respected and known for cool bravery under fire, daring in judgment when a crisis occurred in battle, [and] leading charges in front of his command direct into the lines of the enemy regardless of personal danger. . . .

September 3, 1862

Fine day and quite warm. All were up by sunrise, cooking breakfast, smoking and cleaning up arms, saddles, [and] bridles. General Heintzelman went off at 10 a.m. to see General Pope at Alexandria, and with him went to see [General Henry] Halleck at the War Department at Washington. . . . I made a careful sketch of these headquarters this forenoon and by the maps got all necessary information from our staff and cavalry officers who visited us today relative to the last movements of this army and began a plan of battle of Chantilly for the general. I had made myself a drawing board of large size from part of a walnut door which I took from the large white house nearby on King Street. . . . Our men had demolished the furniture and had broken or carried off everything of value. . . . I worked by the light of four candles which were stuck into bayonets and then stuck into the drawing board. . . . General Pope resigned his command of the army this evening. . . .

Sneden would spend no more time in the field for the next thirteen months. The Union army, again under the command of George McClellan, pursued Lee into Maryland and ultimately fought a brutal stalemate battle at Antietam Creek on September 17. But Heintzelman's corps, depleted by weeks of almost continuous fighting, was held back to man the fortifications of Washington. Then in mid-October, Heintzelman was relieved from command of the III Corps by McClellan, part of a wholesale removal of high-ranking officers in the Army of the Potomac.

Heintzelman was immediately appointed commander of the military district of Washington,

* Contrary to Sneden's comment, there is no evidence that Stonewall Jackson's men robbed or mistreated Kearny's body. Lee ordered his aide-de-camp, Major Walter H. Taylor, to escort the body through the lines. Noted Taylor: "There was no place for exultation at the death of so gallant a man."

† Michel Ney was one of Napoleon's most aggressive generals.

Headquarters on the Old Fairfax Turnpike in foreground

Large house at head of King Street gutted by Zouaves in 1861
Owned by Captain Faulkner, C.S.A., of Black Horse Cavalry

Slave pen (deserted)

HEADQUARTERS OF MAJOR GENERAL HEINTZELMAN, III CORPS
Head of King Street and slave pen, Alexandria, Va., September 3, 1862.

supervising all of the fortifications surrounding the capital. With this new assignment, the general took most of his staff with him, including Sneden. Life as a soldier improved dramatically. Although he still spent long hours making maps, Sneden prepared them in the comfort of the indoors, first at headquarters in Alexandria, then at Robert E. Lee's home, Arlington, and eventually at a large office in Washington. He enjoyed reading many of the books in Lee's library and drawing a copy of the Custis and Washington family genealogies that hung on the wall. He spent evenings in the theater, at concerts, and on one occasion at Barnum's circus. He frequently played tourist, taking detailed notes of trips to see government buildings, the White House, the murals in the unfinished Capitol dome, and "the ugly looking Washington monument." Hastily prepared rations in the field were replaced by elegant meals in some of the city's finest restaurants or by sumptuous dinners at headquarters often attended by the wives of officers. When the weather was fair, he noted that "baseball matches and cricket are now played every day by the department clerks on the grounds back of the White House. Large crowds of ladies, citizens, and [soldiers] attend. A tent is pitched wherein refreshments are served after the games close." He frequented hotel bars, but he especially enjoyed the club near his headquarters in town, which he wrote "is very gay with song, speech, and the large punch bowl is well patronized."

THE "CONTRABAND" CAMP below Arlington House, Va. November 1862.

While life was good, Sneden could not escape observing the realities of a hard war. He commented on the large number of former slaves who had crowded into the nation's capital to escape not only bondage but also the brutality of life in war-torn Virginia. On occasion he talked to some of them. According to Sneden, some of General Lee's former slaves said "that Lee was a hard taskmaster." Nevertheless, like many of his fellow northern whites, Sneden showed little sympathy for these African Americans.

Of greater concern was the outcome of battles fought by the Army of the Potomac and the fate of his comrades in the field. He listened anxiously for news from Fredericksburg in December and Chancellorsville in May, only to be disappointed each time. In early July 1863, when Lee again invaded the North and ran into the Union army at Gettysburg, Sneden reported that "great excitement prevails in the city. Troops were marching through all of last night. Orderlies with clanking sabres were galloping through the streets. . . . All manners of rumors were circulating at the hotels." A few days later he exclaimed "the battle of Gettysburg has been fought and a glorious victory has been gained for the Union. . . . The crisis is over." He then noted that "the forces here are prepared for anything and eager for battle."

By early fall 1863, Sneden was ready for a new assignment in the field.

Chapter Five

Captured

Few enlisted men ever hoped to match Sneden's experience of wartime Washington. The Yankee private enjoyed access to the latest military intelligence, escape from the hardships and dangers of the front lines, and not least, the satisfaction of contributing to a great national cause. In October 1863, however, the army put an end to his evenings at Ford's Theatre and his gossiping with fellow soldiers in the bar of Willard's Hotel. New orders sent Sneden back into the field—still a private, still doing a staff officer's work. Once again he would make maps at a general's headquarters. This time he would be with David Birney, commander of Phil Kearny's old division in the III Corps, which then occupied the rolling Virginia farmland along the Rappahannock River.

Sneden's orders, in fact, resulted from a feud between generals. Since at least May, the contentious Birney had waged a war of red tape to secure the mapmaker's services. Thomas W. Egan, Sneden's friend and now colonel of the 40th New York, lent his support to Birney's effort. In repeated memoranda to the adjutant general of the army, they criticized Samuel Heintzelman for keeping Sneden on his staff after he left the III Corps.

Bad blood between the two generals may have played a part. The army had tried Birney for failing to obey Heintzelman's orders at the battle of Fair Oaks the previous year. But the tribunal exonerated him of the charges, and he went on to distinguish himself under fire several times over. Heintzelman fended off the requests for Sneden for six months. To counter Birney's appeal for the services of "this intelligent man," he praised the topographer's abilities as "much needed" in Washington. In the end, though, Birney won the argument.

For his part, Sneden asserted that he was "glad to leave the monotonous duty of map making, for the excitement of the field," although it is unclear whether he wrote these sentiments in his original diary or added them in his memoir written during the comfort of peacetime.

He packed up the maps and sketches he had copied for himself while working for Heintzelman and shipped them home. During a fifteen-day leave of absence, he went to New York and outfitted himself with new gear—boots, field glasses, a Remington pistol, and a set of new drafting instruments. Then, after one last indulgence of Ford's Theatre, he set off for the front.

On the day he left, he and some other soldiers missed the regular troop train and hopped on another one carrying fodder for the cavalry. It was an ill-omened choice. The hay caught fire, and the unscheduled passengers nearly burned alive. After they put out the fire, Sneden remarked at the destruction visible everywhere in the desolate counties of northern Virginia that they passed through. After two years of war, all he saw were "ruins of houses, blackened chimneys, and ruined cellars . . . where once perhaps had been a happy home."

When he reached the army, he visited his old regiment but hardly recognized the 40th New York. Hard fighting at Chancellorsville and Gettysburg had thinned the ranks of the soldiers of '61 and replaced them with strangers. He did find Ed Marshall, a quartermaster sergeant he knew from the early days of the regiment, and tented with him until he could report to General Birney and learn his specific duties.

Birney's triumph over Heintzelman proved to be short-lived. A day after reaching camp, Sneden discovered that yet another general wanted him. General William H. French's adjutant tracked down the mapmaker and told him his commanding officer desired his services. "French commands the III Corps," Sneden wrote with satisfaction at this news, "and I can do better there than at division [headquarters]."

While he waited for his superiors to decide what to do with him, other generals contrived at a grander rearrangement. The morning after Private Sneden and Sergeant Marshall "sat up most of the night recounting our experiences," Robert E. Lee began a sweeping move to turn the Union army's flank and interpose his Army of Northern Virginia between the Federals and Washington. The Southern force advanced, its left wing brushing up against the Blue Ridge Mountains, but under George G. Meade the Union forces retreated toward the capital and denied Lee his objective.

Meade repulsed the Confederates at Bristoe Station with heavy losses. The main outcome for Sneden was badly blistered feet. "I got on one of the wagons," he confessed after the retreat, "and rode the rest of the way to Alexandria. My civilized living in Washington made me as tender as a raw recruit." The first thing he did back in the capital was to buy a pair of boots "fit to march in."

After Bristoe Station the armies reversed roles. Then it was the Confederates' turn to give ground, with the Army of the Potomac in pursuit. Back where they had begun along the Rappahannock a month before, Meade forced a crossing at a place called Kelly's Ford. In this action, Sneden accompanied Birney's staff when they came under fire from Rebel artillery across the river. "Solid shot and shell struck and burst in the woods in all directions," he wrote. When a cannonball struck a tree right in front of his horse, the tree "came near falling on me."

After this skirmish, engineers threw pontoon bridges across the river, and Lee let the Union army advance, uncontested for the moment. As the temperature dropped and the hours of daylight shortened, both armies began the preliminaries of yet another campaign before they went into winter quarters. It would prove inconclusive as well. A cautious man, Meade wisely declined to attack Lee's strong defenses in what became known as the Mine Run campaign at the end of November—but not before the action ruined the reputation of the slow, incompetent General French.

In his last assignment for Birney, just before transferring to French's headquarters at the beginning of the Mine Run campaign, Sneden went over the battleground at Kelly's Ford to map the terrain in the autumn chill. He knew he was venturing into dangerous territory. Despite nominal Union occupation, that part of Piedmont, Virginia gave willing aid to partisan rangers, led by the most successful and feared Confederate practitioner of irregular warfare, John Singleton Mosby.

November 18, 1863

Cloudy and cold. Large fires were kept up in all the headquarters and camps. The trees and fence rails were being freely used by everyone. General Birney ordered me today to ride over to Kelly's Ford and make a survey and plan of the late battlefield there, to accompany his report of it to Washington.

I started about 10 a.m., went over to headquarters of Major General French commanding III Corps, and got Sergeant Alexander there to accompany me, as he had a theodolite and chain. We took one cavalryman with us, then rode to Rappahannock Station. . . . Part of the VI Corps were encamped around it. Riding three miles down river we came to Kellysville.

The woods were very dense and the roads narrow. Only two or three deserted houses of mean appearance were met with on the way. I made sketches of the Rebel works and rifle trenches, and chained the different distances between them. The two gun battery on the hill above was only partly finished. It was like the rest of the works, built of logs, with earth thrown up from the outside—parapet 4'6" high.

Our pontooniers were laying a third bridge below the mill. The few inhabitants kept

KELLY'S MILL
Kelly's Ford,
Rappahannock River, Va.,
November 8, 1863.

(*Left to right*) Kelly's house, cotton factory showing shot through chimney. Kelly's grist mill showing effect of artillery. Mill dam. Rappahannock River. Two deserted houses. Earthworks.

themselves shut up in their houses. No children were seen or any cattle or poultry, as the troops had cleaned the latter pretty well out after the battle of 7th November.

We met "Old Man Kelly," at the mill. He looked gloomy and sullen, and he being a rabid Rebel denounced our men in loud and futile oaths for stealing all his cattle and hogs. The mill was not in operation but two or three of our commissary wagons were at the entrance filling up with bags of corn meal and flour. Whether he was paid for it, I did not learn.

Lieutenant [William N.] Haymaker, quartermaster of [the] 63rd Pennsylvania Regiment was in charge of several hundred Rebel muskets which were stacked in the mill. These had been secured when the enemy threw them away in the stampede during the battle. They were very hastily and roughly made. The stocks were only partly finished. The barrels had "Richmond" stamped in the metal. They were probably made at the Tredegar Works, Richmond. While going through several deserted shanty looking houses, we unexpectedly came across a dead Rebel soldier. He laid on the side of the road near the mill dam wall. His leg had been wrenched off at the knee, exposing all the arteries and tissues, which had turned black. His face showed terrible agony. A black silk handkerchief was tightly bound around his leg above the wounded part. He was covered with dust and dirt, and his long yellow hair was matted with blood, presenting a terrible sight. A shell must have struck him and he had bled to death. Along the wall on the river bank laid two or three more dead Rebels. All had been shot in the back of the head, and must have died miserably. They were also covered with red mud, and lay in puddles of coagulated blood.

As these dead men had been overlooked by our surgeons and ambulance corps, Lieutenant Haymaker at the mill promised to have them buried at once. As our march from the ford to Brandy Station had been hurriedly made, during a thick fog, many of the Rebels must have crawled into the woods over the hills and died miserably. Several of their sharpshooters had been shot in the advance, and no one had ever searched for their bodies.

They disputed our advance, lying flat on the ground, with small piles of stones to shelter their heads, which remained there still, but no one went over the ground to ascertain whether they all got back or no. During the battle of [the] 7th a shot from one of our batteries then stationed at Mount Holly Church across the river had struck the chimney of the mill, carrying it half away. Others had struck the brick walls on [the] top story, shattering them for twenty feet downwards. The roof was riddled with shell. Part of the front wall had fallen down at the eaves. . . . Still another had struck the chimney of Kelly's house at [the] second story, passed through it, and went out at the other end, carrying away with it a clock on the mantel, just over the heads of several wounded Rebels who were then in the room. The fallen brick and dust covered them.

The cotton factory, a small building with [a] piazza at the head of the only street was shattered very much, while one side of the roof had been shot away. The only stove in the place was badly damaged by [a] shell which had torn its way through and had burst in the cellar. All the fences had been torn down and burnt by our troops when they bivouacked in the place [the] night of 8th November. After making the necessary measurements and sketches, we mounted and returned to headquarters.

As we left the ford at 6:30 p.m. night overtook us in the dark woods. We had eight miles to go, and we were very hungry and tired. We lost our way several times, although the cavalryman who came with us was supposed to know the roads.

We let our horses go as they would for two hours and at last came out on clear upland. The wagon tracks crossed each other, and bothered us as it was very dark with a light fog, so that roads were hard to be seen. The camp fires of the army however lit up the sky, and we rode straight as we could for it, and struck the railroad and then headquarters at 11 p.m. Having the countersign, we had no trouble with the rear picket line. After getting a hearty meal we sought our bunks as usual. I stayed with Alexander in his tent at corps headquarters that night.

Miller's house was a large plantation building on a high and commanding knoll about 1,000 yards from the Orange & Alexandria railroad. About two and one half miles [from] Culpeper which could be seen amid the trees over a long plain. . . .

Several log houses were in close proximity to Miller's house, which had been slave quarters. The staff of General W. H. French occupied the whole front ground of the rising knoll. A few trees were around the house whose sides showed bullet marks, and the front porch had been carried away by shells. It was painted white, and could be seen for miles over the plain below. The railroad embankment, crossed by a muddy stream and stone arched culvert,

"AUBURN," RESIDENCE OF JOHN MINOR BOTTS
Near Culpeper Court House, Va., October 10, 1863.

was perhaps twenty-five feet high. No cars were running as yet. Everything had to be hauled by teams from Kelly's Ford where were several pontoon bridges. General French occupied the first floor of the house. Not a vestige of furniture had been left in it by the owner.

John Minor Botts' house was in the plain below.* Our troops were now encamped around it. A cavalry battle had been fought around it, and his garden was all torn up by horses' hoofs, and ruined of course. John Minor Botts had been a congressman and since the war began declared himself to be "neutral." So his property and person was respected by both sides, and no plundering was allowed by either army of any of his property or stock. General Birney moved his headquarters to another house near Miller's, and I returned there on [the] morning of [the] 19th.

[I] reported, and set about making a large plan of the battle of Kelly's Ford for [Birney], and by 10 p.m. had it completed. General French wanted me to make another for him. And Adjutant General O. H. Hart of his staff made out an order transferring me to headquarters of [the] corps, which Captain Briscoe, of Birney's staff objected to, as I relieved him of making any drawings whatever as long as I was at Birney's headquarters. Both Briscoe and Sergeant Alexander at French's headquarters were very indifferent draughtsmen, though

*John Minor Botts (1802–1869), Whig congressman, Unionist, and warm hater of Jefferson Davis, tried to prevent Virginia's secession. With the declaration of martial law in 1862, the Confederate government imprisoned Botts in Richmond and then released him on parole on a farm he purchased in Culpeper County.

they had practical knowledge of civil engineering. Briscoe served as topographical engineer to General Phil Kearny during the second Bull Run campaign, was captured and sent to Libby Prison and afterwards exchanged when he was placed on General Birney's staff. I had first met Sergeant Alexander of [the] 5th Michigan, while in camp at Harrison's Landing, during the Peninsular Campaign and given him lessons in drawing and topography. (He was made lieutenant of engineers afterwards.)

November 19 and 20, 1863

Rainy, but warmer weather. A strong cavalry reconnaissance was made yesterday towards the fords of the Rapidan as ordered by General Meade which returned this afternoon, after some heavy skirmishing with the enemy. They report that Lee is now entrenching strongly along Mine Run, which is an affluent of the Rapidan River . . . between Jacob's Mill Ford and Germanna Ford. It runs south, through a valley bordered on both sides by gradual slopes, with here and there a farm house.

The enemy were seen felling trees along the front of the ridge on the farther side of the run. The main force of the enemy under General Lee were at Orange Court House with their pickets thrown forward to near Stevensburg and Richardsville, confronting our cavalry pickets there. The turnpike which ran out from Orange Court House was fortified by rails and low stone walls. The position at Mine Run was well chosen for defense. Its natural strength is of a formidable character, being a succession of ridges overlooking the northern bank by which an enemy must approach. These ridges are from thirty to one hundred feet above the level of the water. In front the ground is quite level, with but little woods affording cover, presenting every disadvantage for strategic movements. The enemy have transferred their line from the south side of the Rappahannock to the south side of the Rapidan, and blocks the Orange Turnpike and [the] plank road leading to Ely's Ford.

A council of war will be held at General Meade's headquarters today ([the] 20th) to determine further operations. I went over to General French's headquarters today, saw Adjutant General O. H. Hart there and delivered my map, returning at 11 p.m. The band played at General French's and Meade's quarters from 9 to 10:30 p.m.

November 21, 1863

I was ordered by General French to make [a] survey and plan of [the] battlefield at Rappahannock Station and started at 8 a.m. with Sergeant Alexander, with four detailed soldiers, and an army mule to carry the theodolite. The same route was gone over as when we went to make the Kelly's Ford survey.

We got there about 10 o'clock. The mule delayed us somewhat, as he wanted to throw off his load or climb a tree. After finishing up work, we went to Kelly's Ford again to verify some measurements made when last there. We halted on the outskirts of Kellysville at a small weatherbeaten shanty, which was occupied by an old woman and two young women. They were thorough "Secesh," and gave short defiant answers to several questions. We fastened up the mule in the front yard, built a fire and cooked our coffee and had dinner.

Alexander and the men went off to run the lines, taking their instruments and the mule, leaving myself and horse in the front yard of the house. As my Remington pistol wanted oiling and cleaning, I took it apart for this purpose. The three women of the house chaffed me, but finally begged for a chew of tobacco. I gave them half a plug, which they gnawed on voraciously. The old woman wanted then to borrow my horse, to cross the river to get her shoes mended at a shoemaker's at Wheatley village, a mile or so above the ford, and on being refused opened a tirade of abuse mixed with slang and oaths. I was so pestered with them, that I mounted and rode up on the hills back of the mill where I had an extended view of the country for miles on the other side of the river. . . .

The old woman wanted the horse to get word to the Rebel bushwhackers on the other side of the river to cross over and capture us. At a place known as "the stepping stones," 500 yards above Kelly's Mill, anyone could cross at low water on them. The river was high now, but a horse could ford it there. There [were] only five men [on] guard at the mill. The pontoon had been taken up, and had gone towards Brandy Station at 3:30 p.m. Lieutenant Haymaker had sent off all the captured muskets and other stuff from the mill, and was about leaving. So any armed party could have either shot or captured us easily, as the party were all strung out measuring the ground between the deserted Rebel works, and a corporal's guard was all of our force left at the ford to watch it until cavalry pickets could be established there later on.

I had finished sketching when a mounted man rode up near me on a fine horse and halted in the deserted work and without speaking or making any demonstration, began to survey intently the woods on the opposite side of the river. Alexander and his party were on the slope measuring towards us. The horseman wore blue trousers, rough gray overcoat, and slouch hat. He was a Rebel no doubt. No others were in sight. He rode slowly off to the woods in the rear while I hurried to the surveying party, who were finishing their work. And we all hastened down the hill and made preparations to leave at once.

It was now quite dark, and as the party left the house where we had been in the morning the women chaffed and said that "Mosby would pick us up before morning." We hurried on through the wood roads, and were lost several times. At one place we came across a dead mule or horse lying in the road, with its feet sticking up in the air as usual, when my horse shied, falling on his knees and nearly pitching me over his head. As all the rest of the party were on foot, they belabored the old mule with heavy sticks until they got him into a gallop for a mile. Here we met several crossroads in the woods, and were lost again for a long while. We had not a match in the party and could not see our compass.

We halted, and listened to what we supposed to be horses marching in our rear, and thinking that Mosby might be pursuing we hurried up that mule for all he was worth along some road on our left. My horse shied again at something and threw me off sideways into a clump of underbrush where trees had been felled.

I fell into a lot of wires, which had been strung from one stump to another, and was not hurt. It was a little lighter here, as some trees had been cut and we could get light from the sky. Examining these wires, we concluded that soldiers had strung them crosswise from tree stumps to make a dry bed. They were of telegraph wire, and we soon saw the poles and knew about where we were. I recognized a ruined barn, after riding several hundred feet in three or four different directions as one which we had passed in the morning and in a little while we got out of the woods on the clear ground.

The lights and fires at headquarters guided us, and we reached Miller's house about midnight. Lanterns with different colored glass are hoisted on the flagpoles at the several headquarters at night to enable orderlies and others to find them readily while carrying despatches. They served us now in good turn.

November 25, 1863

Fine day but cold. A general inspection of the whole army under General Meade was had this forenoon on the wide plateau in front of the range of hills where headquarters were located. The troops were in fine condition and looked fine, arms and bright uniforms glistened in the sun, bands playing while the whole marched past in review. It was 4 p.m. before the pageant was over. Several British officers were here to see it, who pronounced the whole army in fine condition. They were entertained by the officers of different headquarters, with great conviviality until a late hour, while the band played several English army tunes in the evening at headquarters of Generals Meade and French, where they were staying.

After seeing the review, I went with a friend to Culpeper Court House, about three miles up the railroad, it being the next station to Brandy Station. I made a good sketch of the town from the plain outside of the place first. . . . Our troops occupied the town. Few inhabitants were on the streets. It was a nice place, and had not suffered from the ravages of war thus far. I made a sketch of the quaint and ancient court house, which then was being used for a hospital for our troops. After going over the place we rode back to Brandy Station where I made another sketch. Also one of John Minor Botts' house, and got to headquarters at 6:30 p.m. and worked on maps with the help of four candles until 11:30 p.m. . . .

Some time after midnight an orderly dashed into these headquarters with despatches for General French. "Old Blinky," as we call him was asleep, but his Adjutant General O. Hart got him up and I think that the whole staff had a drink or two, as news came of a great Union victory at Chattanooga and at Lookout Mountain, Tennessee, where Grant had whipped Bragg completely, driving him out of sight beyond Missionary Ridge.* Hooker had

* General Ulysses S. Grant inflicted a stunning defeat on the Confederate army of General Braxton Bragg at Chattanooga, Tennessee.

View of Culpeper Court House, Va., 1863

carried the rocky mountain, driving out the enemy, capturing guns and over 4,000 prisoners. All were in good humor and spirits at the news, while maps were called for by the general, which I could not furnish.

I and Alexander were working on the Kelly's Ford map in our tents at the time by the light of five candles. We did no more work when the news came. The map is all finished except the view. The orderly rode post haste from General Meade's headquarters here. There they have a telegraph station, which connects directly with the War Department at Washington. So the news came very quick to us here. . . .

I made a sketch of these headquarters and that of General Meade's today. I had moved into a new tent, and had comfortable quarters for some days, hoping to finish up my maps at leisure, when an order was given to prepare for a forward movement tomorrow at daybreak. At a recent council of war held at General Meade's quarters this had been decided on. So after the review of the army yesterday this was made known to the troops, who were now cooking ten days' rations for the march while thousands of camp fires made the air smoky from plain to hill tops all around.

Adam's Express [a package delivery service], which ran regularly once a week, had brought thousands of boxes of good things for tomorrow would be Thanksgiving Day in camp. Now everyone was getting ready for a battle. I sent to my home at New York all my sketches, diary, memos, etc., as we had expected to have made a move towards the enemy some days ago, but the *New York Herald* published the fact at the time! and General Meade countermanded the order, as the enemy got the New York papers nearly as regularly as we did! The press was therefore denounced in no complimentary language by all the officers who knew of the movement and correspondents were now "snubbed" everywhere.

I was up most of the night at work on maps for the use of Generals Birney and French and at about 2 a.m. woke up Adjutant General Hart to give them to him. As I had work yet

MILLER'S HOUSE, HEADQUARTERS OF MAJOR GENERAL WILLIAM H. FRENCH, III ARMY CORPS
Brandy Station, Va., scene of raid by Mosby's guerrillas, November 27, 1863.

unfinished on the Kelly's Ford map, I was ordered to stay behind and try to complete it. All the clerks and most of the headquarters baggage would be left behind with a provost guard of ten men under a corporal.

I packed up my instruments however, and Alexander took some of my maps and other things in the wagon, as he was going forward with the corps in the morning. All were busy around . . . several staff officers' tents, packing up until a late hour. Colonel Thomas W. Egan of [the] 40th New York Regiment called to see me in the evening. He had yesterday presented General Birney with a new headquarters flag (a red flag with white Maltese cross). I showed him the route of march on the map. Artillery were moving and rumbling over the plain below us from midnight until 3 in the morning, when I turned in to get some sleep.

November 26 and 27, 1863

The bugles and drums aroused the whole army this morning at 4 a.m., while it was yet quite dark. The soldiers cooked their breakfasts and fell into line at 5 o'clock and long lines of wagons filed over the plain towards Culpeper Court House and to the several fords on the Rapidan where they would cross over and march against the enemy. The scene was splendid as the infantry, artillery and cavalry moved over the ground in three or four columns, stretching three or more miles with arms glistening in the sun which just began to show himself over the hill tops. Custer's cavalry passed close to our headquarters, with

"THE SHEBANG," QUARTERS OF THE U.S. SANITARY COMMISSION, BRANDY STATION, VA.

himself at the head, his long golden hair flowing over his shoulders much like a Rebel officer's style.* General French and staff moved off at the head of the III Corps. Birney's troops had the lead. They continued marching all day over the vast plain, losing themselves in the woods beyond Culpeper. Part of the V Corps did not break camp until near sundown. Soon the canvas tops of the wagons were seen moving in lines from all directions. The bugles of the artillery were heard, the bands did not play, but the men looked fine and went forward with vigor.

The canvas had been taken from the staff headquarters' shanties in front of Miller's house. They were built up at the sides with boards, logs and sods. They now looked like a lot of pig pens without roofs. Stoves, desks, broken chairs and stools were mixed in with straw beds, bags of oats, valises, and frying pans, kettles, barrels of pork and cracker boxes. Of those who were left behind at Miller's house were five or six officers' cooks, who occupied several log houses near the house. About ten clerks, who occupied the house, among two belonging to the 40th New York Regiment (Chamberlain and Brown); two clerks of the adjutant general, Thomas Walsh of [the] 74th New York Regiment, George Rhineheart of [the] same regiment, [Patrick V.] Halley, and others, including myself, all had orders to stay where they were until next day, when they were to go with the wagon train to Jacob's Mill Ford, thence to the

*Cavalry commander George Armstrong Custer was the youngest general in the Union army.

front. Ten armed soldiers under a sergeant and corporal were left as provost guard over the stores, officers, baggage, etc., which were lying loose in piles in front of the house.

Alexander had gone forward with the advance, and had taken my unfinished map of Kelly's Ford battlefield with him. So I finished up some loose sketches which I had made of General Meade's headquarters, the telegraph operator's camp, and the Sanitary Commission camp at a half demolished house known as "The Shebang." After a good dinner of roast beef, etc. I cleaned my Remington pistol, got my things together and going to the upper floor of the house made a good bed on the floor and slept until near sundown.

The day was bright and clear, but quite cold. The clerks built large fires in the wide fireplaces on the first floor, and brought their desks (which are portable and were carried in the wagons) into the house with their other baggage. There was no furniture in the house whatever but stools were taken from the deserted officers' shanties, and with a broken chair or two, we were housed and made comfortable. We had lots of good food, plenty of hot strong coffee, but not a thimble full of whiskey to keep Thanksgiving Day with. Two of the provost guard were on duty, the rest all slept or played cards on the straw beds left in the officers' shanties, now roofless.

Long lines of wagons were filing over the plain towards Culpeper at 5 p.m. The sun set finely, and a construction train of about 200 wagons, which contained pickaxes, shovels, etc., for entrenching purposes came to a halt and parked the wagons in rows, across the railroad embankment about 500 yards below the house, while the mules were unhitched and watered. The V Corps wagons in the woods in our rear started about sundown when we knew that all had gone forward and that we were isolated, with only ten muskets to protect us from any enemy.

This made me uneasy, and I proposed to the clerks to quit and join the construction train below in the plain who evidently were going to camp there all night. They had a guard on the wagons of course which with our provost of ten men would probably amount to thirty or forty muskets. None of the clerks were armed, neither were the cooks. I had the only pistol in the lot, but I was chaffed at by them, and they concluded that no enemy would disturb them. It was at the ensuing night that troubled me, as I remembered what the old woman at Kelly's Ford said on our leaving there "that Mosby would pick us up." About sundown we were nearly all engaged in pitching quoits near the house using horseshoes for that purpose.

Twilight had nearly gone, when as I looked at the woods across a small field in rear of the house I saw a line of horsemen behind the trees coming towards us at a walk, in column by twos. As they filed off to their left into the woods again, I noticed that they did not look like our cavalry, although they all wore blue overcoats like ours. Some wore slouch hats. More than half of them walked their horses slowly, as if to reconnoitre our position. I concluded that they were either Mosby's gang or Rebel cavalry of some sort, but on telling the boys, who saw them as well as myself, they laughed at my fears. Still I had a premeditation that something would happen before morning. A cold fog shut down at 7 p.m. so thick that objects fifty feet from the house could not be seen. This made it worse.

I warned the clerks that we had better start for the [wagon] train while we could find it in the fog, but it was of no use. Brown strung his banjo, and most of us sang songs in the large front room before a large log fire until 10:30 p.m. Before sundown I noticed three or four broken down horses (one of them was lame) around the house. I gave them lots of oats in a blanket which they ate voraciously. They then huddled together close to the rear of the house, out of the wind, seeming afraid of being left alone. Five men were on guard in front and rear of the house, but not twenty feet away from it, on account of the heavy fog which prevailed at 11 p.m.

I went upstairs and was about to make my bed on the floor in one of the empty rooms, but changed my mind, as if the enemy should come upon us I would be caught napping. I returned to the first floor where the fire was yet blazing in the large room, and concluded to keep awake all night. I made a good blanket bed in one corner on the floor. Walsh sat up with me. All the other clerks but [Charles] Colvin and Rhineheart had bunked on the floor across the hallway in another room. There was no fire in their room. I bid them "good night" about 11 p.m. saying in way of a joke "to look out for Mosby" or he would get them all before morning, and returned to the other room where the fire was, and smoked [my] pipe until midnight.

I went out and around the house at that hour. The cooks were snoring in one of the log houses. Only two men were on guard close to the house. They were very sleepy. The rest of the guard were asleep in the deserted officers' quarters. The fog was very cold and so thick that the trees around the house twenty feet off could hardly be seen. The corporal of the guard, Thomas Taber promised to rouse the men up and put eight on guard anyhow. I returned to Walsh. I got a fresh log for the fire, which blazed up brightly, and smoked half an hour, when going towards one of the windows in [the] rear of house, I was surprised to see ten or fifteen small fires of brush, which were built quite close to each other. They seemed to be not more than 500 feet away and appeared to be smothered or kept down. This showed a cavalry picket, and as no cavalry of ours should be there, as all had gone in advance of the army in the morning, I was confident that they must be of the party whom we all saw at sundown filing through the field and woods in our rear.

It was now 2 o'clock of the morning of 27th November. The fog was not so heavy, while the moon, scarcely perceptible, was struggling through masses of scud overhead. I awoke up all hands in the next room, explained what I had seen, and my reasons for quitting the house at once under cover of the fog, and gain our construction train. None were inclined to move from their comfortable beds of blankets. So I returned to the large room again. About 3 a.m., I went out and around the house saw but three guards, two of whom were very sleepy, and noticed that all the small fires which I had seen were now extinguished. I laid down on my blankets fully dressed with exception of overcoat, hat and boots. My satchel, containing clothing, razors, mathematical instruments, and several large roast beef sandwiches, put between two new tin plates, hung on the wall near me. My field glass [was] on the door knob, [my] pistol under my blanket pillow . . . in its holster. I kept my belt on as my prismatic compass was attached to it. Colvin and Rhineheart laid down in another corner of the room, and soon were sound asleep. Walsh dozed over the fire which was now very low, seated in an old broken chair, with pipe to console him.

I was very nervous and could not sleep for a long while. I dozed off in a cat nap at 3:45 a.m., and knew nothing more until awakened by a rough tap on the head with a pistol barrel. I was instantly awake, and was amazed to find a soldier kneeling beside me who wore blue clothes, and who cocked his pistol at once and pressing the muzzle to my head ordered me to "be silent or he would blow a hole through me." Then, in an undertone he told me to "get into my clothes right smart" as Mosby wanted me. At the same instant five or six other soldiers came in and immediately covered Walsh and Rhineheart with pistols demanding silence, then greenbacks. As they were all dressed in our army cavalry overcoats, I thought it was a huge joke at first played on us by our own cavalry, but was soon convinced that the enemy were upon us in reality. I got on my boots and coat the quickest I ever did, while one Rebel seized my pistol from under my pillow which he found fully loaded. . . .

Mosby himself interrogated me at once. He wanted to know where our cavalry were! And how many of them. He opened his blue cavalry overcoat, showing a Rebel uniform underneath. Of course I knew nothing about our cavalry and told him so, which he did not believe. After some hard words, he said, "it would be an easy thing for him to hang me up to one of the trees in front of the house." I said that it only showed a coward to treat unarmed men so. One of his officers . . . hearing me say that I would not give any information as to our forces, struck me with his pistol barrel over the right eye which stunned me for a minute. Then others rushed into the room and ordered me out with the rest advising haste, and I was hustled out by the gang to the front of the house.

Mosby was an undersized, thin visaged looking fellow, with a sickly looking yellow moustache. He wore a United States officer's blue overcoat over a uniform of gray, had on fine silk stitched top boots, which he had probably relieved some sutler's wagon of in some of his raids. On the outside of the house, I found the line of stationary cavalrymen, while eight or ten others were riding around the prisoners, some partly dressed or bareheaded, pointing their pistols, swearing, and demanding greenbacks.

The fog was quite thick yet. The scud was flying low and the air was quite cold and damp. Some of the prisoners handed up to the Rebels all they had. They did not get any of mine, as I dodged around in the crowd without being seen distinctly in the fog by the Rebel horsemen. I had only $8, as I did not see our paymaster when he was at headquarters some days before. Walsh, and several other clerks had been paid and he had to surrender his $86 quickly or be shot. I noticed that all the Rebel cavalry wore U.S. blue army overcoats over their gray uniforms underneath, and that they had two pistols in each holster beside those worn in their belts. These were without doubt the cavalry which we all had seen filing into the woods in [the] rear of the house while we were pitching at quoits at sundown. The capture was made so easily that it maddened me beyond conception and I bitterly regretted not going to the train alone.

The enemy were in a bad humor, as they had ridden some miles to capture us and got no valuable plunder. There was much officers' baggage in another room in the house, blankets, valises, etc., but in the darkness they were not discovered. There were piles of oats, and provisions, out of doors, some in the log houses near the house. These were not seen either by the enemy on account of darkness and fog. The Rebel troopers only came into the large room to capture three of us. As there were no blinds to the windows [they had] walked their horses up to them, and of course could look right in as the fire lit up everything plainly in it. I thought at one time that I heard a horse's step, and laid it to one of the wounded horses which were lying near the front door. . . . The Rebels had counted us and had heard the songs, but were now in a hurry to get away to attack the construction train, which was still parked across the railroad while all were yet asleep.

It was now near daybreak, and the fog was yet dense in the low grounds. All the rebel troopers mounted, and ordered us prisoners to march towards the railroad without noise or we would be instantly sabred. There were eleven of us and we started off in a line in front of the Rebel horsemen. We came to the high bank near the culvert on the track, clambered over it, and gained the level plain beyond. The faint glimmer of two or three camp fires through the fog showed where the train was parked. Some of us had left coats, hats, and shoes behind. There were five only who had overcoats. We were now crowded into a mass, and the dim outline of the wagons could be seen about 200 feet away.

The Rebel horsemen formed a long single line, when some one of them said to us "get in thar quick and loose them ar mules or get cut down where you are." There was no help for it, as we knew the Rebels would not scruple to murder us at once. So everyone made a rush for the wagons and mules while I heard Mosby give orders, "draw sabre, forward, charge." They came on at a sharp trot, driving us before them on the train like sheep. Not a sound came from the sleeping guard as we ran in upon the unsuspecting line of wagons. These were parked in three or four long lines, about twenty feet apart, about 200 wagons with the mules unharnessed, and all tied to the wagon poles with short ropes or halters. The guard on the train were in front about 200 feet distant. We struck the wagons in the rear and flank. The guard were all asleep. So were the teamsters, most of whom were Negroes and who were snoozing away inside the wagons.

As we struck the train, the Rebels yelled, and charged at full gallop between the wagons shooting into them: Everything now was uproar and confusion. The mules kicked and brayed. Pistol shots, yells, and curses were heard on all sides, all at once. Our guard on the wagons began firing right into the wagon train, while two or three wagon tops caught fire and the blaze soon made everything visible, while the Rebels yelled to the mules and shot at every teamster who showed himself. This continued for some minutes. I jumped in among four mules who were hitched with snap halters, [and] let two of them loose. They ran off into the fog to join many others who were running to the ditch at the foot of the railroad bank for water. They followed the "bell mule" as was their habit.

The firing from our guard now increased. A bullet whizzed past my right ear [and] struck the mule which I was trying to loosen from the pole, who let both hind legs go high in the air just missing me. I let go, and dodged under the wagon. The ground was level, and the bullets struck and whizzed past me, or hit the wheels. My eye was now so swollen that I could hardly see, while the blood covered my face, neck, and clothes. In the excitement I had taken little notice of the wound before. The pistol barrel had cut clear to the cheek bone. I had a white pocket handkerchief and bound it around my head.

The wagon tops were now burning, as was [the] hay and fodder inside. The Rebels were driving off all the mules in sight, while pistol firing and musketry from our wagon guard made it lively enough. I got under another wagon, when hearing a rumbling overhead, was somewhat surprised to see a large fat Negro drop from it to the ground, all in a heap quite close to me. He rolled his eyes, and seeing me, yelled "Lor gor amighty Massa don't burn my wagon."

At the same moment a Rebel horseman rode up, and pointing a pistol through the spokes of the wagon wheels, yelled to me "get out from under thar an ketch them mules." I got out quick, grabbed a mule at the wagon pole but he had tangled up his rope so that I could not unfasten him. I tried another, who broke his rope and dragged me off twenty feet or so. When he let go his hind feet, his hoofs fanned my face with the wind made by them. I had been covered with the Rebel's pistol until the mule got away with me tugging at the halter. He now rode on, and as I was in the fog now and out of the range of our rear guard musketry thought only of escape. The mules were yet in frantic fright braying, kicking, and streaming all over the ground in the fog on the gallop. I struck off towards the culvert in the railroad embankment where I knew there was a chance to get through, and good cover. This culvert was built of masonry, about fifteen feet wide and eight to ten high with a shallow stream running through it. I caught one of the runaway mules but could not mount him as he was so restless.

Just then a mounted Rebel came up and ordered me to mount or be shot. I asked him to "give me a foot," which to my surprise he did, having first dismounted himself to do so. He followed me up however and drove my mule clean over the embankment, with the flat of his sabre, where I found myself among a hundred or more mules, with Rebel horsemen guarding them, while upon some of the mules sat all my late companions who had been captured with me all looking woe begone and "tuckered out." Munson had escaped on muleback, however, but there were several new men who had just been captured from the train guard, five in number, also seven or eight Negro teamsters also captured. These were holding the mules, and all in mortal terror.

The firing of the wagon guard now died away. One or two balls came towards hitting some of the mules, and scaring the others, and at one time it looked like a general stampede. The Rebels now made haste to get away, as it was getting quite light, and their small numbers would soon be discovered to our men. The mules were driven loose, with the bell mule ahead as usual. There were over a hundred of them, all fat and in prime condition, for they only had to draw wagons filled with picks, shovels, ropes, etc., and made short marches with plenty of time for frequent rests. Part of the Rebel cavalry rode to the front. Some on each side, others in the rear to drive the mules up. All us prisoners were mounted on mules. The Negro teamsters had to walk or run, and keep up or be shot in their tracks. There were twenty-three of us prisoners now, all told. Streaks of light appeared in the east but a thin fog was in all the low grounds. The cavalcade headed straight for our late headquarters at Miller's house on the hill where we had left an hour or so before.

We passed within 100 feet of Miller's house. All was dark and quiet within. The rest of the clerks were not with us, and we wondered how they had been overlooked by Mosby, and were glad that they had time to hide or escape. I had left my horse in one of the log houses used for a stable. I did not say anything of this of course. Mosby did not know of it. Some of our fellows would get him instead. We crossed the field and woods at the rear of the house at a walk and took the wood road towards [the] Hazel River.

We had to ride the mules bareback, without halters. Some had broken their halters, others had a small piece of rope tied around the head. This was looped by us over the noses of the animal which served in a measure to hold him in, but they would very frequently slip off, and the army mule would have his own sweet will, and dash off sideways, endways and all kinds of way, while the luckless rider had to regain the dangling rope as best he may. To dismount or fall off was sure death from a Rebel pistol. The large drove of mules were driven in a herd loosely. They would break away on a gallop and a general stampede was had every few minutes while we had to follow suit. The Rebels cut long switches in the woods to drive up the stragglers.

My wounded face had now become very painful and swollen so that I could not see but with the other eye. The mule I rode was not a fat one, and the chafing was irksome. I was terribly thirsty too which was enhanced by my chewing up several small plans while it was yet dark. They were very important sketches of the routes to be followed by the III and V Corps now on the march to Mine Run.

Mosby was very anxious to get away, as he feared a cavalry pursuit. He hurried us up for several miles, as fast as the mules could be driven. I noticed when it got to be light that Mosby or any of his gang had not been hit or wounded at all, by the continuous firing of thirty or forty of our wagon guard indiscriminately in among, mules, wagons, and mounted rebels numbering 200 or more. It was wonderful bad shooting.

The Rebels were nearly all young men. Some looking not more than eighteen years old. They were dressed in home made jeans or wool, had very fine light built horses, good arms, and made long marches mostly at night, while a few ears of shelled corn was fed to the horses on the march. All the Rebels had on good top boots, the plunder of some unfortunate sutler's shop or wagon. There was little or no discipline in Mosby's gang. Captains and lieutenants were called Bill, Sam or Jim as the case might be, by the privates who seemed to be independent of the officers. Nothing but plunder kept them together. They seldom showed fight when attacked by our cavalry, and as they knew every bye road and short cuts through the woods from Loudoun County to Warrenton Junction managed to get away, when surprised or pursued. Their general rendezvous was at Aldie's Gap, in the Blue Ridge Mountains. . . .

One young horseman paid particular attention to me as we rode together conversing freely. He said that Mosby had been down to the construction train after sundown and in the dense fog then prevailing was taken for a Union officer. (He wore a U.S. blue overcoat.) He learned from the officer in charge of the train that it would hitch up and move at daylight. He rode through the camp, counted the wagons and guard and made up his mind to have most of them by attacking. He, unfortunately for us, scooped our party in at the same time.

After leaving our late headquarters at Miller's house the cavalcade of horsemen and about 117 loose mules went due westward three or four miles when we struck [the] Hazel River, a small stream branching from the Rappahannock.

The sun was just above the hill tops when we reached Woodville, a collection of a dozen houses, weatherbeaten and depopulated except at one or two houses where several women and Negroes were gathered to see us come up. Mosby had been here for a week or more only a short distance in our rear where he had made the place his headquarters. I noticed now that the mules were all very fine ones, all fat, and many were spotted light yellow, while others were all cream colored or dark red. The light colored ones were the most valuable. The Rebels were in high glee at the capture of so fine a lot. They were afraid that our cavalry would pursue them at daybreak or during the day and hurried both the mules and prisoners by roads only known to themselves. We waded the Hazel River, here only about 200 feet wide. The Negro teamsters who were prisoners like ourselves had to wade through it holding on to the mules. The water was breast high and cold, of course, as ice had made some days before.

A young Rebel rode alongside me all the way. He was not over seventeen. We conversed freely on the situation. He admired my waistcoat and sleeve buttons so much that I cut them off and gave them to him. They were staff buttons double gilt. He could sell them to the Rebel officers for $10 apiece in Confederate money. I reserved only two on my waistcoat, so he got ten. In return he kept the rest of the Rebels away from annoyance, saying that I was his prisoner. I had only $8 in greenbacks. My Rebel companion said that they were worthless in Richmond and offered me $10 in Confederate bills for them, knowing that I would be robbed by some of the gang at the first place we stopped at. I exchanged money with him. (When I did get to Richmond I found out that it took $25 of Confederate money to equal one of ours!) We arrived at Woodville about 5 a.m. and halted to count mules and prisoners.

The Rebel cavalrymen yelled and threw up their slouch hats, while the mules kicked, brayed and plunged in all sorts of ways. Mosby went into the best looking house and brought out a lot of women and Negro servants or slaves to look at us. We were a hard

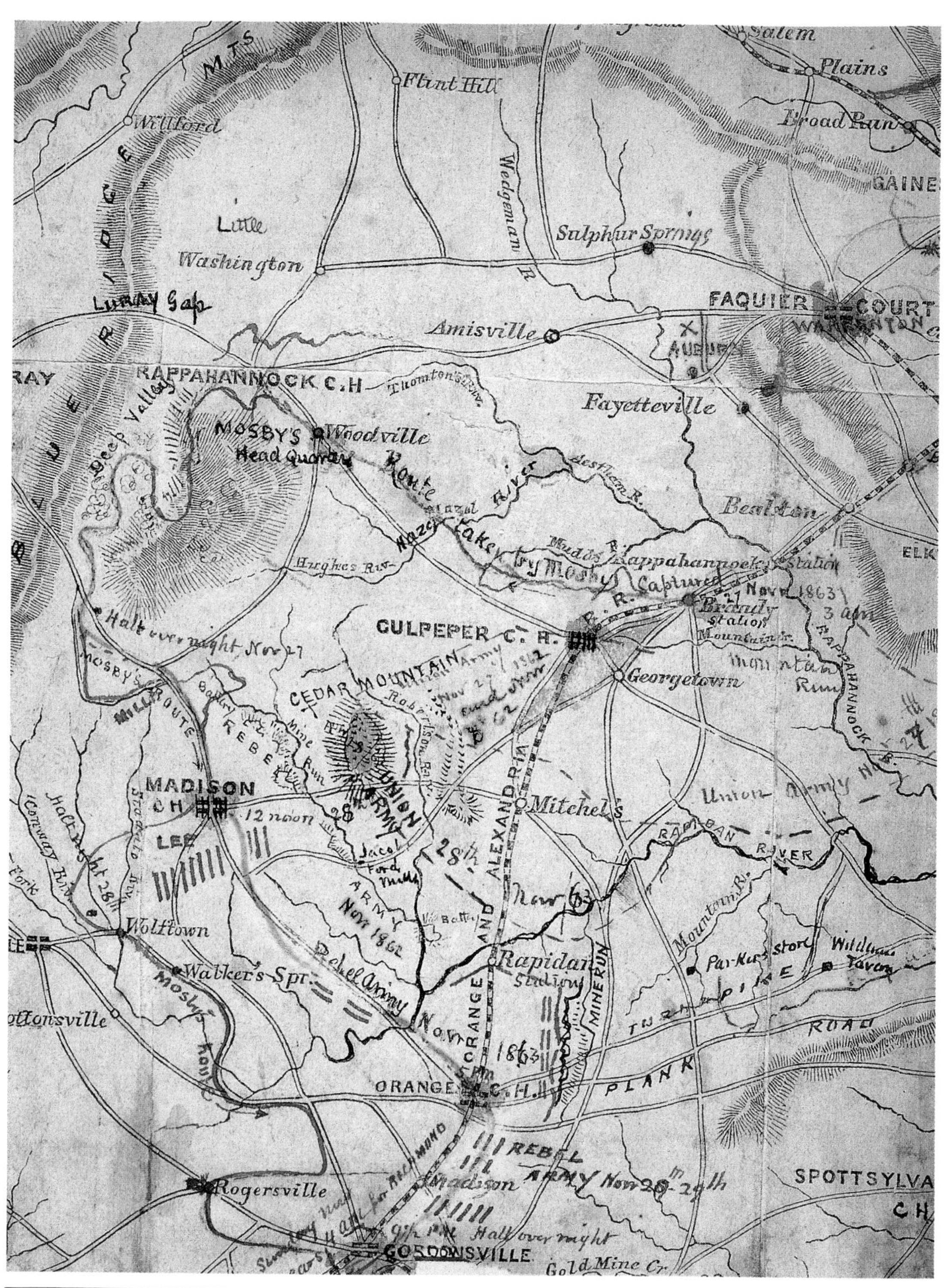

MAP SHOWING ROUTE TAKEN BY MOSBY WITH HIS PRISONERS

November 27 to 29, 1863. Route = red line.

looking crowd, some without shoes or hats, jaded and hungry. Walsh had no hat, so he had tied his blanket over his head, [which, with] his white hair and moustache, gave him the appearance of a mounted Arab. He scared the Negroes, who got away in the rear, especially when one of the Rebels yelled out, "say Yank where's your horns?" I must have made a sorry appearance, with eye all swollen up and the dried blood all over my face and neck. Mosby sent one of the gang to say that a "doctor would fix up my face" if I wanted him to do so. I declined his services however. With a wet handkerchief I now washed off most of the blood. [I] got a piece of rock salt from one of them. This I put in the wet handkerchief and bound it over the eye.

After staying a few minutes in which we were not allowed to dismount, the drove of mules were driven off ahead while we took another road, crossed fields and bye roads and went at a sharp trot. About sixty Rebels guarded us. The rear Rebel was a brutal looking fellow dressed in Zouave uniform, and a deserter from our army. He kept his pistol pointed at us, swearing he would shoot the first one of us who should get off, or be thrown by the mules we rode. Before reaching [the] Hazel River, during the darkness, I had stealthily managed to tear up all my papers, letters, and small plans, which I always carried, and had strewed the route with the pieces for a mile or more.

I also managed to unbuckle my belt, and throw it into some bushes while the mules were stampeding. This was to give a clue to any of our fellows who might come after us in pursuit. None came at this time. We all clung to our mules and went at a hard gallop two or three miles, when the pace was slackened. A Rebel lieutenant was in charge of the party and I rode next to him for some miles. He said that they had made a good haul and had been scouting along the Rappahannock at Kelly's Ford and above for over a week. When it was known that our army had marched they came in on our rear as was usual to pick up all they could get.

He said that he was going to take us to Madison Court House. I told him that our army would be there before we could get there. Mosby was not with us now or perhaps the line of march would be changed. Having made several maps of this region I was conversant with the situation of the towns in the vicinity but not the topography. I now told the lieutenant what he had missed in stores, private baggage, etc., left at Miller's house, which riled him much, and he was inclined to return there only that our fellows would now be waiting for him.

He informed me that all the headquarters clerks in the Rebel army had horses and carried either pistols or muskets. It was customary in our army for all soldiers who were detailed from their regiments to serve as clerks at headquarters to turn over all their arms and accouterments to the quartermasters before leaving camp. And none were allowed horses but march and keep up with the headquarters trains. So the Rebel custom was better than ours. For had we horses or arms, we would have all gotten away from Miller's house to the train before capture.

We were now approaching the high hills near Rappahannock Court House. The Blue Ridge Mountains were in plain view for miles on [the] right and left of us. Dense woods came up close to the road and the sun shone warm and brightly. We still kept hurrying on however, much to our discomfort, for we were now hungry, tired and chafed badly by riding bare-backed mules. We got a drink or two from the brooks which ran across the road, but had nothing to eat. The rest of the Rebels with the mules joined us while going through a large field about noon. They followed on behind for a mile. When they would stampede and come rushing on at full gallop we could not hold in our mules and the whole were on a dead run for a mile before we could hold up. The sun came out hot, which made us perspire freely, and we were thirsty too but could not stop for water. At 1:30 p.m. our pace was quickened to a gallop and we went several miles without holding up.

The road up the hills was narrow and full of stones. We could only go slow, and walked the mules all the way to the summit. This was a great relief, as by friction many of us had chafed off the skin on our legs from which blood had soaked through to the mules' hide. The road wound up to the steep summit when all held up to give men and animals a breathing spell. The summit was nearly level for hundreds of acres, covered with a short grass yet quite green, which the horses and mules ate voraciously. The sun had gone down and the air grew chilly. Out of the grassy surface grew hundreds of small hillocks covered with pine trees, light green in color. They looked like so many islands in a lake. The view was for many miles in extent, but the dark shadows were in the deep ravines below, and slight wreaths of fog were forming in them. The Blue Ridge stood up against the sky like a black wall. I was sorry that we could not have got here during the earlier part of the day so as to have a better view.

We had passed only three or four tumble down half ruined houses since leaving Woodville, and had not met a single human being or animal thus far. After the mules and horses had eaten of the grass for twenty minutes or so, without dismounting we started off in single file to descend into the lowlands. Mosby, and most of his men with the loose mules had left us, but the twenty-three Rebel cavalry with the lieutenant guarded us closely. The Negroes captured rode on mules since leaving Woodville. They, knowing the country, were liable to get away, or drop off their mules while going through the woods. They were eight in number, and two cavalrymen rode close to them all the time, pistol in hand ready to shoot them instantly if they fell off their mule or tried to run away. These Negroes were in mortal terror all the time, rolled their eyes, but said nothing. The Rebels questioned them closely but could get no information of the Union army. They were all contrabands however and had run away from their masters in Culpeper and vicinity, and had just been put at work driving teams when captured. A mule will travel faster and do more pulling when a Negro yells or talks to them, than any white man ever was known could make do.

We now filed down through a deep mountain gorge with ragged sides covered with trees and huge boulders. . . . We found a good hard road at the bottom of the hills, and after many turnings came upon large level fields which were cut up into wide ditches eight or ten feet wide, and full of water. There was nothing left but to jump these on our mules. The Rebel cavalry horses went over easily, but our mules balked of course, pitching us over their heads, and running every way but the right one. The Rebels covered us with their pistols, and we had to catch the mules again and mount. My mule cleared three or four of these ditches in good style, so I had no trouble. It was now 9:30 p.m. starlight and quite cold fog in the low grounds. We came up to a farm house with several outbuildings and log houses around it.

After a short halt in which the Rebel lieutenant consulted with the snuff colored proprietor about keeping and feeding us overnight, we moved on to the next farm house to try there. The party were too much for this old farmer to feed so he recommended us farther on. This farmer had good reasons for not entertaining us, as his payment would be made in a promissory note charged to the Confederate government payable "After the War" he did not "see it" in this light. So we had to gull the next farmer to board us at the bogus government's expense. After a ride of a mile or more, we came to another farm house. He, hearing the tramp of horses, was at his front gate. We halted 150 feet away while he and the lieutenant signalled by motions of arms. Everything was all right here. So we all dismounted, led our respective mules to a fenced in enclosure or corral, and left them for the night.

It was now 11 p.m. and we were all fagged out, sore, hungry and thirsty. A large log house near the dwelling which had been used as a kitchen was assigned to us. We were marched in and left to ourselves for a while. A large fire was built of large logs in the huge fireplace. Buckets of well water were brought with gourds to drink out of. Then those who had pipes and tobacco smoked, passing the pipes to those who had none. I had a good stock of tobacco, and shared it all with my companions in misery. The Negro prisoners were taken somewhere else. There were two or three long benches in the room, and [a] pine table. The windows were covered with solid board shutters tightly closed and nailed from the outside. There were five or six Rebel guard kept on the outside all night. The place was very clean anyhow.

About midnight there came two Negroes bringing a large wooden trencher of fresh boiled beef cut into small junks, with several large loaves or "pones" of hot corn bread. No knives or forks were had so we used our fingers as old Adam had to do. The rations were divided as equally as could be guessed and we ate like wild animals as long as the food lasted. Then five Rebel guards came in not armed as far as we could see and said that "we must sleep on the flo" and that they would sleep with us. Those who had overcoats or blankets soon lay down on the clean floor and being thoroughly exhausted were all asleep in a little while. I could not sleep for hours and as I listened to the pacing up and down of the Rebel guard outside, thought over all the things which had happened since the night before.

November 28, 1863

We were all up at break of day about 4:30 a.m. and after washing in the horse trough, and then getting a light breakfast of pieces of fat bacon and a small corn pone, were marched to the corral to catch our mules. These were all frisky enough, plunging and kicking when we went into the pen to catch them. I could not get the mule I had ridden yesterday, and took my chances with another one. The Rebel cavalry horses were fed on shelled corn. We saw the Negroes again this morning, who were shelling the corn very fast by rubbing one ear upon the other in their hands. We were all on muleback by 6 a.m., and started south towards Madison Court House. The road was good and we all felt much better, still the bare backs of the mules cut us terribly. Blankets and overcoats were used for saddles. My mule was fractious as [were] many more. . . .

We passed several large plantation houses which were a long distance from the road. Log barns were numerous. Good fences were met with as the contending armies had not yet passed over the ground. A stranger joined us at where we last left. He was a thick set ferocious looking Rebel, and was on a scout. The others called him major. He outranked the lieutenant, and now took command of the party. He was dressed in gray home made cloth, but had a fine spirited horse. He carried two large old fashioned pistols in the holsters, and two revolvers in his belt. He soon introduced himself to us by ordering us "to keep closed up" or he would blow holes through us. He led the whole party at a fast trot for miles without stopping which shook us up in a bad way. He swore like a dragoon all the time, and appeared to be half drunk on the vile pine top whiskey made by the farmers in these parts. He was uncertain as to the roads we were on and halted many times. [He] sent a cavalryman over the hills to scout, and when he returned and reported we would move on again. He gave the guard orders to "shoot the first Yank who should tumble off his mule" and we were all afraid of the bully while he was with us. . . .

It was now 4:30 p.m. and the sun was going down behind the mountain tops. We turned back in our tracks, taking short cuts across fields, halting to let the gate bars down, and struck into a narrow road through the woods, which was full of stumps and wagon ruts. The mules stumbled, throwing the prisoners over their heads, and hurting them badly. They were instantly covered with pistols and told to "get up thar lively and catch a mule." Many got on other mules than which they had ridden before. My mule was a light colored one and better trained. All I could do was to hold on by his mane and let him run. Walsh was thrown two or three times, as were Halley and others. The road was so blocked with old fallen trees that a halt was called several times, during which we distinctly heard the booming of cannon far to the south of us. I knew that our army were now fighting on the Rapidan somewhere near Mine Run and told the Rebel lieutenant so. We now had only twenty-three Rebel cavalrymen as guard as the rest turned off to the left just before getting through half of the woods. We kept on at a walk for a mile or so when we came to a hill at sundown at the bottom of which was a shallow river or run, with a village on the other side. . . .

We forded several other small streams and by 4:30 p.m., approached near to Madison Court House, whose white houses and steeples came in view. We passed through it on the outskirts only, [and] could see nice gardens and handsome dwellings, but very few inhabitants. We halted near a hotel or tavern of some kind, while the major and lieutenant went in "to liquor up." Many of the Rebel privates went in also to get their canteens filled. These canteens were unlike those used in the Union army, being small kegs made of wood with a strap attached. They were plugged either by a wooden bung or a corncob. They held about half a gallon, some a gallon. These were filled with the best pine top whiskey at a rate of $20 a gallon. About $200 had been taken from those captured, so the Rebels had plenty of money. Mosby got none of this, only those of his gang who had robbed us before leaving Miller's house. We sat on our mules in the street while several old men and Negroes stood looking at us, while women were seen at the windows. Soon we heard distant cannonading, and the major and lieutenant came out and ordered us to march.

The major left us here, much to our relief. The lieutenant now rode ahead, and we struck off to the right, and were soon in woods and rough ground. We had to ford several wide but shallow streams and came to the outskirts of Wolftown, a miserable collection of weather-beaten houses at about 9 p.m. it being quite dark. Here we were put into a log barn or out-house near a good sized dwelling, where we got corn pone in small quantities, one small cake for each, as large as a breakfast roll, some water, but nothing else. We slept on the barn floor with no light but a lantern with one Rebel guard inside, who was relieved every two hours. The weather was milder and it began to rain about 10 p.m., continuing all night. The mules which we had ridden were put into a corral or somewhere by two Negroes belonging to the place. The Negro prisoners were confined in some other barn under guard.

There were two or three guard on the building where we were confined. We slept on a pole floor as best we could, and could not smoke our pipes as the guard would not give us a light and our matches were all gone. The windows were high up, so that we could not get out or reach them. We passed a miserable night but had some sleep as we were very tired. The dirty paned lantern threw an uncertain light on beams hanging with cobwebs, but there was no hay or anything softer to lie on than our overcoats and blankets spread on the corrugated floor, composed of poles laid close together. One of the guard who came on duty towards morning was pretty well filled up with pine whiskey, and got to be quite talkative to several of us who could not sleep. He said that there was a big fight going on down the plank road and the Yanks were "getting whipped out of thar boots," which of course we would not believe. He finally got sleepy and dozed off on a horse block until relieved by another guard. The rain pattered on the roof, and we were soon all asleep.

November 29, 1863

We were all up at 6 a.m. and were served with some cold corn bread and a thick slice of bacon. We had to catch our mules in the corral about 200 feet from the house, and mount as usual. It rained and drizzled all day. The lieutenant in charge had a long conversation with the old butternut clothed proprietor, who pointed to [the] southwest. We struck a good road leading to Walker's Spring and got there in an hour. There was evidences of a recent encampment here, as the numerous brush shelters showed. We had but one canteen in the party. This was filled, and we all had a drink of fine water, which was handed up to us on muleback by the Negro prisoners. Soon we heard artillery firing and met several Rebel scouts coming towards us during the next three or four miles of our journey. A halt was had every time while they talked to the lieutenant, far away not to be heard by us.

The scouts were dressed as citizens, in gray homespun clothes, with antiquated cartridge belts around the waist. All had muskets but no bayonets. Several had powder horns slung round them, and carried double barreled shotguns. The lieutenant had filled pretty well up with pine top whiskey, as well as nearly all the guard. They grew insolent, and ordered us to keep closed up or be shot. At one time while going at a sharp trot the lieutenant, being ahead drew his pistol, and pointing it at us swore he would shoot us off the mules. We all laid along the neck of our mules flat, and for a mile it was rather uncomfortable riding.

We struck into a wooded road, and went lively for some time, when all at once several pistol shots were fired in succession at the rear of our cavalcade. We kept on at the gallop for a while, when two of our mounted guard rode up from behind, and reported to the lieutenant that they had shot "two of the coons, who fell off their mules purposely to escape." These were two of the Negro prisoners, who knowing the country had made an attempt to escape and were at once riddled with bullets. We were warned not to fall off our mules or we would be treated in the same way. We kept on, and reached a small collection of houses called Rogersville.

We did not stop here, but pushed on, it now rained hard, and we were pretty well wet through. We left the main road, going over fields and along several sunken roads, some of which were mere gullies on the hillsides fringed with scrub oak and pine trees, when rounding a turn in the road came again upon the drove of captured mules, which were being driven by about thirty Rebel cavalry of Mosby. Some of these had long whips, others switches. As we came up the whole drove stampeded down the road at [a] full gallop, while our mules ran away with us into the mass and we were all mixed up for a long time. Amid yells, curses, and cracking of whips we rode through the mass as best we could.

We approached the wooded bluffs of Gordonsville and soon rode through part of the town towards the railroad depot, where we turned into a large field of red mud and water and were halted a while. Then moved into a small clump of gnarled trees and bushes, while the lieutenant, with the drove of mules, went to see the provost marshal to turn us over to his custody. We were surrounded by lots of Negroes, and the rebel citizens and Negroes stared at us in wonder. One of the guards told them that we were "a lot of Yankee devils goin ter Richmond." They thereupon fell farther back, while the Negroes rolled their eyeballs in a frightened way. We were now ordered to dismount and as we tumbled off the mules were so sore and tired, that it was some minutes before we could walk a step. The blood had come through our trousers, sticking to the mules' hide. We all presented a jaded and dejected appearance and were splashed all over with red mud. Wet and hungry as we were, we could get nothing to eat or drink.

Chapter Six

"On to Richmond!"

Taunted by curious civilians, the prisoners shuffled through the small but busy crossroads of Gordonsville, sixty miles northwest of Richmond. At a shack by the rail line, the local provost marshal took charge of the exhausted men in blue. When a Confederate officer wrote their names "in a ragged book, the leaves of which were of brown wrapping paper," Sneden took the first formal step into the Confederate prison system.

With him were twelve other men captured near Brandy Station. Their guards herded them into a barn for the night with twenty more recent Union captives, who told them all about the first day of the Mine Run campaign. Later their jailors returned carrying "a half cask of water, with two rusty tin dippers [and] a lot of ship biscuit and several junks of raw pork. . . . We were all very hungry and the rye flour biscuit was a luxury." In good spirits despite their fatigue and blisters, the prisoners stayed up late smoking their pipes and swapping capture stories.

The next morning, guards marched them to the rail yard and put them on two empty gunpowder cars made of sheet iron nailed to wooden frames, with one tiny ventilation window. Sneden elbowed his way to the door and watched through the crack while they waited on a siding. He saw that the stationmaster had coupled their cars onto the tail end of an ammunition train consisting of other powder cars and flatcars loaded with gun carriages and artillery shells. With a piece of chalk, one of the prisoners managed to write the Union slogan on the outside of the door: "On to Richmond!" This, Sneden said, infuriated the guards.

When the signal came at mid-morning, the wood-burning engine labored to pull its heavy load into motion, one swaying, squealing car after another. As they rolled slowly to the southeast, Sneden noted that the countryside appeared "very flat and swampy in many places, with patches of woods or deserted corn fields."

The ammunition train entered Richmond from its least attractive approach. Travelers often remarked on the splendid aspect of the city when they first viewed it from the James River, either coming from the west on canal boats or from the east by steamer. The road from the south showed off the city even better. From that perspective, the state capitol, a colonnaded Roman temple designed by Jefferson, towered over the business district that sloped down to the riverfront. Sneden saw none of that as his train chugged in from the north, over the Chickahominy swamp and through vast areas of felled trees and earthworks built by impressed African Americans and ringing the city three times over. Still, he said, "the city looked charming to us who had been so long living in the dark woods."

After two years of war, Richmond was beginning to fray about the edges. The seceded states had moved their capital there in 1861 not only for political reasons but also because the city boasted the largest concentration of heavy industry in the South. It became the workshop of the Confederacy as well as its political center. In addition to the national legislature and the bureaucracy that sprang up with it, Richmond hosted the largest military hospital complex in the world. Refugees poured into town from every Union-occupied county in the state.

Also among the residents were war profiteers, blockade runners with pocketfuls of London gold, civilians who had finagled exemption from military service, and soldiers who had eluded the provost marshal for some fun in town. These and other adventurers rubbed shoulders in the seamier precincts below Capitol Square and provided ample patronage for the brothels and bars and gambling dens that did a thriving business despite wartime inflation.

As a result, the city's prewar population of under forty thousand had more than doubled. Sneden and his friends represented yet another source of congestion, for in the waning days of 1863, Richmond housed thousands of prisoners of war. It put Union officers in the best-known prison, Libby, a ship chandler's warehouse on the waterfront. Southern civilians accused of disloyalty saw the inside of a warehouse named Castle Thunder. The unluckiest Union enlisted men shivered in tents on Belle Isle in the middle of the river. More fortunate ones lived in converted tobacco warehouses, the main one being Sneden's new home one block north of Libby.

In prison Sneden found it harder to keep his diary. Still, he managed to find enough loose pages and pencil stubs to keep writing. He later supplemented these with a partially used notebook and a New Testament, in the margins of which he made shorthand notations. After the war, these aids to memory enabled him to fill thousands of manuscript pages.

November 30, 1863

. . . We were hustled out of the cars, and put under a detachment of the home reserve guard, who were dressed in homespun clothes, dirty slouching looking young men and old men mixed together. They were forty in number under an officer of some kind for he wore nothing to denote his rank. We were surrounded by a mixed crowd of citizens and Negroes. The guard soon marched us off in single file to Libby Prison. We halted in front of another prison known as Castle Thunder on Cary Street and 18th Street which was a gloomy dirty looking brick building with a high wall on one side and a large arched entrance, where stood held by a chain an immense fierce looking dog, a species of Russian bloodhound. On the second story on a sort of gallery or platform paced two Rebel guards, all the windows were heavily barred. Some of the loungers around the entrance crowded around us, saying "What did you uns come to Richmond for," etc., etc. One of our fellows said we had come to steal niggers. This made them howling mad, and one fellow cocked his musket, intending to shoot but just then we were ordered to move on, going a few hundred yards we came to Libby Prison, a dingy three story brick building facing Cary Street with the canal dock in the rear. Guards were pacing all around it on the sidewalk and were a slovenly looking set, with slouch hats, long hair and old fashioned muskets.

We were ushered into a small room, in which at a desk sat Major Thomas P. Turner,* head jailor, one of the most villanious looking rebels to be met with anywhere. With scowl-

*Like other prisoners of war writing afterward, Sneden sometimes confused Thomas Pratt Turner with Richard R. Turner, commonly called Dick Turner, a private soldier in charge of counting prisoners.

Castle Thunder, Richmond, Va.
19th and Cary Streets.
Captain Alexander, C.S.A., jailor. 1863.

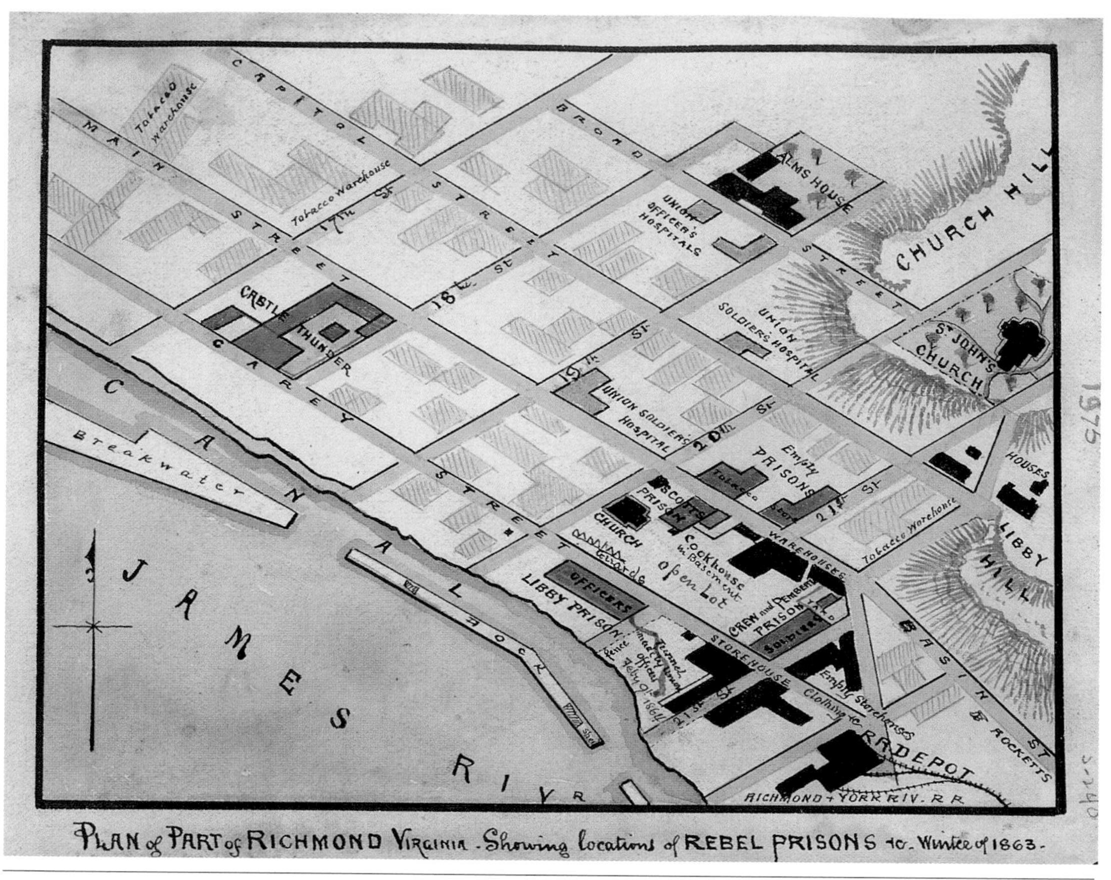

PLAN OF PART OF RICHMOND, VA.
Showing locations of Rebel prisons. Winter, 1863.

ing black countenance he sat in an armchair, while around him were a dozen or so prisoners just arrived, some of whom were sailors of [the] U.S. Navy. Several piles of greenbacks and coins were on the desk, and as he entered the names of the different owners from whom they had been taken, he scooped up the money, put it in his trouser pocket, and told the deluded prisoners that "it all would be returned to them when they were exchanged"!

Turner now entered all our names in a large book, with name, regiment, and rank of each. We were then searched by a tall Rebel, who was dressed in a clean new uniform, with a gilt cord around his hat. Two other Rebels in citizens' clothes with pistols in their belts went among us and felt the seams of our clothing for money. They got none however. I had a small pocket compass which I had thus far kept secreted in my boot, some plug tobacco, two lead pencils, and [a] small memo book. These I was allowed to retain. I was examined separately by the tall Rebel sergeant in an adjoining room. He did not see the compass. The others were taken into this room and were forced to take off their shoes even. When

CREW AND PEMBERTON PRISON, RICHMOND, VA.
1,600 prisoners of war confined December to February 1863.
The building was owned by Majors Crew and Pemberton and used as a tobacco factory.

Turner learned that Mosby had captured us by the written report sent, he relaxed his scowling visage, and secretly felt elated probably at the large capture of mules.

We filed out on the sidewalk, and waited some time. All the windows on [the] second and third floors were open, at which we could see our officers who asked questions about the army. We told them that the Rebels were being whipped at Mine Run yesterday, when many of them cheered. Some were in red shirts, others had none apparently, but kept their coats buttoned up close to the throat although it was a warm day. We asked how many of them were in there. They said eleven hundred. There were no iron bars on the windows at this time excepting on the first or ground floor. The officers did not look out, but kept back some feet from the window. In the letter sent by Mosby to Turner, he had the assurance to say that he nearly captured General French. We all laughed at this while Turner swore at us and ordered a new guard to "take us to Pemberton." We were forthwith marched up the street and nearly opposite to a large five story brick building known as Crew and Pemberton tobacco factory now used as another prison. . . .

As we passed out of the Libby, many heads were stuck out of the windows on the upper stories wanting to know where we were from, and the army news. We shouted back all we knew which encouraged them, as we could hear cheering about the hubbub of voices. They were our officers as we saw by their uniforms, though many were in their shirt sleeves. We told them "that Meade was after Uncle Bob" (meaning Lee, as the Rebels called him) and meant business too. Soon we filed into the building and ascended steep stairs, at the head of which was a double planked door, secured by large bolts and chains. Two loopholes were in this door that muskets could be fired through into the room. Here we met a hundred or so of our boys. Cavalry, infantry, and artillery, some in torn and patched uniforms, others in shirt sleeves, others half naked, all looking dirty, squalid, dejected and half starved in appearance. We were assailed with "fresh fish. What army do you belong to? Where were you captured? What news? Will there be exchange?" Amid cat calls, and "stand back give them air," and numberless others tramping over head, and tumbling down another stairs from the upper floors to ask us the same questions, in return [we] wanted to know ourselves if we could get anything to eat, and where.

We were told that "the grub had been given out in the morning, and that nothing more was to be had until the morrow." We did not relish this much, as we had nothing to eat since 4 o'clock in the morning and that was only some scraps which only some of us had served from the rations at Gordonsville. Some of us however were given something to eat . . . which however consisted of a few sweet potatoes boiled to mush, and half rotten at that.

I, with three others, went up to the top story, and finding a lot of men-of-wars men who were prisoners also, got acquainted soon, and made my bed on the floor with my only blanket, and for my pillow had a block of cedar wood which I had picked up at Gordonsville, and which had served thus far for a seat, by setting it on end. This was handy for the same purpose, and I stuck to it for a long while. On the second floor were numerous tobacco presses through the centre of the room, but all the other floors were devoid of any seat, bunk, or other accommodation. The men sat huddled on the floor in groups. Some were playing cards, others sleeping on the bare plank floor, others walking up and down listlessly, all wearing a haggard, starving, and sickly appearance. We were shouted to "keep back from the windows," as the Rebel guards below would shoot us if seen.

So we passed the time wandering around among the masses, "getting the hang of things" as they say at Boston. There were about 500 of us prisoners cooped up on these three floors. The building was about 50 feet front by 200 deep, and was divided in the middle throughout by a twelve inch brick wall excepting on the top floor. The arches in this wall had been bricked up, which effectually separated us from the other half. A long rough plank table was on the top floor where the rations were distributed by one of our sailors who seemed to be "boss," and a general inspector over us. The men were divided into messes of ten each and we had roll call every morning.

When darkness came on, we sat in groups on the floor. Some sang songs, others talking loudly, and as no lights were allowed, we "worried it out" until 9 p.m., when I, with others, sought our hard beds on the floor. The cry of "lights out" at the Libby just across the street by the guards was heard, and we of our party lay down dejected, sore, and fearfully hungry to go through the long and cold night. The windows on the floors below us had been all broken out, sash and all in many places, having been used for divers purposes, and the cold air towards morning chilled us through. Some time previous we had two or three jets of gas allowed us, but some of the prisoners had been up all night cooking "scouse"* in tin pans over the flame, which when the Rebels found out had turned the gas off, and now we had to spend the long evening in darkness.

[We selected] our sleeping places as the shades of evening closed around us, our places being in many instances marked with chalk in numbers on the brick wall. Many had pried bricks out to use for pillows. After midnight all was quiet, except the snoring of the rows of sleeping men, and the hours being called by the guard on the sidewalk of ours and Libby Prison's with the accustomed "All's well." I was so excited by the last three days' incidents that despite fatigue did not get asleep until far into the morning.

December 1, 1863

Dull and cloudy day, making it dismally dark and cheerless for us. I awake stiff and sore enough, and for the first time in a prison found out what "sleeping on the soft side of a plank" meant! About 8 o'clock we were formed in long lines on each floor, and Ross,† the prison clerk for Libby, came in to call the roll. He was a little "cuss" dressed in a homespun jacket much too large for him but was full of importance and swagger. He cursed and swore at short intervals calling us d____ Yankees, etc., while the sailors laughed and made fun of him. He counted us over three times to be sure that none had escaped, and went down on the other floors to do the same while a guard was put at the head of the stairs to keep us from mixing with those below.

Soon after, a detail of four sailors went out for rations and came back about 9 o'clock carrying large tubs of grub, which consisted of black goober bean soup, which had been boiled with the hulls on, and was as salty as pickle and boiling hot, corn bread, made of unbolted meal; and sweet potatoes half rotten, of all colors and sizes. The tubs were put on the long table and our "sergeant of the floor" ladled out the soup to those who had anything to hold it. About half of us had no cups and had to go without, consequently the others lent their cups, for they could not eat the stuff, and each mess man got his own quantum which was to be equally divided among the ten composing the mess. And each was the possessor of three sweet potatoes, about six ounces of corn bread, and [a] half pint of the black villainous smelling soup if he had anything to hold it in. I was fortunate in having a quart measure, which I had got from the Negro cook at the place where we had stopped overnight the first day of our capture. Others had cups made of cans which had contained preserved fruits or vegetables.

The sailors, who were the only privileged ones allowed to go out for "grub," had

* "Scouse" was slang for a soldier-cooked dish.

†E. W. Ross, Thomas Pratt Turner's chief clerk at Libby, was the nephew of Franklin Stearns, one of the wealthiest Unionists in Richmond. Some historians think Ross was part of the Unionist underground and feigned hostility to war prisoners while secretly helping them. If so, he played his part so well that many prisoners never realized the truth.

brought in lots of these which were in the vacant lot on their way to the cook house, which was in the basement of Scott's building near us. The Rebel officers were using the canned meats, etc., sent to us by the U.S. Sanitary Commission and stored opposite in the large warehouse, and by throwing away the empty cans had thus furnished us with something very valuable to hold water, soup, or anything else in. There was not a tin plate among us, nor a spoon but what the prisoners had themselves made of wood, or bones found in the soup. Some few had knives, but the greater portion had wooden spoons and forks. A piece of tin split and turned up at the edges served for plates.

I learned from the sailors that there were about 1,100 officers imprisoned in Libby, and that Castle Thunder was full of Rebel deserters, spies, and the very worst scum of Rebeldom. The poor devils there were tried by a military court, and hung or shot as the case might be, cut off from all outside interference or aid in proving their innocence to the charges brought against them. There were twenty-eight sailors and marines with us as prisoners, they having been captured in the night attack on Fort Sumter September 7th last in which they were badly repulsed. From the coxswain of Ensign Benjamin Porter's boat, who was there at the time, I learned . . . the particulars of the affair. This coxswain's name was Littlefield* from Somerville, near Boston, Massachusetts. He and I were chums now, and as he went out for rations would always bring in something for our mutual comfort, such as tobacco, tin cups and plates, spoons and forks, which he "hooked" in the cook house. . . .

December 2, 1863

Cold and raw day with appearance of snow. Ross called the roll as usual this morning, but not before 10 o'clock so we had to wait until nearly noon for our rations, which caused much grumbling. Something had gone wrong with the Rebels, and Ross was very abusive and cursed us vehemently. We heard our prisoners in the Libby singing songs last night, and "Rally round the Flag" sounded the loudest. We waited anxiously for the detail to come with the rations, and news if any: our rations were the same as yesterday, only the corn bread was half raw, and rice and meal gruel substituted for the vile black goober bean soup. From the front windows I got a fine view of the Libby Prison, the bridges across the James River, Manchester, with its tall cotton factories, etc., and could see away down the river several miles towards Fort Darling. I made a long and careful sketch . . . and another of Castle Thunder, from my rough lines I had taken when we halted in front of it. . . . Our men could not tell us anything new when they came in with the grub, but something was the matter with the Rebels, which was intended to be kept from us.

With Walsh and Littlefield, I made a close survey of our prison and surroundings from the rear and side windows of [the] top floor, one being on the watch to give notice. When

*Probably Austin Littlefield, a landsman serving in the Navy on the USS *Lodona*. He took part in the attack on Fort Sumter on September 8, 1863, was captured and later served in prison in Andersonville.

Libby Prison, Cary Street, Richmond, Va.
1,100 to 1,500 Union officers confined February 1863. Sketched from Scott's prison.

the Rebel guard on the sidewalk pointed his musket upwards at us, we would dodge back and try another point. The sinks* were built on the outside of the rear wall, as is common in factories, and on each floor, and by the small windows we could see into the rear yard, and had a good view of the city towards Capitol Hill and "the Rocketts" which were quite near. The roof of the capitol was plainly in sight with a Rebel flag flying at each end. Church steeples and large hotels showed above groves of trees. Fine residences were numerous, relieved by the dark brick factories and warehouses in the lower ground.

Manchester stood out on a hill on the other side, the high bridges crossing the James . . . with sparkling waters below the falls made a fine view, while a redoubt, with a Rebel flag flying on the highest point in Manchester showed where "Fort Winder" was, the guns of which covered Belle Isle in the river below where 1,700 of our fellow prisoners laid in the mud, protected from the weather by a few old ragged tents only. The smoke from the Tredegar Works near here showed that the Rebels were busy forging cannon to be used against our army yet in the field. In the afternoon some of our fellows, led by two stalwart sailors, piled the mess tubs on the table and with pieces of iron taken from the presses on the lower floor, broke the ceiling and forced their way into the attic, which thus far had not been invaded. Soon through the opening came a quantity of short boards, bottles and iron hoops, which were eagerly seized by those below, and all put to some use. A broken file was the most valuable of all. . . .

The men were seated on the floor most of the day with blankets (if they had them) over

* Sink was the name for a latrine.

CAMP OF UNION PRISONERS OF WAR ON BELLE ISLAND, JAMES RIVER
Opposite Richmond, Va., 1863. Area of island: six acres. 6,000 to 8,000 prisoners.

their shoulders playing "checkers." The squares being chalked on the floor or a small board, and the men composed of buttons and bits of leather. Others were playing with dice made of beef bones shaken up in a small tin cup. There was but one pack of greasy cards in the room which one of the sailors had got from the guard somehow, and as they were in much demand the figures thereon were nearly obliterated causing much discussion and angry talk incessantly. We had plenty of water, which was the only comfort to those who used it. Two faucets were on each floor near the sinks.

The sailors washed the floors with buckets of water, then broomed it, same as on board ship every morning. All had to gather his blankets and wait until the floor dried before occupying his place or berth. If any were too lazy to get up, they got a bucket of cold water thrown over them. On the floor below us they did not wash the floor as we did. Consequently the place was very dirty, and helped to breed vermin. Great many Germans and Irish were on this floor and they always were dirty and unkempt. Many never even washed their faces for a week or more, just wiped a wet rag around their eyes which gave them a cadaverous and more dirty appearance. The sick lay upon the dirty floors crawling with vermin and too lazy or helpless to keep themselves clean as they had lost all ambition to do so. No soap was issued to us, and a piece was of great value. If laid down anywhere it was instantly stolen by someone. . . .

Paper was very scarce with us at all times. I had marked and written all over every scrap which I possessed, and was lucky to get a small though thick memorandum book from a newcomer with only a few pages written on in pencil. This I cleaned off with corn bread crumbs and made new entries of my diary from the scraps. I made in it plans of Rebel forts, etc., which I had passed, and most of the writing was in short hand, which no Rebel could ever decipher. I used an alphabet of numbers also which was intelligible only to myself. A copy of the Rebel newspaper found its way into the prison and we were all glad when the enemy admitted that he was whipped badly at Lookout Mountain and Missionary Ridge in November last.* We sang songs from dark to 11 or 12 o'clock at night. "Rally round the Flag," "Star Spangled Banner," and others. We heard songs over at Libby too during the fine moonlight night. The officer of the guard yelled to us to "stop that infernal howling" but we did not mind him and sang the louder. . . .

December 4 to 10, 1863

We made another raid into the attic this morning and got a lot of boards and stuff for fuel. Some crawled out on the flat roof and tore off the tin roofing which they threw down to us and which was eagerly scrambled for. Soon many were making tin pans or plates to hold our food. The wind blew hard which deadened the noise made ripping off the tin. The guards being close under the walls of the building did not see the operators on the roof who worked with spikes. The hole was closed up again while those hammering on the tin on the second floor where the tobacco presses were made a great noise for an hour or more. I made a deep tin pan with much difficulty, hammering the cut ends together with a large spike.

Our rations of rotten sweet potatoes have given out. Now we get boiled rice with grease of some sort mixed with it. It was brought in by the detail of sailors sent for it in a pine box with handles. This mess of swill was very hot. Some beef bones were found in it, but whether of an ox or mule we could not tell. The pine box gave the mess a flavor of some kind like "resin sauce." It was far preferable to the black rotten sweet potatoes however, and satisfied the cravings of hunger for a longer time. Each man got about a pint of the stuff. Many set about making wooden spoons, while others used strips of tin.

The high tides in the river drive the wharf rats up into the building in great numbers. These brutes run over us while we lay on the floor at night. They are pelted with tin cans, sticks or anything that comes handy amid curses and yells. Many a sleeper gets struck instead of the rats, which brings on renewed cursings. Two of our number died today of cold or pneumonia. They were on the floor below us. I saw them after they had lain on the floor all day. They were much discolored, and emaciated. The skin had worn off to the bone nearly from their hips and elbows by lying so long on the floor. After roll call this morning there was great excitement among us as a long row of new prisoners [from Belle Isle] were in the street; and who soon began to file into the doors in the other half of this building. . . .

We heard them rushing up the stairs, yelling and making a great din like beasts in a menagerie after being locked in. Soon we heard them hammering on the walls which divided

*The battle of Missionary Ridge, Tennessee, occurred on November 25, 1863.

[us] and four or five holes were soon made, six or eight bricks being taken out of each, and we could communicate and see each other. All crowded to the holes to hear what they had to say and trading in pipes, bone rings, and other things began. They were a hard and ragged set, and had suffered the most horrible privations to make them so. . . .

December 16 to 19, 1863

Cold and northeast rain storm. Old Cunningham the jailor came in this morning with four Rebel guard. They brought in another large iron stove which was put up on [the] fourth floor. We have two on our floor now. A lot of green cord wood was brought in and the stoves put up. He saw the new boards and stuff which we had got up in the attic, and wanted to know where we got them. Nobody knew of course. He made an inspection of the walls and found three or four of the holes. He never thought to look at the ceiling.

We broke up the stuff, and soon had two good fires at which hundreds crowded around and the stove tops were soon covered with all sorts of pans, half canteens, and tin plates made from the roofing. Everyone was cooking some kind of a mess. The wood, being green, soon filled the room with a dense smoke which set everyone coughing, and made our eyes watery. Only a few could get any heat from the stove and there was much wrangling and pushing to get near it. The smoke was so unbearable that the fire was put out in an hour or two, as we preferred the cold to the smoke. . . .

December 19, 1863

The stove smokes yet at a terrible rate. Everyone has sore eyes and the coughing is constant. We have to open all the windows and the Rebel guard down below thought we had set the building on fire. A thick East River fog in New York is nothing to it. A large rat was taken out of the mess bucket among the bean soup. At the bottom of course. It was in a boiled condition, and caused some merriment. We had eaten all the soup. So our stomachs did turn on us. We thought it gave the stuff an extra flavor. Cries of "Heathen Chinee" were heard. The rat was thrown out of the window and hit one of the guards on the sidewalk square in the face. There was considerable swearing down there for a time. . . .

December 21 to 24, 1863

Fine clear cold weather. Thin ice formed on the canal in rear of Libby Prison while down on the second floor of this prison there is good sliding which the prisoners indulge in to keep themselves warm. The rain beats in at all the sashless windows which soon makes a skating rink of the long room, but many have no shoes, and cannot slide with the rest. The scout to whom I had sold my pocket compass escaped last night, with three other prisoners who belonged to West Virginia.

There was a high old time at roll call this morning when Ross, the Libby Prison clerk called the roll, three men short every time the count was made. He counted and recounted five or six times before it dawned through his thick head that they probably had escaped. He was nearly frantic with rage and cursing. . . .

Nearly all of us prisoners have "exchange" on the brain. Groups of twenty or more sit on the floor and discuss the probabilities. The sailors and marines don't believe that there will be any exchange of prisoners until the spring campaign opens in April. I, with a few others, have the same opinion, as Uncle Sam won't exchange good fat Rebels who are confined in the North for the sickly, emaciated and physically wrecked soldiers confined here.

Both armies are in winter quarters on the Rapidan and Rappahannock and will probably remain so until warm weather and dry roads permit them to kill one another again. Sickness and dejection is visible on two thirds of the 600 prisoners confined here. Typhoid fever has broken out among us! Five or six cases in one room. Alarm is generally felt that this terrible disease should get headway, as we know that we will get no medicine or doctor's attendance, and will be left to die like dogs. To escape is hopeless. The smoke from the green wood in the stoves made the sick cough worse than ever while nearly everyone had sore eyes from the same cause. The sick lay on the floor covered with lice they being too weak to keep them under by "skirmishing." We can expect nothing from our brutal jailors, while the Rebel newspapers gloat over our situation, and advocate a further reduction in the miserable rations which a hog would not eat, for fear that we may get strong enough to try to escape!

Major Dick Turner gloats over our misery, and John Mitchel,* the editor of the Richmond *Enquirer* is the most rabid Rebel of the whole lot. He daily advocates starving us, so that we cannot run away. . . .

The sailors returned about 5 p.m. bringing us good news which cheered up many of us. They have unloaded or helped unload two barges which had come up from Aitken's Landing on the James about fifteen miles down river with clothing which was sent to us prisoners by flag of truce from our government and the Sanitary Commission. They recounted how hundreds of boxes and bales had been landed and most of them carted by mule teams to Scott's building on Main Street, which can be seen from any of the windows here facing north. Lots of provisions were landed also, hams, canned vegetables, boxes of all kinds and sizes. The sailors managed to break the ends of some of these boxes while unloading and "sequestered" several packages of real coffee, sugar and canned milk. So the sailors' mess lived sumptuously while this lasted. The smell of the coffee alone set the rest of us nearly crazy.

My sailor chum Littlefield got a pint cup of it for me, which I divided up among three who were captured with me. The sailors pick up much information from the Rebels when out helping unload vessels as they are looked upon much more favorably than soldiers. They have met two or three old sailors who were once in the U.S. Navy before the war,

*John Mitchel (1815–1875), an Irish nationalist and editor, was transported by the British to Van Diemen's Land (Tasmania), from which he escaped in 1853. Strongly pro-Confederate, he moved to Richmond and became an editor with the *Enquirer* and then the *Examiner*.

who help them in all ways but escape. My chum Littlefield is a general favorite among all of us prisoners, and being very intelligent and a good looking lad of nineteen years he asks for information from the Rebels and generally succeeds.

December 24, 1863

The Rebels wanted to detail some of the prisoners to go out to sweep the street in front of Libby and this prison and clean up the guard room on the ground floor of this building but could not get one of us to go, although double rations to those going were offered. This lasted a week when four or five consented to go. They hid themselves in the cook house under Scott's building, eating all they wanted, but were caught by the guard while trying to escape by the Rocketts' wharves and brought back here. So no more are allowed to go out. . . .

There is a rumor that we will be permitted to write a letter home, and the Rebels will furnish paper and some pencils. We will have to pay the Rebel postage of 10¢ Rebel scrip. We can only write twenty or twenty-five words and leave them open so that Turner, or some other Rebel cuss can read them before they are sent. The officers have always had the privilege of writing home, and often get money safely, which of course goes to feed the Rebel sutler or to bribe the guards to give a chance to escape as they all can be bought.

December 25, 1863

Fine clear and cold. As our "grub" did not come in to us until 3:30 p.m. we thought the delay was caused by getting a good Christmas dinner of some kind. Turkey or beef could not be expected of course, but when it did come in we were not served until 4:30 p.m. It consisted of six or eight ounces of heavy corn bread and half boiled rice in a big pine box with a pint of the old strong smelling goober bean soup. We were ravenously hungry and the small ration was swallowed in a minute, when we were as hungry as ever. The Rebel cooks were all drunk, and the vile food was kept from us purposely by Turner's orders, as we learned afterwards.

The sailors had brought in yesterday some coffee, sugar, and beef tea. They had these within our mess only. I got some of the beef tea, however, which was a luxury. It comes in thin cakes, and looks much like glue in color and appearance. Hot water soon dissolves it, when we can get at the stove to heat it. We have lots of tin tomato cans as the sailors bring them in from the empty lot near us, where they are thrown by the Rebels after they have devoured the contents. This canned vegetables, etc., were sent to us prisoners but the Rebels are not so gullible as to give it to us. So the U.S. Sanitary Commission at home are actually feeding the Rebel officers with hams and all kinds of good things. Jeff Davis no doubt has his share. . . .

All the guards and their officers were more or less drunk all day. Many fell down helplessly drunk while on post, when another fellow was put in his place. Several fired their muskets right into the upper stories of Libby. I watched one fellow aim a dozen times before he fired. Some of our officers put [an] old hat out on a stick when three of the guards fired at it thinking that there might be a head behind it.

It got to be very cold in the afternoon, while a thin skim of ice was seen in the river close in shore and in the canal back of Libby. Several of us tried to make a fire in the big stove, and succeeded after a while, but here the stove having no pipe, sent the smoke out in the room in thick volumes choking us, and making it impossible to see twenty feet. All the windows were thrown open on our floor amid yells, curses, and coughing. The Rebels seeing the smoke pouring out of the windows thought the building was on fire. The officer of the guard with twenty or more came rushing upstairs, but did not stay any longer than was necessary to see the cause, and went down again cursing us for "ignorant blue bellied Yankees." Water had to be used to put the fire out and we sat on the floor all night in the cold. Two sentry boxes were put in the enclosed yard in the rear of this prison after the scout and his comrades escaped. (We have heard nothing of them since.) The Rebel guard are generally asleep in these boxes while the officer or corporal of the guard have to yell to them many times to keep them awake.

Tonight there seemed more trouble than ever. And the guard was relieved before his time was up on his post. These fellows snooze away most of their days and many wear the blue overcoats and have the blankets which once belonged to the prisoners here as they traded them off for food and tobacco long ago. Many prisoners are now in rags, and have to lie on the bare floor shivering with cold all night, unable to sleep at all, until the morning sun comes into the room, when they try to get some sleep in its warmth. We have yet five or six cases of small pox among us. These poor fellows are compelled by the others to stay down on the second floor where there are no stoves, and all the windows broken out sash and all! They walk up and down, ragged, shoeless and crawling with vermin! All the others shun them, and about twenty or more sick fellows lie on the floor helpless, with sometimes no friend to bring him his miserable daily rations. Gloom and despair [are] seen on all countenances.

Two men died of small pox last week, and the Rebels let the corpses lie on the floor nearly two days. And still not taking them out for burial they were thrown out of the windows by their companions on the heads of the Rebel guard fifteen feet below on the sidewalk! The putrefying corpses could not be left lying among the sick ones any longer. It was night time when they were thrown out. It caused much commotion in the guard room below on the first floor, but they were carried off somewhere out of sight. The dead men were unknown, but were both Germans. . . .

December 26 to 30, 1863

Very cold weather for the past two days. Half an inch or more of ice is on the canal opposite us. All who had nerve and strength walked the floors night and day to keep warm. All the cracks and crevices were stuffed up on our floor, but the cold draughts came up the open stairway as from the North Pole. The cold really was about 30 degrees, but with confinement and thin poor blood in our veins we felt it to be about zero.

We made loud calls on the officer of the guard to refit up our stoves and get us some wood. After several hours he sent in a lot of old rusty stovepipe with some wire, and we got the stove in order again. The pipe did not fit however, and the smoke at the joints soon filled the room so as to compel us to open all the windows to let it out. About six or eight sticks of green cordwood was brought in, but it would not burn. So we got on the mess table and broke a hole in the ceiling, clambered up into the attic and threw down a large pile of dry stuff found there. Some of it was flooring. Soon we had the stove hot, while forty or fifty of us stood around it to keep warm. Those on the outside got no warmth from the stove, but they imagined they did, which to a prisoner is all the same. Everyone now tried to heat up his soup ration while the poor fellows downstairs came up to get warm.

December 28, 1863

There was a great commotion among us this morning at seeing thirty or forty prisoners all in citizens' clothes or gray homespun filing into our side of the prison. There were cries of "fresh fish," "make room for the Johnnies," etc. They proved to be a lot of old gray haired men and several youths from seventeen to twenty years old. They were sent from Castle Thunder here because the Rebels could find no earthly cause for shooting or hanging them. They will not be exchanged, nor will they be set free. So they must remain in captivity until they die or the Confederacy "bursts up.". . .

We had no roll call this morning. Ross is on his Christmas spree it is said. We don't want him here anyhow. Five or six of us prisoners got down into the cellar of this building today. A hole was first made in the chimney stack at the lower end of the room on the second floor, and by means of a twisted blanket rope they slid down to the bottom fireplace.

The guards are full of whiskey all day and are shouting and quarreling among themselves in the guard room while several lay snoozing in the sun around the entrance in front. The noise made by breaking the chimney flue was not noticed. The men stayed down an hour, and found the place full of bins, some of which were full of bran or what they thought was corn meal. A bushel or two was brought and as there seemed to be corn husks or ground corn cob in the stuff, many began cooking it into a mush and ate it greedily. At night all those who had eaten the stuff were sick with dysentery and colic pains. The sailors have not been out to work for some days. The warehouse nearly opposite to us contains a large quantity of soldiers' boxes, sent here by their families or friends but never delivered.

The Rebel officers go over there every day in numbers [to] break open the boxes, and help themselves to the ham, canned stuff, and anything that they can find. They don't intend to feed Yankees on the good things which they get for nothing. One of us yelled to a Rebel officer as he stood with others in the doorway, with his pockets bulged out with plunder, and a ham under his arm, "Drop that ham," "Johnny stole the ham," etc. But he did not do it of course. . . .

Large archways once led from one half of the rooms on each floor to the other half. These had all been bricked up solid before we came here. Numerous holes had been made, about six bricks taken out, through which we conversed and traded with the other prisoners in the other half of the building. Blankets were pinned up over these places, the bricks being first replaced, and a very sick looking fellow laid on the floor with two improvised nurses during the inspection of walls. Several holes were found on the third floor however, and two Negro masons came in with brick and mortar and built them solid again. The prisoners stole the masons' trowels however during the operation. The Negroes made no fuss over the loss, but they rolled their eyes at the two Rebel guards who stood over them during the operation. They were not allowed to speak a word with us while bricking up the holes. Two pistols in the hands of the guard were pointed at them. Yet many of our fellows asked them all sorts of questions, merely to see the guards kill them if they answered them!

The prisoners were getting selfish, cruel, and demoralized by their privations, every one was for himself. All cohesion as army comrades was broken up, thieving from one another was common, but no fighting of any account had yet taken place among the large crowd of 600 men. All were intensely loyal to the flag, which although in desperate want, kept a sort of fellow feeling among us which the Rebels could not destroy. . . .

December 31, 1863

This is the last day of the eventful year and a general despondency prevails among us. Many are talking of the good old times we used to have at home about this time, or in camp. Storytelling among us occupies the dark lonely hours from 6 to 10 p.m. A sickening feeling comes over us as we realize that we are prisoners with no immediate prospects of being released by exchange. . . .

The Rebel guard say that the "Yankees are dying right smart now at the hospitals." We learned that they were buried in trenches out back of Libby Hill, which is next to Church Hill, east of us. So we die like dogs, and are buried like dogs! The Rebels furnished us with 300 sheets of coarse paper and brown paper envelopes so that we could write home today. We are limited to twenty words, envelopes to be left unsealed so that Turner may read them first before posting. We advise those to whom we write to enclose a 10¢ silver piece by return mail if they answer our letters or they would not be received over the Rebel lines. Pieces of lead pencil were furnished us also to write with. Very few of us wrote at all. Many had forgotten the addresses. Others would not let their friends or relations know how they were suffering. Nothing could be sent us by our friends, for the Rebels would appropriate the things to their own use. And, knowing that Turner would inspect and read

Rear of Rebel Redoubt at Belle Island, James River, Va., 1863

every letter, many would not give him the grim satisfaction of doing so. Walsh, Halley, Rhineheart, and myself wrote home. We just said that we were captured by Mosby 27th November last at headquarters General French at Brandy Station, and that we were all well and in good heart looking for an early exchange. . . .

January 1, 1864

Clear day and warmer. There was some unusual excitement last night over at Libby. Singing was heard by our prisoners over there, lanterns flashed on the upper stories, which showed that the Rebel officers and guards were "stirring up the animals" in some manner. We kept up our singing last night until after 12 p.m. in spite of the Rebel guard who did not molest us. The scene was novel as 300 men sat on the floors in a bright moonlight singing in chorus to "Rally round the Flag," etc., in which the line "Down with the traitor, up with the Stars" were loudly emphasized for the benefit of the traitor guard on the front sidewalk. When Ross came in this morning to call the roll, he said that "if any more howling was heard at night we would all be sent to Belle Island to cool off." We jeered and chaffed him in return, and by shifting our places in line, he was compelled to call the roll four times before he satisfied himself that none had escaped.

The mess detail were a long time getting the food at the cook house, as it was nearly 2:30 p.m. when they came in with our New Year's dinner! Three large pine boxes with handles to each were carried in which contained mule meat and rice boiled together! Junks of this villainous meat stuck up in the rice which proved to be as tough as rubber, while the rice had been strongly impregnated with pine resin. All the pots and pans were brought into requisition to hold this boiling hot mixture which a hog would not eat unless very hungry. Loud calls were made for turkey, during the time occupied in serving this vile mess out, but as the majority of us were very hungry we swallowed the stuff with avidity, as it was a new dish to us and a change from the vile black "loud smelling" goober bean soup and we had meat in some shape. . . .

January 2, 1864

We have clear cold weather, with fine moonlight nights. As no lights are allowed, the moonlight shines in the windows upon five to six hundred prisoners all seated or lying in the floor, who tell stories, or sing songs until past midnight. We hear a military band nearly every evening about 9 to 10:30 playing "Dixie," and other Rebel tunes. Probably they are serenading "Jeff Davis" or some other high toned Rebel on Capitol Hill. The music is not like that which we were wont to hear in our army, but it recalls the glorious old times at headquarters. . . .

About noon Colonel [James M.] Sanderson,* and Captain Chamberlain, both of the 123rd Ohio U.S. Volunteers, came in here from Libby under guard of ten Rebel soldiers and went among us looking for intelligent men to act as clerks to open the boxes of clothing stored in Scott's building on Main Street, which would now be delivered to us prisoners. Great excitement ensued at once as they passed through the rooms inspecting the prisoners. They were asked a thousand questions which of course they could not answer. They had no idea of the misery and deaths among us. Eight sergeants were called for to go out and do the work. These were selected in about half an hour, while I volunteered to go out with them to act as invoice and entry clerk.

We joyfully packed our few belongings in five minutes, and had our names entered on the officer's book, bid goodbye to our comrades in misery and tramped downstairs to the street. Here we breathed the free air of heaven for the first time since November. We were all willing to go anywhere, as long as we got out of the cursed prison in which we had been so long confined.

We met the Rebel guard at the door under a young lieutenant and with Colonel Sanderson and Captain Chamberlain were marched past Libby up 20th Street to Main Street and in a short time came to Scott's, where we were met by Captain Munroe of the Rebel army who had charge of the contents of the building. Our officers showed us a large pile of boxes

*Lieutenant Colonel James M. Sanderson was falsely accused by Brigadier General Neal Dow, a fellow Union prisoner in Richmond, of showing sympathy for the Confederates and acting against the best interest of the Union prisoners. Sanderson marshaled overwhelming testimony from his fellow captive officers to refute Dow's attacks.

and cases, and after giving us our instructions to open them and lay out their contents for delivery, invoice each box, etc., we were left "like cats in a strange garret" to ourselves, while our two officers were marched back to Libby under guard about 5 p.m. Captain Munroe was a good natured elderly Rebel and showed us what to do on the morrow.

We were on the second floor of the building which contained about 150 large cases, or boxes, had three or four hammers and cold chisels to open them with, while the boxes were piled eight or ten feet high on the floor, leaving gangways between. We were warned not to attempt to try to escape as we would all be shot at once, even if one of us got away. We gave no parole whatever, only our word of honor as soldiers that we would not attempt escape but "liberty is dear," and I was the only one of the lot to forfeit my word of honor! There were two Rebel guards in front of the building the entrance to which was through a narrow door in Captain Munroe's office on the first floor to the street, the other doors being all locked and barred. One Rebel sentinel paced the second floor on which we were, between the gangways made by the piles of boxes. At this time not one of us would have escaped if told that we could do so, as in the rear end of the second floor was a large room, piled high with boxes which contained all kinds of cooked and raw provisions.

Here also was a large cook stove, two or three tin pans, and nearly a dozen of new very large coffee pots. We were given to understand that we could help ourselves to the canned goods in the boxes, and cook and eat to our hearts' content in return for the work of opening and assorting the clothing for delivery to our comrades who would be marched in to get them by squads after a dozen or so boxes had been opened for them. We soon had a good fire going in the stove, made from broken boxes, and we deputized a sergeant from some Ohio regiment among us to act as cook and do no more work on the boxes than he could help, provided a good square meal was always to be found cooked for us. Captain Munroe left us about dark, and we hunted among the piles of boxes until we found a box of candles. We broke open recklessly dozens of small boxes, and soon found canned tomatoes, corned beef, brandied peaches, and a large crate of aerated wheat bread. We sat on boxes and ate until midnight! We got a lot of coffee, also sugar, and canned milk, and had the first "square meal" since we had been captured. . . .

January 4, 1864

Light snow all day. We were all up at 7 a.m. and made a royal good breakfast on canned turkey, canned tomatoes, bread steamed, canned peaches and apple sauce. These were all found among the stores and we ate until we could hardly move. Then we found [a] plug of tobacco and had a good smoke until 9 a.m. when Captain Munroe came up from his office on the first floor and set us all at work opening boxes of clothing. All the provisions were stored in an enclosed room at the end of the second floor which was partitioned off from the main room, and was probably used for offices and counting room of the factory. It was about twenty-five feet by fifty, fitted with broad shelves on which were stored hundreds of small boxes, soldiers' boxes not yet delivered, and large boxes all over the floor. During the night we had broken open lots of these boxes and many of us were greedy to get at what was better to us than a gold mine.

The guard was relieved by Captain Munroe and no other guard was substituted in his place inside the building. Two guards were on the sidewalk in front only. We opened twenty or thirty cases of clothing, invoiced and laid out piles of overcoats, drawers, trousers, undershirts, and 300 pairs of stockings. No shoes could be found as the Rebels had a few nights ago stolen seven cases of shoes and carried them off by a row boat to Manchester across the James River. They were worth $250 per pair Confederate, so some Rebel made a good speculation. We worked hard until noon when we stopped to get another good dinner. Our cook had seven large coffee pots on the stove at once all containing canned meats and vegetables. We found tin cans of brandied peaches and we soon felt the effects of the brandy as they had been put up a long time. How the Rebel officers overlooked them was a wonder to us. Most of the provisions were marked U.S. Sanitary Commission. The clothing were marked U.S. Army. So we had no compunction in helping ourselves liberally to everything found.

About 1 o'clock the tramp of prisoners was heard and old Cunningham the jailor of Crew and Pemberton Prison marched in the head of 300 or more prisoners. He carried an old gun barrel for a cane, with which he prodded the laggards. Eight of us stood at the boxes [and] as they passed us in single file [we] delivered an overcoat, blanket, shirt, blouse, trousers and socks to each. . . . Another 100 were marched in about 3 p.m. and another at 4 p.m. All were under a strong guard of fifty men and two officers sent by Turner from Libby.

We had a fine supper at 7 p.m., having found a cooked ham in one of the soldier's boxes. We found lots of pies, cakes, etc., but they were all mouldy and spoilt. We found several white shirts and nice clean underclothing, and numerous suits of citizens' clothes in the seams of which were sewn greenbacks, about $60 in small sums, generally $5 notes. These of course were appropriated by us as we knew well that the owners of these boxes would never get them. We found jackknives, books, mouldy hams and spoilt puddings, cakes, and pies, with letters or notes from those at home to the owners of the boxes. We had good fresh canned stuff, and did not bother with the eatables. No liquor was found in any of the soldier boxes. We had plenty of good genuine coffee and canned milk by the dozen cans. We ate, drank and smoked until nearly midnight, while several kept on breaking open provision boxes nearly all night. We all provided ourselves with two suits of new clean clothes and underwear, which was valued above all things. One sergeant put on three white shirts one over another. I got two white starched shirts, needles and thread, two knives, $20 in greenbacks, and other nice things for my share.

We kept candles burning until long after 10 p.m. when the guard in the basement yelled to us to put them out. We were so intent in breaking open and plundering the boxes that we paid no attention until they threatened to fire on us through the floor. We jumped on the boxes and yelled to "fire and be d______." They did not fire however, and we worked on the boxes until 2 or 3 o'clock in the morning screening the windows with two army blankets each. We found more peaches but they were not put up in brandy as the others were. We devoured ten cans or more of them however and were surfeited for once anyhow. We knew that this fat job would last only as long as it would take us to deliver the clothing, and we made the most of the opportunity. We bunked down on layers of army blankets and kept the fire in the stove going all night. Some of us were eating at intervals until daylight! We called the place "Heavenly Rest" and dreaded when we should have to go back to prison again when our work was finished. Several Rebel officers came in to see us about dark, and as they were a mild gentlemanly set, we filled their pockets with canned milk and other good things, including genuine coffee, which they thought much of. Three of them had supper with us, and they enjoyed the good things as well as ourselves.

January 5, 1864

Raining hard all day. Squads of 100 men were marched in at intervals all day. We opened clothing boxes and delivered as on the previous days. At my suggestion we cooked a lot of chicken, turkey, ham, and other good things and wrapped them in paper and put them in the pockets of the clothing given away. But as there were so many to feed that although the stove was piled full of cooking food it soon was given away, and a few only got it. We scraped the mold off some of the hams, cut them into junks and gave them to the first comers hidden in the clothing. . . .

January 8 to 10, 1864

. . . We work at the boxes and deliver clothing every day and have supplied over 1,500 of our men so that the stores are beginning to run out. All the blouses, trousers, and overcoats have been delivered. Captain Munroe with two other Rebel officers took away and carried off two cartloads of provisions from our inner room. The Rebel officers say that the provisions are sent to the hospitals for the use of our sick men, but we cannot be made to believe this. The Rebel officers get the stuff, and Jeff Davis is supplied of course with the nice things which money cannot buy in this city at any price. I had time to explore the upper stories of Scott's building this morning. We are confined to a wing which fronts on the street. Two doors lead to the main building four stories high, which has been occupied by the Belle Island prisoners, but which is now empty.

The floors were covered with rags, remnants of blankets, and dirt an inch thick. The top rooms had been once whitewashed, now they are stained with dirt in all colors. From the top rear windows I had a fine view of Manchester and the James River with the bridges crossing it. Libby Prison was in plain sight and not far off. The canal and breakwater with

VIEW OF SCOTT'S PRISON, RICHMOND, VA.
Main Street, December 1863. Occupied by prisoners from Belle Island. Captain Munroe, C.S.A., jailor.

Rocketts a part of the city below Libby. Several schooners were tied up here at the wharves. The guards were marching their beats around Libby, while I saw several of our prisoners through the grated windows, several of whom wore red shirts. The river sparkled in the sunlight. Mayo's Bridge and the railroad bridges above it to Manchester, the huge Haxall's flour mills nine stories high, the tobacco factories in which is stored nearly a million dollars' worth of tobacco owned by the French government, all loomed up in the morning sun. The low hills along the Manchester shore showed a streak of red clay on the summits, which were earthworks without any mounted guns or sentries. These swept around the bend of the river until lost in clumps of low trees below. There are two or three falls in the river, both above and below the bridges. The railroad bridges looked to be about eighty foot high, and the tracks run to Norfolk and Petersburg.

Down river the low hills were dotted with white houses, and the view was shut out by another bend in the stream and haze. The Rebel flag was flying over "Fort Winder" opposite Belle Island, while the black smoke from the furnaces of the Tredegar Ironworks rose high in the air, showing that they were making cannon and gun barrels over there to kill our fellows in the time to come. Down river, towards Drury's Bluff and "Fort Darling," the sun shone brightly on the crooked stream, beyond was hazy. Some coal barges were unloading coal along the canal, the workmen all being Negroes. Few people could be seen in the streets, while the Rebel guard opposite Libby in dirty blankets and slouch hats were warming themselves around a small fire. Everyone passing in front of all the Rebel prisons must walk in the middle of the street, not being allowed on the sidewalks at all. . . .

I could hear drums beating in the different Rebel camps out beyond Church Hill. I had all my companions come up to see the fine view and surroundings. This was about 6 a.m. before Captain Munroe got to the building. I had found some good white paper in the boxes, and cut the stiff paper into small squares for sketching purposes, so that they would fit into the crown of my cap to escape Rebel curiosity. We had a splendid breakfast of boned turkey, aerated bread toast, stewed tomatoes, pickles, cold ham, and apple butter or apple sauce in tin cans of about two quarts' capacity. I found in one of the soldier boxes a tin quart measure, which I kept for coffee. This was a great thing too, as we have had to use tomato cans for all kinds of purposes, and they soon blacken up and are hard to keep clean. We made a heavy meal, no talking being allowed, when at 9 a.m. we were at our posts delivering out the clothing as usual.

A lot of poor miserable sick ragged soldiers came in today. Several had sticks to help them walk. We gave them cans of good things, hidden in their clothing issued to them. Colonel Sanderson comes from Libby now every day to superintend our work, and returns as usual before sundown under guard. He gets all that he can eat here, and we fill his pockets with small cans of milk, sugar, coffee, etc., to take back to his brother officers at Libby. Turner does not search him for a wonder. . . .

January 11 to 15, 1864

While looking out of the front window today, I noticed that only one Rebel guard paced in front of the building. The sash was up and I could see up and down the street which was deserted, not even a wagon or cart. All at once I heard the musket click of the guard and he [was] looking up at me [and] said something twice over which I did not understand. I asked him "what he was trying to do," when in a surly tone he said, "Keep your head in dar Yank or I'll shoot." I got back out of range quick enough. I forgot all about Rebel proclivities to shoot "Yanks." We have now grown strong again with the help of eight or ten meals in every twenty-four hours, and good sleep, and know that this "soft snap" can't last long but have formed no plan to escape, in fact we would not escape if we had the chance, or as long as the "luxurious feeding" continues. Still no one can tell what he may do until the certain moment arrives to risk all or nothing on chances which look to an escape from the pangs of hunger and terrible treatment in the accursed prisons in Richmond. I went up to the top floors of the main building, and had good views of the whole city from the attic windows which I opened, and made several sketches from there. I could see the camps of the Rebels out towards Fair Oaks road, and the smoke of numerous camps out over Shockoe Creek and beyond Capitol Hill.

A light snow lay on the ground, through which protruded the red earthworks along Shockoe Creek and the Chickahominy River beyond. I thought over the good old times at General Heintzelman's headquarters at Savage's Station prior to the battle of Fair Oaks, and made a small map of the roads from memory leading from thence to Mechanicsville, which I could dimly see on the hill over the tree tops. I had made so many copies of these roads while at Savage's Station that I knew most of them by heart, and if I could . . . find my way to Williamsburg, Virginia, that is if I were not stopped on the road by some Rebel, that was the question. I had now thirteen days of good living and felt strong and hearty.

We delivered all the remaining clothing today and helped move the other things from rear to front of this building while four Negroes carried them off somewhere else. We had supplied about 1,800 men with clothing sent by "Uncle Samuel" and took mighty good care to supply ourselves at the same time. About twenty boxes of provisions remained, with about as many more of soldiers' boxes which we had rifled. We were "fat and saucy" and had good clean clothes and underclothes and lots of "greenbacks" in our pockets and did not care much about the biggest Rebel in Richmond.

Between 12 and 1 o'clock while the seven sergeants were eating and drinking in the rear room, I went to the front windows and looked casually out of the open windows. An old dilapidated ragged Rebel guard was pacing his beat in front of the building. I opened the door at the head of the stairs out of curiosity and saw that Captain Munroe had gone out of his office on the first floor and that the front door to it was wide open. After waiting some few minutes, a thought struck me that now or never was the time to escape, where to I never thought. A Rebel gray coat with gilt chevrons hung on a peg in Captain Munroe's office. I said nothing to the seven wise sergeants eating their dinner, but went downstairs and put the coat on, with my new blue overcoat over it, leaving it open in front so as to show the coat buttons. It was a fine sunny day, quite warm and I felt like getting away somewhere or anywhere rather than go back to Pemberton. Upon second thought I took off my blue overcoat and threw it up the stairway to the top step. Then lit my pipe and went to Captain Munroe's desk, where I "hooked" a lead pencil. The old Rebel guard saw me handling papers on the desk. I let him look all he wanted to as I wanted to pass for a clerk, which in one sense I was.

It got to be 12:30 p.m. and Captain Munroe would soon be back from his dinner. So no time was to be lost, and grasping a small bundle of receipts I walked to the door and told the guard to tell Captain Munroe that I would be back at half past 1 o'clock and stepped out boldly, went up the street and turned the first corner into 20th and Main streets. I expected to feel a bullet under my ribs every second, as the guard looked suspiciously at me all the while. I had on dark blue cavalry trousers, a gray embroidered Rebel coat and a glazed cover on my cap. Lots of Rebel officers dressed the same way at this time. Why should I not palm myself off for one?

I had no fixed plan, but I knew the roads on the other side of the Chickahominy, and concluded to get over that river by Mechanicsville Bridge. I had come into the city at midday and saw all the earthworks in the vicinity last November. Amid hopes and fears I now walked several blocks hastily, not meeting a single person. This part of the city had no residences whatever. Large warehouses and factories filled the space for many blocks. They were all shut up and deserted by owners or occupants. I turned into some street on my right and soon came among shops and stores. Some of which were closed but saw no men anywhere. I stopped in front of a large dry goods store, where three Negro women were looking in the show windows. I did the same, to recover my thoughts. I remembered seeing a good sized full dressed doll in this window with the price card on it, $1,000. Confederate of course. Cotton dresses were marked $10, $12, and $16 a yard. While wondering who bought these things, I saw a Rebel guard turn a corner two blocks away. I went on faster in the opposite direction along 4th Street, and towards the Capitol and followed the Virginia Central Railroad some time.

I met an old ragged looking citizen and asked the way to Broad Street as I knew that the Fredericksburg & Potomac Railroad ran through it. And I might get over the creek to the city limit. He directed me with a suspicious look, and I did not stop to argue. I saw that the low grounds were all overflowed with water but met nobody but a few Negro women and children, though I saw several seedy looking men behind, and in front of me on the opposite side of the street. I got into Capitol Street, and up to Broad Street, saw the depot on the other side of the hill, and went towards Shockoe Creek. Here I saw the earthworks. No guards anywhere in them and no guns mounted. The swamp was all overflowed here too. So I turned east again towards the Virginia Central, which I knew led to Sexton's Junction but ran between several forts on the outside of Richmond. The crooked creek headed me off several times, and I thought of getting into the yard of an empty warehouse and remain until night, as I knew that there would be a full moon then.

I was getting very thirsty, and seeing a street pump, with no one near it at a corner of the street I ran plump into a Rebel patrol guard composed of about twenty boys under a sergeant who yelled out, "Hello Yank! where are you going? halt thar." The sergeant eyed me suspiciously and wanted to know if I had a pass? I said that I was an officer and had a pass, but the fellow wanted to see it. I was in a quandary and gave him some of Captain Munroe's receipts to look at which I had taken from his desk before leaving. I could not make the fellow understand that I was on duty at Scott's building with Captain Munroe. I had to fall in with the guard and go there anyhow. I went to some guard house where three men and a corporal were detailed to see me back safe to Scott's building and see my pass, which I said must be there.

So we trudged through muddy streets until we got to Scott's, where I met Captain Munroe in the doorway in a rage, and swearing at the old guard for stealing his coat! As I came marching up with it on, he saw through "my little game," and then I got the curses. I argued the case, while he dismissed the guard, and told me to "at once pack up my kit and go to Libby with the whole detail of men in ten minutes." It was now about 5 p.m. and we were all surprised at so short a notice. I argued that it was all fair in war, but Captain Munroe said that I had broken my word of honor and that if I had got away the seven sergeants, my comrades, would have been sent to Castle Thunder and shot according to agreement when we first came in. I had not thought of this, and felt mean enough.

We then hastily got our things together, while a guard was sent from Libby to escort us there to see Major Turner whom we all dreaded. Captain Munroe went with us and on the way I talked him into a better humor for he was a kind hearted Rebel anyhow. We grabbed our bags of plunder already kept full for an emergency like this which we all expected, as our work was finished. And we had to leave five coffee pots full of good things all cooking on the stove! We sorrowfully marched to Libby and came before Turner, who had a big black dog, a big nigger and a sergeant (who had deserted from our army) in the office with him.

After Captain Munroe had consulted with Turner in an undertone we were all told to "give up our bags and go into the next room to be searched." Turner was in a bad humor, and there was no help for it. We were searched by the sergeant two at a time. I came last. Briggs, the sergeant, preceded me to an inner room. On the way there he picked up a coil of manila rope from the floor [and carried] it with him. Visions of hanging or binding came before me at once, which made me very nervous. But he hung the rope up on a nail in the wall and we entered a small room with one barred window overlooking the canal.

Here Briggs felt my pockets, felt the seams of all my clothes except the overcoat, which I had recovered at Scott's building. He found needles and thread, two knives, my tin quart measure, and two cans of condensed milk. He took the milk but not the other things. I had left my overcoat on the floor of Turner's office. In it were some cakes, a flat can of corned beef and $20 in greenbacks sewed in under the cape at the neck. I had $30 Confederate. This he confiscated, and gave to Turner with the milk. I found my comrades all in line while Turner was folding and putting into a wooden box the money taken from them, about $15 greenbacks in all and a few dollars in Confederate. We had got this money (the greenbacks) out of the boxes sent [to] soldiers. None but myself took the precaution to sew it in our clothes. All at once Turner asked Briggs "if he had taken off and searched our shoes?" He said no! When Turner cursed him roundly and we had to remove our shoes and stockings before him: nothing was found however.

Turner then vented his wrath on one of our sergeants who belonged to the 1st New York Dragoons, because he had on four nice white shirts, one over another! He hesitated whether to take them off or not, but as it was growing dark he did not order him to do so. A guard of ten men were waiting on the sidewalk for us and we were all remanded to Crew and Pemberton except myself, who was consigned to No. eight dungeon under Libby. I spoke up at this and said that "All prisoners had a right to escape if they could," while Captain Munroe put in a good word for me, and that we had all worked hard and done our work faithfully. Turner thereupon changed his mind, and I was told that I could go with the others.

We filed out of the narrow door and went across the street to Crew and Pemberton when old Cunningham unlocked the door at the head of the stairs and we found ourselves among our old comrades in arms whom we had left thirteen days ago. And found it the same old place surrounded by the sick, dying and filth of every description as when we had left it. The Rebel guard on the sidewalk were lounging around, sitting in the doorway and took us for a lot of new prisoners. They wanted to know "where we uns came from?" and "where we got our new clothes," etc. We chaffed them until the doors were opened for us. Nearly all the guards wore our new blue overcoats over their dirty, greasy gray homespun clothes, with horn buttons instead of metal ones. We were received joyously by the sailors, marines, and our personal friends on the top floor, and shared with them the needle thread and stuff which we had managed to secrete from Briggs.

Some of us had secreted money in our pipes with tobacco on top. Some had money in the linings of their caps. Many of the seams in their clothing had been cut, to find money, without success. I kept two large needles and a big hank of black thread, which was invaluable. I had lots of paper too, which was very scarce in prison, and from which I made a diary, making entries all in short hand. I found a Testament in one of the boxes, which was not taken from me. I used the margins of the pages for a diary, mostly in short hand. I had three lead pencils and two knives, and with a piece of india ink, and seven or eight steel pens taken from Captain Munroe's desk found myself well fitted out for sketching. As no rations were served us, we grew ravenous hungry even at the thought of the splendid supper which we had to leave cooking on the stove when we left Scott's building.

I divided up my canned meat and cakes with Walsh, Halley, Rhineheart, and Colvin, and sat on the floor with the others telling all about the glorious old times we had over at Scott's. Our officers confined in Libby hailed us from the windows as we came out, and thought that we were "fresh fish" or new prisoners, as our good living and new clothes furnished by the Sanitary Commission at Scott's building showed on our now fat ribs and jaunty appearances. We talked ourselves hoarse during the moonlight night, recounting our adventures, and everyone wiped his mouth who listened to us, when we mentioned the quantities of canned beef, milk, brandied peaches, apple sauce, turkey, chicken, etc., which eight of us had devoured for thirteen days over in Scott's building. . . .

January 20, 1864

Three Rebel surgeons came in among us today, and after going through the rooms gave [the] order that "All those who had never been vaccinated for the small pox were to go down on the second floor." There was some commotion among us as hundreds formed lines under the direction of Ross, the Libby prison clerk, and the roll was called. They were met by several surgeons and ten Rebel guards. All had to be vaccinated excepting those who could show a scar of former vaccination. Those who had never been so vaccinated had to be now, as the guard forced them whether or no. About 300 of us could show scars and were sent back. I was not vaccinated as I showed my scar. Some resisted the operation, but were held by two strong Rebels while the surgeon operated. Afterwards we were told by the guard outside that "we Yanks had good nigger blood put into us." This we understood to be virus taken from Negroes whether healthy or not we did not learn. The surgeons were cursed before they got half through the operation while many resisted with all their strength but the Rebel guards generally threw them on the floor and held them there until they were vaccinated. . . .

The Rebels had allowed seven or eight corpses at a time to lay among us on the floors, and we had been more than once compelled to throw them bodily out of the windows because they would not take them out! Now it looked as if they took a fatherly interest in us by vaccination. Arguments were kept up among us for days and nights as to the chances of being vaccinated with good or diseased virus.

As money was mighty scarce among us, a plan was started by which a $1 greenback could be turned into a $100 bill to pass on the guards. Not one in ten of these Rebels could read anyhow but they recognized United States in German text and the denomination of the bill. This always had satisfied them as they wasted no time in examining the bill further. I was called on by certain parties and agreed to make the attempt if they would furnish me the india ink and camel's hair brush with red ink. The oldest sailor had a large piece of india ink which he used for tattooing arms and legs on board ship and which they had not taken from him. Someone among us had a printed advertisement gotten up like United States money. Mustang liniment or something of the sort. There were about six of them. I blotted out the medical part, wrote in [the name of the] Secretary of Treasury, and changed it to $100, using blood for the red seal part of it. I then tried on a $1 greenback . . . but made seven or eight others so that they would pass for $10 each. As it took $25 Confederate to equal $1 United States currency, a nice profit was made on the $1 notes. These all passed eventually the guard giving change in Confederate money of course. I made $150 Confederate out of the job, and went up in the attic to do it, where in the daytime only a few prisoners were.

The money was always passed on the guard at dusk so that he could not see to read very well. Still the numbers or denomination was the only thing he satisfied himself with. And soon we bought lots of things from the guard, who procured them from the Rebel sutler over in the lot opposite Libby. We never heard anything more of the bogus money, whether the sutler or guard were "stuck on it" or not. Nobody among us knew who did make the stuff, as I worked secretly at it at different times. I changed eight or nine genuine $1 bills to $10 each and six advertisements to $100 each which made me rich. I bought all I could from the sailors, who bought from the guard, and shared the potatoes, onions, bread, etc., with my intimate friends, giving away my daily rations of goober bean soup and corn pone to those who would have them. This lasted twenty days. . . .

A day or two ago we saw from our front windows some high toned Rebel dressed in citizen's clothes and wearing a high silk hat. Two Rebel officers were with him showing him around. They all went into Libby prison to see Turner. As they passed our fellows yelled out of the windows "Hi there Jeff. Let us out of this." "What are you doing with that ham," "Drop it," etc. Many of us thought it must be Jeff Davis. We see Rebel officers very often coming out of the warehouse on the other side of the street with their pockets full of canned food and a ham or so under their arms. . . .

February 1, 1864

Snow and fog. The Rebels put up a printed handbill on the entrance door on second floor of this prison which offered $500 in Confederate money and a suit of clothes to anyone of us who would enlist in their army! Yelling and curses greeted the Rebel sergeant who put it up. It was torn down whenever he turned his back and another one was put up in the passage way at the stair landing outside the door which we could see but not reach. A crowd of prisoners were around the door all day who chaffed the Rebel sergeant and guard. Amid yells and curses the thing was taken down in the afternoon. They got no recruits here. If any one of us had showed any symptoms of recruiting to the Rebels, he would have been murdered at once by his comrades. Ragged, half starved, and miserable as we were, not one of us would fight for Jeff or any of his gang. . . .

February 15, 1864

I have just recovered from typhoid fever and came near dying. My friend Littlefield stayed by and nursed me in the best way he could. I was delirious for five days and during this time knew nothing of my horrid surroundings. I thought I was inside an immense water wheel and strove to keep my footing on the buckets as it went round and round. The ceiling of the room here being cross bridged must have reminded me of a water wheel. I remembered seeing three or four Rebel surgeons who were looking and examining me as the last thing in the room. My friends say that I sprang at them with great strength, threw one on the floor and nearly tore the clothes off the other one. It took three strong men to hold me to the floor for three or four hours. The surgeons ordered me to be taken to the Rebel hospital and I resisted all their efforts to move me downstairs. I laid on the floor with a brick under my head insensible for two days. When I came to I was as if in a dream. Littlefield had made some weak beef tea and was trying to force it down my throat. I was so weak as not to be able to stand alone for two days more, so I consider that I had a "close call.". . .

Chapter Seven

Prison Train to Andersonville

While typhoid fever prostrated Sneden, the greatest prison break of the war took place a few dozen yards away across the street at Libby. On February 9, 1864, more than a hundred Yankee officers escaped under cover of darkness through a tunnel they had dug to a shed in the adjoining vacant lot. Though the Confederates recaptured nearly half of them, fifty-nine reached Federal lines. Sneden later took sardonic pleasure in describing how the event electrified Richmonders—"a grand scare for the old maids no doubt." Certainly it confirmed the predictions of those who had warned all along against trying to house so many prisoners in their city.

If the escape terrified Richmonders, it emboldened the men at the Pemberton and Crew Prison to attempt their own break. After the news from Libby, they planned and schemed excitedly about digging their own tunnel to an empty warehouse across the street. But as Sneden lamented, "it all ended in talk."

The new year brought increasing privation, not just to the prisoners of war but to their jailers as well. In the early weeks of 1864, the South faced narrowing, though not yet fatal, prospects. Hope faded that Britain and France would recognize the Confederacy. The happy times of Southern victories that had energized home front and soldiers alike had passed. The war in the West piled disaster upon disaster. In the East, Lee's great days of carrying the fight to the North had vanished.

And yet Confederates hoped that spring campaigning might yet reverse the tide. Despite the belt-tightening at home and the ominously growing disparity of strength between the opposing forces, hopes for a Southern republic endured while the armies hibernated in their winter camps in the Virginia Piedmont and on the Tennessee-Georgia border. The Confederacy still harbored great reservoirs of strength, and Union prisoners knew they were still in the hands of a determined enemy.

The Libby escape confirmed to the Confederate military hierarchy the wisdom of its plans to open a new prison in a remote area. There, they hoped, the prisoners of war would not pose as great a threat to security and presumably would be easier to guard and feed. By late February, the new camp in southwest Georgia neared completion. It first touched the lives of Sneden and his fellow captives in Richmond—though they did not yet know it—on February 22. On that day they received orders to pack up their few, pitiful belongings and prepare to leave for an undisclosed destination.

After three months of close confinement, they took heart. Any movement, they reasoned, was better than languishing in the detested Rebel capital. Their six-hundred-mile journey south in filthy cattle cars filled many of them with an excitement all out of proportion to their wretched circumstances. The much hoped for prisoner exchange seemed close at hand.

During the trip and during his months of confinement, Sneden was able to scratch out only a shorthand account, but these accumulated jottings, along with his sketches, gave him the basis for his memoir.

February 22, 1864

After we had roll call this morning Ross gave us notice to be "ready to leave by the [rail] cars for the south at any hour of the day." There was great excitement and everyone began to pack up what few things he had. The sick could not go and they bewailed their situation as all they could see before them was the Rebel hospital and sure death. Ross would not say where we were going but the Rebel guard told us that we were all going to Georgia to be exchanged. Some believed this, but most of us did not. At 4 p.m. a detachment larger than usual went out to the cook house for extra rations, and an hour later, all were served with a loaf of corn bread double the size of the usual ration. Many thought that we were going to Savannah for exchange, as our gunboat fleet were below that city. Songs and shouting were heard all over the building, and a new life seemed to take possession of most of us.

We waited until midnight, when Ross came from Libby and told us to "pack up right smart and get down on the lower floor." Such yells, cat calls, and confusion [were] never seen here before. We filed down stairs by the hundred at a time, and on to the sidewalk, where we stood in line four files deep for nearly an hour before moving on. It was very cold with snow and we were thoroughly chilled through. . . . We were guarded by over 300 Rebels, who carried pine torches, and had old muskets, but no bayonets.

The Rebel officer shouted out to shoot every d____d Yank who tried to escape and the column about 450 of us started up Cary Street and kept along the streets which bordered the river and canal. Hundreds of the Belle Island prisoners in the other half of the building were left behind. They shouted and yelled like wild animals when they saw us moving off in the darkness. As we passed Libby Prison the officers there shouted to us, and wanted to know where we were going. Of course we could not say. Many yelled out "Exchange."...

After a long wait we were marched over the railroad bridge to Manchester, where we were packed sixty to seventy into cattle cars and boxcars which stood on the track. These cars were all in a filthy state, and the manure was some inches deep in the cattle cars. There were no seats, and we had to stand pretty close together. Here we were left for the rest of the night. It must have been 3 o'clock in the morning. Rebel guards were posted on the roofs of the cars, and were strung out on both sides of the track. We munched on our corn bread and shivered with the cold until sunrise. There was no water to be had. I and a few others had taken the precaution to fill our canteens before leaving. Canteens were very scarce among us and many suffered from thirst. Some of the sick fellows had come with us too, and they had to squat down on the filthy floors of the cattle cars. There was no sleep for any of us as we were so closely packed together that there was no room to lie down. We worried through the remainder of this miserable night. The snow made the ground white, but stopped about daylight, though we were numbed with the cold wind from off the river. My comrades, Walsh, Rhineheart, Halley, Colvin, and most of those who were captured with me managed to get into a boxcar, when we shut the doors on both sides, but could not sleep for sixty-two of us were packed in it.

We passed this miserable time in eating our corn bread, smoking and conjecturing where we were going. There were thirteen cars; part of the train stood on a high trestle work. We never gave a thought to try to escape, and we were strongly guarded. We chaffed the guard on the roof, but could get no information whatever.

February 23, 1864

Cold and windy. An old, wheezy locomotive pushed the train up to the end of the high trestle. Two or three cars more were added to the train and we waited here until 10 a.m. before starting. The doors of the cars were kept closed except an opening of about three feet wide. Four guards were stationed in each car at the door. We crowded to the opening for light and fresh air. I pushed my way into the first row and had a good view of the surroundings. Belle Island lay below us in the river, now deserted, a few ragged tents and a mud embankment full of sticks and debris of a camp was all that could be seen. The flagstaff was crooked and showed where the battery had been....

A thin skim of ice was along the shores of the river, and the Tredegar Ironworks were in full blast. Richmond, with the capitol and church steeples were in full view. Hotels, factories and huge flouring mills were all along the river and canal. Fort Winder flew a dirty old

Rebel flag. It was built on clay or mud with log breastworks, faced on the outside with clay. Manchester, with its numerous mills and factories was in full view, and the rocks stuck up in the James River in all directions above the rushing current and falls, around Belle Island and under the three bridges.

About 9 a.m., a long line of prisoners were seen coming over the bridges under a strong Rebel guard, who soon joined us and clambered into the empty cars near the engine. They all came from Crew and Pemberton Prison. About 10 o'clock the whistle blew and we started on our unknown journey amid yells and much noise. I had brought my piece of hardwood log with me, which now served as a seat, no one else had anything to sit on. I got near the door, which was now shoved more than half open and saw the country which we passed through. We got to Petersburg, where the locomotive took water, and could see that it was a pretty place on the Appomattox River. We saw no signs of any earthworks or fortifications. The citizens crowded around the cars to see the "Yanks" and some school girls threw some apples in among us which created a great scuffle when the doors were closed on us by the guard.

We left Petersburg and came to Lawrenceville, Virginia, crossing a railroad bridge over the [Meherrin] River. The guards were on the roof, and on the ground twenty feet or so from the cars, with their muskets at a "ready" to shoot any one of us who would try to escape. This was a pretty place. A large stone building on the outskirts looked like a college or an arsenal. The tender of the engine leaked badly, and the rickety old engine puffed and wheezed all the while, so we had to make many stops to take wood and water. No coal was burnt by the engines on the southern railroads. Long piles of cordwood were met with at every station, and along the tracks.

We started again about 3 p.m. The guard got down from the roof of the car and came inside with us. They sat on a board supported at either end by a block of wood. Two to each door. They were a lot of old ragged dirty Rebels [who] had percussion locks to their muskets and were not abusive or ugly with us. We were not allowed to leave the car when at a stopping place on any account. Our water had given out in the morning, and we were all thirsty of course. One old ragged guard took all the canteens that we had in our car and filled them with water for us at the pumping station. Old darkies do the work at all of these "wood up" stations. Cutting the cord wood and pumping the water into the tender by hand, they have no syphon water pipe as we have in the North. The railroads were very rickety, the cars jolted and did not run smooth. They swayed right and left all the time. The tracks are laid on wooden rails which are then spiked to the sleepers, not spiked to the sleeper on each side of the rail as in the North. All the insulators on the telegraph poles were made of brown or red earthenware instead of glass. On the front of the train were two or three platform cars on which were two or three pieces of artillery, sent from the Tredegar Works for some fort south.

Here the officer of the guard with eight or ten soldiers were seated. All were dressed in homespun gray clothes, no mark of any kind on them. We came to Hicksford, a small town with many log houses in it. Then we crossed the Roanoke River over a long trestle bridge at Gaston. The opposite side was fortified by a redoubt and a series of rifle trenches extending along shore. The hills were low and scrub oak was plentiful. We had sixteen cars in our train, and before we crossed over the engineer must have thought that we would break through the bridge, as he and two others walked down to see the timbers before risking going over. After some delay he started again, and we went over as fast as the wheezy old engine could pull us. Several Rebel officers and some soldiers came out of the fort or redoubt on the other side to see us Yanks. Red clay banks were seen in all directions and the country had a desolate look, very few houses were seen, and these were nearly all small ones. Our rations had all been eaten up and now we were ravenously hungry but no fresh rations were given us.

Gaston is near the state line of Virginia and North Carolina, and a strategic point. A branch road runs from thence to Weldon. We left Gaston about sundown and got to Raleigh the capital of North Carolina about 11 p.m. Here we were switched off on a side track and remained there for the rest of the night. The doors were shut nearly close and we were nearly suffocated for want of air. None of us were allowed to leave the cars on any pretense whatever. We had to sit down on the car floor, or try to sleep standing up. The engine left us, and we were on the outskirts of the city about one half mile from it. . . .

February 24, 1864

Rain. We were all taken out of the box and cattle cars at 5 a.m. and marched towards Raleigh, where at the depot we were all put upon platform cars. Three or four of us had escaped during the night, but were caught and brought back covered from head to foot with red mud. We had eight Rebel guards on each car with us. We got three crackers apiece of the same kind as last night. Another old battered engine took us in tow, and we pulled out of the station about 7 a.m. Very few people were about, as it was a freight station. A cold rain storm set in, while we switched back and forth for a long time before starting. The red mud banks and deep cuts with a great number of tracks and switches at Raleigh put us in mind forcibly of Jersey. The train passed slowly through the outskirts of the city.

At one place we passed back of the rear gardens and lots and were surprised to see twenty or thirty young girls and women looking over their back fences at us, and to get a shower of apples and sweet cakes from them as we slowly drew out of the city. There was a grand scramble for these things, in which the sick were trampled on, while the women and girls laughed loud at our efforts to secure the apples and cakes. The North Carolina people are not as rabid secessionists as the Virginians and a strong Union sentiment prevails among them.

We had a new guard too, and most of them were North Carolinians. They were all old

Union Prisoners of War Crossing the Yadkin River on Platform Cars
Near Salisbury, N.C., February 24, 1864.

men of the home guard. They would not talk but wanted to trade buttons, or anything else we had. They kept a sharp eye on us however, and no one was permitted to leave the car on any pretense. Those among us who had blankets could keep dry, but those who had foolishly sold them to the Rebel guard in Richmond now had to get thoroughly wet in the drizzling rain. We came to Greensboro, where we stopped for wood and water for the engine and our water tubs were refilled. Here a lot of Negro women crowded around us. They had sweet potato pie for 50¢ and cold chicken for $1, but we had very little or no money. The guard kept them off from the cars with their guns. (They had no bayonets either.) And would not let them sell us anything even if we had any money.

We crossed the Yadkin River about 3 p.m. on a trestle bridge, and after waiting an hour to let another train pass, continued on and arrived at Salisbury, N.C. about 6 p.m. Here the engine broke down, and we were switched on a side track which ran past the prison fence, which looked to be twenty feet high. Another engine pulled off most of the train of ten flatcars with the prisoners on them, while two cars were left behind. We were marched into the prison yard for the night. There were about eighty of us. Here we met several hundred of our fellow prisoners who were dirt begrimed, ragged and in a deplorable state, covered with mud from the yard which looked and smelt like a hogpen. They shouted "fresh fish, Where did you come from? What army do you belong to? Where is Meade?" and a hundred other questions all at once. There were five or six ragged Sibley tents in the yard with the mud a foot thick all around them and dozens of skeleton looking prisoners crowded around us.

Cook house and yard for prisoners, five acres of ground — Cotton factory prison about 1,350 men — Hoisting steps to second story — Gate — Well

REBEL PRISON AT SALISBURY, N.C.
Commanded by Major John H. Gee. February 25, 1864.

We entered the prison yard through a strong gate in the high plank fence, on the top of which were posted the Rebel guard. Two small pieces of artillery were mounted on scaffolding outside the fence. These guns could sweep the yard with grape and canister from end to end. The yard was overcrowded with the most abject, dirty, ragged lot of prisoners that we ever saw. It was hard to believe that these grimy skeletons of men were once in our army. There were mostly men captured from the army of the West. There were lots of Negro soldiers here too. In October last there were 10,000 prisoners confined here, now there were about 3,000, hundreds of whom had died. The place was so crowded that many had to sleep and live in the filthy yard which was trampled into a muck which went over our shoes, and smelt just like a pig pen. Very frequently one or more detachments of 800 men would get no rations at all for twenty-four and thirty hours. Bread was from $5 to $15 a small loaf (Confederate) and the prisoners having no money, sold their overcoats and blankets, blouses, buttons and anything they had for food.

For weeks the prisoners in the yard had no shelter whatever. All were thinly clad, thousands were barefooted, and not one in twenty had a blanket, blouse, shirt or shoes! One Sibley tent and one A tent were furnished to each squad of 100 men. There were only a few of these standing now, all were torn, ragged, and very dirty. The cloth had been cut from them to patch clothes with. The rest burrowed in the ground, or under the buildings, having first torn away the foundation stones. The main building was crowded to suffocation from the second floor to the attic. The windows of the ventilator on the roof was partially boarded up to keep out the cold.

The prison was originally a cotton factory. . . . A smaller building was near it in the yard which had been a boiler and engine house. All were of brick. The main building had a tower with doors on each story. . . . At one time no prisoners were confined on the first floor of the factory. A novel contrivance was made so that the prisoners could get access to the rooms above the first floor. This was a mast, holding a movable gangway or boardwalk which worked by a rope and pulley. When it was hoisted close to the mast all access was cut off from the second floor to the ground. There were two old broken stoves, which filled the rooms with dense smoke, and the whole place was infested with vermin, while ragged clothes, bed quilts, and blankets, all reeking with vermin hung up on nails and strings in every room. The mud and other filth in the yard was horrible. All the prisoners were covered with red mud and filth, ragged and half starved.

The head devil or jailor was Major John H. Gee, CSA.* He believed in starving the prisoners so that they were too weak to get away. He even would not allow the commissary to issue full rations, small as they were. No light of any kind was furnished. Vermin swarmed everywhere, and the prisoners were tortured night and day with them, cold and hungry, amid noxious smells and smoke from the fires, thousands died and were buried like dogs. . . .

The Rebel surgeons were generally humane and attentive but the authorities at Richmond and Salisbury took no notice of the atrocities, while the citizens generally deplored the situation but could do nothing to help, as long as the fiend Major Gee was in command of the prison. Many of the prisoners were farmers, citizens, sutlers, and other non-combatants, who had been sent from other prisons. They looked on us in astonishment, as we had on new clean clothes which were issued to us at Richmond, while they were only half clad in dirty, ragged, homespun clothes, while hundreds were barefoot and bareheaded, having rags tied around their feet, bound with strings. . . .

February 25, 1864

Fine day, cold east wind. Many of us were up and about at daylight, for it was too cold to sleep. Many of us had no overcoats or blankets, stockings, or underclothing. These foolish fellows had sold these things to the guard at Richmond, and now they had to shiver. About

*Here Sneden adds an editorial note on the overall history of conditions at Salisbury based on his postwar knowledge of the prison. Conditions at Salisbury began reasonably well for prisoners early in the war, but by the time Sneden's train passed through, sanitary conditions had worsened dramatically. After he left, the mortality rate eventually exceeded that of Andersonville. Major John H. Gee, the commandant at Salisbury who gained a notorious reputation, perhaps unfairly, because of the bad conditions over which he presided, was not put in charge until after Sneden's time there.

7 a.m. we were all marched out of the gate, and were met by a guard of about 100 men who belonged to the "City Battalion." Old men and young boys, all of whom were dressed in gray homespun or jeans. There were only five bayonets in the crowd, and many of the guns were old flintlocks. Some had double barreled shotguns. The railroad track ran pretty close to the fence on the outside of the yard. We were marched a long way down this track to a curve, when we saw on the switch our train of the night previous waiting for us. They had lain there all night, and another engine pulled us off.

I had made a good sketch of the prison before leaving there. We were all now in box-cars and cattle cars, another guard was posted on the roofs and two inside with us, each sat at the door on a board supported by two blocks of wood. They faced outwards and had their muskets between their knees. Before going far some of us removed the gun caps from off their muskets, which we kept on the "half-cock." We passed lots of Negroes, who were cutting wood. Long piles of cordwood for the engine were on both sides of the track for several hundred yards. The trees were all cut and tapped for balsam and resin looking much like the maple trees in the North when tapped for syrup. Large iron pans and charcoal heaps were near the tracks. We came to a pretty village called Concord where the trees were very thick and numerous, [and] women were on the track waiting to see us pass. We went very slow, as the old engine had all it could to draw thirteen cars. We came to Charlotte which was a nice place, did not stop here, but continued on to Columbia, the capital of South Carolina. This was a very handsome city with many fine buildings. . . .

Lots of mulatto women surrounded us in the cars. They had sweet potato pie, and other things for sale, but the guard kept them off on the sidewalk line and we had very little money among us to buy anything, but [the doors] were pulled open by us and again shut several times by the guard. Long trains of cotton were standing on the tracks for transportation to Charleston or Wilmington, North Carolina. It was after 5 p.m. before we pulled out of Columbia. Seven or eight of our fellows had escaped from the train while we waited in the streets, but they were all caught by the guards and the provost, and brought back just before we started. It came on a dark cold night, with a drizzling rain. . . .

About 10 p.m. we crossed the Edisto River on a high bridge of some length. When we got to about the middle of the bridge, by a concerted movement the two guards in our car were pushed clean out simultaneously from each open door where they sat as usual! They must have fallen sixty or more feet down among the rocks in the river, one of their muskets fell inside the car, but it was thrown out too. The train was going very slow over the bridge, but when we got to the land side the speed was increased and we went on for a mile nearly. When it came to a dead stop in a clump of trees, it was very dark and raining hard. The wheezy old engine was taking water at a roadside tank. A Rebel officer came along, and noticed that no guard was visible in our car. When he asked where the guard was we told him that "they had stopped at the bridge to get a drink!" He could not understand why they were not in the car. Two more guards were therefore put in our car to replace the others thrown out! We never heard what became of them, but they must surely have been killed or drowned, for we could hear the rushing water below us but could not see anything for darkness. The deviltry which prompted our fellows to throw out the guard came from the fact that several of them had cut a hole in the floor of the car with their knives, which was large enough to crawl through for a small man. Several of them were getting ready to escape while the cars were not in motion. Two Rebel officers now came alongside the car in the darkness, and ordered us to give up our knives.

One of our fellows yelled at him with an oath to "come in and take them." They did not try to. After a while we continued on, going very slow, as the engine did not seem able to pull us any faster, one extra guard had been put on the roof of each car before starting. We stopped a few minutes every little while, and soon we could hear the musket shots from the guard in the other cars in front of us. Our fellows were escaping to the woods on either side of the track. None got out from our car, as the guard was on the alert and did not sit in the doorway. One of them fell partly asleep and let his musket drop on the floor. It was a wonder that it did not go off among us as it was at half cock. After this our fellows got the caps off the nipples of both guns without the owners knowing it. They were very old men, and quite communicative, said that they were conscripted, and cursed Jeff Davis thoroughly. They were North Carolina home guards. After this the cars kept at a better speed, so that it was impossible to get away by the holes in the floors of the cars. After we had crossed two or three rivers on bridges we came at daylight to Augusta. . . .

February 27, 1864

Fine and cold. At 10 o'clock we were visited by Bradford, the Rebel provost marshal with several well dressed citizens who seemed very gentlemanly, and sympathized with us in our misery and hard luck to be prisoners of war. They told us that efforts were being made by the Confederacy to have us soon exchanged, but that our government would not consent, as the Rebels would not exchange Negro soldiers captured. General Butler being our exchange commissioner wanted his niggers exchanged. Butler got the cursings of the whole lot of us. We learned too that medicine was contraband of war, and that the Rebels had very little of it in the Confederacy. They could only get it through the blockade runners at Wilmington. A large laboratory was in operation at Augusta where medicines of some kinds were made principally from herbs and roots. Quinine was worth fabulous sums, owing to its scarcity. Some citizens brought us food, but the guard would not let them pass it in to us. The provost marshal told us that we were going to a fine place near Macon where we would all camp out, and get enough to eat. Our spirits rose in proportion to the nice yarns which he told us. This was to make us docile, and not to try to escape while under his care. Rations were furnished us which consisted of three large ship biscuit made of wheat flour and about one half pound of boiled beef each. About noon we were all marched out again to take the cars. The dandy officer of the guard called them carriages! On the way many citizens crowded on the sidewalks to see us and many plugs of tobacco were thrown by them to us.

We boarded boxcars or freight cars, where we were so thickly packed that it was hard to get enough air; sixty-two were in each car! The guards were on the roofs while two were inside with us stationed at the doors. We broke the siding off the cars for more air with the pieces of iron picked up in the foundry. One of the guards thrust his musket through, swearing he would shoot. The barrel was seized by those inside and pulled inward so that the guard was nearly pulled off the roof. He did not fire, however. We had air enough now in our car. One of the Rebel guards fell off the roof of another and [was] hurt. He was picked up insensible and taken into the cab next to the engine. After the train had started, several of us hung up a blanket inside, while others began cutting the floor to make a hole to escape by when the train should stop. After working for hours the enterprise was given up as we had no saw and many knives had been broken. We passed through a fine hilly country, and saw many rice fields flooded with water by the wayside.

About 7 p.m. we came to Goreham Junction. . . . The cars were sidetracked and we all had to get out in a rain storm, when we were marched a few hundred feet until we came to a deep hollow made by the embankments of the railroad where two tracks crossed each other. Down in this muddy hole which was partly covered with tree stumps and loose brushwood we bivouacked for the night. Small fires were made, but would not burn much on account of being wet. We got plenty of pitch pine smoke however. We huddled in small groups in the hollow, while the Rebel guard were posted above us on the railroad tracks on the embankment. About midnight we were served with three crackers and a slice of raw bacon. We pulled our blankets over our heads and sat on stumps and stones until daylight through a drizzling rain. We had gotten one good night's sleep in the foundry, and not many of us slept at all here. The place was called "Hell's Delight" by the guard and before morning the red mud was nearly over our shoes. The guards built quite large fires on the side of the railroad track above us. These enabled them to see us all the time to prevent escape. This hole had been used some weeks ago by a detachment of our prisoners who had preceded.

February 28, 1864

Rain and fog. We were aroused very early by the guard firing on some of our fellows who had crawled up the embankment and rushed through their line. There was a long strip of woods not far off and the Yanks had run the line. Someone of our fellows had been hit in the leg and was recaptured. Another had been badly wounded in the arm. Several got away. The guard were cross and surly, of course no roll call was had since leaving Richmond, so we never knew how many got away, seven or eight anyhow, as their friends and comrades missed them.

Shortly after 10 a.m. we were all put into freight cars and old cattle cars and started for Macon. The manure in some of the cattle cars had not been removed. I and my friends fortunately got into the freight car. We had a new guard. They thought more of trading with the Yanks than anything else. Consequently several of our fellows escaped by jumping out of the car doors while going slow though the woods. As most of the guard were lying flat on the car roofs, they had not much time to get up and fire at the escaping prisoner before he had struck the underbrush. We passed through the outskirts of Milledgeville, about noon. This was a fine city, the public buildings were fine and costly. It was a very fashionable center for the high toned families of the Confederacy and the inhabitants were very aristocratic and wealthy. It is the capital of Georgia at the head of navigation on the Savannah River. Our old engine took water for a long time at a tank on the outside of the city. It seemed to leak out of the tender as fast as they pumped it in. Negroes did the work by a hand pump, while here three of our fellows jumped out of the half closed car doors and getting over a rail fence made for a hill and strip of woods. One guard fired, then they all fired. The guard were as usual lying flat on the roofs of the cars, trading and talking with us. One of our fellows fell and was slightly wounded as he straddled a fence. Five of the guard ran and recaptured him. He wore green plaid trousers, such as the 79th New York Highland regiment used to wear. I heard that this was the fourth time he had got away and was caught again. . . .

When Sneden's train arrived at Andersonville on the last day of February 1864, the Confederates had just finished the stockade and received the first contingent of prisoners only four days before. General John Henry Winder, the provost marshal in Richmond, would arrive that summer to take command—first of Andersonville and eventually of all Confederate prisons east of the Mississippi. The local commandant for most of Andersonville's notorious history was Captain Henry Wirz, a profane, controversial Swiss native whose iron regime repeatedly enraged the prisoners. Wirz was given pitiful resources and a hopeless situation to manage. Fairly or not, he became the universal object of loathing on the part of Union prisoners and the Northern public in general. Because Wirz was such a prominent presence at Andersonville, Sneden, writing his memoir years later, mistakenly places Wirz on the scene when his train arrived. Wirz, in fact, did not reach the prison until early March, as Sneden later notes.

February 29, 1864

. . . Our guards told us on leaving Macon that we were going to Anderson, where there was a nice large field all fenced in, which was full of shade trees and grass with a brook running through it, and that "it was too good for you Yanks anyway." And as the train drew up in front of a long row of log houses on the track, we were informed that we must "tumble out

THE SOUTH GATE FROM THE OUTSIDE, ANDERSONVILLE PRISON, GA.

right smart away." The log house was the depot, and we were at our journey's end. We had been five days and nights on the cars and all were glad enough to get out of them, over twenty were so sick and feeble that their companions had to lift them out of the filthy cars and lay them on the ground. Out beyond a clearing in the woods we saw a high fence between two hills, but no trees in the enclosure. In a few minutes a long line of Rebel guards perhaps 500 strong filed along the track, headed by a round shouldered black visaged officer on an iron gray horse. This was Captain Wirz, the Rebel jailor and commandant of the prison. He wore an old slouch hat, his beard and hair was black, mixed with gray, and he had a villainous look of authority. As with many oaths he ordered us all out of the cars to form [a] line. He and all the guard were dressed in common gray homespun clothes with horn buttons, and no military insignia whatever. From a belt, Wirz carried two large revolvers.

All the guards had muskets with bayonets fixed. The guard formed [the] line in a bungling unmilitary way, and we were formed in columns of fours, and started across over the sand hills towards the prison, while Wirz rode at the head of the column swearing and cursing at us for not going faster, and at the guard for not making us do so. "Pick up the damned Yanks with your bayonet" he would order. We struggled down and into ravines which were full of loose sand, and up small hills covered with stumps and fallen trees, until we were all out of breath. Many a comrade had to hold up and support his fellow in misery before we had gone the distance to the gate of the prison, which was about 800 to 1,000 feet. As we all had been robbed when captured and by Turner in Richmond, there was nothing left for Wirz. We had among us some greenbacks yet, which he did not suppose we had, so nothing was taken from us. We were about 750 men all told, all tired, hungry, weak, and depressed mentally. We could hardly drag one foot after the other; our confinement of five days in the boxcars, crowded in like sheep, cramped our limbs so that they ached all over. We reached one of the gates of the prison and were marched into the enclosure at dark. And the high strong gates shut us out from the world!

Here we were met by three or four hundred of our comrades who had arrived here before us, getting here on 15th February.* They had come from Richmond and Belle Island before we had started. It was so dark in a few minutes that we could do nothing but build little fires from the pine brush which lay all around us, and crouch in groups over them all night. There were hundreds of tree stumps from two to three feet high sticking out of the ground and a great many trees whose branches had been lopped off by the Negroes while building the stockade. By building a fire against one of these stumps we had one that lasted for many hours without replenishing it as the pitch pine gave out a great heat and made a good blaze. All the prisoners who came here before we did were in a half starved, ragged and dirty condition. The pitch pine smoke made them look like Negroes. All had tales of the horrible situation and the brutal treatment by Wirz. The night was cold but starlit, lanterns flashed once in a while from where the headquarters of Wirz were on a hill in a double log house which was surrounded by a log breastwork and a battery of eight guns. A dismal swamp ran through the middle of the enclosure through which ran a sluggish brook. Many of our fellows during the night got stuck in the mud while getting water. We had no rations and were very hungry.

We slept on felled trees and on the ground around our fires as we were cramped and tired out. Many kept talking all night to our newfound companions in misery. None seemed to have met before in any other of the Rebel prisons. I with Walsh, Halley, Rhineheart and Colvin slept on our blankets with overcoats on, shoes under our heads (army style) before a large blazing pine stump and kept warm all night. Rebel sentinels on top of the stockade called the hours and all's well from the number of his post all night.

March 1, 1864

The camp was astir by sunrise, everyone gathering pine brush to replenish the fires. We had a blustery cold day but we kept warm by piling up small trees and logs for fuel at night—fires were built alongside a fallen tree until it was burnt through. This was repeated until we had piles of short logs. We heard a Rebel drum beating on the hill about 7 a.m., which was for the guard to be relieved, and soon a long file of Rebel soldiers were seen coming down towards the south gate, while those who had been on duty all night returned in the same

*The early arrivals gave Sneden slightly incorrect information. The first contingent had arrived about February 24, 1864, making Sneden's party one of the earliest to be sent to the new prison.

manner to their camp of tents and log houses on the hill among the trees. Wirz came down an hour or so later on his white horse. This he left on the outside and came in among us. He ordered us into line then subdivided us into detachments of 270 men each.

These were again divided into nineties, with twenty-five men each to a mess. We had our own sergeants appointed to the detachments of 270, to those of the nineties, and corporals to the messes of twenty-five. I and my friends were put into the second thousand, third hundred. So, when 2.3. was called by the sergeants, those belonging to it fell in line for roll call.

This was done by our men. This was to see how many rations were called for. Wirz went along the lines of men inspecting them and heard all the roll calls. He was a tall round shouldered man with a very foul mouth, for he swore at anything and everything. He wore a gray Rebel jacket with leaden buttons, a slouch hat, and had his two revolvers strapped behind to his belt. We numbered 2,660 men.

About 10 a.m. two wagons, drawn by two mules each, with Negro drivers, drove in with hundreds of bags of corn meal. These bags were thrown on the ground all along the line of shanties on the route, when the sergeants of the 270 would open and measure out as near as he could guess a pint to each man. These were given to the other sergeants and corporals of the messes. Some got a little more, some less, though it was measured by a tin cup, which are not all the same size. This was all we got. When the wagons drove out a Rebel sergeant came in with each wagon fully armed, with another Rebel who acted as commissary.

The meal was very coarse, and the cob had been ground with it! Besides it was not bolted. Out of this we made mush, or corn cakes, which were baked by the fires in tin pans which we had made ourselves in Richmond from the tin roofing, cut at the corners with turned up edges, or in split canteens. We got water from the brook to mix the meal with. We had not a particle of salt, and everyone now went at work cooking the stuff as he best knew how. Many corn cakes were upset and lost in the fires while many were burnt hard and black as bricks.

It was "root hog or die" with us now, and the new occupation turned our thoughts for the moment from the miserable surroundings. The corn bread or cakes were found to be more substantial than the mush however, though hundreds did not know how to cook either. There were thousands of big and little fires smoking all over our enclosure all day, the black pitch pine smoke making us as black as niggers. We had no matches, so we never let a fire go entirely out. We could always borrow coals, and the fire burnt down to the roots of the big stumps, when they looked like great red hot stoves. When we had finished this mealy meal! all hands went at work constructing shelter. The underbrush was overhauled on both sides of the swamp and all got crotched sticks and poles, or sticks five or six feet long. Some of these were stuck in the ground and bent over to make an arch, the other end being stuck in the sandy soil also. On this were then spread blankets or overcoats fastened with strings. Others made regular shelters of crotched sticks five feet high, with ridge poles on which blankets were put. Two or four clubbed together what they had in the way

Union hospital outside / Causeway across swamp — Caves in bank — Stockade and dead line / Rifle trench at foot of hill — Wirz's log house and eight gun battery — Brook and swamp — Camp of Rebel guard / South gate

VIEW IN ANDERSONVILLE PRISON
Looking south from the swamp, April 1864.

of blankets who all slept together under them. Others made a wicker work of saplings and brush for one end of their shelters. (I did so and wove the pine tops in the interstices.) I fortunately had a rubber blanket, which came in for a roof. I had no other one but my chum had: this we laid on at night, pine tops being put under it next the ground.

The camp was not laid out in any order or shape, everyone had built his tent or shanty where he thought would be a good place, all along the road which ran from the north gate straight through the camp. Huts and shelters had been built by those who got here first of pine boughs, sticks, and mud taken from the swamp. There was not a single stone in the whole place larger than a marble. Old tattered overcoats and ragged dirty blankets were propped up on three sticks with just room enough to crawl under while some had dug holes in the ground three or four feet deep and made a slanting roof over them of poles and pine top boughs. The whole camp looked like a collection of pig pens. Walsh and Colvin made a shelter and shared it together. Halley and Rhineheart did the same. . . .

I made a bed of sand a foot or two from the ground to serve as a seat and a bed. On this I placed pine tops all laid one way. Over this was part of a blanket with a log of wood for a pillow. I made a pitch roof of my india rubber blanket and filled the three sides in with wicker work or boughs. It was six feet high inside and about 4 x 6 feet square. The stump of a tree served for a table. All the other stumps around were used for fires and I was smoked out several times. We had no soap or grease of any kind, and the smoke blackened us so that we looked like charcoal men or niggers. It was very hard to get the black off. Sand at the brook was the only thing to do it, with some corn meal mixed with it. All were unshaven and dirty, ragged, hungry and did not care how he looked. . . .

Having constructed thousands of shanties and shelters, we all slept the second night more comfortable than at first. Many were in good spirits and kept talking and joking most of the night, but after midnight it came on to be very cold with a strong north wind. Many had to get out and build fires, at which they laid until morning. We laid to windward of the smoke as a rule. Those who did not looked like chimney sweeps in the morning. One young fellow slept inside the trunk of a large pine tree, by crawling into it. The heart of the trunk had been burnt out with fire previously.

He was tall, lanky, and thin as a rail from starvation. He was a pitiable object in daylight, being as black as a crow all over. He was sick too, and his pallid face showed in blotches where he had rubbed the dirt off. He was known as "Skeleton Jim." He did not live many weeks. Today I inspected our prison pen and made a plan of it. . . . Walked all over the ground but did not go near the stockade as the guard had orders to shoot us [if] we did so.

Some of our fellows went right up to it and talked with the guard on the fence or stockade. The guard would trade for money or buttons off our clothes, giving tobacco in return which now was a great luxury. Thousands of us having none at all. Corn meal burnt black on a tin pan was smoked by many. Ice made on the brook last night one eighth of an inch thick while hoar frost was on the ground all over. There was not a single blade of grass to be seen anywhere inside the stockade, nor a single tree excepting three scraggy pines which stood on the south side of the brook which the workmen had overlooked when they built this place in January last.

March 3, 1864

A cold wind blew all last night. Fires were kept burning around which we shivered until daybreak. Not many got asleep. I took a chum in with me today, Tom Taber. He was one of our guard at Miller's house [at] Brandy Station and was captured with us. He belonged to a Massachusetts regiment and lived near Boston when at home. With his help our shanty was made more comfortable. We drove in pegs at the bottom, laid in pine sticks lengthwise and rammed in sand and earth a foot or more high on three sides.

This kept out the cold wind. We thatched both ends with pine tops by means of cross sticks and tearing up an old shirt for strings. We had roll call about 10 a.m. Some changes were made in the messes. A Rebel sergeant came in for each thousand detachment, and stood by while our sergeant of detachment called the roll. We had to all form [a] line for

Dead man's hollow

Clay oven
Stockade in distance

R. K. Sneden's Shanty at Andersonville Prison, Ga.

Well St. and Broadway, Squad 6. 300.
(Original sketch made there July 15, 1864 and retouched afterwards.) Sketched while outside the Prison getting firewood.

Telegraph operator's tent
End filled with pine tops

Dying prisoners

this operation. Many could not stand in line for nearly three quarters of an hour while the roll was being called which made W. S. Winder* swear considerably. Wirz came into the stockade with two others. They were forming the lines for roll call at the other end of the street. Our ration of corn meal came in about noon, when all set to work making mush and corn cakes. This took up all of our time for two or three hours every day.

Wirz gave orders for us to lay out our camp in streets or squares on each side of the main street which runs straight through from the north gate. So our sergeants were directing the moving or tearing down of many hovels and blanket shelters and rebuilding them in camp shape. Before this everyone had pitched his shanty anywhere thought to be a good place on the side hill and no one seemed to know where to find his comrade among the large collection of pig pens and holes in the ground.

A detachment of about 500 prisoners arrived by train this afternoon and were marched in as we had been. They were guarded by nearly a whole regiment of the 55th Georgia and another detachment of home guards. . . .

The new prisoners were formed into detachments and messes as we had been by the adjutant. Among them came . . . about fifteen sailors and seventeen marines whom we had left at Richmond.

Some of the prisoners came from Salisbury Prison and among these were eight or nine small sailor boys of the U.S. Navy the oldest of whom was not more than eighteen years of age! They had belonged to some of our gunboats which had been captured on the Mississippi River. My old chum Littlefield rejoined us. All set to work making shelters in which nearly all the serviceable pieces of brush and poles had been now used up. The tree stumps and a few felled trunks of trees still served us for firewood, while hundreds hauled the brush and logs over from the south side of the swamp. Here laurel roots were found in abundance and many employed themselves making pipes, forks, and wooden spoons. The wood was first boiled in water, which makes it the consistency of old cheese. Then it is easily cut and carved to suit the fancy. Many pipes were made with eagles, cannon, etc., engraved on the bowls. We had wood carvers among us, and some of these pipes were very handsome.

The day passed as usual, many of us gossiping with the newcomers to learn any news, more especially about "Exchange." Iron skillets were issued to us by the Rebels in the afternoon to bake our corn bread in.

One was given to every mess of fifty men. Four or five would contribute his whole meal ration, make a cake, then hand the skillet over to four or five more. This took a long time, so more than half the mess could not wait and cooked their meal ration as before. I, or any of my friends could not get the skillet at all as it was so much in demand that we would have

*Captain William Sidney Winder had selected the site for the new prison at Andersonville on orders from his father, General John Henry Winder, provost marshal in Richmond. In June General Winder arrived at Andersonville, and, as Sneden has already noted, he was later was given command of all Confederate military prisons east of the Mississippi.

to wait until midnight for it. Some tried their hand at making pancakes on half canteens and pieces of tin roofing. Most was miserable failures for we had no soda or salt. We had a cold rain which lasted all night and put the fires out. All were huddled over small fires and getting well smoked with the black pitch pine faggots. Some of us fashioned wooden shovels from the tree branches.

They were rudely cut with jackknives and partly burnt in the fires, which hardened them nearly as though they had been made [of] iron. These were used to throw the earth up around our shanties, or to dig holes over which a bough shelter would be built.

March 5, 1864

Rain all day, everyone was wet and miserable. The small brush wood being all used up, great trouble was had to keep any of the fires going. Many a ration was spoilt, and had to be either thrown away or eaten half raw and sodden. I and my chum started to build a Dutch oven alongside the shanty. The mud was brought from the swamp in an old haversack having been previously kneaded there into the consistency of mortar. A frame of sticks was built about 2 x 4 feet on the ground, on which the clay and sand were put. Then a small fire was built inside to harden it. A flue two feet high was built at one end, while for a door we had a piece of tin roofing from Pemberton. . . .

[Wirz and his adjutant] gave new orders and regulations as to roll call in [the] future. At the hour of 7:30 a.m. drummers would beat the roll at the gate, when the whole lot of prisoners must at once form into lines at the same time. We had been in the habit of forming in no hurry whatever when the Rebel sergeants came to the several detachments and many men who belonged to a certain detachment had his shanty or shelter a long way from the others. These had to be hunted up by their comrades so as to form the line with the rest. Sometimes the missing ones would be away several hundred feet or over on the south side of the swamp and keep the others standing a long while. Now everyone had to form [a] line and stay there until inspected by Wirz, or his adjutant in person. Orders were given also for no one to approach nearer the guards on the stockade than thirty feet as he would shoot to kill.

This was afterwards found out to be a rule to prevent the guards speaking or trading buttons, pipes, or anything we had for tobacco or anything to eat. There were three to five hundred of our fellows who had shelters on the south side now. They had constructed a roadway over the brook and swamp on the west side of the stockade, where the stream came in to us of logs, mud and brush wood so that now one could cross dry shod, though hundreds preferred walking through the water to cleanse the dirt from their feet at the same time. Hundreds were without any shoes or stockings, having them bound up sometimes with rags and string. A dam was constructed by our fellows about fifty feet from where the water comes into us, which was divided in two parts by another dam of logs or trees.* The first pool was for drinking water and the other for washing purposes. This narrowed the stream which ran through the prison to three or four feet wide and three or four inches deep. The water was very black in color, of a sweetish taste and wholly unfit to drink. On the side hill outside up where the Rebel camp was all the drainage of it ran into the stream before it came in to us. Even their sinks ran into it! If the sand purified the water before it reached us, the taste alone of it would turn anyone's stomach except that of an ostrich.

All along the sandy banks of the swamp prisoners had burrowed quite large holes or caves, propping up the roofs with brushwood. There they lived as well as they could, but a heavy rain would drive them all out every time. Little springs of water oozed out of these banks. Holes were made and then water used instead of the main supply. No one could get this spring water but those who made and owned them, so the great mass of prisoners had to use that which came in to us through the stockade though it was filthy.

March 6, 1864

Fine and cold. At 7:30 a.m. this morning three drummers and one fifer entered the stockade by the small door in the south gate and began playing and drumming "Dixie" and "Bonny Blue Flag." This was the Rebel roll call as we all knew. Such a yelling, cursing, and swearing I never heard from so many throats at once. The sergeants with Wirz on his gray horse came in by the north gate in a minute or two and rode through the main street of the camp. On all sides only parts of detachments were getting ready to form [a] line. Wirz was furious at the delay, drew his pistol, and ordered many a poor fellow to get up and into line or be shot. When a line was formed by our fellows a minute or so all would sit down on the ground. Wirz insisted that all should stand in line until all the detachments were formed. This took fully two hours for us to do, as whenever Wirz would ride from one detachment to another, the line behind him would all sit down again! Wirz cursed, swore and went nearly frantic. The little adjutant who was with him on a small pony looked scared half to death. Our fellows laughed and bothered the sergeants all the time. Some were in their holes in the ground and would not come out at all. Fortunately Wirz could not see or find them or he would have shot them sure.

After a long delay of two hours or so Wirz had to give in and ordered the roll call to proceed. We were all stood up then, but many were absent. Comrades were sent to hunt them up. Some came, some did not. Wirz kept riding around among us, flourishing his revolver and swearing all the while until he was out of breath, when he and his little adjutant rode out. The drummers had gone back to their camp on the hill long before. Rations did not come in until 3 or 4 o'clock in the afternoon, and when they did come it was discovered that we only had one half rations all around. This brought our corn meal down to a

*Sneden misdates the construction of this series of dams. The prisoners did not build them until later that spring.

teacup full each, nothing else! Then there was more cursing among us. Our fellows would not fall in to a Rebel roll call anyway, [and] much discussion was had all day and night on it. But Wirz got the best of us by only allowing one half ration. What if he should further reduce it! After much discussion most of us agreed not to fall in until after the Rebel music had ceased.

It was nearly dark before we had cooked and eaten our miserable corn cob meal. There was much quarreling among ourselves over the matter. Several schemes are in progress among us to dig our way out by tunneling under the stockade. We have lots of old coal miners among us, who all think it easy enough as the soil is all sand and the only obstructions are the roots of the pine trees. These often are twelve to fourteen feet in the ground, and spread fifteen to twenty feet around the trunk. There are no stones. There was great demand for pieces of pine which would be made into scoops or shovels.

Two of our number died today. Their bodies were carried by their comrades to the south gate and the guard allowed them to carry them to the dead house which has just been built of pine boughs about 200 feet from the western end of the stockade. . . .

All along both sides of the brook where it runs outside eastward the ground is used for a sink. There are many sick among us who can only lie on the ground, cough or groan with no human help except for their comrades. They have no shelter at all but lie alongside a big tree stump, with a little brush on each side of them. They are too sick to do anything, even to cook their miserable ration of corn meal. This is generally brought to them by a comrade, and the sick man eats it raw! as he has no pan to cook it in and won't wait for others to cook it for him as he is famishing with hunger! This increases his bowel complaint, and he grows worse every day. Every other one of us have terrible colds, and the coughing is very distressing. . . .

Large quantities of brick have come here by the cars. They are piled up in stacks near where the new cook house will be built 300 feet or so from the stockade near the north gate. Several Negro workmen have been at work hewing the timbers hauled there for its construction. It will be built on the stream known as the northwest branch of the creek or brook which runs through the stockade for our use. The sides of the hills near there have been cleared up of the stumps and felled trees which has been chopped up for fuel for the brick ovens which will be built in the cook house. A trestle bridge spans the stream now and another road made from it up to Wirz's headquarters on the hill and a branch road off to the railroad depot.

The best part of the 11th Georgia Regiment who came here a few days ago as guard have been working on the cook house material, while the Negroes do all the hardest work of course. They often get lashed by their masters or overseers, as we can hear their cries of pain plainly over at the log house village of Andersonville on still nights. When the Rebels capture a Negro soldier, if he is already wounded they either shoot him instantly [or] if not badly wounded they capture him so that he may work for them when he recovers. All the others have to work, on fortifications, felling trees, making roads, etc. . . .

March 7, 1864

. . . Although we like the outdoor situation better than being confined in buildings in Richmond, the cold winds and heavy rains offset it. All energy for escape is lost. Not a hope left for exchange. Every one is despondent except the rougher class of prisoners. Hunger gnaws our vitals day and night. All are impressed with the terrible fact that the Rebels will slowly starve us to death, and we are shut completely out from the rest of the world where our armies can never reach us. Among us are large numbers of roughs, who steal anything from each other or from a sick and weak comrade, taking his shoes, blanket, tin pan or anything coveted by sheer brutal force. There are over thirty of these desperate villains among us who make it a practice to prowl around a sleeping prisoner in the middle of the night and steal anything and everything he has. If he resists they club him into a state of insensibility, but generally get away with what they come for. They travel and prowl about at night like hyenas, three or four in a gang. Many of us know this and have made clubs, hardening them in the fire, so as to be ready for them. Many have been robbed of their overcoats, blankets or shoes, and money. Some of us have money yet, both Confederate and greenbacks. This is the main desire for these scoundrels to get. Something must be done to stop this villainy. Some of us are talking about establishing a patrol or police among ourselves, but no one volunteers to be chief and act.

Among the prisoners are all sorts and grades of men, from the Bowery toughs (the worse class of all) to mechanics, clerks, lawyers, doctors, gamblers, and thieves, who do not hesitate to strangle or club to death any weak, sickly prisoner who resists or makes an outcry while being forcibly robbed of what little the Rebels have not previously taken from him.

The terrible privations and long imprisonment had made two thirds of the men cruel, selfish, unscrupulous to do anything to gain their ends. A few who still preserve their gentlemanly principles kept together, and stood aloof from the great mass of uneducated, rough, demoralized and reckless companions in misery. The educated class stood the privations of prison life very much better than they of the rougher sort, and we were always in fear that the reckless portion of the prisoners would do something against the prison rules, which would give our Rebel jailors cause to open fire on the whole lot of us indiscriminately, as Major Gee had done at Salisbury.

Wirz had threatened to open fire from the battery with grape and canister in case he found out a systematic plan of escape by us, and added that he "would keep on firing until every d_____d round had been expended."

Several of us had already began the construction of deep holes in the ground around our shanties, to get into in case the batteries did open fire. From their position on the ridge south of us, they could rake the whole hills on both sides of the swamp and slaughter us wholesale. On a small hill opposite the gates and within easy gunshot about fifty Rebel guard were stationed. They had constructed a rifle trench nearly all around their tents there.

Another guard of more than 300 men were posted on another hill in our rear, and north of us. They had constructed rifle trenches around their encampment also. The guard was relieved daily by another set from the battery where Wirz's headquarters were on the hill.

We could see all their movements plainly from the inside of the stockade on the north side, as also the railroad depot, Rebel camps, and the small collection of log houses now called Andersonville. Several new houses had been built there within the past week and more are being built. The Rebel officers are quartered over there. Another storehouse of logs is being built at the depot station, and from here we can see the meal bags piled up in great heaps. All this work is done by gangs of Negroes under an overseer, and we hear their axes going all day until after dark. All the small young sailors have been taken out of the stockade by Wirz. They were so delicate and young that they could not live here among us more than two weeks.

They should be exchanged at once. The other sailors among us are a good lot of fellows, several of them being old man of war's men. The marines have a lot of tough men among them. They are a quarrelsome set, but they fight the sailors only. This is always the case, whether they are ashore or afloat. I have made good friendship among them. One, named Leonard, is from New York and he helps me in many ways. "Old Jack" is another good fellow. On the 5th March, seven prisoners died. On 6th March, four died.

Lieutenant Colonel Parsons or Peissons [Alexander W. Persons] who commands the guard of the 55th Georgia Regiment came in this afternoon with two or three others. They inspected the camp for two hours then went out of the north gate. He was a good looking and mild mannered officer, was very conversant and promised to build sheds for us. He was the first commandant of the post before Wirz came here this month. Winder is yet at Richmond but will be here in April so the colonel said "to take charge of us."* He was dressed in gray homespun suit, with a strip of blue braid on collar and cuffs, wore big boots, and was unarmed. Hundreds gathered around him asking all manner of questions. He seemed surprised at our miserable situation, more especially the twenty or thirty sick ones lying in a cluster, with no shelter but dirty tattered blankets and overcoats, smoke begrimed faces and naked legs and arms, splashed with red mud and sand, and skeletons in appearance. He said that a hospital would be built outside the stockade for us but there was great difficulty in procuring axes and saws, and that he had ordered lumber to be brought here by the cars to build the hospital. . . .

March 15, 1864

. . . There have been five or six tunnels started by the prisoners here so as to escape at night. They are started in some fellow's shanty and carried under the stockade forty or more feet outside. As the soil is sandy, the cutting is not so hard as the want of pure air during the operation.

* General Winder, in fact, was not appointed to the post by Jefferson Davis until June.

Iron skillets, half canteens, wooden scoops, and shovels are used. It was a slow but sure way of getting out, but when out, nobody knew the country at all and must be eventually recaptured while begging food from some house. . . . The shaft was only large enough for one to dig at a time, and that upon his hands and knees.

The miner would first cut the clay out with a case knife, then scoop the earth between his legs behind him, where another man put it into an old haversack, or bag made out of an old blanket and crawl with it backward out to the shaft from the surface where others would haul it up, and scatter the earth along the sinks on the swamp. The bag of earth was sometimes hauled out by a rag rope from the first operator's feet, and pushed in by poles lengthened as the work progressed. An empty bag was pushed in as the full one came out.

Several haversacks of dirt might be carried from the mouth of the shaft without attracting attention from the guard on the stockade, but to carry them at regular intervals all night required the utmost caution and strategy. The dirt carriers started for the swamp in no hurry and in different directions, hiding the bag of earth under his ragged blanket or overcoat.

The one who operated in the hole had to be relieved every twenty minutes or so on account of the foul air, when another one took his place. Many times the head operator was dragged out by the feet the whole way in an insensible condition, but the cold fresh air soon revived him. Gangs of twelve, fourteen, or sixteen generally composed the workmen. Great secrecy was enforced and it took several weeks of night work to construct a tunnel sixty to eighty feet long, which was the required length, though some were much longer on account of having to dig the entire distance around huge roots of the trees which were underground. Then when the tunnel had progressed to a sufficient distance, the entrance was carefully concealed from those who had huts near by. Very frequently the first hole sunk would be from some comrade's shanty, who had a pole floor to it and slept over the shaft in the daytime. There was always a risk of its being told of by another man not concerned in the construction to the Rebel sergeant at the gate, when he would receive double rations and some tobacco for his information, when a guard all armed would march in and by sounding the earth with crowbars soon discover its course and destroy it before our eyes. Two Negroes generally came in and did this work with shovels. Work on a tunnel would not occur for over two nights when many knew of its location and progress of construction. No one of the prisoners would "give it away," but the meanest and most miserable prisoner. If found out he would be beaten with sticks until he could not stand. . . .

Just near my tent is a barber shop. The owner lives, or exists in a sunken shanty, he has a barber pole too—made of a long stick with the bark cut out in serpentine shape like any barber pole in a city. . . . Some of the prisoners who last came in managed to secrete the razors somehow—everything else was taken from them by Wirz at his headquarters on the hill before they were marched in the gate. The barbers do a good business on fine warm days only. We have been having very cold blustery weather for nearly a week. Several have died from hunger and exposure as hundreds have no shelter at all only the ragged clothes on their backs. They mope all day and night over little fires. All are woe begone, ragged, dirty, and black with pitch pine smoke. . . .

March 17 to 31, 1864

Walsh and the rest of us who were captured together are still in middling good health, by daily washing and taking the best possible care of ourselves. We grow thin but can get around and cook the coarse rations which a hog would not eat unless very hungry. Among the new prisoners were many cripples and those who had lost an arm or leg in battle. If they are captured while wounded, the Rebel doctors cut off an arm or leg high up and where there is no actual necessity for doing so. Thus if a soldier was wounded in the foot or below the knee, the Rebel doctor or butcher would cut off the whole limb close up to the hips! or if wounded in the hand or forearm he would cut off the limb close up to the shoulder! If the owner made any resistance he was held down by Rebels until the limb was taken off! They thus made sure that the soldier would never be able for any further fighting.*

Sixteen have died in the hospital within two weeks. A ghastly lot of half naked skeletons, wallowing like hogs in the sand and tattered blankets. Old gray headed men and the young recruit of nineteen or twenty years are mixed up in one common pest hole. The dead bodies are piled up one on top of each other at the rough bough shelter built outside the stockade, and we from the inside can plainly see the ghastly pile of corpses sticking out of the so called dead house all the time. When there is enough for a "load" the same wagon which brings in our corn meal rations carts off the dead like so much cord wood to a graveyard not far away in the woods where they are dumped on the ground and buried after a fashion by three or four of our men who are paroled for this purpose. . . .

April 1, 1864

Rain hard all day and night. It came down in sheets of water which flooded out all those who had their hovels and burrows along the swamp and side hills. The mud hovels in the swamp collapsed entirely and all their occupants had to seek other places higher up to rebuild again. The brook rose to four feet deep, sweeping away the artificially constructed dams—and there was quite a waterfall where the water forced its way through the interstices of the logs which formed the stockade at that point. The blanket, tents, now getting rotten, leaked like sieves. Everyone was wet and the rations were wet also. The rain put out the fires too and it was with great persistency that anything could be cooked. . . .

There are one or two Bibles among us. And several Testaments. I have one. On the margins of pages or leaves, I make my notes and sometimes plans of earthworks which we have passed through while coming here from Richmond. The Rebels won't rob one of his Bible or Testament—not one in ten can read either print or writing. It serves as a good pocket

*There is no evidence to corroborate Sneden's accusation of such inhumane treatment by Confederate doctors.

book for money. That is if the owner has any: this is about the last place where a thief or any Rebel will look for it. I read mine daily, and lend it to others whom I know. Since March 1st when I and comrades came here from Richmond up to 31st March there have been 282 deaths! Of these 262 died in the so called hospital. Five from small pox and fifteen among the shanties and burrows along the swamp. The dead at the hospital are carted out by the ration wagon, piled up like cordwood, with arms and legs hanging over the wheels, glassy eyes, and open mouths. The sight is horrible! They are buried like dogs too while Wirz gloats over the corpses and makes coarse jokes on them. The others lie alongside the shanty sometimes two days at a time when their comrades carry them in an old blanket to the south gate where they are dumped on the ground until the Rebel officer there thinks there are enough of them to make a load!

The dead house on the outside of the stockade is only made of pine branches and we can see the corpses in it piled up several feet high just like cordwood! Sometimes the officer of the guard permits two or three comrades to carry the corpse out to the dead house—one armed guard goes with them. On their return to the stockade gate they are permitted to gather and bring in branches of pine or sticks which are on the ground for firewood, etc.

My tent mate Thomas Taber died yesterday.* We carried him down to near the north gate and left him among a pile of a dozen other poor emaciated corpses! which the ration wagon would carry out whenever the number amounted to a load of thirty or more! Taber died from gangrene in the foot. He stubbed his toe against a root some time ago, being barefoot at the time, and caught cold, bathing it with the brook water which was sure to fester the wound and turn ultimately to gangrene. All those who came in here wounded are dying of the same thing. Many are already dead. We are horrified at the death rate in March. And we implore the Rebel doctors to have the hospital moved outside, as over a dozen cases are of small pox which spreads among us every day. All the sick fellows are huddled together over on the south side of the brook—with nothing to shelter them but a few old meal bags propped up on sticks. Doctors don't come in to see them for a week at a time. And when they do come, [they] can do no good as they have no medicine. So the poor fellows die and live as best they may! The raw corn meal which they have to eat soon kills them. Some have friends or comrades who try to help and attend to their wants. Some have not and lay grovelling in the sand staring at the sky in their own filth and vermin! which is a horrible sight.

April 3 to 6, 1864

Drizzly rain and fog both yesterday and today. After roll call Wirz's adjutant gave out at the various detachments that prisoners were wanted to go outside to help build the cook house. None but good carpenters and masons were wanted. They were to be paroled and fed outside until the building was completed. All the timbers and boards were on the ground with

*Taber died at Andersonville on October 11, 1864. Sneden does not indicate why he placed Taber's death in April.

THE COOKHOUSE AS SEEN FROM OVER THE STOCKADE

bricks and lime for the ovens two weeks ago. Colonel [Persons] came in the stockade and selected about twenty men to go out as workmen. It was wonderful to see how many hundreds of carpenters and masons offered their services. Not one in twenty knew anything about the business in reality, but it was a grand chance to get out of this hell hole and get enough to eat outside. . . .

April 7, 1864

After roll call this morning a four mule team came in driven by a Negro on the off mule which was loaded with short stakes and strips of scantling or narrow boards. Wirz accompanied by two Rebel carpenters from the cook house came in the stockade at the same time. They measured off from the foot of the stockade a line twenty feet wide all the way around. The short stakes were driven in the ground and the scantling nailed on top of them forming a rail around the whole camp inside. Stakes were about ten feet apart and the rail about four feet high. Wirz now went all over the camp and informed us that this was the dead line which no prisoner could approach nearer than ten or twelve feet or the guard on the top of the stockade would shoot him at once. No more trading was to be had with the guard. All of them had orders to fire on anyone near the dead line etc. While driving the stakes, Wirz and his men stumbled [on to] two or three tunnels. This made him in a furious rage. He cursed and swore all the while and the tunnels were filled up of course. One led clean under the stockade for over twenty feet outside. The ragged tent from which it started on the inside was quickly vacated by its occupants and Wirz could not find out whose shanty it was. He was so mad that he knocked down two prisoners and stamped on them with his heavy boots. He had his pistol in hand all the while. Many of us laughed at him.

It took the best part of the day to put the dead line up. Negroes were on the outside felling the trees for thirty or more feet beyond the stockade so as to form a clear space to see when anyone should make an exit for a tunnel. Fires were built of all the branches and stumps at night which lit up the ground for several hundred of feet. Still there was a dense forest left on the outside of the stockade on the east side where the brook ran through it. We are having warmer weather but it rains every day for an hour or two. The Rebel quartermasters are very wroth because several axes and shovels which they lent us to build the causeway across the swamp cannot be found. They threaten to stop our rations if not found and returned to them. The prisoners want them to chop stumps with. And at night sounds of three or four axes are heard in the swamp. The nights are still cold and damp, many sleep during the day in a sunny place on the ground and keep working at the tree stumps for fuel most of the night, while hundreds lay on the bare ground shivering with the cold until they can start a small fire next morning. I went all over the camp today—made several acquaintances who were educated men—and heard their stories of capture. Found several lawyers and doctors among them, and some of the III Corps, but not one from my regiment. I am the only one of them here.*

April 8 to 20, 1864

During the nights of 7th and 8th the prisoners tore all the rails from off the dead line and are using them for firewood: many of the stakes on which the rail was supported have gone the same way. The nails are very useful for constructing shanties. Wirz was furious and made the air blue with oaths. We only laughed at him. Nobody took the rails of course. He went into several shanties trying to see some signs of them—but they had all been broken up in short pieces and hidden in the sandy ground. Parts had been left intact, near the north and south gates and where the brook enters the stockade. In some places all traces of it had disappeared. One of the prisoners was killed last night by some of the Raiders with clubs. He was of course robbed of his overcoat and money. His head was smashed in with a pine club which had been hardened in the fire recently as the black smut left its mark. He was an old Belle Island prisoner who had his miserable hovel near what is known as Raider's Island, a small spit of sand on the brook and swamp near the sinks. As it was very foggy at the time the Raiders got away and are not known. About thirty of these scoundrels keep together and rob prisoners nearly every foggy night.

*In fact, by the end of the war other men of the 40th New York became Andersonville prisoners. Sneden's comment is understandable because many of these soldiers arrived after he left the camp and many had joined the regiment after he left it and so were strangers to him.

THE DEAD LINE, ANDERSONVILLE PRISON, GA.
Shot by the guard while taking a part of the dead line for firewood.

The new cook house is nearly completed being all boarded in and shingled. Large iron kettles are being set in brick work and ovens are built to bake our corn bread for two or three days. Large quantities of cordwood have been hauled there by Negroes and mule teams. The chimney stack is a few feet above the roof. Ventilators are yet to be put on the roof. Several of those who went out to work on it attempted to escape and were caught. These were sent back into the stockade, the Rebels first taking all the homespun clothes . . . from them and sending them back in their original ragged clothes. Some of these "Galvanized Yanks" act as cooks and servants for the Rebel officers at the village, being paroled of course. If they should be sent in the stockade for some misdemeanor committed outside, they would not live here long, as the majority of prisoners denounce them as traitors and deserters. The whole number of prisoners are intensely loyal to our government in here.

The prisoners organized a police force among us. They will be known as "The Regulators." About fifty of the largest and strongest men among us were by common consent thus formed. These men will deal with the "Raiders" and use club force to keep them under. A squad of twenty men will always be moving about the camp during the day while twenty-five will stand at prominent points all night to head off and club those "hyenas" who murder their comrades in their sleep to get their money and miserable possessions. A certain portion of each man's ration is to be allotted them, so that they will get more to eat than the others to keep them in fighting trim. The chief is a large man, six feet high, a good natured fellow and is known as "Big Pete." He will decide all cases of theft and other crooked acts among the prisoners and owns a cat-o-nine-tails to lash those found guilty of theft, etc.

The Raiders are a desperate set of thieves and murderers who were Belle Island prisoners and came from the slums of the cities to which they belong. Most of them have served time in [a] penitentiary or prisons before they enlisted. Most of them are Irish, or Irish Americans. There are a lot of hard fellows too among the police force, but they are supposed to be honest, and no one's life is safe among us as long as these Raiders have their own way. There are nearly 200 of these fiends, who live always in groups so that one can help the other in a fight. They are given a "wide berth" and no right minded prisoner will venture into their quarters knowingly, as he is sure to be robbed of everything he has if he does.

The daily routine in camp is monotonous enough. Roll call at 7 a.m. (no drums now), delivery of rations—bags of corn meal and a thronging of men around where they are delivered—everyone cooking his mush or corn bread in little pieces of tin, or half canteens, washing at the brook, getting water and hunting for firewood. Some sleeping, others clustered around smoky fires talking "exchange," some playing cards or checkers. Some fighting among themselves, yelling and swearing, although they are so weak that they can hardly stand up to it. Hundreds lying on the ground sleeping, dozing in the sun, or dying from diarrhea. Then at night huddled around the small fires or at work on tunnels until daylight.

I have taken in a new "chum" into my shanty whose name is Brock. He having two poles and two pieces of board, with a blanket and two half canteens and knife for cutting large sticks, made it quite an object for me to have to share my shanty. Together we moved the site and moved up nearer the north gate fifty or sixty feet inside the dead line and erected a much more comfortable shanty than I had before. . . .

The death rate for this month is very large, over 300 have died since 1st April! Sixty or more are lying helpless, and there is not much chance for them. The hospital (so called) will be soon moved out of the stockade to the hill east of the battery on the hill. Walsh and Colvin who were captured with me are very low with diarrhea and cannot walk. The other friends attend to their wants and cook their rations for them as best they know how. As life is very uncertain in this hell hole, and our families at home have no conception of the horrors of this place, we have made contracts with each other in case any of us who were captured together are exchanged or escape to do all we can to let our folks at home know our fate and have written each other's addresses and residences so that we may personally apprise those who as yet do not know our destiny or fate. The letter which I wrote home from Crew and Pemberton Prison must never have reached my folks in New York or I would have had an answer of some kind. Turner probably has seized on the 10¢ silver piece which must have been sent in the letter for postage to me. . . .

April 21, 1864

It has been very sultry and foggy for the past two days. This afternoon a terrific rain storm deluged the whole camp.* The rain came down in sheets of water while it blew a gale. The thunder and lightning was a constant roll and nearly blinded us. I had never seen such a terrific storm before since that one on 24th June just before the battle of Fair Oaks at Savage's Station. The brook rose in half an hour to the size of a small river overflowing all along both sides of the swamp washing away all the shanties and burrows at once, the occupants fleeing for their lives to the high ground. . . .

Among us there was great excitement, all fearing that the battery on the hill would open on the camp with grape and canister. The rain beat down thousands of shelters and shanties flat to the ground. Those who were in burrows or in any kind of a sunken tent had to be pulled out by their comrades to prevent drowning as every hole was full of rain water in ten minutes' time. In the streets leading to the swamp, which now were good sized brooks, were floating down hill clothing, pans, hats and caps, shoes, and any and everything which had been in the tents. All were scrambling to recover these, yelling and swearing—while the wind blew everything flat and the crashing of the thunder was terrific. The swamp was turned into a lake, and in the current floated stockade timbers with here and there two or more prisoners astraddle them and who floated clean outside to be picked up there by the guard. Wirz and several of his men were at the eastern gap swearing above the storm and fearing that we would now make a break. The artillery men on the hill had lighted fuses alongside their guns—ready on signal to open fire. Many of us plunged into the gullies made by the rushing water to get out of sight of the gunners. The whole camp was in an uproar but no one thought of breaking away or escape. . . .

April 22 to 30, 1864

The camp presented a very curious scene this morning. The debris of tents and shanties were spread all over the side hills and looked like a great junk shop, remnants of tattered blankets, clothing, tent poles, tin pans, etc., etc., covered the ground by the acre, amid which were men vainly trying to find what once belonged to them. Although the brook had fallen somewhat, it was yet a broad wide shallow stream six or eight feet deep with a good current of water still running out, all yellow mud color mixed in with branches of trees and debris washed down the steep side hills from the camps of the Rebel guards on the other branch of the creek. The flood did one good thing however, for it washed the filthy swamp clean out from end to end. The Rebel guard were kept on the ends of the brook all day, while the Negroes and several white men repaired and set up the stockade again where it was broken down. We had no roll call until nearly noon, and did not get

*Although there were many thunderstorms that spring, the one that washed away part of the stockade and destroyed many prisoners' shanties took place later that summer, not in April.

our rations until 4 p.m. So it was nearly dark before any of us got anything to eat as the wood was all so wet that we had the greatest difficulty to make fires. Many had lost all their tin pans and stocks of firewood in the flood.

The rations of corn meal were wet, and the bacon [was] slimy from being left somewhere where the rain could get at them. In addition and to sweeten our appetites there was issued today two tablespoonfuls of sorghum to go with our mush to each man. This sugar cane grows in large quantities in South Carolina and from it a kind of molasses is made which entirely outranks the blackest and dirtiest of cane syrups. It has a sweetish sour taste and when mixed and eaten with corn meal with the cob and all ground in as ours is. It acts as a cathartic to the stomachs of those afflicted with the diarrhea like a dose of Epsom salts. It is wonderful how it will gripe and twist one's insides! Everyone was eager to get his ration nevertheless. I had made its acquaintance before and gave my ration to Brock my tentmate. Before the storm broke on us he and I had stripped the blanket roof off our new shanty and secured the ridge and other poles. We got several poles by the flood and another piece of board which was [a] great help to lay on instead of the wet ground. Everyone was at work reconstructing their shelters blown down by the storm. And many filled up their sunken tents level with the ground in case of another flood. . . .

April 30, 1864

. . . Men were up all night over little fires cooking pancakes and bread of corn meal to sell in the morning. All the ovens were in full blast, though wood was very scarce—nearly all the tree stumps have been dug up and the roots used for fuel. This was laborious work as the roots go ten or twelve feet in the ground. The swamp is fast filling up again with filth. Still the men delve in it to get at the roots which are dried in the sun and sold. Tent poles, fuel, and other things were sold to the new prisoners who paid high prices for them to the others. $1.50 in greenbacks was paid for three tent poles the size of bean poles. Nearly all the new prisoners had blankets, some had rubber blankets too, which were not to be bought for less than $50 each. The prisoners had packs of cards and bought all the wooden pipes which the old prisoners had made. They bought sites for shelters too and erected their shanties or blanket tents on them. The new prisoners seemed to keep by themselves and could not be brought to fraternize with the ragged, emaciated dirty set of comrades who once were in the ranks as smart and clean as any of them. They bewailed their lot. Some even cried at the horrible sights around them and the hundreds of half naked men lying on the ground without any shelter whatever waiting for death! As my new shanty was now built on a larger scale than formerly, and could hold three comfortably, I took a "boarder" who was captured at Plymouth. He was a sutler, was comfortably dressed, had some money, and a gold watch,

*On April 20, 1864, the Confederates captured the Federal garrison at Plymouth, N.C., a major victory in that part of the state for the South.

which he managed to secrete from Wirz. So now Brock and I had someone to talk to and learn all the particulars of the fight and surrender of Plymouth* from one who was there. . . .

May 3 to 8, 1864

The cook house is now finished at last and we will have corn bread and soup made for our rations instead of the raw meal. The ovens were fired up today, great clouds of black smoke came from the chimneys. It is seen from nearly every part of the prison as it stands on a hill at the edge of the stream which branches off from the main brook that supplies us with water.

The carpenters and others who went out of the stockade to help build the cook house were all sent back again to the stockade much to their disgust. I saw several of them and got the particulars and dimensions of the building from them. Some had gone to be servants to the Rebel officers! "Great Scott," who would have thought that this would be the destiny of the Union Volunteer in 1861–2 while marching down Broadway to the tune of "John Brown's Body," etc! Privation and hunger had worked wonders. The majority of prisoners, though, would scorn even to go out to work for the Rebels, nearly all were true to the flag yet. Only the Raiders, and other thieves would sell their honor to help the enemy, [but the others] died by scores with the Union cause strong in them to the last breath. Walsh, Colvin, and the rest of us who were captured together met very often and discussed matters, and as the death roll was so large this month, we all wondered how much more so it would be when the terrible hot weather of July and August came. . . .

There are yet in the stockade a dozen or more Negroes, all prisoners of war. They were captured at Olustee, and are of the 8th U.S. Colored Regiment.* Nearly all are minus an arm or leg, and their wounds are yet unhealed. Many of them are gangrened and they will all surely die. They keep by themselves and are very quiet. The Rebels have removed every vestige of any uniform they once wore, and they have nothing on but old cast off jean trousers and cotton shirts. All are bareheaded, barefooted, and as thin as skeletons. Those captured who were able to work are kept at work outside by the Rebels, felling trees, making roads, etc., etc. The white officers who were captured with them have been all put in the dungeons of Libby and Castle Thunder at Richmond, and are made to eat and sleep with Negroes. . . .

May 12 to 25, 1864

We have had fine warm days for a fortnight. The pine woods look greener, but the filthy swamp smells so that we cannot smell the buds on the trees. We are supplied now with rations from the cook house outside, a loaf of corn bread about the size of half a brick, made

*The battle of Olustee (or Ocean Pond), on February 20, 1864, was the largest engagement of the war in Florida. A Union raid into the interior of the state ended in defeat at the hands of an inferior Confederate force.

of unbolted meal with the cob and all ground in. No salt in it either. And about two ounces of rusty bacon raw. The bread is either burnt black on one side or not half baked, the inside being nearly raw. Only one half of us get the cooked bread. The other half get raw corn meal and bacon with two tablespoonsful of "sorghum" or sour molasses every second day. The bread is piled up in a wagon seven or eight feet high and drawn in by a two mule team driven by a Negro. The rations are delivered to the mess sergeants and divided by them as usual. There are nearly 14,000 prisoners now here! Small squads of twenty men each were allowed to go out of the north gate every day from 10 a.m. to 4 p.m. to gather and bring in for fuel the loose chips, sticks, branches, etc., which strewed the ground where the trees had been cut to form the stockade. About 200 or 250 men in all would go out in squads of tens and twenties. A Rebel armed guard of fifteen went with them. . . .

Walsh has been at the point of death. He seems to be the oldest aged prisoner in here. Wirz wants him to be his clerk at the log house on the hill, and we advise him to go so that he may live, for in here he won't live long. Over fifty have died in the stockade since the 1st May. About fifteen have been shot by the guard.

Chapter Eight

This Hell on Earth

Conditions at Andersonville worsened with the approach of summer. The Confederates crowded more and more prisoners into the stockade to bake in the heat of the Georgia sun. A decision made far to the north compounded the problem. General Ulysses Grant believed that exchanging prisoners prolonged the war because of the relative disparity of manpower between North and South. As a result, for more than a year there had been no general exchange of prisoners as there had been earlier.

From the first arrivals at Andersonville in February 1864, the number of inmates swelled to its maximum of almost 33,000 in July. Sneden's periodic count peaks at 35,000 and thus overstates the numbers only slightly. Indeed, for a time Andersonville became the fifth largest city in the Confederacy. The original stockade of sixteen acres, a third of them occupied by the swamp and deadline, was enlarged in July. Nevertheless, as historian William Marvel has calculated, this enclosure gave each prisoner about the square footage of a grave. With overcrowding and the lack of sanitation, the death rate skyrocketed. Smallpox, dysentery, scurvy, malnutrition, and infections that turned gangrenous all took their toll. The Confederate prison doctors protested the conditions and their lack of medicine, but to no avail. They began ascribing some deaths to "nostalgia," their word for the abject despair that caused some men to give up hope and wither away. By the end of the war, nearly thirteen thousand Union soldiers would lay their bones in the common graveyard just outside the stockade. Some sources set the death toll even higher.

Confederate regulations provided for prisoners to receive the same rations as guards. Sne-

den and his comrades would never believe Wirz carried out these orders. If bad food and disease were not enough tribulation, the prisoners turned on one another like the caged animals they had become. The camp descended into a Hobbesian cesspit of brutality against the weakest.

Sneden described all of these conditions, as well as the daily monotony of the captives. Sometimes he gave up attempting a day-by-day accounting and lumped his stories together by the week or half-month. Sometimes he got his chronology wrong. Sometimes he conflated stories, as when he placed Confederate General Howell Cobb at Andersonville on the Fourth of July, a week before the general actually visited the camp. Like nearly every other Union prisoner of war who wrote afterward about his experience, Sneden exaggerated the hardships and described the Southern guards as more vicious, callous brutes than the facts warranted. Still, for all its quirks, his account paints a convincing picture of desperate times and parlous conditions, based on notes he made continuously while a prisoner. Though he wrote his memoir several decades later, Sneden still burned with hatred for his jailors and with a desire to bear witness to their crimes.

June 26 to 30, 1864

We have now a surgeon's call for the sick every Sunday forenoon at the south gate. Hundreds crawl, or are carried there by their comrades on blanket litters or on their backs. They cross the dead line and go through the small gate to the enclosure recently built on the outside of the main gates. Here they are given bark decoctions or camphor pills by two Rebel doctors—[Isaiah H.] White and [Randolph] Stevenson. They had no other medicine to give. If the prisoner is in a dying state he is taken to the hospital on the hill outside. Only 150 are admitted there anyhow as the place now is overcrowded. Otherwise he is returned to the stockade to take his chances which many prefer, as the pest house known as the hospital is a perfect "Golgotha." The sick there lie or wallow like hogs in the sand which is teeming with lice and maggots by the million! They only get a little broth made of flour and water with rusty bacon grease! . . .

I got a long letter from Walsh who went out as clerk to Wirz some time ago. The sergeant who calls the roll in our detachment brought it in to me. I get all the vital statistics from Walsh who is in a position to know. Colvin keeps the death book at Wirz's office.*

On Sunday June 6th there were five prominent Raiders caught while clubbing and robbing. They all got twenty lashes, were half shaved and ridden through the camp and dumped into the filthy swamp. Some of them contrived to get out at the gate and complained to Wirz. He sent them immediately back saying it served them right, and if we had killed them he would not interfere. Two Catholic priests Fathers [Peter] Whelan and

*Like Thomas Walsh, Charles Maxwell Colvin was captured with Sneden at Brandy Station. His unpublished account of working as a paroled prisoner keeping the hospital books is at the Chicago Historical Society.

[William] Hamilton come into the stockade on Sundays. They visit and shrive the dying. They cause many of the thieves to return their ill gotten gains to their owners too for many of these thieves are dying among the rest of us. From Father Hamilton I got a piece of crude opium about as large as a walnut which I kept chewing on and it relieved a bad diarrhea very much of which I have been suffering for a long while. This was caused by my swallowing the saliva when I had scurvy in the mouth. The youngest of the telegraph operators who tented near me died recently of fever and ague. He literally shook himself to death.

More than half of the sailors and marines are dead as also the Massachusetts battery who came in with the Plymouth prisoners.* All the officers who belonged to Negro regiments and who were put in here sometime ago are dead with the exception of Major Bogle† of [the] 17th Massachusetts Regiment. Corpses are now piled up near the dead line at the south gate inside to be taken out at sundown. The sight is sickening and horrible beyond conception. All are nearly naked, black as crows, festering in the hot sun all day, covered with lice and maggots—while thousands of big flies swarm on the bodies filling their mouth, nose, and ears! The stench is sickening too—worse than any battlefield. Some are so decomposed as to have to be shovelled into the dead wagon! The dead and dying lie alongside each other in the shelter tents until someone rolls the corpse out a few feet away. Sometimes the dead lie there a day or more. I have counted twenty-six dead in one day who lay in the sun festering until an hour before sundown, which is the only time the Rebel officer at the gate permits them to be carried out to the bough shanty outside known as the dead house. Here they are loaded up in the ration wagon like cordwood and carried to [the] graveyard.

These horrible sights were so common that the prisoners got hardened to it. Nearly all of us had given up all hopes of being exchanged or seeing our homes again. They were reckless as to anything and everything while all the bad qualities in a man showed themselves prominently. The brutal natures of the ignorant and uneducated men gave itself vent in inhuman conduct to their comrades in misery. Two or three would sit around a dying man waiting to grab his blanket, tin cup or canteen and clothes before life was out of him. Many were groaning or crying in pain during the night which prevented sleep to those near them. Sometimes the sick man was clubbed to death or kicked in the stomach by his nearest companion! with the exclamation of d___n you why don't you die! Some one of us were dying every hour when his tent poles, blanket, or anything which he had was quickly taken by these ghouls; everyone was for himself regardless of consequences. . . .

The flies are now here in millions. Everything is covered with them, dense swarms like a cloud settle on the pile of dead which are daily seen near the gates. The ground in the thickest part settled in the camp is fairly alive and moves with maggots or lice! The filthy swamp undulates like small waves with them, while the insufferable stench nearly takes away one's

*Prisoners at Andersonville often called their comrades captured by the Confederates at Plymouth, North Carolina, the "Plymouth Pilgrims."

†Probably Major Archibald Bogle, 1st North Carolina Colored Infantry, captured at the battle of Olustee, Florida.

THE HUT FOR THE BLOODHOUNDS KEPT BY HARRIS, OUTSIDE THE STOCKADE, ANDERSONVILLE PRISON
Sketched while outside the prison getting firewood.

breath! In the morning hours the ground is covered with white maggots for hundreds of feet on each side of the swamp like a snow storm. The sun comes out hot and kills them by the million. On foggy days, especially in the morning, the whole camp is infested with a species of white winged moths by the million. They get into one's nose and mouth so we have to swallow them! They all disappear when the sun comes out.

We have hot days now, it must be 80 degrees. We have no way of knowing how hot it is. Dozens of poor ragged half starved prisoners lie along the brook in the hot sun. Some are naked. They paddle in the filthy black water all day to keep cool. The water is only three or four inches deep below the artificial dam. Only the framework of the sinks built on the brook now stands. The Rebels began to board over the roof, but the prisoners took the boards for firewood as fast as it was put on. They carried off some of the frame work too. . . .

There were about 27,000 prisoners now here. One half still get raw rations of corn meal and two ounces of rusty bacon. The other half get the corn bread baked in the cook house with half pint of the black goober bean or cowpease. Trading for rations still goes on daily on Main Street, and the cries of vendors of corn beer or bones with no meat on them equals pandemonium. Speculators have bought up all the fuel, and one stick of cordwood now must be divided among twenty-five men.

For the past six weeks many tunnels have been built and over forty have got away through them. None of them have been heard from so far. Wirz, with [Benjamin] Harris [a local hunter] and the dogs, go around the stockade every morning to find the burrows sometimes with success. There are over thirty tunnels on the east side of the stockade. Six Negroes with crowbars came in the stockade with three Rebel officers who held pistols in each hand. They sounded the ground with the crowbars all around the stockade inside the death line or death space, and found fifteen tunnels, some large and some small. Nine of these went clean under the stockade which is sunk five feet in the ground. Seventeen prisoners went through one hole last night. Wirz was furious, and the rations were stopped for forty-eight hours in the detachments to which the men belonged. The hunters are now out with the dogs. They are generally recaptured and brought back within two days from their leaving. The red peppers which the sutler sells are now ground fine and put in the tracks of those who escape to destroy the dog's scent. One sniff of this makes the dog useless for a week, so the recaptured ones say who have tried it. . . .

July 1, 1864

Fine dry weather but very hot, 90 to 95 degrees. Clothes are cumbersome and thousands go nearly naked on account of the sweltering heat. The majority keep inside their shanties or blanket shelters from noon to 3 p.m. The sun beats down on the red sand so as to dazzle one, while it helps to breed the maggots, so that the ground actually heaves with them. The stench from the swamp is stifling. All along its edges the dried filth is crusted a foot thick while the center heaves like a sea with festering rottenness and live maggots! It can be smelt ten miles away, and nearly takes away one's breath. This swamp covers an area of three acres. No conception can be had of the smell.

The Rebels say that the smell makes them sick. About eighty of the guard outside have died, and many more are in the hospital at Andersonsville. General Winder moved his headquarters from the hill near the stockade to the outskirts of the village. The smell from the swamp was too much even for him and [his] staff. The Rebel doctors are afraid to come into the stockade now on account of the sickness among us. Every Sunday morning all those who are sick and can hobble to the south gate are attended to by the doctors, or given some bark decoction for diarrhea or scurvy. So many go there that not half of them are seen by the doctors or given anything. Many die on their way there or while waiting for two hours or more to be attended to. They fight and scramble among themselves very often, while they are trampled on and pushed about roughly by their companions in misery. They resemble a lot of wild animals, though half of them are sent back without any help. Many of them give up in despair, and lie along the brook where they can die and get water without help from their comrades. Fifteen to twenty can be seen there day and night dying!! Many crawl up to the dead line in a half delirious state when they are sure to be shot by the sentry on the stockade, who gets four weeks furlough for it.* . . .

Notice was given us by the Rebel sergeants who call the roll that the new stockade is ready for us, and today twenty or more Negroes began tearing down the intervening stockade between the new and old. By noon large openings were made and the prisoners rushed

*Sneden here repeats the prisoners' universal belief in this story, even though it was untrue.

through by the thousands, amid yells, and all kinds of shouting. The men scrambled and fought for sites on which to build their new shelters. Several fights took place among them, when black eyes and bloody faces were plentiful. Crowds would gather round the fighters and cheer them on. Only fists were allowed. The combatants were too weak to hurt each other much. All the sticks of the intermediate stockade were pulled out of the earth by the Negroes and then thrown down anywhere. This was given to us for fuel. But how to cut or split up the long sticks twenty-five feet was a puzzle as no axes were furnished to us. There were four or five axes which had been stolen from the quartermaster when we built the corduroy roads across the swamp in May, but no one could use them but those who had them, so the men hauled or shouldered the sticks and carried them to the location of their several messes.

Despite the vigilance of these Rebels, forty-seven of the prisoners have dug out or escaped during June. A few have been recaptured and torn by the dogs sent in pursuit. None of the rest have been heard from. Whether they have been killed or escaped to our lines no one knows. This has given a great impetus to tunnel digging, and hundreds will avail themselves of the new ground in the additional space of six acres now occupied by us to dig and keep at it. The new ground has a dead line, stronger built than the old one (which has nearly disappeared being used for fuel): The ground is rising all the way up to the northern barrier or stockade, and hundreds of tree stumps stick out of [the] ground which will be rooted up for fuel in a week or two. Many are burrowing in the ground like rabbits, as they have neither blankets or brush to make a shelter. The sand is clean however, not full of lice and maggots as in the old stockade. As my shanty is very comfortable, except in wet weather, I and my chums have concluded not to move into "the new stockade," as it is now called. . . .

We were very much crowded, the narrow streets which were only six to eight feet wide made it impossible for anyone to go through them without jostling each other. South Street on the other side of the swamp, and Main Street or Broadway on this side, are [not] much under about ten feet, so as to allow room for the mule teams to bring in the rations. Main Street now is thronged from early morning until dark by thousands of prisoners, who all have rations of some kind to sell or exchange for money or other rations not cooked. One half of us yet get raw ration. The barbers and others buy up all the goober beans which they cook and sell for 5¢ a cup, or half pint. Wood has been so scarce that enough could not be had to cook one's own ration.

The sailors have taken by force enough sticks of the dismantled stockade to build them a good shanty twenty feet long on Main Street near my tent. The roof is covered with these sticks too, and it is the best one in camp. All the sailors and marines, about twenty in number, live together now. Old Jack does a good and profitable business by pricking flags, shields and figures in the arms and legs of those who can pay him from $1 to $5 each. India ink is used and raw vermillion. Six or eight fine needles are bunched together and put into a pine stick securely tied around with thread. The ink is pricked into the flesh on arm or leg on the design painted there. The jabbing takes an hour or more. The arm soon swells up and inflames which is painful for a few days only. The ink appears in blue lines. Anchors, hearts, men's names and regiments are the favorite designs, with crossed flags and muskets. Old Jack is quite an artist, and the oldest of the men-of-wars-men here. The sailors have lots of money, and seem to live well on sutler's supplies. They get whiskey once in a while from the sutler, paying 50¢ greenbacks for a tablespoonful. They have managed to buy a fiddle from the Rebel guard and all take turns at scraping on it. Only one of them can play a tune anyhow.

Many are splitting up the stockade timbers with pine wedges which are first hardened in the fire. Pails are being made of the wood to hold water or beer in. The corn beer peddlers are doing a good business. Several barrels of the stuff [are] constantly being fermented in the sun and made for sale. Hundreds are yelling all day, "Here's your fine cold beer; coldest in the stockade for only 5¢ a cup," etc., or "Who'll swap beans for soup?" or "Who'll give a chew of tobacco for half a raw ration?" Some carry their wares of a few potatoes, onions, tobacco, etc., on little boards slung around their necks. Others have little stands on four sticks with their half dozen potatoes, or a few onions, some salt and pieces of plug tobacco cut in inch squares which sell for 25¢ each. Others are trading rations, raw for cooked or vice versa. All yelling and making a great noise all day. The noises and yells in the Gold Room* at New York is nothing in comparison. Many who win a stake at cards speculate in tobacco, salt, potatoes, onions, etc., which can be had from the sutler at wholesale prices and in a week or two have hundreds of dollars made from a start of a dollar or two. There is a perfect mania for trading and swapping.

All the vacant sites of shanties left by those who moved into the new stockade have been seized and held by some who lived nearby and held for real estate, which they expect to sell to the next lot of new prisoners who arrive here. Thread is carefully picked out of the old dirty clothes thrown away, or from some dead man. With needles got from the sutler at $1 each, numbers of tailors have started business, mending and patching the clothes of others who pay from 10¢ to 50¢. Trousers made from stolen meal bags are cut out by the sailors for 50¢ each [and] made up by the tailors, and sell readily for $2.50 per pair. All the sailors and marines wear them now. Gamblers are playing cards all day or throwing dice into a tin cup for a box, and games of Honest John, euchre, or poker are going on all day, while crowds of others stand by to watch the piles of money change hands. Among the gaping crowd stand the half starved, ragged skeleton like forms of some of the prisoners, who have no money, and don't ever expect to have any, who beg 10¢ or so from the lucky ones when the game breaks up. Stakes are from $1 or $5 per game to $100 greenbacks.

The Raiders are also in the crowd, watching the lucky winner pocket his gains then follow him to his shanty which is marked by the gang for a midnight raid that night. These

*Sneden uses the popular term for the raucous trading floor of the New York Gold Exchange, located at William Street and Exchange Place. (Gold dealers scandalized patriotic Northern opinion by hoping for Confederate victory.)

raiders have been making desperate attacks lately on all those who are known to possess any money, watches, rings, or other valuables. They have grown so bold as to attack and rob prisoners in broad daylight, regular highway robbers. They select their victim and two or three of them club the unfortunate man either in his tent or in the streets, rob him so quickly that before he can cry out the thieves generally have escaped by dodging in behind the tents in the narrow crooked streets, or in a tent of a confederate thief and robber near-by. Out of sixteen robberies reported to Big Pete who is chief of the police or Regulators, not one of the scoundrels have been arrested. Seven or eight prisoners have been known to have been murdered by the gang within the past month!* As they have suddenly disappeared and must have been killed and buried for plunder. The Regulators seem to be in with the gang and a new force of police has recently been organized which come in the place of the old ones although "Big Pete" is still chief. While excavating for a tunnel last week the workmen exhumed two dead prisoners who had been buried seven feet deep together, entirely naked and in a decomposed state. The owner of the tent or shanty which was over the dead men hastily tore it down and moved away to some other locality before he could be identified. This was on the south side of the swamp.

The new police was organized by Sergeant Leroy S. Key, of the 16th Illinois Cavalry, who is a man of great nerve and strong will. Ned Carrigan, and one large fellow known as "Limber Jim,"† Goody Larkin, Jim Johnson, and about 100 others comprise what is now known as "Key's Regulators." The men were formed into companies, each commanded by a sergeant. All the men were selected from the strongest and most respectable of the prisoners. Most of them being of the prisoners who were captured at Plymouth, North Carolina. Each man of them was armed with a long heavy pine wood stick, which was full of sap and nearly as heavy as lead. They had three pistols among them and about twenty cartridges which had been smuggled into the stockade secreted in their blankets when they first arrived here. These billies were secured to their wrists like a policeman's club, a detail of these men under a sergeant was posted at night at different places through the camp not being at the same place always, and by a system of low whistles could concentrate at any one point. There were two captains and three lieutenants, commissioned U.S. officers among them.

They did not interfere with Big Pete who was honest enough, but the men under him were bribed by the Raiders, and some of the very Raiders were in the Regulators. Sergeant Key now determined to have men that he could depend on, and put the Raiders down if his force had to attack them in open day. He saw Wirz at the north gate, who for a wonder asserted to the new organization among us as he was powerless to help us in any way. Wirz

* Sneden's count of prisoners murdered by the Raiders is high and based, like the accounts of other prisoners, on hearsay as well as firsthand evidence.

† Sneden, like some other Andersonville prisoners, assumed Key and Limber Jim were two people, when in fact it is likely that Limber Jim was Key's nickname.

had never attempted to preserve order in the camp. His whole business was to keep the Yankees inside the stockade, he and the Rebel guard cared nothing of what was done inside, provided we did not escape and [kept] away from the dead line space.

The 35,000 men and boys who were prisoners inside the stockade were nothing more than a mob, all ranks alike, and hitherto no one had attempted to organize a force on military principles of respectable and reliable men and assume command before Sergeant Key did so. Of course he was backed up by every well meaning prisoner in the stockade, for no one's life was safe either day or night now, whether he had money or not. The Raiders on the other hand were well organized, had certain signals by which they could concentrate, and were led by five or six ruffians who stopped at nothing to gain plunder by robbing and killing if any resistance was offered by the victims they selected to pounce upon. These Raiders were known by the names of their leaders, as Curtis' Raiders, Delaney's Raiders, Sarsfield's Raiders, Collins' Raiders, or Mosby's Raiders. Collins was known as "Mosby."

They numbered nearly 200, and were composed of bounty jumpers and natural born thieves and ruffians who had graduated from the slums of the Bowery and Water streets, New York. They travelled in bands of from five to twenty, and were armed with sand bag clubs, tough pine clubs, brass knuckles, dirk and bowie knives, and carried pine roots which had sharp points, and which had been hardened to the consistency of ebony in a slow fire. One blow of this weapon would fracture a man's skull at once. About twenty of them lived in a large shelter or tent made from blankets which they had stolen from the other prisoners, on the Main Street which ran through the camp on the south side leading from the south gate, west to east. Over 100 were clustered near the southwest corner of the stockade on the south side of the swamp. Thirty or more had shelters on a dry sand knoll known as Raiders Island near the sinks, while others were scattered within whistle call of the headquarters of the five chiefs in the large tent near the south gate.

These Raiders were all strong, as they bought food from the sutler and other dealers with stolen money, or robbed some poor prisoner of his whole stock of food exposed for sale in front of his miserable ragged shelter. If the victim made any outcry, he was visited during the night by some of the gang and beaten nearly to death. These Raiders were feared by all of us and were thought to be invincible against anything we could do to stop their robbery or murders. Of course Wirz was often appealed to for help, but he could do nothing. We were a mob without any leaders. I had witnessed these robberies and beatings ever since last March with others who had got here at the same time. Then few if any had money. Now there was nearly $20,000 greenbacks in the hands of the newcomers, but mostly held by a few men. . . .

Sometimes the yell of "Raiders," "Stop thief," is heard among the thickly crowded shanties and tents when all is commotion among the dwellers. The thief, with his plunder of cooking utensils, blankets, etc., dodges among the low built shelters to get to the swamp which he crosses not by the causeway but plunges into the filth and dirty water above the sinks to regain Raiders Island, when he is lost to view among his fellow thieves. No one dare to follow him up there, for twenty clubs would soon be flourished in his defense. The thieves on the north side make raids on the south side and visa versa. . . . Many thieves have now moved into the new stockade where the tents and shanties are not so thickly built and fewer men are met to oppose them. Lately they knock down and rob in broad daylight but escape generally before a force can be gotten to head them off. . . .

We are dying inside the stockade at the rate of about thirty a day. I have been sick for some time. Rheumatism in [the] legs compels [me] to use a crutch, and am so weak that I have to rest for a minute to get breath if I go fifty feet. Scurvy in [my] mouth troubles me again. Raw potatoes help somewhat. I wash every day in well water but am getting thin, weak and ragged. I often dream of eating roast beef or oysters, and can actually taste them in my sleep. . . .

Wirz has sent Rebel soldiers in here among us as spies, to see if we have any organization among ourselves which will tend to our breaking out in force. These spies are dressed in Union soldiers' clothes taken from the dead ones who die out in the hospital, and of course they mingled with the newcomers and were not recognized. They would only stay two or three days at a time, when others took their place. One of them was taken for a Raider, and cries of "here's a Raider" "look out for him" followed him through the camp for some time.

Wirz is very much afraid that we will make an attempt to break out. It is known that he stands at the door or window of his log house for hours during the night, watching us, and has the artillery men on duty day and night ready to open fire on the stockade in a moment's warning. He does not trust his own men either, as many lately have deserted the camps and probably gone home. Most of the guards who get furloughs for twenty or thirty days for shooting a prisoner in the stockade never come back again. These are not of the regular Georgia regiments who guard us but of the Georgia Reserves, who are mostly comprised of old men and boys, and known as "the Home Guard." . . .

*July 3, 1864**

The morning of 3rd July was fine and sunny and not as hot as usual. There was no roll call, and no rations came in at all! The consequence was that those who had not saved food from yesterday or had no money to buy had to go hungry, but the excitement of the coming battle furnished nervous excitement and all were anxious to see and help win. All the respectable and orderly prisoners wished to see the gang of murderers killed with clubs just where they were and make an end of them and a terrible example to those yet not known to be as bad

*Sneden probably gives the wrong date for the uprising against the Raiders. Although several former prisoners writing after the war say it began on July 3, the evidence suggests that the initial attack took place on June 29.

as they were. Great excitement prevailed throughout the prison as the Regulators began to form lines of battle about 11 a.m. Even the sick crawled out of their miserable holes in the ground and ragged tents to witness the battle. 25,000 prisoners were crowded among the narrow streets and shanties along Main Street or Broadway on the north side of the prison: All the occupants of the new stockade ground joined in, while for hundreds of feet around the street which led through the prison from the south gate all the shelters and shanties were empty. Raiders Island and the whole of the swamp were deserted.

Sergeant Key formed his men about 250 strong along the Main Street on the north side of the prison. The Raiders could be seen drawn up two deep in line on the south side about 11:30 a.m. Key's men began the attack; his whole line moved forward in open skirmish order about ten paces apart, and as they gained the sand hills along the brook on the other side of the swamp, all closed up. Filing through the crooked lanes and streets, [they] rushed for the opposing line of Raiders with yells and cheers. Instantly tents were leveled with the ground, clubs flourished in [the] air, and a fierce hand to hand fight took place. Key, when he had gained the other side of the swamp made a flank attack on the Raiders' line with about one half of his force. After about ten minutes' hard fighting the Raiders broke and ran every one for his life, dodging in among the upturned and wrecked shelters, and being closely pursued by the Regulators. Scores were bleeding and crying for mercy, others fought on hopelessly.

Many tried to cross the swamp to the north side but they had stationed a reserve force to meet this and they were driven back, cursing and yelling with bloody heads and arms. All were in shirt sleeves and the clubs told heavily on the heads of both sides. Wirz had lent Key several lengths of rope; those who surrendered were bound with them and marched out of the south gate where the Rebel guard took charge of them. These were only a dozen or so. All the others had scattered so among the shanties that they could not be caught. And as many of the Regulators had been much hurt the battle came to an end. The victorious Regulators crossed the swamp to their own quarters, enough had been done for one day. The battle would be renewed on the morrow. Key gave his orders in the evening for the capture of the remaining Raiders to his men. . . .

July 4, 1864

We had a fine sunny day but very hot! At early morning bands of Key's men with clubs tied to their wrists marched through the prison stockade in all directions, hunting up the Raiders and arresting a large number of them. Many of them made a fierce resistance but they were clubbed without mercy and hauled out of wells, holes and sunk tents amid the wildest excitement. The big tent of the most prominent Raiders was stormed and demolished. The stolen blankets taken and the ground dug up to find the hidden plunder. Several watches, with chains, knives, piles of rubber ponchos, and other stolen articles were found, and it was said that four or five decomposed bodies were found also. Key's men went through the whole south side, then scoured through the north side and the new stockade. Many dozens of prisoners armed with clubs helped them and pointed out many of the Raiders.

Short quick fights soon settled them however and by sundown 125 of them had been arrested and marched into the enclosure at the north gate where they were confined under a strong Rebel guard. These were to be tried for their lives. Eighty-six of the strongest and most desperate of these were bound with ropes before they could be pulled to the gate. All were more or less cut or hurt. Blood was running down their arms and heads. All were cursing and swearing, making desperate resistance, but the ropes cut them, and they were pulled along without mercy to the gate. Intense excitement prevailed among the prisoners. . . .

The determination and quick action of Key and his men had destroyed their confidence by being defeated, and many other Raiders still in the stockade had not joined them in the second day's fighting as anticipated. Sergeant Key will now confer with Wirz so as to try all the principal ones and hang or shoot them if necessary for their many murders. We have good lawyers among us, and good solid men for a jury. So they will be tried for their lives, in the enclosed space outside the north gates. They were jeered and cursed by the other prisoners.

The sun grew very hot at noon and beat down upon the red earth so as to dazzle the eyes. The rations did not come in at the usual time and everyone was hungry who could not buy from the sutler. We saw lots of carcasses of beef lying all day in the hot sun over by the cook house but none of it came in to us until near sundown, then we found it to be boiled beef and mule meat, rotten, and full of great white maggots nearly 1/8 of an inch long! It was quite dark before each man got his miserable ration of about two ounces each. Some had bones. All the meat had turned blue, green, yellow, and black. Some of it was boiled to a mush and some quite raw. Maggots were thick and plentiful. Much of it was thrown away. I got just two mouthfuls of good solid meat out of my ration. Hundreds kept on eating it however, despite the maggots, and in three or four hours were seized with cramps and violent diarrhea which kept them running to the sinks all night. Those who got bones broke them up and made soup. The corn bread was burned black on the outside and raw inside, while the goober beans were only half boiled and were full of bugs, which had to be skimmed off in water. The cattle and mules must have been killed for three or four days before being cooked, and they laid out in the sun and rain all the while.

Today being Independence Day several educated comrades made short speeches to small crowds of willing listeners. Our desperate condition was fully discussed and as there was no prospect of being exchanged and seeing our far off homes again we were advised to keep orderly and abide our time when Sherman's army might reach us, as it was known that he was marching with 100,000 men through Georgia. The fearful monthly death roll was commented on and prayer meetings would be held if any would attend. The Raiders were now vanquished and would meet just and quick punishment. Some of them must die for their brutal murders and they would be tried by judge and jury composed of our own men. All those Raiders yet in camp were cautioned to stop their work at once, or they would be clubbed and arrested like the others. Three rousing cheers from 200 or more prisoners were given for "The Old Flag," while hundreds of others sang "Rally round the flag boys" and "Star Spangled Banner." One of the sailors who was good at sewing made a small American flag from some red flannel and part of a white shirt. This was waved as the crowd sang, and cheers went up all over the northern part of the stockade. All was quiet and orderly again in a few minutes. Small crowds of twenty to fifty discussed the case of the Raiders now confined outside the north gate.

In the meantime Wirz had been watching the crowds and must have heard the singing and cheering [at] his headquarters at the fort. He was now in mortal fear that we would attack the guard and try to break out of the stockade. At about 9 a.m. he rode over to the depot on the gallop and sent an engine which happened to be there off at full speed for General Howell Cobb at Macon sixty miles away to come here at once. About 10 a.m. all were startled by a gun being fired from the fort on the hill and as the round shot "swished" through the air overhead a panic seized many of us, who ran for the holes in the ground dug previously. All thought that the Rebels were now going to fire grape and canister into the whole mass of 35,000 men as threatened by Wirz. But only one shot was fired. The ball went clean over the stockade into the woods beyond at the height of about fifty feet, so the Massachusetts artillerymen who came in with the Plymouth men said. This shot brought in all the outlying picket guards on the full run. They were joined by a large force from near the fort of three guns on the north side of the stockade and all went on "the double" into the rifle trenches and fort at Wirz's headquarters. The whole Rebel forces was turned out at their camps, about 3,000, and formed lines of battle. Wirz was thoroughly scared, but all was quiet and order among us.

Wirz went over to see General Winder whose headquarters was near the depot, and between it and Andersonville, and with an escort all the Rebel staff went to the depot where they waited an hour or so for the coming of General Cobb who commanded the 8th district of the state, with headquarters at Macon. About 11 a.m. the engine returned with Cobb on it. After a confab, General Cobb went along the lines of the Rebel troops and came down the hill towards the cook house and within 100 yards of the stockade. General Winder ordered the troops to file past General Cobb, who stood on a tree stump inspecting them, and ordered a hollow square to be formed. This was very clumsily executed for the "square" was a crooked oblong. Wirz and Generals Cobb and Winder were near its center. The sun came out red hot and the resin almost boiled out of the tree stump on which General Cobb stood.

After some delay Cobb made a speech* in a husky voice to those around him in this wise: "Officers and Soldiers of the Southern Confederacy: If you are surprised to see me here today, it is mine to confess a greater surprise that there should be deemed such a necessity for my presence. Can it be true that Georgians are deserting their posts in the face of a disarmed enemy? Can it be true that Georgians are refusing in safety to guard the Vandal horde within that den, whom your more valorous brothers have captured on a hundred bloody fields? Can it be true that there are Georgians here today, who are ready to turn loose upon their mothers, sisters, daughters and wives, that multitude of robbers who are panting for opportunities to burn and ravage our land as they wander back to rejoin their comrades, who are pressing us at every point?!"

Just at this part of the speech the songs from the stockade were heard. "The Star Spangled Banner," etc., and "Long may it wave," etc. As the chorus ended the speaker resumed. "Is there a man here who would so fail of his duty? Hear me, I announce in your hearing—and let no one be deceived by the hope of escape. The next and every other deserter from this post, who is captured will be immediately tried by drum head court martial, and executed on the spot. And I announce further, that the commander of this post is fully vested with authority to carry out this order into execution." The last of these words were almost drowned by the sounds from the stockades and General Cobb turned to Captain Wirz and said "Have the prisoners stop that noise." As Wirz was moving off, that sound grew tenfold louder than before. From 10,000 to 20,000 voices were now singing, "The Star Spangled Banner," etc. All the Rebels turned their heads towards the stockade, even Wirz stood stock still until the chorus had ended. General Cobb shouted sternly to have the prisoners "stop that noise."

For a minute he essayed to continue his speech until the chorus was a third time reached [and] his voice was completely drowned out by the booming tornado of sound and melody. The Rebel guard in [the] square stood still from astonishment. One of the sentries on the stockade wall was so scared that he let his musket fall inside the stockade. Cobb could say no more and General Winder ordered the troops to march to their camps, while the corpulent figure of Cobb was helped down from the tree stump and he with others walked up to Wirz's headquarters to get a drink probably. The singing was very good considering that so many thousand voices without any leader [were] doing it. Good time was kept too throughout. Poor half starved prisoners, cripples and sick fellows caught at their comrades who helped them to stand, and waving their bony hands united their hollow voices with enthusiasm in vocation. This was about noon time.

*As with other passages citing speeches, Sneden adds quotation marks to indicate where he inserted text taken from sources outside his notes. He does not indicate his source for Cobb's speech. In a letter to his wife dated July 11 and now at the Cobb papers in the University of Georgia Library, Cobb downplayed the seriousness of desertion by camp guards and said he "gave the men a talk of a half hour in the sun—and then came away leaving both officers and men perfectly content and satisfied."

After this, when the Rebel troops were seen to go to their camps, every one quieted down. The sailors had managed to get some whiskey, and a fiddle from somewhere outside and they kept up a noisy jubilee as long as the whiskey lasted. Singing and dancing until rations came in after 6 p.m. when all were hungry enough to eat some of the mule or rotten meat. . . .

July 5 to 10, 1864

Sergeant Key went around among us to get men to serve as jurymen in the trial of the Raiders. The judge has been selected but his name is kept secret. Many of the men are afraid to serve as they fear violence from the Raiders yet among us. The deaths in the stockade for the past week have been over sixty. I managed to send a letter to my friend Walsh, who is clerk at Wirz's headquarters by the Rebel corporal or something, who calls the roll. I ask for much information which is against the rules, but hope to get it nevertheless, as one can bribe a Rebel always. From a recaptured prisoner I obtained part of a map of [the] state of Georgia showing from here to Atlanta, copies of which I am making in india ink to sell to those who are digging tunnels to escape. I have to keep very secret about it and draw a blanket across the entrance to prevent observers. Wilson, the recaptured prisoner, cut a piece out of a map hanging in a Rebel house, where his captors took him to get something to eat while bringing him back here. He got six days in the foot stocks outside the stockade for running away. . . .

The trial of the Raiders was finished 8th July. The judge was selected by ballot, and the jury was drawn from a panel of 1,000 prisoners from the stockade. The murderers were given the privilege of rejecting jurors, and they exercised that privilege till they were tired of it and allowed a jury to go on. They had also the privilege of pleading their own case, or of employing anyone within the stockade to plead for them. Two attorneys were selected, from a number of that profession among us to proceed against the prisoners. The trial was conducted as fairly and honorable as was possible under the circumstances. The court martial consisted of thirteen sergeants, taken from the late arrivals, in order that they may not be prejudiced against the prisoners. The whole trial, which lasted six days was conducted with all the formality that could be had and the prisoners had the privilege to cross question all witnesses until satisfied. Six of the number were clearly found guilty of murder in the first degree and sentenced to be hung within the stockade next day 11th July, between sunrise and sunset. These were the chiefs of the several gangs, viz. William Collins, alias "Mosby" of [the] 88th Pennsylvania Regiment, John Sarsfield, 154th New York Regiment, Charles Curtis, 5th Rhode Island Battery, Patrick Delaney, 83rd Pennsylvania, Terrence Sullivan,* 72nd New York and Andy Muir, of U.S. gunboat *Watch Witch*. Of the 125 of the

*John Sullivan was his correct name. That Sneden called him "Terrence" suggests he relied on another postwar memoir written by Andersonville prisoner John McElroy, who also incorrectly called him "Terrence."

most noted Raiders arrested, six were sentenced to be hung, eighty-six were sentenced to "run the gauntlet" inside the stockade, twenty or more to be "bucked and gagged," fifteen to have ball and chain for thirty days, and a dozen or more to get twenty lashes each with the cat-o'-nine-tails, then sent into the stockade to "run the gauntlet."

Those who had been sentenced to ball and chain had the irons fitted to them at once, and were taken up near the stocks. Each had thirty-two pound balls riveted to his legs with a heavy ox chain. These Wirz playfully termed "Confederate watches." Wirz refused to guard any more than those sentenced to death. So today the eighty-six who had to run "the gauntlet" were thrust through the small gate which is in the large gate, one by one and they had to run the whole length of Broadway, or Main Street from one end of the prison to the other.

We got word of this about noon. On 9th July about 2 p.m. long lines of prisoners were drawn up all along the street, each armed with a pine stick or club, and as the Raiders ran between the double lines of men they were showered with blows without mercy. Three of them were knocked senseless with broken skulls, and died in an hour! Others had their arms broken, all were beaten until the blood ran from their arms, or heads, and were terribly bruised all over. The culprits held their heads down and ran as fast as they could. The ranks were so packed with prisoners that they could not go anywhere but through the long lane of uplifted clubs.

Many of the men who had thus to "run the gauntlet" were those who had robbed and maltreated the prisoners and we considered this the only chance to get even with them. It was not generally known among the prisoners in the stockade that six of the most prominent Raiders were to be hung until at night. I with my chums looked on the terrible punishment inflicted on those who had to run the gauntlet. Wirz and several other Rebel officers viewed "the run" from the sentry boxes on top of the stockade.

July 11, 1864*

Fine day but very hot, about 110 degrees in a cool place! About 8 a.m. a Rebel guard came in the stockade armed only with revolvers and stood near the dead line at the south gate. Wirz was with them and other officers. A mule team came in soon after drawing a wagon load of timbers, five or six carpenters unloaded it and in an hour or so they constructed a rough gallows to hang the Raiders on. . . .

As the time approached for the execution the excitement both inside and outside the stockade was intense. Many of the prisoners would not even look at the hanging and lay in their tents. Others formed long lines along Broadway five or six deep, but did not cross the swamp. All those from the new stockade crossed over, and with the thousands on the

*When he sat down to write his own account, Sneden used his diary fragments as an aid to memory, but he could not resist adding colorful embellishments gleaned from memoirs published after the war by other prisoners. Most of the direct quotations he cites in the long entry under July 11 have been appropriated from those other accounts. He also incorrectly identifies the priest as Father Hamilton when in fact it was Father Whelan.

south side gathered in a dense crowd around the scaffold. Sergeant Key had formed his Regulators around the scaffold in a hollow square facing outwards, each man of them had their clubs drawn to repel any attempt made by the Raiders to prevent the execution. Up at the fort and battery on the hill the Rebel 1st Florida artillerymen stood to their pieces, with lighted fuses. The whole Rebel guard were turned out fully armed. They occupied the rifle trenches and batteries and other earthworks which encompassed us. All the artillery in the three forts were trained on the stockade to fire on us at the command and all were shotted of course.

All along the slopes of the hill around Wirz's headquarters, were farmers with their wives and children even, who had come from the country around in wagons, buggies, and all kinds of carts to see the execution. Many of these spectators were strung along the slope of the hill back of the rifle trenches with the eight gun battery behind them. All the sentry boxes on the south side of the stockade were occupied by four or five Rebel soldiers and officers who were all fully armed. I went over to the swamp and got within forty feet of the scaffold.

About 2 p.m. all was in readiness and 30,000 prisoners lined the slopes on the north side of the stockade among the ragged tents and shanties looking intently across the swamp with the glaring hot sun in their faces. Quietness and order was everywhere.

A line of Regulators were posted twenty feet apart all along the margin of the swamp on the north side with clubs, and none were allowed to cross the swamp to the south side after 2 p.m., as fully 6,000 were now there packed in a close throng all around the gallows. About 2:15 p.m. one half of the big south gate was opened and Wirz came riding in on his white horse. Behind him walked Father Hamilton, the old gray haired priest, who used to visit the sick and dying men in the stockade on Sunday.

He was reading the service for the dying from a missal. Then came the six condemned men. William Collins, alias Mosby, John Sarsfield, Patrick Delaney, Terrence Sullivan, Charles Curtis, and the sailor Andy Muir. Each had their arms bound with small rope fastened behind and around the elbow. They slowly walked in single file between a double row of Rebel guard, all fully armed. Key, having formed his Regulators in a hollow square around the scaffold, took his position inside it, with the six men who were to act as hangmen. As soon as the culprits had come inside the square, the two barrels were then fixed under the drop plank, and the pull rope stretched on the ground while three stout men stood ready to jerk the barrels from underneath it when the time came.

Wirz now said "Prisoners I return to yo dese men so goot as I got dem. You have tried dem and found dem guilty. I haf had noting to do wit it. I vash mine hands of everyting connected wid it. Do wid tem as you like, and may Got haf mercy on you and on dem. Garts, about face, forwarts march!" With this the guards marched out at shoulder arms. Wirz followed on horseback.

For a moment the condemned men looked dazed. They seemed to realize for the first time that the "Regulators" were in terrible earnest. They had thought all along that the trial and all the talk was a "bluff" to frighten them or that they would be rescued by their comrades. One of them exclaimed, "My God! men you don't really mean to hang us up there?" "That's about the size of it. You and the rest of the d___d gang have now to swing," said Key.

At this they all burst out in protestations, pleadings, and imprecations, until one of them said "All stop now, and let the priest talk for us." At this Father Hamilton closed the book which he had constantly read aloud since entering the gate. And turned to the crowd, began an earnest plea for mercy. As soon as the crowd caught the first few words, and realized their import, they began to shout, "No, No, No." "Hang the murderers." "Hang them," "Never let them go," etc., etc. Then [Collins] a low set heavily built man when he saw the hopelessness of any appeal for mercy, exclaimed, "By God, I say die this way first."

(He had managed to loosen the rope which bound his elbow.) Lowering his head he made a dash through the line of the "Regulators" on the east side of the square with such powerful force as to take several of them clean off their feet, in a trice, tents were upset, men in the crowd [thrown] down and trampled on, and a panic lasted for a full minute. Curtis dashed through the crowd and ran with all his might towards the sinks on the swamps. Delaney, a great brawny Irishman started to follow, but "Limber Jim" strode in front of him, and with a big upraised bowie knife said: "You dare to move another step, and I'll open you from one end to the other." Delaney stopped, being yet bound, and this checked the others until the Regulators got them inside the square again which now was reformed. In the meantime the guards on the stockade scrambled down from their boxes in a great hurry. While Wirz, seeing the panic and the immense crowd surging to and fro, thought the dreaded outbreak of all the prisoners in the stockade would now take place, rushed from his log house headquarters to the battery near it, shrieking "Fire! Fire! Fire!" The artillerymen were held in check by the captain of the battery who saw that the rush was away from and not toward the stockade. So he did not fire.

The crowd of citizens, farmers, men, women, and children who had pushed up directly on the slope below the eight gun battery outside on the hill to get a good view of the scaffold, hearing the order of Wirz to "fire," and knowing themselves to be directly in range, were panic stricken, and ran screaming and tumbling over each other towards the western slope, where their horses and wagons were, to get out of danger.

During all this confusion two of the Regulators were in hot pursuit of Collins, who had run down to the swamp, plunged in, and forced his way to the north side, although he sank into the filthy ooze up to his hips. Here he was met by the line of Regulators placed there previously by Big Pete. He was knocked down by their clubs, and carried bodily by four strong men across to the south side again by the causeway at the west end where the brook came through the stockade, and brought once more into the square formed around the gallows. On the way over he begged piteously for his life, cursed and swore, kicked, and struggled with all his strength, but it was of no use. He was covered from head to foot with the filth of the swamp, [and] so were his captors. During the rush and panic, the crowd in front of me surged suddenly back. I, with many others were forced violently in among the ragged sunk tents on the side hill which were instantly wrecked.

I fell into a sunk tent on top of a sick man, I suppose, for he was lying down in there. I scrambled out just in time, for a big Irishman made a blow at me with a long wooden shovel. As it was made of sappy pine, it might have been as heavy as one made of iron. "Git out of here d__n you" was all I heard. I regained a place about twenty feet from the scaffold in a few minutes though much excited.

I got there just as Collins was being carried over the causeway from the north side. Collins was allowed to sit down on the ground a few minutes to rest as he seemed in an exhausted condition. The sentry boxes on top of the stockade were reoccupied by several of the guards in each. The ladder had been put up, and the culprits were ordered by Key to "get up on the plank."

Collins went up last, being helped up by two Regulators who were the hangmen. The priest had during this time continued to read the service for the dying, to which Delaney gave little attention. Delaney seemed to think that Collins was suffering more from fright than anything else, and advised him to "stand up like a man and die game," and he kept calling out to his friends, making dispositions of different articles of his stolen property, telling one to "take his watch to his mother in New York," and other articles he distributed among his fellow Raiders in the stockade.

The priest admonished him to turn his attention from things of this earth to those of heaven. The whole six then began to talk, saying their farewells, and sending messages to their friends. During this short time the six hangmen were placing the prisoners in position directly under the six nooses on the beam overhead. Sergeant Key took out his watch and said "Two minutes more to talk." Well good-bye said Delaney. "If oive hurted any of yez I hope yez'll foregive me. Shpake up now!" But no one seemed to be in a forgiving mood and a dead silence followed, which in fact prevailed among all the 35,000 lookers on in the stockade. "Time is up," said Key, and he raised his right hand as signal.

The two men who were to pull the barrel supports from under the planks on which the prisoners stood took hold of the rope. The hangmen then pulled a small meal sack over each of the culprits' heads. Their arms were securely tied back of the elbows previously, then [the hangmen] tightened the nooses, and sprang to the ground, the priest all the time praying aloud. Key dropped his hand. The men at the rope snatched the barrel supports from under the planks, which fell, and the culprits dropped suddenly the length of their ropes. Five struggled violently for a minute, drawing their knees up to their bodies. Collins, alias Mosby broke his rope and fell to the ground in a heap. He was a large heavy man weighing nearly 200 pounds. The meal sack was at once removed from his face. The rope was cut off his neck: he was hurt only by shock, in a few minutes he recovered consciousness, and gasped out "Where am I? Am I in eternity?" Limber Jim, whose brother he was said to have killed said, "We'll soon show you where you are d___ you," and began to fix up the scaffold.

Battery on hill and Wirz's headquarters | Brook and swamp | South gate | Spectators outside | Rebel camp by railroad

HANGING OF THE RAIDERS, ANDERSONVILLE PRISON
July 11, 1864.

Collins was now aware that he would be shown no mercy and began begging piteously for his life, but without avail. The scaffold was soon adjusted and he was carried up and out on the fatal plank.

A new rope noosed around his neck, and the barrels kicked from under him. He struggled violently but in ten minutes all the bodies were swaying at the end [of] their ropes. They fell about seven feet. After hanging about twenty minutes, they were examined and found to be dead. The ropes were cut, and the meal bags taken from their heads. They laid on the ground until sunset while hundreds of the prisoners filed past, two abreast to see them between two rows of Regulators. Their faces were much distorted, one only had his neck broken. All the remainder died by slow strangulation. The immense crowds of prisoners dispersed slowly to their shelters all glad that the terrible example had been made of the murderers, while the remaining Raiders yet in the stockade were cowed at once, and thieving, robbery, and murder stopped for a time. After sundown the bodies of those hung were carted out by the ration wagon to the graveyard, and they were all buried close together, near the centre of the place, no mark or stake was allowed to be put over them. The gallows was left standing a day or two, for a holy terror to all thieves and Raiders yet among us, over whom a strict watch will be kept. . . .

Down by the north and south gates are daily brought dead men, mostly entirely naked, who lay piled on top of each other, all swollen up, dirt stained and as black as Negroes from exposure to sun and rain, while millions of flies hover over the ghastly corpses! These are waiting for the ration wagon to carry to the graveyard! At night, the scene is solemn enough for the most hardened sinner. The ragged skeleton forms clustered around a small fire singing hymns or a comrade prays. The pile of naked corpses in the firelight, etc. The solemn looks of haggard men. A perfect stillness of all noises in the vicinity gives an impression never to be effaced from one's memory. All around were sick or dying men lying in their ragged shelters, or without any shelter; propped up by their comrades to hear and listen to the singing, some crying, others cursing in delirium, others joining in singing the old familiar hymns of long ago when they were then in their happy homes far away, little thinking that they would be in such a hell upon earth as this place! Sometimes four or five groups were having prayers and singing at one time among us.

One of the last batch of prisoners who came in on 12th July gave information to the Rebel officer at the gate as to the locality of a large tunnel which had been in course of construction in the high sand bank on the west side near the sinks. He was also one of the "Union League" and had given Wirz all the information about the proposed "break" which was to be made. . . . He was pounced upon by four or five of "the League," carried to "Big Pete's" shanty and sentenced by him to thirty lashes on the bare back with the cat-o'-nine-tails. "Old Jack" the sailor was sent for, who by orders, pricked a large T (for traitor) on his forehead, and was not very gentle about it either, with a bunch of needles and india ink. The thirty lashes were about to be given him when Wirz sent in a guard of thirty or forty soldiers and took the traitor out of the stockade. The man was known as a bounty jumper, an Irishman belonging to some New York regiment, and he betrayed the plot for two plugs of tobacco and extra rations to the Rebel sergeant at the south gate, being overheard as he made the bargain by two other prisoners near him.

During this month I had a terrible attack of chronic diarrhea which lasted two weeks. My comrades helped me to walk for some days so that I could answer roll call, but after a while I lay on the ground or in my tent perfectly helpless and at some times insensible to all my horrible surroundings. I rinsed my mouth only with water and ate nothing for several days. . . .

Several of my friends began anew to make holes in the ground large enough for one man to get below the surface in anticipation that the battery would open fire on us some day or night. As to enquiries the other fellows were told that the hole was to be a new well, etc. Yet those who knew of the order all felt anxious about it and worried much over it. Wilson's gang of sixteen or more men have been for a long time tunneling on the east side. Many times have they been ready to "break ground" and escape but they have been discovered by some traitor among themselves and Wirz being informed has filled up the holes again.

Wilson himself came to me with a genuine Rebel pass issued by Winder to see if I would make him some counterfeit ones. After assuring myself that he acted on the square I engaged to do so for "$2 greenbacks" each. He then furnished me the paper. I had the india ink and a steel pen which I stuck in a piece of split pine for a handle, and in a broiling sun with a blanket propped up on one stick so that I was completely covered from sight, I made several, which passed as good as the genuine. I changed the names only in each one. The men certainly got away somehow two or three in a day sometimes, and rations were stopped in several squads until they could be accounted for. . . .

The 55th Georgia regiment were in the force of Rebel guards of course. If I had been detected by Wirz he would in all probability have had me shot. The chain gang would have had a new recruit sure. I was not suspected, and the men all proved true. Later on, one man was recaptured and one of my passes was found on him. I got notice of this from Walsh at headquarters. The man would not tell where he got the pass. Wirz was furious and put the man in the stocks. I never heard what became of him. Wirz then dressed a Rebel in our uniform and put him in the stockade to "find out the 'Yank' who made the passes." The Rebel went out of the stockade every night. Another one was tried but did not get at me. I had cut off my moustache and wore my clothes turned inside out for a week or more to change my identification. Kept much in my tent and "laid low" for a long while. I had $60 in greenbacks with which I bought things to eat from the Rebel sutler, which being just after my dangerous sickness served me to a good purpose. I gave many dollars away to my sick comrades, bought potatoes to give away to those who had the scurvy in mouth and also invested with Brock in stolen meal bags which were made into trousers by others and which sold for $2.50 greenbacks each. . . .

August 2 to 10, 1864

There were numerous country wagons seen up at Wirz's headquarters today which contained several women. Three or four of these climbed up into the sentry boxes from the outside to have a look at the "Yanks." Some of these women stayed for a long while. They talked and chaffed with the prisoners, who crowded up to the dead line as close as they dared. I saw one woman near where I had my shanty. She was cursing us and shaking her fists. Our fellows yelled "Bull Run" and "Gettysburg" which made her frantic and she soon got down and away. At one place near the south gate two women were in the box with the sentry. There seemed to be a sort of picnic up at the fort. A Mrs. Reed* is at Winder's headquarters. She is seen on horseback riding around the stockade with the dogs. No other women are seen by us. I hear that there are none in the village but Negro women.

One of the prisoners was shot dead by the guards on top of the stockade near the south gate while dipping water from the stream which ran through it there on August 4th. . . .

*Probably the wife of Winder's provost marshal, Captain W. Shelby Reed, who once violently rebuffed a deputation of kindly civilians who brought a donation of food for the prisoners.

Prayer meetings were held in several places tonight by the light of a pine knot torch or two and a smouldering smoky fire through which the emaciated ragged prisoners looked like ghosts. Hymns were sung and prayers were fervently made by some one of us for our speedy delivery from the daily horrors of this cursed place. A terrible awe filled every one at the prospect of dying in such large numbers and in such a horrible manner. Even the most hardened and reckless among us kept quiet for once. And very little noise was made by those who bought and sold rations on Main Street or Broadway. . . .

September 1, 1864

Raining hard all day and most of the night. Thick fog set in at daylight. Cold and wet. Everyone [was] drenched through and the mud soon made in the camp several inches thick. I, with hundreds of others sat up all night bailing out our shanties and trying to stop the leaks in the rotten blankets which served us for roofs, but the rain came through as through a sieve, wetting all our clothing and food. Those who lived in holes were drowned out and the sick men had to be pulled out of them by their comrades. No fires would burn and every one was in a wretched state at sunrise. I had moved from my larger shanty some days ago, and now had for shelter only a rotten army blanket propped up on sticks and had to crawl into it on hands and knees and lie on two pieces of board on the wet red sand. I had to move from Wall Street because the whole ground for thirty feet about me was teeming with vermin and disgusting white worms which came through the sand and got into everything.

The dying men laid on the ground there and died at all hours of day and night, and to hear the . . . shrieks, oaths and moans of the poor fellows in their delirium was horrible. Many were kicked to death by the ghouls who sat around them, waiting to strip them of clothes or anything of value, and could not wait for them to die as best they could. And because some would make much noise while dying those sleeping near would kick them in the side or head saying "why don't you die quietly you!" Corpses, entirely naked, were lying on the ground in every direction. Some were side by side with the yet living, who were too weak to crawl away from them, while the large flies were in clouds on both dead and living filling their mouths and noses. It was sickening to see it. I counted sixty-two dead lying around camp today, their comrades being too weak to carry them to the gate for burial outside in that ever yawning graveyard! Many of us feel the awful situation which we are now in, but many again are reckless and think not much of our horrible surroundings. All sounds of hilarity have long since ceased. Even the Raiders seem more quiet. When they do prowl around, the guard of our own men run them off to Raiders Island, or over the creek and swamp to the south side hills.

Several prayer meetings are held every evening around a small fire, while good men exhort the prisoners, and hymns are sung too, amid the groans and cries of those who are dying all around them. A dim light through a fog from the fire makes the group of ragged

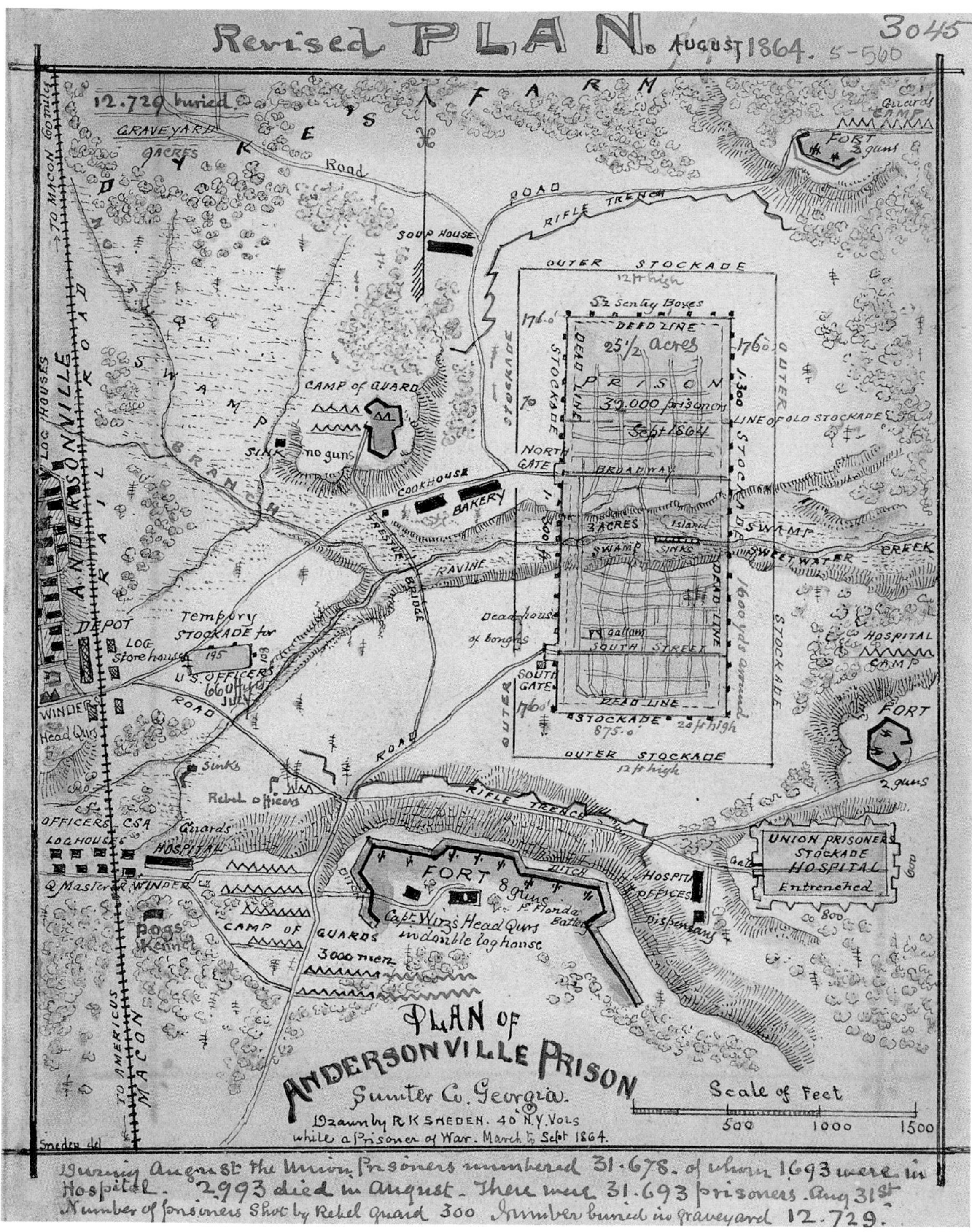
Revised PLAN. August 1864.
3045
5-560
12.729 buried
GRAVEYARD
6 ACRES
DYKES FARM
Road
ROAD
RIFLE TRENCH
Guards CAMP
FORT 3 guns
TO MACON 60 miles
SOUP HOUSE
OUTER STOCKADE
12 ft high
52 Sentry Boxes
DEAD LINE
25 1/2 acres
PRISON
32.000 prisoners
Sept 1864
1.300
LINE OF OLD STOCKADE
STOCKADE
DEAD LINE
OUTER
SWAMP
CAMP of GUARD
SINK
no guns
BRANCH
RAILROAD
LOG HOUSES
ANDERSONVILLE
NORTH GATE
BROADWAY
COOKHOUSE
BAKERY
TRESTLE BRIDGE
3 ACRES
Island
SINKS
SWAMP
SWEETWATER CREEK
RAVINE
Dead house
of boughs
1600 yds around
DEPOT
Tempory STOCKADE for U.S. OFFICERS
LOG Store house
195
660 offrs JULY
SOUTH STREET
SOUTH GATE
HOSPITAL CAMP
WINDERS Head Qurs
ROAD
STOCKADE
875.0
20 ft high
OUTER STOCKADE
12 ft high
FORT
2 guns
Sinks
Rebel officers
RIFLE TRENCH
OFFICERS CSA
LOG HOUSES
Guards
HOSPITAL
UNION PRISONERS STOCKADE HOSPITAL
Entrenched
800
FORT 8 guns
DITCH
HOSPITAL OFFICES
Dispensary
Q Master & WINDER
Capt. Wirz's Head Qurs in double log house
Fla. Florida Battery
Dogs Kennel
CAMP OF GUARDS
3000 men
TO AMERICUS
MACON
PLAN OF
ANDERSONVILLE PRISON
Sumter Co. Georgia.
Drawn by R.K. SNEDEN. 40th N.Y. VOLS
while a Prisoner of War. March to Sept 1864.
Scale of Feet
500
1000
1500
Sneden del
During August the Union Prisoners numbered 31.678. of whom 1693 were in Hospital. 2993 died in August. There were 31.693 prisoners Aug 31st
Number of prisoners Shot by Rebel Guard 300 Number buried in graveyard 12.729.

emaciated prisoners look like spectres, and the singing and preaching coming from the dark places throughout the camp give a very impressive and melancholy aspect to the whole. The singing is sometimes interrupted by yells, oaths, and a scuffle nearby, which shows that some Raider is at work robbing some poor sick fellow, and is being clubbed by others. . . .

Nearly all the prisoners are in rags—shoeless—and half naked—bareheaded—and covered with dirt and vermin. Some wear ragged waist coats with no shirt of any kind—no shoes or stockings—no blankets—and have to burrow in the ground like rabbits.

Small squads of men still go out under guard to gather sticks, chips or pine tops for fuel. Sometimes they get away from the guards, but are soon after followed by Harris or Turner with the hounds and are recaptured for they don't know in which way they are trying to escape. Five got away last night and were brought back this afternoon. Two of them were badly torn by the dogs in arms and legs. They had to "run the dead line" as usual but were not hit by the Rebel guard on top of the stockade at the south gate because they ran and tumbled on the ground over the prescribed twenty foot spaces. Six guards fired at them, but the bullets all went into the ground.

I made a careful observation of the new works and rifle trenches which the Rebels have lately thrown up outside the stockades, but those on the east side cannot be seen from the inside of the stockade as this shuts off the view even when standing on the other hill across the swamp. I made a plan of what I saw, however, which I sewed in the knee of my trousers, under a patch there. Davis keeps much to himself at Wirz's log house and is afraid to come inside the stockade at all.

September 5, 1864

The Rebel doctors, Isaiah H. White and another one, with several assistants, have recently put up some ragged tents outside the north and south gates where they dispense medicine such as it is to crowds of prisoners daily. Roots and herb decoctions are dispensed to those only who are in the last stages of disease and who are actually dying on their feet, so that in nearly all cases the medicine does them no good at all, as they are past caring for. From noon to 5 p.m. hundreds of poor emaciated prisoners are wending their way to either gate to be relieved. Some are carried in old blankets tied to poles by their comrades. Others crawl all the way to the gates on hands and knees—many of the lame and crippled hobble along on crutches made out of tent poles—while hundreds cannot go at all—being too weak to walk there or get there any how. Two or three at a time pass the dead line and the gates to get the decoctions for scurvy rheumatism—or what not. Hundreds are kept waiting in the hot sun all day—huddled on the ground—all struggling to get out. Many die on their way there while being carried, and they die on the ground when they do get there. The doctors are afraid to come inside the stockade. . . .

September 7, 1864

Fine weather, but very hot, 110 degrees anywhere in the shade. This terrible heat helps to kill us off at the rate of 100 per day inside the stockade. Dead men may be seen by the score lying all along the brook which runs through the filthy swamp, while others are tearing off their soiled clothes to get thread from the seams, or patches to put on their own ragged clothes. The swamp is literally dried up from the intense heat and presents a sickening mass of decomposed human filth which actually moves in big waves by the immense number of large white maggots, while the stench is overpowering all over the whole stockade. The sinks along the lower end of the swamp always overflow, when there is a heavy rain, and the contents are washed out and piled up against the south end of the stockade three and five feet high as it cannot escape through the small slits cut in the logs to let the water run through, while the flies hover over the whole disgusting ground in immense black swarms—a species of white fly, or miller breeds amid this filth—which gets into one's nose and mouth when the swamp is crossed.

Four or five prisoners escaped last night by secreting themselves with the connivance of the Negro teamster who drove the wagon out, being paid for it of course. Turner, Harris, and Dunn started early this morning for the pursuit, accompanied by five or six bloodhounds. They struck through the woods west of us. The baying of the hounds could be heard by us for a long while. Wirz on his white horse rode ahead of them.

A lot of boxes of clothing sent by the U.S. Sanitary Commission of New York came to Wirz's headquarters today via railroad from Macon. Some blankets came also. About 150 of our men who are working in the cook house, who are called paroled men by the Rebels, and "Galvanized Yanks" by us, marched up the hill and got a whole suit of clothes, except shoes. About fifty pairs of shoes came, but these were all taken by the Rebel officers and Wirz's immediate attendants. Some of the colored men got clothes too, but not all who worked for Wirz or his officers. Wirz sold a pair of trousers to the Rebel sergeant who had command of the Negroes, for $5 greenbacks.

Nearly all the boys who were first put in the stockade in April last, and afterwards transferred to the hospital outside as helpers, are dead long ago. These were mostly ship boys on U.S. vessels captured. They were about forty of them the ages averaged fifteen to nineteen years. The state of the hospital now is terrible. Men are huddled on the sandy ground by the hundred, their only shelter being rotten blankets or meal bags propped up with sticks. Two or three sheds are used by the doctors and their attendants who are under Dr. Isaiah H. White. The boy prisoners sometimes had leave to go into the woods to get blackberries and the roots for the sick. The doctors got the roots, but the cooks used all the blackberries to make pies for themselves. The dead lay among the living wallowing in their own filth like hogs. The Rebel students were constantly employed cutting up all those who died out there, sawing open their skulls, etc. in search of medical knowledge. Over 600 sick men have died at the hospital during the past week, while the small pox is also increasing. The prisoners are all vaccinated with "Negro pox"! Drs. White and Stevenson are the ones in charge there. . . .

September 10, 1864

Rainy, sultry weather with heavy fogs and dew after 9 p.m. The prayer meetings are well attended now as the terrible death rate among us daily overawes most of us. A private called "Boston Corbitt"* and Lieutenant Tracy make the most energetic discourses, while many Germans, who cannot understand much English, sing songs together of their native land.

Last night after sundown, the whole camp was infested with millions of large mosquitoes. They bit through our thin clothing and kept us all up until sunrise beating them off—no sleep for anyone. They were larger and fiercer than any Jersey mosquitoes that I ever saw. We were in pain and agony all night. Only around the small fires were they smoked off, and hundreds lay on the ground around the fires to get relief. Wood is very scarce with us yet, and those who could not get enough to make a fire, used pine splints. This is the first time that we were so annoyed by mosquitoes, and their bites smarted for days afterwards.

Several large mud ovens built of wet mud and pine sticks have been erected in camp. One notably on Broadway, near Wall Street, and two others on the south side of the swamp. These average ten feet in diameter and eight or nine feet high. Those who cannot get wood have their [corn pones] baked in these ovens for 2¢ each, but money is very scarce now—it being all in the hands of speculators in food or wood, sutler supplies, and the gamblers, who compose the roughest and toughest among us. . . .

September 12, 1864

Wilson, with thirty others, got away by a tunnel last month. Some of these were recaptured but not Wilson himself. Twenty-three have escaped since the 1st September, and others are digging holes like beavers in spite of all precautions taken to prevent. The Rebel guards on the stockade are bribed with money of which there is now considerable among us, but it is all in the hands of a few men. The foggy nights favor those who get away by tunneling, and the gaps through which they must pass through between the inner and outer stockade are not guarded at all, as they are near the Rebel fort on the hill. But we get away all the same, and Wirz is nearly frantic with rage. I interviewed some of Wilson's gang who were recaptured and who were put in the stocks afterwards. Others were put in the chain gang, where they still are. Wilson's men clubbed a Rebel guard, took his musket cartridges and everything else he had and got off into the swamp region on the Flint River near here. They kept together for miles when they scattered, going towards West Point, Georgia, they heard the dogs baying after them for two days. They destroyed the dogs' scent by sprinkling ground

*Celebrated later as the soldier who killed John Wilkes Booth.

red peppers in their tracks where they crossed water. The four who were recaptured were betrayed by a Rebel farmer's wife, who put them in a barn and got other farmers to come armed and recapture them. . . .

September 11, 1864*

We have heavy rains for some days. The Rebel sergeants who came in with the food wagons declare that we will move to a splendid new stockade in the woods, where we will have plenty of water and better rationing. We don't believe a word of this however as it may be a new ruse to keep us quiet as we know by the new prisoners just arrived that Stoneman's† cavalry 10,000 strong is raiding the country between us and Macon, which is only sixty miles west and north of us. We notice however that both the cook house buildings outside the stockade [are] being worked night and day cooking rations for some purpose. The chimney stacks send up large quantities of pitch pine black smoke continually. The Rebel guard are noticed to gather in groups on the outside of the forts, and look as if they were listening to someone talking to them. They are very quiet and sullen looking about the gates of the prison, while a newspaper of any kind cannot be bought anywhere for love or money. The Rebel camp fires on the hill are kept going most of the night.

There was much excitement in camp all day as distant artillery firing was plainly heard by us during the forenoon. The cry arose that "Sherman was coming" and everyone was packing what valuables he possessed and some took down their miserable blanket tents or shelters, selling the poles and sticks to others who were too sick to travel anywhere. The roll calls lasted longer than usual, and the Rebel sergeants told us to keep quiet as we were all going to a new stockade for exchange. This last part we did not of course believe, but thought that Stoneman was coming to free us at once. The Rebel guards were doubled at the forts on [the] south side and the fort in our rear on [the] east side. Lists of men were made out by our sergeants of messes as to the number of men who were thought able to travel by cars.

About 8,000 men were found to be in a dying condition, all laying on the ground, ragged skeletons, covered with vermin and mud and filth without any shelter whatever! About 7:30 p.m., a large number of Rebel guards from the fort and camp on our rear or east side marched in a straggling column up to near Wirz's log house, which is inside the large fort, and halted in a ravine, where soon many fires were seen which continued until after dark. The police inside the stockade knew the whole program, and several managed by bribes, or otherwise to go along too. Money was the talisman, as it always was with the Rebels, no matter whether officer or privates. The same rotten putrid meat was served out as rations again today, but a great many would not eat it. Only the poor demented fellows ate it vora-

*It is unclear whether Sneden inverted the entries for September 11 and 12 or just switched the dates.

†Sneden's news is behind time here. Union General George Stoneman's cavalry did make a raid deep into Georgia in July 1864, but it failed to rescue the prisoners at Andersonville. Stoneman himself was captured near Macon and later released.

ciously which only hastened their death. Several hundred head of cattle were seen to be driven into what was once the officers' stockade, between us and the railroad depot. (The officers, who were only sixty in number, have long since been sent to a prison at Macon.) Those who bring the rations say that the meat spoils in the sun before it can be cooked, as the capacity of both cook houses is too small to accommodate the number of prisoners. There are now about 34,700 of us here! No small amount of meal and meat to handle and cook. The bread has improved in size and quality, salt being used in it, but half is yet made of unbolted meal with cob all ground in. Deaths still average 80 to 100 inside the prison. Many of the Rebel guards died last month so the Rebel sergeant says.

The Rebel officers and doctors are afraid to come in the stockade for fear of catching disease of some kind, and well they may. Some of the prisoners who came in recently had just left the prison at Salisbury, North Carolina. They were dying at a fearful rate there. The hospitals and prison was much overcrowded, there being over 9,000 there, half of whom had no shelter whatever even by burrowing under the buildings. The tales of cruelty inflicted by Major Gee the Rebel commandant were only equalled by our treatment here. The rations for a thousand men at a time were often withheld for forty-eight hours.

One Sibley tent and one A tent was furnished to each squad of 100 men. The rest burrowed in the ground or shivered in the open air. The buildings were crowded, and infested with all kinds of vermin. Many preferred the cold and exposure in the open. The prisoners said this was a much better place, as the rations were regular and more room to walk about. I, with others had shared the privation at Salisbury in February last though fortunately for a short time, and could form an idea of how much worse it now was, and was even thankful that I did not have to stay there. The mosquitoes came down on us again tonight as on the 6th, only more of them, and no rest was had by thousands who were about until daylight fighting them off. I noticed that they did not alight on the sick and dying men who lay around.

September 13, 1864

. . . This afternoon a long line of prisoners were marched down from the fort and into the stockade by the south gate, and we were surprised to find that they were of the same party who left here on the 7th for exchange. They had been taken to Rough and Ready, a small shanty village near Atlanta, where under a flag of truce Sherman had selected only his own command for exchange, and sent all the rest back to captivity! All hope of exchange was now abandoned, and amid hearty curses on the government, and Sherman, Butler, and others, the camp was wild with excitement, anger, and gloom. The returned prisoners had fared well in the way of getting enough to eat, but not an article of clothing was given them, which was the least thing that Sherman could have done. Now 740 were sent back! and they looked like a lot of skeletons in rags. Our death rate is still sixty to eighty per day, and this act of Sherman's will kill hundreds, as all hope of ever getting out of this is gone. Many of the last lot of prisoners who came in on the 5th have been robbed of their shoes while sleeping with them under their heads by Raiders, who still prowl around at night. I came very near losing mine, but caught the fellow and clubbed him well.

All the gamblers, sutlers, bakers, etc. who had paid Wirz or the Rebel officers large sums of money to go to Rough and Ready were sent back. They grumbled and swore the loudest at their non-exchange, as well they might, for they lost all they had acquired by fair or foul means, and must begin over again. The Rebel quartermasters, Duncan and Hume, come in with the mule loads of rations daily, and say, "that we will soon be exchanged at Savannah," but we don't believe them. They always talk this way to keep us quiet, and many think that our army at Atlanta will come this way and set us free. Very few of them know of Winder's order for the batteries to open on us indiscriminately if they should come within seven miles of this charnel house!

Many of the last lot of prisoners are down on the ground sick. No shelter of any kind have they, as their blankets were thrown away in battle when captured. Several of the 40th Regiment are already dead. Captain Stevens of D Company with many others are prisoners at Libby in Richmond.

The camp was never in a dirtier state than now, as many are sick that nobody is left to clean streets. The smell is fearful! The rains washes the prison filth by the natural declivity of the ground on both sides of the brook which by constant tramping of the men, kneaded the filth into a muck several inches deep of sand, feces, decomposing vegetable matters, and grease from the cook house outside, in which maggots and flies germinated, and worms, and other species of vermin festered and fattened all about the camp proper. The same filth accumulated while naked skeleton like corpses lay around in every direction, encroaching on the living, who lay helplessly sick in holes covered partly by ragged blankets, parts of old overcoats, or any other shelter which they had erected from the fierce heat of the sun. We still think the spring is poisoned by arsenic, put in by the Rebels, and we are once more compelled to use the filthy water in the brook, on which clots of solid grease can be seen floating, as they wash the kettles in it from the cook house and as it also receives the filth of the Rebel camps outside before it comes in to us!

Many are digging new wells. I am engaged in one which is fifteen feet deep. There are several deeper than this. The Rebel quartermaster has furnished us a few boards to cover them with when finished. The spring water runs to waste. It is inside the western dead line and is led by a trough of boards 200 feet down the hill. Sheds, open on all sides have been built in the entrenched hospital outside. We hear that the wild hogs are rooting up the dead bodies in the graveyard which is outside near the railroad. Negroes are employed to bring the dead there, which is very imperfectly done, as there are so many per day, and the rain washes many out again, who are seldom reburied and as the place is not enclosed, the hogs and other animals have a horrid feast. . . .

Chapter Nine

Freedom

Ever since his capture nearly a year before, Sneden had learned from repeated disappointments to doubt rumors about release. He could hardly believe it when the guards told the prisoners one morning in September to pack up their belongings. But the commotion that the announcement caused and reports of events beyond the stockade convinced even skeptics that a move was at last afoot.

The war news that summer had offered some encouragement, but only at a distance. Far to the north, Grant pinned down Lee's army to begin the siege of Petersburg and Richmond. But the stalemate in Virginia showed little sign of ending. Closer at hand, the Union push from Tennessee into northern Georgia offered the best hope for the Andersonville captives. That effort too dragged on for months. Then word reached the prison that General William T. Sherman had finally captured Atlanta. No one knew what Sherman intended next, but the Confederates frantically began to move the prisoners to other camps.

At the last minute, on the very eve of departure, an unexpected personal threat confronted Sneden. He saw on the camp notice board a request that "If R. K. Sneden, of the 40th N.Y. Vols. is in camp, he will immediately report to the Officer at the Gate as there are important papers for him at headquarters." Sneden feared that someone had told Wirz he had fabricated counterfeit papers for escaping prisoners. Three friends captured with him at Brandy Station worked as paroled clerks for the prison administration. Had Thomas Walsh, Patrick Halley, or Charles Colvin betrayed him?

He took no chances and moved to a friend's shanty until time to leave. "I now began

THE PRISON PEN AT SAVANNAH, GA.

secreting my sketches, maps, etc. in my clothing, sewed patches over some, made a false top to my cap, sewing the smallest between the linings, and . . . made soles for my shoes in which I sewed the most important." He was satisfied that no one could decipher his eccentric shorthand journal—"unintelligible to anyone but myself"—and hoped no one could tell that he had used pitch pine gum to glue together pages of his New Testament to conceal other sketches.

His fears proved unfounded, and on September 17 he boarded a train with hundreds of comrades. "We were packed," he wrote, "into boxcars, and open slat cattle cars, with the manure still on the floors." The train might not take them to freedom, as the more gullible prisoners hoped, but at least it would take them away from Andersonville.

As they approached Savannah, they passed sidings filled with shabby passenger cars that gave a home of sorts to hundreds of refugees from the fighting. Crossing a rickety trestle over the swamps on the city's outskirts, the prison train finally squealed to a stop, and the tired, hungry prisoners tumbled out. They were still hopeful, though. In the morning sunlight, even skeptical Sneden remarked that "the city itself looked beautiful embowered in trees, with the numerous church steeples clear against a cloudless sky."

When they reached their destination, the prisoners found a new stockade just completed for them. They immediately jockeyed for position in the enclosure to stake out the best location and grab the most useful bits of lumber left by the construction workers in order to make new shanties. It was nearly sundown before they received their rations of corn bread, ship biscuit, and raw bacon, thankfully in generous portions for once.

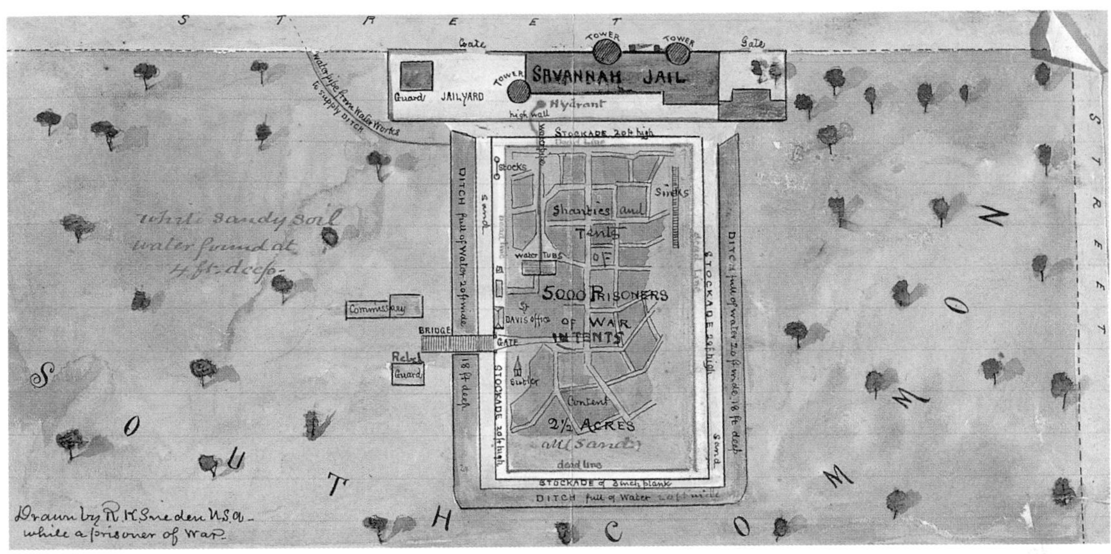

PLAN OF THE REBEL PRISON PEN AT SAVANNAH, GA.
September 1864.

The prisoners took heart when the guards announced orders to send the small number of sailors in their midst to Charleston for exchange. Many of the army prisoners of war took the opportunity to write letters home for the sailors to deliver. Sneden sent one by way of his friend, the young Bostonian Littlefield, and also gave him most of his diary to take with him. At first, mild weather and better sanitation made the Savannah camp a welcome change. There was even a gesture of sympathy from the citizens. "Several boxes of provisions and some good clothing [were] sent into the stockade by the Masonic fraternity of the city," Sneden reported, "and those who were Masons got them after an equal division. Hams, pies, fruit, etc. made the recipients happy for days."

Prison was still prison though. To discourage tunneling, the Confederate guards placed a dozen large locomotive headlights on the stockade and set several hundred slaves to digging a trench around the perimeter. Despite the vigorous efforts of prison official Edward Anderson, overcrowding, hunger, disease, and death preyed on the luckless prisoners. Anderson despaired of providing for them. By mid-October orders came to move the prisoners to yet another location. The Confederate commander in Savannah, Lafayette McLaws, ordered Anderson to destroy the stockade so that he would never have so many prisoners of war in his city again. Disgusted, Anderson called McLaws "a worthless incubus . . . who has risen to prominence . . . as scum rises in a cauldron."

But after a month, the prisoners were moved. The guards packed them into filthy hog cars, and Sneden and his companions headed back in the direction they had come, this time to a brand-new prison, Camp Lawton at Millen, Georgia.

Throughout his months in Southern prisons, Sneden had often disparaged "Galvanized Yanks," men who gave their word of honor not to escape in return for the chance to work outside the stockade, eat better food, and perhaps survive. He had encouraged his friend Thomas Walsh to make just such a commitment, however, when Walsh's health failed. It was Walsh, in fact, who worked as a clerk in Wirz's office and gave Sneden some of the statistics about Andersonville that he peppered his narrative with. When the prisoners headed back into the Confederate interior rather than to Charleston for exchange, Sneden would face the same moral dilemma as Walsh. Should he give his oath and work for the Confederates in order to ensure he had enough to eat?

October 16, 1864

We arrived at Millen about daylight, and went three miles nearly north, when we stopped at a rough looking collection of log shanties and barns in a thick pine woods. We "tumbled out" as fast as possible, and formed into column, guarded by Rebel soldiers who were stationed near the new stockade, which could be seen through the trees on the left. On our way, we marched within 200 feet of a gallows, upon which hung a dead Negro, who had been there for some time. The carrion crows were fluttering in the air, and the stench sickening. We could not learn what he had been hanged for, as the guard were a surly set, and would not answer questions. Davis* was not with us anyhow, and we trudged along in hopes and fears as to our new situation. After marching about a quarter of a mile through woods, we came to a large clearing when the stockade came in view, with several log houses and wall tents outside all along the ridge, and a large earthwork and fort on a bluff which overlooked the interior, while several pieces of cannon were visible over the parapets.

Camps of Rebel guards were in the woods, and nothing could be heard but the sighing of the wind through the trees, until we entered the gate, when the noise of a large camp of prisoners who were already here shouting to us across a small stream broke the monotony, and all was confusion in our ranks. Guards were posted along the brook and we were kept on one side of it all night, until we could be counted and messes formed properly, no communication being allowed with the other prisoners until next day.

On the side near the entrance were large numbers of pine and scrub oak trees, and from branches and underbrush we made large fires and cooked our corn pones and rice, making temporary shelter at night of boughs and blankets, and sleeping very well after the cramped and unpleasant journey. . . .

*Possibly Lieutenant Samuel B. Davis, who had succeeded Wirz when he fell ill in August at Andersonville.

October 20, 1864

Cold rain storm. We who came into the stockade were this morning moved across the brook, and soon were lost to each other by mixing up with the prisoners already here. All day was occupied in making new shelter. Those who had first come found numbers of felled trees on the ground with which some good shanties had been made. Now all the small sticks had been used up by them, and we had to put up with anything we could collect for the same purpose. Many large trunks of trees were left however, but having no axes, could not be of use, except for building fires against. Numerous stumps of pine trees were about the ground which made good fires, which were kept going night and day. We were not allowed to use the trees which grew on the other side of and along the brook, and they served for shade for those who had no blankets to make shelter with. The brook was of good clear water, and about twelve feet wide and in some places four feet deep. This was the greatest luxury we had, as for about thirty feet we could use it for bathing. . . .

November 1, 1864

. . . The weather has been rainy and very cold at nights. Many prisoners have died from exposure, as not more than half of us have any shelter but a ragged blanket propped upon sticks, under which the rain drizzles through like spray, completely wetting the occupants before many hours. Our rations have grown smaller in bulk too, and we have the same hunger as of old. Disease and starvation together are decimating us daily, and the average deaths are twenty to thirty-five per day. There is a hospital outside but very few are taken out, and those who do go are in the last stages of dissolution, and have to be carried on blanket stretchers. No medicine is given to any of us inside, and no doctor comes into the stockade to see the terrible mortality daily making our numbers less—scurvy, rheumatism, and diarrhea, while many are perfect imbeciles and idiots, who don't know how to take care of themselves and sleep on the ground anywhere. . . .

November 5, 1864

I made a sketch of the interior of the prison today from a spot near the entrance gate . . . and another of my shanty, showing brick ovens, etc. The guard on the stockade did not interfere, and wanted me to "take his picture," but I told him "I could not do it as I had not pencil enough" which so tickled him that he threw me a plug of tobacco.

No tunnels have been dug by us since the first one was discovered some weeks ago. The strength of many is exhausted, and rheumatism prevents those who would if they could. Captain Vowels* comes in sometimes on Sundays for a half hour, and being a mild

*D. W. Vowles, formerly assistant adjutant general under Winder at Andersonville.

Rebel fort outside Sutler's shanty and brook Stockade and dead line Prisoners' camp Brick ovens

VIEW OF CAMP LAWTON, MILLEN, GA.

lenient kind of man, is besieged by the men asking questions. This is the best camp any of us have yet been in, as far as plenty of room, good water, and regular rations go, and the captain says he would give us more if he had them, and supplies have been prevented from coming to the station because "the Yankees have destroyed the railroad."

Many of us are willing to go on short rations at this welcome news, but as there are no newspapers, and the guards being dumb on the subject, we cannot tell where the railroad is cut or where our forces may be, and Winder may issue an order to his artillery men similar to that at Andersonville to fire indiscriminately on us from the fort if our army approaches Millen. The subject is discussed at all our camp fires today, and several have again determined to start a new tunnel.

From the Negro teamsters who drive in with the rations, two or three axes have been obtained, which have been hired out at 10¢ per hour by their owners for cutting stumps only after dark however, with a party who hired both axes. I volunteered to help on a tunnel, which starts from a log shanty near mine. The dead line here is full twenty-five feet from the stockade, and much wider than at Andersonville or Savannah. The tree stumps are deep in the ground, and the forest has been cleared for a good space all around the outside of the stockade, but there is a large swamp not far off, and there are no blood hounds outside to follow us, and the chances are good if we can overcome the natural obstacles. The guard are generally sleepy on windy nights, and there is nothing like trying. We made confidants of twenty of the strongest and will break ground this afternoon, inside the log shanty, and continue on with the tunnel abandoned two weeks ago.

November 8, 1864

We worked hard at the tunnel in reliefs of ten men each, and struck the foundations of the stockade by daylight, when we stopped, all completely used up. We will have to dip three or more feet to clear it. The night was windy and dark, which favored operations. A great quantity of tree roots had to be cut through, but we went around the stumps in all cases, which makes "the hole" very crooked. The earth and roots were carried down to a part of the enclosure not much frequented, and packed between two large felled trees which still lay there about six feet apart. It was carried in the boxes with handles, used for policing the camp. I went into the hole for twenty minutes or more to scoop sand, but the want of air, made me glad to get out. I carried earth in the barrows the rest of the night, and must get sleep during the day.

Several Rebel sergeants have been in the stockade yesterday and today to persuade the prisoners to take the parole advertised on the 3rd and by the roll call over twenty are unaccounted for, and as the Rebel sergeants don't make a row as usual, these men must have gone out after dark. The gates can hardly be seen from where we have our shanties, for the trees are quite numerous along the brook, and the only crowd in camp are around the bridge and sutlers. So the recruiting must have been done there, when not one in twenty but those interested would know if anyone went out or not. They are gone however, and probably more will follow. . . .

November 10, 1864

The weather is very cold, though fires are kept up day and night. The brick ovens have not been yet used for cooking rations for us as intended when built, and are filled by night by shivering prisoners who lie close together to keep warm. All the smaller firewood in camp has been long ago used, and but few large trees are about, which have two or more fires built along their trunks, at which prisoners cook their scanty rations, or huddle around for warmth. Several tree stumps are being dug around to get the roots and fibres for making fires. Someone among us betrayed the tunnel now constructing to the Rebels, and today, Duncan and Hughes are sounding the space between the stockade and dead line for it with crowbars.

In the meantime we are destroying the entrance, which is inside a log shanty, by first bracing sticks across the hole or well, three feet from the surface, stretching an old blanket over, with brush wood, and filling up level with sand. The whole shanty is then taken down, the occupants move off to some other part of the camp, and when the Rebels trace the tunnel to its former site, "nobody knows anything about it," and the fellows have moved away and lost in the crowd, so the tunnel is left for another enterprising party to recommence operations.

Today I made another sketch of the camp . . . which is much better than the former one, as it shows the interior plainer with brook, fort, ovens, etc. A German prisoner died in camp a few days ago who was somewhat of an artist with figures. He left me his small stock of pencils and a few colors, which helped me in this line very much.

November 11, 1864

Weather still very cold and windy, the ice formed on the edges of the brook and many of the prisoners had to walk about camp all night to keep from freezing. What fires were kept going were surrounded by prisoners in crowds, while the smoke blackened the faces and hands of all of them, which without soap, is impossible to get off. We have no soap issued to us, as at Savannah, and sand is used instead. At roll call this morning the Rebel sergeant wanted a man to go out as clerk at headquarters to the surgeon, work to be all writing, full rations and a parole offered. I was selected at my own request and given ten minutes to pack up, which I did, and went out of the gate soon after, though the guard pointed his musket at me while crossing the dead line, and would have fired, had I not kept the sergeant in front of me well covered while he shouted that I was a "paroled Yank." The guard was green or stupid, and probably thought it was a Yankee trick to escape. I passed through the gate however, and with the sergeant walked up a long road to General Winder's headquarters, which were at a log house on the hill.

Winder was seated at a table covered with papers, while seven or eight officers stood around him. After several questions of how long I had been a prisoner? Whether I could write a Latin invoice of medicines? etc. I was accepted and a written parole given me to read over, which I must first take. It was as follows.

"I, ____ ____, a prisoner of war to the Confederate States of America, do pledge my word as a military man, that I will not attempt to escape from the prison authorities nor pass beyond the prison limits without the proper leave to do so, under penalty of being shot with musketry, without a court martial, if recaptured."

I had several objections to offer to this, and as I told Winder that I did not recognize any "Confederate States of America" he sprang up with a volley of oaths, and said "he'd damn soon show me," etc. I argued that I had a right to escape when opportunity offered, in fact, that "it was my business to run away, and their business to catch me." And that as yet, "the meanest nation on earth had not recognized them or their bogus Confederacy." Winder was now infuriated and called on the provost marshal to read a document of some kind to me, which that individual proceeded to do after a delay to adjust his spectacles.

The room had in the meantime filled up with officers, and others whose rank it was hard to determine, as they were all dressed in common country made homespun clothes, devoid of shoulder straps or insignia of any rank, excepting a strip of blue or red braid on collar and cuff. Winder was similarly dressed, and looked like an old farmer, or bushwacker; none were over clean either in their personal appearance, while all swore and chewed tobacco.

The shaky and tremulous voice of the provost marshal was drowned in the noise of talking, so that I heard very little of what it was about, until the words "shot to death by musketry" (which he pronounced mus-quetry) arrested my attention, when I surveyed him closely for the first time. He was an old man of about sixty, with iron gray hair, wore a pair of iron rimmed spectacles, dressed in dirty homespun, with a red worsted sash across his breast, which being much too short, was tied close under his arms. The back part of his trousers at the bottom were scorched from standing too near a fire, rough cowhide shoes encased feet which would cover the "Devil's half acre," and a very dirty shirt completed the costume of this antiquated personage. A Colt's revolver stuck in a sheepskin belt, and a dirty slouch hat gave him a reckless look. He had to spell most of the words first before reading. I could not help laughing heartily. And before he had finished the document, I asked Winder "if that scarecrow was really a provost?" This broke up the court, as Winder yelled with many oaths to "take the prisoner away," when two Rebel guards entered and marched me off.

At the same time, an officer, who was dressed much better than anyone else, caught my hand as he passed out, giving a Masonic sign of some kind. . . . It was of course not understood, still I thought it singular. I must have found a friend of some importance. He wore a black cloth frogged overcoat precisely similar to that worn by officers in our army, which puzzled me still more. I was marched past the line of log houses and tents which composed the Rebel officers' quarters, and thence to a swamp near the hospitals, when I was chained to a felled tree by leg irons attached to a heavy iron bar. And two Rebel guards placed over me. I had not calculated on this treatment and of course felt uneasy enough, as I had not heard half of what the provost marshal had read previously. And I knew that it would be just like Winder to have me shot in the morning as well as not.

The guards were young fellows of the 53rd Georgia Reserves and were good natured and green at soldiering, for they sat on the tree on each side of me, and conversed freely on the situation, and cursed Winder for a drunken tyrant. It was now sundown, and the guards brought me some fried bacon, corn bread and sweet potatoes, when I made a "good square meal," lit my pipe, and thought gloomily over the situation. After dark it began to rain, and continued in light showers until morning; a fire was built near me, and as I could not sleep a wink, was awake all night. The most vexatious feelings with me were that I would be probably shot in these dark woods, far away from home, where my true fate would never be known. And for what, I could not determine, excepting refusing the parole, and giving Winder to understand that I was not afraid of him or his Baltimore plugs,* and resolved to stand up and die honorably at any rate if the thing had to be done, which is the best way in all cases.

*Ever since his appointment as provost marshal in Richmond, Winder had employed private detectives from Baltimore, popularly known as "Baltimore plug uglies."

After 9 p.m. the guard halted someone, who giving the countersign approached my position. By the light of the fire I soon perceived it to be the same person who had given me the secret sign in the morning. He sat on the tree alongside me and the first words he asked me "Whether I was a Yankee or not" I answered by asking him "What he called a Yankee?" when he said that "all those who came from Massachusetts, Vermont, Connecticut, etc. were," I told him I belonged to neither, and for some time I bluffed all his questions as I thought he was a spy, and the forged passes which I had circulated at Andersonville loomed up before me.

Finally I told him "I was a 'Blue-nose'* from Nova Scotia but had lived much at New York." To other enquiries I learned that he was a chum to a friend of mine whom I used to often visit at the New York College of Surgeons then in 13th Street in 1859. To prove this I asked my friend's name, which he gave correctly. Of course I saw that he intended to befriend me, and asked "why I was ironed and what for, etc." He said that Winder was very cross that morning being pretty well "set up" with whiskey. And as I had talked disrespectful, and denounced the Confederacy, a sentence of death had been read to intimidate me, which would not be carried out probably; as no papers were signed by him authorizing the execution of the sentence.

He further added that he would see "the old man" in the morning and see what could be done. Also that he was Surgeon White of Winder's staff,† and wanted a clerk himself, and would have me, if I came out all right. This altered my position very much, and he soon after left for his quarters. I had seven or eight of the Rebel soldiers keep me company until after midnight. Their camp was a few rods away, and I told them all about moose hunting, salmon and herring fishing, wild geese shooting, etc., as we practice them in Nova Scotia. And although not one of them ever heard of such a country, [they] were interested, and even volunteered to shoot over my head in case they would be detailed for my execution. This I objected to, [and] I told them to aim true, as I did not want my head blown off by the officer in charge at close quarters (which is done if the victim is not killed outright by the volley first fired). I had more to eat at midnight, and smoked my pipe until daylight without sleeping a wink all night.

Several of the soldiers were fairly educated, and were "gentlemen's sons," others of the "poor whites" were ignorant as mules but not bad hearted in the main. Many of their muskets were old flint locks. No bayonets were visible. They were a scarce article in their army, and they told me that sometimes the bayonets in the rear files had to be passed to those in front rank when the Yankees looked like making a bayonet charge on them.

As to war news, they knew nothing, as newspapers were very few in camp, and many

* Bluenose was the nickname for natives of the Canadian Maritime Provinces, especially Nova Scotia.

† Isaiah H. White, a twenty-five-year-old Virginian, had been chief surgeon at Andersonville. Sneden mentions him earlier but apparently had not met him until Millen. When an inspector toured the Andersonville camp, White submitted a scathing report on the inadequate supplies at the hospital.

could not read if they had them. The papers came from Savannah and Charleston. They thought that if Sherman advanced on Macon and Savannah from Atlanta (which I told them he would) that "Georgy was clean gone up," and that we could not stay here. Thick fog settled down after midnight, and all was quiet in camp but the sentry's calling the hour, and "all's well" from the fort near me and the stockade a few hundred feet away. The irons hurt my ankle by chafing and I passed a miserable night, thinking of my dangerous situation, but resolved "to die game" anyhow.

The drums in the Rebel camp for "reveille" awoke me from a stupor, and after a breakfast poor in quality, but large in quantity, I was unshackled and at 9:30 a.m. marched up to the provost's again.

November 12, 1864

Fine bright morning but cold. I found but few Rebel officers at the log shanty. Winder was absent; but Surgeon White was on hand as also the antique looking provost marshal, whom I did not laugh at this time; being in a different mood. Surgeon White had probably made it all right for me and offered me a parole which I signed without any questioning from the other officers, as follows. "I, ____ ____, a prisoner of war to the Confederate States of America, do pledge my parole as a man of honor, and as a military man, that I will not attempt to escape, nor pass beyond the prison limits, nor within 500 feet of the stockade, without permission from the authorities, or until regularly exchanged, under penalty of being shot without court martial."

I was then given a star cut out of tin, with two holes though it, so that it could be sewn on cap or collar, which was for a protection against the guard firing on me in case I was within the prescribed limits unconsciously. And [I] went to Dr. White's tent with him. Here, he threw off all reserve, and was very kind and gentlemanly, saying "I should stay with him until exchanged," relying on me to keep the parole, which if broken would certainly put me in a bad position, when his influence with Winder would be of no avail to save my being shot without mercy.

Declining breakfast with him, I was led into a wall tent twenty feet from his own, which I found filled up as an office, such as desks, stools and medicine in numerous bottles, dried herbs, etc., etc. The tent had a plank floor, and an army cot in one corner which was for my use. Surgeon White's tent was of the largest hospital size, with plank floor, and a large brick chimney and fireplace which completely filled up one end. [It had a] four posted bed with fancy bed quilt, white pillows, etc., and [was] partly carpeted. I had not seen anything so handsome and cleanly among any field quarters in our army; and now I made up my mind to do what was expected of me, and eat all I could get. I cut some fresh pine tops and made a good soft bed, for which I got new blankets in the afternoon, and did nothing but eat and smoke, while I could look into the stockade in the distance and watch the poor fellows there.

November 13, 1864

Yesterday afternoon, with Surgeon White, I went to the hospitals used for Rebel soldiers which [are] below the fort . . . more or less filled with sick. In the storeroom were numerous boxes and piles of bed quilts which the Confederate army use as blankets. I was much surprised to see lots of boxes filled with clothes sent by the U.S. Sanitary Commission for the use of the Union prisoners which never had been given to them, but feloniously appropriated by the Rebels, and more surprised when I was told to "help myself" to anything I wanted. I soon got a fit out of drawers, undershirts, flannel shirt, shoes, socks, pants, and coat (there were no overcoats), and with two new blankets returned to my quarters to divest myself of my ragged suit. The trousers were of a mixed pattern for civilians. The coats [were] of the regular army blouse, with horn buttons instead of military. The Rebels had refused to accept military clothing for prisoners from the commission. I got a new felt hat also, and soon was dressed once more clean and comfortable.

I ripped my old clothes to get at my sketches and other papers, then burnt them up. I was set to work copying invoices, which were in Latin which occupied me all day. I have taken my meals thus far at Surgeon White's table, but it was very unpleasant as there presided a Mrs. Shely Reed,* a violent Rebel, who continually insulted me by referring to the "nasty dirty Yankees," etc. I asked, and got leave from Surgeon White to detail a cook for my special benefit from the prisoners in the stockade.

After due consideration, I called for a man who went by the name of "Reddy." (He had red hair, and I never learned his right name.) So when the sergeant went in, he was forthcoming, and after being paroled, reported to me for duty. I had noticed much playing of cards by the Rebel soldiers since yesterday, and knew that they did not play for nothing. So I thought to make good use of Reddy, as he was the most accomplished and lucky gamester in the stockade, and more than a match for the best of players. He was very grateful for being detailed by a perfect stranger, and set about building a shanty of boughs, with old blankets I had brought out with me for [a] roof to be used for a kitchen. He made a bunk and slept in the tent I occupied.

Together we now drew from the commissary as rations one quart meal, one pint rice, two pounds beef, salt, and potatoes, about two dozen per diem, a frying pan, skillet, and tin coffee pot was also furnished. We were fitted out to cook anything and everything which could be bought, borrowed, or stolen (for Reddy had a way of appropriating anything in the eating line whenever he had a chance.) About fifty feet in the rear of the line of officers' quarters were log huts used by Negroes who were officers' servants for cooking the mess. And many a ham, and other articles of provender was given me by them. I walked round the prescribed limits today, but did not wear the tin star for protection. I carried it in my pocket however in case a guard should stop me. I saw several of our fellows, who were

* Probably the same woman Sneden mentions at Andersonville, wife of Captain W. Shelby Reed, on Winder's staff.

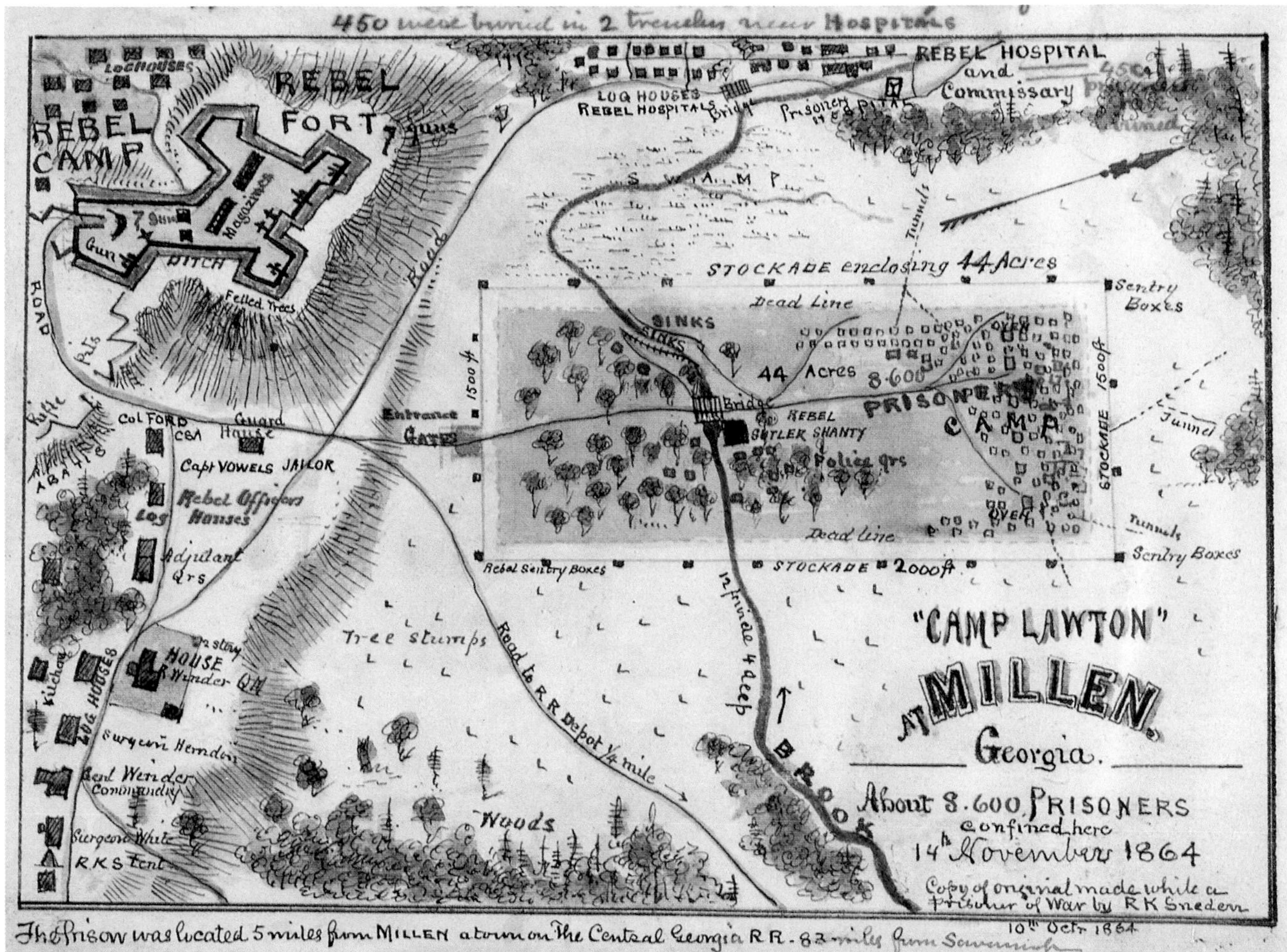

paroled clerks to [the] commissary and Quartermaster's . . . they had been clerks at Wirz's quarters in Andersonville when moved here and had left Walsh, Colvin, and Halley there all right last September. I was refused admittance to the fort, and after going all around elsewhere, I made a careful plan of the grounds and stockade. . . . So I did not work at anything for the Rebels today, and after three good square meals and a pipe, turned in.

November 14, 1864

Rainy weather but [I] have none of the uncomfortable consequences as when in the stockade for here [I] am warm and dry, with clean new clothes and blankets, a soft bed, and plenty to eat, and as "Reddy" is a good cook, enjoy the meals very much. Such a vast change from life in the stockade! And which puts me in mind of the good times we had in Scott's building in Richmond, makes me think as then, that it is too good to last long. "Reddy" has been playing cards with Rebel soldiers in the kitchens in our rear, and last night brought in a ten pound bag of wheat flour, two bushels sweet potatoes, and two old silver watches (regular bulls eyes) won from Negroes. This with ham and onions, we made four heavy meals today and both of us are content and even happy.

At my suggestion Surgeon White consented that I should keep the death book, or record of the number of our men who die and are buried by men who are paroled for this purpose. It had been kept by somebody from 1st October to 1st of this month. During this time it showed that 926 had died in the stockade. Of these 370 were unknown. These were buried in a trench near the railroad, 491 and 450 in two trenches near the hospitals, which were about 2,000 yards from it. The hospitals for our men were old condemned tents, leaky, and unserviceable for the guard, and were near the Rebel hospitals west of the stockade. The grave diggers brought me every evening the names, regiment, etc., of those buried by them, which were written on slips of paper attached to the corpses as brought out. Very many were unknown however; and I entered them on the book as such. From seventeen to twenty-three were buried daily. The Rebel soldiers had lost three by death since 15th September and 120 were in hospital. Of prisoners there were 200 in hospital, as few were taken out of the stockade except in a dying condition.

I had several arguments with Surgeon White and Dr. Herndon (who was doctor to the guard) but they said there was very little medicine in the Confederacy, and I knew myself that most of it were simple herbs, and the only laboratory in the state was at Augusta from whence it came. So the prisoners had to die! White had been stationed at Andersonville before coming here, and said that Wirz was always in mortal terror that the prisoners there would break out of the pen "en masse." And that he would be sought for first if successful on which to wreak their vengeance, and used to go to the windows of his house several times during the night to see if we were safe.

November 16, 1864

I am getting quite strong again on the regular system of feeding and sleeping, and as "Reddy" continues to bring in provisions captured from the Rebel soldiers by card playing, we have more than we can eat, and sell the surplus back to the soldiers or Negroes. "Reddy" has five watches won at play and sold two besides, for $300 Confederate money last night. He divides the spoil with me fairly, and is delighted at his situation. The wheat biscuit, rye coffee, sweet potatoes and ham, are delicious, and the quantity devoured amazing. He cooks for Surgeon White also, and can go to any of the Rebel soldiers' camps to buy supplies or win them from them by card playing. I keep pretty well to my quarters, and have nothing to do but enter the poor dead fellows' names on the death book. I am revising part of my diary, but do not let even White know that I have sketches or memoranda. I have confiscated [twenty-four sheets] of good foolscap paper for my own particular use hereafter. The paper made in the Confederacy is most miserable in quality, mostly very thin and quite yellow. Good paper is hard to get, and even the newspapers are printed on dingy straw paper, rough in texture and full of imperfections.

November 17, 1864

Cold weather and snow. Three of our men were frozen to death last night in the stockade! Large fires are going, but many are so reduced in vitality that they easily froze notwithstanding. There was great excitement among the Rebels today in consequence of an order received by General Winder to remove the prisoners as soon as possible! Where to, nobody knew. It was reported in the afternoon, that Sherman had cut loose from Atlanta and was marching on Macon, Augusta and Savannah!* No papers were to be had, but Winder believed it, for the Rebel soldiers were given three days' rations to cook this evening, and their camp fires were burning nearly all night. The Rebel officers whom I saw looked anxious and much discussion was carried on among them as to the probable truth of the rumor. I entered forty-seven names in the death book today and fifty-two yesterday, of these sixty were unknown. Mrs. Reed left camp today for good, much to my relief. This was the woman who opened and destroyed soldiers' letters at Andersonville, first taking the 10¢ silver piece which was enclosed for return postage. The letters never were delivered.

November 18, 1864

There fell about two inches of snow last night, and today we have cold winds, which must make the poor fellows in the stockade suffer terribly. The excitement continues, and Sherman's moving this way hurries up matters with the Rebels who look rather scared, and want to get away anywhere. From Surgeon White I got a *Charleston Courier* of the 14th, and it sounds the alarm all over the country, while the governors of Georgia, North and South Carolina, and Alabama are making frantic calls for men, and impressing even aged men into their army. . . .

November 22, 1864

Fine weather but very cold. Snow is on the ground yet and several men were frozen to death in the stockade two days ago, and are there yet, as all other prisoners have been sent off by railroad. There is no one to bury them either, for the Rebels are getting away themselves as fast as possible. Detachments of prisoners were marched out and sent to

*After occupying Atlanta for about ten weeks, on November 15, Sherman's army set out on its "March to the Sea," foraging and burning as it went.

Charleston, and to another stockade recently built at Florence, South Carolina. Winder with other Rebel officers left here last night for Savannah, and Surgeon White and Herndon go today. I will have to go with them, and have everything packed up. "Reddy" went with the "Galvanized Yanks" who were clerks in commissary and quartermaster's departments yesterday. He first gave me $600 Confederate money which he had won from the Rebel soldiers at euchre, etc. The tents are all struck. Rebel guard all gone, and the whole place deserted with the exception of the artillery company who have been stationed at the fort, and a few Rebel officers and quartermasters, who are dismantling the shanties and preparing to follow. I have charge of the medical stores, while one of the Rebel clerks named Prendergast oversees the transportation. He was one of the new conscripts who came into camp a day or two ago.

At 4 p.m. we all left for the railroad station leaving behind the empty fort, and log houses, the gloomy and weatherbeaten stockade. All seemed relieved when we were on the cars and ready to start an hour later. We had five cars loaded with hospital stuff, carpenters' tools, saws, etc., and three platform cars on which the field artillery (seven pieces) were lashed. One old dirty battered passenger car was kept for officers and the dozen or so Rebel artillerymen. We soon went three miles to Millen, where we switched off for two hours to allow continuous trains to pass, loaded with household furniture, cotton, women and children, and lots of Negro slaves. Alarming news that "the Yankees were coming" hurried up the Rebels wonderfully. . . .

Large clouds of black smoke in the woods on both sides of the track showed where storehouses and bales of cotton were being burnt to prevent them falling into "Yankee hands." . . . About 6 p.m. we switched on the main track and started for Savannah where we arrived at about 6 a.m. next morning. I had a large quantity of wheat biscuits, and a raw ham, from which I made three or four good "square meals" before morning, but got no sleep but smoked and twitted Drs. White and Herndon on "the situation." . . .

November 23, 1864

Leaving Prendergast and Stubbs to hunt up Negroes and teams for moving the hospital stores, I went with Dr. White to our new quarters which were to be at the "Screven House."* First stopping into the Pulaski House we had drinks at $10 Confederate apiece. The "Screven House" had been a large hotel but was now devoid of furniture or occupants, save General Winder, whom I found here with other Rebel officers. All the stores under the house were empty and when the stuff came from the railroad depot it was put into one of them, where I spent the rest of the day in directing how it should be piled. Among the stuff I noticed twenty or more boxes which were sent by U.S. Sanitary Commission for the

*When the Screven House opened on Johnson Square in 1857, it supplanted the older Pulaski House as the most fashionable hotel in Savannah.

use of Union prisoners, but which had been kept for the Rebel use. And the contents of many more had been appropriated by Rebel officers on Winder's staff. . . .

November 24, 1864

This morning on awaking I found the Rebel officers laying all around in a drunken sleep, and the front door wide open, which on reporting to Surgeon White he gave me authority to turn them all out in [the] future if they stayed over 9 p.m. or to lock them all in and hide the key. So now I was to be jailor over the Rebel officers instead of being a prisoner myself to them. Dr. White acknowledged that "he had a white elephant" on his hands [because there was no longer a military prison hospital in Savannah], and gave me leave to live at the Pulaski or any other hotel in the vicinity. I gladly accepted the offer, and engaged a room at the Pulaski at $38 per day Confederate. Board was to be had there from $40 to $60 per day! I therefore selected a new suit of clothes from the Sanitary [Commission] stores, as I had more right to them than the Rebels, and was fortunate to find in the lot some white shirts which I also appropriated. I had about $800 in Confederate money, $600 of which had been given me by "Reddy."

So I felt easy as to "the situation." There was nothing for me to do but eat and sleep. Not even a death book to keep: So I determined to see the sights and get all the information from the Rebels possible, and found the whiskey barrel a good auxiliary to help me in this respect. On the second floor of the Screven House General Winder had made his quarters and furnished a bedroom off from his office. There was nothing for him to do here, as there were no prison pens in the city or vicinity. . . .

[The] pen in which I was confined on my first visit in September had been demolished. So he would not stay here long I thought, and made the best of my time while it lasted. Prendergast was Winder's head clerk. I went to the office to hear the Rebel officers who congregated there talk of army matters, etc. Winder had a ten gallon cask of good brandy in his rooms, which probably drew many officers there to sample. As I was dressed in many respects similar to them (for they were wearing the Sanitary Commission clothes), [I] was taken for a Rebel officer of some kind, when in fact I was the only "Yankee" in the city. I therefore made application for a pass which would enable me to go anywhere within the city limits. . . .

November 25, 1864

I opened all the Sanitary [Commission] boxes remaining this morning by Dr. White's direction, and the contents were distributed to a dozen or more Rebel officers. I managed to keep back a case of shoes which I proposed to sell for my own benefit when my money gave out (for who had a better right?). The storeroom was filled all day with officers drinking and playing cards, as all the ingredients were there free to the initiated: a stove was put up and now they even had hot water for punches. Dr. White seldom came in the place: while I had to stay to keep property from being taken away without proper vouchers. Many stores were furnished from here to the hospitals for Rebel soldiers in the city. The provost marshal had headquarters at the Oglethorpe Barracks, which was owned by the U.S. Government, and formerly used by them for troops. I received my pass today which was as follows.

"Surgeon I. H. White of General Winder's staff in charge of 2 men, in charge of hospital train, will not be interrupted in the discharge of his duties.

Jn Cunningham Maj. Comm. Post & [Assistant Provost Marshal] Headqrs Oglth. Barr. Sav[annah] 25th Nov 1864. Official Isaiah H. White chief surgeon."

Armed with this document I could go anywhere within the city limits, but "Fort Pulaski" was too far away for me to escape there. I put in an appearance at the dinner table of the Pulaski House today, and was not quizzed by the boarders, or even asked to what Rebel regiment I belonged to. The table fare was good, though corn meal and rice, sweet potatoes and ham formed the principal dishes. Sweet potato pies were a new thing to me however, and I thought $38 a day was not exorbitant taking into consideration that it took twenty of them to make one greenback of our money. In Winder's office I saw today copies of the *New York World* and *Times* only four days old, and wondering how they got there, was informed that they came pretty regularly before Sherman had left Atlanta! I read them both before leaving, as Winder was down the harbor somewhere on a short visit.

Prendergast showed me where he kept his brandy, which was under his bed, but as there was no way of getting it out of the bung hole of the cask without spilling and betraying its use, the clerk was unable to use it. I soon found a way, for I bought a flexible smoking tube at a cigar store, with which [I] made a syphon; and we soon had it running into both of our canteens. It was a prime article, and had been smuggled by the blockade runners at Wilmington, North Carolina. After this I did not touch the whiskey in my charge in the hospital storeroom, but filled up my canteen from Winder's cask as long as it lasted. I shared it with only particular Rebel acquaintances who could keep a secret.

I went through several streets and squares in the city today and visited the site of the old pen, where Lieutenant Davis had a short but profitable reign. The ditch was still there, but the stockade had been removed and was being used for gun platforms in the fortifications outside the city. The buildings were fine throughout the city, and much more architectural than those of Richmond. . . . At the depot of Charleston Railroad were immense piles of cotton which Negroes were loading on platform cars for Wilmington, where they would be shipped to England by blockade runners. This is the only route now left the Rebels to replenish them with arms, ammunition or luxuries. There was little or no business doing and the people were few in the streets. Nothing doing on the wharves, where vessels lay tied up, deserted by their crews. I heard that there was about 50,000 bales of cotton in the city, many of the prominent men were leaving for Wilmington or going south to St. Augustine, Florida to be out of Yankee reach.

November 26, 1864

We have had fine clear weather with moonlight nights since I have been in [the] city, and after 9 p.m. very few are in the streets, and the sandy soil prevents all noise from carriage wheels. There is an open market here, where Negro hucksters abound, and who bring their vegetables, etc. in by small carts driven by mules. This morning a raid was made by the military on the premises, and all the Negroes there found were impressed to work on the fortifications. While returning from breakfast, I met a frightened crowd of Negroes running in every direction to hide themselves from the military, while mule teams were running away without drivers, spilling vegetables and other articles through the streets. The most alarming news prevailed for the Rebels this morning, as their troops had been defeated at Griswoldville* by Sherman's army, losing over 1,000 men. . . .

The provost guard were today very active, forcing citizens to work on the fortifications. I saw them in several instances arresting young men in Confederate officers' uniform, stripping them of their gold laced jackets in the square, and marching them off to Oglethorpe Barracks, where they will have to answer for wearing officers' uniform[s] without any commission.

These fellows never held commission[s] in the Rebel army, but had been "playing officer" in the city ever so long, no wonder the hotel bars were full of them. I was taken for one of them but my pass made it "all right." When the popinjay looking officer had halted me asking "if I had a pass," I pretended to have lost it. When he immediately ordered me to "fall in and go to barracks," I asked "what for?" When he said "if I had never done any digging before I would have to do so now." I told him I was a good hand to dig tunnels and produced my pass. He read only the first line . . . and asked if "I was Surgeon White?" I told him that the paper told the whole story. He immediately apologized, thinking I was White, returned my pass without reading more than the first line, and marched on. From him I learned why he took the coats off the officers, which was as I have written and that they were political skulkers, and that the city was full of them.

The fact was that a large quota of the inhabitants had Union sentiments, and sought every way to escape being enrolled in the hated Confederate army. General [William Joseph] Hardee had a review of all the troops today. Some artillery firing in the harbor in consequence created a panic among the Negroes, who have kept indoors as much as possible in consequence of the raid this morning. And I heard that all those employed loading cotton had mysteriously disappeared and work had been stopped. On the opposite corner from the "Pulaski House" was a restaurant in the basement. I had noticed horses tied in front belonging to scouts or Rebel cavalry of some sort, and today I ventured down to get some oysters, etc. The place was full of [General Joseph "Fightin' Joe"] Wheeler's cavalry,

*One of many small engagements in Sherman's march from Atlanta to the sea took place at Griswoldville, Georgia, on November 22, 1864.

who were discussing army reports, and I kept on eating and listening to all they knew of the positions of troops and was unnoticed by them meanwhile.

They verified the newspaper reports as to Sherman's positions and victory at Griswoldville, which made a corresponding feeling of dismay to the other customers in the place, while I enjoyed it much in secret. As the oysters were $1 apiece, or $7 per plate, rye coffee $3 per cup (Confederate) I could not keep eating very long at this rate. So paid my bill, and left the soldiers in angry discussion. As I did not want recognition of any kind, I went to Winder's office, and he being still away, I filled my canteen with his best brandy by the syphon process which I carried under my coat to give away to the "right kind" of Rebels I might meet during my walks. As several Rebel officers were "too much gone" to walk home I locked them all in the hospital storeroom and left them happy enough, as they had lots of whiskey, sugar, lemons, and hot water to help themselves from in my absence.

While standing outside deciding where I should go, a provost guard passed, having in charge a dozen or more citizens, carrying belts and cartridge boxes in their hands. One asked the guard "what he should do with them" who answered "that they would d____d soon show them the use of them when they got to the trenches." I pitied the poor devils, who had probably to dig stumps all night.

November 27, 1864

Fine and cold. I intended to go to church, but Winder was getting ready to move, and I had to superintend the sending off of nearly all the rest of the hospital stores, including his office desks, etc. I had kept the Rebel officers locked up all night and they complained to Surgeon White who only laughed at them. As my money was getting low, I bethought me of the shoes hidden away, which I unearthed and sold six pairs at $100 per pair to some Negroes in an alleyway opposite the storeroom. They promised to find purchasers for all I had. I dined in good style at the Pulaski, and was not spoken to by any save the Negro waiters. I was probably taken for some officer of importance, as most of the crowd generally there had been sent to the trenches. I heard the words "Winder's staff" several times during dinner. After dark, I took my canteen and went down on the waterfront, and wandered I don't know where, until I came to the Albany & Gulf Road Railroad Depot. In conversation with the watchman, I soon perceived that he was Union in sentiment, and after giving him a good drink of brandy, learned further that there were organized over 700 men, all Union, who were waiting Sherman's approach to rise and help in its capture.

Many of these men were employed in the various railroad depots. And shammed lame and blind, so as not to be conscripted in the Rebel army. Anything but that. And by political influence and strategy had thus far escaped soldiering. They were all of the laboring class but had good leaders, Irishmen principally. I offered to sell them shoes, which was taken up, promising to bring them another time. I returned to the hotel after midnight having had to show my pass very often to provost guards. General Winder left this evening for Charleston and Florence. There is a large stockade at the latter place, where all the prisoners from "Camp Lawton" had been removed. . . .

November 28, 1864

Weather cold but clear. Some days ago I obtained a map of the city and environs, and with the help of a Rebel doctor who visits the forts and batteries often, I marked these places down, and from it constructed a map showing the position and strength of same. I gave him the printed map in return for information given, and secreted the duplicate in my clothing. . . . I went to the restaurant again this afternoon, and found the place full of Wheeler's scouts. They were much afraid that the Yankees could not be stopped in their advance toward the city, and were telling of the immense destruction of mills and depots by the "Yankees" and the impossibility of getting men from Augusta as the railroad had been torn up, and the city isolated from help from that quarter.

I went after this to the barber's shop adjacent, which was elegantly fitted up with marble, glass, and gilt frescoes, etc., where five mulatto men were shaving as many Rebel officers. I took the sixth chair, and in a few minutes heard the distant sound of artillery. Soon it seemed nearer and heavier cannonading. The Rebel officers sprang out of their chairs half shaved, and rushed out to mount their horses which were at the door, leaving me the sole occupant of a single chair. The Negroes were much excited, and wondered why I did not leave also. When I told them I was a Yankee, and had been here a week this surprised them so much that they all ran out of the shop rolling their eyes wonderfully. One remained only to finish his work. He would not take pay on any account (the price was $10 Confederate) and I was shaved free gratis.

Going down to the vicinity of the old custom house and exchange I saw accidentally a large store with Anthony Barclay & Company on the sign. As this gentleman was a relation to my family I did not hesitate to enter (Mr. Barclay was British consul at New York for over twenty years and left there in consequence of favoring the enlistment of men there for the Crimean War, when he moved to Savannah).* I had a very pleasant meeting, and told him [I] had been a prisoner of war a year, and advised him to get his slaves away or they would get away themselves. He had a plantation some miles below the city which he wanted me to visit, but this being impossible for me on parole. I had to decline. One of his sons was an officer on board of one of the Rebel rams in the harbor . . . I could not even visit

*Anthony Barclay was godfather to Sneden's father, John Anthony Sneden. Barclay had left New York, where he had been British consul for many years, and set up business in Savannah. After Sherman occupied the city, Barclay approached him for compensation for British cotton the Union soldiers had destroyed. Sherman indignantly wrote Secretary of War Edwin Stanton that he told Barclay, "I was unwilling to fight for cotton for the benefit of Englishmen openly engaged in smuggling arms and instruments of war to kill us; that on the contrary it would afford me great satisfaction to conduct my army to Nassau and wipe out that nest of pirates."

him. So the old gentleman insisted on my taking a few hundred dollars Confederate which I did, and left him wondering how he could save his property from the "Yankees" (his plantation was afterwards utterly destroyed by Sherman's army and all the buildings burned to the ground).

Returning to Screven House I got as many shoes as I could conceal about me, and went to the railroad depot to sell them to the watchman there whom I had previously encountered. I went with him to his house, when after bringing in several men, I sold five pairs at $100 a pair, and exchanged four pairs for a pair of good boots. I was well entertained during the evening, and discovered that all these men belonged to the "Union League." I defined my position to them also.

After leaving them, and while crossing a park by moonlight, I was pounced on by four men, strangers to me, who cocked pistols at my head and bade me "stand!" I thought they were highwaymen, but was asked for my pass, and questioned as to whether I was a Union man or a spy. I soon satisfied them that I was all right, when they as suddenly left me to pursue my way unmolested. I then concluded that they were of the "Union League," and were afraid I would betray the organization to the authorities. I had been watched, and had satisfied them that their secret was safe. I now had about $1,700 Confederate money, and did not stint myself in buying anything I wished. I gave $300 for a secondhand pistol for one thing, bought blank books, pencils, etc. at enormous prices. All the stores were closed where dry goods or luxuries were sold. Provision stores were the only ones open and doing any business. The market is closed and deserted.

November 29, 1864

All was excitement this morning at the Screven House as Surgeon White had left for Florence last night leaving orders for the remainder of the hospital stores to be shipped this morning by 6 a.m. Assistant Quartermaster Stubbs and myself were to go in the same train. Dr. Herndon and Prendergast stayed behind. As they wore citizens' clothes they were safe from our troops if the city was captured. There seems to be a policy with the Rebels in not having their army in uniform, as in time of danger all that was needed was to tear off the strips of blue or red braid on collar or cuff, when they immediately become citizens. When the Army of the Union had passed through the vicinity the braid was sewed on, and again they were soldiers, or bushwhacking farmers! This practice was invariably done on the Virginia Peninsula during McClellan's campaign.

While Stubbs went to hunt up Negroes to remove the goods, I packed up my traps and was ready for a "change of base." Stubbs came back without help, as since the recent raids made on them by the military very few were to be seen. They had hidden themselves somewhere evidently. We had to leave all the stores behind us, with the exception of several cross cut saws and carpenter's tools, which Stubbs managed to get to the depot. I had no further charge of the stores, as Dr. Herndon was left behind with Prendergast to look after them.

The depot was crowded with Rebel troops, and as we had to go by the same train, Stubbs and I got the saws into the car next the engine, and about 7 a.m. started with twenty-seven cars full of Rebel soldiers, by the Savannah & Charleston railroads. General Hardee was on board the train, and reports were that "fighting was going on up the road." Most of the Rebel soldiers were half drunk before many miles had been travelled, and between singing songs and fighting among themselves the whole train was in an uproar for hours. In the car in which Stubbs and I sat several fights occurred, and bayonets were used to quell the disturbance by the guard, while several had to be bound hand and feet. The soldiers were all dressed in homespun and butternut clothing, dirty slouch hats, and smelt of pine top whiskey villainously. All had parti colored bed quilts instead of army blankets. And the crowd sang "We'll hang Abe Lincoln to a sour apple tree" in maudlin tones. If they had known that a "Yankee" sat in the front seat of the same car, I would have been bayoneted without ceremony by them!

After we passed the suburbs of Savannah, the railroad makes a wide sweep or curve as the river was crossed, which brought the city waterfront in view, and it looked very handsome on this side. The rams, *Savannah* and *Georgia** were at anchor with steam up and Rebel flags floated from the several forts away down river. No flags were on any of the buildings of the city, or shipping. With the exception of the capitol at Richmond, and the flag on Fort Winder on the Manchester side, I had never seen any other Rebel flag flying until now. The Rebels never had their flags flying in their forts erected around our stockade prisons, and though staffs were on Libby, and other prisons in Richmond, no flag was ever hoisted to my knowledge since I have been in the Confederacy. They knew that we would break through the roofs of any of these prisons to get at it, and are afraid to tempt us by flying their bogus bunting.

We passed the earthworks, which cross the railroad outside the city. Several hundred Negroes were at work on them, no white men to be seen but overseers. They were very crooked in shape, and only three feet high as trees were scarce. There was no abatis, but the ground in front of them was very swampy and intersected by numerous ditches. Our train consisted of twenty passenger cars, which were old and battered in appearance, which were filled to repletion by soldiers and six platform cars loaded with field artillery. An engine was at each end of the train, which were also rusty, and leaking badly. We went very slowly, about eight miles an hour, as the train was heavy for the worn out locomotives.

About 11 a.m. we came to a standstill near Parrisburg on the state line, where General Hardee and staff left the train to review and inspect the Georgia Militia and Reserves. The

* Sneden misnames the Confederate ironclads. The CSS *Georgia* had been captured several months earlier. The CSS *Savannah*, however, was there when Sneden was.

troops, about 5,000 in number were drawn up in lines on each side of the railroad, in open fields, and looked far better than any Rebel forces I had yet seen. They were neatly uniformed in cadet gray, and had military buttons, bayonets, and cross belts. The officers all wore red sashes, and looked very well. These troop were the best in the state as to appearance and drill, but had never been in any engagement, and were composed of "gentlemen's sons." Several hundred Negroes attended them and probably "toted their muskets for them" while on the march, as I had been before informed. Hardee merely passed down their lines, while he was cheered, and a band played "Bonnie Blue Flag," etc.

After an hour's delay we were again on our way, passed Grahamsville, crossing the Coosawhatchie River at 1 o'clock. While getting wood and water here, we distinctly heard artillery firing ahead. And the Rebel soldiers were much excited, and their officers tried to keep them in order without much success. They all seemed to be as good as the officers, and discipline was very lax among them.

Shortly after passing Pocataligo station the train was slowed and finally stopped, while a battle was going on in the woods just ahead of us.* Shells were flying over the tree tops, and a heavy fire of musketry in a continuous roar on the left of the track. The Rebel soldiers were all ordered out of the train, and went into the woods on the right on "the double quick." The telegraph wires were cut, and the Yankees might be in front and capture the train, and the engineer refused to go farther, [so] we backed down a short way for an hour.

I got on the roof of the car but could see nothing but smoke over the tree tops, while the musketry fire grew heavier. Away up the railroad I saw a man on horseback making flag signals. The whole train was uncoupled soon after, leaving the engine and tender with one baggage car into which Stubbs and I scrambled just in time, for another engineer was going to run through to Charleston at all risks. With a shrill whistle we started off like a rocket, and ran a mile or more under fire. I was at the open door of the baggage car all the time, but could only see a battery of horse artillery, and large numbers of cavalry on the edges of a clearing; all else was woods and white smoke. The shells flew all over and about the locomotive, and I hoped every one would hit, or disable the cars, but we passed through safely, going very fast, and did not stop until we reached the Big Salkehatchie River twenty miles away. No one knew of any part of Sherman's army being near where we saw them, and the Rebels must have been taken by surprise.

There were now only five of us in the boxcar, which had been cut off from the rest of the train, which was left on the tracks. Stubbs had a lot of cross cut saws and his carpenter's tools, etc. Two or three unloaded torpedoes, intended for sinking in Charleston harbor, and a few boxes and barrels. About 3 p.m. we passed Ashepoo bridge, at the further end of which was an old time cannon mounted on cart wheels and surrounded by a lot of old

* The battle of Honey Hill, or Grahamsville, occurred on November 30, not November 29, 1864.

country militia in homespun gray clothes, long hair and very dirty in appearance. The engineer now put on all the steam he could make, and we went through for some miles at a lively rate. The old engine and boxcar, which now constituted the train rocked from side to side on the rickety engine and track. Stubbs and I now had something to eat for the first time today. We had some good whiskey, too, which I took care to secure before we left the storeroom at Savannah. We crossed the Edisto River before sundown. Here we met two mounted guns at the bridge head and a lot of old artillery men, who looked very much like farmers. They wore no uniform, all were dressed in home made homespun and jeans. Home guard I supposed.

We arrived at the Wappo forts and railroad station on the Ashley River opposite Charleston a little after sundown. There was no hotel, or any other house in sight. So Stubbs got out his old saws and tools which he put in the deserted railroad station and we made our blanket beds on the floor and slept soundly until "sunup." The Wappo forts near [the] depot were not occupied by any Rebel forces now. The red clay earthworks were washed down to a few feet high by the recent rains. The corduroy roads leading to them were broken up and rails stuck up in all directions. There were no platforms for guns in the fort. . . . They were intended to defend the head of the Ashley River bridge.

During the night our forces on James and Morris Island down the harbor shelled Charleston . . . until daylight. I could see the trail of the burning fuses on the sky, and heard plainly the bursting shells, and the dull roar of the falling walls in Charleston. Two or three small fires were burning at the same time, which flickered against the dark sky, but died out after a while. . . .

November 30, 1864

Fine clear day. I was up at sunrise, and soon after went to Wappo Creek on the Ashley, where I made a sketch of the city, showing the West Point Mills, etc. . . . I then went all over the deserted Rebel forts, which never seemed to have had any occupants, though several log huts were standing near for soldier's quarters. The main redoubt was of sand. . . . The embrasures were all badly washed out by rain, no platforms for guns were visible, and loose sand was everywhere. A large mill in the vicinity was deserted, and as only freight came by railroad, but a few persons were to be seen anywhere.

After building a fire in one of the deserted log houses Stubbs and I got breakfast, and about 10 o'clock started to cross the Ashley bridge into the city. This is a fine structure built on piles, with large draw of modern construction, and is for carriages only, with footpaths on each side. From it I got a fine view of the lower harbor. Fort Sumter, still defiant, though half in ruins, long embankments of white sand lined both sides of the harbor, over which black guns pointed seaward, while Rebel flags were flying at Moultrie, and Fort Sumter, Castle Pinckney, Johnson, etc., bright in the morning sun. Black specks on the shining waters away down the harbor showed our monitor fleet at anchor, while a successful blockade runner was blowing off steam, having come in during the night, which accounted for the firing heard by us. . . .

On arriving on the Charleston side, the bridge gates were shut, and the only egress was by a toll house and turnstile just wide enough for one person at a time. A very large man stepped into the space thus left and demanded my pass. I told him that "I was an officer and needed none," and pointing to Stubbs some fifty feet behind me, told him that he had all the necessary papers." [I] went through the opening unmolested. It took Stubbs twenty minutes or more to convince this official that it was "all right." As he had to dive into all his pockets to show papers, etc., while I stood on the curbstones 200 feet away watching the result. Stubbs said that it was the hardest thing to convince this official that I was the "paroled Yankee," while he insisted that Stubbs must be the Yankee, and was not inclined to let him pass. I had grown absolutely fat on good living for the past month, and my strength had come proportionately, and I would have forced my passage anyhow if interrupted.

Stubbs was a cripple, and was of no count. He was a drunken fellow also, but as he was one of Winder's Baltimore pets. . . . He was under Wirz at Andersonville, and told me that he had disguised himself in our dead soldiers' clothes by Wirz's orders, and had been in the stockade over a week trying "to discover the Yankee who forged the passes." I thanked heaven that he was unsuccessful, as I would have had a short shrift if discovered. Wirz was frantic with rage at the time at the discovery of them, and offered $500 to any one of the detectives to find out the forger. Others besides Stubbs were in the stockade for the same purpose, and if those to whom I sold them had not proved true, my fate had been settled long ago.

Stubbs rejoined me, and we went through the city, where we put up at a small cheap hotel, and as I had plenty of money, ordered a good dinner. After which I treated everyone to all the whiskey they wished. This and the dinner cost me $200 but I made good friends with everybody, but did not of course let on that I was a Yankee, and only that I was attached to Winder's staff in some way or other. . . .

December 2, 1864

Foggy morning. Our guns on Morris Island were shelling the city all night and until 7 a.m. one shot in every fifteen or twenty minutes. I was up until a late hour watching the immense 200 pound missiles as they came screeching toward the city. Several exploded before striking any building. Three were killed during the night. One buried itself in the yard next to the hotel where I am staying! It first knocked a coal shed into kindling wood. There is no sign of Stubbs yet, and I begin to think he has given me the slip and gone on to Florence. He has the transportation order, and I doubt if the Rebel authorities would give me a passage in the cars there. I think they would send me to the jail or racecourse where our prisoners are, or take me for a spy, as I have numerous plans and sketches which they could soon get at if I was arrested. I kept in doors all day until towards sundown, when I went to the Wilmington, or North Eastern railroad depot but could not find Stubbs.

December 3, 1864

Fine weather. The Swamp Angel* and Fort Wagner threw shells and solid shot at the city all night. I could hear them crashing among houses all the while [though] very few exploded. King and Queen streets seemed to have been favored. Our artillerists are complimented by the Rebels for their accuracy; and no place is esteemed safe in the city from their missiles. I kept indoors today as much as possible. I saw two men and a Negro boy who had been killed while unearthing one of our shells. They tried to break off the copper ring with an axe! The thing burst, tearing them to pieces. I hear that several boys have been killed in this way—they pay dearly for their stupidity. The city will be fired before surrendering, and much powder is at the "Citadel Arsenal" near the Wilmington Depot, which is but two blocks off from where I am staying, and I feel rather anxious at night for fear one of our shells should burst there.

The Roper Hospital on Queen Street has been used to imprison our officers in September last: it had been struck once at that time. Last night another shell passed through the roof, and going through to the cellar had there exploded, tearing out the main rear wall, and knocking down many of the iron columns which supported the floors. Fortunately the building was empty, the officers having long ago been sent to Columbia, S.C. The Charleston jail and workhouse is in the immediate rear of Roper Hospital, and is now full of our prisoners, Negro soldiers, and Rebel deserters.

Going to the depot this afternoon I was much surprised and pleased to see Mr. Stubbs pushing his saws and tools into a boxcar, ready to go by train. I hurried back to the hotel, paid my bill, and packing my valuables in a small satchel, got to the train just in time, as it was already in motion. Stubbs has met old friends over on the other side of the Ashley River, and had been having a "hard old drunk." We left the depot about sundown with a train of thirteen passenger cars, which were full of men, women and children, who were all going to Wilmington, N.C. There were several Jews, women speculators, captains of blockade runners, but no soldiers. . . . As we left the suburbs we passed over much marshy ground on the Cooper River side. I got a good view of the lower harbor from the rear platform of the train. The conductor got no fares from either Stubbs or myself, and this is the only part of the United States where one can ride as a "deadhead."

We crossed the Santee River thirty-eight miles from Charleston before dark. The coun-

* The Swamp Angel was a celebrated artillery battery constructed by Union forces in the siege of Charleston.

FORT WAGNER SHOWING POINT OF ASSAULT

Fort Moultrie Fort Gregg

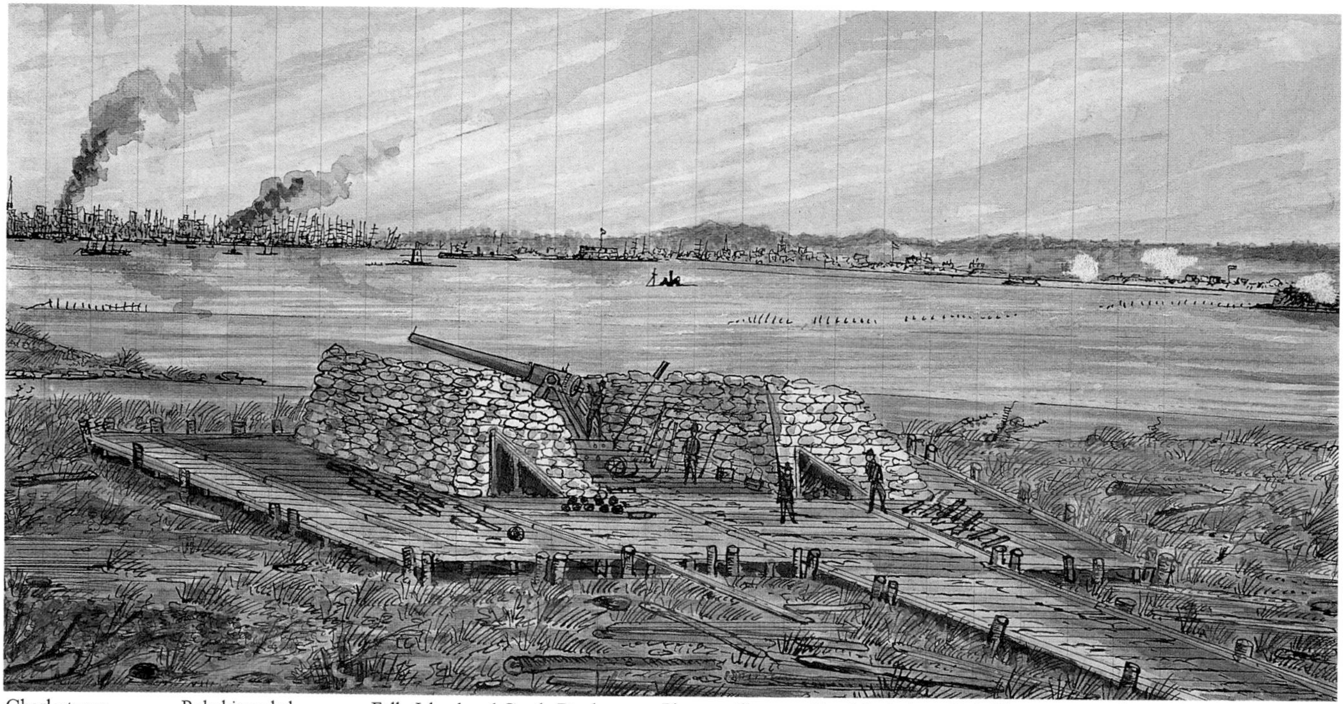

Charlestown Rebel ironclad Folly Island and Castle Pinckney Pleasantville Fort Moultrie Rebel batteries on Sullivan Island Fort Sumter

"THE SWAMP ANGEL GUN," MARSH BATTERY, MORRIS ISLAND, CHARLESTOWN HARBOR, S.C.

U.S. monitor fleet

try here is very swampy on both sides of the river which is covered with a dense undergrowth of pine and cypress trees of very large size. "Hell Hole Swamp," which is some miles east, floods the country for miles in every direction and affords concealment to vast numbers of alligators. I could see the black waters of the swamp for hundreds of yards under the trees, whose stumps and gnarled roots stuck up in every direction, and which in olden time afforded concealment effectually for "Marion and his men."* We took wood and water at St. Stephen's, on the Santee, and from thence went very slow, going over many trestle bridges which seemed very shaky and dangerous for a heavy train. We crossed Lynches Creek, an affluent of the Great Peedee River, at midnight and arrived at Florence about 2 o'clock in the morning ninety-two miles from Charleston.

As the railroads branch off here to Columbia, Cheraw, and Wilmington, there are a great number of switches, and we ran back and forth for nearly an hour on them before finally stopping. Many passengers got off here by the light of numerous pine torches, which lighted up the dark pine forest on both sides of the track. Many trunks and packages were recklessly thrown out at the station, several of which bursting open, disclosed large quantities of cigars loosely packed. Soon every other man was smoking them. I was not behind hand, and secured a bundle of them; for as they belonged to Rebels, I had as good a right to confiscate as any of the others. . . .

*A reference to Revolutionary War hero Francis Marion.

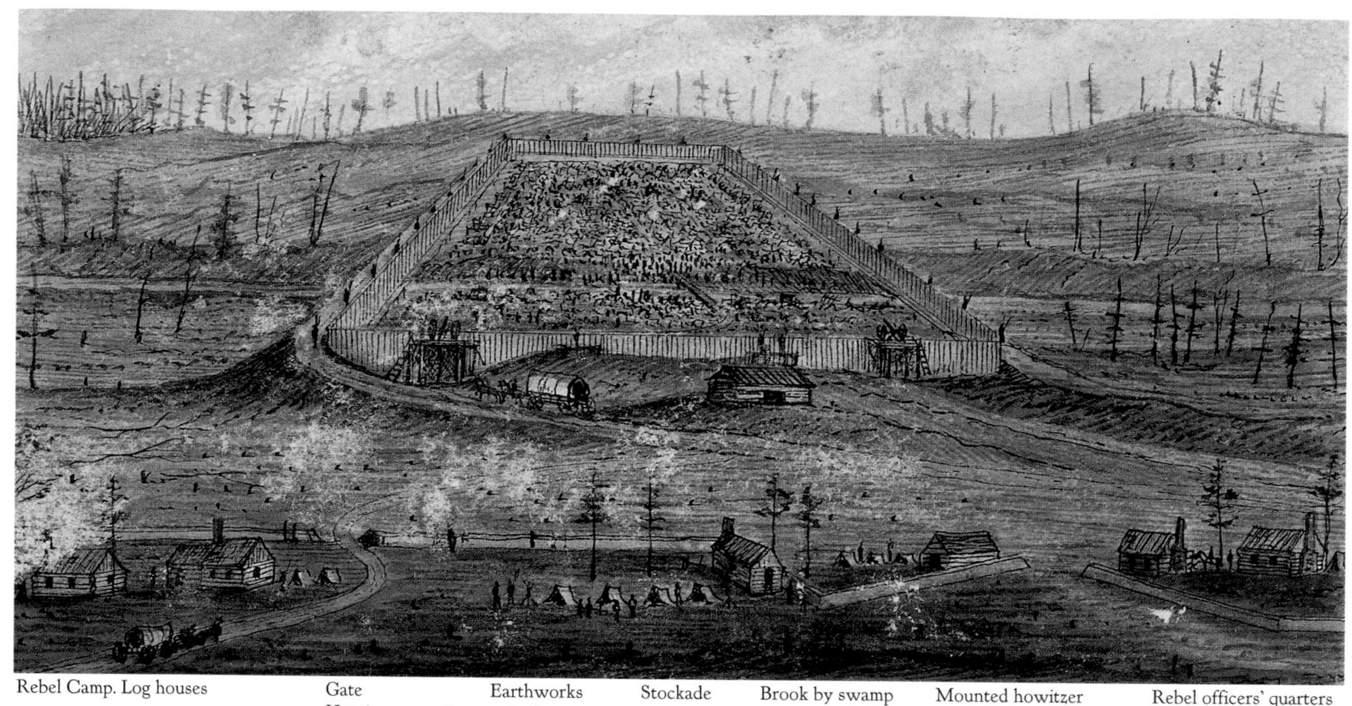

THE REBEL PRISON NEAR FLORENCE, S.C.

December 4, 1864

Stubbs and I made our way through the darkness to a large frame hotel some distance from the town, where General Winder and staff were supposed to have their headquarters. But as everybody was asleep, and after an ineffectual ringing of doorbells, we were now compelled to make our beds on the piazza floor, which we did and slept soundly until sunrise; disturbed only by the ceaseless hootings of owls in the adjacent woods. After making a toilet, I presented myself at the breakfast table of the hotel and surprised Surgeon White and Winder; who soon came in for breakfast, this being the first notice they had of our arrival. The meal cost me $15, and I took care to eat this much worth, if not more. Stubbs was brought to account by Winder for coming without the stores, which had been left at Savannah, and was put in arrest for several days. . . .

December 8, 1864

Weather still cold, another large detachment of prisoners left this morning for Charleston and this evening I will go also. I told Surgeon White that as there was no use for me to board any longer on the Confederacy I would like to go home, where I could get turkey for

Christmas dinner at any rate. He said that I ought to be satisfied with Confederate beef, etc. but after a while consented to give me an order on Colonel Iverson,* so that I could be put on the cartel [for exchange] today. I took the valuable paper, although it was written on a fly leaf torn out of a book, and hurriedly packed up my traps in a happy state of mind. As the shoemakers had gone early in the day, I would have to walk up the track 2½ miles alone. So everything being ready I started about 3 p.m. and as I had not walked so far for more than a year, I found it very tiresome, and the sun in my face all the way made me very warm. I was heavily laden too, and it was near sundown when the stockade log houses, rifle pits, etc. showed themselves ahead which accelerated my walking so as not to be too late.

As I had followed the railroad track all the way from Florence, I came towards the stockade and in the rear of the Rebel log houses and rifle pits and as the interior of the prison which was on a side hill came into view, long lines of men in single file were coming out and forming in front of the log houses. I had an opportunity to make a careful sketch of the prison and the surroundings which I did. . . . As I came nearer I saw that the head of the column of prisoners were giving their paroles at a shanty some ways off. I did not go there, but presented my order at another log house where several Rebel officers were making out the cartel for the day. After some delay in finding Iverson and showing him the order, he looked at me in hesitancy, and seemed to doubt my identity. I was dressed better than any of the officers present and put on all the assurance of an important personage. He hesitated upon putting my name on the cartel, telling me to wait until the morrow. I told him "I had walked from Florence with the order and did not intend to be bluffed off, and that if I was not put on the cartel I would report him to Winder." This changed his mood, and he pointed to a log house where I had presented myself at first. My name was entered at the bottom of the list, when I immediately got into line with the other prisoners, and we filed into a large field in the rear and were surrounded by [a] strong guard of Rebel soldiers on all sides.

Soon after, we were marched past a wagon where every man was given a loaf of corn bread of pretty good size. I divided mine with the others, as I had a good supply of wheaten biscuit which I had brought with me. Here again I met the same crowd of ragged, half naked prisoners, halt and blind, struggling to keep alive as usual, who looked at me in wonder when I told them where I had been since 11th November.

They did not believe in the exchange, until I told them how I had read it in the New York newspapers. And when I told them the army news they raised a faint cheer of rejoicing. After sundown, the weather grew very cold, and as the ground was frozen hard, and nothing but dried grass to make fires, we suffered terribly, and had to keep walking all the time to prevent freezing to death. And although there was quite a patch of woods a little way off, we were not allowed to gather any fuel from it. And the consequence was that seventeen of the prisoners who could not keep moving about were frozen to death before

*Lieutenant Colonel John F. Iverson was commander of the Florence prison camp.

10 p.m.! The cars which were to take us away and which should have been here on the usual time (6 p.m.) did not arrive until 10:30 p.m. and when they did come, we crowded into them sixty to a car by the light of pine torches, leaving the dead lying on their backs with glazed eyes and feet bound up in dirty rags, to be buried by the Rebels when they could find time. There was no excuse for the Rebels at this barbarity in refusing us firewood only for a few hours, but with their former hatred they intended to kill as many Yankees as possible, knowing that we were about to escape from their clutches.

The packed cattle cars soon reached Charleston, but not before nine more prisoners died. A city battalion marched the survivors to the Roper Hospital, a large, handsome building damaged by shelling and now used to house Federal prisoners. The guns were temporarily silent. The two sides had declared a truce until December 17 in order to complete a large exchange of prisoners. From the roof, Sneden took in a panoramic view of the harbor, including the Union fleet in the distance, and made a sketch.

On December 10, guards marched the prisoners down to the waterfront toward freedom. On the way, they passed many African American women who threw corn cakes, sweet potatoes, and biscuits to the prisoners. To Sneden, they had "warm hearts as they sympathized with us in our ragged and forlorn condition." When the prisoners reached the wharf on the Cooper River, they could see the damage done to the lower part of the city by months of shelling. For more than an hour, they huddled on the deck of a tugboat tied to the pier. Then word came that the sea was running too heavily to effect a transfer, and the dejected men had to shuffle back for another night at the Roper Hospital.

December 11, 1864

Fine and clear. We all slept soundly as the city was not shelled during the night. I, with others went on the roof very early, and from there saw several steamers at anchor quite near Sumter. We were all in good spirits at the prospect of getting away from the "cursed Confederacy," and visions of good square meals haunted most of us during the night, and all were packed up by sunrise expecting to move at any moment.

About noon, a new guard halted in front of the gates and we were ordered to "fall in"; which we were not long in obeying; as this was the only welcome order we had ever heard the Rebels give. We went this time to the Ashley River, and passed the Rebel battery of six guns at Chisholm's mills which I had seen and inspected at my former visit to Charleston. A much larger steamboat was lying near, and we were packed on board like sheep, and soon after much blowing of steam whistles started. We passed a blockade runner of rakish build

CHARLESTON, S.C., FROM THE ROOF OF ROPER HOSPITAL
December 1864.

and fine model, whose crew stared at us in wonder. We were "human cattle" to them no doubt. I secured a good place to note the course of the steamer through the lines of spiles and obstructions, and made [a] sketch of Fort Sumter from the side next the city before passing it. . . .

Soon we descried our fleet of transport steamers with large white flags at the fore, and "the stars and stripes" at the peaks and three feeble cheers were raised by us, which was responded to by waving of handkerchiefs from our vessels. The steamer *New York** was the flagship of the commission, and the name on her paddleboxes was enough to raise our spirits.

We soon came alongside another large river steamboat to which our steamer was lashed, and we walked over the fore and aft gangplanks in single file, being counted by one of our officers and one Rebel officer until all had been transferred, when the Rebel steamer cast off and returned to the city for more prisoners. Large tubs of warm water were at the gangways. And every prisoner was compelled to take a thorough wash, while every article of clothing of which they had divested themselves was thrown overboard, which went floating in an irregular line towards the city carried by the tide. New clothing was distrib-

*The steamer *New York* had been engaged in flag of truce activity in Virginia as well as South Carolina. On this occasion it served as headquarters for Lieutenant Colonel John E. Mulford, the U.S. assistant agent for exchange.

uted to the prisoners, and after a while all were in clean new clothes from head to foot; while three or four barbers cut hair, and shaved until night. Many of the prisoners could not realize the new situation, and were wild with joy and excitement.

We were formed in long lines and served with canned beef, wheat bread and coffee, in small quantities, as it would cause death to have made a hearty meal in our half famished condition. Many nevertheless got double rations by shifting positions in line. This was done three or four times before 10 p.m., so our appetite was diminished by degrees. The smell of real coffee alone made us very impatient, and every man of us must have drank two or more quarts apiece. We were now provided with new blankets, and bunked down on the main deck. Another load of prisoners were undergoing the washing and clothing process at the tubs, while several of our surgeons stood by noting the skeleton forms and half idiotic expressions of delight of the majority.

At midnight all were comfortably asleep; and the only noise was that made by the ship bell striking the hours. I went on deck from 10 to 11 and the appearance of the fleet with lights streaming the waters of the harbor was charming, while a solitary red light at Sumter alone showed where the Rebel stronghold lay in our path, sullen and still defiant. We had not been the first lot in the exchange, and there were on board many of our officers who had been prisoners, and their dirty, ragged, faded uniforms to which they still clung, showed that they had endured privations and poverty equal to the rest of us. They kept by themselves, and did not condescend to converse with any below their rank, probably not knowing that a private is equal to an officer of any grade when a prisoner of war.

December 12, 1864

Fine and clear with strong wind from northeast. At 7 a.m. all had a ration of whiskey, and breakfast at 8 a.m. We were given more to eat but not as much as we craved for sanitary causes. About 11 a.m. we slipped anchor and [were] towed to the steamer *Varuna** near us when we all embarked on board. Here we were placed on the second deck which had been cleared of all obstructions to give us room. We were about 700 in number including a dozen or more officers who had also been prisoners. The *Varuna* was a screw steamer, and the cabins were built on deck which were occupied by our officers, and those belonging to the vessel.

From the upper deck I made a careful sketch of "Sumter" with the city of Charleston in the background. Our monitor fleet lay off a mile or more toward the harbor entrance behind us, and looked like dogs of war keeping guard on both Rebels and us. We were formed in line every two hours during the day to get something to eat, and the quantity increased in

*Launched in 1863, the steamer *Varuna* served as a troop transport. The prince of Korea bought the *Varuna* in 1866, and a year later it went down off the China coast in a typhoon.

EXCHANGE OF 10,000 UNION PRISONERS OF WAR UNDER FLAG OF TRUCE
Charlestown Harbor, S.C., December 11 and 12, 1864.

proportion in every meal. Many were still unable to move about, and kept below deck. I did not throw my clothing away until I had unwrapped all the portions in which I had sewed my sketches and papers, but still stood in Rebel shoe leather as my boots were as good as could be desired though I had to confiscate some of the Union stores at Savannah to pay for them. I did not see any of my former companions in misery on board the *Varuna.*

December 13, 1864

Fine day, blowing heavy from eastward all day. We had a good breakfast and whiskey rations as usual, and I spent most of the day watching the Rebel works and finishing sketches. About 3 p.m. we were towed alongside the steamer *New York* and made fast, though the sea ran very high. Captain Chisholm* came on board in quest of me, as his wife saw my name on the register last night, and I was actually lifted on board by him over the rails, and at once found myself among friends who I had not before seen for twenty years! The surgeon examined me, ordered brandy, and I spent several hours in conversation until it was time to regain the *Varuna* as she was about to haul off again. About sunset we "cast off" and resumed our former position at anchor, after getting sundry stores and other necessaries from the *New York*. I was urged to stay with my friends until the quota of prisoners had been exchanged, but it would take probably a week or more, and I concluded to go home by the first chance. Before leaving the *New York*, I was given a pillow case half full of cake and fruit, and one bottle of whiskey and two of brandy for use on the home passage. These were furnished by my friend Captain Chisholm of the *New York*.

* Sneden provides no other evidence to identify his friend from before the war.

December 14, 1864

Steamer *Varuna* December 14th. Fine, but blowing half a gale with a "heavy cross sea on." About 8 a.m. we tripped anchor and headed seaward. We passed within fifty feet of our monitors soon after, which were laboring heavily in the sea at anchor, the spray was making clean breaches over the turrets and smoke stacks. The seamen were cheering loudly while holding on the life lines on deck. We hailed to know the cause of the excitement, when we were informed that Sherman was at Savannah and had captured Fort McAllister by storm! At this we cheered in return, and passed out of hearing. I, with others, kept the deck all day, and as we kept the South Carolina coast in sight was interested as we passed Cape Romain, and other headlands of less altitude.

We passed several steamers carrying stores to the fleet and army before Charleston during the day, their crews cheered us as we passed them in a heavy sea. The *Varuna* rolled very much and nearly all of the prisoners were sea sick. I was too old a sailor for that, and enjoyed the open sea, and thanked heaven that I was at last out of the cursed Confederacy. There was not much sleep among the prisoners, as the vessel labored heavily. The crew set the foresail and jib at midnight which eased her head considerably. . . .

December 16, 1864

Cloudy, blowing hard with heavy cross sea. Since leaving Charleston the officers of the ship have kept secluded. No order having been enforced among the large number of prisoners, many do just as they like. The meals have not been given regularly, and much grumbling the consequence. Last night however a lot of prisoners took matters into their own hands by getting down the fore hatch, carelessly left unfastened, and helping themselves to anything and everything fit to eat, while not a sailor or ship's officer was 'tween decks to prevent them.

We were off Cape Hatteras about 3:30 p.m. The wind and sea had been increasing since morning, all sail had to [be] taken in, and we were rolling fearfully though the vessel behaved well. Most of the prisoners were lying down " 'tween decks" as nobody but a sailor could "keep his legs." I went on deck at this time, and was seated alone at the stern, and as we rose on the waves could see the lighthouse at Hatteras Inlet to starboard.* At every plunge the steamer made into the sea the screw whirled around in air. And every time she rose, I could almost put my hands into the foam astern. The wind was blowing a gale, whistling loud through the rigging, while three or four seamen were at their posts on deck and in the pilot house forward.

All at once a thin white smoke rose well forward near the windlass which soon turned to a heavy puff of dense black, and the terrible fact struck me that we were on fire!! Soon, several seamen came running aft . . . while the ship's bell sounded the alarm. The black smoke continued to escape up the hatchways, while the frantic prisoners were yelling, and

*The lighthouse would have been to port rather than starboard for ships sailing north up the coast.

THE U.S. STEAMER *VARUNA*
600 exchanged prisoners of war, off Cape Hatteras, homeward bound, December 12, 1864.

trying to reach the deck, both gangways were soon blocked up with a crowd of prisoners, while others were ineffectually trying to get on deck by the hatchways. After twenty minutes of active work the fire was extinguished. Both steam pumps on the lower deck were luckily in order. But for this, we would have been all burnt or drowned!

When I saw the continued volume of black smoke, I thought it was "all up with us" and I was thoroughly afraid for a minute or so. There was no discipline enforced, as the officers were continually out of sight in their cabins (playing cards or drinking in all probability). The prisoners were like so many wild animals; nobody could enforce orders among them. As they were so demoralized by imprisonment that every one did just as he liked, despite remonstrance. The boats which hung at the davits would not hold one tenth part of us. And a horrid fate stared me in the face, after going through the long imprisonments and Rebel cruelties safely for over a year. When I took in the situation I immediately, with a good knife, cut the lashings of the small ladder which reached to the poop deck, intending to jump overboard with it when the fire got well aft. And as another steamer (which proved to be *The Star of the West*) was but a few miles to leeward, I calculated upon being picked up by her boats, but it was nearly dark before *The Star of the West* came within hail, and during this time we would have burnt to the water edge had the fire not been put out.

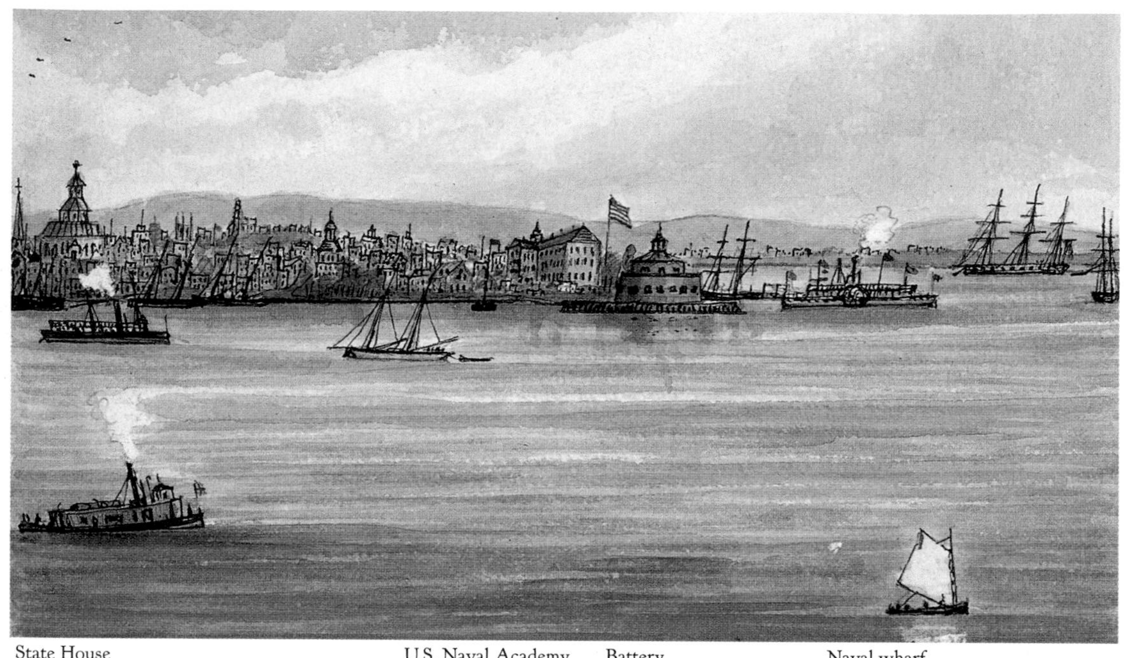

"CAMP PAROLE," ANNAPOLIS, MD., 1864

Afterwards I went down between decks, where I saw six or seven of our fellows who had been killed by suffocation, [beneath] the feet of the other prisoners, while trying to get on deck by means of the main hatch. A panic had ensued during the fire; crowds rushing for the hatch, which being eight feet or more in height from the main deck they were unable to reach. . . .

The cause of the fire was that someone of the prisoners had gone into the hold in quest of something to eat or drink, and no doubt thought the barrels of pork were whiskey, and having a small piece of candle (for it was very dark down there) had set the forage on fire. I had looked down this hatch myself, and saw numbers of bales of pressed hay on top of barrels down there. The hay was much burnt, but fortunately the wet and salty barrels did not have time to take fire before it was put out. It was out of this hatch where the provisions were gotten last night. After this narrow escape better order was observed, and the ship's officers kept a look out on the reckless crowds of prisoners.

The gale went down after midnight, and we passed Point Comfort, and in the morning we were running up Chesapeake Bay with sail again set, making for Annapolis, Maryland, our destination. There was no doctor on board the *Varuna*, and several of the prisoners die daily on the passage and before we reached the wharf a dozen or more of the poor fellows were lying on [the] deck dead, and in rough boxes hastily made by the ship's carpenter. It was sad to think that after long imprisonment and suffering that they could not live to see liberty. We had a head wind and heavy chopping sea all night.

December 17, 1864

Rain most of day. We had a good fair wind and easy sea, and the steamer made good speed. We passed several vessels and steamers laden with troops and horses for the army, and the whole bay was dotted with sailing vessels and steamers. As the bay is studded with numerous islands, the voyage up it was very pleasing, I remained on deck many hours. There was an excitement among the prisoners as we grew near the end of our voyage, and discussions as to what would be done with us on landing. About 4 p.m. we made the harbor of Annapolis and came to anchor, while we were taken off by a large tugboat, and landed about dark at the wharf near the Naval Academy. A band of music, and about 200 people were waiting here to receive us, who escorted us to "Camp Parole" in the vicinity, where we were all put into long barracks, in which bunks were fitted up, [and] where after rations were issued we smoked and discussed matters to a late hour.

December 18, 1864

The heavy rain storm cleared off during the night and after a good breakfast I went all over the camp. The grounds were level but the mud was deep and sticky as about 2,000 returned prisoners are here who tramped most of the ground into a quagmire, especially around the log house cook houses which were built about 150 feet from the barracks buildings. A high stone wall with open iron gates separated us from the academy buildings with the waterfront on one side and a guard on the other two sides. Outside we could see a large stockade in which are confined over 12,000 deserters from our army, mixed in with bounty jumpers, "Galvanized Yanks," over a thousand of whom were desperate characters, raiders and murderers. They killed six of their fellow prisoners a few days ago, and threw them all into a deep well, where they were recovered. A court martial was held and they were sent to the Dry Tortugas prison for a number of years, two of them were shot.

Colonel Chamberlain* has charge of this stockade, and has a regiment of soldiers under him for guarding it. He has shot six or seven of these desperadoes himself inside this stockade while resisting his authority. The guard are encamped near the stockade in log houses and tents. The academy buildings which now serve for hospitals for the returning prisoners of war are of brick with hipped slate roofs. The surgeons are busy night and day with the sick, wounded and dying, for many die there daily after being operated on. Many have to lose their legs, arms, and feet, on account of the incurable scurvy. Photos are being made of the worst cases by order of the U.S. government. Ambulances are seen daily carrying sick and wounded men there. A ship load of prisoners of war arrives every day, which anchors in the river until room can be made for them ashore here.

*Samuel E. Chamberlain, 1st Massachusetts Cavalry, commanded the College Green Barracks at Camp Parole.

All the sick came ashore today and were brought here in ambulances. Most of them were afterwards removed to the Naval Academy buildings, which now is a vast hospital. There is a bureau of officers here who have numbers of clerks employed in making out furloughs for us to go home. Several of the Regulators, or police, who were in power at Andersonville and "Camp Lawton" have been arrested for cruelty towards us while there, and Stanton, who was the most cruel, is in irons. We are quartered in several barracks which are built on a dreary waste of mud and about 200 are in each building. There is a sutler here too, where we can buy luxuries at a reasonable price, and the large wood stoves are surrounded by men cooking eggs, cheese, ham, and all kinds of messes from morning to night. As fast as the papers can be made out, detachments are furnished with [a] thirty day furlough, and advanced all their legitimate ration money accumulated during their imprisonment, which in many cases amounts to over $150. They are then sent home.

December 19, 1864

Several detachments of prisoners were paid off yesterday, and many were robbed of their money while at the sinks last night. The same old robbers are among us who infested the Rebel prisons, and are as yet undiscovered. The mode adopted is for one to pull the capes of the overcoat over a man's head, holding it fast, while the confederate "goes through him." Another is for a gang to enter the barracks when all are asleep in the bunks and take by force from those who are too weak to defend themselves. As there is no other guard except that on the boundaries of the camp these fellows have all their own way. And if resistance is made, [they] club the victim, so that he is afraid for his life to identify the scoundrels. In the barrack where I am quartered men were making clubs all day to use on these fellows if they "try it on us." I got ammunition for my pistol today, and am ready for them.

The weather is cold, and as the men are huddled around the stoves cooking as usual, it is hard work to keep warm. Opposite every barrack is a cook house, where the army ration is cooked and issued three times a day, when all have to form [a] line with tin cup and plate, which the men beat continually on with a spoon, making a great clatter. The rations are very liberal, and much more than can be used without waste.

December 20, 1864

Fine and clear. I, with others was paid off today, and after investing heavily at the sutler's in boots, hat, satchel, and a few luxuries, took the cars for Washington by the evening train on thirty days' leave of absence. Last night the Raiders made an attempt to rob those in the next building adjoining where I was, when they were set upon and clubbed unmercifully by the inmates. Some will die. Others are arrested, and perhaps this will break up the gang. At the sinks, which are a long way from the barracks, many men were "mugged" and robbed.

The thieves got over $1,000 from the different men who had to go there, and who had been paid off in the morning. I have searched all through the barracks and elsewhere without success to find those who were captured with me at Brandy Station, Virginia. Walsh, Colvin, Halley, etc. They must still be at Andersonville, or on their way home. I got New York files of papers, and have read them continually while in camp and [am] much satisfied with army news. . . .

December 21, 1864

I arrived at Washington at 7 a.m. and after putting up at "the National" ordered a uniform suit of clothes. I then went to our old headquarters corner 15½ Street and Pennsylvania Avenue, where I was received by my old friends still here on duty as one risen from the dead. General [Christopher Columbus] Auger had now headquarters here. The officers attached were all strangers to me. Several of the old clerks were here still, and with them I had a grand time in the evening.

My object in coming here is to investigate and secure my pay, as I had not drawn any in the field before I was captured. And my last payment had been made here by Major Pratt. I had hard work to identify myself. Even with the official papers given me at Annapolis Major Brock at the War Office did not recognize me as I had been away over a year, and finally after much delay I was identified at the War Department, after a clerk had been sent to the archives to find my name on the regimental muster roll, [whereupon] I was furnished a certificate. In the evening I met J. Munson, who was one of those in our party when captured by Mosby who succeeded in escaping in the fog, after slipping off his mule, who gave me the story while with a number of old friends I recounted some of my adventures.

December 24, 1864

Snow and rain. For the past three days I have been searching through piles of paymasters' books to find my last payment. And finally today [I] found my name against which was written "missing or killed" to which I added "found alive," in pencil. I had not drawn pay since September 1st, 1863, when I had left headquarters here for my first absence from the army since 1861. After this, I was furnished with proper documents and transportation home. I went to the theatres and capitol, seeing sights, and meeting old friends, very few of whom could believe the horrors of Rebel prisons as set forth by my experiences. . . .

After making calls on friends at headquarters, and investing heavily in "steamed oysters," I took the train for Baltimore, where I arrived in due time and put up at the Eutaw House. Provost guards came on board the train at every place, in search of soldiers who were trying to desert, or go north without passes. Everyone had to show passes who wore military clothing, but there were numbers of soldiers among us who were in citizen's clothes who escaped.

December 25, 1864

Snow two inches. I went over the principal streets of the city this forenoon, visited the battle monument and Barnum's large hotel. Baltimore Street was crowded with people and many handsome women could be seen there shopping. I met some army officers at the Eutaw House bar and had a very enjoyable time "swapping stories."

December 26, 1864

Three inches of snow on [the] streets but fine and clear. I took the evening train for New York, and arrived about midnight. Put up at [the] Mansion House [in] Brooklyn and next day about 2 p.m. found my family who had long given me up for dead.

Epilogue

In New York on October 21, 1865, *Frank Leslie's Illustrated Newspaper* printed an unusually large, panoramic engraving that covered a whole page. The editors declared that it gave "the only correct view . . . ever published" of the most notorious Southern military prison. They described how the artist endured seven months there and barely escaped detection as he made his surreptitious drawing. This view of Andersonville and other sketches "were secreted between the soles of his shoes, and brought out of the Confederacy, with drawings of the prisons of Salisbury, Millen, or Camp Lawton, Florence, and the bull pen of Savannah." The illustration was based upon "a drawing made by R. K. Sneden, of the Topographical Engineers."

Through four years of war, *Leslie's* and its rival, *Harper's Weekly*, had fed the public a steady diet of graphic images—thousands of engravings that depicted every conceivable story about the conflict, from battles and sieges to celebrated leaders and the hardships of the common soldier. But by autumn 1865 the war and the victory parades were over. The nation turned its attention eagerly to peacetime pursuits. Why, then, did *Leslie's* devote a whole sheet to the unpleasant subject of Andersonville six months after Appomattox? One last piece of wartime business being tidied up in Washington held the answer.

Since late August, a military tribunal had met in the nation's capital under the presidency of General Lew Wallace to try Henry Wirz for the real sins of Andersonville and for a good many imagined ones besides. Prosecution witnesses included Private Thomas Walsh, who had been captured with Sneden at Brandy Station. He knew something about the running of the Confederate prison from his perspective as a paroled clerk working outside the

ENGRAVING IN *FRANK LESLIE'S ILLUSTRATED NEWSPAPER*
October 21, 1865, based on a Sneden drawing.

stockade. Other, less credible witnesses also stepped forward to catalogue the brutalities of Wirz.

Wirz alone would pay for Andersonville. General Winder died before the war ended. Sneden's medical patron, Dr. Isaiah White, and other Confederate officials were lucky the government dropped their names from the indictment. Only vile, repellent, hapless Wirz remained. Testimony stretched on into autumn as the prosecution bullied Wirz's lawyers and presented dubious evidence of its own. The truth of Andersonville was horrific enough, but the army did not distinguish itself with its conduct of the trial.

Even so, it is unlikely Sneden or his friends would have objected to the prosecution's arguments, so great was their hatred of Wirz and all he represented. They would never forget the privations they endured or the comrades who had died. Sneden's sketch appeared in *Leslie's* at the height of publicity over the trial. Three days later the tribunal sentenced Wirz to death. They hanged him within sight of the United States Capitol.

By the time his sketch of "The Great Rebel Prison Pen at Andersonville" drew national attention, however fleeting, Sneden had been back in New York for almost a year. He had arrived home from prison at Christmastime 1864, alone, in the snow, in broken health, given up for dead by his family. Despite this dramatic homecoming, which must have seemed nothing short of miraculous to his parents, he did not stay long at their Brooklyn home. Instead, he went up the Hudson to Tarrytown, where a physician cousin supervised his gradual recovery. "By good living, and [a] little phisic," he boasted, "[I] was all right in three months." He regained his weight and then some. A large mop of dark brown hair, parted in unequal, lopsided mounds, added a little to his height. But at five feet six and a half inches and 155 pounds, he was still the average, ordinary-looking man who had wandered in an extraordinary odyssey through the Confederate prison system and survived to tell his story.

The 40th New York Regiment formally mustered him out of the service on the last day of January 1865, barely two months before the war ended. Sneden was probably still in Tarrytown and not present among the teeming crowds who gathered spontaneously in Wall Street on April 3 to celebrate the fall of Richmond, sing the Doxology, and give thanks for Union victory. But a few weeks later he did join the far greater number of New Yorkers who stood along the rail line to watch Lincoln's funeral train pass by.

About that time he began working for the promising young architect Carl Pfeiffer, a recent German immigrant and founding member of the American Institute of Architects. He only stayed with Pfeiffer a few months. By the end of the year he joined the firm of architect William B. Olmsted. His employment there, lasting twelve years, provided the longest period of financial stability in Sneden's postwar career.

In a superficial sense, he picked up where he had left off in 1861. Olmsted gave 50 Wall Street as his business address, the same location that Sneden listed for himself, both before the war and again in 1865. Because he described it as "50 Wall Street (top floor)," he may have rented quarters over the office. If he lived there at the time he enlisted, perhaps Olmsted had employed him before the war.

Sneden freelanced while he worked for Olmsted. On his business cards, he described himself as a "Topographical Engineer and Landscape Artist" who could execute "Architectural and Perspective Drawings, Plans of Hotels and Manufactories, and Fire Surveys of same. Hydrographical and Land Surveys, and Machine Drawings for Patents." By the end of the decade, a few of his maps and engravings based on his watercolors appeared in atlases of New York and the surrounding area.

For Sneden, though, it was not simply a matter of picking up where he had left off before enlisting in the Mozart Regiment. The promise of his draftsmanship, recognized by so many Union generals during the war, never really flourished in peacetime. No evidence survives that any of the grand projects advertised on his business card existed anywhere beyond Sneden's imagination. By the late 1880s he still styled himself a civil engineer and architect, though neither the American Institute of Architects nor the American Society of

Civil Engineers admitted him to membership. Like many other marginal practitioners, he seems to have been left out in the cold as both occupations became increasingly professionalized. In all, he executed only a few minor building projects and derived some income, though not much, from surveys of rural mills and farms upstate and in New England.

As it did for so many veterans on both sides, the war branded him for life. He survived it but he did not get over it. And when professional success eluded him, reliving the war through the compiling of a vast illustrated memoir filled up more and more of Sneden's hours. Perhaps his lonely ways explain his hours of solitary drafting and sketching during the war. Perhaps too they explain his willingness to be paroled to work for a Confederate surgeon—a move that may well have spared his life, yet must have been extraordinarily unpopular among his fellow prisoners. Now, after the war, Sneden turned inward and spent many obsessive hours creating his memoirs.

In 1883 assistant editor Clarence Buel of *Century Magazine* proposed a scheme to revive the fortunes of the troubled monthly. His boss, Richard Watson Gilder, enthusiastically supported Buel's plan to publish accounts of Civil War battles as told by surviving officers on both sides. A colleague called the idea "a flash of divination." The timing was perfect. Enough of the leading commanders were still alive. A new generation had grown up that had only known the war as children and were eager to learn more about the great events of their parents' day. Most crucially for sales, the veterans were well into middle age and beginning to reflect on those same great events that had molded their youth.

Beginning in November 1884, each monthly issue of *Century* carried an installment in the series called "Battles and Leaders of the Civil War." Circulation doubled. Veterans mailed a blizzard of letters to the editors. They wanted to correct errors, add details, and have their say.

The illustrations were as important as the writing. According to Buel's co-editor, Robert Underwood Johnson, "contemporary views on both sides were discovered and a dragnet search was made for authentic materials . . . all over the country."

None of the images the editors accepted, however, came from the hand of Robert Sneden—none, that is, until the very last issue of the series. The final article, "Grant's Last Campaign," featured a small engraving based on a Sneden watercolor of Appomattox Court House. It did not matter that the artist probably never visited Appomattox: his work caught the editors' attention, and that was enough to give Sneden hope for greater recognition.

In the meantime, even before that last installment appeared in November 1887, the editors were rushing a four-volume hardcover compilation into print, also called *Battles and Leaders of the Civil War*. They added even more illustrations than appeared in the original version. By the time they were done, they assembled contributions from more than 200

Appomattox Court House, Va., April 1865

Union and Confederate veterans. More than 1,700 images illustrated the expanded edition. This time they did not wait until the last chapter to include Sneden's work. Nearly three dozen engravings appeared that were based on Sneden watercolors.

Sneden's work was still at the *Century* offices when disaster struck. According to Richard Watson Gilder, "the fire that we have always feared, coming down from those confounded binderies, burnt us out last night." Happily for Gilder, he rescued most of his authors' manuscripts. Unhappily for Sneden, "most" did not include all of his work. Some of it was "very badly damaged by smoke and water." Worse, one of his volumes—the one covering the Peninsula Campaign from Williamsburg to Fair Oaks—was entirely destroyed.

Much remained. Approximately four hundred large watercolors survived, as well as five of the six huge memoir volumes containing thousands of manuscript pages and another four hundred original watercolors, maps, and pen-and-ink sketches. Together these items constitute the powerful testament of one soldier about the greatest event of his life and of his country's. His contributions to *Battles and Leaders*, however, amounted to only 5 percent of his total Civil War watercolors. And despite Sneden's hopes, they were his last known publication. The public saw no more of them for more than a hundred years after the *Century* project. And they knew nothing at all about his mammoth illustrated memoir.

A month after *Century* began its "Battles and Leaders" series in 1884, Sneden started what would become a long-running correspondence with bureaucrats in Washington. He asked for back pay never received while he had been a prisoner of war and reimbursement for personal property confiscated by the Rebels when they captured him. No evidence survives that he convinced the authorities of his argument. Three years later, he began the lengthy process of applying for a disability pension. He admitted he had recovered his health enough to work at least part-time, but he attributed chronic problems to his year of imprisonment. He cited rheumatism and kidney trouble as the most debilitating ailments. But he also never failed to mention the slight scar under his right eye, a souvenir from that long ago foggy Virginia night when one of Mosby's soldiers pistol-whipped him. He also laid his bad memory for figures to the prison experience. Concluding his argument, he said that serious infirmities resulting from diseases he suffered in the line of duty "have unfitted me ever since to withstand changes in the weather and travelling in my profession, and I have generally to abandon all business in the winter's months, go home to the country and thereby lose work, and money."

By that time Sneden had long since left the Olmsted firm. He had done so in 1877, the year his father died. He moved in with his mother, first in Greenwich, Connecticut, and then in Monsey, a village in Rockland County, New York, that boasted of "six stores, two blacksmith shops, one carpenter shop, a lumber and coal yard, a steam feed mill, and a hotel." In Monsey, he continued to pursue his as yet unsuccessful application for a disability pension. He was, he wrote, "partly supported by my Mother, who has a small income since the death of my Father." It cannot have amounted to much. Insurance broker John Anthony Sneden owned no real estate. He left Ann Knox Sneden an estate consisting of a gold watch, a few sticks of furniture, and little more than $800 in two savings accounts.

In the last decades of the century, Sneden continued part-time employment "engaged in making Plans and Surveys of Mills &c" and dabbled in genealogy. Though he compiled a scrapbook about the Spanish-American War, his obsession with *his* war never flagged. He joined Rankin Post No. 10 of the Grand Army of the Republic, composed mostly of veterans of the 40th New York Regiment. He augmented his memoir with a collection of newspaper clippings that showed special relish for the obituaries of prominent Confederates. One concerned Major John H. Gee, former commandant of the prison at Salisbury, North Carolina, where the mortality rate exceeded even that of Andersonville. When Gee died in a Florida hotel fire, Sneden gleefully scribbled in the margin of the clipping that he had "burned to a crisp." On the other hand, this veteran who had enjoyed theatergoing so much when he was stationed in wartime Washington kept a framed carte de visite of actor Edwin Booth, brother of the assassin.

The quest for a pension assumed greater urgency as surveying commissions dried up. Henry Gotleb, former captain in the 40th New York Regiment, lent a hand. According to his service records, Sneden was recruited by Gotleb for the regiment in 1861. A quarter century later Gotleb certified that he had known the artist since before the war, that Sneden indeed suffered from wartime disabilities, and that these infirmities received in the service of the republic entitled him to a government pension. Another friend testified that Sneden "earns a very precarious living" because chronic illness prevented him from attending to business "with any regularity." Precarious, indeed. In a five-year period at the end of the century, Sneden said he designed "2 school Houses here [in Monsey] and 2 Dwellings," all apparently of modest dimensions.

The surgeons who examined Sneden found the scar under his eye but no evidence of rheumatism or kidney problems. He may have contracted typhoid fever in Richmond, and scurvy may have cost him three teeth at Andersonville. But the doctors judged him to be in reasonable health for a man in his seventh decade. They nevertheless approved him for a tiny pension based on general disability that was "not due to vicious habits." At $8 a month, raised to $10 in 1903, it could hardly support him, even assuming he inherited his mother's meager assets when she died.

By the turn of the century, Sneden's financial problems pushed him toward an unappealing decision. He wrote the commissioner of pensions that he could "see nothing in view to help me financially but to go to the 'Soldiers Home' at Bath, N.Y. unless you grant me an increase of pension. I do not want to go to the 'Home' if I can possibly help it." But there was no livelihood to sustain him in Monsey, "this miserable slow town."

On June 22, 1905, he finally made that move to the Soldier's and Sailor's Home at Bath in Steuben County. There he joined nearly two thousand other Union veterans in the idyllic

ROBERT KNOX SNEDEN
Taken at South Beach Resort, Staten Island, N.Y., July 11, 1911.

Finger Lakes district of western New York, far from the bustling metropolis of his young adulthood. The move did not spare the pension office in Washington from Sneden's long letters importuning the commissioner for increases in his meager monthly check. Clerks who opened the mail at the pension bureau, as well as the commissioner himself, would readily have agreed with Sneden's great-niece, Elizabeth Phelps Sneden. Years later, she remembered the veteran in old age, his dark hair intact but now faded to iron gray. He was, she recalled, a cranky old man, peculiar in his ways, still very much the solitary survivor.

He seems to have had little to do with his siblings—a brother and three sisters. At least he mentions them only in passing in the few letters that survive from the turn of the century. It is tempting, nevertheless, to speculate about his relationship with his brother's son. Arthur Durant Sneden graduated from New York University and was attracting favorable comment in the architecture section of the Paris Salon the same year that his uncle made the unwanted move to the Soldier's and Sailor's Home. Could it really have been only a coincidence that the relative who inherited the watercolors and memoir was Arthur Sneden, the nephew who built the successful architectural career that had always eluded his uncle?

In 1917 America joined the European conflict that people called the Great War. By the next summer, the last German offensive exhausted itself, and the Allies dared to hope for victory. At home, the worldwide influenza epidemic threatened to overshadow even the titanic struggle on the Western Front. In Bath the *Farmer's Advocate* gamely promoted the annual Steuben County Fair that September. But side by side with stories of prize bulls and blue-ribboned pies, the paper was compelled to announce, week after week, the deaths of local doughboys far from home and of flu victims across the country.

Transfixed by these dramatic events, county residents paid little notice to the death in their midst of an aged veteran of another war. On September 18, 1918, at the Soldier's and Sailor's Home, Robert Knox Sneden finally succumbed at the age of eighty-six. He had survived Confederate bullets on half a dozen battlefields and endured starvation rations in as many Southern prisons, even the squalor and anarchy of Andersonville. They laid his bones to rest in the neat rows of graves that compose the national cemetery at the Home, in section J, row 11, grave 4.

A bachelor all his life, he once told a local historian inquiring about the Sneden family that "I leave no posterity, but a good WAR RECORD."

War Record.
BATTLE RECORD of the 40th N.Y. Regt
THIRD CORPS
ARMY of the POTOMAC
HEINTZELMAN - KEARNY
HOOKER - BIRNEY
THE GETTYSBURG MEDAL 1893.
GETTYSBURG VETRAN
1863 1893
G.A.R.
RANKIN POST
No. 10.
OF BROOKLYN, N.Y.
COMMANDERS of the 3rd CORPS.
ARMY SERVICE of R.K. SNEDEN.
Record of R.K. SNEDEN.
40th N.Y. VOLS (MOZART REGt)
Topographical Engineer. of 3rd CORPS. A.P.
BATTLES,
PENINSULAR CAMPAIGN. 1862
YORKTOWN. Va April 6th to May 4th
WILLIAMSBURG. Va May 5th
FAIR OAKS. Va May 31st
SKIRMISHES on the CHICAHOMINY June.
SAVAGE'S STATION. Va June 29th
WHITE OAK SWAMP. June 30
GLENDALE. and CHARLES CITY CROSS ROADS JUNE 30.
MALVERN HILL. Va July 1st and 2nd
BRISTOE STATION. Va Aug 27
KETTLE RUN. Va Aug 26th
2nd BULL RUN. 30th and 31st Aug.
CHANTILLY. Va Sept 1st
1863.
GETTYSBURG. Penna July 2nd + 3rd
and KELLYS FORD. Va Nov. 7th
CAPTURED.
Novr 27th 1863 - 3 a.m.
at Head Quarters of Maj Genl FRENCH
of 3rd CORPS. A.P.
AT BRANDY STATION - VIRGINIA.
By MOSBY'S GUERRILLAS. C.S.A.
REBEL PRISONS.
LIBBY.
CREW & PEMBERTON PRISON &
SCOTTS PRISON - RICHMOND.
ANDERSONVILLE - GEORGIA.
from March 1st 1864. to Sept. 15th 64.
MILLEN. or "CAMP LAWTON". Geo.
SALISBURY. S.C. SAVANNAH.
CHARLESTON. (under fire.) AND
FLORENCE. S.C. Exchanged
from Charleston. S.C. 11th Decr 1864.
DULCE ET DECORUM EST PRO PATRIA MORI
KEARNY'S MOTTO.
THE BROOKLYN WAR MEDAL 1866.
THE KEARNY CROSS
FIRST DIVISION BADGE of 3rd CORPS 1862 1863.
2nd and 3rd CORPS COMBINED
THE KEARNY MEDAL 1862.
SIEGE of YORKTOWN Va 1862.
WILLIAMSBURG
FAIR OAKS
SAVAGE'S STATION
WHITE OAK SWAMP
GLENDALE
MALVERN HILL
2nd BULL RUN
CHANTILLY
ANTIETAM
FIRST FREDERICKSBURG
1863
CHANCELLORSVILLE
GETTYSBURG
BRISTOE STATION Oct. 14th 1863.
KELLYS FORD
MINE RUN
1864
BATTLES of the WILDERNESS
SPOTTSYLVANIA
NORTH ANNA
COLD HARBOR
PETERSBURG
BATTLE OF STRAWBERRY PLAINS
BOYNTON PLANK ROAD
1865
HATCHER'S RUN
DEEP BOTTOM
DETONSVILLE
SAILOR'S CREEK
FARMVILLE
History of the 40th N.Y. Vols Mozart Regiment
STATE of NEW YORK
EXCELSIOR
CITY of NEW YORK
DESIGNED and DRAWN by R.K. Sneden.
NOTE.

Note on Sources

We know Robert Knox Sneden intimately during the Civil War through his own words,but the rest of his life, both before and after the war, remains a mystery illuminated by the barest of details. Other than his voluminous memoir and collection of watercolor drawings, the limited extant sources on Sneden make it difficult to piece together a complete biography. Attempts to locate personal papers or any other original documentary materials on him at various repositories and with family descendants proved unsuccessful. The fate of the diaries he kept during the war, including the shorthand versions from his months of imprisonment, upon which he based his memoir, is unknown. His letter-writing campaign regarding his pension, located at the National Archives, provides the only known collection of any size of Sneden correspondence and documents. The library of Palisades, New York, has a few letters in Sneden's hand from the turn of the century. The New-York Historical Society owns five of his watercolor drawings, two of them pre–Civil War landscapes, the others postwar. The Library of Congress and the National Archives hold a small number of his manuscript maps from the war.

Background information on Sneden's ancestry and early life came from several sources. Most helpful were Pat Wardell, compiler, *Ancestry of Robert Knox Sneden: The Sneden/Snethen Family Newsletter* (Annandale, New Jersey, 1996); Cornelia F. Bedell, compiler, *Now and Then and Long Ago in Rockland County, New York* (New City, New York, 1968); Alice Munro Haagensen, *Palisades and Snedens Landing* (Tarrytown, New York, 1986); Frank B. Green, *History of Rockland County, New York* (New York, 1886); and David Cole, *History of Rockland County, New York* (New York, 1884).

Sources consulted for Sneden's Canadian background included A. W. Savary, *Supplement to the History of the County of Annapolis* [Nova Scotia] (Toronto, 1913); and marriage bonds and church records at the Public Archives of Nova Scotia in Halifax. A few sketchy details of the Sneden family's move back to New York appear in the following sources consulted at the New York City Public Library and New York State Library: New York state census records, Federal census records, and various New York City and Brooklyn city directories beginning in the early 1850s. For example, a question in the 1905 New York state census provided the date for the Sneden family's move to the United States in 1851. For information on antebellum New York City, *Gotham: A History of New York City to 1898* (New York, 1999), by Edwin G. Burrows and Mike Wallace, and *The Civil War and New York City* (Syracuse, New York, 1990), by Ernest A. McKay, were especially helpful.

Our knowledge of Sneden's education must remain frustratingly speculative. Even so, some published sources provide a useful background. For his Canadian years, J. Donald Wilson et al., *Canadian Education: A History* (Scarborough, Ontario, 1970) was consulted. There is little scholarship on the education and training of American engineers and architects in the nineteenth century, especially relating to apprenticeships. Information gleaned on this subject came from the following: William H. Wisely, *The American Civil Engineer, 1852–1974: The History, Traditions, and Development of the American Society of Civil Engineers* (New York, 1974); George S. Emmerson, *Engineering Education: A Social History* (New York, 1973); James G. McGivern, *First Hundred Years of Engineering Education in the United States, 1807–1907* (Spokane, Washington, 1960); Dell Upton, *Architecture in the United States* (New York, 1998); Judith A. McGaw, ed., *Early American Technology; Making and Doing Things from the Colonial Era to 1850* (Chapel Hill, 1994); James M. Fitch, *American Building: The Forces That Shape It* (Boston, 1948); and Leland M. Roth, *A Concise History of American Architecture* (New York, 1979).

Sneden's memoir provides voluminous details about his Civil War experience. The following materials proved helpful in checking the accuracy of his information, filling in details, and putting his narrative in a broader context. Fred C. Floyd's *History of the Fortieth Mozart Regiment New York Volunteers* (Boston, 1909) and Joseph Murphy's "Record of the Mozart Regiment 40th New York Volunteers," typescript (c. 1900), at the New York State Archives provided useful background information on Sneden's unit and his probable involvement early in the war. Sneden's frequent references to fellow Nova Scotian Bluenoses serving in the Union army may surprise some readers. Greg Marquis's *In Armageddon's Shadow: The Civil War and Canada's Maritime Provinces* (Montreal, 1998), however, suggests that as many as fifty thousand native-born Canadians served under the Stars and Stripes during the war.

The following sources provided background on topographical engineers and mapmaking: Frank N. Schubert, ed., *The Nation Builders: A Sesquicentennial History of the Corps of Topographical Engineers, 1838–1863* (Fort Belvoir, Virginia, 1988); Garry D. Ryan, "War

Department Topographical Bureau, 1831–1863: An Administrative History" (Ph.D. dissertation, American University, 1968); Daniel D. Nettesheim, "Topographical Intelligence and the American Civil War" (M.A. thesis, Command and General Staff College, Fort Leavenworth, Kansas, 1978); Harold E. Gulley, "Maps in the Civil War: An Examination of Map Use During the Peninsular Campaign" (M.A. thesis, University of Georgia, 1985); and Christopher Nelson, *Mapping the Civil War: Featuring Rare Maps from the Library of Congress* (Washington, D.C., 1992).

General reference sources providing background information on people, places, and events Sneden discussed in his account include Mark M. Boatner III, *The Civil War Dictionary* (New York, 1959); E. B. Long, *The Civil War Day by Day, An Almanac, 1861–1865* (New York, 1971); Ezra J. Warner, *Generals in Blue: Lives of the Union Commanders* (Baton Rouge, 1964) and *Generals in Gray: Lives of the Confederate Commanders* (Baton Rouge, 1959); and Vincent J. Esposito, ed., *The West Point Atlas of American Wars*, vol. 1 (New York, 1959). Other useful secondary sources include: Stephen W. Sears, *George B. McClellan: The Young Napoleon* (New York, 1988) and *To the Gates of Richmond: The Peninsula Campaign* (New York, 1992); Bruce Catton, *Mr. Lincoln's Army* (Garden City, New York, 1951); John Hennessy, *Return to Bull Run: The Campaign and Battle of Second Manassas* (New York, 1993); Martin F. Graham, *Mine Run: Campaign of Lost Opportunities, October 21, 1863–May 1, 1864* (Lynchburg, Virginia, 1987); James A. Ramage, *Gray Ghost: The Life of Col. John Singleton Mosby* (Lexington, Kentucky 1999); John E. Simpson, *Howell Cobb: The Politics of Ambition* (Chicago, 1973).

William Marvel's *Andersonville, The Last Depot* (Chapel Hill, 1994) is the best modern account of the subject. Marvel's work was the most valuable resource for sorting out Sneden's sometimes confusing and inaccurate account of his imprisonment at Andersonville. Other secondary accounts of imprisonment during the Civil War include: Sandra V. Parker, *Richmond's Civil War Prisons* (Lynchburg, Virginia, 1990), and Edward F. Roberts, *Andersonville Journey* (Shippensburg, Pennsylvania, 1998). Some of the published prisoner of war accounts that Sneden consulted as he expanded his wartime notes into his memoir include the exaggerated tales written by John L. Ransom, *Andersonville Diary, Escape, and List of the Dead . . .* (Auburn, New York, 1881), and John McElroy, *Andersonville: A Story of Rebel Military Prisons* (Toledo, Ohio, 1879).

In addition to containing nearly three dozen engravings based on Sneden originals, editors Robert U. Johnson and Clarence C. Buel's four-volume *Battles and Leaders of the Civil War* (New York, 1887–88) provides detailed accounts of the war by the men who fought it. Volume 2, covering the Peninsula and Second Bull Run campaigns, was especially helpful. Other useful nineteenth-century sources include William Swinton's *Campaigns of the Army of the Potomac* (New York, 1866) and Alexander Webb's *The Peninsula: McClellan's Campaign of 1862* (New York, 1881).

An engraving of the Andersonville prison appeared in *Frank Leslie's Illustrated Newspaper* in October 1865. This is the first image identified by the publisher as being by Sneden ever to appear in print. Earlier, in August 1862, *Leslie's* published an engraving of the battle of Willis' Church in the Seven Days campaign. Sneden clipped this article for his scrapbook and appended a note claiming it was based on one of his drawings, but the newspaper caption attributes it only to an unidentified Union soldier. From time to time Sneden mentions in his memoir that he sent drawings to *Leslie's* or its main competitor, *Harper's*. Through the thousands of engravings that appeared in these two weekly newspapers, the Northern public formed a visual image of the war. The main iconographic study is Mark E. Neely, Jr., and Harold Holzer, *Mine Eyes Have Seen the Glory: The Civil War in Art* (New York, 1993).

Among printed primary sources, the most significant was, of course, the monumental War Department publication *The War of the Rebellion: A Compilation of the Official Records of the Union and Confederate Armies* (Washington, D.C., 1880–1901). Other important manuscript sources examined include the diary of General Samuel P. Heintzelman (Library of Congress), the papers of Howell Cobb (University of Georgia), the papers of Dr. Isaiah H. White (Duke University), the Charles Maxwell Colvin diary (Chicago Historical Society), the records of the 40th New York Regiment and the Grand Army of the Republic (New York State Archives), and Civil War pension and service records (National Archives).

Editorial Method

The original manuscript of Robert K. Sneden's sprawling memoir runs to thousands of pages. He compiled this massive account over a period of more than a decade, from the late 1870s through the 1880s and possibly into the early 1890s. *Eye of the Storm* presents less than a third of the original text and reproduces about a tenth of the watercolors. These proportions, however, actually represent a much larger part of Sneden's most important work—both art and narrative—than they at first suggest. Sneden frequently repeated himself, both in the subject of his watercolors and in relating stories in the memoir. We have not included more than one watercolor of the same subject (for example, only one plan of Andersonville among the half-dozen or so he sketched), and we have omitted the repetition in his narrative.

More important, the reader should keep in mind that Sneden wrote a combination of memoir and overview of the whole war. We have omitted all of the latter passages, which Sneden based on secondary sources and in any case deal with places and events he did not observe firsthand. For example, he wrote an aside of more than a hundred pages on the battle of Gettysburg, which took place while he was in Washington, D.C. *Eye of the Storm* is limited to Sneden's firsthand experiences, based on his diary.

Our editorial method can be summed up thus: we modernized some of Sneden's text but still retained much of its original flavor and style. This book does not attempt to present a literal rendering of his original manuscript, filled as it is with erratic punctuation, inconsistent abbreviations, nonexistent paragraphing, confusing marginal notes, and elaborate, artistic running heads. At least his penmanship was consistently clear and regular throughout—a happy circumstance for transcribers—and his excellent spelling reflects a solid educational background. Nevertheless, numerous elements of his style are impossible to render in published form and stand in the way of the reader's comprehension. Readers interested in seeing the complete work may examine photocopies of each original page in the reading room of the Virginia Historical Society in Richmond. What follows is a list of the main ways our transcription altered his original text.

Sneden wrote his memoir in the form of a diary because he based it on original diaries and notes written during the war and expanded afterward. We have kept that format but have standardized each "diary" entry to give the month, day, and year in a consistent manner and to begin the narrative following each date as a new paragraph, something Sneden did not always do. Because Sneden did not employ indenting, either at the beginning of a daily entry or within it, we have introduced paragraph breaks to relieve his long blocks of text. Similarly, we have imposed on his manuscript the nine chapter divisions that we believe represent the major episodes or turning points of his wartime career.

Military titles are spelled out rather than abbreviated ("general" not "genl"), as are many other words that Sneden commonly but erratically truncated. We have standardized certain frequently repeated terms that he spelled in many ways (for example, "headquarters," instead of "head quarters" or "head qrs" or "hd qrs"). Sneden liked to use arabic numbers and ampersands in his text; these have been written out where appropriate. If we could determine the full name of an individual mentioned for the first time in the text, we have added any missing elements in brackets (for example, "[John] Sedgwick").

Ellipsis points indicate omitted text. We have silently corrected Sneden's occasional misspellings. Perhaps Sneden's most erratic usage is capitalization. He employed it in the same way he did his quirky underlining—to give most pages in the memoir an extravagant and distinctive design appeal. (He often went back and used a rose, crimson, or purple pencil or watercolor to underline and highlight certain words.) Because we have modernized the capitalization and omitted the colorful underlining, the text in *Eye of the Storm* is less visually flamboyant than the original—but, we hope, easier to follow.

Because Sneden painted his watercolors on pages considerably larger than those of this book, most of the art required reduction in size and cropping of the broad expanse of sky that is typical of his scenes. The picture legends and identifying labels are his own words.

The reader should realize that nothing we have done alters either the facts or the sentiments expressed in Sneden's diary/memoir in any way. The book that you hold in front of you allows the most important aspects of Sneden's writing to shine through—his powers of description and his skill as a teller of compelling firsthand stories about the greatest conflict in American history.

Acknowledgments

Eye of the Storm benefited from the kindness, advice, and assistance of many people. We wish to thank them all, one in particular, Dr. James C. Kelly, assistant director for museums at the Virginia Historical Society. When the Robert Sneden watercolor scrapbooks first came to his attention, he immediately recognized their importance and campaigned for the Historical Society to acquire them. Once it did, he began to investigate this exceedingly obscure artist. We knew little about Sneden beyond fragments in his military service record and nothing at all about him before or after the war. That lack of information did not deter Jim. After some false starts and disappointing leads, his diligence paid off in a spectacular way, for he discovered Sneden's huge memoir of several thousand pages illustrated by hundreds more watercolors. Among the many links in the long chain of events that led to this publication, then, Jim Kelly is the crucial one for bringing the two halves of this singular body of Civil War soldier art together again.

Two people helped Jim in his detective work with vital bits of information. The first was art historian David Meschutt, who wondered whether Robert Sneden might have been connected in some way with Sneden's Landing, New York. The second was Alice Munro Haagensen, a historian and genealogist familiar with that locality. She made the connection for Jim between Sneden's Landing and the artist, and she put him on the trail of the memoir.

Of course, discovering Sneden's lost artwork and recollections was not enough. Without the financial resources to acquire and conserve these artifacts, our story would be at an end. And that is where we would be if it were not for generous contributions from Mr. and Mrs. Floyd D. Gottwald, Jr., of Richmond. They came forward at a crucial moment and enabled the Society to purchase both Sneden collections—both the watercolor scrapbooks and the illustrated memoir. Without their gifts, we could never have hoped to acquire either collection, and this book could never have appeared. It has been our great good fortune to have such splendid patrons willing to come forward and support the Society. We cannot thank them enough and are only too happy to dedicate *Eye of the Storm* to them as a small expression of our esteem for their willingness to help so generously.

Ed Crews, who wrote two articles in *Colonial Williamsburg* magazine on the Sneden collection, first encouraged us to think expansively about the kind of publication that would best showcase these remarkable Civil War artifacts. Of all the members of the Virginia Historical Society who read about Sneden in our own newsletter, Alice Everett without question played the most crucial role. She thought her friend, New York literary agent Julian Bach of IMG Literary, might have an interest in Sneden and sent him the newsletter. She guessed right. Like Ed Crews, Julian also encouraged us to think expansively. We are very grateful for his encouragement and his wonderful guidance as our agent. Julian worked the legendary magic for which he is known in the publishing world and helped us secure a contract with The Free Press. His associate, Carolyn Krupp, ably seconded him in the process and eventually succeeded him as our agent on his retirement. Since then she and Sophia Seidner, also of IMG Literary, have continued to offer sage advice. Our attorneys, Hugh White and Steve Demm, gave us the kind of wise counsel that every lawyer's client dreams of.

Bruce Nichols, our editor at The Free Press, came to the Virginia Historical Society to inspect the Sneden watercolors and manuscripts before he committed his company to bid on the contract. He left entirely energized by what he saw. Since the summer of 1998, Bruce and his assistant, Dan Freedberg, have generously invested their time and advice so that as a team we all could make *Eye of the Storm* the best publication possible. Loretta Denner, Fred Chase, and Kim Llewellyn have been exceptionally able producers of copyediting and design. We are very grateful to them indeed.

Many people at the Virginia Historical Society have contributed to this book. At times it seemed like the whole staff was working on Sneden. For helping with conservation, transcription, editing, proofreading, photography, and general research, we especially thank the following Historical Society employees and volunteers: Libby Anderson, Sara B. Bearss, Carol Betsch, Melanie Christian, Giles Cromwell, AnnMarie Price, Kelly Henderson Hayes, Crista LaPrade, Michelle McClintick, Frances S. Pollard, William R. Rasmussen, Joanna Riedel, Doug Rodman, Janet Schwarz, Jacquelyn M. Shopland, and Mary Studt.

The quality of the images in this book is the result of splendid work on the part of two people in particular. Ron Jennings produced beautiful photographic images of the original art, and Stacy Rusch shepherded a complex conservation project to a successful conclusion. Throughout the process of putting this complicated story together, we relied heavily on Graham T. Dozier to check both Sneden's account and our interpretation of it.

We would also like to thank the following institutions and individuals: Alan C. Aimone at the United States Military Academy Library; Mary Ellen Brooks at the University of Georgia Special Collections Library; Charles Brownell of Virginia Commonwealth University; Linda Davison-Landymore at King's Edgehill School, Windsor, Nova Scotia; William R. Erwin, Jr., at the Rare Book, Manuscript, and Special Collections Library, Duke University; Dale Floyd at the National Park Service; Betsy Gotbaum at the New York Historical Society; Richard Hart at the Greenwich, Connecticut, Library; Philip L. Hartling at the Public Archives of Nova Scotia; Mike Musick at the National Archives; Shawn Purcell at the New York State Library; John V. Quarstein at the Virginia War Museum; Eric Reinert at Andersonville National Historic Site; Susan Richardson at the Historical Society of the Town of Greenwich, Connecticut; Emily Todd for research at the Chicago Historical Society; Benjamin H. Trask at the Mariners' Museum, Newport News, Virginia; and Pat Wardell, editor of the *Sneden/Snethen Family Newsletter.*

Editing Sneden's memoir on top of full-time jobs has put us deeply in debt to colleagues and friends for their help and indulgence. Charles Bryan thanks Betty and Battle Haslam for kindly allowing him the use of their lake house in South Carolina to work on Sneden in solitude. He also thanks his wife, Cammy, who became very well acquainted with Private Sneden. In addition to serving as an able research assistant, including slogging through numerous reels of microfilm and New York census records, she spent long hours as a volunteer cataloguing and renumbering the Sneden drawings. Charles Bryan also extends his appreciation to his board of trustees for generously granting him a three-month sabbatical to work on this project and be a practicing historian again.

Nelson Lankford hopes readers of the *Virginia Magazine of History and Biography* will forgive him for allowing Sneden temporarily to divert his attention from his regular editorial duties at the journal. He thanks his wife, Judy, for her enthusiasm and support for the Sneden story and, even more important, for her sense of proportion: she reminded him from time to time that the world did not, contrary to what he sometimes thought, revolve around Sneden.

Both of us thank the trustees and members of the Virginia Historical Society for the chance to make the work of this obscure Union private better known. Robert Sneden spent much of his long life after his release from prison obsessed with recording his experiences in words and watercolors. He saw only a few of his paintings appear in print, and those were in the pale, derivative form of engravings. His giant narrative remained unpublished. We hope he would be pleased with *Eye of the Storm.*

Charles F. Bryan, Jr.
Nelson D. Lankford
Virginia Historical Society
November 1999

Index

Index

Oxford School *Shakespeare*

the Merchant of Venice

edited by
Roma Gill, OBE
M.A. *Cantab.*, B. Litt. *Oxon*

OXFORD
UNIVERSITY PRESS

OXFORD
UNIVERSITY PRESS

Great Clarendon Street, Oxford OX2 6DP

Oxford University Press is a department of the University of Oxford. It furthers the University's objective of excellence in research, scholarship, and education by publishing worldwide in

Oxford New York

Auckland Cape Town Dar es Salaam Hong Kong Karachi Kuala Lumpur Madrid Melbourne Mexico City Nairobi New Delhi Shanghai Taipei Toronto

With offices in

Argentina Austria Brazil Chile Czech Republic France Greece Guatemala Hungary Italy Japan Poland Portugal Singapore South Korea Switzerland Thailand Turkey Ukraine Vietnam

Oxford is a registered trade mark of Oxford University Press in the UK and in certain other countries

First published 1979; second edition published 1979; first revised edition published 1992; third revised edition published 2006.

Reprinted in this new edition 2010

British Library Cataloguing in Publication

Data available

ISBN 978 0 19 832867 4

20 19 18 17 16 15 14

Printed in Italy by L.E.G.O. SpA.

The Publisher would like to thank the following for permission to reproduce photographs:

Donald Cooper (Photostage): pp. vii, xviii, 8, 17, 22, 36, 74, 78, 84, 88, 105. Richard Kalina: pp 110. Capital Pictures: pp xxvii.

Cover artwork by Silke Bachmann
Illustrations by Alexy Pendle

Oxford School Shakespeare
edited by Roma Gill

Macbeth
Much Ado About Nothing
Henry V
Romeo & Juliet
A Midsummer Night's Dream
Twelfth Night
Hamlet
The Merchant of Venice
Othello
Julius Caesar
The Tempest
The Taming of the Shrew
King Lear
As You Like It
Antony and Cleopatra
Measure for Measure
Henry IV Part I
The Winter's Tale
Coriolanus
Love's Labour's Lost

Contents

Introduction

About the Play

A pound of flesh. You may know the expression, meaning 'the full and exact repayment of some debt or duty'. It's part of the English language, and the common property of people all over the world who have never heard of *The Merchant of Venice.* But this is where it began.

Money

The play is all about money – and as soon as you say that word, clichés come tumbling out. Money is not the most important thing in life, won't bring you happiness, can't buy me love, and is the root of all evil (a common misquotation[1]). For Portia, who has lots of it, wealth is almost an embarrassment and certainly an obstacle when it comes to finding a husband. For Shylock (who loses his daughter but complains more loudly about the ducats – Venetian gold coins – that she has stolen from him), money still means less than the opportunity to be revenged on his rival. And at the beginning of the play Antonio, a prince among Venetian merchants and a successful dealer in sumptuous luxury goods, is unspeakably and unaccountably depressed. Only Bassanio, broke and reckless, is reasonably cheerful: he has a plan, and just needs funding. His crazy idea – shoot another arrow in the direction of the one you've lost and you'll find both – triggers the action, and sets both of the play's main plots in motion.

Bassanio can be sure of a loan from his affectionate friend Antonio, but Antonio's money is all tied up in his business ventures, and so he turns to Shylock, a professional moneylender, who demands an unusual security for the loan – a pound of Antonio's flesh.

Shylock the Jew

Shylock is a Jew, a member of a race feared and despised by the Elizabethans for reasons that are complex and historical, and only partly religious. The Jews were hated for their biblical role in the

[1] 'for *the love of money* is the root of all evil', 1 Timothy 6:10.

crucifixion of Jesus and European countries from the twelfth century onwards had used this as a pretext for expelling them from their shores. Those who remained were often forbidden to own property, or to engage in any of the professions, and were thereby forced into the business of usury – lending money for profit. And mercantile societies need moneylenders. Some Jews prospered, and in England their success intensified the distrust of the native English, although Queen Elizabeth numbered a Jewish woman among her ladies-in-waiting, and even, for a time, had a Jewish doctor as her private physician – although Dr Lopez was eventually (in 1594) charged with trying to poison her, and executed.

All through the play we are aware of anti-Semitic prejudice in many of the characters, but Shakespeare himself takes no sides. His plot, based on a narrative fiction, demanded a Jewish villain – but Shakespeare understood human suffering and that Jews had for centuries been subject to humiliating discrimination, and he allows Shylock to speak for all persecuted minorities:

> Hath not a Jew eyes? Hath not a Jew hands, organs, dimensions, senses, affections, passions? Fed with the same food, hurt with the same weapons, subject to the same diseases, healed by the same means, warmed and cooled by the same winter and summer as a Christian is? If you prick us, do we not bleed?

If we can appreciate this argument, then it is hard not to agree with its logical extension –

> And if you wrong us, shall we not revenge?

Antonio is in serious danger when the underdog (Shylock) tries to seize his opportunity for triumph – but this is a comedy, and the good fairy comes to his rescue in the person of Portia, the first of Shakespeare's truly great female roles.

A woman's role

Most modern girls would find Portia's situation intolerable: a wealthy heiress, she has to obey the wishes of her dead father and agree to the test he has arranged to choose a husband for her – though not without showing a shadow of resentment that 'the will of a living daughter [should be] curbed by the will of a dead father'. She can only act, however, as every daughter of that time, never questioning a man's right to the ownership of all his wife's possessions, and resigning herself happily into the protection of Bassanio – who has won the lottery:

But now, I was the lord
Of this fair mansion, master of my servants,
Queen o'er myself; and even now, but now,
This house, these servants, and this same myself
Are yours, my lord's.

Only for the past hundred years or so has a woman in England been allowed to keep her own property after marriage – and sexual discrimination is still felt and practised even today.

A modern tragedy

The *Merchant of Venice* deals with topics and social issues that belong as much, or even more, to the twenty-first century as they did to Shakespeare's own day – fathers and daughters, racial discrimination, colour prejudice, love and friendship. And to all of these there is some financial aspect. Altered attitudes in the twentieth century shifted the emphasis of Shakespeare's play so that it nearly became the *tragedy* of 'The Jew of Venice' (always an alternative title), but the magic of the final Act is powerful. The serious issues and complex figures of the trial scene dissolve into the moonlit serenity of Belmont, and laughter returns the characters and the audience to the real world with Gratiano's final bawdy joke.

Leading Characters in the Play

Antonio The merchant of the play's title. He is a good and generous man, who promises to pay Shylock the money borrowed by Bassanio or else allow Shylock to cut off a pound of his flesh. His part in the play is rather a passive one, and he reveals his character mainly in his generosity to his friend and in his hatred of the Jew.

Bassanio A young man who has already spent all his own money and now hopes to restore his fortunes by marrying an heiress. He needs to borrow money so that he can make a fine display when he courts Portia, and it is for his sake that Antonio enters into the bond with Shylock. Bassanio shows good judgement in his choice of caskets, and wins Portia for his wife.

Gratiano A young man with a reputation for wild behaviour. He accompanies Bassanio to Belmont, and wins the love of Portia's lady-in-waiting, Nerissa.

Lorenzo He is in love with Jessica, Shylock's daughter, and plans to steal her from her father's house.

Portia The most important character in the play. She is an heiress, and is in love with Bassanio; but her father has devised a test involving three caskets, and Portia must marry the man who chooses the right casket. Portia is intelligent as well as beautiful; dressed as a lawyer she goes to Venice and saves Antonio from being killed by Shylock. Her home is Belmont, and the peace and harmony here contrast with the tense business world of Venice.

Nerissa Portia's lady-in-waiting, who falls in love with Gratiano. When Portia goes to Venice as a lawyer, Nerissa accompanies her, dressed as a lawyer's clerk.

Shylock A money lender, who is hated for his greed and because he is Jewish. He is Antonio's enemy, and when Bassanio's money is not repaid he demands the pound of flesh that Antonio promised as a forfeit.

Jessica Shylock's daughter; she disguises herself as a boy in order to run away from her father's house, where she is unhappy. She is in love with Lorenzo, a Christian.

Lancelot Gobbo The comedian of the play. He is at first Shylock's servant, then goes to work for Bassanio. His clowning often takes the form of misusing the English language; it is sometimes a welcome break from the tense or romantic scenes.

Synopsis

Act 1

Scene 1 Antonio is very depressed; he is willing to fund Bassanio's expedition to Belmont, but must try to borrow money from Shylock to do so.

Scene 2 Portia longs to find a husband, but all her suitors must submit to a test arranged by her father before his death.

Scene 3 Shylock agrees to lend money to Antonio – but he demands an unusual bond.

Act 2

Scene 1 Portia interviews a new suitor, the Prince of Morocco, and explains the terms of her father's will.

Scene 2 Lancelot Gobbo wants to leave Shylock, his master, and find employment with Bassanio, who is preparing for his trip to Belmont.

Scene 3 Lancelot says goodbye to Jessica, Shylock's daughter, who gives him a letter for Lorenzo, the Christian man she is in love with.

Scene 4 Lorenzo is planning some late-night entertainment when Lancelot brings Jessica's letter.

Scene 5 Shylock leaves Jessica in charge of his house.

Scene 6 Lorenzo and his friends rescue Jessica from her father's house.

Scene 7 The Prince of Morocco examines the caskets and makes his choice.

Scene 8 Salarino and Solanio gossip about the news: Lorenzo and Jessica are missing, Shylock has been robbed, and Antonio is in trouble.

Scene 9 Another suitor makes his choice – and Portia learns that Bassanio is coming to Belmont.

ACT 3

SCENE 1 Trouble for Antonio: Shylock rejoices in his power over the merchant – and laments the loss of his daughter.

SCENE 2 Bassanio makes his choice of caskets, winning Portia for his wife. Nerissa agrees to marry Gratiano, and both marriage contracts are sealed with rings. Lorenzo and Jessica arrive in Belmont, bringing a letter from Antonio.

SCENE 3 Antonio has been arrested and Shylock threatens him.

SCENE 4 Portia and Nerissa plan a visit to Venice.

SCENE 5 Lancelot teases Jessica.

ACT 4

SCENE 1 The trial. Antonio is prepared to die when Shylock refuses to show mercy, but Portia, disguised as a young lawyer, tricks Shylock out of his bond and asks Bassanio for his ring as a reward.

SCENE 2 Portia gets Bassanio's ring – and Nerissa plans to get her own from Gratiano.

ACT 5

SCENE 1 Lorenzo teases Jessica as they wait in the moonlight. Portia and Nerissa return from Venice, followed by Bassanio and Gratiano – who are embarrassed when their wives demand to see the rings. All is explained, and Portia has good news for Antonio.

The Merchant of Venice: Commentary

The action of the play takes place in Venice and in Belmont. Belmont is imaginary, but Venice is real. The city is located on the sea coast in the north of Italy, and is in fact built over a lagoon. Its main streets are canals, and the only vehicles are boats. In the sixteenth century, Venice was the centre for international trade, importing goods from all corners of the earth, and exporting them in the same way. We are told that Antonio, the greatest of the merchants, is waiting for his ships to return

> From Tripolis, from Mexico, and England,
> From Lisbon, Barbary, and India. (3, 2, 266–7)

To be successful, a merchant had to invest his money wisely – and have luck on his side. Trading by sea was hazardous, and a sudden storm, or unseen rocks, could easily wreck a ship and drown the merchant's hopes along with the cargo.

Act 1

Scene 1 When his friends see that Antonio is depressed, they immediately think that he is worried about his ships at sea. They are sympathetic, and Solanio does his best to make light of the situation by exaggerating his fears to make his friend smile. But Antonio is sad for some other reason, and when we meet his dearest friend, Bassanio, we begin to guess at this reason. Bassanio is a carefree young man, who cheerfully admits that he has spent all of his own money and a good deal of Antonio's. However, Bassanio now has a scheme for increasing his wealth. Before he gives any details, he explains his theory: a lost arrow (he says) can often be found by shooting another arrow in the same direction, and watching carefully to see where it falls. The theory is, as Bassanio acknowledges, a 'childhood proof'; he believed it when he was a schoolboy, and now he wants to put it to the test again, spending more money in the hope of winning back what he has lost. This is not a very sensible, or responsible, way to act, but Bassanio emphasizes his youth and innocence. Perhaps he hopes that Antonio will treat him as though he were a child, and ignore the irresponsibility of his demand for more money to spend.

Bassanio next tells Antonio of an heiress, who has already given him some unspoken encouragement. Her name is Portia, and Bassanio claims to have fallen in love with her. He may be speaking the truth, but it is clear that the lady's wealth is a very attractive feature for him. Antonio promises to help him, but all the money he has is tied up in his own business ventures. Still, his 'credit' is good, and Bassanio can borrow all the ducats he needs to present himself to Portia as an eligible suitor, giving Antonio's name as security – that is, promising that Antonio will repay the debt if he himself is unable to do so.

Our feelings towards Bassanio at the end of this scene cannot be very warm, despite his youthful optimism. He has wasted a lot of money, both his own and his friend's. It seems that he wants to marry Portia not just for love, but also for her money. But he himself, perhaps unconsciously, shows what we should feel about him when he explains that his youth has been 'something too prodigal'. Repeated phrases throughout the play compare Bassanio with the Prodigal Son of Christ's parable (St Luke 15:11–32), who spent all his inheritance in 'riotous living'. When he was penniless and starving, he went repentantly back to his father's house, where he was welcomed with rejoicing. Bassanio has been 'prodigal'; now he asks for a chance to redeem himself.

Like the Prodigal Son's father, Antonio has shown the loving and forgiving generosity of his nature, but he remains a mysterious character. Early in the scene he tells Gratiano that he thinks of the world as 'A stage where every man must play a part, / And mine a sad one'. It is his changing relationship with Bassanio that causes his melancholy. Some Elizabethans thought – as the Greeks and Romans did – that the friendship between two men was a more spiritual bond, and should be more highly esteemed, than the love between a man and a woman. Knowing that Bassanio is interested in a lady (see lines 119–21), Antonio may be secretly grieving for the inevitable end to a friendship.

SCENE 2 From the hearty, but anxious, masculine world of Venice, we move to the feminine peace of Belmont. Even here there is anxiety, as Portia's opening sigh indicates. It is now Nerissa who tries to cheer Portia, but she cannot take her mistress's mind off the situation where she is surrounded by suitors and yet 'cannot choose one, nor refuse none'. Shakespeare has to communicate to his audience a lot of information about the test that Portia's father devised for the men who wish to marry her. The information is given gradually, in five separate scenes, so that we seem to discover the facts just as the suitors do. For the moment, we are just told that each candidate must make a choice between three caskets.

Nerissa explains why Portia must obey this somewhat ridiculous order when she says that 'holy men at their death have good inspirations'. Proverbially, at this time, it was believed that a good man would be divinely inspired, and might even speak prophetically, when he was close to death. To disobey or disregard such a prophecy was considered almost sacrilege.

The two young women amuse themselves by gossiping about the suitors who have already assembled at Belmont. Although Portia and Nerissa are Italian, they share a sense of humour which is undoubtedly English. As they laugh about each man's peculiarities, we can learn something of what the Elizabethans thought of their continental neighbours – and also of how they could laugh at themselves. The 'young baron of England' is a caricature of the Englishman abroad, in the twenty-first century as well as in the sixteenth: the English have never been good at speaking foreign languages! Nor is there a 'national dress' for England, such as many other countries possess; the English were always content (it seems) to imitate the costumes of other countries. The joke about the Scottish lord would have a topical significance for Shakespeare's audience. At this time England and Scotland were separate kingdoms, and in their frequent quarrels the French always promised to aid the Scots (but rarely kept their promises).

We are never allowed to see this 'parcel of wooers', for Nerissa tells Portia that they have all decided to return home, not trying their luck with the caskets. There is no doubt that Portia is glad they are leaving. Nerissa reminds her of a young Venetian whom Portia met whilst her father was alive, and the speed with which Portia recalls Bassanio's name is enough to tell us that she remembers him with pleasure. Bassanio is described by Nerissa as 'a scholar and a soldier'. These qualities made up the ideal courtier in Elizabethan eyes, and the description may help to prepare us for a Bassanio who is rather different from the one we left in Venice.

Portia's enthusiasm dies away, and her weary resignation returns, when she is told that a new suitor is approaching Belmont. It is the Prince of Morocco, and the title arouses her prejudice as she goes inside to prepare for his arrival.

SCENE 3 Meanwhile, in Venice, Bassanio has found a usurer who can lend the money he needs. Shylock is very cautious, repeating each of Bassanio's demands to make sure that they are perfectly understood. His deliberation makes Bassanio nervous, and he shows irritation when Shylock says that 'Antonio is a good man'. The word 'good' has different implications: Bassanio thinks that it refers to Antonio's character, and he is angry that such a man as Shylock should presume to judge his friend. Shylock, having succeeded in annoying Bassanio, hastens to explain that by 'good' he meant only 'sufficient' – financially sound. The two disagree again over the interpretation of 'assur'd', by which Bassanio means that Shylock may trust Antonio; Shylock says that he will indeed be 'assur'd', meaning that he will take all precautions to protect himself and his money.

Bassanio's polite invitation to dinner is refused by Shylock in words that introduce the theme of racial hatred: he thinks he would be asked 'to smell pork', a meat forbidden to Jews by their religion. Shylock perhaps speaks these words '*aside*', not talking directly to Bassanio but uttering his thoughts aloud for the audience alone to hear them, just as only the audience hears the soliloquy in which Shylock reveals his attitude to Antonio. Religious feeling has some part to play in this attitude, but a minor one compared with the hostility he bears towards a business rival.

We learn that Antonio disapproves morally of lending money for interest (and it is a mark of his affection for Bassanio that he is prepared now to break his own rules). Shylock justifies his activities by telling the story of Jacob from the Old Testament (Genesis 30:31–43). Jacob was angry with Laban, his uncle, and tried to outwit him, using his skill as a shepherd. He believed that the ewes, seeing the striped twigs in front of them when they conceived, would give birth to striped or spotted lambs, which Laban had agreed should become Jacob's wages. This indeed happened, but whereas Shylock applauds Jacob's cunning, Antonio (and most devout Jews) ascribed the success to the hand of God.

The merchant and the usurer engage in passionate argument. Shylock reveals the cruel insults he has had to suffer from Antonio in the past, but Antonio stands firm in his contempt for the Jew. He refuses to borrow the money as a friend, but urges Shylock, with words that he will regret, to

> lend it rather to thine enemy,
> Who if he break, thou may'st with better face
> Exact the penalty.

Shylock proposes 'a merry sport' which Antonio, surprisingly, is willing to accept. He agrees to the forfeit that Shylock suggests – 'an equal pound of your fair flesh' – to be given if the money cannot be properly repaid.

The words 'kind' and 'kindness' are repeated several times at the end of this scene. They have a surface meaning – 'generous' and 'generosity' – which Antonio accepts, and an ironic double meaning. If Shylock 'grows kind' in this second sense, he will become even more like himself, true to his nature. And we have already, in his soliloquy, seen what this is.

Act 2

Scene 1 Prejudice is the subject of the short episode in Belmont, where we see Portia's reception of the Prince of Morocco. The prince's appearance shows that he is an exotic figure: the stage direction, probably written by Shakespeare himself, describes him as 'a tawny [brown] Moor, all in white'. His first speech reinforces our sense that he is excitingly different from the Europeans that we have seen so far, but it does not change Portia's mind. She is polite, but we understand, better than Morocco can, what she means when she tells him that, in her eyes, he is 'as fair / As any comer I have look'd on yet'. We have heard what Portia thought of her other suitors. The Prince's reply to this ambiguous remark does not encourage our good opinion of him. He boasts of his own courage and achievements in a very exaggerated language, and so loses some of our sympathy.

We are given a new piece of information concerning the casket test. The men who choose wrongly must never again think of marrying. It is now clear why the earlier suitors left Belmont without trying their luck; Morocco, however, is not deterred, and prepares to make his choice.

Whilst Morocco is taking his oath in the 'temple' – many great houses at this time had their own private chapels – Shakespeare returns us to Venice. The next five scenes will bring Bassanio from Venice to Belmont, and develop the romance of the plot through the introduction of Jessica, Shylock's daughter. But first, Shakespeare must create a role for the leading comic actor in his dramatic company – the part of Lancelot Gobbo, Shylock's servant.

Scene 2 Comedy scenes such as this are the most difficult and unrewarding to read; they need to be performed, so that the actor can introduce the visual effects that the lines demand. When Lancelot pretends to be torn between his conscience and the devil, he might (for instance) jump to the left when the devil is speaking – because devils traditionally appeared on the left – and to the right when 'conscience' replies. There could be humour in the difference between Lancelot's appearance (as the miserly Shylock's servant he would not be well dressed) and his grand manner of speech to the old man; this would emphasize the comedy of the 'mistaken identity' situation. When Old Gobbo feels his son's head and comments on his 'beard', it is obvious from Lancelot's reply that he has got hold of the hair tied at the back of his neck; and if Lancelot passes his father's hand across his fingers, implying that they are his ribs ('You may tell every finger I have with my ribs'), the comedy will increase with the old man's confusion.

The English language is a very complicated one, and even English people make mistakes when they speak it. There are many words that sound grand – but sometimes those who use them do not understand their meanings, or else confuse one word with another that sounds similar. This is especially likely to happen when the speakers are trying to create a good impression of themselves. Lancelot and his father are doing this when they address Bassanio. They are conscious that Bassanio is a gentleman, whilst they are only peasants, and they try to use what they think is the proper language of gentlemen. Even in the twenty-first century, when class distinctions are much less clearly marked than they were in the sixteenth, the writers of television comedy still find subjects for laughter in our linguistic snobbishness. Lorenzo's comment is valid today: 'How every fool can play upon the word' (Act 3, Scene 5, line 38).

Bassanio is in a good temper, and responds well to Lancelot's fooling; he agrees to employ him and give him 'a livery / More guarded than his fellows'. A 'guarded' uniform – one decorated with yellow braid – was often worn by the professional fool in a gentleman's household; perhaps this is the function that Bassanio intends for Lancelot when he becomes 'The follower of so poor a gentleman'.

Even though he admits he is poor, Bassanio is already behaving with his former extravagance now that he has got Shylock's money. He is planning to give a party before he leaves Venice. However, he shows a more sedate side of his character when Gratiano asks to accompany him to Belmont. Gratiano turns Bassanio's solemn warning into comedy. He promises to behave in a way that is very sober, but at the same time quite ridiculous, and he probably accompanies his speech with exaggerated gestures.

SCENE 3

When Jessica gives Lancelot the letter for Lorenzo, the short scene takes the plot a stride further – and also serves to increase our dislike for Shylock. We learn that his 'house is hell', and that Jessica is 'asham'd to be [her] father's child', although she recognizes that it is a 'heinous sin' for a daughter to have such feelings.

SCENE 4 The letter is delivered to Lorenzo as he and his friends are discussing their costumes for Bassanio's party. It was quite usual, in Shakespeare's time, for a small band of the guests at a grand feast to disguise themselves in elaborate costumes and entertain the other guests with a masque – a performance with singing and dancing. Page-boys carried torches for the masquers, and Lorenzo suddenly realizes how he can steal Jessica away from her father's house: she can be disguised as his page.

SCENE 5 There can scarcely be a greater contrast than that between the lively young men planning their evening's entertainment, and the surly Shylock. He takes no pleasure in the feast, but has decided to 'go in hate, to feed upon / The prodigal Christian' (yet another comparison of Bassanio with the Prodigal Son). Shylock is determined to do all he can to ruin Bassanio, and he even considers that Lancelot's change of employer might 'help to waste / His borrow'd purse'.

SCENE 6 Gratiano's reference to the 'penthouse' under which they are standing is one of many remarks in Elizabethan drama that help us to reconstruct, in imagination, the kind of stage that Shakespeare was writing for. It seems that there was always a balcony, which allowed 'split-level' acting. In this scene the young men assemble on the main stage, underneath the 'penthouse' formed by the balcony on which Jessica appears, dressed as a boy. She is shy, because in Elizabethan times women *never* wore men's clothes. Her embarrassment is expressed with great delicacy, and it is easy to forget that Shakespeare and his contemporaries would probably have been a little amused by the situation. In many plays of this period the female characters put on masculine clothing, and a gentle comedy arises out of the fact that female characters were always played by boy actors: the boys dress up as girls, and then the 'girls' turn into boys.

Waiting for Jessica has made the masquers late for the feast, and now Antonio comes in search of Gratiano. The wind has changed, and it is time to set sail for Belmont.

SCENE 7 Whilst all the activity of Jessica's elopement has been taking place in Venice, the Prince of Morocco at Belmont has dined, and sworn an oath never to look for a wife if he fails the casket test. At last we see the caskets that we have heard so much about. Each one bears an inscription, which Morocco reads aloud. The gold and silver caskets make promises, but the leaden one is menacing. Morocco refuses to be threatened, and passes to the silver casket, which assures him that he

'shall get as much as he deserves'. We heard in Act 2, Scene 1 that he has a good opinion of himself, and he is naturally tempted to choose silver. The golden casket, however, offers 'what many men desire', and Morocco decides that this refers to Portia, because 'all the world desires her'. It would be an insult to Portia (he concludes) to associate her with lead, or even with silver; so he opens the golden casket.

The casket contains a skull, the emblem of death – which indeed many unhappy men do desire. Shocked and saddened, the Prince of Morocco departs immediately.

SCENE 8 In Venice, Shylock has discovered that his daughter is missing – and she has taken a lot of his money with her. Solanio gives a comical account of the Jew's confusion, when Shylock apparently did not know which loss to lament more. It is important that we do not *see* Shylock here, because his distress might create too much sympathy for him. Instead, we join Salarino and Solanio in their laughter.

But not everything in this scene is comic: there is bad news for Antonio. A ship has been wrecked in the English Channel, and it may well be his. The conversation becomes sober, as the two friends think of Antonio's generosity – 'A kinder gentleman treads not the earth' – and remind us of his great affection for Bassanio: 'I think he only loves the world for him'.

SCENE 9 Yet another suitor, the Prince of Arragon, has arrived at Belmont; he repeats the three promises that he has sworn to keep, and goes to make his choice of the three caskets. Like the Prince of Morocco, he reads the inscriptions, and speaks his thoughts aloud. The Prince of Arragon is excessively conscious of his social position, and insists that he is different from other men: he will not 'jump with common spirits', and look in the golden casket for 'what many men desire'. He is attracted by the promise of the silver casket: 'Who chooseth me shall get as much as he deserves'. For a time he meditates on the subject of nobility and merit, deploring the fact that 'low peasantry' (people of humble birth) can be found among noblemen – 'the true seed of honour'. Having convinced *himself* that he deserves to win Portia, he opens the silver casket. We are not surprised that this is the wrong choice, for Arragon has convinced *us* that he is far too conceited – although perhaps he deserves something better than 'the portrait of a blinking idiot'.

As soon as the Prince of Arragon has left, news is brought that another suitor is approaching. He has already made a good impression on Portia's servants with the 'Gifts of rich value' that he has sent to announce his coming; and we recognize the extravagance that is characteristic of Bassanio. Portia and Nerissa are hopeful.

Act 3

SCENE 1 The optimism of Belmont gives place to the darkening atmosphere of Venice. There is still no confirmation that the ship wrecked in the English Channel is indeed Antonio's, but Solanio believes the rumour to be true. Shylock also has heard the report, and his anger over his daughter's flight is forgotten for a moment as he voices his hatred and resentment of Antonio. He has had to suppress his feelings for years, but now they explode violently. His passion increases, and so too does the sympathy of the audience. He appeals to common humanity: 'Hath not a Jew eyes? hath not a Jew hands . . . If you poison us, do we not die?' He becomes almost a hero, and certainly a human being – then suddenly he changes back into a monster: 'And if you wrong us, shall we not revenge?'

Salarino and Solanio are fortunately saved from having to reply to this tirade; they leave Shylock with another Jew, Tubal, who has news of Jessica.

Shylock experiences another confusion of emotions as Tubal imparts various pieces of information in an incoherent manner. Jessica is spending her father's money recklessly, and in exchange for a pet monkey she has given away the ring that was a token of betrothal from her mother to her father. Grief and anger conflict with malicious glee when Shylock hears of Antonio's misfortunes, and it is clear that he will take revenge for the loss of his daughter and his ring when he claims the forfeit from Antonio.

SCENE 2 Portia is happy in Bassanio's company, and she tries to persuade him to stay at Belmont for a few days before making his choice of the caskets. Her happiness is mingled with modesty, as she is too shy to tell Bassanio that she loves him. Bassanio too has fallen in love, but he cannot endure the uncertainty and feels that he must try his luck as soon as possible. Nerissa and the servants stand aside, leaving Portia and Bassanio almost alone on the stage. Music plays, while Portia watches the man she loves as he tries to make the decision that will bring happiness to both of them.

The song that helps to create a magic atmosphere also introduces Bassanio's meditation on appearance and reality. He is speaking only to himself – Portia does not hear him (just as he did not hear her words before the song). The audience, of course, knows which casket Bassanio must choose, because Shakespeare has already shown us the contents of the gold and silver caskets.

Portia is almost overcome with delight when Bassanio selects the 'meagre lead'; and when Bassanio finds 'Fair Portia's counterfeit' in the casket he is ecstatically happy. He praises the picture rapturously, and for a time cannot believe his luck.

A rather more materialistic note is heard in the metaphorical language when Portia wishes to 'stand high in [Bassanio's] *account*', and offers him 'the full *sum*' of herself; it is repeated when Gratiano refers to the '*bargain*' of their faith. But to balance this there is the ritual moment when Portia gives away all that she owns (including 'this same myself') and as a token places a ring on Bassanio's finger. Bassanio accepts the token, and binds himself to Portia:

> when this ring
> Parts from this finger, then parts life from hence.

Gratiano and Nerissa announce their intention of imitating Bassanio and Portia; and the happiness of the moment is complete.

It is now time to change the direction of the scene, and Shakespeare switches the mood with a bawdy joke (in prose).

The arrival of Salerio, Lorenzo, and Jessica is a welcome surprise, but the letter that Salerio has brought from Venice 'steals the colour from Bassanio's cheek'. Things have gone very badly for Antonio: he is ruined. Salerio tells of Shylock's eagerness to claim his bond from Antonio, and Jessica is able to bear witness to her father's fiendish malice: 'he would rather have Antonio's flesh / Than twenty times the value of the sum / That he did owe him'. Portia is more than able to pay back the three thousand ducats, but we can take no comfort from her offer. The situation seems hopeless, and when Antonio's pathetic letter is read aloud it destroys the last remaining scrap of the happiness established in the scene.

SCENE 3 A short scene shows us what the letter described. Antonio, in the custody of a jailer, meets Shylock. The Jew will hear no pleas for mercy, and Antonio knows that it is useless to speak to him. Solanio hopes that the Duke will be able to intervene in the dispute, but Antonio knows the importance of strict justice in the mercantile world of which Venice is the head. This is a subject that will be mentioned at Antonio's trial.

SCENE 4 Lorenzo has been telling Portia about Antonio, and Portia has decided that she and Nerissa will go away for a few days, leaving Belmont in the care of Lorenzo. She sends a servant to her cousin in Padua, asking for some 'notes and garments'. We understand the request for clothes when Portia explains to Nerissa that they are going to dress up as men, and that she herself will imitate all the mannerisms of a brash young man – including the voice that is 'between the change of man and boy'.

Scene 5 The next scene, still at Belmont, does nothing to develop any plot. But it encourages the audience to imagine that enough time has passed to allow Portia and Nerissa to travel from Belmont to Venice; on a practical level, it gives the actors time to change from their female dresses to the male costumes required in the following scene. In addition, it provides an opportunity for the comedian to deliver some more of his word-play jokes in the part of Lancelot Gobbo – who of course accompanied his new master when Bassanio came to Belmont.

Act 4

Scene 1 The trial scene in *The Merchant of Venice* is one of the most famous scenes in English drama. It has given a phrase to the English language: people who have never heard of the play understand what it means to want one's 'pound of flesh'.

The conversation between the Duke and Antonio, before Shylock comes on to the stage, shows the hopeless resignation with which Antonio faces Shylock's wrath. The Duke makes a further plea for mercy, but Shylock is unmoved. He will admit that his hatred for Antonio is irrational and emotional: just as some people hate cats, or the sound of bagpipes, so (he says)

can I give no reason, nor I will not,
More than a lodg'd hate and a certain loathing
I bear Antonio.

Antonio is not intimidated, and shows his contempt for Shylock's 'Jewish heart'. Bassanio offers to repay twice the money that he borrowed, but Shylock will not yield, and reminds the court that the pound of flesh is his by law. If the Duke refuses to grant this, it will appear that 'There is no force in the decrees of Venice'. We remember Antonio's words (Act 3, Scene 3, lines 26–31), and realize that, if the law is not observed, Venice will suffer in its reputation as the centre of international trade.

The Duke has made a final attempt to save Antonio legally. He has asked for the opinion of a famous lawyer, Bellario, and the court waits to hear this man's judgment. Bassanio is optimistic, but the tension of the situation has made Antonio even more resigned to his fate; he almost feels that he deserves to die.

The lawyer's clerk has brought a letter from Bellario, and whilst the Duke reads the letter, Shylock sharpens his knife. Gratiano cannot bear to see this sight, and he begins to abuse Shylock. The Jew appears to be unaffected by his insults, for he knows the strength of his position: 'I stand here for law'.

Bellario is sick, and cannot come to Venice; instead he has sent a legal colleague, 'a young doctor of Rome', who is fully acquainted with the case. The audience recognizes this 'doctor': it is Portia, and her 'clerk' is Nerissa – but, needless to say, the other characters of the play cannot see through the disguise.

Portia upholds Venetian law, but she urges Shylock to show mercy. She describes the 'quality of mercy' as a divine blessing, which benefits both the man who shows mercy and the man who receives it. The petition in the Lord's Prayer, 'forgive us our trespasses', comes to mind when Portia explains how mercy belongs to God; if this were not so, the whole human race would be damned for its sins. But this is Christian doctrine, and Shylock's religion is that of the Old Testament, which emphasizes the importance of the law, just as Shylock does now: 'I crave the law'.

Once again Bassanio offers the money; again Shylock refuses it; and once more we are reminded that a general principle lies beneath this particular instance: any deviation would be

> recorded for a precedent,
> And many an error by the same example
> Will rush into the state.

The statement is harsh, but it is correct. Portia has earned Shylock's praise: 'A Daniel come to judgement'. Daniel was 'a young youth', according to the 'Story of Susannah' in the *Apocrypha*. He was inspired by God to give judgement when the chaste Susannah was accused of adultery by two lascivious 'elders' who had tried to rape her.

Portia continues to win Shylock's approval as she instructs the court about the penalty that Antonio must pay. The knife is sharpened, and the scales are ready; Antonio prepares for death. He speaks a few words of comfort to Bassanio, ending with a wry jest about the debt:

> For if the Jew do cut but deep enough
> I'll pay it instantly with all my heart.

The tension is broken, but only for a moment, when Bassanio and Gratiano refer to their wives. The 'lawyer' and his 'clerk' are amused.

Just when Shylock is ready to cut into Antonio's flesh, Portia stops the proceedings. She reveals to Shylock the single flaw in his carefully worded bond: he is entitled to his pound of flesh, but has made no provision for a single drop of blood.

Gratiano exults over Shylock, repeating ironically all the words of praise that the Jew bestowed on the 'learned judge', and agreeing that he is indeed 'A second Daniel'. Like Portia, Daniel was not expected in the court, and the verdict he gave saved Susannah and condemned her accusers. The comparison is more apt now than it was when Shylock introduced it.

Shylock realizes that he cannot have his pound of flesh, and he tries to take the money that Bassanio is still offering. Now it is Portia's turn to be inflexible, and she insists that Shylock can have 'merely justice, and his bond'. When Shylock proposes to leave the court, Portia calls him back. The law of Venice has a strict penalty that must be paid by any 'alien' – foreigner – who tries to murder a Venetian. Shylock has thus offended, and for this crime his possessions are confiscated and his life is in danger. Antonio, of course, shows his generosity. Half of Shylock's wealth is forfeited to him, but he is willing to renounce his personal share and take the money on loan, keeping it in trust for Lorenzo, 'the gentleman / That lately stole his daughter'. He makes two conditions: firstly, Shylock must become a Christian; and, secondly, he must make a will leaving all that he possesses to Jessica and Lorenzo. Shylock is utterly defeated. He asks for permission to leave the court, and indicates his agreement to Antonio's conditions: 'send the deed after me / And I will sign it'.

It is now the function of Gratiano to swing the mood of the scene and the audience from near-tragedy to an almost light-hearted acceptance of the situation: this is only a play, and we are in England, where twelve 'godfathers' would make a jury.

It is only necessary now to pay the 'lawyer', and then Bassanio can take Antonio home to Belmont, to meet his new wife. The 'lawyer' refuses payment, then suddenly catches sight of a ring on Bassanio's finger, and requests this as a keepsake. It is the ring that Portia gave to Bassanio, telling him that if he should ever part with it for any reason, it would 'presage the ruin of [his] love'. Remembering this, Bassanio refuses; the 'lawyer' departs, apparently angry. Antonio begs Bassanio not to withhold the ring, and Bassanio cannot refuse the friend who risked so much for him.

Scene 2 Gratiano hurries after Portia to give her Bassanio's ring. Nerissa, still disguised as the lawyer's clerk, whispers to Portia that she will use a similar trick to get her own ring from Gratiano. The two girls laugh in anticipation of their husbands' embarrassment when they return to Belmont.

Act 5

Scene 1 Moonlight and music emphasize the tranquillity of Belmont and its contrast with the harsh legal world of Venice. Lorenzo and Jessica are relaxed here, and Jessica's escape from the 'hell' of her father's house seems to be almost as remote in time as the mythological lovers who are recalled by the moonlight. The mood of the scene is saved from being over-romantic when the couple start to tease each other, and when the messengers break in with their news. Harmony is restored, however, when Lorenzo and Jessica are alone again. Lorenzo starts to explain the theory of the music of the spheres, made by the planets in their constant motion but beyond the hearing of human ears, which are deafened by the noises of earthly life.

Portia's musicians appear, probably on the balcony, to 'draw [their mistress] home with music'. The beauty of Lorenzo's speech (when he describes the 'patens of bright gold', and the 'young-eyed cherubins') blends with the

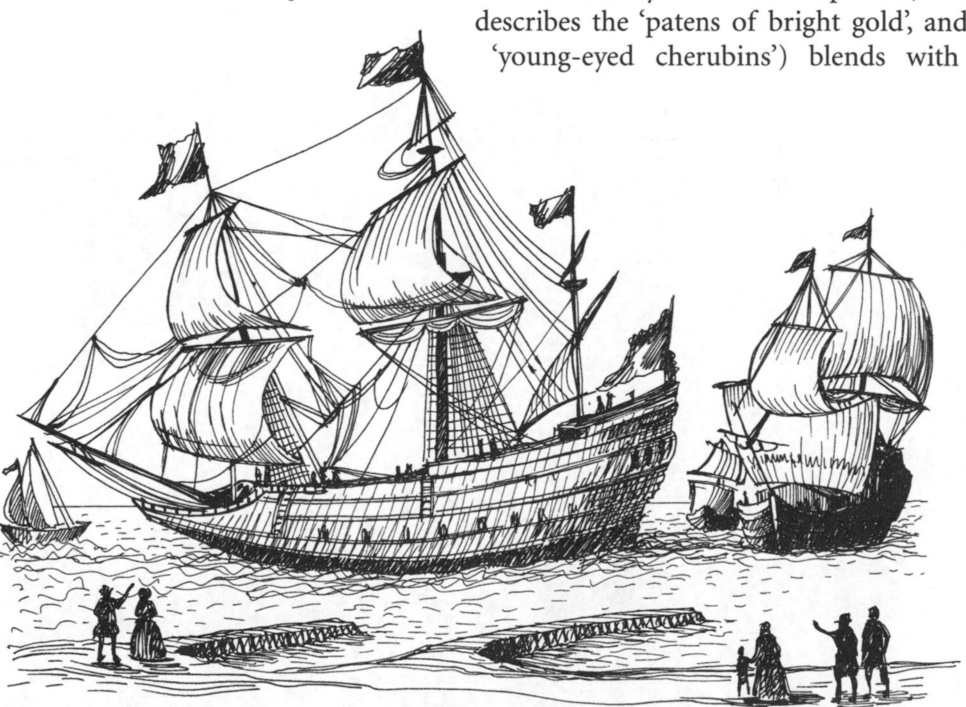

playing of the musicians to recreate, in human terms, the heavenly harmony. Lorenzo and Jessica fall silent; perhaps they are asleep.

Portia and Nerissa come from the opposite side of the stage as they approach Belmont from Venice. Their chatter breaks into the music, and the dream world becomes real. A trumpet announces the arrival of Bassanio, just as day is breaking. The missing rings provide a final gentle comedy, as the two embarrassed husbands try to justify their actions to wives who are trying to hide their amusement.

In the end, of course, all is happiness. Lorenzo and Jessica join the other two couples, and Portia gives Antonio a last surprise – the news that three of his ships 'Are richly come to harbour suddenly'. There can be no reaction from the audience other than Antonio's 'I am dumb', and final applause for Shakespeare. He has taken three main strands – the casket story, the bond story, and the ring story – and woven them into a single plot, which brings all three stories to a successful conclusion, and ensures that all the characters (with one exception) 'live happily ever after' – just as fairy-tale characters ought to do.

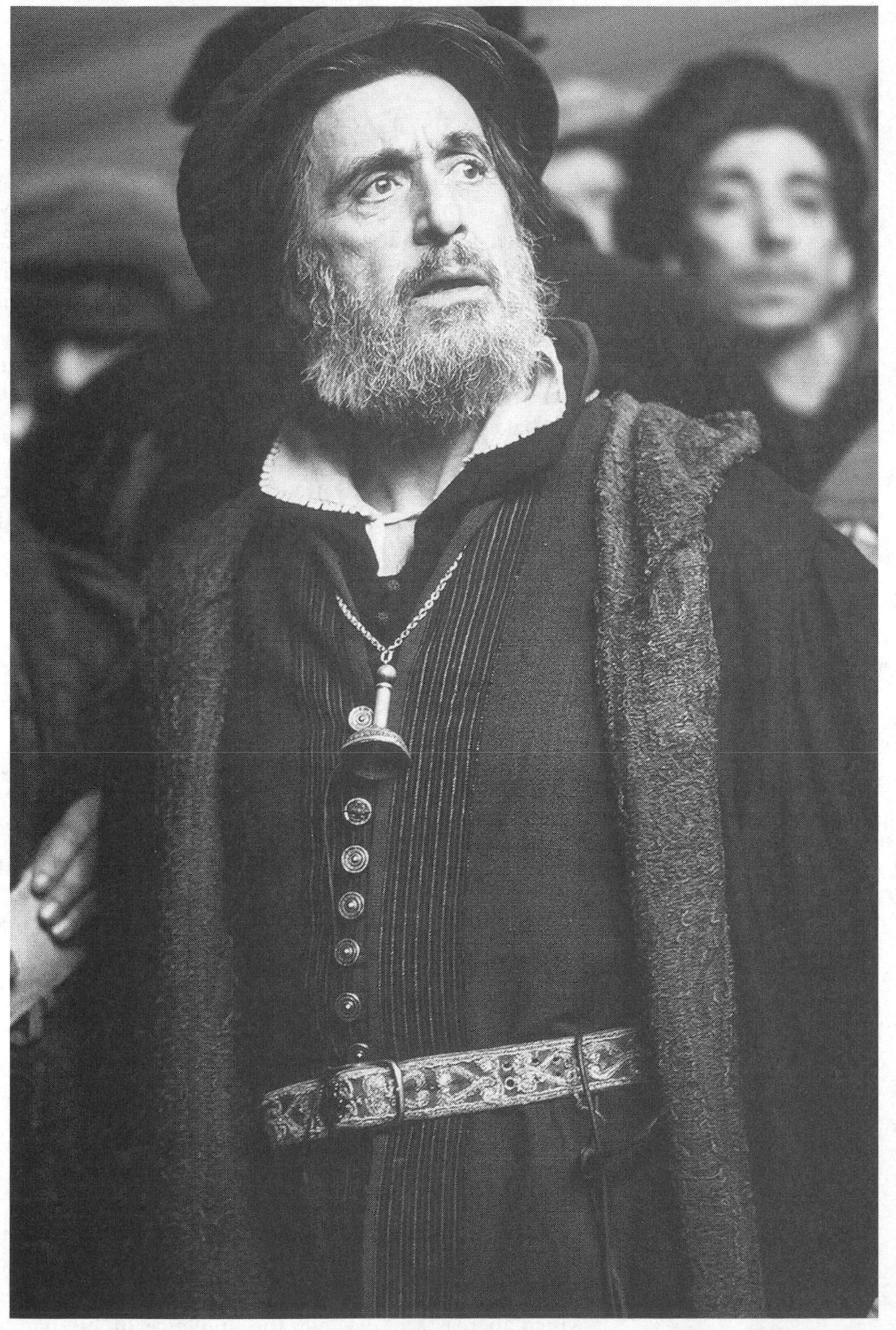

Shylock

A happy ending for the leading characters is essential for a romantic comedy such as *The Merchant of Venice.* But one very important character is left out of the general rejoicing in Act 5. Shylock has been defeated of his bond, robbed of his ducats, and deserted by his daughter; he is even compelled to give up his birthright, his Jewish religion, and become one of the Christians whom he so much hates. Does he deserve this fate? Is *The Merchant of Venice* a comedy for all the other characters, but a tragedy for Shylock?

Shakespeare took the story of Shylock's bond from an Italian novel, but the money-lending Jew in this source has no personality, and no daughter. Consequently we can assume that Shylock is Shakespeare's own creation: all the personality traits that we find in him were deliberately worked out by the dramatist, and not borrowed accidentally along with the plot.

Shylock the Jewish moneylender

Shylock starts from a double disadvantage, as far as an Elizabethan audience was concerned. He is a Jew, and he is a moneylender. There were not many Jews in England in the Middle Ages, but English Christians hated them, and this feeling was still strong in the sixteenth century. The Elizabethans also hated the traditional Jewish profession of usury – the lending of money for profit. Jews were often forbidden to own land or to engage in trade in England; consequently the only lucrative profession open to them was money lending. The Christians deplored this – in theory. In practice, the expanding economy of the times demanded that money should be readily available. Francis Bacon, who was Lord Chancellor of England in 1618, claimed that

> to speak of the abolishing of usury is idle. All states have ever had it, in one kind, or rate, or other. So as that opinion must be sent to Utopia. (Essay 'Of Usury')

Certainly, the usurer is necessary to the world of *The Merchant of Venice.* Shylock's wealth is evidence of his professional success, which could only come from satisfying a social need.

Shylock first appears as a cautious businessman, thinking carefully before he invests his three thousand ducats in Bassanio's enterprise. His reaction to the polite invitation to dinner is unexpected in its venom, which increases as he tells the audience of his hatred for Antonio.

Religious differences seem to be less important than professional jealousy:

> I hate him for he is a Christian;
> But more for that in low simplicity
> He lends out money gratis.

To some extent Shylock justifies his hostility when he describes how he has been treated by Antonio – insulted, spat upon, and kicked out of the way like 'a stranger cur'. Because of this, we sympathize with him. When the scene ends, we are left with two conflicting opinions of Shylock and his 'merry sport'. Are we to share Antonio's surprise, 'And say there is much kindness in the Jew'? Or is Bassanio right to be suspicious of 'fair terms and a villain's mind'?

Shylock the father

The scene with Antonio and Bassanio shows Shylock in his professional, public, life. Next, we hear what he is like at home. His comic servant, Lancelot Gobbo, exaggerates (with a characteristic misuse of the English language) when he says that 'the Jew is the very devil incarnation'. But this opinion is echoed by Shylock's daughter, Jessica, when she sighs 'Our house is hell'. Jessica is 'asham'd to be [her] father's child', although she knows that it is a 'heinous sin' for a daughter to have such feelings. We can understand Jessica's misery when her father gives instructions about locking up his house whilst he is away. Jessica is forbidden even to look out of the window to watch the masquers going to Bassanio's feast. Shylock is a killjoy – and he has also killed his daughter's natural affection for him.

Shakespeare does not let us see Shylock in his first frenzy of distress when he finds that Jessica is missing, because this would surely arouse our sympathy. Instead, Solanio describes the scene, and the audience is encouraged to share in his laughter. From Solanio's account, it seems that Shylock's grief over the loss of his daughter is equalled (perhaps even surpassed) by his anger at the theft of his money. He utters 'a passion so confus'd':

> My daughter! O my ducats! O my daughter!
> Fled with a Christian! O my Christian ducats!

Shylock the victim

When Shylock next appears (Act 3, Scene 1) the passion is subdued into an intense and malevolent bitterness; yet the jesting of the two Christians is cruel. The loss of a daughter is a real cause for sorrow, and

Shylock earns some pity (from the audience) when he tells Solanio and Salarino that 'my daughter is my flesh and my blood'.

It is with very mixed feelings, then, that we are led up to the powerful speech in which Shylock catalogues the abuses he has had to suffer from Christians in general, and from Antonio in particular. There is only one reason that he can see for this treatment: 'I am a Jew'. It is easy to respond to the rhetorical questions that follow:

> Hath not a Jew eyes? Hath not a Jew hands, organs, dimensions, senses, affections, passions? Fed with the same food, hurt with the same weapons, subject to the same diseases, healed by the same means, warmed and cooled by the same winter and summer, as a Christian is? If you prick us, do we not bleed? If you tickle us, do we not laugh? If you poison us, do we not die?

Shylock appeals to our common humanity. To give a negative answer to his questions would deny not *his* humanity, but our own. The speech, however, continues:

> and if you wrong us, shall we not revenge? If we are like you in the rest, we will resemble you in that . . . The villainy you teach me I will execute, and it shall go hard but I will better the instruction.

Common humanity ignores all limitations of colour, race, or creed; and this is strongly asserted in the first part of Shylock's speech. But the assertions of these last lines show that the individual – Shylock – is determined to ignore the limits of humanity. He will 'better the instruction', and prove himself to be not the *equal* of the Christians in inflicting suffering on others, but their *superior*.

Shylock's downfall

The events that follow do nothing to moderate the presentation of Shylock in the terms used by the Duke when he warns Antonio, before the trial begins, that his adversary is

> an inhuman wretch
> Uncapable of pity, void and empty
> From any dram of mercy.

During the trial, Shylock loses the audience's sympathy, by his words and by the action of sharpening the knife on the sole of his shoe (which Gratiano observes in Act 4, Scene 1, line 123). Neither insults nor pleading spoil the enjoyment of his triumph, and when sentence is

given against Antonio, he repeats the words of the bond with a lingering relish:

> Ay, his breast.
> So says the bond, doth it not, noble judge?
> 'Nearest his heart': those are the very words.

Shylock demanded a strict observance of the law, and (in poetic justice) it is precisely this that defeats him. Gratiano exults over his downfall, but the other characters in the court speak no unnecessary words and show no satisfaction until Shylock has left the court. Even then, conversation is formal, occupied only with thanks and payment. It does not obliterate the memory of Shylock's parting words:

> I pray you give me leave to go from hence;
> I am not well.

A snarl of frustrated wrath can deliver this line; or else it can be spoken with the anguish of a man who has lost everything – his daughter, his wealth, his religious freedom, and the engagement ring given to him by his wife.

Shakespeare's Shylock

Recent English productions of *The Merchant of Venice* have emphasized the suffering human being, but I do not think that this is what Shakespeare intended. Shylock is more complex than any of the other characters in the play: we can think of him as a 'real' person, whose words and deeds are motivated by thoughts and feelings that we can discover from the play, and that we can understand when we have discovered them. We cannot think of Bassanio (for instance) in this way. Yet in admiring Shakespeare's achievement in the creation of Shylock, we must beware of danger. Often, when we know a person well, and understand why he acts as he does, we become sympathetic to him; in *The Merchant of Venice* we are further encouraged to sympathize with Shylock by the fact that other leading characters (such as Bassanio) do *not* compel our sympathies. Sympathy can give rise to affection, and affection often tempts us to withhold moral judgement, or at least be gentle in our censure. Shylock's conduct merits condemnation. We can only refrain from condemning it because we know that he has suffered for being a Jew; and this, surely, is another form of prejudice?

Shakespeare's Verse

Blank verse

Easily the best way to understand and appreciate Shakespeare's verse is to read it aloud – and don't worry if you can't understand everything! Try not to be influenced by the dominant rhythm, but decide which are the most important words in each line and use the regular metre to drive them forward to the listeners.

Shakespeare's plays are mainly written in 'blank verse', the form preferred by most dramatists in the sixteenth and early seventeenth centuries. It is a very flexible medium, which is capable – like the human speaking voice – of a wide range of tones. Basically, the lines, which are unrhymed, are ten syllables long. The syllables have alternating stresses (one stress followed by one unstressed), just like normal English speech; and they divide into five 'feet'. The technical name for this is 'iambic pentameter'.

Iambic pentameter

Solanio

Beliéve me, sír, had Í such vénture fórth,
The bétter párt of my afféctions woúld
Be wíth my hópes abróad. I shoúld be stíll
Plúcking the gráss to knów where síts the wínd,
Píring in máps for pórts, and piérs, and róads;
And évery óbject thát might máke me feár
Misfórtune tó my véntures, oút of doúbt
Would máke me sád.

Salarino

My wínd coolíng my bróth
Would blów me tó an águe whén I thoúght
What hárm a wínd too gréat might dó at seá. (1, 1, 15–24)

Here the pentameter accommodates a variety of speech tones – Solanio starts with the simple, conversational expression 'Believe me'; then his speech becomes more dramatic as his imagination takes hold of the subject. Salarino, speaking on the same theme, joins in halfway through a line, as though he were singing the same tune as Solanio.

In this quotation, the lines are fairly regular in length and mostly normal in iambic stress pattern. Solanio's 'every' must be given only two syllables ('ev'ry') as in much modern English speech; and the stresses on 'Plucking' and 'Piring' are not iambic – an irregularity which adds dramatic emphasis.

Sometimes the verse line contains the grammatical unit of meaning – 'Piring in maps for ports, and piers, and roads' – thus allowing for a pause at the end of the line, before a new idea is started; at other times, the sense runs on from one line to the next – 'I should be still / Plucking the grass to know where sits the wind'. This makes for natural fluidity of speech, avoiding monotony but still maintaining the iambic rhythm.

Source, Text, and Date

Popular fiction (see '*The Merchant of Venice*: the Source', p.101) provided the plot outlines, and a rival dramatist's play gave inspiration for the character of Shylock in *The Merchant of Venice.* The play must have been written at some time after June 1596, when an English expedition made a surprise attack on four richly appointed Spanish galleons in Cadiz harbour. In the fighting, these cut adrift and ran aground, and two of them, the *San Matias* and the *San Andrès*, were captured and brought in triumph back to England. It is, almost certainly, this event that Salarino is referring to in Act 1, Scene 1, lines 25–9:

> I should not see the sandy hourglass run
> But I should think of shallows and of flats,
> And see my wealthy Andrew dock'd in sand,
> Vailing her high top lower than her ribs
> To kiss her burial.

The merit of Shakespeare's comedy was already recognized by 1598, when it was praised by Francis Meres in his account of the best contemporary English writing, *Palladis Tamia* (registered for publication September 1598).

The earliest text of the play, published in 1600, was probably based on Shakespeare's own manuscript, and reproduces the author's own detailed (but often imprecise) stage directions. The present edition is based on the text established by M. M. Mahood for the Cambridge Shakespeare in 1987.

the Merchant of Venice

Characters in the Play

The Duke of Venice	
The Prince of Morocco The Prince of Arragon	*suitors to* Portia
Bassanio	*an Italian lord, suitor to* Portia
Antonio	*a merchant of Venice, friend of* Bassanio
Solanio Salarino Gratiano Lorenzo	*gentlemen of Venice, friends of* Bassanio
Shylock	*the rich Jew, a moneylender*
Jessica	*his daughter*
Tubal	*another Jew,* Shylock*'s friend*
Lancelot Gobbo	*servant to* Shylock
Old Gobbo	Lancelot*'s father*
Portia	*a rich Italian lady*
Nerissa	*her lady-in-waiting*
Stephano	*a messenger*
Leonardo	Bassanio*'s servant*
Salerio	*a messenger from Venice*
Balthazar	Portia*'s servant*
Jailer	
	Other serving men, messengers, merchants, officers, court officials, musicians

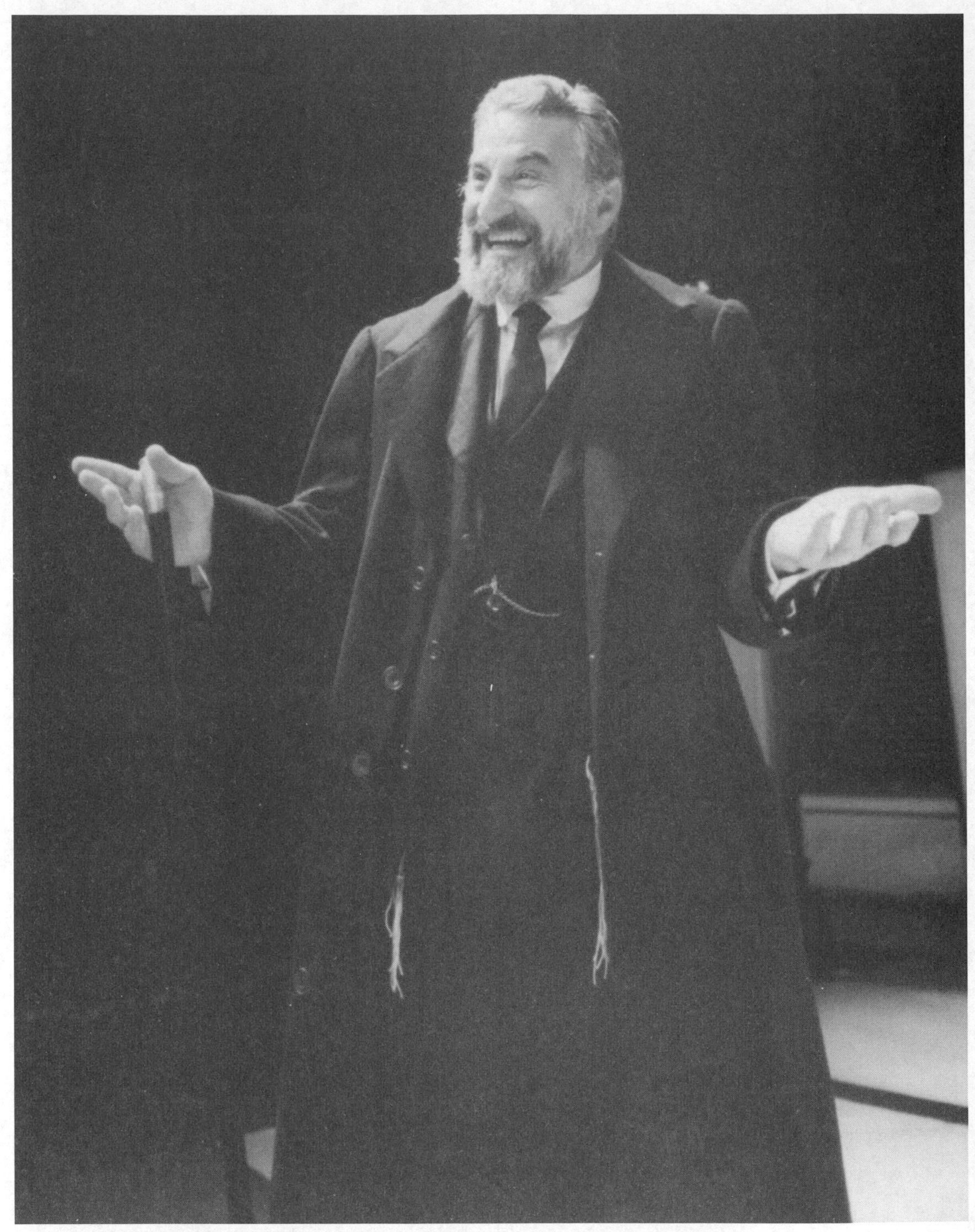

'Rest you fair, good signor! Your worship was the last man in our mouths' (1, 3, 54–5).
Henry Goodman as Shylock, Royal National Theatre, 1999.

ACT 1

Act 1 Scene 1
Antonio is depressed; his friends cannot cheer him, but he is only too willing to lend his money to Bassanio.

0s.d. *Salarino*: Some editors print 'Salerio' here, doubling Antonio's business colleague with Portia's messenger.
1 *In sooth*: truly.
2 *It*: his sadness.
3 *came by*: got.
5 *am to learn*: do not know.
6 *want-wit*: idiot.
7 *ado*: trouble.
9 *argosies*: merchant ships.
portly: stately.
10 *signors*: gentleman (the modern Italian word is *signori*).
burghers: citizens.
flood: sea.
11 *pageants*: decorated carts in carnival processions.
12 *overpeer*: look over the heads of.
petty traffickers: small commercial boats.
13 *That . . . reverence*: that bob up and down, as if they were showing respect.
15 *had . . . forth*: if I had such business abroad.
16 *affections*: concerns.
17 *still*: always.
18 *Plucking . . . wind*: holding up a blade of grass to see in which direction the wind is blowing.
19 *Piring in*: looking closely at, poring over.
roads: anchorages.
21 *out of doubt*: without doubt.
22 *wind*: breath.
broth: soup.
23 *ague*: fit of shivering.
25 *sandy hour-glass*: the sands in the hour-glass.
26 *shallows*: shallow waters.
flats: sandbanks.

SCENE 1

Venice: a street. Enter Antonio, Salarino, *and* Solanio

Antonio
In sooth I know not why I am so sad.
It wearies me, you say it wearies you;
But how I caught it, found it, or came by it,
What stuff 'tis made of, whereof it is born,
I am to learn.
And such a want-wit sadness makes of me,
That I have much ado to know myself.

Salarino
Your mind is tossing on the ocean,
There where your argosies with portly sail
Like signors and rich burghers on the flood,
Or as it were the pageants of the sea,
Do overpeer the petty traffickers
That curtsy to them, do them reverence,
As they fly by them with their woven wings.

Solanio
Believe me, sir, had I such venture forth,
The better part of my affections would
Be with my hopes abroad. I should be still
Plucking the grass to know where sits the wind,
Piring in maps for ports, and piers, and roads;
And every object that might make me fear
Misfortune to my ventures, out of doubt
Would make me sad.

Salarino
My wind cooling my broth
Would blow me to an ague when I thought
What harm a wind too great might do at sea.
I should not see the sandy hourglass run
But I should think of shallows and of flats,

And see my wealthy Andrew dock'd in sand,
Vailing her high top lower than her ribs
To kiss her burial. Should I go to church
And see the holy edifice of stone
And not bethink me straight of dangerous rocks,
Which touching but my gentle vessel's side
Would scatter all her spices on the stream,
Enrobe the roaring waters with my silks,
And (in a word) but even now worth this,
And now worth nothing? Shall I have the thought
To think on this, and shall I lack the thought
That such a thing bechanc'd would make me sad?
But tell not me: I know Antonio
Is sad to think upon his merchandise.

Antonio

Believe me, no. I thank my fortune for it,
My ventures are not in one bottom trusted,
Nor to one place; nor is my whole estate
Upon the fortune of this present year:
Therefore my merchandise makes me not sad.

Solanio

Why then, you are in love.

Antonio

Fie, fie!

27 *my wealthy Andrew*: my own richly-laden vessel; see 'Source, Date, and Text', p. xxxii.
28 *vailing her high top*: lowering her mast.
ribs: the wooden sides of the ship.
29 *burial*: burial-ground.
31 *straight*: immediately.
32 *touching but*: only by touching.
gentle: a) delicate; b) noble.
33–4 *spices . . . silks*: The luxury goods of Venetian trade.
34 *Enrobe*: clothe.
35 *in a word*: briefly.
35–6 *but . . . nothing*: highly valuable just a moment ago, then worth nothing.
36 *thought*: imagination.
38 *such . . . bechanc'd*: such a (disastrous) thing happening.

41 *fortune*: a) wealth; b) luck.

42 *ventures*: business.
bottom: ship.

44 *fortune*: chance.

46 *Fie, fie*: nonsense; two syllables are missing from this line—perhaps allowing for an embarrassed pause.

50 *Janus*: the two-heading Roman god of doorways and openings, who faced both directions at once.

52 *evermore*: always.
peep . . . eyes: screw up their eyes.

53 *laugh like parrots*: squawk with laughter.
bagpiper: Bagpipes make a melancholy, droning music.

54 *other*: others.
vinegar aspect: sour looks; 'aspect' is stressed on the second syllable.

56 *Nestor*: an old and wise Greek general who fought in the war against Troy.

57 *kinsman*: In Shakespeare's main source, the merchant ('Ansaldo') was the godfather of the younger man ('Giannetto').

61 *prevented*: forestalled, anticipated.

62 *regard*: esteem.

63 *calls on*: needs.

64 *embrace th'occasion*: welcome the opportunity.

66 *laugh*: meet together for fun.

67 *strange*: distant, unfriendly.

68 *We'll . . . yours*: we'll be free when you are.

71 *have in mind*: think about.

72 *I will . . . you*: This half-line could allow Lorenzo some gesture of farewell.

Solanio
Not in love neither? Then let us say you are sad
Because you are not merry; and 'twere as easy
For you to laugh and leap, and say you are merry
Because you are not sad. Now by two-headed Janus,
Nature hath fram'd strange fellows in her time:
Some that will evermore peep through their eyes,
And laugh like parrots at a bagpiper;
And other of such vinegar aspect,
That they'll not show their teeth in way of smile
Though Nestor swear the jest be laughable.

Enter Bassanio, Lorenzo, *and* Gratiano

Here comes Bassanio, your most noble kinsman,
Gratiano, and Lorenzo. Fare ye well;
We leave you now with better company.

Salarino
I would have stay'd till I had made you merry,
If worthier friends had not prevented me.

Antonio
Your worth is very dear in my regard.
I take it your own business calls on you,
And you embrace th'occasion to depart.

Salarino
Good morrow, my good lords.

Bassanio
Good signors both, when shall we laugh? Say, when?
You grow exceeding strange; must it be so?

Salarino
We'll make our leisures to attend on yours.
[*Exeunt* Salarino *and* Solanio

Lorenzo
My Lord Bassanio, since you have found Antonio
We two will leave you, but at dinner time
I pray you have in mind where we must meet.

Bassanio
I will not fail you.

Gratiano
You look not well, Signor Antonio.

You have too much respect upon the world:
They lose it that do buy it with much care.
Believe me, you are marvellously chang'd.

Antonio

I hold the world but as the world, Gratiano:
A stage where every man must play a part,
And mine a sad one.

Gratiano

Let me play the Fool.
With mirth and laughter let old wrinkles come,
And let my liver rather heat with wine
Than my heart cool with mortifying groans.
Why should a man whose blood is warm within
Sit like his grandsire cut in alabaster?
Sleep when he wakes? And creep into the jaundice
By being peevish? I tell thee what, Antonio—
I love thee, and it is my love that speaks—
There are a sort of men whose visages
Do cream and mantle like a standing pond,
And do a wilful stillness entertain,
With purpose to be dress'd in an opinion
Of wisdom, gravity, profound conceit,
As who should say, 'I am Sir Oracle,
And when I ope my lips, let no dog bark!'
O my Antonio, I do know of these
That therefore only are reputed wise
For saying nothing; when I am very sure
If they should speak, would almost damn those ears
Which, hearing them, would call their brothers fools.
I'll tell thee more of this another time.
But fish not with this melancholy bait
For this fool gudgeon, this opinion.
Come, good Lorenzo. Fare ye well awhile;
I'll end my exhortation after dinner.

Lorenzo

Well, we will leave you then till dinner time.
I must be one of these same dumb wise men,
For Gratiano never lets me speak.

Gratiano

Well, keep me company but two years moe,
Thou shalt not know the sound of thine own tongue.

74 *respect upon*: regard for.

75 *They . . . care*: those who worry too much about the world lose the ability to enjoy it.

76 *you . . . chang'd*: you have changed a lot.

77 *hold*: think of.

78 *A stage . . . part*: This Elizabethan commonplace became the motto of Shakespeare's Globe Theatre (*Totus mundus agit histrionem*—all the world plays the actor).

79 *Let . . . Fool*: 'Gratiano' was the name of a comic doctor in the Italian *commedia dell' arte*.

82 *mortifying groans*: Sighing was supposed to shorten life.

84 *his . . . alabaster*: a monumental statue of his grandfather.

85 *Sleep . . . wakes*: be still and silent all day.
jaundice: yellow sickness, thought by the Elizabethans to be of psychological origin.

87 *it is . . . speaks*: I'm saying this because I love you.

88–9 *whose . . . pond*: whose impassive faces are like stagnant ponds filmed over with algae.

90–1 *do . . . opinion*: maintain an obstinate silence in order to get a reputation.

92 *conceit*: thought.

93 *Sir Oracle*: a noble oracle (speaking with divine authority).

94 *ope*: open.
let . . . bark: don't interrupt.

95–7 *know . . . nothing*: know some of these men who are thought to be clever only because they never say anything.

99 *call . . . fools*: 'whosoever shall say to his brother . . . Thou fool, shall be in danger of hell fire' St Matthew, 5:22.

101–2 *fish . . . opinion*: don't use your melancholy to catch yourself an easy and worthless reputation; 'gudgeon' was a particularly gullible fish.

104 *exhortation*: sermon.

108 *moe*: more.

Antonio

Farewell; I'll grow a talker for this gear.

Gratiano

Thanks, i'faith, for silence is only commendable
In a neat's tongue dried, and a maid not vendible.

[*Exeunt* Gratiano *and* Lorenzo

Antonio

It is that anything now.

Bassanio

Gratiano speaks an infinite deal of nothing, more than any man in all Venice. His reasons are as two grains of wheat hid in two bushels of chaff: you shall seek all day ere you find them, and when you have them they are not worth the search.

Antonio

Well, tell me now what lady is the same
To whom you swore a secret pilgrimage
That you today promis'd to tell me of.

Bassanio

'Tis not unknown to you, Antonio,
How much I have disabled mine estate
By something showing a more swelling port
Than my faint means would grant continuance.
Nor do I now make moan to be abridg'd
From such a noble rate, but my chief care
Is to come fairly off from the great debts
Wherein my time, something too prodigal,
Hath left me gag'd. To you, Antonio,
I owe the most in money and in love,
And from your love I have a warranty
To unburden all my plots and purposes
How to get clear of all the debts I owe.

Antonio

I pray you, good Bassanio, let me know it,
And if it stand as you yourself still do
Within the eye of honour, be assur'd
My purse, my person, my extremest means
Lie all unlock'd to your occasions.

Bassanio

In my schooldays, when I had lost one shaft,
I shot his fellow of the selfsame flight

110 *grow . . . gear*: become more talkative for this reason.

112 *a neat's . . . vendible*: an impotent old man and an unmarriageable woman.
neat's tongue: ox-tongue, preserved for eating.
vendible: marketable.

113 *It is . . . now*: peace at last.

115 *reasons*: ideas.

117 *ere*: before.

122–34 *'Tis . . . I owe*: Bassanio is rather inarticulate in his embarrassment.

123 *disabled*: damaged.

124–5 *By . . . continuance*: by flaunting a rather more extravagant lifestyle ('port') than my limited means would allow me to continue.

126 *make . . . abridg'd*: complain about being forced to cut back.

127 *noble rate*: grand style.
care: concern.

128 *come fairly off*: extricate myself honourably.

129 *my time . . . prodigal*: my past, when I was spending rather too lavishly; Bassanio seems to compare himself with the Prodigal Son who spent his inheritance on riotous living (St Luke, chapter 15).

130 *gag'd*: owing.

132 *from . . . warranty*: your love authorizes me.

133 *unburden*: disclose to you.
purposes: plans.

136–7 *if . . . honour*: if your plan looks honourable, as you yourself have always been.

139 *occasions*: needs.

140 *shaft*: arrow.

141 *his fellow . . . flight*: an identical arrow of the same weight ('flight').

142 *advised*: advisèd; careful.
143 *find . . . forth*: to find out where the other was.
adventuring: risking.
144 *urge . . . proof*: I'm offering you this childhood example.
145 *innocence*: ingenuity.
148 *self*: selfsame.
150 *aim*: direction.
150–1 *or . . . Or*: either . . . or.
151 *hazard*: risk, gamble.
152 *rest debtor*: remain in debt.
153 *spend but time*: only waste time.
154 *To . . . circumstance*: in going such a roundabout way to make use of my love.
156 *making . . . uttermost*: doubting that I will give you every assistance.
157 *made waste of*: destroyed.
160 *prest unto*: ready to do.
161 *richly left*: who has inherited a fortune.
162 *fairer . . . word*: even better than that: Bassanio sets wealth, beauty, and virtue in ascending order of desirability.
163 *Sometimes*: at one time, formerly.
164 *speechless*: unspoken.
165–6 *nothing . . . Portia*: no less worthy than the historical Portia, daughter of a distinguished Roman tribune and the wife of Brutus, who led the conspiracy against Julius Caesar.
169 *Renowned*: renownèd.
sunny locks: golden hair.
170 *golden fleece*: In Greek mythology, Jason led an expedition to Colchis in search of the golden ram's fleece.
171 *seat*: house.
strand: shore.
172 *quest*: search.
173–4 *had I . . . them*: if I could become a rival with these suitors.
175 *presages*: prophesies.
thrift: profitable success.
176 *questionless*: without doubt.
177 *fortunes*: wealth.
178 *commodity*: merchandise.

The selfsame way, with more advised watch
To find the other forth; and by adventuring both
I oft found both. I urge this childhood proof
Because what follows is pure innocence.
I owe you much, and like a wilful youth
That which I owe is lost; but if you please
To shoot another arrow that self way
Which you did shoot the first, I do not doubt,
As I will watch the aim, or to find both
Or bring your latter hazard back again
And thankfully rest debtor for the first.

Antonio

You know me well, and herein spend but time
To wind about my love with circumstance;
And out of doubt you do me now more wrong
In making question of my uttermost
Than if you had made waste of all I have.
Then do but say to me what I should do
That in your knowledge may by me be done,
And I am prest unto it: therefore speak.

Bassanio

In Belmont is a lady richly left,
And she is fair, and—fairer than that word—
Of wondrous virtues. Sometimes from her eyes
I did receive fair speechless messages.
Her name is Portia, nothing undervalued
To Cato's daughter, Brutus' Portia.
Nor is the wide world ignorant of her worth;
For the four winds blow in from every coast
Renowned suitors, and her sunny locks
Hang on her temples like a golden fleece,
Which makes her seat of Belmont Colchos' strand,
And many Jasons come in quest of her.
O my Antonio, had I but the means
To hold a rival place with one of them,
I have a mind presages me such thrift
That I should questionless be fortunate.

Antonio

Thou know'st that all my fortunes are at sea;
Neither have I money nor commodity

179 *a present sum*: some ready money.
180 *Try . . . do*: see what you can borrow on my credit in Venice.
181 *rack'd*: stretched.
182 *furnish . . . Belmont*: provide what you need to go to Belmont.
183 *presently*: immediately.
184–5 *I . . . sake*: I'm sure you will get it either on my credit or for the sake of my friendship.

To raise a present sum; therefore go forth,
Try what my credit can in Venice do,
That shall be rack'd even to the uttermost
To furnish thee to Belmont to fair Portia.
Go presently enquire, and so will I,
Where money is, and I no question make
To have it of my trust or for my sake. [*Exeunt*

Act 1 Scene 2
Portia is rich, but she has not yet found a man who can pass her father's test to be her husband.

0s.d. *waiting-woman*: lady-in-waiting—a companion and confidante.
1 *troth*: faith.
aweary: tired; Portia seems to be as melancholy as Antonio.
1–2 *my . . . world*: Portia invokes the routine Elizabethan comparison between the little human world (microcosm) and the physical universe (macrocosm).
4 *in . . . abundance*: as plentiful.
5 *aught*: anything.
surfeit: eat excessively.
6–7 *no mean . . . mean*: no small happiness to be set in the middle; Nerissa plays on two senses of 'mean'.
8 *superfluity*: excess.
9 *competency*: adequacy.
10 *sentences*: proverbs.
pronounced: delivered.
11 followed: obeyed.
12–20 *If . . . cripple*: Portia can provide 'sentences' of her own.
13 *had been*: would be.
14 *divine*: preacher.
17 *blood*: will, passion; Portia recognizes the conflict between head and heart.
18–20 *such . . . cripple*: crazy young love, like a hare, easily eludes the snares of well-meaning but unfeeling advice.
20–1 *reasoning . . . husband*: talking like this isn't the right way to find myself a husband.
22 *I would*: I like.

Scene 2

Belmont: Portia*'s house. Enter* Portia *with her waiting-woman* Nerissa

Portia
By my troth, Nerissa, my little body is aweary of this great world.

Nerissa
You would be, sweet madam, if your miseries were in the same abundance as your good fortunes are; and yet for aught I see, they are as sick that surfeit with too much as they that starve with nothing. It is no mean happiness, therefore, to be seated in the mean—superfluity comes sooner by white hairs, but competency lives longer.

Portia
Good sentences, and well pronounced.

Nerissa
They would be better if well followed.

Portia
If to do were as easy as to know what were good to do, chapels had been churches, and poor men's cottages princes' palaces. It is a good divine that follows his own instructions; I can easier teach twenty what were good to be done, than be one of the twenty to follow mine own teaching. The brain may devise laws for the blood, but a hot temper leaps o'er a cold decree—such a hare is madness the youth, to skip o'er the meshes of good counsel the cripple. But this reasoning is not in the fashion to choose me a husband. O me, the word 'choose'! I may neither choose who I would, nor refuse

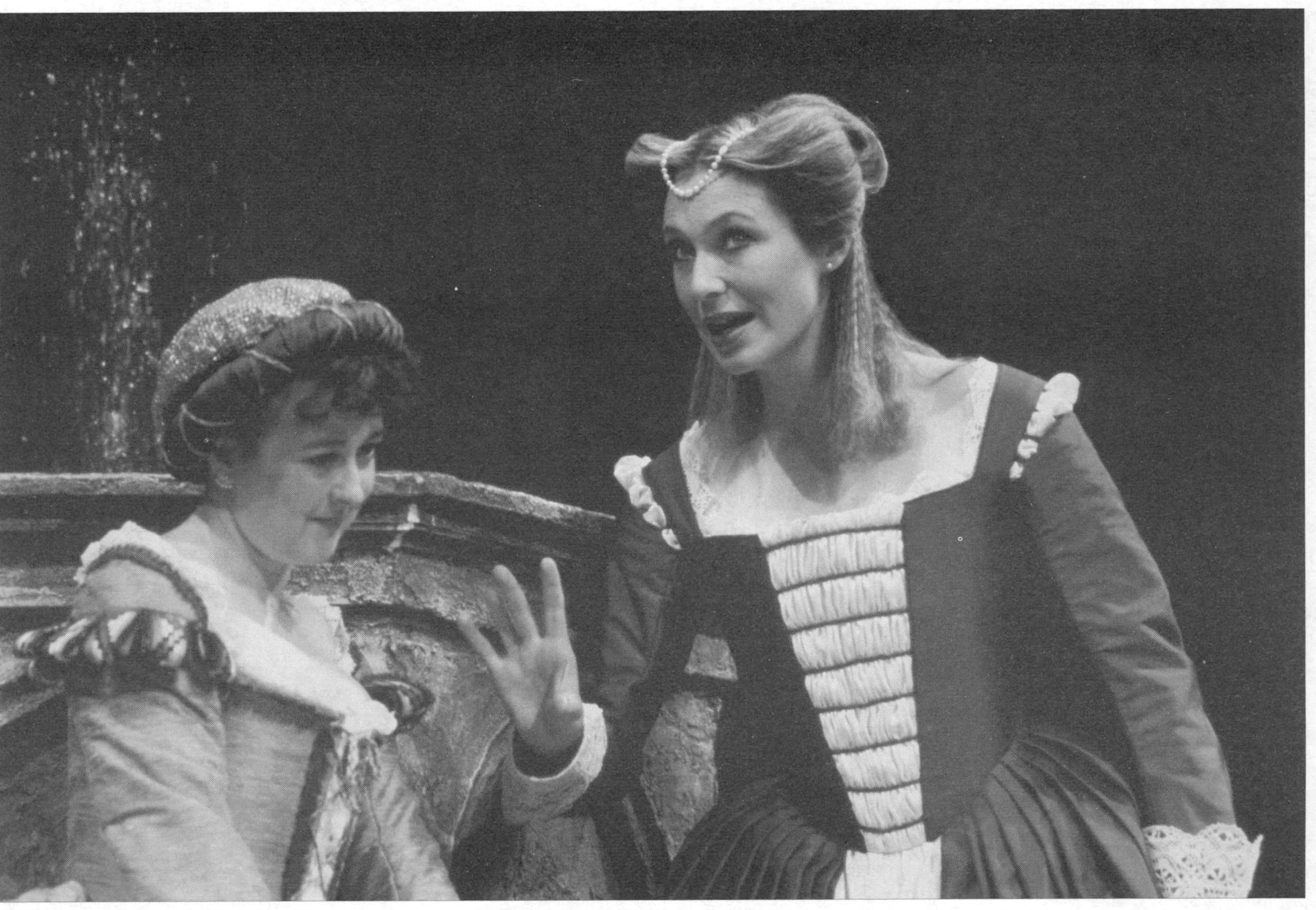

‘I may neither choose who I would, nor refuse who I dislike’ (*1*, 1, 22–3) Jane Carr as Nerissa and Joanna McCallum as Portia, Chichester Festival Theatre, 1984.

who I dislike, so is the will of a living daughter curbed by the will of a dead father. Is it not hard, Nerissa, that I cannot choose one, nor refuse none?

Nerissa

Your father was ever virtuous; and holy men at their death have good inspirations. Therefore the lottery that he hath devised in these three chests of gold, silver, and lead, whereof who chooses his meaning chooses you, will no doubt never be chosen by any rightly but one who you shall rightly love. But what warmth is there in your affection towards any of these princely suitors that are already come?

Portia

I pray thee over-name them, and as thou namest them I will describe them—and according to my description, level at my affection.

Nerissa

First, there is the Neapolitan prince.

Portia

Ay, that's a colt indeed, for he doth nothing but talk of his horse; and he makes it a great appropriation to his own good parts that he can shoe him himself. I am much afeared my lady his mother played false with a smith.

Nerissa

Then is there the County Palatine.

Portia

He doth nothing but frown, as who should say, 'And you will not have me, choose.' He hears merry tales and smiles not; I fear he will prove the weeping philosopher when he grows old, being so full of unmannerly sadness in his youth. I had rather be married to a death's head with a bone in his mouth than to either of these. God defend me from these two!

Nerissa

How say you by the French lord, Monsieur Le Bon?

Portia

God made him, and therefore let him pass for a man. In truth I know it is a sin to be a mocker, but he!—why, he hath a horse better than the Neapolitan's, a better bad habit of frowning than the Count Palatine: he is every

23 *will*: a) wish; b) sexual desire; c) testament.
curbed: restrained.

26 *ever*: always.

28 *these*: Apparently the caskets are already on the stage.

29 *his meaning*: the one he intended.

30 *rightly*: a) correctly; b) truly.

34 *over-name*: run through their names.

36 *level*: guess.

37 *Neapolitan*: Portia's suitors are all national stereotypes.

38 *colt*: uncouth young man.

38–9 *nothing . . . horse*: The southern Italians were famous for their horsemanship.

39–40 *appropriation . . . parts*: addition to his accomplishments.

42 *smith*: blacksmith.

43 *County Palatine*: i.e. a nobleman with royal privileges, holding jurisdiction over a province within an empire.

44 *as . . . say*: as if to say.
And: if.

45 *choose*: have it your own way.

46 *prove*: turn out like.
the weeping philosopher: Heraclitus of Ephesus, who surrendered his throne and became a melancholy recluse because he was distressed by human stupidity.

47 *unmannerly*: impolite, inappropriate.

48 *death's head*: skull.

51 *How . . . by*: what do you think about.

52 *pass for*: be accepted as.

55–6 *he is . . . no man*: he imitates everybody and is nobody himself.

56 *throstle*: thrush.
56–7 *falls . . . a-capering*: immediately begins to dance around.
61 *Falconbridge*: The character of this name in Shakespeare's *King John* is a model of English conduct.
65 *come . . . court*: bear witness.
66 *have . . . English*: have very little knowledge of English.
66–7 *proper man's picture*: the appearance of a handsome man.
68 *dumbshow*: mime.
suited: dressed.

69 *doublet*: sleeveless tunic.
round hose: padded breeches.
70 *behaviour*: manners.
71 *Scottish*: When James I (James VI of Scotland) came to the throne, this was discreetly changed to 'other'.
72 *neighbourly charity*: 'Charity worketh no ill to his neighbour' (Romans 13:10).
73 *borrowed . . . of*: received a blow on the ear from.
74–6 *the Frenchman . . . another*: the Frenchman also promised to repay the Englishman for another blow and added his signature and seal to the (imaginary) bond.
82–3 *fall . . . fell*: befall (= happen) . . . befell.
83 *make shift*: contrive.
84 *offer*: attempt.
85 *you . . . perform*: you would be refusing to comply with.
88 *Rhenish*: Rhineland; white wine from this district was highly esteemed.
contrary: wrong.

man in no man. If a throstle sing, he falls straight a-capering; he will fence with his own shadow. If I should marry him, I should marry twenty husbands. If he would despise me, I would forgive him; for if he love me to madness, I shall never requite him.

Nerissa
What say you then to Falconbridge, the young baron of England?

Portia
You know I say nothing to him, for he understands not me, nor I him: he hath neither Latin, French, nor Italian, and you will come into the court and swear that I have a poor penny-worth in the English. He is a proper man's picture, but alas who can converse with a dumbshow? How oddly he is suited! I think he bought his doublet in Italy, his round hose in France, his bonnet in Germany, and his behaviour everywhere.

Nerissa
What think you of the Scottish lord his neighbour?

Portia
That he hath a neighbourly charity in him, for he borrowed a box of the ear of the Englishman and swore he would pay him again when he was able. I think the Frenchman became his surety and sealed under for another.

Nerissa
How like you the young German, the Duke of Saxony's nephew!

Portia
Very vilely in the morning when he is sober, and most vilely in the afternoon when he is drunk. When he is best he is a little worse than a man, and when he is worst he is little better than a beast. And the worst fall that ever fell, I hope I shall make shift to go without him.

Nerissa
If he should offer to choose, and choose the right casket, you should refuse to perform your father's will if you should refuse to accept him.

Portia
Therefore, for fear of the worst, I pray thee set a deep glass of Rhenish wine on the contrary casket, for if the

devil be within, and the temptation without, I know he will choose it. I will do anything, Nerissa, ere I will be married to a sponge.

Nerissa

You need not fear, lady, the having any of these lords. They have acquainted me with their determinations, which is indeed to return to their home, and to trouble you with no more suit unless you may be won by some other sort than your father's imposition, depending on the caskets.

Portia

If I live to be as old as Sibylla, I will die as chaste as Diana unless I be obtained by the manner of my father's will. I am glad this parcel of wooers are so reasonable, for there is not one among them but I dote on his very absence; and I pray God grant them a fair departure.

Nerissa

Do you not remember, lady, in your father's time, a Venetian, a scholar and a soldier, that came hither in company of the Marquis of Montferrat?

Portia

Yes, yes, it was Bassanio!—as I think so was he called.

Nerissa

True, madam; he of all the men that ever my foolish eyes looked upon was the best deserving a fair lady.

Portia

I remember him well, and I remember him worthy of thy praise.

Enter a Servingman

How now, what news?

Servingman

The four strangers seek for you, madam, to take their leave; and there is a forerunner come from a fifth, the Prince of Morocco, who brings word the prince his master will be here tonight.

Portia

If I could bid the fifth welcome with so good heart as I can bid the other four farewell, I should be glad of his approach. If he have the condition of a saint, and the

92 *the having*: having to accept.
93 *determinations*: decisions.
96 *sort*: means, way.
98 *Sibylla*: In classical mythology the sibyl (= prophetess) of Cumae was granted as many years of life as she could hold grains of sand in her hand.
99 *Diana*: the classical goddess of chastity.
100 *parcel*: bunch.
104 *a scholar . . . soldier*: This was the Renaissance idea of a perfect man.
105 *Marquis of Montferrat*: The contemporary holder of this title was the Duke of Mantua, who had fought against the Turks in 1595.
106 *as I think*: Portia attempts to conceal her interest.
112 *four*: Shakespeare probably forgot that there were *six* suitors.
113 *forerunner*: herald.
118 *condition*: character, disposition.

119 *complexion*: appearance.
119–20 *I had . . . wive me*: would rather have him for a priest than a husband.
119 *shrive*: give absolution (after confession).

complexion of a devil, I had rather he should shrive me than wive me.
Come, Nerissa; sirrah, go before:
Whiles we shut the gate upon one wooer, another knocks at the door. [*Exeunt*

Act 1 Scene 3
Shylock will lend the money—but he demands an unusual bond.

Scene 3

Venice: a public place. Enter Bassanio *with* Shylock *the Jew*

1 *ducats*: Venetian gold coins.
5 *bound*: as security.
6 *stead*: supply.
pleasure: oblige.
11 *good*: financially secure; but Bassanio takes the word to mean ‘honourable’.
14 *sufficient*: adequate security.
15 *in supposition*: to be assumed.
argosy: merchant ship.
17 *the Rialto*: the Venetian Stock Exchange.
19 *squandered*: scattered lavishly.

Shylock
Three thousand ducats, well.

Bassanio
Ay, sir, for three months.

Shylock
For three months, well.

Bassanio
For the which, as I told you, Antonio shall be bound.

Shylock
Antonio shall become bound, well.

Bassanio
May you stead me? Will you pleasure me? Shall I know your answer?

Shylock
Three thousand ducats for three months, and Antonio bound.

Bassanio
Your answer to that?

Shylock
Antonio is a good man—

Bassanio
Have you heard any imputation to the contrary?

Shylock
Ho no, no, no, no: my meaning in saying he is a good man is to have you understand me that he is sufficient. Yet his means are in supposition: he hath an argosy bound to Tripolis, another to the Indies; I understand moreover upon the Rialto he hath a third at Mexico, a fourth for England, and other ventures he hath squandered abroad. But ships are but boards, sailors but

men; there be land rats, and water rats, water thieves and land thieves—I mean pirates—and then there is the peril of waters, winds, and rocks. The man is notwithstanding sufficient. Three thousand ducats: I think I may take his bond.

Bassanio

Be assured you may.

Shylock

I will be assured I may; and that I may be assured, I will bethink me—may I speak with Antonio?

Bassanio

If it please you to dine with us—

Shylock

Yes, to smell pork, to eat of the habitation which your prophet the Nazarite conjured the devil into. I will buy with you, sell with you, talk with you, walk with you, and so following; but I will not eat with you, drink with you, nor pray with you. What news on the Rialto? Who is he comes here?

Enter Antonio

Bassanio

This is Signor Antonio.

Shylock

[*Aside*] How like a fawning publican he looks!
I hate him for he is a Christian;
But more, for that in low simplicity
He lends out money gratis, and brings down
The rate of usance here with us in Venice.
If I can catch him once upon the hip,
I will feed fat the ancient grudge I bear him.
He hates our sacred nation, and he rails
Even there where merchants most do congregate
On me, my bargains, and my well-won thrift
Which he calls interest. Curs'd be my tribe
If I forgive him!

Bassanio

Shylock, do you hear?

Shylock

I am debating of my present store,

21 *pirates*: These were terrorists to shipping in the Adriatic.

25, 26 *assured*: a) reassured; b) financially secure.

27 *bethink me*: give the matter some consideration.

29 *pork*: A meat forbidden to the Jews.

29–30 *the habitation . . . into*: Jesus of Nazareth ('the Nazarite') ordered the devils possessing the mind of a madman to enter into a herd of pigs (St Mark 5:1–13).

32 *and so following*: etcetera.

36 *fawning publican*: servile tax-collector.

37 *for*: because.

38 *low simplicity*: humble foolishness.

39 *gratis*: interest-free.

40 *usance*: usury, money-lending.

41 *upon the hip*: at a disadvantage.

43 *rails*: speaks abuse.

45 *bargains*: business deals. *thrift*: success.

46 *interest*: profit.

48 *debating of*: reckoning up. *present store*: ready money.

And by the near guess of my memory
I cannot instantly raise up the gross
Of full three thousand ducats. What of that?
Tubal, a wealthy Hebrew of my tribe,
Will furnish me. But soft, how many months
Do you desire? [*To* Antonio] Rest you fair, good signor!
Your worship was the last man in our mouths.

Antonio

Shylock, albeit I neither lend nor borrow
By taking nor by giving of excess,
Yet to supply the ripe wants of my friend
I'll break a custom. [*To* Bassanio] Is he yet possess'd
How much ye would?

Shylock

Ay, ay, three thousand ducats.

Antonio

And for three months.

Shylock

I had forgot, three months; [*To* Bassanio] you told me so.
Well then, your bond; and let me see—but hear you,
Methoughts you said you neither lend nor borrow
Upon advantage.

Antonio

I do never use it.

Shylock

When Jacob graz'd his uncle Laban's sheep—
This Jacob from our holy Abram was
(As his wise mother wrought in his behalf)
The third possessor; ay, he was the third—

Antonio

And what of him, did he take interest?

Shylock

No, not take interest, not as you would say
Directly interest. Mark what Jacob did:
When Laban and himself were compromis'd
That all the eanlings which were streak'd and pied
Should fall as Jacob's hire, the ewes being rank
In end of autumn turned to the rams,
And when the work of generation was
Between these woolly breeders in the act,

---

49 *near*: close.
50 *gross*: whole sum.
53 *furnish*: supply.
soft: wait a minute.
55 *in our mouths*: that we were talking about.
56 *albeit*: although.
57 *excess*: interest, anything above the sum lent.
58 *ripe*: pressing, urgent.
59 *possess'd*: informed.
60 *would*: want.
65 *Upon advantage*: with interest.
I . . . use it: I never do so.
66–83 *When Jacob . . . Jacob's*: Shylock conflates two stories: Genesis 27 tells how Jacob, with the help of 'his wise mother', tricked his brother out of his birthright; and Genesis 30 describes the deception of Laban as Shylock recounts it here.
66 *graz'd*: shepherded.
67 *our holy Abram*: The patriarch Abraham was the founder of the Jewish race.
68 *wrought*: devised.
73 *compromis'd*: agreed.
74 *eanlings*: new-born lambs.
streak'd and pied: with fleeces of two colours.
75 *fall as Jacob's hire*: be counted as Jacob's wages.
rank: on heat, ready for mating.
76 *turned*: turnèd.
77 *work of generation*: mating.

79 *pill'd . . . wands*: went and stripped the bark of some twigs; 'me' is used purely for emphasis.
80 *deed of kind*: act of breeding.
81 *fulsome*: passionate.
82 *eaning*: lambing.
83 *Fall*: gave birth to.
85 *thrift*: profit.
86 *venture*: speculation; Antonio approves Jacob's calculated enterprise.
serv'd for: worked for; usury was condemned partly because no work was involved.
88 *sway'd*: governed.
fashion'd: shaped.
89 *Was . . . good*: did you bring up this story as a justification of usury.
93 *cite*: quote.
100 *beholding*: indebted.

101 *oft*: often.
102 *rated*: scolded.
103 *usances*: financial deals.
104 *Still*: always.
105 *suff'rance*: long-suffering, forebearance.
badge: a) characteristic; b) distinguishing mark: Venetian Jews at this time were compelled to wear a yellow O.
106 *misbeliever*: heretic, unbeliever.
dog: The Jews believed that dogs were unclean.
107 *gaberdine*: long loose coat, worn traditionally by Jews.
110 *Go to, then*: and now what are you doing (an expression of exasperation).
111 *monies*: The plural form may be Shakespeare's attempt to indicate some Jewish speech habit.
112 *void your rheum*: spit.

The skilful shepherd pill'd me certain wands
And in the doing of the deed of kind
He stuck them up before the fulsome ewes,
Who then conceiving, did in eaning time
Fall parti-coloured lambs, and those were Jacob's.
This was a way to thrive, and he was blest;
And thrift is blessing if men steal it not.

Antonio

This was a venture, sir, that Jacob serv'd for,
A thing not in his power to bring to pass,
But sway'd and fashion'd by the hand of heaven.
Was this inserted to make interest good?
Or is your gold and silver ewes and rams?

Shylock

I cannot tell, I make it breed as fast.
But note me, signor—

Antonio

Mark you this, Bassanio,
The devil can cite Scripture for his purpose.
An evil soul producing holy witness
Is like a villain with a smiling cheek,
A goodly apple rotten at the heart.
O what a goodly outside falsehood hath!

Shylock

Three thousand ducats, 'tis a good round sum.
Three months from twelve, then let me see, the rate—

Antonio

Well, Shylock, shall we be beholding to you?

Shylock

Signor Antonio, many a time and oft
In the Rialto you have rated me
About my monies and my usances.
Still have I borne it with a patient shrug
For suff'rance is the badge of all our tribe.
You call me misbeliever, cut-throat dog,
And spit upon my Jewish gaberdine,
And all for use of that which is mine own.
Well then, it now appears you need my help.
Go to, then, you come to me, and you say,
'Shylock, we would have monies'—you say so,
You that did void your rheum upon my beard,

113 *foot*: kick.

114 *suit*: request.

118 *key*: tone.

119 *With bated breath*: anxiously.

120 *Say this*: The pause in the line, allowing time for a gesture of mock-humility, throws emphasis on Shylock's conclusion.

125 *as like*: just as likely.

129 *A breed . . . friend*: an increase in the sum of sterile money from a friend.

131 *break*: go bankrupt.

136 *doit*: a Dutch coin of little value.

137 *usance*: interest.

138 *kind*: kindness; Bassanio takes the word in its normal sense—but Shylock will pun on the meaning 'natural inclination'.

140 *notary*: solicitor.
seal me: sign for me.

141 *single*: simple.
in a merry sport: as a joke.

144 *the condition*: the terms of the bond.

145 *nominated for*: named as.
equal: exact.

And foot me as you spurn a stranger cur
Over your threshold: monies is your suit.
What should I say to you? Should I not say
'Hath a dog money? Is it possible
A cur can lend three thousand ducats?' Or
Shall I bend low, and in a bondman's key,
With bated breath and whisp'ring humbleness,
Say this:
'Fair sir, you spat on me on Wednesday last,
You spurn'd me such a day, another time
You call'd me dog: and for these courtesies
I'll lend you thus much monies.'

Antonio

I am as like to call thee so again,
To spit on thee again, to spurn thee too.
If thou wilt lend this money, lend it not
As to thy friends, for when did friendship take
A breed for barren metal of his friend?
But lend it rather to thine enemy,
Who if he break, thou mayst with better face
Exact the penalty.

Shylock

Why look you how you storm!
I would be friends with you, and have your love,
Forget the shames that you have stain'd me with,
Supply your present wants, and take no doit
Of usance for my monies, and you'll not hear me.
This is kind I offer.

Bassanio

This were kindness.

Shylock

This kindness will I show.
Go with me to a notary, seal me there
Your single bond, and, in a merry sport,
If you repay me not on such a day,
In such a place, such sum or sums as are
Express'd in the condition, let the forfeit
Be nominated for an equal pound
Of your fair flesh, to be cut off and taken
In what part of your body pleaseth me.

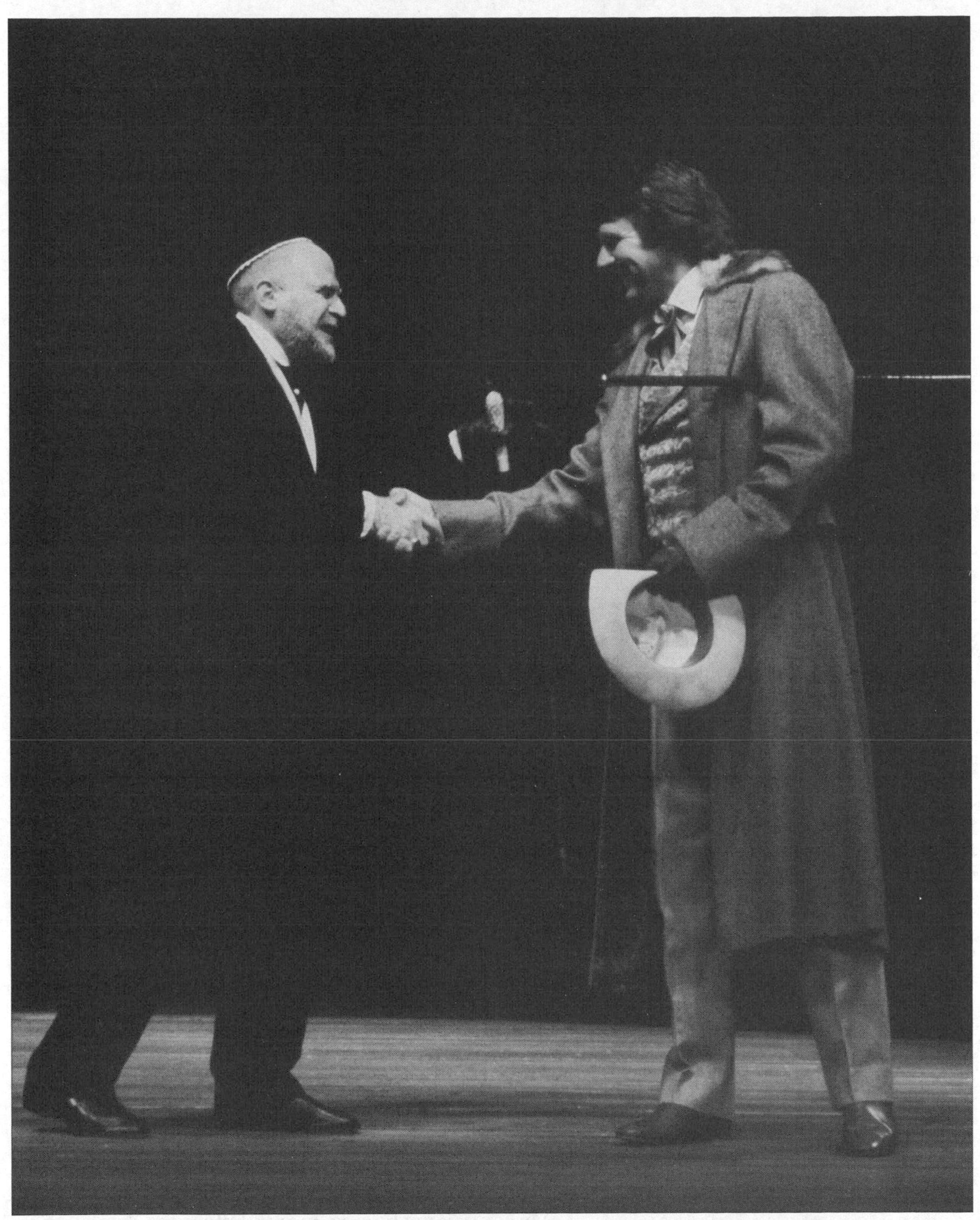

'Yes, Shylock, I will seal unto this bond.' (*1*, 3, 167). David Suchet as Shylock and Tom Wilkinson as Antonio, Royal Shakespeare Company, 1981.

Antonio
Content, in faith! I'll seal to such a bond,
And say there is much kindness in the Jew.

Bassanio
You shall not seal to such a bond for me;
I'll rather dwell in my necessity.

Antonio
Why, fear not, man, I will not forfeit it.
Within these two months, that's a month before
This bond expires, I do expect return
Of thrice three times the value of this bond.

Shylock
O father Abram, what these Christians are,
Whose own hard dealings teaches them suspect
The thoughts of others! Pray you tell me this:
If he should break his day what should I gain
By the exaction of the forfeiture?
A pound of man's flesh, taken from a man,
Is not so estimable, profitable neither,
As flesh of muttons, beefs, or goats. I say
To buy his favour, I extend this friendship.
If he will take it, so; if not, adieu,
And for my love, I pray you wrong me not.

Antonio
Yes, Shylock, I will seal unto this bond.

Shylock
Then meet me forthwith at the notary's.
Give him direction for this merry bond,
And I will go and purse the ducats straight,
See to my house left in the fearful guard
Of an unthrifty knave, and presently
I'll be with you. [*Exit*

Antonio
Hie thee, gentle Jew.
The Hebrew will turn Christian, he grows kind.

Bassanio
I like not fair terms and a villain's mind.

Antonio
Come on, in this there can be no dismay,
My ships come home a month before the day.

[*Exeunt*

151 *dwell . . . necessity*: remain in need; Bassanio emphasizes his meaning with his rhyme.

157 *hard*: tough.
suspect: to be suspicious.

159 *break his day*: fail to pay on the agreed date.

163 *muttons, beefs*: sheep, oxen; Shylock's usage seems to emphasize his status as an 'outsider'.

170 *purse . . . straight*: get the money ready immediately.

171 *fearful*: untrustworthy.

172 *unthrifty*: careless.
knave: lad, servant.

173 *gentle*: Antonio makes a pun with 'Gentile' (= a non-Jewish person).

ACT 2

Act 2 Scene 1
Portia interviews a new suitor, and explains the conditions of her father's will.

0s.d. *flourish*: fanfare.
0s.d. *a tawny Moor . . . accordingly*: The details and the vagueness about numbers, are typical of an author's own manuscript.
accordingly: in the same way.
1–3 *Mislike . . . bred*: 'Marvel not at me that I am so black, for why? the sun hath shined upon me' (Song of Solomon).
1 *Mislike*: dislike.
2 *shadow'd*: darkened.
livery: uniform.
3 *near bred*: closely related.
4 *fairest*: most light-skinned.
5 *Phoebus*: the god of the sun.
6 *make incision*: cut ourselves.
7 *reddest*: Red blood showed courage.
8 *aspect*: aspèct.
9 *fear'd*: terrified.
10 *best-regarded*: most admired.
clime: part of the world.
12 *steal your thoughts*: win your affections.
13 *In . . . choice*: when it comes to choosing.
led: influenced.
14 *nice*: fastidious, over-particular.
16 *Bars*: forbids.
17 *scanted*: restricted.
18 *hedg'd*: confined.
18–19 *to yield . . . wife*: marry that man.
20 *renowned*: renownèd.
then . . . fair: would then have stood as good a chance; Portia plays on 'fair' = light-skinned.
21 *any comer*: any other suitor.
24 *scimitar*: short curved sword.

Scene 1

Belmont: Portia*'s house. A flourish of cornets. Enter the* Prince of Morocco, *a tawny Moor all in white, and three or four followers accordingly; with* Portia, Nerissa, *and their train*

Morocco
Mislike me not for my complexion,
The shadow'd livery of the burnish'd sun,
To whom I am a neighbour and near bred.
Bring me the fairest creature northward born,
Where Phoebus' fire scarce thaws the icicles,
And let us make incision for your love
To prove whose blood is reddest, his or mine.
I tell thee, lady, this aspect of mine
Hath fear'd the valiant; by my love I swear
The best-regarded virgins of our clime
Have lov'd it too. I would not change this hue,
Except to steal your thoughts, my gentle queen.

Portia
In terms of choice I am not solely led
By nice direction of a maiden's eyes.
Besides, the lottery of my destiny
Bars me the right of voluntary choosing.
But if my father had not scanted me,
And hedg'd me by his wit to yield myself
His wife who wins me by that means I told you,
Yourself, renowned prince, then stood as fair
As any comer I have looked on yet
For my affection.

Morocco
Even for that I thank you.
Therefore I pray you lead me to the caskets
To try my fortune. By this scimitar,

That slew the Sophy and a Persian prince
That won three fields of Sultan Solyman,
I would o'er-stare the sternest eyes that look,
Outbrave the heart most daring on the earth,
Pluck the young sucking cubs from the she-bear,
Yea, mock the lion when a roars for prey,
To win thee, lady. But alas the while,
If Hercules and Lichas play at dice
Which is the better man, the greater throw
May turn by fortune from the weaker hand.
So is Alcides beaten by his rage,
And so may I, blind Fortune leading me,
Miss that which one unworthier may attain,
And die with grieving.

Portia

You must take your chance,
And either not attempt to choose at all
Or swear before you choose, if you choose wrong,
Never to speak to lady afterward
In way of marriage: therefore be advis'd.

Morocco

Nor will not. Come, bring me unto my chance.

Portia

First forward to the temple; after dinner
Your hazard shall be made.

Morocco

Good fortune then,
To make me blest—or cursed'st among men!

Cornets. [*Exeunt*

25–6 *slew . . . Solyman*: The Moroccans owed allegiance to the Turks who, under Solyman the Magnificent, fought against the Persians in the mid-sixteenth century—but no Shah ('Sophy') was killed in the fighting.
26 *fields*: battlefields, battles.
of: over.
27 *o'er-stare*: outface, defy.
30 *a roars*: he roars.
32 *Hercules and Lichas*: In classical mythology, the superman (grandson of Alceus) and his servant.
play at dice: toss dice, gamble.
35 *So . . . rage*: just as Hercules was destroyed by his own frenzy.

42 *In way of*: on the subject of.
be advis'd: consider, be careful.

43 *Nor will not*: I certainly won't.
chance: fate, trial.

44 *forward . . . temple*: Oaths of such magnitude were customarily taken at an altar.

46 *cursed*: cursèd.
46s.d. *Cornets*: Another fanfare to mark the Prince's departure.

Act 2 Scene 2
Lancelot Gobbo teases his blind father, who asks Bassanio to give employment to his son. Bassanio is preparing for Belmont, and Gratiano wants to accompany him.

0s.d. *Scene 2*: The action of Scenes 2–6 can be made continuous, provided that the three stage entrances are clearly identified—the door of Shylock's house, the direction of Gratiano's lodging, and the opening (perhaps the central, curtained space) for Bassanio's house.
0s.d. *the Clown*: An indication that the part was played by the company's professional comedian (Will Kemp).
1 *serve me*: a) assist me; b) obey me.
2 *The fiend*: the devil; Lancelot imagines himself as the central character of a Morality Play.
8 *scorn*: despise—with a play on the sense 'kick aside'.
9 *courageous*: encouraging.
pack: be gone.
Fia: on your way (Italian).
12 *hanging . . . heart*: clinging to my heart.
14 *honest woman*: virtuous woman.
15–16 *my father . . . taste*: Lancelot hints at his father's sexual activities.
17 *budge*: move, leave.
21 *God . . . mark*: if I may say so; Lancelot apologizes for his language.
23 *saving your reverence*: if you'll excuse me.
24 *incarnation*: incarnate; mistaken words ('malapropisms') are Will Kemp's speciality.
25 *in my conscience*: to speak truly.
26 *hard*: strict.
offer: presume.

Scene 2

Venice: the street outside Shylock*'s house. Enter* Lancelot Gobbo, *the Clown, alone*

Lancelot
Certainly, my conscience will serve me to run from this Jew my master. The fiend is at mine elbow and tempts me, saying to me 'Gobbo, Lancelot Gobbo, good Lancelot', or 'Good Gobbo', or 'Good Lancelot Gobbo, use your legs, take the start, run away.' My conscience says 'No: take heed, honest Lancelot, take heed, honest Gobbo'—or (as aforesaid)—'honest Lancelot Gobbo; do not run, scorn running with thy heels.' Well, the most courageous fiend bids me pack. 'Fia!' says the fiend, 'Away!' says the fiend. ''For the heavens, rouse up a brave mind', says the fiend, 'and run.' Well, my conscience, hanging about the neck of my heart, says very wisely to me, 'My honest friend Lancelot, being an honest man's son, or rather an honest woman's son' (for indeed my father did something smack, something grow to; he had a kind of taste): well, my conscience says 'Lancelot, budge not!' 'Budge!' says the fiend. 'Budge not!' says my conscience. 'Conscience', say I, 'you counsel well.' 'Fiend', say I, 'you counsel well'. To be ruled by my conscience, I should stay with the Jew my master who—God bless the mark!—is a kind of devil; and to run away from the Jew, I should be ruled by the fiend who—saving your reverence—is the devil himself. Certainly the Jew is the very devil incarnation, and, in my conscience, my conscience is but a kind of hard conscience to offer to counsel me to stay with the Jew. The fiend gives the more friendly counsel: I will run, fiend, my heels are at your commandment, I will run.

Enter Old Gobbo *with a basket*

Gobbo
Master young-man, you, I pray you, which is the way to Master Jew's?

'Master young-gentleman, I pray you, which is the way to Master Jew's?' (*2*, 2, 35–6). Rob Edwards as Lancelot Gobbo and Jimmy Gardner as Old Gobbo, Royal Shakespeare Company, 1981.

32 *true-begotten father*: Another deliberate confusion.
33 *sand-blind*: half-blind.
high . . . blind: almost stone (= completely) blind.
34 *try confusions*: test him out, give him some riddles.

37–40 *Turn . . . house*: This is an old joke, made more effective if Lancelot turns his father about until he faces Shylock's door.
38 *Marry*: by the Virgin Mary (a mild oath).

41 *Be . . . sonties*: by God's saints; Old Gobbo speaks a rural dialect.
hit: find.
42 *one*: a certain.
dwells with him: is a member of his household.
42–3 *dwell with him*: lives with him.
45 *raise the waters*: bring tears to his eyes.

49 *well to live*: well-to-do, prosperous; another malapropism.

50 *a*: he.

52 *Your . . . Lancelot*: just call him plain Lancelot.

55 *an't*: if it.

56 *ergo*: therefore; Lancelot wants to confuse his father with the Latin word.
57 *father*: A courteous way of addressing an old man—making for more comedy here.
58 *sisters three*: The Fates—three sister-goddesses of classical mythology who controlled human destiny.

Lancelot
[*Aside*] O heavens! This is my true-begotten father who being more than sand-blind, high gravel-blind, knows me not. I will try confusions with him.

Gobbo
Master young-gentleman, I pray you, which is the way to Master Jew's?

Lancelot
Turn upon your right hand at the next turning, but at the next turning of all on your left. Marry, at the very next turning turn of no hand but turn down indirectly to the Jew's house.

Gobbo
Be God's sonties, 'twill be a hard way to hit! Can you tell me whether one Lancelot that dwells with him, dwell with him or no?

Lancelot
Talk you of young Master Lancelot? [*Aside*] Mark me now, now will I raise the waters. Talk you of young Master Lancelot?

Gobbo
No 'master', sir, but a poor man's son. His father, though I say't, is an honest, exceeding poor man and, God be thanked, well to live.

Lancelot
Well, let his father be what a will, we talk of young Master Lancelot.

Gobbo
Your worship's friend and Lancelot, sir.

Lancelot
But I pray you, *ergo* old man, *ergo* I beseech you, talk you of young Master Lancelot?

Gobbo
Of Lancelot, an't please your mastership.

Lancelot
Ergo Master Lancelot. Talk not of Master Lancelot, father, for the young gentleman, according to fates and destinies, and such odd sayings, the sisters three, and such branches of learning, is indeed deceased, or as you would say in plain terms, gone to heaven.

Gobbo

Marry, God forbid! The boy was the very staff of my age, my very prop.

Lancelot

Do I look like a cudgel or a hovel-post, a staff or a prop? Do you know me, father?

Gobbo

Alack the day, I know you not, young gentleman, but I pray you tell me, is my boy—God rest his soul!—alive or dead?

Lancelot

Do you not know me, father?

Gobbo

Alack, sir, I am sand-blind, I know you not.

Lancelot

Nay indeed, if you had your eyes you might fail of the knowing me: it is a wise father that knows his own child. Well, old man, I will tell you news of your son. [*Kneels*] Give me your blessing; truth will come to light, murder cannot be hid long, a man's son may, but in the end truth will out.

Gobbo

Pray you, sir, stand up; I am sure you are not Lancelot my boy.

Lancelot

Pray you, let's have no more fooling about it, but give me your blessing; I am Lancelot your boy that was, your son that is, your child that shall be.

Gobbo

I cannot think you are my son.

Lancelot

I know not what I shall think of that; but I am Lancelot the Jew's man, and I am sure Margery your wife is my mother.

Gobbo

Her name is Margery indeed. I'll be sworn if thou be Lancelot thou art mine own flesh and blood. Lord worshipped might he be, what a beard hast thou got! Thou has got more hair on thy chin than Dobbin my fill-horse has on his tail.

63 *hovel-post*: main timber support of poor dwelling.

71–2 *a wise . . . child*: Lancelot inverts the proverb 'It is a wise child that knows his own father'.

88 *thou*: Old Gobbo shifts from the respectful form 'you' to the familiar form of address.

86–7 *Lord . . . be*: the Lord be praised.

87 *what . . . got*: Old Gobbo (unaware that his son is kneeling) has grasped the hair of Lancelot's head.

89 *fill-horse*: carthorse ('fills' = the shafts of a cart).

Lancelot

It should seem then that Dobbin's tail grows backward. I am sure he had more hair of his tail than I have of my face when I last saw him.

Gobbo

Lord, how art thou changed! How dost thou and thy master agree? I have brought him a present. How 'gree you now?

Lancelot

Well, well; but for mine own part, as I have set up my rest to run away, so I will not rest till I have run some ground. My master's a very Jew. Give him a present? Give him a halter! I am famished in his service; you may tell every finger I have with my ribs. Father, I am glad you are come; give me your present to one Master Bassanio, who indeed gives rare new liveries: if I serve not him, I will run as far as God has any ground. O rare fortune, here comes the man! To him, father, for I am a Jew if I serve the Jew any longer.

Enter Bassanio *with* Leonardo *and a follower or two*

Bassanio

You may do so, but let it be so hasted that supper be ready at the farthest by five of the clock. See these letters delivered, put the liveries to making, and desire Gratiano to come anon to my lodging.

[*Exit one of his men*

Lancelot

To him, father.

Gobbo

God bless your worship!

Bassanio

Gramercy; wouldst thou aught with me?

Gobbo

Here's my son, sir, a poor boy—

Lancelot

Not a poor boy, sir, but the rich Jew's man that would, sir, as my father shall specify—

90 *backward*: i.e. shorter.

91 *of*: on.

94 *agree*: suit each other.
'gree: agree.

96 *for . . . part*: so far as I am concerned.

96–7 *set . . . rest*: made up my mind; 'rest' = final gambling stake.

98 *ground*: distance.
very: real (an intensifier).

99 *halter*: rope (to hang himself).

100 *tell . . . ribs*: count all my ribs with your fingers; traditionally, Lancelot puts his father's hand on his own fingers, spread out to represent his ribs.

101 *give . . . present*: give your present on my behalf.

102 *rare new liveries*: splendid fashionable uniforms.

104–5 *a Jew*: i.e. 'someone I could not possibly be' (compare the modern 'I'm a Dutchman').

106 *hasted*: speeded up.

108 *put . . . making*: get the uniforms made.

109 *anon*: at once.

110 *To him*: speak to him.

112 *Gramercy*: may God reward you (derived from Old French *grant merci*).

Gobbo
He hath a great infection, sir, as one would say, to serve—

Lancelot
Indeed, the short and the long is, I serve the Jew, and have a desire, as my father shall specify—

Gobbo
His master and he, saving your worship's reverence, are scarce cater-cousins—

Lancelot
To be brief, the very truth is that the Jew having done me wrong doth cause me—as my father being I hope an old man shall frutify unto you—

Gobbo
I have here a dish of doves that I would bestow upon your worship, and my suit is—

Lancelot
In very brief, the suit is impertinent to myself, as your worship shall know by this honest old man, and though I say it, though old man, yet poor man, my father—

Bassanio
One speak for both. What would you?

Lancelot
Serve you, sir.

Gobbo
That is the very defect of the matter, sir.

Bassanio
I know thee well, thou hast obtain'd thy suit.
Shylock thy master spoke with me this day,
And hath preferr'd thee, if it be preferment
To leave a rich Jew's service to become
The follower of so poor a gentleman.

Lancelot
The old proverb is very well parted between my master Shylock and you, sir: you have the grace of God, sir, and he hath enough.

Bassanio
Thou speak'st it well; go, father, with thy son;
Take leave of thy old master, and enquire
My lodging out. [*To a follower*] Give him a livery
More guarded than his fellows'; see it done.

116 *infection*: Gobbo's mistake for 'affection' (= desire).

118 *the short and long*: all that needs to be said; Lancelot inverts the usual phrase.

120 *saving . . . reverence*: if you'll allow me to say this.

121 *cater-cousins*: close friends who eat together.

124 *frutify*: Lancelot combines 'notify' and 'fructify' (= bear fruit)—which Old Gobbo takes as the cue for his gift.

125 *dish of doves*: doves prepared for eating.

127 *impertinent*: Lancelot means 'pertinent' (= relevant).

132 *defect*: i.e. 'effect' (= purpose).

133 *thou . . . suit*: your request is granted.

135 *preferr'd*: recommended.
preferment: promotion.

138 *old proverb*: 'The grace of God is gear enough (for salvation)'.
parted: divided.

142–3 *enquire . . . out*: make your way to my house.

144 *more guarded*: with more (gold) braid; the extra trimmings might suggest that Lancelot is to act as a jester.

Lancelot

Father, in. I cannot get a service, no, I have ne'er a tongue in my head! [*Looks at palm of his hand*] Well, if any man in Italy have a fairer table which doth offer to swear upon a book!—I shall have good fortune. Go to, here's a simple line of life, here's a small trifle of wives: alas, fifteen wives is nothing, eleven widows and nine maids is a simple coming-in for one man. And then to 'scape drowning thrice, and to be in peril of my life with the edge of a featherbed: here are simple 'scapes. Well, if Fortune be a woman, she's a good wench for this gear. Father, come, I'll take my leave of the Jew in the twinkling. [*Exeunt* Lancelot *and* Gobbo

Bassanio

I pray thee, good Leonardo, think on this.
These things being bought and orderly bestow'd,
Return in haste, for I do feast tonight
My best esteem'd acquaintance. Hie thee, go.

Leonardo

My best endeavours shall be done herein.

Enter Gratiano

Gratiano

Where's your master?

Leonardo

Yonder, sir, he walks. [*Exit*

Gratiano

Signor Bassanio!

Bassanio

Gratiano?

Gratiano

I have a suit to you.

Bassanio

You have obtain'd it.

Gratiano

You must not deny me, I must go with you to Belmont.

Bassanio

Why then, you must. But hear thee, Gratiano:
Thou art too wild, too rude, and bold of voice—
Parts that become thee happily enough,

145–56 *Father . . . twinkling*: Lancelot, rejoicing with heavy irony in his success, takes his father upstage towards Shylock's door, while Bassanio and Leonardo confer downstage.
147–8 *table . . . fortune*: Lancelot pretends to read his fortune in the lines of his hand—which would be laid on the Bible to swear an oath.
148 *Go to*: come along (an expression of exasperation).
149 *simple . . . life*: straightforward lifeline (ironic).
small trifle: trivial matter.
151 *simple coming-in*: only a (sexual) beginning.
152 *'scape*: escape.
153 *'scapes*: adventures.
153–4 *if . . . woman*: Fortune is pictured as being female and fickle.
154 *gear*: business.
155–6 *in the twinkling*: in the twinkling of an eye.
158 *orderly bestow'd*: stowed neatly on board.
159 *feast*: give a banquet for.
161 *endeavours*: efforts.
165 *have . . . you*: want to ask a favour.
You . . . it: it's yours.
167 *you . . . thee*: Bassanio drops into the familiar form of address for his admonishment.
168 *rude*: uncouth, outspoken.
169 *Parts*: qualities.
become thee: suit you.

And in such eyes as ours appear not faults;
But where thou art not known, why there they show
Something too liberal. Pray thee take pain
To allay with some cold drops of modesty
Thy skipping spirit, lest through thy wild behaviour
I be misconster'd in the place I go to,
And lose my hopes.

Gratiano

Signor Bassanio, hear me:
If I do not put on a sober habit,
Talk with respect, and swear but now and then,
Wear prayer books in my pocket, look demurely,
Nay more, while grace is saying, hood mine eyes
Thus with my hat, and sigh and say 'amen',
Use all the observance of civility
Like one well studied in a sad ostent
To please his grandam, never trust me more.

Bassanio

Well, we shall see your bearing.

Gratiano

Nay, but I bar tonight, you shall not gauge me
By what we do tonight.

Bassanio

No, that were pity.
I would entreat you rather to put on
Your boldest suit of mirth, for we have friends
That purpose merriment. But fare you well,
I have some business.

Gratiano

And I must to Lorenzo and the rest;
But we will visit you at supper time. [*Exeunt*

171 *show*: appear.
172 *Something too liberal*: rather too free-and-easy.
pain: care.
173 *allay*: moderate.
modesty: decorum.
174 *skipping*: boisterous, effervescent.
175 *misconster'd*: misconstrued, misinterpreted.
177 *sober habit*: a) decent costume; b) restrained behaviour.
178 *but*: only.
180 *saying*: being said.
hood: cover; Elizabethan men kept their hats on indoors, even for meals.
182 *Use . . . civility*: maintain all forms of good manners.
183 *one . . . ostent*: someone who is thoroughly accustomed to showing a serious appearance.
184 *grandam*: grandmother.
185 *bearing*: conduct.
186 *bar*: make an exception of.
gauge: measure, judge.
187 *were pity*: would be a pity.
189 *suit of mirth*: a) entertaining manner; b) party dress.
190 *purpose*: intend.

Act 2 Scene 3
Lancelot says goodbye to Jessica, Shylock's daughter.

SCENE 3

Venice: outside Shylock*'s house. Enter* Jessica *and* Lancelot *the Clown*

Jessica
I am sorry thou wilt leave my father so.
Our house is hell, and thou a merry devil
Didst rob it of some taste of tediousness.
But fare thee well: there is a ducat for thee.
And, Lancelot, soon at supper shalt thou see
Lorenzo, who is thy new master's guest;
Give him this letter, do it secretly.
And so farewell: I would not have my father
See me in talk with thee.

Lancelot
Adieu; tears exhibit my tongue. Most beautiful pagan, most sweet Jew, if a Christian do not play the knave and get thee, I am much deceived. But adieu; these foolish drops do something drown my manly spirit. Adieu!
[*Exit*

Jessica
Farewell, good Lancelot.
Alack, what heinous sin is it in me
To be asham'd to be my father's child!
But though I am a daughter to his blood
I am not to his manners. O Lorenzo,
If thou keep promise, I shall end this strife,
Become a Christian and thy loving wife. [*Exit*

3 *taste*: feeling.
10 *Adieu*: goodbye (French); Lancelot's high-flown language contrasts with Jessica's simple words.
exhibit my tongue: a) inhibit me from speaking; b) express what I can't say in words.
12 *get*: get hold of, steal.
13 *something*: somewhat, rather.
15 *heinous*: monstrous, abominable.
18 *manners*: behaviour.
19 *keep promise*: keep your promise.

Act 2 Scene 4
Lorenzo is planning some late-night entertainment when Lancelot brings a letter from Jessica.

SCENE 4

Venice: outside Shylock*'s house. Enter* Gratiano, Lorenzo, Salarino, *and* Solanio

Lorenzo
Nay, we will slink away in supper time,
Disguise us at my lodging, and return
All in an hour.

Gratiano
We have not made good preparation.

1 *supper*: A meal eaten around 5.00 p.m.
2 *Disguise us*: Lorenzo is urging his friends to join him in a masque—which usually involved a spectacular entry with music and torches.

5 *spoke us*: made arrangements for.

6 *quaintly order'd*: done with style.

9 *furnish us*: get ourselves ready.

10 *And*: if.
break up: unseal.

10–11 *seem to signify*: appear to indicate.

12 *hand*: handwriting.

12, 14 *fair hand*: a) elegant handwriting; b) beautiful hand.

15 *By your leave*: please excuse me (a phrase to excuse one's departure).

17 *sup*: come to supper.

19 *this*: i.e. a tip.

23 *provided of*: supplied with.

24 *straight*: immediately.

26 *some hour*: in about an hour.

Salarino
We have not spoke us yet of torchbearers.
Solanio
'Tis vile unless it may be quaintly order'd,
And better in my mind not undertook.
Lorenzo
'Tis now but four of clock; we have two hours
To furnish us.

Enter Lancelot *with a letter*

Friend Lancelot! What's the news?
Lancelot
And it shall please you to break up this, it shall seem to signify.
Lorenzo
I know the hand; in faith, 'tis a fair hand,
And whiter than the paper it writ on
Is the fair hand that writ.
Gratiano
Love news, in faith!
Lancelot
By your leave, sir.
Lorenzo
Whither goest thou?
Lancelot
Marry, sir, to bid my old master the Jew to sup tonight with my new master the Christian.
Lorenzo
Hold here, take this. Tell gentle Jessica
I will not fail her; speak it privately. [*Exit* Lancelot
Go, gentlemen:
Will you prepare you for this masque tonight?
I am provided of a torchbearer.
Salarino
Ay marry, I'll be gone about it straight.
Solanio
And so will I.
Lorenzo
Meet me and Gratiano
At Gratiano's lodging some hour hence.

Salarino
'Tis good we do so.
[*Exeunt* Salarino *and* Solanio

Gratiano
Was not that letter from fair Jessica?

Lorenzo
I must needs tell thee all. She hath directed
How I shall take her from her father's house,
What gold and jewels she is furnish'd with,
What page's suit she hath in readiness.
If e'er the Jew her father come to heaven,
It will be for his gentle daughter's sake;
And never dare misfortune cross her foot,
Unless she do it under this excuse
That she is issue to a faithless Jew.
Come, go with me; peruse this as thou goest.
Fair Jessica shall be my torchbearer. [*Exeunt*

29 *I . . . all*: I've just got to tell you everything.
directed: instructed.
31 *furnish'd with*: in possession of.
34 *gentle*: Lorenzo seems to make a pun with 'Gentile' (see *1*, 3, 173).
35 *foot*: path.
36 *she do it*: misfortune trips her up.
under: with.
37 *issue . . . Jew*: the child of a Jew lacking Christian faith.
38 *peruse*: study.

Scene 5

Act 2 Scene 5
Shylock leaves Jessica in charge of his house.

0s.d. *Clown*: i.e. the company comedian—see *2*, 2, 0s.d. note.

Venice: outside Shylock*'s house. Enter* Shylock *the Jew and* Lancelot *his man that was, the Clown*

Shylock
Well, thou shalt see, thy eyes shall be thy judge,
The difference of old Shylock and Bassanio—
What, Jessica!—Thou shalt not gourmandize
As thou hast done with me—What, Jessica!—
And sleep, and snore, and rend apparel out.
Why, Jessica, I say!

Lancelot
Why, Jessica!

Shylock
Who bids thee call? I do not bid thee call.

Lancelot
Your worship was wont to tell me I could do nothing without bidding.

2 *of*: between.
3 *gourmandize*: gorge yourself with food.
5 *rend . . . out*: wear out your clothes by tearing them.
8 *wont*: accustomed.

Enter Jessica

Jessica

Call you? What is your will?

Shylock

I am bid forth to supper, Jessica.
There are my keys. But wherefore should I go?
I am not bid for love, they flatter me;
But yet I'll go in hate, to feed upon
The prodigal Christian. Jessica my girl,
Look to my house. I am right loath to go;
There is some ill a-brewing towards my rest,
For I did dream of money bags tonight.

Lancelot

I beseech you, sir, go; my young master doth expect your reproach.

Shylock

So do I his.

Lancelot

And they have conspired together—I will not say you shall see a masque; but if you do, then it was not for nothing that my nose fell a-bleeding on Black Monday last, at six a clock i'the morning, falling out that year on Ash Wednesday was four year in th'afternoon.

Shylock

What, are there masques? Hear you me, Jessica,
Lock up my doors, and when you hear the drum
And the vile squealing of the wry-neck'd fife,
Clamber not you up to the casements then
Nor thrust your head into the public street
To gaze on Christian fools with varnish'd faces;
But stop my house's ears—I mean my casements—
Let not the sound of shallow foppery enter
My sober house. By Jacob's staff I swear
I have no mind of feasting forth tonight:
But I will go. Go you before me, sirrah;
Say I will come.

Lancelot

I will go before, sir.

[*Aside to* Jessica] Mistress, look out at window for all this:

11 *bid forth*: invited out.

12 *wherefore*: why.

15 *prodigal*: wastrel; see *1*, 1, 129 note.

16 *Look to*: take care of.
right loath: very reluctant.

17 *There . . . rest*: something is being plotted to harm my peace of mind.

18 *tonight*: last night.

20 *reproach*: Lancelot means 'approach'—but Shylock takes his word, not his meaning.

23–6 *it . . . afternoon*: Lancelot mocks Shylock's interpretation of his dream; 'Black Monday' = Easter Monday, and 'Ash Wednesday' is the first day of Lent (40 days *before* Easter).

29 *wry-neck'd fife*: a small pipe played sideways, giving the musician a twisted ('wry') neck.

30 *casements*: windows.

32 *with . . . faces*: wearing painted masks.

34 *shallow foppery*: frivolity.

35 *Jacob's staff*: Jacob, Shylock's hero (see *1*, 3, 66–83), had only one staff when he crossed the river Jordan, yet he returned a rich man (Genesis 32:10).

36 *forth*: away from home.

41 *worth . . . eye*: The expression (= something very valuable) was proverbial; 'Jewès' is an old inflected genitive (= Jew's).

42 *Hagar's offspring*: Abraham rejected Hagar and her son (his child), who were driven into the wilderness to live as outcasts (Genesis 21:9–21).

44 *patch*: fool.

45 *profit*: learning his job.

46 *wildcat*: a nocturnal animal which rests by day.
Drones . . . me: non-working bees do not live in my beehive.

48–9 *waste . . . purse*: squander the money he has borrowed.

52 *Fast . . . find*: keep what you've got, and you'll soon get more.

54 *cross'd*: thwarted.

There will come a Christian by
With be worth a Jewès eye. [*Exit*

Shylock
What says that fool of Hagar's offspring, ha?

Jessica
His words were 'Farewell, mistress', nothing else.

Shylock
The patch is kind enough, but a huge feeder,
Snail-slow in profit, and he sleeps by day
More than the wildcat. Drones hive not with me,
Therefore I part with him, and part with him
To one that I would have him help to waste
His borrow'd purse. Well, Jessica, go in;
Perhaps I will return immediately.
Do as I bid you, shut doors after you.
Fast bind, fast find:
A proverb never stale in thrifty mind. [*Exit*

Jessica
Farewell, and if my fortune be not cross'd,
I have a father, you a daughter, lost. [*Exit*

Scene 6

Act 2 Scene 6
Lorenzo and his friends rescue Jessica from her father's house.

0s.d. *masquers*: Fantastic costumes, grotesque masks, and torches help to create the Carnival atmosphere that Shylock feared.

1 *penthouse*: projecting upper storey of building; Gratiano may indicate the balcony above the stage doors, or the stage roof.

5 *lovers . . . clock*: lovers always come before their time (a near-proverbial saying).

6 *Venus' pigeons*: doves drawing Venus's chariot.

7 *seal . . . made*: make sure of new engagements.

7–8 *than . . . unforfeited*: than they usually do in keeping marriage vows ('obliged faith') unbroken.

8 *obliged*: obligèd.

9 *ever holds*: is always true.

Venice: outside Shylock*'s house. Enter the masquers,* Gratiano *and* Salarino

Gratiano
This is the penthouse under which Lorenzo
Desir'd us to make stand.

Salarino
His hour is almost past.

Gratiano
And it is marvel he outdwells his hour,
For lovers ever run before the clock.

Salarino
O, ten times faster Venus' pigeons fly
To seal love's bonds new made than they are wont
To keep obliged faith unforfeited!

Gratiano
That ever holds: who riseth from a feast
With that keen appetite that he sits down?

Where is the horse that doth untread again
His tedious measures with the unbated fire
That he did pace them first? All things that are
Are with more spirit chased than enjoy'd.
How like a younger or a prodigal
The scarfed bark puts from her native bay,
Hugg'd and embraced by the strumpet wind!
How like the prodigal doth she return
With overweather'd ribs and ragged sails,
Lean, rent, and beggar'd by the strumpet wind!

Enter Lorenzo

Salarino
Here comes Lorenzo; more of this hereafter.

Lorenzo
Sweet friends, your patience for my long abode.
Not I but my affairs have made you wait.
When you shall please to play the thieves for wives,
I'll watch as long for you then. Approach—
Here dwells my father Jew. Ho! Who's within?

Enter Jessica *above, in boy's clothes*

Jessica
Who are you? Tell me, for more certainty,
Albeit I'll swear that I do know your tongue.

Lorenzo
Lorenzo, and thy love.

Jessica
Lorenzo certain, and my love indeed,
For who love I so much? And now who knows
But you, Lorenzo, whether I am yours?

Lorenzo
Heaven and thy thoughts are witness that thou art.

Jessica
Here, catch this casket, it is worth the pains.
I am glad 'tis night, you do not look on me,
For I am much asham'd of my exchange.
But love is blind, and lovers cannot see
The pretty follies that themselves commit;

11 *untread*: retrace.

12 *measures*: steps, paces (in a riding-school display of dressage).
unbated fire: undiminished energy.

14 *chased*: chasèd.

15 *younger*: younger son.

16 *scarfed bark*: scarfèd; ship with all flags flying.

17 *embraced*: embracèd.
strumpet: unfaithful (like a prostitute).

18 *the prodigal*: The Prodigal Son wasted his inheritance on prostitutes and riotous living (see *1*, 1, 129).

19 *over-weather'd ribs*: weather-beaten timbers.

20 *rent*: torn.

22 *long abode*: staying away so long.

26 *father*: father-in-law; Lorenzo is sarcastic.

36 *exchange*: change into male clothing.

For if they could, Cupid himself would blush
To see me thus transformed to a boy.

Lorenzo

Descend, for you must be my torchbearer.

Jessica

What, must I hold a candle to my shames?
They in themselves, good sooth, are too too light.
Why, 'tis an office of discovery, love,
And I should be obscur'd.

Lorenzo

So are you, sweet,
Even in the lovely garnish of a boy.
But come at once,
For the close night doth play the runaway,
And we are stay'd for at Bassanio's feast.

Jessica

I will make fast the doors, and gild myself
With some moe ducats, and be with you straight.

[*Exit* Jessica *above*

Gratiano

Now by my hood, a gentle and no Jew!

Lorenzo

Beshrew me but I love her heartily.
For she is wise, if I can judge of her,
And fair she is, if that mine eyes be true,
And true she is, as she hath prov'd herself:
And therefore like herself, wise, fair, and true,
Shall she be placed in my constant soul.

Enter Jessica

What, art thou come? On, gentleman, away!
Our masquing mates by this time for us stay.

[*Exit with* Jessica

Enter Antonio

Antonio

Who's there?

Gratiano

Signor Antonio?

40 *transformed*: transformèd.

43 *good sooth*: goodness knows.
light: a) apparent; b) immodest.

44 *'tis . . . discovery*: the torchbearer's job is to show light on things.

45 *obscur'd*: concealed.

46 *garnish*: costume.

48 *close*: secretive.
doth . . . runaway: is speeding by.

49 *stay'd*: waited.

50 *make fast*: lock up.
gild myself: provide myself with (more) gold.

51 *straight*: immediately.

52 *by my hood*: upon my word.
gentle: a) well-bred girl; b) Gentile.

53 *Beshrew me*: damn me (a mild oath, added for emphasis).
heartily: with all my heart.

55 *be true*: see truly.

58 *Shall . . . soul*: she will always have a place in my faithful heart.
placed: placèd.

59 *gentleman*: Lorenzo laughingly addresses Jessica in her page's costume.

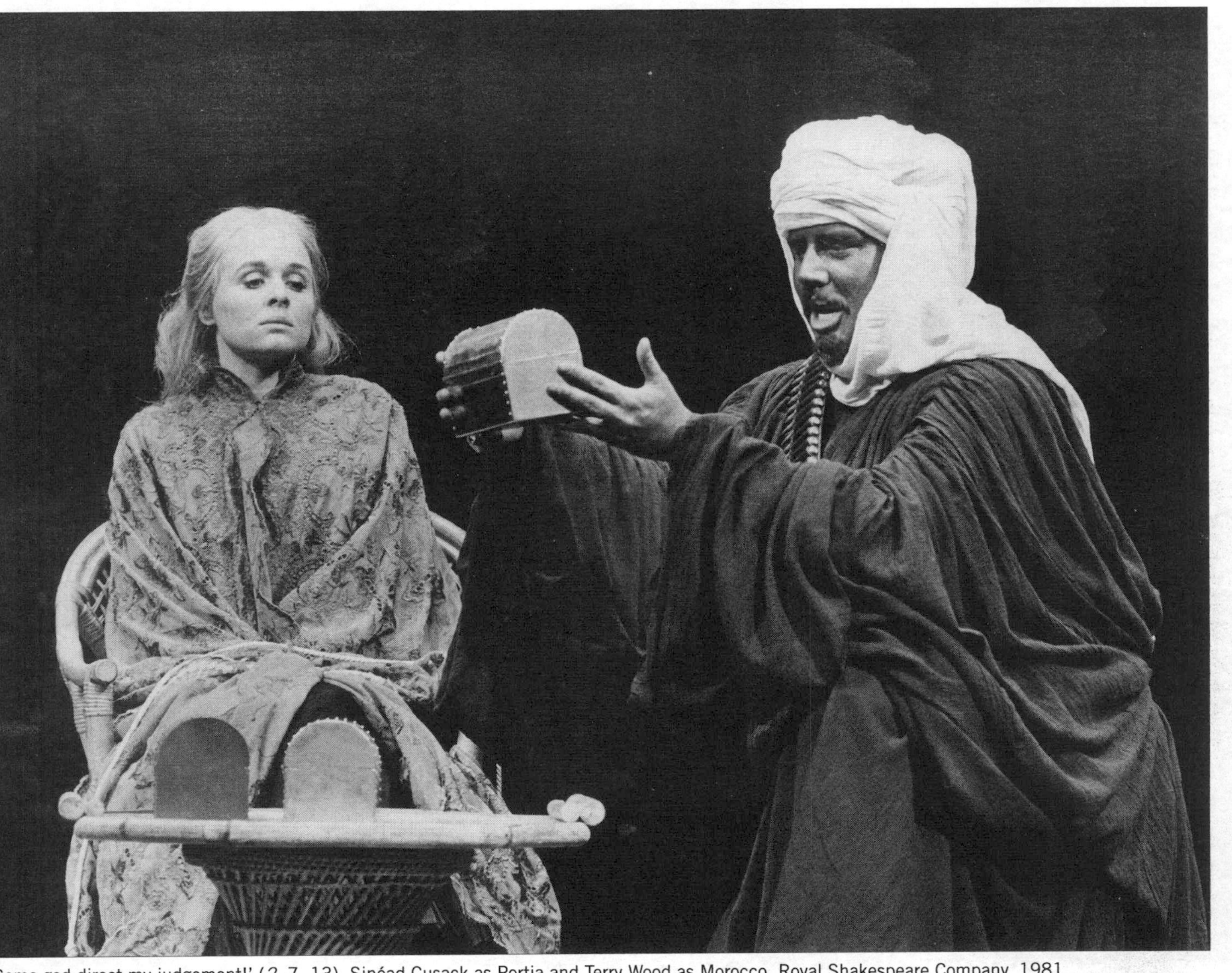

'Some god direct my judgement!' (*2*, 7, 13). Sinéad Cusack as Portia and Terry Wood as Morocco, Royal Shakespeare Company, 1981.

Antonio
Fie, fie, Gratiano, where are all the rest?
'Tis nine a clock, our friends all stay for you.
No masque tonight: the wind is come about,
Bassanio presently will go aboard.
I have sent twenty out to seek for you.

Gratiano
I am glad on't; I desire no more delight
Than to be under sail and gone tonight. [*Exeunt*

65 *is come about*: has changed direction.
66 *presently*: immediately.
69 *to . . . sail*: to sail away.

Scene 7

Act 2 Scene 7
The Prince of Morocco examines the caskets and makes his choice.

Belmont: Portia*'s house. Enter* Portia *with the* Prince of Morocco *and both their trains*

1 *discover*: reveal.
2 *several*: different.

Portia
Go, draw aside the curtains and discover
The several caskets to this noble prince.
Now make your choice.

Morocco
This first of gold, who this inscription bears,
'Who chooseth me, shall gain what many men desire.'
The second silver, which this promise carries,
'Who chooseth me, shall get as much as he deserves.'
This third dull lead, with warning all as blunt,
'Who chooseth me, must give and hazard all he hath.'
How shall I know if I do choose the right?

8 *as blunt*: as plain as the metal.
9 *hazard*: risk.

Portia
The one of them contains my picture, prince.
If you choose that, then I am yours withal.

12 *withal*: with the casket.

Morocco
Some god direct my judgement! Let me see:
I will survey th'inscriptions back again.
What says this leaden casket?
'Who chooseth me, must give and hazard all he hath.'
Must give—for what? For lead? Hazard for lead!
This casket threatens: men that hazard all
Do it in hope of fair advantages.
A golden mind stoops not to shows of dross;
I'll then nor give nor hazard aught for lead.
What says the silver with her virgin hue?

14 *back again*: in reverse order.
19 *fair advantages*: good returns.
20 *dross*: rubbish, impure metal.
21 *nor . . . nor*: neither . . . nor.

'Who chooseth me, shall get as much as he deserves.'
As much as he deserves—pause there, Morocco,
And weigh thy value with an even hand.
If thou be'st rated by thy estimation
Thou dost deserve enough; and yet enough
May not extend so far as to the lady;
And yet to be afear'd of my deserving
Were but a weak disabling of myself.
As much as I deserve: why, that's the lady.
I do in birth deserve her, and in fortunes,
In graces, and in qualities of breeding:
But more than these, in love I do deserve.
What if I stray'd no farther, but chose here?
Let's see once more this saying grav'd in gold:
'Who chooseth me, shall gain what many men desire.'
Why, that's the lady; all the world desires her.
From the four corners of the earth they come
To kiss this shrine, this mortal breathing saint.
The Hyrcanian deserts and the vasty wilds
Of wide Arabia are as throughfares now
For princes to come view fair Portia.
The watery kingdom, whose ambitious head
Spits in the face of heaven, is no bar
To stop the foreign spirits, but they come
As o'er a brook to see fair Portia.
One of these three contains her heavenly picture.
Is't like that lead contains her? 'Twere damnation
To think so base a thought; it were too gross
To rib her cerecloth in the obscure grave.
Or shall I think in silver she's immur'd,
Being ten times undervalu'd to tried gold?
O sinful thought! Never so rich a gem
Was set in worse than gold. They have in England
A coin that bears the figure of an angel
Stamped in gold; but that's insculp'd upon:
But here an angel in a golden bed
Lies all within. Deliver me the key:
Here do I choose, and thrive I as I may.

Portia

There take it, prince, and if my form lie there,
Then I am yours.

25 *even*: impartial.

26 *rated*: judged.
estimation: reputation.

29 *afear'd . . . deserving*: unsure what I deserve.

30 *disabling*: belittling.

36 *grav'd*: engraved.

40 *mortal breathing*: living.

41 *Hyrcanian deserts*: The classical name for a savage region south of the Caspian Sea.
vasty wilds: immense wildernesses.

42 *throughfares*: main roads.

44 *The watery kingdom*: Neptune's realm, the ocean.

44–5 *whose . . . heaven*: whose waves surge up to the sky.

45 *bar*: obstacle.

46 *spirits*: men of courage.

49 *like*: likely.

50–1 *it were . . . cerecloth*: lead would be too coarse to enfold the shroud.

51 *obscure*: dark; the emphasis is on the first syllable.

52 *immur'd*: walled in.

53 *ten . . . gold*: of ten times less value than pure ('tried') gold.

54–5 *Never . . . gold*: jewels as precious as Portia are never set in anything but gold.

56 *A coin . . . angel*: The coin, called an 'angel', depicted the archangel Michael.

57 *Stamped*: stampèd.
insculp'd upon: engraved.

61 *form*: picture.

Morocco unlocks the gold casket

Morocco

O hell! What have we here?
A carrion death, within whose empty eye
There is a written scroll. I'll read the writing.
'All that glisters is not gold;
Often have you heard that told.
Many a man his life hath sold
But my outside to behold.
Gilded tombs do worms infold.
Had you been as wise as bold,
Young in limbs, in judgement old,
Your answer had not been inscroll'd.
Fare you well, your suit is cold.'
Cold indeed, and labour lost;
Then farewell heat, and welcome frost.
Portia, adieu; I have too griev'd a heart
To take a tedious leave: thus losers part.

[*Exit* Morocco *with his train*

Portia

A gentle riddance! Draw the curtains, go.
Let all of his complexion choose me so. [*Exeunt*

A flourish of cornets

63 *A carrion death*: a death's-head, a skull.

65 *glisters*: glitters.
72 *Your . . . inscroll'd*: you would not have got the answer on this scroll.
73 *your . . . cold*: your hopes are dead.

79 *of his complexion*: like him.

SCENE 8

Act 2 Scene 8
Salarino and Solanio gossip about the news: Lorenzo is missing, Shylock has been robbed, and Antonio is in trouble.

Venice: a street. Enter Salarino *and* Solanio

Salarino

Why, man, I saw Bassanio under sail,
With him is Gratiano gone along;
And in their ship I am sure Lorenzo is not.

Solanio

The villain Jew with outcries rais'd the duke,
Who went with him to search Bassanio's ship.

Salarino

He came too late, the ship was under sail.
But there the duke was given to understand

1 *under sail*: sail away.

4 *rais'd*: roused.

That in a gondola were seen together
Lorenzo and his amorous Jessica.
Besides, Antonio certified the duke
They were not with Bassanio in his ship.

Solanio

I never heard a passion so confus'd,
So strange, outrageous, and so variable,
As the dog Jew did utter in the streets:
'My daughter! O my ducats! O my daughter!
Fled with a Christian! O my Christian ducats!
Justice! The law! My ducats and my daughter!
A sealed bag, two sealed bags of ducats,
Of double ducats, stolen from me by my daughter!
And jewels—two stones, two rich and precious stones,
Stolen by my daughter! Justice! Find the girl!
She hath the stones upon her and the ducats!'

Salarino

Why, all the boys in Venice follow him,
Crying his stones, his daughter, and his ducats.

Solanio

Let good Antonio look he keep his day,
Or he shall pay for this.

Salarino

Marry, well remember'd:
I reason'd with a Frenchman yesterday
Who told me, in the Narrow Seas that part
The French and English, there miscarried
A vessel of our country richly fraught.
I thought upon Antonio when he told me,
And wish'd in silence that it were not his.

8 *gondola*: a flat-bottomed boat used on the canals of Venice.

10 *certified*: assured.

18 *sealed*: sealèd.

19 *double ducats*: worth double the value of ducats.

24 *his stones*: a) jewels; b) testicles.

25 *look . . . day*: be sure to pay his debt on the appointed day.

28 *reason'd*: spoke.

29 *the Narrow Seas*: the English Channel.

30 *miscarried*: miscarrièd; perished.

31 *fraught*: laden.

Solanio
You were best to tell Antonio what you hear.
Yet do not suddenly, for it may grieve him.

Salarino
A kinder gentleman treads not the earth.
I saw Bassanio and Antonio part:
Bassanio told him he would make some speed
Of his return: he answered, 'Do not so.
Slubber not business for my sake, Bassanio,
But stay the very riping of the time;
And for the Jew's bond which he hath of me,
Let it not enter in your mind of love.
Be merry, and employ your chiefest thoughts
To courtship, and such fair ostents of love
As shall conveniently become you there.'
And even there, his eye being big with tears,
Turning his face, he put his hand behind him,
And with affection wondrous sensible
He wrung Bassanio's hand, and so they parted.

Solanio
I think he only loves the world for him.
I pray thee let us go and find him out
And quicken his embraced heaviness
With some delight or other.

Salarino
Do we so. [*Exeunt*

40 *Slubber not business*: don't be hurried and careless with your affairs.
41 *stay . . . time*: wait until the time is exactly right.
42 *for*: as for.
43 *mind of love*: love-schemes.
45 *ostents*: demonstrations.
46 *conveniently become you*: make you appropriately attractive.
47 *even there*: just at that point.
49 *affection . . . sensible*: amazingly powerful emotion.
51 *he . . . him*: Bassanio is all he lives for.
53 *quicken . . . heaviness*: brighten up this misery that he's indulging in. *embraced*: embracèd.

Act 2 Scene 9
Another suitor makes his choice—and Portia learns that Bassanio is coming to Belmont.

0s.d. *Servitor*: servingman.
1 *draw*: pull back. *straight*: immediately.
3 *to his election*: to make his choice.

Scene 9

Belmont: Portia*'s house. Enter* Nerissa *and a* Servitor

Nerissa
Quick, quick, I pray thee, draw the curtain straight.
The Prince of Arragon hath tane his oath,
And comes to his election presently.

A flourish of cornets. Enter the Prince of Arragon, *his train, and* Portia

Portia
Behold, there stand the caskets, noble prince.

6 *solemniz'd*: performed.

9 *enjoin'd*: bound.
observe: promise.

10 *unfold*: disclose.

14 *do . . . choice*: make an unlucky choice.

17 *hazard*: gamble.

18 *address'd me*: prepared myself (by taking the oath).
Fortune: good luck.

24–5 *be . . . By*: refer to.

25 *show*: appearance.

26 *fond*: foolish.

27 *pries not*: doesn't look into.
the martlet: the swift, or house-martin.

28 *Builds . . . weather*: builds its nest exposed to the weather.

29 *Even . . . casualty*: right in the power and path of destruction.

31 *jump*: go along with.

32 *rank me*: class myself.

36–7 *go . . . cozen*: try to cheat.

38 *Without . . . merit*: without the legal authorization ('stamp') of merit.

39 *wear*: hold; positions of rank and authority are usually indicated by the wearing of some badge or garment.
undeserved: undeservèd.

40 *estates . . . offices*: estates of the realm (e.g. nobility), ranks within these estates (e.g. earls, barons), and official appointments (e.g. the chancellorship).

41 *deriv'd*: obtained.

42 *the wearer*: the bearer.

If you choose that wherein I am contain'd,
Straight shall our nuptial rites be solemniz'd;
But if you fail, without more speech, my lord,
You must be gone from hence immediately.

Arragon

I am enjoin'd by oath to observe three things:
First, never to unfold to anyone
Which casket 'twas I chose; next, if I fail
Of the right casket, never in my life
To woo a maid in way of marriage; lastly,
If I do fail in fortune of my choice,
Immediately to leave you and be gone.

Portia

To these injunctions everyone doth swear
That comes to hazard for my worthless self.

Arragon

And so have I address'd me. Fortune now
To my heart's hope! Gold, silver, and base lead.
'Who chooseth me, must give and hazard all he hath.'
You shall look fairer ere I give or hazard.
What says the golden chest? Ha, let me see:
'Who chooseth me, shall gain what many men desire.'
What many men desire: that 'many' may be meant
By the fool multitude that choose by show,
Not learning more than the fond eye doth teach,
Which pries not to th'interior, but like the martlet
Builds in the weather on the outward wall,
Even in the force and road of casualty.
I will not choose what many men desire,
Because I will not jump with common spirits,
And rank me with the barbarous multitudes.
Why then, to thee, thou silver treasure house:
Tell me once more what title thou dost bear.
'Who chooseth me, shall get as much as he deserves.'
And well said too, for who shall go about
To cozen Fortune and be honourable
Without the stamp of merit? Let none presume
To wear an undeserved dignity.
O, that estates, degrees, and offices
Were not deriv'd corruptly, and that clear honour
Were purchas'd by the merit of the wearer!

43 *cover*: keep their hats on (instead of doffing them in respect to superiors).

45 *glean'd*: picked out.

47 *Pick'd . . . times*: sorted out from what the modern age rejects and spoils.

48 *new varnish'd*: a) polished up (like grains of corn); b) newly-painted (as a coat-of-arms).

50 *I will . . . desert*: I will claim to be deserving ('assume' = put on the ceremonial insignia of).

52 *Too . . . pause*: Arragon is speechless.

53 *blinking*: goggle-eyed.

54 *schedule*: written scroll.

60–1 *To . . . natures*: Portia cannot comment on the offence she has (unwittingly) given Arragon.

61 *opposed*: opposèd.

62 *The . . . this*: this silver was tested seven times in the furnace.

64 *amiss*: wrongly.

65 *shadows kiss*: embrace illusions.

67 *iwis*: assuredly.

68 *Silver'd o'er*: covered in silver (with decorations, or with white hair).

69–70 *Take . . . head*: whatever wife you marry, you will always be a fool.

71 *sped*: finished.

72–3 *Still . . . here*: I shall appear an even bigger fool the longer I stay here.

How many then should cover that stand bare!
How many be commanded that command!
How much low peasantry would then be glean'd
From the true seed of honour, and how much honour
Pick'd from the chaff and ruin of the times
To be new varnish'd! Well, but to my choice.
'Who chooseth me, shall get as much as he deserves.'
I will assume desert. Give me a key for this,
And instantly unlock my fortunes here.

Arragon *unlocks the silver casket*

Portia

Too long a pause for that which you find there.

Arragon

What's here? The portrait of a blinking idiot
Presenting me a schedule! I will read it.
How much unlike art thou to Portia!
How much unlike my hopes and my deservings.
'Who chooseth me, shall have as much as he deserves.'
Did I deserve no more than a fool's head?
Is that my prize? Are my deserts no better?

Portia

To offend and judge are distinct offices,
And of opposed natures.

Arragon

What is here?
[*He reads*] 'The fire seven times tried this;
Seven times tried that judgement is
That did never choose amiss.
Some there be that shadows kiss;
Such have but a shadow's bliss.
There be fools alive iwis
Silver'd o'er, and so was this.
Take what wife you will to bed,
I will ever be your head.
So be gone, you are sped.'
Still more fool I shall appear
By the time I linger here.
With one fool's head I came to woo,
But I go away with two.

Sweet, adieu; I'll keep my oath,
Patiently to bear my wroth.

[*Exit* Arragon *with his train*

Portia

Thus hath the candle singed the moth.
O, these deliberate fools! When they do choose
They have the wisdom by their wit to lose.

Nerissa

The ancient saying is no heresy:
'Hanging and wiving goes by destiny.'

Portia

Come draw the curtain, Nerissa.

Enter a Messenger

Messenger

Where is my lady?

Portia

Here. What would my lord?

Messenger

Madam, there is alighted at your gate
A young Venetian, one that comes before
To signify th'approaching of his lord,
From whom he bringeth sensible regreets:
To wit, besides commends and courteous breath,
Gifts of rich value. Yet I have not seen
So likely an ambassador of love.
A day in April never came so sweet
To show how costly summer was at hand
As this forespurrer comes before his lord.

Portia

No more I pray thee, I am half afear'd
Thou wilt say anon he is some kin to thee,
Thou spend'st such highday wit in praising him.
Come, come, Nerissa, for I long to see
Quick Cupid's post that comes so mannerly.

Nerissa

Bassanio, Lord Love, if thy will it be! [*Exeunt*

77 *wroth*: A possible spelling of either 'ruth' (= grief), or 'wrath'.

78 *singed*: burnt.

79 *deliberate*: reasoning, debating.

80 *They . . . lose*: their reasoning ('wit') gives them the wisdom to make the wrong choice.

81 *The . . . heresy*: the old proverb was no mistaken belief.

82 *wiving*: marrying.

84 *what . . . lord*: what do you want (Portia is ironic).

85 *alighted*: landed, dismounted.

87 *signify*: announce.

88 *sensible regreets*: tangible greetings (i.e. gifts).

89 *commends . . . breath*: compliments and polite speeches.

91 *likely*: a) promising; b) handsome.

92 *A day in April*: In England.

93 *costly*: rich (in flowers).
at hand: near.

94 *forespurrer*: herald (who spurs his horse ahead of the main party).

95 *afear'd*: afraid.

96 *anon*: presently.

97 *highday wit*: well-dressed language.

99 *post*: messenger.
mannerly: courteously.

100 *Bassanio . . . be*: O Lord Love, let it be Bassanio.

ACT 3

SCENE 1

Act 3 Scene 1
Trouble for Antonio: Shylock rejoices in his power over the merchant—and laments for the loss of his daughter.

Venice: a street. Enter Solanio *and* Salarino

Solanio
Now, what news on the Rialto?

Salarino
Why, yet it lives there unchecked that Antonio hath a ship of rich lading wrecked on the Narrow Seas; the Goodwins I think they call the place—a very dangerous flat, and fatal, where the carcasses of many a tall ship lie buried, as they say, if my gossip Report be an honest woman of her word.

Solanio
I would she were as lying a gossip in that as ever knapped ginger or made her neighbours believe she wept for the death of a third husband. But it is true, without any slips of prolixity, or crossing the plain highway of talk, that the good Antonio, the honest Antonio—O that I had a title good enough to keep his name company!—

Salarino
Come, the full stop.

Solanio
Ha, what sayest thou? Why, the end is, he hath lost a ship.

Salarino
I would it might prove the end of his losses.

Solanio
Let me say 'amen' betimes, lest the devil cross my prayer, for here he comes in the likeness of a Jew.

Enter Shylock

How now, Shylock, what news among the merchants?

2 *it lives*: the rumour persists.
unchecked: without contradiction.
3 *lading*: loading, cargo.
the Narrow Seas: the English Channel.
4 *the Goodwins*: The Goodwin Sands in the middle of the Channel are a major hazard for shipping.
5 *flat*: sandbank.
tall: fine.
6 *my gossip Report*: my old friend Rumour ('gossip' = godmother).
8 *in that*: in that report.
9 *knapped*: munched; ginger (also associated with old women in *Measure for Measure*, *4*, 3, 7) is good for flatulence.
11–12 *without . . . talk*: without falling into garrulousness or deviating from a straightforward account; Solanio illustrates the fault he claims to avoid.
15 *Come . . . stop*: a) finish your sentence; b) rein in your horse (from a full gallop).
19 *betimes*: quickly.
cross: a) frustrate; b) sign with a cross.

Shylock

You knew, none so well, none so well as you, of my daughter's flight.

Salarino

That's certain; I for my part knew the tailor that made the wings she flew withal.

Solanio

And Shylock for his own part knew the bird was fledged, and then it is the complexion of them all to leave the dam.

Shylock

She is damned for it.

Salarino

That's certain—if the devil may be her judge.

Shylock

My own flesh and blood to rebel!

Solanio

Out upon it, old carrion! Rebels it at these years?

Shylock

I say my daughter is my flesh and my blood.

Salarino

There is more difference between thy flesh and hers than between jet and ivory; more between your bloods than there is between red wine and Rhenish. But tell us, do you hear whether Antonio have had any loss at sea or no?

Shylock

There I have another bad match: a bankrupt, a prodigal, who dare scarce show his head on the Rialto, a beggar that was used to come so smug upon the mart. Let him look to his bond. He was wont to call me usurer; let him look to his bond. He was wont to lend money for a Christian courtesy; let him look to his bond.

Salarino

Why, I am sure if he forfeit thou wilt not take his flesh. What's that good for?

Shylock

To bait fish withal; if it will feed nothing else, it will feed my revenge. He hath disgraced me, and hindered me half a million, laughed at my losses, mocked at my gains, scorned my nation, thwarted my bargains, cooled

25 *withal*: with.

27 *fledged*: had feathers.
complexion: nature, disposition.

28 *dam*: mother.

30 *the devil*: i.e. Shylock himself.

32 *Out . . . carrion*: get away with you, you dirty old man; Solanio pretends that Shylock is referring to his own body.

36 *Rhenish*: expensive white German wine.

39 *match*: bargain.

41 *smug*: pleased with himself.
mart: stock exchange.

42 *look to*: take care of.
wont: accustomed.

43–4 *for . . . courtesy*: out of Christian charity.

47 *bait*: use as a bait for.

48 *disgraced*: done me disfavour.

48–9 *hindered . . . million*: prevented me from making half a million ducats profit.

50 *bargains*: business deals.
cooled: alienated.

my friends, heated mine enemies—and what's his reason? I am a Jew. Hath not a Jew eyes? Hath not a Jew hands, organs, dimensions, senses, affections, passions? Fed with the same food, hurt with the same weapons, subject to the same diseases, healed by the same means, warmed and cooled by the same winter and summer as a Christian is? If you prick us, do we not bleed? If you tickle us, do we not laugh? If you poison us, do we not die? And if you wrong us, shall we not revenge? If we are like you in the rest, we will resemble you in that. If a Jew wrong a Christian, what is his humility? Revenge. If a Christian wrong a Jew, what should his sufferance be by Christian example? Why, revenge! The villainy you teach me I will execute, and it shall go hard but I will better the instruction.

Enter a Servingman *from* Antonio

Servingman
Gentlemen, my master Antonio is at his house, and desires to speak with you both.

Salarino
We have been up and down to seek him.

Enter Tubal

Solanio
Here comes another of the tribe; a third cannot be matched, unless the devil himself turn Jew.

[*Exeunt* Salarino *and* Solanio *with the* Servingman

Shylock
How now, Tubal, what news from Genoa? Hast thou found my daughter?

Tubal
I often came where I did hear of her, but cannot find her.

Shylock
Why there, there, there, there! A diamond gone cost me two thousand ducats in Frankfurt! The curse never fell upon our nation till now, I never felt it till now. Two thousand ducats in that, and other precious, precious

51 *heated*: enraged.

53 *dimensions*: bodily parts, limbs. *affections, passions*: Elizabethan psychology distinguished between 'affections' (= strong sensuous responses of attraction or revulsion) and 'passions' (= disturbances of the mind).

61 *what . . . humility*: what is the response of his Christian humility.

62 *sufferance*: forebearance (see *1*, 3, 105).

64–5 *it . . . instruction*: unless something serious prevents me, I will improve on what you have taught me.

68 *up . . . him*: looking everywhere for him.

69–70 *cannot be matched*: cannot be found to equal these two.

76 *Frankfurt*: A great jewel fair was held here annually.

76–7 *The . . . nation*: The Jews were cursed and condemned to eternal exile because they disobeyed God's law (Daniel 9:11).

jewels! I would my daughter were dead at my foot, and the jewels in her ear: would she were hearsed at my foot, and the ducats in her coffin. No news of them, why so? And I know not what's spent in the search. Why thou loss upon loss—the thief gone with so much, and so much to find the thief, and no satisfaction, no revenge, nor no ill luck stirring but what lights o'my shoulders, no sighs but o'my breathing, no tears but o'my shedding!

Tubal

Yes, other men have ill luck too. Antonio as I heard in Genoa—

Shylock

What, what, what? Ill luck, ill luck?

Tubal

—hath an argosy cast away coming from Tripolis.

Shylock

I thank God, I thank God. Is it true, is it true?

Tubal

I spoke with some of the sailors that escaped the wreck.

Shylock

I thank thee, good Tubal: good news, good news! Ha, ha, heard in Genoa!

Tubal

Your daughter spent in Genoa, as I heard, one night four score ducats.

Shylock

Thou stick'st a dagger in me; I shall never see my gold again. Four score ducats at a sitting! Four score ducats!

Tubal

There came divers of Antonio's creditors in my company to Venice that swear he cannot choose but break.

Shylock

I am very glad of it. I'll plague him, I'll torture him. I am glad of it.

Tubal

One of them showed me a ring that he had of your daughter for a monkey.

80 *hearsed*: laid in her coffin.

82–3 *Why . . . loss*: Shylock's angry grief makes him inarticulate.

85 *lights o'*: lands upon.

86 *but o'my breathing*: except those I sigh.

91 *argosy*: trading vessel.
cast away: wrecked.

96 *one night*: in one night.

99 *at a sitting*: on a single occasion.

100 *divers*: several.

100–1 *in my company*: along with me.

102 *break*: go bankrupt.

105 *of*: from.

107 *Out upon her*: A common expression of impatience.
108 *had it of Leah*: it was a present from Leah; Shylock's wife is presumably dead.
110 *undone*: ruined.
111–12 *fee . . . officer*: hire a sheriff's officer at my expense (to arrest Antonio).
112 *bespeak . . . before*: order him to be ready two weeks before the debt's repayment is due.
114 *make . . . will*: drive whatever bargains I like.
115 *synagogue*: The Jewish moneylenders will confirm their dealings with an oath.

Shylock

Out upon her! Thou torturest me, Tubal: it was my turquoise, I had it of Leah when I was a bachelor. I would not have given it for a wilderness of monkeys.

Tubal

But Antonio is certainly undone.

Shylock

Nay, that's true, that's very true. Go, Tubal, fee me an officer, bespeak him a fortnight before. I will have the heart of him if he forfeit, for were he out of Venice I can make what merchandise I will. Go, Tubal, and meet me at our synagogue, go, good Tubal, at our synagogue, Tubal. [*Exeunt*

Act 3 Scene 2
Bassanio makes his choice of caskets, winning Portia for his wife. Nerissa agrees to marry Gratiano, and both contracts are sealed with a ring. Lorenzo and Jessica arrive in Belmont, bringing a letter from Antonio.

0s.d. *trains*: attendants.
1 *tarry*: delay.
2 *hazard*: take the risk.
5 *I would not*: I don't want to.
6 *Hate . . . quality*: hatred does not give advice in this manner.
8 *a maiden . . . thought*: maidenly modesty won't let me speak my thoughts.
10 *venture for me*: try to win me.
11 *am forsworn*: have broken my vow.
12 *miss*: lose.

Scene 2

Belmont: Portia*'s house. Enter* Bassanio, Portia, Gratiano, Nerissa, *and all their trains*

Portia

I pray you tarry, pause a day or two
Before you hazard, for in choosing wrong
I lose your company; therefore forbear a while.
There's something tells me, but it is not love,
I would not lose you; and you know yourself
Hate counsels not in such a quality.
But lest you should not understand me well—
And yet a maiden hath no tongue but thought—
I would detain you here some month or two
Before you venture for me. I could teach you
How to choose right, but then I am forsworn.
So will I never be. So may you miss me;

13–14 *wish . . . forsworn*: wish I had sinned and broken my vow.
14 *Beshrew*: a curse upon.
15 *o'erlook'd*: bewitched.

18–19 *these . . . rights*: these wicked times bar owners from claiming what belongs to them.
20 *Prove it so*: if it happens that I am lost to you.
21 *Let . . . hell*: let Fortune go to hell for depriving you of what is yours.
22 *peize*: weigh down, prolong.
23 *eche it*: stretch it out.
24 *stay . . . election*: hold you back from making a choice.

25 *the rack*: an instrument of torture, stretching out the victim's body (as Portia is trying to stretch out the time) until he confessed his treason.

28 *mistrust*: anxiety.
29 *fear . . . love*: afraid that I shall not be able to have you as my wife.
30 *amity*: friendship.

33 *enforced*: enforcèd; compelled (by torture).

36 *Had . . . confession*: would have been my full confession.

38 *deliverance*: release.

42 *aloof*: at a distance, upstage.

But if you do, you'll make me wish a sin,
That I had been forsworn. Beshrew your eyes!
They have o'erlook'd me and divided me:
One half of me is yours, the other half yours—
Mine own, I would say: but if mine then yours,
And so all yours. O these naughty times
Puts bars between the owners and their rights!
And so though yours, not yours. Prove it so,
Let Fortune go to hell for it, not I.
I speak too long, but 'tis to peize the time,
To eche it, and to draw it out in length,
To stay you from election.

Bassanio

Let me choose,
For as I am, I live upon the rack.

Portia

Upon the rack, Bassanio? Then confess
What treason there is mingl'd with your love.

Bassanio

None but that ugly treason of mistrust
Which makes me fear th'enjoying of my love.
There may as well be amity and life
'Tween snow and fire, as treason and my love.

Portia

Ay, but I fear you speak upon the rack
Where men enforced do speak anything.

Bassanio

Promise me life and I'll confess the truth.

Portia

Well then, confess and live.

Bassanio

'Confess and love'
Had been the very sum of my confession.
O happy torment, when my torturer
Doth teach me answers for deliverance!
But let me to my fortune and the caskets.

Portia

Away then! I am lock'd in one of them:
If you do love me, you will find me out.
Nerissa and the rest, stand all aloof.
Let music sound while he doth make his choice;

Then if he lose he makes a swan-like end,
Fading in music. That the comparison
May stand more proper, my eye shall be the stream
And watery deathbed for him. He may win,
And what is music then? Then music is
Even as the flourish when true subjects bow
To a new-crowned monarch. Such it is
As are those dulcet sounds in break of day,
That creep into the dreaming bridegroom's ear
And summon him to marriage. Now he goes
With no less presence, but with much more love,
Than young Alcides when he did redeem
The virgin tribute paid by howling Troy
To the sea-monster. I stand for sacrifice.
The rest aloof are the Dardanian wives,
With bleared visages come forth to view
The issue of th'exploit. Go, Hercules!
Live thou, I live. With much much more dismay
I view the fight than thou that mak'st the fray.

Here music. A song the whilst Bassanio *comments on the caskets to himself*

Tell me where is fancy bred,
Or in the heart, or in the head?
How begot, how nourished?
 Reply, reply.
It is engend'red in the eye,
With gazing fed, and fancy dies
In the cradle where it lies.
Let us all ring fancy's knell.
I'll begin it—Ding, dong, bell.

All
 Ding, dong, bell.

Bassanio
So may the outward shows be least themselves:
The world is still deceiv'd with ornament.
In law, what plea so tainted and corrupt
But, being season'd with a gracious voice,
Obscures the show of evil? In religion,
What damned error but some sober brow

44 *swan-like end*: It was an old belief that the mute swan sang once before its death.
45 *Fading*: dying, vanishing away.
46 *stand . . . proper*: fit more exactly.
46–7 *my eye . . . him*: I shall weep, and he will seem to drown in my tears.
49 *flourish*: trumpet fanfare.
50 *crowned*: crownèd.
51 *dulcet*: sweet.
54 *presence*: noble bearing.
55 *Alcides*: Hercules (grandson of Alceus) rescued a Trojan princess, Hesione, who was being sacrificed to a sea-monster.
56 *howling*: lamenting.
57 *I . . . sacrifice*: I represent the sacrificial victim.
58 *Dardanian wives*: Trojan women; Dardanus was the legendary founder of Troy.
59 *bleared visages*: blearèd; tear-stained faces.
60 *issue*: outcome.
61 *Live thou*: if you live.
62 *fray*: fighting.
62s.d. *comments . . . himself*: ponders silently over the caskets; the words of the song seem to articulate his thoughts.
63 *fancy*: attraction.
64 *Or . . . or*: either . . . or.
65 *nourished*: nourishèd.
67 *engend'red*: generated.
69 *in the cradle*: i.e. in its infancy.
70 *knell*: funeral bell.
73 *shows*: appearances.
least themselves: not what they are.
74 *still*: continually.
76 *season'd . . . voice*: presented with eloquence (like rotten food disguised with spices).
78 *damned error*: damnèd; heresy, false belief.
sober brow: solemn-faced person.

79 *approve . . . text*: confirm it with a quotation from the Bible (see *1*, 3, 93).
81 *simple*: a) uncomplicated; b) foolish.

84 *stayers*: ropes; many editions have 'stairs' (= sandbanks).
yet: nevertheless.
85 *Hercules . . . Mars*: the superman and the god of war in classical mythology.
86 *inward search'd*: intestinally examined.
livers . . . milk: The liver, believed to be the seat of courage, should be red with blood.
87 *valour's excrement*: the outgrowth of a brave man—i.e. a beard.
88 *redoubted*: terrible, fearsome.
89 *purchas'd . . . weight*: Cosmetics and false hair (taken from dead bodies or from prostitutes) could be bought by the kilo.
91 *lightest*: a) most dissolute; b) most light-weight (morally).
92 *crisped*: crispèd; curled.
snaky: flowing.
93 *wanton*: promiscuous.
94 *supposed fairness*: supposèd; presumed beauty.
95 *dowry*: endowment, gift.
97 *guiled*: guilèd; treacherous.
99 *Indian beauty*: A contradiction in terms: Elizabethans thought there was beauty only in fair skins.
102 *Hard . . . Midas*: Food became a problem when Apollo granted the mythological king's wish that all he touched might turn to gold.
103 *common drudge*: general servant.
106 *paleness*: lack of colour.
109 *As*: such as.
110 *green-ey'd jealousy*: Compare the proverbial 'green with envy'.
111 *allay*: diminish.
112 *measure*: moderation.
scant: restrain.

Will bless it and approve it with a text,
Hiding the grossness with fair ornament?
There is no vice so simple but assumes
Some mark of virtue on his outward parts.
How many cowards whose hearts are all as false
As stayers of sand, wear yet upon their chins
The beards of Hercules and frowning Mars,
Who inward search'd have livers white as milk,
And these assume but valour's excrement
To render them redoubted. Look on beauty,
And you shall see 'tis purchas'd by the weight,
Which therein works a miracle in nature,
Making them lightest that wear most of it.
So are those crisped snaky golden locks
Which maketh such wanton gambols with the wind
Upon supposed fairness, often known
To be the dowry of a second head,
The skull that bred them in the sepulchre.
Thus ornament is but the guiled shore
To a most dangerous sea; the beauteous scarf
Veiling an Indian beauty; in a word,
The seeming truth which cunning times put on
To entrap the wisest. Therefore thou gaudy gold,
Hard food for Midas, I will none of thee,
Nor none of thee, thou pale and common drudge
'Tween man and man. But thou, thou meagre lead
Which rather threaten'st than dost promise aught,
Thy paleness moves me more than eloquence:
And here choose I. Joy be the consequence!

Portia

[*Aside*] How all the other passions fleet to air:
As doubtful thoughts, and rash-embrac'd despair,
And shudd'ring fear, and green-ey'd jealousy!
O love, be moderate, allay thy ecstasy,
In measure rain thy joy, scant this excess!
I feel too much thy blessing: make it less
For fear I surfeit.

Bassanio *opens the leaden casket*

Bassanio

What find I here?
Fair Portia's counterfeit! What demi-god
Hath come so near creation? Move these eyes?
Or whether riding on the balls of mine
Seem they in motion? Here are sever'd lips
Parted with sugar breath; so sweet a bar
Should sunder such sweet friends. Here in her hairs
The painter plays the spider, and hath woven
A golden mesh t'entrap the hearts of men
Faster than gnats in cobwebs. But her eyes—
How could he see to do them? Having made one,
Methinks it should have power to steal both his
And leave itself unfurnish'd. Yet look how far
The substance of my praise doth wrong this shadow
In underprizing it, so far this shadow
Doth limp behind the substance. Here's the scroll,
The continent and summary of my fortune.
[*He reads*] 'You that choose not by the view
Chance as fair, and choose as true.
Since this fortune falls to you,
Be content and seek no new.
If you be well pleas'd with this,
And hold your fortune for your bliss,
Turn to where your lady is,
And claim her with a loving kiss.'
A gentle scroll! Fair lady, by your leave,
I come by note to give, and to receive.
Like one of two contending in a prize
That thinks he hath done well in people's eyes,
Hearing applause and universal shout,
Giddy in spirit, still gazing in a doubt
Whether those peals of praise be his or no—
So, thrice-fair lady, stand I even so,
As doubtful whether what I see be true,
Until confirm'd, sign'd, ratified by you.

Portia

You see me, Lord Bassanio, where I stand,
Such as I am. Though for myself alone
I would not be ambitious in my wish

115 *counterfeit*: picture.
116 *Move . . . eyes*: do these eyes move.
117 *riding . . . mine*: fixed on my eyes.
118 *sever'd*: parted.
119 *bar*: barrier (i.e. Portia's breath).
121 *painter . . . spider*: the painter has been like a spider.
123 *Faster*: more securely.
125 *power*: i.e. like the sun; Bassanio uses a conventional conceit.
126 *unfurnish'd*: without a mate.
how far: by the extent to which.
127 *substance*: body.
shadow: semblance.
128 *underprizing it*: failing to describe it adequately.
so far: to the same extent.
130 *continent*: container.
132 *Chance . . . true*: may you have such good fortune and always choose as well.
136 *hold . . . bliss*: account your fortune happiness.
140 *by note*: with a bill of dues.
141 *prize*: match.
143 *universal*: general.

To wish myself much better, yet for you
I would be trebled twenty times myself,
A thousand times more fair, ten thousand times
More rich, that only to stand high in your account
I might in virtues, beauties, livings, friends,
Exceed account. But the full sum of me
Is sum of something: which to term in gross
Is an unlesson'd girl, unschool'd, unpractis'd;
Happy in this, she is not yet so old
But she may learn; happier than this,
She is not bred so dull but she can learn;
Happiest of all, is that her gentle spirit
Commits itself to yours to be directed
As from her lord, her governor, her king.
Myself, and what is mine, to you and yours
Is now converted. But now I was the lord
Of this fair mansion, master of my servants,
Queen o'er myself; and even now, but now,
This house, these servants, and this same myself
Are yours, my lord's. I give them with this ring,
Which when you part from, lose, or give away,
Let it presage the ruin of your love,
And be my vantage to exclaim on you.

Bassanio

Madam, you have bereft me of all words.
Only my blood speaks to you in my veins,
And there is such confusion in my powers
As after some oration fairly spoke
By a beloved prince there doth appear
Among the buzzing, pleased multitude,
Where every something being blent together
Turns to a wild of nothing, save of joy
Express'd, and not express'd. But when this ring
Parts from this finger, then parts life from hence:
O then be bold to say Bassanio's dead!

Nerissa

My lord and lady, it is now our time,
That have stood by and seen our wishes prosper,
To cry 'good joy'. Good joy, my lord and lady!

155 *That only*: only in order to.
156 *livings*: material possessions.
157 *account*: estimation.
158 *to . . . gross*: in gross terms.
159 *unpractis'd*: inexperienced.
160 *Happy*: fortunate.
162 *bred so dull*: born so stupid.
166–7 *Myself . . . converted*: I, and everything I possess, have now become your property.
167 *but now*: just a moment ago.
174 *vantage*: opportunity.
exclaim on: denounce.

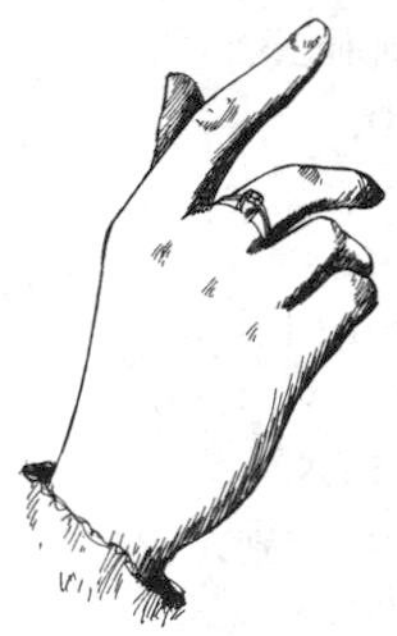

175 *bereft me of*: stolen from me.
176 *my blood speaks*: Bassanio blushes.
177 *powers*: faculties.
178–83 *As . . . express'd*: Bassanio compares his mixed feelings to a happy mob of citizens after a well-delivered speech from their popular ruler.
179 *beloved*: belovèd.
180 *buzzing*: murmuring.
pleased: pleasèd.
181 *something*: little thing.
blent: blended, mixed.
182 *wild of nothing*: indistinguishable wilderness.
save: except.

Gratiano

My lord Bassanio, and my gentle lady,
I wish you all the joy that you can wish;
For I am sure you can wish none from me.
And when your honours mean to solemnize
The bargain of your faith, I do beseech you
Even at that time I may be married too.

Bassanio

With all my heart, so thou canst get a wife.

Gratiano

I thank your lordship, you have got me one.
My eyes, my lord, can look as swift as yours:
You saw the mistress, I beheld the maid.
You lov'd, I lov'd; for intermission
No more pertains to me, my lord, than you.
Your fortune stood upon the caskets there,
And so did mine too as the matter falls.
For wooing here until I sweat again,
And swearing till my very roof was dry
With oaths of love, at last—if promise last—
I got a promise of this fair one here
To have her love, provided that your fortune
Achiev'd her mistress.

Portia

Is this true, Nerissa?

Nerissa

Madam, it is, so you stand pleas'd withal.

Bassanio

And do you, Gratiano, mean good faith?

Gratiano

Yes 'faith, my lord.

Bassanio

Our feast shall be much honour'd in your marriage.

Gratiano

We'll play with them the first boy for a thousand ducats.

Nerissa

What, and stake down?

Gratiano

No, we shall ne'er win at that sport and stake down.
But who comes here? Lorenzo and his infidel!
What, and my old Venetian friend Salerio!

190–1 *I wish . . . me*: I hope you will have all the joy you wish for yourselves, because I am sure you will not wish any of my joy away from me.

192 *solemnize*: formally celebrate.

194 *Even*: just.

195 *so*: provided that.

198 *maid*: lady-in-waiting.

199–200 *for . . . you*: I wasted no more spare time ('intermission') than you.

201 *stood*: depended.

202 *as . . . falls*: as it happens.

203 *until . . . again*: so hard that I was sweating.

204–5 *swearing . . . love*: making vows of love until the roof of my mouth was dry.

205 *if promise last*: if she keeps the promise; Gratiano puns on two senses of a word (also in line 211).

206 *of*: from.

209 *so . . . withal*: provided that you are pleased with it.

210 *mean good faith*: have good intentions.

211 *'faith*: upon my faith.

213–14 *We'll . . . ducats*: we'll wager a thousand ducats on who has the first son.

215 *stake down*: money for the bet laid on the table; Gratiano takes the slang sense 'with a limp penis'.

216 *infidel*: Gratiano refers to Jessica's Jewishness.

Enter Lorenzo, Jessica, *and* Salerio, *a messenger from Venice*

Bassanio

Lorenzo and Salerio, welcome hither—
If that the youth of my new interest here
Have power to bid you welcome. By your leave
I bid my very friends and countrymen,
Sweet Portia, welcome.

Portia

So do I, my lord.
They are entirely welcome.

Lorenzo

I thank your honour. For my part, my lord,
My purpose was not to have seen you here,
But meeting with Salerio by the way
He did entreat me past all saying nay
To come with him along.

Salerio

I did, my lord,
And I have reason for it. [*Giving letter*] Signor Antonio
Commends him to you.

Bassanio

Ere I ope his letter,
I pray you tell me how my good friend doth.

Salerio

Not sick, my lord, unless it be in mind,
Nor well, unless in mind: his letter there
Will show you his estate.

Bassanio *opens the letter*

Gratiano

Nerissa, cheer yond stranger, bid her welcome.
Your hand, Salerio; what's the news from Venice?
How doth that royal merchant, good Antonio?
I know he will be glad of our success;
We are the Jasons, we have won the fleece.

Salerio

I would you had won the fleece that he hath lost.

219–20 *If . . . welcome*: if my very new position here gives me the right to welcome you.

221 *very*: true.

223 *entirely*: heartily.

225 *My purpose was not*: I did not intend.

226 *by the way*: by chance.

227 *past . . . nay*: and would not let me refuse.

230 *Commends him*: sends his greetings.

233 *in mind*: in fortitude.

234 *estate*: condition.

235 *cheer*: welcome.
yond: yonder.

237 *royal*: prince among merchants.

239 *Jasons*: See note on *1*, 1, 170.

240 *fleece*: Salerio puns on 'fleets'.

Portia

There are some shrewd contents in yond same paper
That steals the colour from Bassanio's cheek:
Some dear friend dead, else nothing in the world
Could turn so much the constitution
Of any constant man. What, worse and worse?
With leave, Bassanio, I am half yourself
And I must freely have the half of anything
That this same paper brings you.

Bassanio

O sweet Portia,
Here are a few of the unpleasant'st words
That ever blotted paper. Gentle lady,
When I did first impart my love to you,
I freely told you all the wealth I had
Ran in my veins: I was a gentleman.
And then I told you true; and yet, dear lady,
Rating myself at nothing, you shall see
How much I was a braggart. When I told you
My state was nothing, I should then have told you
That I was worse than nothing; for indeed
I have engag'd myself to a dear friend,
Engag'd my friend to his mere enemy,
To feed my means. Here is a letter, lady,
The paper as the body of my friend,
And every word in it a gaping wound
Issuing lifeblood. But is it true, Salerio?
Hath all his ventures failed? What, not one hit?
From Tripolis, from Mexico, and England,
From Lisbon, Barbary, and India,
And not one vessel 'scape the dreadful touch
Of merchant-marring rocks?

Salerio

Not one, my lord.
Besides, it should appear that if he had
The present money to discharge the Jew,
He would not take it. Never did I know
A creature that did bear the shape of man
So keen and greedy to confound a man.
He plies the duke at morning and at night,

241 *shrewd*: bitter.

244 *constitution*: complexion.

245 *constant*: normal.

246 *With leave*: excuse me.

250 *blotted paper*: spoiled a paper with ink.

252 *freely*: honestly.

253 *Ran in my veins*: was in my blood.

255 *Rating*: valuing.

256 *was a braggart*: boasted.

259 *engag'd*: bound.

260 *mere*: absolute.

261 *To feed my means*: to get the money I needed.

262 *as*: is like.

264 *Issuing lifeblood*: from which his lifeblood pours.

265 *ventures*: speculations.
hit: succeeded.

269 *merchant-marring rocks*: rocks that ruin merchants.

271 *present*: ready.
discharge: pay his debt to.

275 *plies*: urges his case on.

And doth impeach the freedom of the state
If they deny him justice. Twenty merchants,
The duke himself, and the magnificoes
Of greatest port have all persuaded with him,
But none can drive him from the envious plea
Of forfeiture, of justice, and his bond.

Jessica

When I was with him, I have heard him swear
To Tubal and to Chus, his countrymen,
That he would rather have Antonio's flesh
Than twenty times the value of the sum
That he did owe him; and I know, my lord,
If law, authority, and power deny not
It will go hard with poor Antonio.

Portia

Is it your dear friend that is thus in trouble?

Bassanio

The dearest friend to me, the kindest man,
The best condition'd and unwearied spirit
In doing courtesies; and one in whom
The ancient Roman honour more appears
Than any that draws breath in Italy.

Portia

What sums owes he the Jew?

Bassanio

For me, three thousand ducats.

Portia

What, no more?
Pay him six thousand, and deface the bond.
Double six thousand, and then treble that,
Before a friend of this description
Shall lose a hair through Bassanio's fault.
First go with me to church, and call me wife,
And then away to Venice to your friend!
For never shall you lie by Portia's side
With an unquiet soul. You shall have gold
To pay the petty debt twenty times over.
When it is paid, bring your true friend along.
My maid Nerissa and myself meantime
Will live as maids and widows. Come away,
For you shall hence upon your wedding day.

276 *impeach . . . state*: discredit the integrity of Venetian law.

278 *magnificoes*: noblemen.

279 *port*: eminence.
persuaded: argued.

280 *drive him from*: persuade him to give up.
envious plea: malicious claim.

283 *his countrymen*: fellow Jews.

287 *deny not*: do not prevent it.

288 *hard*: badly.

291 *best condition'd*: most good-natured.

292 *courtesies*: acts of kindness.

293 *The ancient Roman honour*: i.e. loyalty to friends and country.

297 *deface*: cancel.

301 *call me wife*: make me your wife.

309 *shall hence*: must go away from here.

310 *cheer*: face.
311 *dear bought*: expensively purchased.
313 *miscarried*: been lost.
316 *cleared*: cancelled.
317 *but*: only.
318 *use your pleasure*: do as you please.
320 *Dispatch*: quickly finish.
321 *good leave*: kind permission.
323–4 *No . . . twain*: no bed will be accused of holding me back, and no rest shall come between the two of us.

Bid your friends welcome, show a merry cheer;
Since you are dear bought, I will love you dear.
But let me hear the letter of your friend.

Bassanio

[*Reads*] 'Sweet Bassanio, my ships have all miscarried, my creditors grow cruel, my estate is very low; my bond to the Jew is forfeit, and since in paying it, it is impossible I should live, all debts are cleared between you and I if I might but see you at my death. Notwithstanding, use your pleasure; if your love do not persuade you to come, let not my letter.'

Portia

O love! Dispatch all business and be gone.

Bassanio

Since I have your good leave to go away,
I will make haste. But till I come again
No bed shall e'er be guilty of my stay
Nor rest be interposer 'twixt us twain. [*Exeunt*

Act 3 Scene 3
Antonio has been arrested and Shylock threatens him.

1 *look to him*: guard him carefully.
2 *gratis*: free of interest.
4 *speak not*: don't argue.
5 *my bond*: Shylock emphasizes the legality of his claim.

SCENE 3

Venice: a street. Enter Shylock *the Jew, and* Solanio, *and* Antonio, *and the* Jailer

Shylock

Jailer, look to him. Tell not me of mercy.
This is the fool that lent out money gratis.
Jailer, look to him.

Antonio

Hear me yet, good Shylock—

Shylock

I'll have my bond, speak not against my bond;
I have sworn an oath that I will have my bond.

Thou call'dst me dog before thou hadst a cause,
But since I am a dog, beware my fangs.
The duke shall grant me justice. I do wonder,
Thou naughty jailer, that thou art so fond
To come abroad with him at his request.

Antonio

I pray thee hear me speak—

Shylock

I'll have my bond; I will not hear thee speak;
I'll have my bond, and therefore speak no more.
I'll not be made a soft and dull-eyed fool,
To shake the head, relent, and sigh, and yield
To Christian intercessors. Follow not!
I'll have no speaking, I will have my bond. [*Exit*

Solanio

It is the most impenetrable cur
That ever kept with men.

Antonio

Let him alone.
I'll follow him no more with bootless prayers.
He seeks my life, his reason well I know:
I oft deliver'd from his forfeitures
Many that have at times made moan to me;
Therefore he hates me.

Solanio

I am sure the duke
Will never grant this forfeiture to hold.

Antonio

The duke cannot deny the course of law;
For the commodity that strangers have
With us in Venice, if it be denied,
Will much impeach the justice of the state,
Since that the trade and profit of the city
Consisteth of all nations. Therefore go.
These griefs and losses have so bated me
That I shall hardly spare a pound of flesh
Tomorrow to my bloody creditor.
Well, jailer, on. Pray God Bassanio come
To see me pay his debt, and then I care not. [*Exeunt*

8–10 *I . . . request*: It would appear that Antonio is being given some unusual privileges.
9 *naughty*: worthless.
fond: foolish.
10 *abroad*: out of the prison.

14 *dull-eyed*: stupid.
16 *intercessors*: pleaders.
18 *impenetrable*: hard-hearted.
19 *kept with*: lived among.
20 *bootless*: unsuccessful.

22 *deliver'd*: rescued.
forfeitures: actions for breach of contract (like that which Antonio now endures).
23 *made moan*: complained.

25 *grant*: allow.

27 *commodity*: privilege.
strangers: foreigners.

29 *impeach*: discredit.

31 *Consisteth of*: depends upon.
32 *bated me*: made me lose weight.

34 *bloody*: bloodthirsty.

Act 3 Scene 4
Portia and Nerissa plan a visit to Venice.

Scene 4

Belmont: Portia*'s house. Enter* Portia, Nerissa, Lorenzo, Jessica, *and* Balthazar *a man of* Portia*'s*

Lorenzo
Madam, although I speak it in your presence,
You have a noble and a true conceit
Of god-like amity, which appears most strongly
In bearing thus the absence of your lord.
But if you knew to whom you show this honour,
How true a gentleman you send relief,
How dear a lover of my lord your husband,
I know you would be prouder of the work
Than customary bounty can enforce you.

Portia
I never did repent for doing good,
Nor shall not now; for in companions
That do converse and waste the time together,
Whose souls do bear an equal yoke of love,
There must be needs a like proportion
Of lineaments, of manners, and of spirit;
Which makes me think that this Antonio,
Being the bosom lover of my lord,
Must needs be like my lord. If it be so,
How little is the cost I have bestow'd
In purchasing the semblance of my soul
From out the state of hellish cruelty!
This comes too near the praising of myself,
Therefore no more of it: hear other things.
Lorenzo, I commit into your hands
The husbandry and manage of my house
Until my lord's return; for mine own part
I have toward heaven breath'd a secret vow
To live in prayer and contemplation,
Only attended by Nerissa here,
Until her husband and my lord's return.
There is a monastery two miles off,
And there we will abide. I do desire you
Not to deny this imposition,

2 *conceit*: understanding.
3 *amity*: friendship.
5 *to whom*: i.e. Antonio.
7 *lover*: friend.
9 *customary . . . you*: your usual generosity must make you feel.
12 *waste*: spend.
13 *bear . . . love*: are joined equally together in love.
14 *needs*: of necessity.
like: similar.
15 *lineaments*: appearances.
17 *bosom lover*: intimate friend.
19 *bestow'd*: spent.
20 *semblance . . . soul*: likeness of the one I love.
22 *comes too near*: is too like.
25 *husbandry and manage*: careful management.
33 *deny*: refuse.
imposition: task.

37 *people*: household.
my mind: what I intend.
38 *acknowledge*: recognize your authority.

44 *wish . . . you*: with the same to you.

45 *Now, Balthazar*: The broken line allows for movement on the stage.
46 *ever*: always.
honest-true: honest and trustworthy.
47 *So . . . still*: may I continue to find you so.
48 *all . . . man*: go as fast as a man can.
49 *render*: give.
51 *what*: whatever.
52 *imagin'd speed*: all the speed imaginable.
53 *the traject . . . ferry*: the ferry, the public transport.
54 *trades to*: communicates with.

56 *convenient*: appropriate.

57 *work in hand*: a plan in my mind.

59 *think of us*: expect to see us.

60 *habit*: costume.
61 *accomplished*: accomplishèd; equipped.

The which my love and some necessity
Now lays upon you.

Lorenzo

Madam, with all my heart
I shall obey you in all fair commands.

Portia

My people do already know my mind,
And will acknowledge you and Jessica
In place of Lord Bassanio and myself.
So fare you well till we shall meet again.

Lorenzo

Fair thoughts and happy hours attend on you.

Jessica

I wish your ladyship all heart's content.

Portia

I thank you for your wish, and am well pleas'd
To wish it back on you: fare you well, Jessica.

[*Exeunt* Jessica *and* Lorenzo

Now, Balthazar—
As I have ever found thee honest-true,
So let me find thee still; take this same letter,
And use thou all th'endeavour of a man
In speed to Padua. See thou render this
Into my cousin's hand, Doctor Bellario;
And look, what notes and garments he doth give thee
Bring them, I pray thee, with imagin'd speed
Unto the traject, to the common ferry
Which trades to Venice. Waste no time in words
But get thee gone; I shall be there before thee.

Balthazar

Madam, I go with all convenient speed. [*Exit*

Portia

Come on, Nerissa; I have work in hand
That you yet know not of. We'll see our husbands
Before they think of us.

Nerissa

Shall they see us?

Portia

They shall, Nerissa, but in such a habit
That they shall think we are accomplished

62 *that we lack*: i.e. male genitals.
63 *accoutred*: dressed up.
64 *prettier*: smarter.
66 *between . . . boy*: as though my voice were breaking.
67 *reed*: squeaky.
mincing: dainty, ladylike.
68 *'frays*: affrays, fights.
69 *bragging*: boastful.
quaint: elaborate.
72 *do withal*: help it.
75–6 *I have . . . twelvemonth*: it's more than a year since I left school (i.e. I'm a real man).
77 *raw*: crude.
jacks: fellows.
78 *turn to men*: change into men. Portia pretends to think that Nerissa means 'take men for lovers'.
80 *lewd interpreter*: someone with a dirty mind.
81 *device*: plan.
84 *measure*: travel.

With that we lack. I'll hold thee any wager,
When we are both accoutred like young men
I'll prove the prettier fellow of the two,
And wear my dagger with the braver grace,
And speak between the change of man and boy
With a reed voice, and turn two mincing steps
Into a manly stride; and speak of 'frays
Like a fine bragging youth; and tell quaint lies
How honourable ladies sought my love,
Which I denying, they fell sick and died—
I could not do withal. Then I'll repent,
And wish for all that that I had not kill'd them;
And twenty of these puny lies I'll tell,
That men shall swear I have discontinu'd school
Above a twelvemonth. I have within my mind
A thousand raw tricks of these bragging jacks,
Which I will practise.

Nerissa
Why, shall we turn to men?

Portia
Fie, what a question's that,
If thou wert near a lewd interpreter!
But come, I'll tell thee all my whole device
When I am in my coach, which stays for us
At the park gate; and therefore haste away,
For we must measure twenty miles today. [*Exeunt*

Act 3 Scene 5
Lancelot teases Jessica.

Scene 5

Belmont: Portia*'s garden. Enter* Lancelot *the Clown and* Jessica

1 *look you*: you see.
1–2 *the sins . . . children*: Lancelot quotes from the Second Commandment (Exodus 20:5).
2 *laid upon*: revenged upon.
2–3 *I fear you*: I fear for you.
3 *plain*: honest.
4 *agitation*: Lancelot means 'cogitation' (= considered opinion).
7 *bastard hope*: a) false hope; b) hope that you are a bastard.
neither: anyway.

Lancelot
Yes truly, for look you, the sins of the father are to be laid upon the children. Therefore I promise you I fear you. I was always plain with you, and so now I speak my agitation of the matter. Therefore be o'good cheer, for truly I think you are damned. There is but one hope in it that can do you any good, and that is but a kind of bastard hope neither.

Jessica
And what hope is that, I pray thee?

Lancelot
Marry, you may partly hope that your father got you not, that you are not the Jew's daughter.

Jessica
That were a kind of bastard hope indeed; so the sins of my mother should be visited upon me.

Lancelot
Truly, then, I fear you are damned both by father and mother; thus when I shun Scylla your father, I fall into Charybdis your mother. Well, you are gone both ways.

Jessica
I shall be saved by my husband; he hath made me a Christian.

Lancelot
Truly, the more to blame he; we were Christians enow before, e'en as many as could well live one by another. This making of Christians will raise the price of hogs; if we grow all to be pork eaters, we shall not shortly have a rasher on the coals for money.

Enter Lorenzo

Jessica
I'll tell my husband, Lancelot, what you say: here he comes.

Lorenzo
I shall grow jealous of you shortly, Lancelot, if you thus get my wife into corners.

Jessica
Nay, you need not fear us, Lorenzo: Lancelot and I are out. He tells me flatly there's no mercy for me in heaven, because I am a Jew's daughter; and he says you are no good member of the commonwealth, for in converting Jews to Christians you raise the price of pork.

Lorenzo
I shall answer that better to the commonwealth than you can the getting up of the Negro's belly: the Moor is with child by you, Lancelot.

9 *got*: begot, fathered.

11 *so*: if that were the case.

12 *visited*: revenged.

14–15 *Scylla . . . Charybdis*: Monsters (a rock-formation and a whirlpool) threatening sailors of classical mythology in the narrow straits between Italy and Sicily.

15 *gone*: ruined, damned.

16 *saved . . . husband*: Jessica can quote St Paul: 'the unbelieving wife is sanctified by the husband' (1 Corinthians 7:14).

18 *enow*: enough.

19 *e'en . . . another*: just enough to live comfortably together.

21 *pork eaters*: Jews are forbidden to eat pork.

21–2 *not . . . money*: soon not be able to afford a rasher of fried bacon.

27–8 *are out*: have quarrelled.

30 *commonwealth*: general public.

33 *getting up*: swelling out.
Moor: Moorish woman (probably a servant).

Lancelot

It is much that the Moor should be more than reason; but if she be less than an honest woman, she is indeed more than I took her for.

Lorenzo

How every fool can play upon the word! I think the best grace of wit will shortly turn into silence, and discourse grow commendable in none only but parrots. Go in, sirrah, bid them prepare for dinner.

Lancelot

That is done, sir; they have all stomachs.

Lorenzo

Goodly Lord, what a witsnapper are you! Then bid them prepare dinner.

Lancelot

That is done too, sir; only 'cover' is the word.

Lorenzo

Will you cover then, sir?

Lancelot

Not so, sir, neither; I know my duty.

Lorenzo

Yet more quarrelling with occasion! Wilt thou show the whole wealth of thy wit in an instant? I pray thee understand a plain man in his plain meaning: go to thy fellows, bid them cover the table, serve in the meat, and we will come in to dinner.

Lancelot

For the table, sir, it shall be served in; for the meat, sir, it shall be covered; for your coming in to dinner, sir, why, let it be as humours and conceits shall govern. [*Exit*

Lorenzo

O dear discretion, how his words are suited!
The fool hath planted in his memory
An army of good words; and I do know
A many fools that stand in better place,
Garnish'd like him, that for a tricksy word
Defy the matter. How cheer'st thou, Jessica?
And now, good sweet, say thy opinion:
How dost thou like the Lord Bassanio's wife?

35 *more than reason*: bigger than she ought to be; Lancelot cannot resist a pun.
36–7 *if . . . for*: if she's not an honest (= chaste) woman, she's certainly more than I thought she was.
38–40 *the best . . . parrots*: silence will soon be the finest display of intelligence, and only parrots will be praised for conversation.
42 *have all stomachs*: are all hungry.
43 *witsnapper*: punster, comedian.
45 *'cover' . . . word*: you should say 'cover' (meaning a) prepare the table; b) put on your hat).
47 *duty*: place, respect; servants stood bare-headed in the presence of superiors.
48 *quarrelling with occasion*: taking every opportunity for quibbles.
55 *as . . . govern*: as your whims and fancies take you.
56 *discretion*: sagacity, judgement. *suited*: matched.
59 *A many fools*: a lot of professional jesters. *stand . . . place*: have higher positions.
60 *Garnish'd*: trimmed up; Lorenzo refers to the extra braid on Lancelot's livery (see *2*, 2, 144) which makes him look like a jester. *tricksy*: clever, playful.
61 *Defy the matter*: contradict the sense. *How . . . thou*: how are you getting on.

Jessica

Past all expressing. It is very meet
The Lord Bassanio live an upright life,
For having such a blessing in his lady
He finds the joys of heaven here on earth,
And if on earth he do not merit it,
In reason he should never come to heaven.
Why, if two gods should play some heavenly match,
And on the wager lay two earthly women,
And Portia one, there must be something else
Pawn'd with the other, for the poor rude world
Hath not her fellow.

Lorenzo

Even such a husband
Hast thou of me, as she is for a wife.

Jessica

Nay, but ask my opinion too of that.

Lorenzo

I will anon; first let us go to dinner.

Jessica

Nay, let me praise you while I have a stomach.

Lorenzo

No, pray thee, let it serve for table talk;
Then howsome'er thou speak'st, 'mong other things
I shall digest it.

Jessica

Well, I'll set you forth. [*Exeunt*

64 *Past all expressing*: beyond words.
meet: proper, right.
65 *upright*: virtuous.

73 *Pawn'd*: gambled.

74 *fellow*: equal, match.

77 *anon*: shortly.

78 *stomach*: a) appetite; b) inclination.

79 *table talk*: mealtime conversation.

80 *howsome'er*: however.

81 *set you forth*: put you in your place.

ACT 4

Act 4 Scene 1
Antonio is prepared to die when Shylock refuses to show mercy, but Portia, disguised as a young lawyer, tricks Shylock out of his bond. Then she asks Bassanio for his ring as a reward.

SCENE 1

Venice: the courtroom. Enter the Duke, *the* Magnificoes, Antonio, Bassanio, Salerio, *and* Gratiano *with others.*

Duke
What, is Antonio here?
Antonio
Ready, so please your grace.
Duke
I am sorry for thee. Thou art come to answer
A stony adversary, an inhuman wretch,
Uncapable of pity, void and empty
From any dram of mercy.
Antonio
I have heard
Your grace hath tane great pains to qualify
His rigorous course; but since he stands obdùrate
And that no lawful means can carry me
Out of his envy's reach, I do oppose
My patience to his fury, and am arm'd
To suffer with a quietness of spirit
The very tyranny and rage of his.
Duke
Go one and call the Jew into the court.
Salerio
He is ready at the door; he comes, my lord.

Enter Shylock

Duke
Make room and let him stand before our face.
Shylock, the world thinks, and I think so too,
That thou but leadest this fashion of thy malice
To the last hour of act, and then 'tis thought

2 *Ready*: present.

3 *answer*: defend yourself against.

5 *void*: barren.

6 *From*: of.
dram: a tiny measure.

7 *qualify*: moderate.

8 *obdurate*: obdùrate; firm, resolute.

10 *envy*: malice.

13 *The . . . his*: all the cruel power and anger of his spirit.

18–19 *thou . . . act*: you intend to carry on with this show of cruelty until the very last moment.

20 *remorse*: pity.
more strange: even more unusual.
21 *strange apparent*: apparently abnormal.
22 *exacts*: demand.

24 *loose the forfeiture*: surrender the forfeit (i.e. the pound of flesh).

26 *Forgive . . . principal*: forgo a certain amount of the sum he borrowed.

29 *Enow*: enough.
royal merchant: even such a substantial merchant prince.
30 *commiseration of*: sympathy for.
31 *brassy bosoms*: hearts as hard as brass.
32 *stubborn*: unfeeling.
32–3 *train'd . . . courtesy*: taught to behave with gentleness.
35 *possess'd*: informed.
36 *Sabaoth*: In Hebrew this word means 'armies'; many editions read 'Sabbath' (= Saturday, the holiest day of the Jewish week).
37 *due and forfeit*: forfeit which is due.
38 *light*: alight, descend.
39 *charter . . . freedom*: city's independence granted by charter.
41 *carrion*: rotten.
43 *humour*: whimsy, fancy.
is it answer'd: will that do for an answer.
46 *ban'd*: poisoned.
47 *gaping pig*: roasted pig's head (with an apple in its mouth).
49 *sings i'the nose*: drones.
50–1 *affection . . . passion*: instinctive (physical) reaction often overcomes emotion (see *3*, 1, 53).
54–6 *he*: this man . . . that man . . . another man.
56 *woollen*: The leather bag of the bagpipes was covered with sheepskin.
of force: involuntarily.

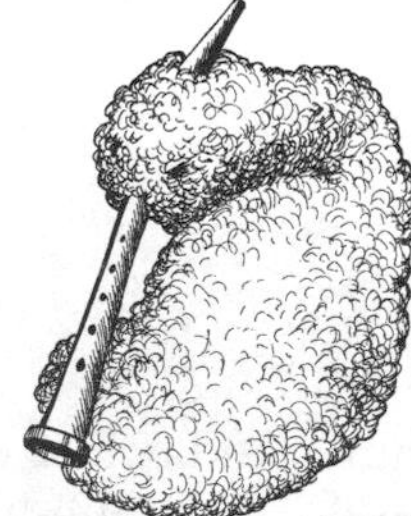

57 *shame*: embarrassment.

58 *to offend*: give offence to others.

Thou'lt show thy mercy and remorse more strange
Than is thy strange apparent cruelty.
And where thou now exacts the penalty,
Which is a pound of this poor merchant's flesh,
Thou wilt not only loose the forfeiture
But, touch'd with human gentleness and love,
Forgive a moiety of the principal,
Glancing an eye of pity on his losses
That have of late so huddl'd on his back,
Enow to press a royal merchant down
And pluck commiseration of his state
From brassy bosoms and rough hearts of flint,
From stubborn Turks, and Tartars never train'd
To offices of tender courtesy.
We all expect a gentle answer, Jew.

Shylock

I have possess'd your grace of what I purpose,
And by our holy Sabaoth have I sworn
To have the due and forfeit of my bond.
If you deny it, let the danger light
Upon your charter and your city's freedom!
You'll ask me why I rather choose to have
A weight of carrion flesh than to receive
Three thousand ducats. I'll not answer that—
But say it is my humour: is it answer'd?
What if my house be troubled with a rat,
And I be pleas'd to give ten thousand ducats
To have it ban'd? What, are you answer'd yet?
Some men there are love not a gaping pig;
Some that are mad if they behold a cat;
And others when the bagpipe sings i'the nose
Cannot contain their urine: for affection
Masters oft passion, sways it to the mood
Of what it likes or loathes. Now for your answer:
As there is no firm reason to be render'd
Why he cannot abide a gaping pig,
Why he a harmless necessary cat,
Why he a woollen bagpipe, but of force
Must yield to such inevitable shame
As to offend, himself being offended:
So can I give no reason, nor I will not,

More than a lodg'd hate and a certain loathing
I bear Antonio, that I follow thus
A losing suit against him. Are you answer'd?

Bassanio

This is no answer, thou unfeeling man,
To excuse the current of thy cruelty.

Shylock

I am not bound to please thee with my answers.

Bassanio

Do all men kill the things they do not love?

Shylock

Hates any man the thing he would not kill?

Bassanio

Every offence is not a hate at first.

Shylock

What, wouldst thou have a serpent sting thee twice?

Antonio

I pray you think you question with the Jew.
You may as well go stand upon the beach
And bid the main flood bate his usual height;
You may as well use question with the wolf
Why he hath made the ewe bleat for the lamb;
You may as well forbid the mountain pines
To wag their high tops and to make no noise
When they are fretten with the gusts of heaven;
You may as well do anything most hard
As seek to soften that—than which what's harder?—
His Jewish heart. Therefore I do beseech you
Make no moe offers, use no farther means,
But with all brief and plain conveniency
Let me have judgement, and the Jew his will.

Bassanio

For thy three thousand ducats here is six.

Shylock

If every ducat in six thousand ducats
Were in six parts, and every part a ducat,
I would not draw them; I would have my bond.

Duke

How shalt thou hope for mercy, rendering none?

Shylock

What judgement shall I dread, doing no wrong?

60 *lodg'd*: deep-rooted.
certain: steadfast.

62 *losing*: unprofitable.

64 *current*: outpouring.

68 *offence*: displeasure.

70 *think . . . Jew*: remember that you are arguing with the Jew.

72 *main flood*: ocean tide.
bate: reduce.

73 *use question with*: ask.

77 *fretten*: blown.

82 *with . . . conveniency*: as quickly and simply as possible.

87 *draw*: take.

90 *purchas'd slave*: slave that you have bought.

92 *parts*: tasks, duties.

97 *Be season'd . . . viands*: be treated with the same food as your own.

101 *fie*: shame.

102 *force*: power.

104 *Upon my power*: with my authority.

106 *determine this*: resolve this dispute.

107 *stays without*: is waiting outside.

114 *tainted*: sick, contaminated.
wether: castrated ram.

115 *Meetest*: most suitable.

118 *live still*: go on living.

You have among you many a purchas'd slave,
Which, like your asses and your dogs and mules,
You use in abject and in slavish parts
Because you bought them. Shall I say to you,
'Let them be free! Marry them to your heirs!
Why sweat they under burdens? Let their beds
Be made as soft as yours, and let their palates
Be season'd with such viands'? You will answer,
'The slaves are ours.' So do I answer you.
The pound of flesh which I demand of him
Is dearly bought; 'tis mine, and I will have it.
If you deny me, fie upon your law:
There is no force in the decrees of Venice.
I stand for judgement. Answer: shall I have it?

Duke

Upon my power I may dismiss this court,
Unless Bellario, a learned doctor
Whom I have sent for to determine this,
Come here today.

Salerio

My lord, here stays without
A messenger with letters from the doctor,
New come from Padua.

Duke

Bring us the letters. Call the messenger.

Bassanio

Good cheer, Antonio! What, man, courage yet!
The Jew shall have my flesh, blood, bones and all,
Ere thou shalt lose for me one drop of blood.

Antonio

I am a tainted wether of the flock,
Meetest for death; the weakest kind of fruit
Drops earliest to the ground, and so let me.
You cannot better be employ'd, Bassanio,
Than to live still and write mine epitaph.

Enter Nerissa *disguised as a lawyer's clerk*

Duke

Came you from Padua, from Bellario?

Nerissa

From both, my lord: [*Presenting letter*] Bellario greets your grace.

Bassanio

Why dost thou whet thy knife so earnestly?

Shylock

To cut the forfeiture from that bankrupt there.

Gratiano

Not on thy sole, but on thy soul, harsh Jew,
Thou mak'st thy knife keen. But no metal can,
No, not the hangman's axe, bear half the keenness
Of thy sharp envy. Can no prayers pierce thee?

Shylock

No, none that thou hast wit enough to make.

Gratiano

O be thou damn'd, inexecrable dog,
And for thy life let justice be accus'd!
Thou almost mak'st me waver in my faith,
To hold opinion with Pythagoras
That souls of animals infuse themselves
Into the trunks of men. Thy currish spirit
Govern'd a wolf, who—hang'd for human slaughter—
Even from the gallows did his fell soul fleet,
And whilst thou layest in thy unhallow'd dam
Infus'd itself in thee; for thy desires
Are wolfish, bloody, starv'd, and ravenous.

Shylock

Till thou canst rail the seal from off my bond
Thou but offend'st thy lungs to speak so loud.
Repair thy wit, good youth, or it will fall
To cureless ruin. I stand here for law.

Duke

This letter from Bellario doth commend
A young and learned doctor to our court:
Where is he?

Nerissa

He attendeth here hard by
To know your answer whether you'll admit him.

121 *whet*: sharpen.

123 *thy sole*: the sole of your shoe.

125 *hangman*: executioner.

127 *wit*: sense, intelligence.

128 *inexecrable*: unspeakably damned.

129 *for . . . accus'd*: only a failure of justice allows you to live.

131 *hold opinion*: agree.
Pythagoras: a Greek philosopher who believed in the transmigration of souls—explained here by Gratiano.

132 *infuse*: pour.

133 *currish*: like a cur—a mongrel dog.

134 *hang'd . . . slaughter*: executed as a murderer.

135 *Even . . . fleet*: let his cruel soul pass straight from the gallows.

136 *unhallow'd dam*: unholy (non-Christian) mother.

139 *rail*: shout.

140 *but offend'st*: are only hurting.

142 *cureless*: incurable.

145 *hard*: near.

148 *give . . . conduct*: escort him courteously.

152 *in loving visitation*: on a friendly visit.

154 *cause*: matter.
controversy: dispute.

155 *turned o'er*: looked through.

156 *is furnished*: has been given.

157 *bettered*: improved.

159 *importunity*: earnest request.

160–1 *let . . . estimation*: do not think poorly of him because he is young.

163–4 *whose . . . commendation*: giving him a trial will show you how much better he is than my praise.

169–70 *the difference . . . court*: the dispute that is at present on trial in this court.

171 *informed*: informèd.
throughly: thoroughly.

Duke

With all my heart. Some three of four of you
Go give him courteous conduct to this place.
[*Exeunt* officials
Meantime the court shall hear Bellario's letter.

[*Reads*] 'Your grace shall understand, that at the receipt of your letter I am very sick; but in the instant that your messenger came, in loving visitation was with me a young doctor of Rome: his name is Balthazar. I acquainted him with the cause in controversy between the Jew and Antonio the merchant. We turned o'er many books together; he is furnished with my opinion which, bettered with his own learning, the greatness whereof I cannot enough commend, comes with him at my importunity, to fill up your grace's request in my stead. I beseech you let his lack of years be no impediment to let him lack a reverend estimation, for I never knew so young a body with so old a head. I leave him to your gracious acceptance, whose trial shall better publish his commendation.'

Enter Portia *disguised as* Doctor Balthazar, *followed by* officials

You hear the learn'd Bellario what he writes,
And here I take it is the doctor come.
Give me your hand. Come you from old Bellario?

Portia

I did, my lord.

Duke

You are welcome; take your place.
Are you acquainted with the difference
That holds this present question in the court?

Portia

I am informed throughly of the cause.
Which is the merchant here and which the Jew?

Duke

Antonio and old Shylock, both stand forth.

Portia

Is your name Shylock?

Shylock

Shylock is my name.

Portia

Of a strange nature is the suit you follow,
Yet in such rule that the Venetian law
Cannot impugn you as you do proceed.
—You stand within his danger, do you not?

Antonio

Ay, so he says.

Portia

Do you confess the bond?

Antonio

I do.

Portia

Then must the Jew be merciful.

Shylock

On what compulsion must I? Tell me that.

Portia

The quality of mercy is not strain'd,
It droppeth as the gentle rain from heaven
Upon the place beneath. It is twice blest:
It blesseth him that gives, and him that takes.
'Tis mightiest in the mightiest, it becomes
The throned monarch better than his crown.
His sceptre shows the force of temporal power,
The attribute to awe and majesty,
Wherein doth sit the dread and fear of kings;
But mercy is above this sceptred sway.
It is enthroned in the hearts of kings,
It is an attribute to God himself,
And early power doth then show likest God's
When mercy seasons justice. Therefore, Jew,
Though justice be thy plea, consider this:
That in the course of justice, none of us
Should see salvation. We do pray for mercy,
And that same prayer doth teach us all to render
The deeds of mercy. I have spoke thus much
To mitigate the justice of thy plea,
Which if thou follow, this strict court of Venice
Must needs give sentence 'gainst the merchant there.

176 *in such rule*: so correctly.

177 *impugn*: oppose.

178 *within his danger*: at his mercy.

180 *must*: is morally obliged to.

181 *must I*: am I forced to.

182 *is not strain'd*: cannot be constrained (= forced).

186 *mightiest . . . mightiest*: the most powerful weapon possessed by the most powerful person.
becomes: suits, is appropriate for.

187 *throned*: thronèd.

188 *temporal*: earthly.

189 *attribute*: proper possession.

190 *Wherein . . . kings*: in which (symbolically) resides the power of kings to command dread and fear.

191 *this sceptred sway*: the world ruled by kings.

192 *enthroned*: enthronèd.

193 *attribute to*: quality belonging to.

195 *seasons*: moderates.

195–200 *Therefore . . . mercy*: Portia reminds Christians of the petition of the Lord's Prayer ('Forgive us our trespasses as we forgive them that trespass against us'), and Shylock should remember Psalm 143:2 ('Enter not into judgement with thy servants: for in thy sight shall no man living be justified').

201 *mitigate . . . plea*: moderate your plea for strict justice.

203 *needs*: of necessity.

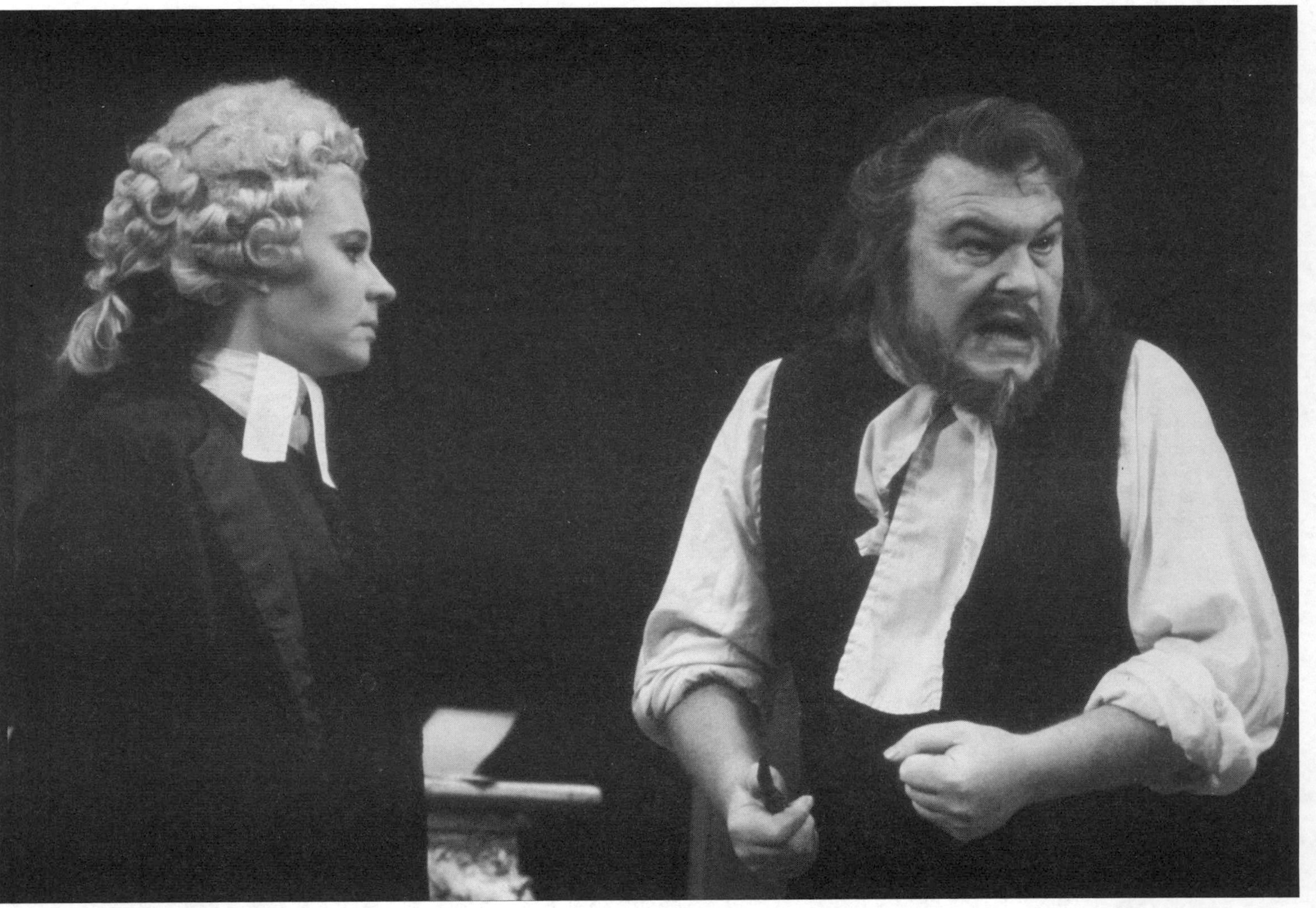

'I crave the law, The penalty and forfeit of my bond.' (*4*, 1, 204–5). Prunella Scales as Portia and Timothy West as Shylock, Old Vic Theatre, 1981.

204 *My . . . head*: I will be responsible for what I am doing.
crave: beg.

206 *discharge*: repay.

207 *tender*: offer.

212 *bears down*: overcomes.

213 *Wrest*: twist.
once: on this one occasion.
to: with.

215 *curb*: restrain.

217 *established*: establishèd.

221 *Daniel*: The story of Susannah and the Elders in the Apocrypha tells how a young man, sent to give judgement when Susannah was accused of unchastity, turned the evidence of the old men against themselves.

225 *thrice*: Portia seems to be raising the offer of line 208.

Shylock
My deeds upon my head! I crave the law,
The penalty and forfeit of my bond.

Portia
Is he not able to discharge the money?

Bassanio
Yes, here I tender it for him in the court,
Yea, twice the sum; if that will not suffice,
I will be bound to pay it ten times o'er
On forfeit of my hands, my head, my heart.
If this will not suffice, it must appear
That malice bears down truth. And I beseech you
Wrest once the law to your authority;
To do a great right, do a little wrong,
And curb this cruel devil of his will.

Portia
It must not be; there is no power in Venice
Can alter a decree established.
'Twill be recorded for a precedent,
And many an error by the same example
Will rush into the state: it cannot be.

Shylock
A Daniel come to judgement; yea a Daniel!
O wise young judge, how I do honour thee!

Portia
I pray you let me look upon the bond.

Shylock
Here 'tis, most reverend doctor, here it is.

Portia
Shylock, there's thrice thy money offer'd thee.

Shylock
An oath, an oath. I have an oath in heaven!
Shall I lay perjury upon my soul?
No, not for Venice.

Portia
Why, this bond is forfeit,
And lawfully by this the Jew may claim
A pound of flesh, to be by him cut off
Nearest the merchant's heart. Be merciful:
Take thrice thy money; bid me tear the bond.

Shylock

When it is paid, according to the tenour.
It doth appear you are a worthy judge,
You know the law, your exposition
Hath been most sound. I charge you by the law,
Whereof you are a well-deserving pillar,
Proceed to judgement. By my soul I swear
There is no power in the tongue of man
To alter me. I stay here on my bond.

Antonio

Most heartily I do beseech the court
To give the judgement.

Portia

Why then, thus it is:
You must prepare your bosom for his knife.

Shylock

O noble judge, O excellent young man!

Portia

For the intent and purpose of the law
Hath full relation to the penalty
Which here appeareth due upon the bond.

Shylock

'Tis very true. O wise and upright judge,
How much more elder art thou than thy looks!

Portia

Therefore lay bare your bosom

Shylock

Ay, his breast.
So says the bond, doth it not, noble judge?
'Nearest his heart': those are the very words.

Portia

It is so. Are there balance here to weigh
The flesh?

Shylock

I have them ready.

Portia

Have by some surgeon, Shylock, on your charge,
To stop his wounds, lest he do bleed to death.

Shylock

Is it so nominated in the bond?

233 *tenour*: actual wording.

235 *exposition*: setting-out, explanation.

237 *pillar*: support.

240 *stay*: take my stand.

241 *Most heartily*: with all my heart.

246 *Hath . . . to*: fully authorizes.

249 *elder*: more mature.

253 *balance*: scales.

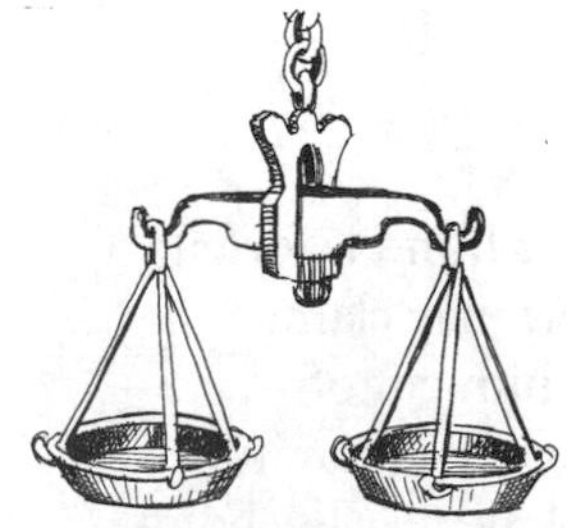

255 *on your charge*: at your expense.
257 *nominated*: specified.

Portia

It is not so express'd, but what of that?
'Twere good you do so much for charity.

Shylock

I cannot find it; 'tis not in the bond.

Portia

You, merchant: have you anything to say?

Antonio

But little; I am arm'd and well prepar'd.
Give me your hand, Bassanio. Fare you well.
Grieve not that I am fall'n to this for you.
For herein Fortune shows herself more kind
Than is her custom: it is still her use
To let the wretched man outlive his wealth,
To view with hollow eye and wrinkled brow
An age of poverty; from which ling'ring penance
Of such misery doth she cut me off.
Commend me to your honourable wife.
Tell her the process of Antonio's end,
Say how I lov'd you, speak me fair in death,
And when the tale is told, bid her be judge
Whether Bassanio had not once a love.
Repent but you that you shall lose your friend
And he repents not that he pays your debt.
For if the Jew do cut but deep enough
I'll pay it instantly with all my heart.

Bassanio

Antonio, I am married to a wife
Which is as dear to me as life itself;
But life itself, my wife, and all the world,
Are not with me esteem'd above thy life.
I would lose all, ay, sacrifice them all
Here to this devil, to deliver you.

Portia

Your wife would give you little thanks for that
If she were by to hear you make the offer.

Gratiano

I have a wife who I protest I love;
I would she were in heaven, so she could
Entreat some power to change this currish Jew.

262 *arm'd*: i.e. spiritually.

266 *still her use*: usually her custom.

269 *age*: old age.

272 *process*: a) manner; b) legal proceeding.

273 *speak . . . death*: speak kindly of me when I am dead.

276 *Repent but you*: you must only regret.

281 *Which*: who.

285 *deliver*: save.

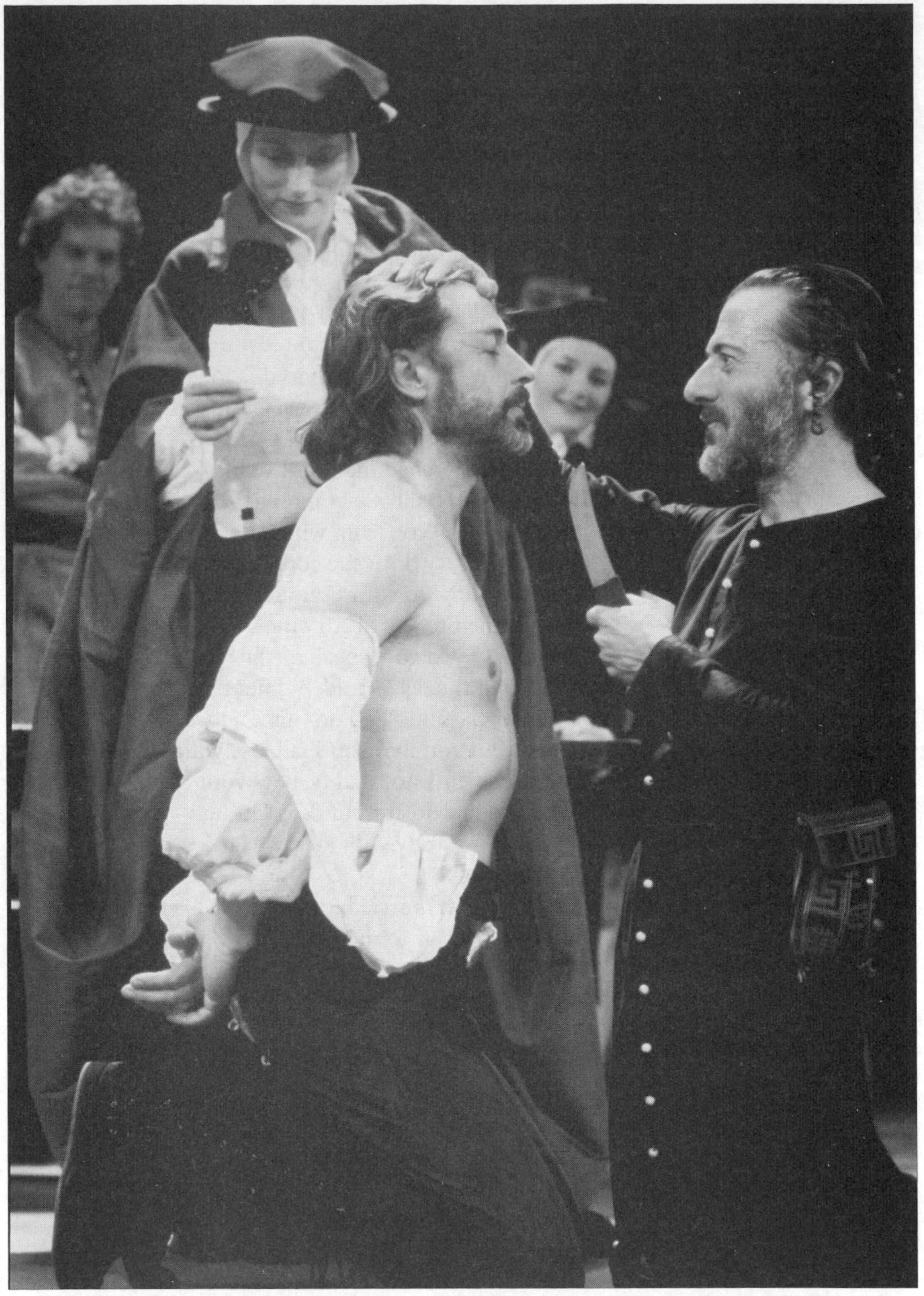

'Most learned judge! A sentence: come, prepare.' (*4*, 1, 302). Geraldine James as Portia, Leigh Lawson as Antonio, and Dustin Hoffman as Shylock, Phoenix Theatre, 1989.

Nerissa
'Tis well you offer it behind her back;
The wish would make else an unquiet house.

Shylock
These be the Christian husbands! I have a daughter:
Would any of the stock of Barabbas
Had been her husband, rather than a Christian!
We trifle time; I pray thee pursue sentence.

294 *stock*: breed.
Barabbas: the thief who was released when Christ was crucified (St John 18:40).
296 *trifle time*: waste time in trivialities.
pursue: go on with.

Portia
A pound of that same merchant's flesh is thine,
The court awards it, and the law doth give it.

Shylock
Most rightful judge!

Portia
And you must cut this flesh from off his breast;
The law allows it, and the court awards it.

Shylock
Most learned judge! A sentence: come, prepare.

Portia
Tarry a little, there is something else.
This bond doth give thee here no jot of blood.
The words expressly are 'a pound of flesh'.
Take then thy bond, take thou thy pound of flesh,
But in the cutting it, if thou dost shed
One drop of Christian blood, thy lands and goods
Are by the laws of Venice confiscate
Unto the state of Venice.

303 *Tarry*: wait.
304 *jot*: drop.

Gratiano
O upright judge!
Mark, Jew—O learned judge!

Shylock
Is that the law?

Portia
Thyself shall see the Act.
For as thou urgest justice, be assur'd
Thou shalt have justice more than thou desirest.

312 *Act*: the legal act confirming the law.
313 *urgest*: demand.

Gratiano
O learned judge! Mark, Jew: a learned judge.

Shylock
I take this offer then. Pay the bond thrice
And let the Christian go.

Bassanio

Here is the money.

Portia

Soft.
The Jew shall have all justice; soft, no haste;
He shall have nothing but the penalty.

Gratiano

O Jew, an upright judge, a learned judge!

Portia

Therefore prepare thee to cut off the flesh.
Shed thou no blood, nor cut thou less nor more
But just a pound of flesh. If thou tak'st more
Or less than a just pound, be it but so much
As makes it light or heavy in the substance
Or the division of the twentieth part
Of one poor scruple—nay, if the scale do turn
But in the estimation of a hair,
Thou diest, and all thy goods are confiscate.

Gratiano

A second Daniel; a Daniel, Jew!
Now, infidel, I have you on the hip.

Portia

Why doth the Jew pause? Take thy forfeiture.

Shylock

Give me my principal, and let me go.

Bassanio

I have it ready for thee; here it is.

Portia

He hath refus'd it in the open court.
He shall have merely justice and his bond.

Gratiano

A Daniel, still say I, a second Daniel!
I thank thee, Jew, for teaching me that word.

Shylock

Shall I not have barely my principal?

Portia

Thou shalt have nothing but the forfeiture,
To be so taken at thy peril, Jew.

Shylock

Why then, the devil give him good of it!
I'll stay no longer question.

321 *upright*: honest.

326 *substance*: weight.

328 *scruple*: a weight unit (used by the old apothecaries) of 20 grains.

329 *estimation*: weight.

332 *on the hip*: at a disadvantage; see *1*, 3, 41.

334 *principal*: the original sum borrowed.

344 *question*: to argue.

Portia

Tarry, Jew:
The law hath yet another hold on you.
It is enacted in the laws of Venice,
If it be prov'd against an alien
That by direct or indirect attempts
He seek the life of any citizen,
The party 'gainst the which he doth contrive
Shall seize one half his goods, the other half
Comes to the privy coffer of the state,
And the offender's life lies in the mercy
Of the duke only, 'gainst all other voice.
In which predicament I say thou stand'st;
For it appears by manifest proceeding
That indirectly, and directly too,
Thou hast contriv'd against the very life
Of the defendant, and thou hast incurr'd
The danger formerly by me rehears'd.
Down, therefore, and beg mercy of the duke.

Gratiano

Beg that thou mayst have leave to hang thyself—
And yet, thy wealth being forfeit to the state,
Thou hast not left the value of a cord;
Therefore thou must be hang'd at the state's charge.

Duke

That thou shalt see the difference of our spirit,
I pardon thee thy life before thou ask it.
For half thy wealth, it is Antonio's;
The other half comes to the general state,
Which humbleness may drive unto a fine.

Portia

Ay, for the state, not for Antonio.

Shylock

Nay, take my life and all, pardon not that:
You take my house when you do take the prop
That doth sustain my house; you take my life
When you do take the means whereby I live.

Portia

What mercy can you render him, Antonio?

Gratiano

A halter gratis—nothing else, for God's sake.

346 *enacted*: decreed.

350 *party*: person (Portia uses the correct legal term, still used today). *contrive*: plot.

351 *seize*: take possession of.

352 *privy coffer*: treasury.

354 *'gainst . . . voice*: without appeal.

356 *manifest proceeding*: quite clearly from what has happened.

360 *rehears'd*: declared.

369 *general state*: general use of the state.

370 *Which . . . fine*: which your good behaviour may reduce to a fine.

371 *not for Antonio*: not Antonio's share of the money.

377 *halter*: rope to hang himself with. *gratis*: free of interest.

Antonio

So please my lord the duke and all the court
To quit the fine for one half of his goods,
I am content, so he will let me have
The other half in use, to render it
Upon his death unto the gentleman
That lately stole his daughter.
Two things provided more: that for this favour
He presently become a Christian;
The other, that he do record a gift,
Here in the court, of all he dies possess'd
Unto his son Lorenzo and his daughter.

Duke

He shall do this, or else I do recant
The pardon that I late pronounced here.

Portia

Art thou contented, Jew? What dost thou say?

Shylock

I am content.

Portia

Clerk, draw a deed of gift.

Shylock

I pray you give me leave to go from hence;
I am not well. Send the deed after me
And I will sign it.

Duke

Get thee gone, but do it.

Gratiano

In christening shalt thou have two godfathers:
Had I been judge, thou shouldst have had ten more
To bring thee to the gallows, not to the font.

[*Exit* Shylock

Duke

Sir, I entreat you home with me to dinner.

Portia

I humbly do desire your grace of pardon.
I must away this night toward Padua,
And it is meet I presently set forth.

378 *So please*: if it pleases.

379 *quit*: be satisfied with.
for: instead of.

380 *so*: provided that.

381 *in use*: on trust—to use as Antonio now describes.

385 *presently*: immediately.

386 *record a gift*: sign a legal deed of gift.

387 *all he dies possess'd*: all that he owns when he dies.

389 *recant*: withdraw.

390 *pronounced*: pronouncèd.

396 *godfathers*: sponsors who would guarantee Christian upbringing (for an infant).

397 *ten more*: i.e. enough to constitute a jury.

402 *meet*: necessary.

Duke

I am sorry that your leisure serves you not.
Antonio, gratify this gentleman,
For in my mind you are much bound to him.
[*Exit* Duke *and his train*

Bassanio

Most worthy gentleman, I and my friend
Have by your wisdom been this day acquitted
Of grievous penalties, in lieu whereof
Three thousand ducats due unto the Jew
We freely cope your courteous pains withal.

Antonio

And stand indebted over and above
In love and service to you evermore.

Portia

He is well paid that is well satisfied;
And I delivering you am satisfied
And therein do account myself well paid;
My mind was never yet more mercenary.
I pray you know me when we meet again.
I wish you well, and so I take my leave.

Bassanio

Dear sir, of force I must attempt you further.
Take some remembrance of us as a tribute,
Not as a fee. Grant me two things, I pray you:
Not to deny me, and to pardon me.

Portia

You press me far, and therefore I will yield.
Give me your gloves, I'll wear them for your sake;
And for your love I'll take this ring from you.
Do not draw back your hand; I'll take no more,
And you in love shall not deny me this.

Bassanio

This ring, good sir? Alas, it is a trifle;
I will not shame myself to give you this.

Portia

I will have nothing else but only this;
And now methinks I have a mind to it.

Bassanio

There's more depends on this than on the value.

403 *your leisure serves you not*: you do not have time to spare.
404 *gratify*: show your gratitude to.
405 *bound*: indebted.
407–8 *acquitted Of*: set free from.
408 *in lieu whereof*: in payment for this.
410 *freely*: most willingly.
cope: reward.
pains: trouble.
411 *over and above*: in addition.
416 *mercenary*: interested in money.
417 *know*: recognize.
419 *of force*: it is necessary.
attempt you further: try harder to persuade you.
420 *some remembrance*: something to remind you.
tribute: token of respect.
423 *You press me far*: you are very insistent.
424 *for your sake*: to acknowledge your politeness.
425 *for your love*: to acknowledge your love.
431 *have . . . it*: really want it.

'In christening shalt thou have two godfathers' (*4*, 1, 396). Nicholas Farrell as Bassanio, Antony Sher as Shylock, and Geoffrey Freshwater as Gratiano, Royal Shakespeare Company, 1988.

The dearest ring in Venice will I give you,
And find it out by proclamation.
Only for this I pray you pardon me.

Portia

I see, sir, you are liberal in offers.
You taught me first to beg, and now methinks
You teach me how a beggar should be answer'd.

Bassanio

Good sir, this ring was given me by my wife,
And when she put it on, she made me vow
That I should neither sell, nor give, nor lose it.

Portia

That scuse serves many men to save their gifts;
And if your wife be not a mad woman,
And know how well I have deserv'd this ring,
She would not hold out enemy for ever
For giving it to me. Well, peace be with you.

[*Exeunt* Portia *and* Nerissa

Antonio

My lord Bassanio, let him have the ring.
Let his deservings and my love withal
Be valu'd 'gainst your wife's commandement.

Bassanio

Go, Gratiano, run and overtake him;
Give him the ring, and bring him if thou canst
Unto Antonio's house. Away, make haste.

[*Exit* Gratiano

Come, you and I will thither presently,
And in the morning early will we both
Fly toward Belmont. Come, Antonio. [*Exeunt*

434 *proclamation*: public announcement.

435 *this*: this one.

436 *liberal in offers*: only generous in making offers (without fulfilling them).

442 *scuse*: excuse.

449 *'gainst*: in balance with. *commandement*: commandèment: a four-syllable word is necessary for the rhythm.

Act 4 Scene 2
Portia gets Bassanio's ring—and Nerissa plans to get her own from Gratiano.

SCENE 2

Venice: a street. Enter Portia *and* Nerissa

Portia
Enquire the Jew's house out, give him this deed,
And let him sign it. We'll away tonight
And be a day before our husbands home.
This deed will be well welcome to Lorenzo.

Enter Gratiano

Gratiano
Fair sir, you are well o'ertane.
My lord Bassanio upon more advice
Hath sent you here this ring, and doth entreat
Your company at dinner.

Portia
That cannot be.
His ring I do accept most thankfully,
And so I pray you tell him. Furthermore,
I pray you show my youth old Shylock's house.

Gratiano
That will I do.

Nerissa
[*To* Portia] Sir, I would speak with you.
[*Aside*] I'll see if I can get my husband's ring
Which I did make him swear to keep for ever.

Portia
Thou mayst, I warrant. We shall have old swearing
That they did give the rings away to men;
But we'll outface them, and outswear them too.
—Away, make haste, thou know'st where I will tarry.

Nerissa
Come, good sir, will you show me to this house?

[*Exeunt*

1 *Enquire . . . out*: find out where the Jew's house is.
this deed: the document in which he promises to make Lorenzo his heir.

5 *well o'ertane*: I'm glad I've caught up with you.

6 *upon more advice*: having thought more about the matter.

15 *Thou . . . warrant*: I'm sure you'll succeed.
old: extraordinary.

18 *tarry*: wait.

ACT 5

Act 5 Scene 1
Lorenzo teases Jessica as they wait in the moonlight. Portia and Nerissa return from Venice, followed by Bassanio and Gratiano—who are embarrassed when their wives demand to see the rings. All is explained, and Portia has good news for Antonio.

Scene 1

Belmont: the garden. Enter Lorenzo *and* Jessica

Lorenzo
The moon shines bright. In such a night as this,
When the sweet wind did gently kiss the trees,
And they did make no noise, in such a night
Troilus methinks mounted the Troyan walls
And sigh'd his soul toward the Grecian tents,
Where Cressid lay that night.

Jessica
In such a night
Did Thisbe fearfully o'ertrip the dew,
And saw the lion's shadow ere himself,
And ran dismay'd away.

Lorenzo
In such a night
Stood Dido with a willow in her hand
Upon the wild sea banks, and waft her love
To come again to Carthage.

Jessica
In such a night
Medea gather'd the enchanted herbs
That did renew old Aeson.

Lorenzo
In such a night
Did Jessica steal from the wealthy Jew
And with an unthrift love did run from Venice
As far as Belmont.

Jessica
In such a night
Did young Lorenzo swear he lov'd her well,
Stealing her soul with many vows of faith,
And ne'er a true one.

4–6 *Troilus . . . night*: In the Trojan War Troilus was separated from Cressida when she was taken to the Greek camp; their love is the subject of Chaucer's *Troylus and Criseyde* and Shakespeare's *Troilus and Cressida*.
7, 10, 13 *Thisbe . . . Dido . . . Medea*: Their stories are told in Chaucer's *Legend of Good Women*.
7 *Thisbe*: When Thisbe, frightened by a lion, failed to keep her assignation, her grieving lover Pyramus killed himself; a (comic) version of the episode is presented in *A Midsummer's Night's Dream*.
o'ertrip: trip across.
8 *ere himself*: before she saw him.
10 *Dido*: The Queen of Carthage, deserted by her lover Aeneas, was the protagonist of a tragedy by Shakespeare's contemporary, Christopher Marlowe.
willow: The traditional emblem of forsaken love.
11 *waft*: beckoned.
13–14 *Medea . . . Aeson*: When she had helped Jason on his voyage to win the Golden Fleece (see *1*, 1, 170 note), the enchantress Medea gave Aeson, his father, a rejuvenating herbal potion.
15 *steal*: a) creep away; b) rob.
16 *unthrift*: a) careless, prodigal; b) penniless.
19 *Stealing her soul*: a) gaining possession of her love; b) converting her away from her Jewish faith.

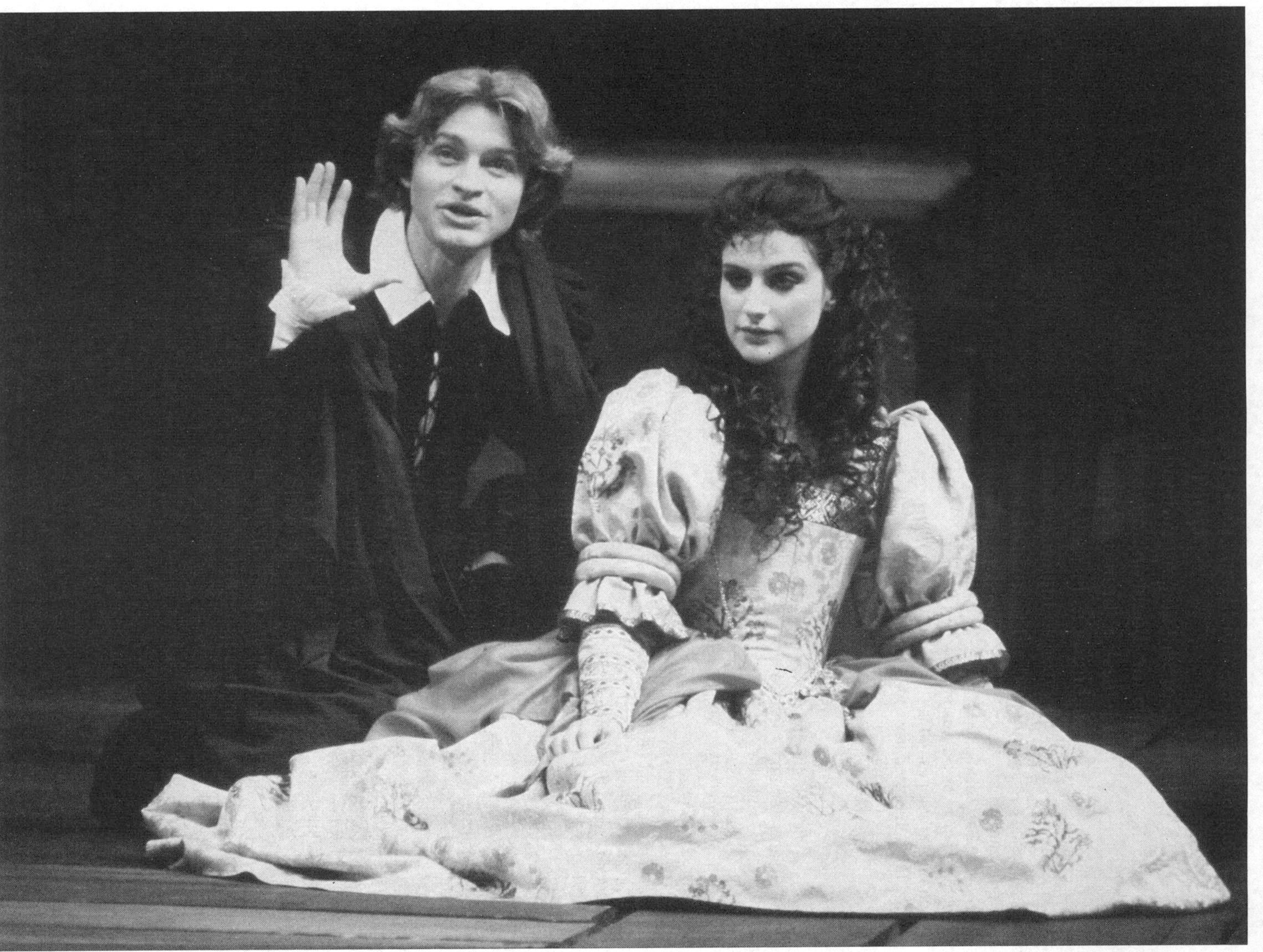

'In such a night Did Jessica steal from the wealthy Jew' (*5*, 1, 14–15). Paul Spence as Lorenzo and Deborah Goodman as Jessica, Royal Shakespeare Company, 1987.

Lorenzo

In such a night
Did pretty Jessica (like a little shrew)
Slander her love, and he forgave it her.

Jessica

I would outnight you, did nobody come:
But hark, I hear the footing of a man.

Enter Stephano, *a messenger*

Lorenzo

Who comes so fast in silence of the night?

Stephano

A friend.

Lorenzo

A friend? What friend? Your name, I pray you, friend?

Stephano

Stephano is my name, and I bring word
My mistress will before the break of day
Be here at Belmont. She doth stray about
By holy crosses where she kneels and prays
For happy wedlock hours.

Lorenzo

Who comes with her?

Stephano

None but a holy hermit and her maid.
I pray you, is my master yet return'd?

Lorenzo

He is not, nor we have not heard from him.
But go we in, I pray thee, Jessica,
And ceremoniously let us prepare
Some welcome for the mistress of the house.

Enter Lancelot, *the Clown*

Lancelot

Sola, sola! Wo ha, ho! Sola, sola!

Lorenzo

Who calls?

21 *shrew*: scolding woman.

23 *outnight you*: i.e. beat you at this game.
did nobody come: if there were not somebody coming.

30–2 *She . . . hours*: This apparent change of plan (*3*, 4, 26–32) passes unnoticed in the theatre.

31 *holy crosses*: wayside shrines.

37–8 *ceremoniously . . . welcome*: let us prepare some ceremony of welcome.

39 *Sola . . . sola*: Lancelot pretends that he cannot find Lorenzo.

Lancelot
Sola! Did you see Master Lorenzo? Master Lorenzo, sola, sola!

Lorenzo
Leave holloaing, man! Here!

Lancelot
Sola! Where, where?

Lorenzo
Here!

Lancelot
Tell him there's a post come from my master, with his horn full of good news: my master will be here ere morning, sweet soul.

Lorenzo
Let's in and there expect their coming.
And yet no matter: why should we go in?
My friend Stephano, signify I pray you,
Within the house, your mistress is at hand,
And bring your music forth into the air.
[*Exit* Stephano
How sweet the moonlight sleeps upon this bank!
Here will we sit, and let the sounds of music
Creep in our ears; soft stillness and the night
Become the touches of sweet harmony.
Sit, Jessica. Look how the floor of heaven
Is thick inlaid with patens of bright gold.
There's not the smallest orb which thou behold'st
But in his motion like an angel sings,
Still choiring to the young-eyed cherubins.
Such harmony is in immortal souls,
But whilst this muddy vesture of decay
Doth grossly close it in, we cannot hear it.

Enter Stephano *with musicians*

Come, ho! and wake Diana with a hymn.
With sweetest touches pierce your mistress' ear,
And draw her home with music.

Music plays

43 *Leave holloaing*: stop shouting.

46 *post*: courier.

47 *horn . . . news*: i.e. like a cornucopia (= horn of plenty).

48 *sweet soul*: Many editors place these words at the beginning of line 49 (which is two syllables short of a regular pentameter).

51 *signify*: announce.

53 *your music*: the resident musicians.

57 *Become*: suit, befit.

59 *patens*: little metal plates (used in Holy Communion).

60–1 *There's . . . sings*: The Elizabethans believed that heavenly harmony was created by the movement of the planets ('orbs').

62 *Still choiring*: always singing together. *young-eyed cherubins*: Elizabethans imagined these angelic creatures (see Ezekiel 10:12) as beautiful winged children.

63 *Such*: the same.

64 *muddy . . . decay*: clothing of mortality made from the dust of the earth (Genesis 2:7).

65 *grossly*: roughly, crudely.

66 *wake Diana*: call out the moon (which seems in line 109 to have gone behind a cloud).

Jessica

I am never merry when I hear sweet music.

Lorenzo

The reason is your spirits are attentive.
For do but note a wild and wanton herd
Or race of youthful and unhandled colts
Fetching mad bounds, bellowing and neighing loud—
Which is the hot condition of their blood—
If they but hear perchance a trumpet sound,
Or any air of music touch their ears,
You shall perceive them make a mutual stand,
Their savage eyes turn'd to a modest gaze
By the sweet power of music. Therefore the poet
Did feign that Orpheus drew trees, stones, and floods;
Since naught so stockish, hard, and full of rage,
But music for the time doth change his nature.
The man that hath no music in himself,
Nor is not mov'd with concord of sweet sounds,
Is fit for treasons, stratagems, and spoils;
The motions of his spirit are dull as night
And his affections dark as Erebus.
Let no such man be trusted. Mark the music.

Enter Portia *and* Nerissa

Portia

That light we see is burning in my hall.
How far that little candle throws his beams!
So shines a good deed in a naughty world.

Nerissa

When the moon shone we did not see the candle.

Portia

So doth the greater glory dim the less:
A substitute shines brightly as a king
Until a king be by, and then his state
Empties itself, as doth an inland brook
Into the main of waters. Music, hark!

Nerissa

It is your music, madam, of the house.

72 *race*: herd, stud.
unhandled: unbroken, untrained.

74 *hot . . . blood*: nature of their excited spirit.

75 *perchance*: perhaps.

77 *make . . . stand*: all stand still at once.

78 *modest*: gentle.

79–80 *the poet . . . floods*: the Roman poet Ovid told how Orpheus, a Greek musician, charmed even lifeless objects with his music.

81 *naught*: nothing.
stockish: stubborn.

84 *concord*: harmony.

85 *stratagems*: plots.
spoils: destruction.

86 *motions*: movements.

87 *Erebus*: the place of darkness in the classical underworld.

88 *Mark*: pay attention to.

91 *naughty*: wicked.

94 *substitute*: deputy.

95 *by*: present.

95–6 *his . . . itself*: his glory vanishes.

97 *main of waters*: sea.

98 *your . . . house*: the resident musicians.

Portia

Nothing is good, I see, without respect;
Methinks it sounds much sweeter than by day.

Nerissa

Silence bestows that virtue on it, madam.

Portia

The crow doth sing as sweetly as the lark
When neither is attended; and I think
The nightingale, if she should sing by day
When every goose is cackling, would be thought
No better a musician than the wren.
How many things by season season'd are
To their right praise and true perfection.
Peace, ho! The moon sleeps with Endymion
And would not be awak'd!

Music ceases

Lorenzo

That is the voice
Or I am much deceiv'd, of Portia!

Portia

He knows me as the blind man knows the cuckoo
By the bad voice.

Lorenzo

Dear lady, welcome home!

Portia

We have been praying for our husbands' welfare,
Which speed we hope the better for our words.
Are they return'd?

Lorenzo

Madam, they are not yet.
But there is come a messenger before
To signify their coming.

Portia

Go in, Nerissa:
Give order to my servants that they take
No note at all of our being absent hence—
Nor you, Lorenzo, Jessica nor you.

A tucket sounds

99 *Nothing . . . respect*: i.e. everything is relative to something else.

101 *virtue*: special quality.

103 *attended*: listened to.

104 *nightingale*: A bird that sings only at night, when all other birds are silent.

107 *by . . . are*: are given a better flavour by coming at the proper time.

109 *the moon . . . Endymion*: Diana, goddess of the moon, slept on Mount Latmos with her love, the shepherd-boy Endymion.

115 *speed*: prosper.

119–20 *take . . . note*: make no mention.

121s.d. *tucket*: personal trumpet call.

Lorenzo

Your husband is at hand, I hear his trumpet.
We are no telltales, madam; fear you not.

Portia

This night methinks is but the daylight sick,
It looks a little paler; 'tis a day
Such as the day is when the sun is hid.

Enter Bassanio, Antonio, Gratiano, *and their followers*

Bassanio

We should hold day with the Antipodes,
If you would walk in absence of the sun.

Portia

Let me give light, but let me not be light,
For a light wife doth make a heavy husband,
And never be Bassanio so for me—
But God sort all! You are welcome home, my lord.

Bassanio

I thank you, madam. Give welcome to my friend.
This is the man, this is Antonio,
To whom I am so infinitely bound.

Portia

You should in all sense be much bound to him,
For as I hear he was much bound for you.

Antonio

No more than I am well acquitted of.

Portia

Sir, you are very welcome to our house.
It must appear in other ways than words:
Therefore I scant this breathing courtesy.

Gratiano

[*To* Nerissa] By yonder moon I swear you do me wrong!
In faith, I gave it to the judge's clerk,
Would he were gelt that had it, for my part,
Since you do take it, love, so much at heart.

Portia

A quarrel ho, already! What's the matter?

127–8 *We . . . sun*: if you were to walk at night, it would be daylight here as well as on the other side of the globe ('the Antipodes').

129 *be light*: be faithless.

130 *heavy*: sorrowful.

131 *for me*: because of what I have done.

132 *sort all*: decide everything.

135 *bound*: indebted.

137 *bound*: in chains as a prisoner.

138 *acquitted of*: repaid for (with the love of Bassanio).

141 *scant*: cut short.
breathing courtesy: verbal politeness.

144 *Would . . . gelt*: I wish he had been castrated.

145 *take . . . heart*: care so much about it.

148 *poesy*: motto engraved inside a ring.

149 *cutler's poetry*: doggerel verse inscribed on a knife-handle.

151 *What*: why.

155 *for me*: for my sake.

158 *wear hair on's face*: grow a beard.

159 *and if*: if ever.

162 *scrubbed*: scrubbèd; stunted.

164 *prating*: chattering.

172 *leave*: part with.

174 *masters*: is master of.

176 *And 'twere to me*: if it had been done to me.

Gratiano
About a hoop of gold, a paltry ring
That she did give me, whose poesy was
For all the world like cutler's poetry
Upon a knife: 'Love me, and leave me not.'

Nerissa
What talk you of the poesy or the value?
You swore to me when I did give it you,
That you would wear it till your hour of death,
And that it should lie with you in your grave.
Though not for me, yet for your vehement oaths
You should have been respective and have kept it.
Gave it a judge's clerk! No, God's my judge
The clerk will ne'er wear hair on's face that had it.

Gratiano
He will, and if he live to be a man.

Nerissa
Ay, if a woman live to be a man.

Gratiano
Now by this hand, I gave it to a youth,
A kind of boy, a little scrubbed boy
No higher than thyself, the judge's clerk,
A prating boy that begg'd it as a fee;
I could not for my heart deny it him.

Portia
You were to blame, I must be plain with you,
To part so slightly with your wife's first gift,
A thing stuck on with oaths upon your finger
And so riveted with faith unto your flesh.
I gave my love a ring, and made him swear
Never to part with it, and here he stands.
I dare be sworn for him he would not leave it
Nor pluck it from his finger for the wealth
That the world masters. Now in faith, Gratiano,
You give your wife too unkind a cause of grief;
And 'twere to me, I should be mad at it.

Bassanio
[*Aside*] Why, I were best to cut my left hand off
And swear I lost the ring defending it.

Gratiano
My lord Bassanio gave his ring away

182 *pains*: care.

189 *void*: empty.

199–202 *If . . . ring*: Portia parodies Bassanio's figure of speech (epistrophe).

199 *virtue*: special quality.

201 *contain*: keep.

205 *terms of zeal*: determination.

205–6 *wanted . . . ceremony*: would have been so indelicate to press for something held sacred.

208 *I'll die for't*: I am ready to die for my belief.

210 *civil doctor*: doctor of civil law.

Unto the judge that begg'd it, and indeed
Deserv'd it too; and then the boy his clerk
That took some pains in writing, he begg'd mine,
And neither man nor master would take aught
But the two rings.

Portia

What ring gave you, my lord?
Not that, I hope, which you receiv'd of me?

Bassanio

If I could add a lie unto a fault,
I would deny it; but you see my finger
Hath not the ring upon it, it is gone.

Portia

Even so void is your false heart of truth.
By heaven, I will ne'er come in your bed
Until I see the ring.

Nerissa

Nor I in yours
Till I again see mine.

Bassanio

Sweet Portia,
If you did know to whom I gave the ring,
If you did know for whom I gave the ring,
And would conceive for what I gave the ring,
And how unwillingly I left the ring,
When naught would be accepted but the ring,
You would abate the strength of your displeasure.

Portia

If you had known the virtue of the ring,
Or half her worthiness that gave the ring,
Or your own honour to contain the ring,
You would not then have parted with the ring.
What man is there so much unreasonable,
If you had pleas'd to have defended it
With any terms of zeal, wanted the modesty
To urge the thing held as a ceremony?
Nerissa teaches me what to believe:
I'll die for't, but some woman had the ring!

Bassanio

No by my honour, madam, by my soul
No woman had it, but a civil doctor,

Which did refuse three thousand ducats of me,
And begg'd the ring, the which I did deny him,
And suffer'd him to go displeas'd away,
Even he that had held up the very life
Of my dear friend. What should I say, sweet lady?
I was enforc'd to send it after him;
I was beset with shame and courtesy;
My honour would not let ingratitude
So much besmear it. Pardon me, good lady,
For by these blessed candles of the night,
Had you been there I think you would have begg'd
The ring of me to give the worthy doctor.

Portia

Let not that doctor e'er come near my house.
Since he hath got the jewel that I lov'd
And that which you did swear to keep for me,
I will become as liberal as you;
I'll not deny him anything I have,
No, not my body, nor my husband's bed:
Know him I shall, I am well sure of it.
Lie not a night from home. Watch me like Argus.
If you do not, if I be left alone,
Now by mine honour which is yet mine own,
I'll have that doctor for my bedfellow.

Nerissa

And I his clerk; therefore be well advis'd
How you do leave me to mine own protection.

Gratiano

Well, do you so. Let not me take him then,
For if I do, I'll mar the young clerk's pen.

Antonio

I am th'unhappy subject of these quarrels.

Portia

Sir, grieve not you; you are welcome notwithstanding.

Bassanio

Portia, forgive me this enforced wrong;
And in the hearing of these many friends
I swear to thee, even by thine own fair eyes
Wherein I see myself—

Portia

Mark you but that?

213 *suffer'd*: allowed.
214 *held up*: saved.
217 *beset*: overcome.
219 *besmear*: stain.
220 *blessed*: blessèd.
candles of the night: the stars.
222 *of*: from.
230 *Lie . . . home*: don't spend a single night away from home.
Argus: A monster of classical mythology who closed only two of his hundred eyes at any one time.
232 *yet mine own*: still intact.
234 *be well advis'd*: take good care.
235 *to mine own protection*: to look after my own honour.
236 *take*: catch.
237 *I'll mar . . . pen*: I'll ruin his equipment.
240 *enforced*: enforcèd.

In both my eyes he doubly sees himself:
In each eye one. Swear by your double self,
And there's an oath of credit!

Bassanio

Nay, but hear me.
Pardon this fault, and by my soul I swear
I nevermore will break an oath with thee.

Antonio

I once did lend my body for his wealth,
Which but for him that had your husband's ring
Had quite miscarried. I dare be bound again,
My soul upon the forfeit, that your lord
Will nevermore break faith advisedly.

Portia

Then you shall be his surety. Give him this,
And bid him keep it better than the other.

Antonio

Here, Lord Bassanio, swear to keep this ring.

Bassanio

By heaven, it is the same I gave the doctor!

Portia

I had it of him; pardon me, Bassanio,
For by this ring the doctor lay with me.

Nerissa

And pardon me, my gentle Gratiano,
For that same scrubbed boy the doctor's clerk,
In lieu of this, last night did lie with me.

Gratiano

Why, this is like the mending of highways
In summer where the ways are fair enough!
What, are we cuckolds ere we have deserv'd it?

Portia

Speak not so grossly; you are all amaz'd.
Here is a letter, read it at your leisure;
It comes from Padua, from Bellario.
There you shall find that Portia was the doctor,
Nerissa there her clerk. Lorenzo here
Shall witness I set forth as soon as you,
And even but now return'd; I have not yet
Enter'd my house. Antonio, you are welcome;
And I have better news in store for you

245 *double*: a) two-fold; b) two-faced.

246 *of credit*: that can be believed.

249 *wealth*: well-being, happiness.

251 *miscarried*: been lost.

252 *My . . . forfeit*: at the risk of forfeiting my soul.

253 *advisedly*: knowingly.

254 *surety*: security.

261 *scrubbed*: scrubbèd.

262 *In lieu of*: in return for.

263–4 *mending . . . enough*: repairing good roads unnecessarily in summertime; Gratiano is saying that this situation is ridiculous.

265 *cuckolds*: men whose wives are unfaithful to them.
deserv'd it: i.e. by showing themselves to be unsatisfactory lovers.

266 *grossly*: crudely.
amaz'd: bewildered.

Than you expect. Unseal this letter soon;
There you shall find three of your argosies
Are richly come to harbour suddenly.
You shall not know by what strange accident
I chanced on this letter.

Antonio

I am dumb.

Bassanio

Were you the doctor and I knew you not?

Gratiano

Were you the clerk that is to make me cuckold?

Nerissa

Ay, but the clerk that never means to do it,
Unless he live until he be a man.

Bassanio

Sweet doctor, you shall be my bedfellow;
When I am absent, then lie with my wife.

Antonio

Sweet lady, you have given me life and living;
For here I read for certain that my ships
Are safely come to road.

Portia

How now, Lorenzo?
My clerk hath some good comforts too for you.

Nerissa

Ay, and I'll give them him without a fee.
There do I give to you and Jessica
From the rich Jew, a special deed of gift
After his death of all he dies possess'd of.

Lorenzo

Fair ladies, you drop manna in the way
Of starved people.

Portia

It is almost morning;
And yet I am sure you are not satisfied
Of these events at full. Let us go in,
And charge us there upon inter'gatories,
And we will answer all things faithfully.

Gratiano

Let it be so. The first inter'gatory
That my Nerissa shall be sworn on is:

275 *soon*: quickly.

279 *chanced*: chancèd.

288 *road*: anchorage.

294 *manna*: the food from heaven that sustained the Israelites starving in the desert (Exodus 16:14–15).

295 *starved*: starvèd.

297 *at full*: in detail.

298 *charge . . . inter'gatories*: interrogate us on oath.

305 *couching*: going to bed.
306 *while I live*: as long as I live.
306–7 *I'll . . . ring*: I'll take care of nothing so much as guarding Nerissa's ring (and also her honour).

Whether till the next night she had rather stay,
Or go to bed now, being two hours to day.
But were the day come, I should wish it dark,
Till I were couching with the doctor's clerk.
Well, while I live I'll fear no other thing
So sore as keeping safe Nerissa's ring. [*Exeunt*

The Merchant of Venice: the Source

The lady, the pound of flesh, and the ring

The most likely source for the main plot in *The Merchant of Venice* seems to have been one of the stories in *Il Pecorone* (= 'the big sheep', or dunce), a collection of tales by Ser Giovanni of Florence, which was published at Milan in 1558. No English version has ever been found – so we must assume that Shakespeare read the original in Italian.

Ansaldo, a wealthy merchant of Venice, financed his godson Giannetto in his attempts to win the Lady of Belmont. This Lady was a rich widow who had agreed to marry the first man who succeeded in making love to her – but she had imposed the condition that all unsuccessful lovers must forfeit everything they possessed. Giannetto twice attempted this task; and both times he failed – because he was given drugged wine to make him fall asleep before the lady came to bed. Because he was ashamed of his failures, he told Ansaldo that he had twice been shipwrecked. Determined to make a third attempt, he begged Ansaldo for more money. This time Ansaldo was forced to borrow ten thousand ducats from a Jew to enable him to equip yet another ship for Giannetto. The Jew made the condition that if the loan were not repaid upon St John's Day, the merchant would forfeit a pound of his own flesh.

Giannetto (warned by a maid not to drink the drugged wine) succeeded in making love to the lady; he married her, and was proclaimed sovereign of all that she possessed. He forgot about Ansaldo's bargain with the Jew until St John's Day arrived, and then he told his wife the whole story. The Lady sent Giannetto to Venice with enough money to repay the Jew; and she herself followed him, disguised as a lawyer.

The Jew refused to accept Giannetto's money, because he wanted to say that he had killed the greatest of all the Christian merchants. The 'lawyer' claimed that she could settle all disputes, and she heard the Jew's case against Ansaldo, with Giannetto's offer to repay the debt. She advised the Jew to take the ten thousand ducats, but he persisted in refusing. She then told him to take the pound of flesh – but, at the last moment, she warned him that if he took more than an exact pound, or shed one drop of blood, he would be executed. The Jew then asked for the money instead of the flesh. When this was refused, he tore up the bond.

Giannetto offered the ducats as a fee to the 'lawyer', but she demanded to be given his ring. He then returned to Belmont, taking Ansaldo with him. The Lady accused Giannetto of giving the ring to one of his former mistresses. He wept, but finally the Lady explained everything – and Ansaldo married the maid who had warned Giannetto about the drugged wine.

The caskets The casket story may have been suggested by the account in History 32 of *Gesta Romanorum*, translated by R. Robinson in 1595, where the heroine was told to make a choice between three 'vessels' in order to win a husband.

'The first [vessel] was made of pure gold, well-beset with precious stones without, and within full of dead men's bones; and thereupon was engraved this poesy: *Whoso chooseth me shall find that he deserveth.* The second vessel was made of fine silver, filled with earth and worms; and the superscription was thus: *Whoso chooseth me shall find that his nature desireth.* The third vessel was made of lead, full within of precious stones; and thereupon was ensculped this poesy: *Whoso chooseth me, shall find that God hath disposed for him.*'

The Jew and his daughter A contemporary play, *The Jew of Malta* (*c.* 1589) by Christopher Marlowe, gave Shakespeare some inspiration for the character of Shylock. Marlowe's Jew, Barabas, is determined to be revenged on the Christians who persecute him; and he too has a daughter who loves a Christian. Shylock's lament – 'My daughter! O my ducats! O my daughter!' (Act 2, Scene 8, line 15) – seems to be modelled on Barabas's cry: 'Oh my girl! My gold, my fortune . . . Oh girl! Oh gold! Oh beauty! Oh my bliss!' (*The Jew of Malta*, Act 2, Scene 2, lines 47–54).

Background

England in 1599

When Shakespeare was writing *The Merchant of Venice*, many people still believed that the sun went round the earth. They were taught that this was the way God had ordered things, and that – in England – God had founded a Church and appointed a Monarchy so that the land and people could be well governed.

'The past is a foreign country; they do things differently there.'

L. P. Hartley

Government For most of Shakespeare's life, the reigning monarch of England was Queen Elizabeth I. With her counsellors and ministers, she governed the nation from London, although fewer than half a million people out of a total population of six million lived in the capital city. In the rest of the country, law and order were maintained by the land-owners and enforced by their deputies. The average man had no vote, and women had no rights at all.

Religion At this time, England was a Christian country. All children were baptized, soon after they were born, into the Church of England; they were taught the essentials of the Christian faith, and instructed in their duty to God and to humankind. Marriages and funerals were conducted only by the licensed clergy and according to the Church's rites and ceremonies. Attending divine service was compulsory; absences (without a good medical reason) could be punished by fines. By such means, the authorities were able to keep some control over the population – recording births, marriages, and deaths; being alert to anyone who refused to accept standard religious practices, who could be politically dangerous; and ensuring that people received the approved teachings through the official 'Homilies' which were regularly preached in all parish churches.

Elizabeth I's father, Henry VIII, had broken away from the Church of Rome, and from that time all people in England were able to hear the church services *in their own language* rather than in Latin. The Book of Common Prayer was used in every church, and an English translation of the Bible was read aloud in public. The Christian religion had never been so well taught before!

Education School education reinforced the Church's teaching. From the age of four, boys might attend the 'petty school' (its name came from the French '*petite école*') to learn reading and writing along with a few prayers; some schools also included work with numbers. At the age of seven, the boy was ready for the grammar school (if his father was willing and able to pay the fees).

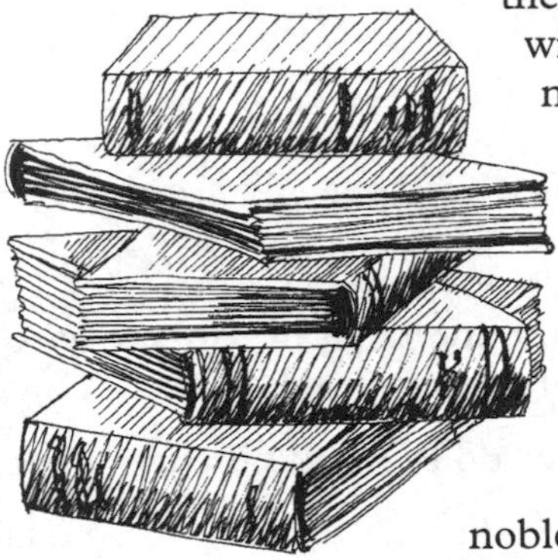

Grammar schools taught Latin grammar, translation work and the study of Roman authors, paying attention as much to style as to content. The art of fine writing was therefore important from early youth. A very few students went on to university; these were either clever boys who won scholarships, or else the sons of rich noblemen. Girls stayed at home, and learned domestic and social skills – cooking, sewing, perhaps even music. The lucky ones might learn to read and write.

Language At the start of the sixteenth century the English had a very poor opinion of their own language: there was little serious writing in English, and hardly any literature. Latin was the language of international scholarship, and the eloquent style of the Romans was much admired. Many translations from Latin were made, and in this way writers increased the vocabulary of English and made its grammar more flexible. French, Italian, and Spanish works were also translated and, for the first time, there were English versions of the Bible. By the end of the century, English was a language to be proud of: it was rich in vocabulary, capable of infinite variety and subtlety, and ready for all kinds of word-play – especially *puns*, for which Elizabethan English is renowned.

Drama The great art-form of the Elizabethan and Jacobean age was drama. The Elizabethans inherited a tradition of play-acting from the Middle Ages, and they reinforced this by reading and translating the Roman playwrights. At the beginning of the sixteenth century plays were performed by groups of actors. These were all-male companies (boys acted the female roles) who travelled from town to town, setting up their stages in open places (such as inn-yards) or, with the permission of the owner, in the hall of some noble house. The touring companies continued outside London into the seventeenth century; but in London, in 1576, a new building was erected for the performance of plays. This was the Theatre, the first purpose-built playhouse in England. Other playhouses followed, including the Globe, where most of Shakespeare's plays were performed, and English drama reached new heights.

There were people who disapproved, of course. The theatres, which brought large crowds together, could encourage the spread of disease – and dangerous ideas. During the summer, when the plague was at its worst, the playhouses were closed. A constant censorship was imposed, more or less severe at different times. The Puritans, a religious and political faction who wanted to impose strict rules of behaviour, tried to close down the theatres. However, partly because the royal family favoured drama, and partly because the buildings were outside the city limits, they did not succeed until 1642.

Theatre From contemporary comments and sketches – most particularly a drawing by a Dutch visitor, Johannes de Witt – it is possible to form some idea of the typical Elizabethan playhouse for which most of Shakespeare's plays were written. Hexagonal (six-sided) in shape, it

had three roofed galleries encircling an open courtyard. The plain, high stage projected into the yard, where it was surrounded by the audience of standing 'groundlings'. At the back were two doors for the actors' entrances and exits; and above these doors was a balcony – useful for a musicians' gallery or for the acting of scenes '*above*'. Over the stage was a thatched roof, supported on two pillars, forming a canopy – which seems to have been painted with the sun, moon, and stars for the 'heavens'.

Underneath was space (concealed by curtains) which could be used by characters ascending and descending through a trap-door in the stage. Costumes and properties were kept backstage in the 'tiring house'. The actors used the most luxurious costumes they could find, often clothes given to them by rich patrons. Stage properties were important for showing where a scene was set, but the dramatist's own words were needed to explain the time of day, since all performances took place in the early afternoon.

A replica of Shakespeare's own theatre, the Globe, has been built in London, and stands in Southwark, almost exactly on the Bankside site of the original.

William Shakespeare, 1564–1616

Elizabeth I was Queen of England when Shakespeare was born in 1564. He was the son of a tradesman who made and sold gloves in the small town of Stratford-upon-Avon, and he was educated at the grammar school in that town. Shakespeare did not go to university when he left school, but worked, perhaps, in his father's business. When he was eighteen he married Anne Hathaway, who became the mother of his daughter, Susanna, in 1583, and of twins in 1585.

There is nothing exciting, or even unusual, in this story; and from 1585 until 1592 there are no documents that can tell us anything at all about Shakespeare. But we have learned that in 1592 he was known in London, and that he had become both an actor and a playwright.

We do not know when Shakespeare wrote his first play, and we are not sure of the order in which he wrote his works. If you look on page 109 at the list of his writings and their approximate dates, you will see he started by writing plays on subjects taken from the history of England. No doubt this was partly because he was patriotic and interested in English history, but he was also a very shrewd businessman. He could see that the theatre audiences enjoyed being shown their own history, and it was certain that he would make a profit from this kind of drama.

He also wrote comedies, with romantic love-stories of young people who fall in love with one another, and at the end of the play marry and live happily ever after.

At the end of the sixteenth century Shakespeare wrote some melancholy, bitter, and tragic plays. This change may have been caused by some sadness in the writer's life (his only son died in 1596). Shakespeare, however, was not the only writer whose works at this time were very serious. The whole of England was facing a crisis. Queen Elizabeth I was growing old. She was greatly loved, and the people were sad to think she must soon die; they were also afraid, because the queen had never married, and so there was no child to succeed her.

When James I, Elizabeth's Scottish cousin, came to the throne in 1603, Shakespeare continued to write serious drama – the great tragedies and the plays based on Roman history (such as *Julius Caesar*) for which he is most famous. Finally, before he retired from the theatre, he wrote another set of comedies. These all have the same theme: they tell of happiness which is lost, and then found again.

Shakespeare returned from London to Stratford, his home town. He was rich and successful, and he owned one of the biggest houses in the town. He died in 1616.

Shakespeare also wrote two long poems, and a collection of sonnets. The sonnets describe two love affairs, but we do not know who the lovers were – or whether they existed only in Shakespeare's imagination. Although there are many public documents concerned with his career as a writer and a businessman, Shakespeare has hidden his personal life from us. A nineteenth-century poet, Matthew Arnold, addressed Shakespeare in a poem, and wrote 'We ask and ask – Thou smilest, and art still'.

Approximate Dates of Composition of Shakespeare's Works

Period	Comedies	History plays	Tragedies	Poems
I	Comedy of Errors	Henry VI, part 1	Titus Andronicus	
	Taming of the Shrew	Henry VI, part 2		
before 1594	Two Gentlemen of Verona	Henry VI, part 3		
	Love's Labour's Lost	Richard III		Venus and Adonis
				Rape of Lucrece
II	Midsummer Night's Dream	Richard II	Romeo and Juliet	
	Merchant of Venice	King John		
1594 – 1599	Merry Wives of Windsor	Henry IV, part 1		
	Much Ado About Nothing	Henry IV, part 2		
	As You Like It	Henry V		Sonnets
III	Twelfth Night		Julius Caesar	
	Troilus and Cressida		Hamlet	
1599 – 1608	Measure for Measure		Othello	
	All's Well That Ends Well		Timon of Athens	
	Pericles		King Lear	
			Macbeth	
			Antony and Cleopatra	
			Coriolanus	
IV	Cymbeline			
1608 – 1613	The Winter's Tale			
	The Tempest	Henry VIII		

Shakespeare's Globe, Southwark, London, England. Photograph by Richard Kalina.

Exploring The Merchant of Venice in the Classroom

Exotic characters and settings as well as electrifying plots and hotly debated themes make *The Merchant of Venice* an excellent choice for study.

This section suggests a range of approaches in the classroom, to help bring the text to life and to engender both enjoyment and understanding of the play.

Ways into the Play

Students may feel an antipathy towards the study of Shakespeare. The imaginative and enthusiastic teacher, with the help of this edition of the play, will soon break this down!

What's in a name?

The names of Shakespeare's characters are often familiar, even without knowledge of the plays themselves. Have any of the students heard the name Shylock? Discuss what sort of character he might be. Give students time to consider the characters behind these names: Antonio, Portia, Lancelot Gobbo. They can compare their ideas with the actual characters as the plays unfolds.

Pictures

Every picture tells a story, so ask your students to look at the picture on page vii and to guess who the characters are and what is happening. Once they are more familiar with the play, ask them to hazard a guess at the exact moment in the play that is depicted.

Navigating the play

Your students may need some help and practice at finding their way around a Shakespeare play. After explaining the division into acts, scenes and lines, challenge them to look up some references as quickly as possible. Refer them to some of the famous lines and those which might lead on to further discussion of the plot. Below are some suggestions:

Act 2, Scene 7, line 65 (*All that glisters is not gold*)
Act 3, Scene 1, line 57 (*If you prick us, do we not bleed?*)
Act 4, Scene 1, line 182 (*The quality of mercy is not strain'd*)

Improvisation

Working on these improvisations may help students access some of the ideas behind the drama.

a) Improvise a scene between two friends – A and B. B is asking A for a loan. B feels embarrassed asking for help, but the loan is for something important and so s/he tries really hard to persuade A. How does A react? Does B get the loan? Are they still friends?

b) Repeat the above improvisation, only this time A is not a friend. In fact B has been rude and horrible to A in the past. How will B try to persuade A? Does B receive the loan?

c) Devise a new TV game show called *Gamble*. In order to win brilliant prizes, participants need to be prepared to gamble things they already have. What would they be prepared to gamble (e.g. their CD collection, all their computer games, pocket money for a year)? Three people play, but only one can win. Students will need to devise the game, and improvise the show.

Setting the Scene

Shylock the Jew

The portrayal of Jews, and in particular Shylock, makes this play controversial. Despite the title of the play, Shylock is the character that makes this play so colourful, and his character is riddled with the stereotypes and prejudices of the Elizabethan Age. Students will need to know that Jews were vilified and expelled from many countries. In those places where they were allowed to remain, often the only occupation open to them was money lending, and in consequence they were even more unpopular.

It has been suggested that because the treatment of Shylock is so grotesque, the play should no longer be performed. But in many ways this is what makes the play so fruitful for study. Use the spotlight of drama to examine prejudices then and now. You can ask how sympathetic Shakespeare is to Shylock. Is the ghastly treatment of Shylock a product of the playwright's own views or Elizabethan society?

Belmont and Venice

There are two main settings for the play:

- Venice: the thriving hub of international trade, inhabited by those involved in the cut and thrust of business and commerce;
- Belmont: an imaginary setting, a civilized and romantic place, home to the gracious Portia.

If you can, show students some pictures of Venice, showing the canals, architecture, markets, etc. Challenge students to design two different sets for Act 1, Scenes 1 and 2. Their designs should aim to illustrate the contrast between the two worlds of the play.

Riddles

The caskets which must be chosen by Portia's suitors bear the following labels:

Gold: *Who chooseth me, shall gain what many men desire.*
Silver: *Who chooseth me, shall get as much as he deserves.*
Lead: *Who chooseth me, must give and hazard all he hath.*

Students can speculate on the possible meanings behind these labels, and decide which casket holds promise and which threatens.

Keeping Track of the Action

It's important to give students opportunities to 'digest' and reflect upon their reading, so that they may take ownership of the play.

Reading journal

As you read through the play, help students to trace and understand the main plot and sub-plots by asking them to keep a journal in which they record what happens. They can also record their reactions and thoughts about the action and the characters. Help them to keep their comments focused by giving them specific questions to answer.

Four stories in one

Shakespeare blends four stories in *The Merchant of Venice.*

The main plot:

- the fortunes of Antonio, Shylock and the pound of flesh.

Three sub-plots:

- Portia and her suitors
- the elopement of Jessica
- the lovers' rings.

Ask the students to use a flowchart to trace each strand of the story. They can look for the links between the stories, as well as analysing how much time Shakespeare devotes to each plot and the relative importance of each part of the overall plot.

Question wall

There are many things that are difficult or puzzling when studying Shakespeare, but asking questions publicly can be daunting for many students. Put blank sticky notes on their desks, and encourage them to write questions or make observations on the notes as the lesson progresses. The notes can then be stuck on a dedicated section of wall in the classroom. At the end of the session, leave enough time to refer to their points and queries. Answer the questions yourself, throw them open to discussion, or promise to do some research if you don't know the answer!

Mini saga

Once the class has read/seen the play, challenge students to retell the story of *The Merchant of Venice* in their own words. Their version should be exactly 50 words long – no more, no less. They might tell the whole story or retell one of the sub-plots. An alternative (possibly extension) activity is to retell the story in verse. See *Shakespeare in a Nutshell: A Rhyming Guide to All the Plays* (listed in Further Reading) for inspiration on Shakespeare in rhyme.

Characters

Students of all ages need to come to an understanding of the characters: their motivations, their relationships, and their development.

Fluctuating fortunes

The fortunes of Antonio and Shylock alternately wax and wane. Ask students to chart the fortunes of both characters, with a simple line graph for each one. With a scale of numbers – say from 1 to 10 – on one axis, and key moments from the play on the other, ask them to plot the fortunes of both.

Suitable points in the play are:

Act 1, Scene 3	Antonio asks Shylock for a loan.
Act 2, Scene 8	Solanio and Salarino gossip about both men.
Act 3, Scene 1	Shylock exchanges views with Solanio and Salarino.
Act 3, Scene 3	Antonio is arrested.
Act 4, Scene 1 (start)	The court seeks the mercy of Shylock.
Act 4, Scene 1 (end)	Shylock is crushed.

The completed graphs can be compared and the fortunes of both characters contrasted.

Thought tracking

This is an excellent way of encouraging students to explore the inner thoughts and motivations of a character. Select a scene where the character's words have hidden meaning, irony or layers of meaning. Ask students to consider and write down the thoughts behind the character's words. Suitable scenes include:

Act 1, Scene 3, lines 133–end	*(Antonio and Shylock agree to the bond.)*
Act 2, Scene 7, lines 1–12	*(Portia leads Morocco to the caskets.)*
Act 4, Scene 1, lines 406–end	*(The disguised Portia asks Bassanio for a ring.)*

A different perspective

Allowing your students the opportunity to think, write and talk as one of the characters gives them a new and illuminating perspective on the character(s). Here are some possible tasks:

a) Act 2, Scene 6: Jessica leaves a note to her father, explaining her decision to run away and take his wealth.
b) Act 3, Scene 2: On his arrival at Belmont, Bassanio makes a video diary disclosing his hopes and fears.
c) Act 4, Scene 1: A television interview with Shylock prior to the trial, asking him about his intentions.

Shylock – sinned against or sinner?

One of the main decisions a modern director must make is how to portray Shylock – an immoral monster or the bruised product of a deeply prejudiced society. The answer, of course, is that he is probably somewhere between the two.

Look for images of Shylock on the Internet (e.g. through an image search on Google). Give a set of images to the students and ask them to discuss the types of person portrayed.

Set up a debate within your class with one half looking for evidence of the stereotypical, money-grabbing character, and the other half looking for evidence of the wronged and abused Shylock. Debate what type of character he is and how they think Shakespeare intended him to be played. How would they depict him in a modern production?

Themes

Front page

There are many themes and key ideas in the play, for example, justice, friendship, religion, money and love. Ask students to produce a newspaper front page which reflects and explores some of the themes throughout the play. Their news stories might cover aspects such as Portia's suitors, the bond and the fate of Antonio's ships.

Fathers and daughters

'…so is the will of a living daughter curbed by the will of a dead father.' Portia's father controls his daughter even after his death, with the lottery of caskets he has set up. Jessica is also under the firm control of her father. The only way she can escape from his control is to renounce him completely and elope. Both women will come under the control of their husbands.

Use the play to look for evidence of the position of women in Shakespearean times, and discuss how things have changed. Ask for two volunteers to take on the roles of Portia and Jessica, and 'hot seat' both characters. Encourage the chosen students to take on an authentic sixteenth-century role and allow the rest of the class to ask them about their positions, their feelings, and hopes for the future.

The two women deal very differently with their situations. Ask the students which one they admire most and why.

Judge a book by its cover

Ask students to design a new cover for this book or for a programme for a performance of the play. The cover should reveal something of the themes of the play as well as giving essential information.

Shakespeare's Language

The language of persuasion

There are several speeches that seek to persuade, the most notable of which must be Portia's lines in Act 4, Scene 1, lines 182ff ('The quality of mercy is not strain'd'). Ask the class to read the speech, with each student reading up to a punctuation mark before the next student takes over.

Ask students to analyse how the speech is persuasive. They can look at the structure of the speech: the build-up from looking at the simple nature of mercy, to mercy in the hands of kings, right up to the mercy of God. Finally there is a direct plea to Shylock for mercy.

Students can also look for ideas and words that are repeated; analogies and associations (e.g. to kings and God); religious references; allusions to power and greatness; and the use of pronouns (e.g. 'us') to establish common ground. Discuss how each of the techniques works.

The language of hate

In Act 1, Scene 3, lines 101–24, Shylock famously relates how he has been abused and insulted. Ask the class to read the speech, with each student reading out one line before moving on to the next student. Ask them to read the speech again, but this time reading only one word from the line – the word that they consider to be the most important or significant. Discuss their choices, then ask them to look at the words and ideas that are repeated (e.g. dog, spit). What is the effect of the words on the reader, and what does this speech reveal about Shylock and Antonio?

The language of love

The words of the lovers are courtly and formalized. Examine the speech where Bassanio opens the lead casket to find Portia's picture (Act 3, Scene 2, lines 114–30). Have some fun with a dramatic reading of this section of the speech by putting students into pairs – one of them reading the lines and the other miming the actions. The reader should aim for an exaggerated and melodramatic presentation which emphasizes the overstated images and tone of the passage.

After students have read the scroll, give them a cloze version of lines 139–48, with some of the end rhymes removed. This will enable them to focus on the rhyming couplets and how rhyme can draw attention to words and ideas.

Exploring with Drama

Book the hall or push back the desks, because the best way to study a great play is through drama. Students of all ages will benefit from a dramatic encounter with *The Merchant of Venice.* They will enjoy the opportunity to act out a scene or two, or to explore the situations through improvisation, for example, putting a character in the 'hot seat' for questioning by others.

Tableaux

Ask your students to create a tableau or freeze-frame involving all the characters in the play. The characters should be grouped together according to their relationships in the play, and their positions should say something about their interactions and status within the scene/play. Bring the tableau briefly to life by having each person saying something in character.

Alternatively, put the students into groups. Each group should create a tableau of one 'family' of characters or one moment in the play. One student from each group should be a 'sculptor' and mould the rest of the group into position.

The trial

Before they read or watch the trial scene from the play, give students a précis of the situation and ask them to prepare an improvisation of the trial. Divide up the parts among the class: jury; Shylock and his prosecution team; Antonio and his defence team; a judge; television reporters. Give them time to prepare their speeches and questions.

Their improvisation will not feature the device of a disguised Portia, of course, but it will enable students to establish and engage with the two sides of the case. It will be also be interesting to see how the judge sums up the case, whom the jury side with, and how the press report the event in a one-minute report 'to camera' (to the class). They can go on to compare their trial with Shakespeare's version.

The director

This is a play of famous speeches. Choose one speech (e.g. Act 1, Scene 3, lines 101–32) and put students into small groups, according to how many people are in the scene. They will also require one student to act as director. The director must then direct the other student(s) to give an action reading of the scene, so they can use their scripts but must act out the lines. Encourage the director to annotate a copy of the script, detailing his or her decisions. View and explore the different interpretations and decisions that different groups make.

Writing about *The Merchant of Venice*

If your students have to write about *The Merchant of Venice* for coursework or for examinations, you may wish to give them this general guidance.

- Read the question or task carefully, highlight the key words and answer all parts of the question.
- Planning is essential. Plan what will be in each paragraph. You can change your plan if necessary.
- Avoid retelling the story.
- *The Merchant of Venice* is a play – so consider the impact or effect on the audience.
- Use the Point, Evidence, Explanation (PEE) structure to explain points.
- Adding Evaluation (PEEE!) will gain you higher marks.
- Keep quotations short and relevant.
- Avoid referring to a film version of the play, unless this is part of your task.

Further Reading and Resources

General

Fantasia, Louis, *Instant Shakespeare: A Practical Guide for Actors, Directors and Teachers* (A & C Black, 2002).

Greer, Germaine, *Shakespeare: A Very Short Introduction* (Oxford, 2002).

Hall, Peter, *Shakespeare's Advice to the Players* (Oberon Books, 2003).

Holden, Anthony, *Shakespeare: His Life and Work* (Abacus, 2002).

Kneen, Judith, *Teaching Shakespeare from Transition to Test* (Oxford University Press, 2004).

McConnell, Louise, *Exit, Pursued by a Bear – Shakespeare's Characters, Plays, Poems, History and Stagecraft* (Bloomsbury, 2003).

McLeish, Kenneth, and Unwin, Stephen, *A Pocket Guide to Shakespeare's Plays* (Faber and Faber, 1998).

Muirden, James, *Shakespeare in a Nutshell: A Rhyming Guide to All the Plays* (Constable, 2004).

Wood, Michael, *In Search of Shakespeare* (BBC, 2003).

Children's/Students' Books

Deary, Terry, *Top Ten Shakespeare Stories* (Scholastic, 1998).

Ganeri, Anita, *What They Don't Tell You About Shakespeare* (Hodder, 1996).

Garfield, Leon, *Shakespeare Stories* (Puffin, 1997).

Lamb, Charles and Mary, *Tales from Shakespeare* (Puffin, 1987).

Williams, Marcia, *Bravo, Mr William Shakespeare!* (Walker, 2001).

Film, Video and DVD

The Merchant of Venice
Directed by Michael Radford (2004)
Starring Al Pacino, Lynn Collins, Jeremy Irons